New Horizons in Comparative Politics
Series Editor: HOWARD J. WIARDA

COMPARATIVE POLITICS IN TRANSITION

FOURTH EDITION

JOHN McCORMICK

Indiana University
Purdue University Indianapolis

THOMSON
™
WADSWORTH

Australia • Canada • Mexico • Singapore • Spain
United Kingdom • United States

THOMSON

WADSWORTH

Executive Editor: David Tatom
Assistant Editor: Heather Hogan
Editorial Assistant: Reena Thomas
Marketing Manager: Janise Fry
Marketing Assistant: Mary Ho
Executive Advertising Project Manager: Nathaniel Bergson-Michelson
Technology Project Manager: Melinda Newfarmer
Editorial Production Manager: Edward Wade

Print/Media Buyer: Rebecca Cross
Permissions Editor: Kiely Sexton
Photo Researcher: Nancy Spellman
Production Service and Composition: Graphic World
Copy Editor: Graphic World Publishing Services
Illustrator: Graphic World Illustration Studio
Cover Designer: Brian Salisbury
Cover Image: Lonny Kalfus/Getty Images
Printer: Transcontinental Printing/Louiseville

Printed in Canada
1 2 3 4 5 6 7   08 07 06 05 04 03

For more information about our products, contact us at
Thomson Learning Academic Resource Center
1-800-423-0563
For permission to use material from this text, contact us by
Phone: 1-800-730-2214   **Fax:** 1-800-730-2215
Web: http://www.thomsonrights.com

Library of Congress Control Number: 2003104460

ISBN: 0-534-50860-X

Wadsworth/Thomson Learning
10 Davis Drive
Belmont, CA 94002-3098
USA

Asia
Thomson Learning
5 Shenton Way #01-01
UIC Building
Singapore 068808

Australia
Nelson Thomson Learning
102 Dodds Street
South Melbourne, Victoria 3205
Australia

Canada
Nelson Thomson Learning
1120 Birchmount Road
Toronto, Ontario M1K 5G4
Canada

Europe/Middle East/Africa
Thomson Learning
High Holborn House
50/51 Bedford Row
London WC1R 4LR
United Kingdom

Latin America
Thomson Learning
Seneca, 53
Colonia Polanco
11560 Mexico D.F.
Mexico

Spain
Paraninfo Thomson Learning
Calle/Magallanes, 25
28015 Madrid, Spain

Foreword

by Howard J. Wiarda, Series Editor

With all the changes taking place in the world at the moment, fresh perspectives on government and politics are ever more important. Hence the development of Wadsworth's New Horizons in Comparative Politics series, which sets out to offer students and professors timely, readable, and current books in this exciting and booming field of political science.

The goal of the series is to provide books that are accessible while enhancing student understanding of the vital themes and approaches in comparative politics. At the same time, we hope that more senior students and scholars will find the conclusions and interpretations of their authors of value as well. Books in the series have been published on politics in Britain (Jorge Rasmussen), France (Ronald Tiersky), Russia (Steve Boilard), Mexico (George Grayson), China and Japan (Peter Moody), Latin America (Howard J. Wiarda), Africa (Carlene Edie), and Eastern Europe (Ivan Volgyes). Other books in the series include *An Introduction to Comparative Politics, European Politics in the Age of Globalization, Comparative Democracy and Democratization, and Non-Western Theories of Development*, as well as recently commissioned books on Germany, the Middle East, and other topics.

In offering this series, we have sought out authors who can balance scholarship with lively, readable writing. We have also made a conscious decision to move to a new generation of scholars who see things from a fresh perspective. Our objective has been to provide short, versatile volumes that can be used in myriad comparative politics courses, and we hope that some of the excitement and enthusiasm that our authors feel for their subject areas will rub off on students.

A lynchpin of this series for several years has been this major introductory comparative politics text by John McCormick, professor of political science at the Indianapolis campus of Indiana University.

It is rare these days for a single author to write a comparative politics text that covers all areas of the world. Most of us in this field are so specialized in our own countries, regions, or topics that we would not even attempt such a feat. Hence, most textbooks are written by teams of authors, each approaching the topic from their own individual perspectives. The multiauthor approach has its advantages, to be sure, but it can also result in anthologies and collections of uneven styles and points of view, with little connection to a common core, or even a sense of integration. McCormick's book avoids all these problems. It is an integrated introduction to the field, with a common set of themes that is woven throughout the manuscript like threads in a tapestry.

McCormick's prose flows nicely, and he includes the most important comparative politics concepts while using a provocative and innovative approach. He is also widely traveled and brings his own personal experiences into an approach that is new and fresh and that moves beyond older cold war thinking. He has updated and rewritten the entire text for this new edition to continue to provide a clear focus on political power and the way it is organized in developed and developing countries, Western and non-Western. His section on Islam has never been more important than it is today.

Moreover, McCormick has included a vast amount of useful information and interpretation. When I first read the manuscript, I was astounded not only at how well he writes but also at the huge storehouse of information he has developed, usefully and coherently organized around his integrating theses and outline. McCormick has true, in-depth expertise, not just in one or two countries but in all of the regions and countries covered in the book.

Adding to the value and utility of the book is the inclusion of suggested reading lists and study questions for each country, the listing of Web sites that will lead students to useful supporting information, the use of boxed features that highlight and draw out key issues and personalities, the inclusion of major country chronologies, and lists of key terms and names. The emphasis on true comparison is most obvious in the Comparative Focus studies at the end of every case, which will help students look across the different cases and compare topics such as executives, legislatures, electoral systems, political parties, constitutions, and bureaucracies. In terms of readability and study aids, this fourth edition is better than ever before.

McCormick's book nicely complements the other books in our series and can be used either as a single text for a course in comparative politics, or as an integrating text that is supplemented by other books—hopefully from our series! *Comparative Politics in Transition*, fourth edition, is a significant accomplishment that continues to be a core part of this series.

Preface

This is a book about political power and about the many ways in which it is defined, given, taken, won, lost, and distributed. As you study the chapters that follow, you will read about the structures of government, the many different ways in which societies are governed, the channels by which people take part in the political process, and the manner in which political decisions are reached and implemented. You will read about presidents and prime ministers, parliaments and congresses, democracies and dictatorships, constitutions and coups, elections and assassinations, and heroes and villains. In short, you will be reading about all the elements that make up government in its many different and intriguing forms around the world.

At the heart of the book is the comparative method. In the nine case studies that make up the book, you will see how politics is approached in societies with values and priorities that are sometimes the same, but sometimes very different. You will see how some countries address similar problems, how other countries have a very different set of priorities, how people relate to politics, and how comparison can help us draw up rules about politics and better understand our place in the global community.

These are the conventional goals of comparative politics, but since I wrote the first edition in the early 1990s, I have taken an unconventional approach to achieving those goals:

- Unlike most other textbooks, which still use the old cold war system of dividing the world into three groups of countries (rich ones, red ones, and poor ones), I have divided the world into six arenas that I believe provide a more realistic and balanced view of the way the world works today.

- Unlike most other textbooks, which devote as much as half their space to Western Europe, I have deliberately sacrificed two of the conventional case studies—Germany and France—to avoid the problems of eurocentrism that color most approaches to comparative politics and to pay more attention to the non-Western world, whose influence in our lives is growing.

- Unlike most other textbooks, which make few distinctions among the 135 countries of Africa, Asia, and Latin America, I argue that we have to distinguish among those that have developed new levels of wealth and stability (and are pulling away from the pack), those that are best understood in light of the political influence of Islam, and those whose progress has stalled.

As you read this book, you will find that politics is constantly changing and mutating and that you will be studying not just one moving target but several, and trying to come to grips with societies that are in a constant state of transition. If there is a single theme that ties the book together, it is change: its causes, it effects, and the impact that it has on the way in which governments evolve.

THE FOURTH EDITION

It has been gratifying to see how widely this book has been adopted for classes across the United States, in Canada, and in several other countries. Because the approach meets the needs of many instructors and students, this fourth edition uses the same basic structure and style, and most of the changes have come from incorporating developments in politics since the third edition went to press in early 2000. Alterations have also been made in response to suggestions from students and instructors.

Case studies This new edition keeps the same nine case studies, each of which has the same basic structure as before: history, institutions, processes, and policies. I have undertaken a thorough edit; tightened up the arguments; inserted new and more recent examples; injected more points of comparison; and updated all the key political, economic, and social data.

The arenas The historical sections in the part openers have been cut back to add more explanation of the features of each group of countries. A number of countries have also been moved from one arena to another in response to changes in those countries. For example, the Czech Republic, Poland, and South Korea are now listed as liberal democracies; Fiji has been moved to the LDC arena; and El Salvador and Panama have been reclassified as NICs.

Boxes These were a popular element in earlier editions, so they have been kept and about half of them cover entirely new topics. Every part opener now has a Checklist that briefly summarizes the key features of the countries in that group, and every case study includes boxes that focus on key personalities in history and/or politics, on key issues that influence government in the different case study countries, and on critical policy issues and political debates of the day. The material in the boxes continues to be overtly comparative, contrasting events, issues, and values across the nine cases.

Key Terms, Key People, and Study Questions The lists of key terms and people at the end of every chapter have been expanded, and—a change on previous editions—the terms have been highlighted in boldface where they appear in the text. Completely new sets of study questions have been developed, designed to encourage students to think about similarities and differences among the case study countries, to guide their analysis as they read, and perhaps to give them ideas for term papers.

Comparative Focus studies These appear at the end of every case study and are designed to illustrate the similarities and differences among countries by looking in depth at specific institutions and processes. They have all been updated for the fourth edition.

Internet sites The lists of Web sites have been completely overhauled and updated. They are all on my home page at *http://mypage.iu.edu/jmccormi/comp.html*, and I will be adding new sites and updating URLs as necessary.

Further Reading These lists have all been fully revised, with many new titles added. The focus continues to remain on the most recent work of the best-known scholars in each area, and a special effort has been made to go beyond the usual mainly American or European sources and to look at the work of local scholars and writers from each of the case study countries.

A NOTE ON SOURCES

In addition to the sources listed in the notes at the end of the book, I rely for news on a mixture of *The Economist*, CNN, MSNBC, BBC World News, National Public Radio, and BBC Online. For basic economic and social data in the book, I mainly used the World Development Indicators database maintained by the World Bank, available on their Web site at *http://www.worldbank.com*.

ACKNOWLEDGMENTS

A book like this demands the help and support of a lot of people. Above all, I want to thank the nearly 1,250 students who have passed through my comparative politics classes at IUPUI since 1989. I wrote the first edition because of concerns that I and they had about the texts we were using, and their comments and questions have encouraged me to constantly refine and rethink my approach to this book. Wadsworth also solicited opinions from specialist outside reviewers, who both fortified my belief in the unconventional approach of the book and made useful suggestions for changes and additions. For their help, input, and often detailed comments, I would like to thank the following:

Dr. Tricia Gray, University of Louisville

Sean K. Anderson, Associate Professor, Political Science Department, Idaho State University, Pocatello, Idaho

Mark A. Cichock, University of Texas at Arlington

Scott Ditloff, University of the Incarnate Word

Joy Chaudhuri, Arizona State University

Rebecca Kingston, University of Toronto

Dr. Samuel B. Hoff, Delaware State University

My particular thanks to Heather Hogan, assistant editor, for ensuring that the process of revision was smooth and efficient. My thanks also to David Tatom, Edward Wade, and the production team—particularly Suzanne Kastner for her excellent work on production, Nancy Spellman for her fine work as photo researcher, and to series editor Howard Wiarda for his help on the project, dating back to 1991. Thanks to my colleague Scott Pegg for reading through the Nigeria chapter and making a number of useful additions. Finally, my love and thanks to my wife Leanne and my sons Ian and Stuart for giving my work its real meaning—this new edition is dedicated to them.

About the Author

John McCormick is professor and chair of political science at Indiana University–Purdue University at Indianapolis (IUPUI). He has studied at Rhodes University (South Africa), the University of London, and Indiana University; has been a visiting professor at Exeter University in Britain; has lived and worked in Britain, Kenya, Zimbabwe, South Africa, and the United States; and has traveled widely through North America, Europe, Southeast Africa, and Southeast Asia.

Before completing his Ph.D. in political science, he worked in the public sector for two environmental interest groups and was a consultant for a number of specialized agencies of the United Nations, including FAO and UNEP. His teaching and research interests lie in comparative politics and public policy, with particular interests in environmental policy, British politics, and the politics of the European Union. His other publications include *Environmental Policy in the European Union* (London: Palgrave, 2001), *Contemporary Britain* (London: Palgrave, 2003), and *The European Union: Politics and Policies* (Boulder, CO: Westview, 3rd edition, 2004).

Brief Contents

Contents

Tables and Figures

Boxed Items

INTRODUCTION

Without comparisons to make, the mind does not know how to proceed.

—Alexis de Tocqueville, French author, 1830s

The future is already here—it's just unevenly distributed.

—William Gibson, science fiction writer

These are exciting times to be studying politics. Over the last decade, the world has been undergoing dramatic change, at a pace almost unparalleled in history. The forces driving these developments are many and complicated and are among the major topics of this book. At their core has been the rapid evolution of new technology, which has made it easier and cheaper for people to communicate. Cell phones, email, and faxes allow us to contact almost anyone in the world in a matter of seconds, at little cost. Digital television and the Internet make it easier for us to find information on almost anything and to be updated on news from around the world almost instantaneously.

Because of these rapid advances in communication technology, events in other parts of the world now have a more direct and immediate impact on our lives. When the United States was in its formative years, it could take weeks and even months for political news to spread across the country, and it could take weeks or months for political leaders to hear about—and respond to—crises. Today, a bomb can go off in Israel, an election can be held in Brazil, the stock market can make gains in London, a politician can make a speech in South Africa, and we can hear about it within minutes and can often watch it live on television or the Web. Also, political leaders can respond to crises as they emerge, no matter how many thousands of miles away they may be happening. The world is a much smaller place than it has ever been, and we are much more immediately affected by what is going on in almost every part of it.

It is links of this kind that now make it critically important for all of us to try to understand what is happening not just at the national level but at the global level. It can be difficult, to be sure, because events move fast and there is much disagreement on the causes of political change, and on the best way of approaching the study of that change. But we must at least *try* to understand and explain what is happening, and one of the tools we have available is comparative politics.

WHAT IS COMPARATIVE POLITICS?

Politics is the process by which two or more people make decisions on issues of mutual interest. It may be that one of those people has control and the others do what he says, or it may be that they decide to negotiate and reach a compromise.

Either way, they have a political relationship, and they need to decide how best to relate to one another and how best to reach decisions. The politics we find within the home is fairly simple, but as we move through communities, cities, states, and countries, it involves more pressures and more decisions and is therefore more difficult to understand.

The study of political science is divided into several subfields. Opinions differ on the definition of these subfields, but most of your professors will probably agree that they include national politics, comparative politics, international relations, political theory, and perhaps public policy. Comparative politics has become increasingly important in recent years because so much of political science now involves comparison. A political science professor may be a specialist in American politics, but the chances are that he or she will make comparisons between the United States and other countries to better understand and illustrate what is happening in the United States.

Comparative politics involves studying the institutions, character, and performance of government and the political process in different countries to (1) better understand how politics works and (2) draw up rules about politics. Unlike physical scientists, social scientists do not have laboratories in which they can study political systems in their search for rules and laws. Instead, they use countries as laboratories and compare politics across those countries. This is the **comparative method,** which is one of the oldest tools of political science. It was used as early as the fourth century B.C. by the Greek philosopher Aristotle, who compared political systems to develop theories about which was best. The underlying argument for the use of comparison is that "knowledge of the self is gained through knowledge of others."[1] We can (and do) study the politics of a single country, but to truly understand its features and characteristics, we need to compare that country with others.

Take the question of political parties. The United States is dominated by just two: the Democrats and the Republicans. Political scientists have developed plenty of explanations for that dominance: The two big parties are good at incorporating the policies of third parties, strongly ideological parties are not popular with American voters, the United States has a tradition of two-party politics, the two big parties control the electoral system to their advantage, and so on. But to fully understand why the Democrats and the Republicans are so strong, we need to study other democracies to establish how many of them also have two-party systems (and why) and how many do not (and why not). One explanation offered by comparison is that the United States lacks the kind of regional, religious, linguistic, or social divisions that have produced multiple political parties in many Western European countries. Another explanation is that the math of the American electoral system tends to produce a two-party arrangement, whereas many European countries use a system known as proportional representation, which makes it easier for small parties to win seats in legislatures.

What are the benefits of studying politics using the comparative method?

- **Comparison can help us make sense of a confusing global system.** Keeping up with political changes in one country is difficult enough, because we are always dealing with a moving target. Keeping up with political developments around the world creates multiple additional layers of complexity, because there are multiple moving targets whose relationships with one another are always changing. One way of trying to sort through the confusion—to better understand the forces that bring political change, to better understand the significance of that change, and to better understand the impact on our own lives of such change—is to undertake a comparative study of different political systems.

- **Comparison can help us understand ourselves.** By studying the ways in which other societies govern themselves, we can better understand the character, origins, strengths, and weaknesses of our own system of government. Comparison can give us more insight into how power is distributed and limited, can give us a broader perspective of our place in the world, and can help us better understand our response to different kinds of problems.

- **Comparison can broaden our options.** Studying other political systems can show us how similar problems are approached by different governments and perhaps offer us ideas that might help us improve the way we do things in our own country or avoid the mistakes made by others. How do other countries manage their education systems and distribute welfare? Which countries have the best record on controlling air and water pollution? Why do voter turnout figures vary so much from one country to another?

- **Comparison can broaden our horizons.** When we think about other people and societies, myths and stereotypes too often come into play and we are too easily influenced by ethnocentrism: regarding our own culture as superior and seeing the world through our eyes rather than through the eyes of others. By studying the way other countries govern themselves and by trying to understand their problems and the way they see the world, we can build a more balanced view of the world, avoiding prejudice and nationalism and better appreciating the variety and complexity of human society.

- **Comparison can help us draw up rules about politics.** Just as no credible zoologist would try to draw up rules about animal behavior without studying and comparing different species, no credible political scientist would try to draw up universal rules about political behavior without studying the structures and values of government in different countries. The study of different political systems can help us develop and test explanations of the trends and underlying principles of politics and help us better understand, explain, and predict political change.

Comparison is not necessarily about deciding which political system is best. Instead, it involves studying different systems with a view to learning more about how and why they are different or the same and what effects the differences and similarities have. If the study of the French bureaucracy can help us understand why it is relatively efficient and professional and provide us with pointers to features that other countries might want to adopt, that is all well and good. But a comparison of the way the bureaucracies of France, Germany, Japan, and the United States are structured would provide us with more insight into the government of each country.

Although the benefits of comparative politics are many, political scientists have yet to agree on the best way of making the comparisons. Things would be easy if there were just a few countries to compare, but there are nearly 190, and although they are similar in some respects, they are different in others. Their political institutions come in varied forms, they organize power in different ways, and their citizens use different channels to influence government. Also, different countries have different economic philosophies, they have remarkable social and cultural variety, and they come in many different sizes. In order to find our way through the maze, we need a system of **classification.** This way we can group countries with similar features and concentrate on how and why these groups are different.

No one system of classification is perfect, mainly because political systems are constantly evolving. The approaches taken by Aristotle (who distinguished between states ruled by one person, by a few people, and by many people) or the 18th century French philosopher Montesquieu (who distinguished between republics, monarchies, and despotic systems) would not tell us much about 21st century political realities because the world is a much more complicated and varied place than it was 2,300 years ago or even 250 years ago.

The ideal system of classification is one that is simple, neat, consistent, logical, and useful. Unfortunately, political scientists have yet to agree on the best approach. Examples of past systems of classification include the following:

- The **structural-functional model,** which sees government as a system made up of structures (institutions) that perform certain functions, and compares how they perform[2]
- The study of **sources of authority,** including traditional (or hereditary) authority, charismatic authority, and legal authority[3]
- A system based around democratic/parliamentary systems (such as the United States or Britain), fascist/authoritarian systems (such as Nazi Germany), and communist systems (such as the old Soviet Union)[4]

These approaches have their value, but they are too narrow and too academic. They may be simple and neat, but they fail to recognize the broader realities of national political systems or of the global environment of which they are a part.

A much broader approach was taken during the cold war (1945–1990), when a **Three Worlds system** of classification was adopted:

- A First World of wealthy, democratic industrialized states, which—by implication—included most of those countries in the Western alliance against communism
- A Second World of communist regimes, which—also by implication—included most of those countries ranged against the Western alliance
- A Third World of poorer, less democratic, and less developed countries, some of which took sides in the cold war, and some of which did not

The system has a strange history. It came out of the *tiers monde,* the "third force" of French political parties in the 1940s that supported neither the government of the Fourth Republic nor the policies of Charles de Gaulle.[5] In 1952, the French demographer Alfred Sauvy borrowed the concept to describe a "third world" of countries that were aligning themselves neither with the West nor with the Soviet bloc during the cold war.[6] The label stuck, and by the late 1960s the so-called developing countries of Africa, Asia, and Latin America were routinely being described as the Third

World. Counting backward, communist states were described as the Second World and industrialized democracies as the First World.

This system was simple and neat and provided evocative labels that could be dropped with ease into everyday conversation. The term *Third World* still elicits powerful images of poverty, inefficiency, underdevelopment, and political instability. The problem, though, is that the system is misleading. The First World always had the most internal logic because its members had (and still have) the most in common. The Second World was always more of a problem because communism was interpreted differently by its members; also, communism was never actually applied as anticipated by its most influential theorist, Karl Marx. As for the Third World, it never had much internal consistency because its 135 members had very little in common: Some were rich, others were poor, some were democratic, others were dictatorships, some had civilian governments, others had military governments, some were industrialized, and others were agrarian. It was little more than a label of convenience.

The fatal blows to the Three Worlds system were struck by the end of the cold war, which not only saw many Second World countries adopting political systems and economic policies at odds with the principles of communism but also revealed many of the inconsistencies in the idea of the Third World. In particular, the logic of the latter was undermined by the emergence of a group of wealthy Asian and Latin American countries whose successes dispelled the popular image of the huddled masses of the Third World. Symbolically, U.S. President George Bush made a speech to Congress in March 1991 in which he spoke of the emergence of a **"new world order,"** and although neither he nor political science gave much definition to the concept, few doubted that he was right.

Despite the new realities, the influence of the Three Worlds system lives on in political science, as a survey of other introductory comparative politics texts reveals. Some still overtly use the three-way classification, for example, dividing the world into industrial democracies, communist and postcommunist systems, and Third World countries. There are others that use the system but have merely changed the labels, presumably to appear more modern. Yet others avoid using a system of classification altogether but still use country case studies, their choice reflecting the three-way division.

The Three Worlds system also lives on in the Western bias evident in the work of many comparative political scientists. The First World has always attracted more study, partly because most political scientists come from the First World and partly because its features are more consistent, making it easier to study. This is why the authors of most comparative politics textbooks published in the United States typically devote as much as half their space to First World case studies, giving the Third World very short shrift—this despite the fact that First World countries account for just 16 percent of the world's population, whereas Third World countries account for 55 percent of the population (or 76 percent if China is included). There is an irony here, because, as noted earlier, one of the principles of the comparative method is that it can help us avoid ethnocentrism, and it should ideally be based on a balanced view of the different shades and varieties in which politics and government are conducted around the world.

To avoid these two key problems—misleading or unrepresentative systems of classification and an ethnocentric view of the world—this text is based on a system of classification that still harks back in some ways to the Three Worlds model, but it makes some significant adjustments.

A DIFFERENT WAY OF SEEING THE WORLD

The inconsistencies in human nature will always make it difficult, if not impossible, to develop a watertight system of comparing political systems. But as we begin a new millennium, we need to approach the study of comparative politics from a perspective that more accurately reflects the realities of a world that is very different from the way it was during the cold war. Also, although there is something to be said for taking the term *comparative politics* literally and studying only the structures and functions of political systems, we need to place politics within its broader context. Thus, we need to look as well at the economic and social pressures on government and at the impact of political decisions on the economy and society. For these reasons, this book uses a system based on a closer reading of the realities of the post–cold war world and on a combination of three sets of variables.

Political Variables

Deciding how to distinguish among different political systems is difficult, because many different measures are available. Should we categorize them on the basis of institutions (for example, presidential versus parliamentary systems), on the basis of philosophy (democratic versus authoritarian), or on the basis of levels of control (unitary versus federal)? This book takes the broad view and is based on the argument that the best way to understand different countries is to look at their records in meeting the basic needs of their people. It does this by examining several different performance indicators:

- The structures of their systems of government
- Their records on human rights and democracy
- The relationship between citizens and government
- Popular ideas about the role of the state
- Relative levels of political legitimacy

These concepts cannot be measured objectively, but one helpful indicator is the index developed by **Freedom House,** an international nonprofit organization (cofounded by Eleanor Roosevelt) that categorizes countries according to their records on political rights (the ability of people to participate in the political process) and civil liberties (including freedom of expression, the independence of the judiciary, personal autonomy, and economic rights). The rating system divides countries into three groups—Free, Partly Free, and Not Free—and gives them scores of 1 to 7 on the scales of political rights and civil liberties. So whereas Canada and the United States do well (a rating of Free and a 1 on each scale), Russia does not do so well (Partly Free and a 5 on each scale) and Egypt does poorly (Not Free and a 6 on each scale) (see Table 1). We can quibble with some of the ratings and the scale is by no means comprehensive, but it is a useful point of reference and discussion.

TABLE 1

Freedom House Ratings

	Political rights	Civil liberties	Freedom rating
United States	1	1	Free
Canada	1	1	Free
Britain	1	2	Free
Japan	1	2	Free
Mexico	2	3	Free
India	2	3	Free
Nigeria	4	5	Partly Free
Russia	5	5	Partly Free
Egypt	6	6	Not Free
China	7	6	Not Free

Source: Freedom House Web site, 2003, *http://freedomhouse.org.*

Economic Variables

Countries are classified according to the size and structure of their economies and according to the nature of their economic policies. The standard measure of the size of economies is **gross domestic product (GDP),** which gives a dollar value to all the goods and services produced by a country in a year.* Not everyone agrees that GDP is the best measure, in part because it is hard to be sure that everything is being counted (for example, we can do no more than guess at the size of the black market in some countries) and in part because it is difficult to give a value to every economic activity (for example, how do you measure the value of intellectual wealth, or of voluntary work, or the potential value of natural resources?). GDP is also criticized because it does not take into account the real value of national currencies, some of which are overvalued relative to the U.S. dollar. To counteract this problem, some economists prefer to convert the figures using **purchasing power parity,** which corrects for anomalies in the value of different currencies.

Despite its problems, GDP is the most common measure of economic wealth. It reveals that the United States is by far the wealthiest economy in the world, with a GDP of more than $10 trillion. The Japanese, the Chinese, and the four big European countries follow, all with GDPs of between $1 trillion and $4 trillion. By contrast, the poorest countries in the world count their GDPs not in the trillions or the billions, but in the *millions* (see Table 2).

GDP provides a measure of the absolute size of national economies but does not take into account population size, so it is only of limited value to comparative politics.

---

*An alternative measure is **gross national product** (GNP), which adds to the total the value of all goods and services produced by a country's government and corporations overseas. It is less popular.

TABLE 2

Comparing Economies

	GDP (in billions of dollars)		Per capita GDP (in dollars)
United States	10,171	Luxembourg	39,840
Japan	4,245	Japan	35,990
Germany	1,846	United States	34,870
Britain	1,406	Britain	24,230
China	1,159	Canada	21,340
Canada	677	Mexico	5,540
Mexico	618	Russia	1,750
India	477	Egypt	1,530
Russia	310	China	890
Egypt	97	India	460
Nigeria	41	Nigeria	290
Kiribati	0.04	Ethiopia	100
WORLD	31,284	WORLD	5,140

Source: World Bank, World Development Indicators database, 2003, *http://www.worldbank.com*. Figures for 2001.

More useful is GDP per person, which gives us a better idea of the relative economic wealth of different countries. If we divide GDP by population, we see that Luxembourg heads the table with a **per capita GDP** at nearly $40,000, that the United States is in the top ten with nearly $35,000, and that countries such as Burundi and Ethiopia share last place with a per capita GDP of just $100. Put another way, it takes 350 Ethiopians to produce as much in a year as one American.

We can also tell much about the differences among countries by looking at **economic structure.** All economic activity falls into one of three categories: industry (which produces tangible, manufactured goods), services (which deal in intangibles, such as insurance, financial services, and retail), and agriculture. Generally speaking, the richer a country, the more it earns from services; the poorer a country, the more it earns from agriculture. Services are more profitable and indicate the existence of a sophisticated economy and an educated workforce. Agriculture is much less profitable, relies on government subsidies in wealthy countries, and is often very low scale in poorer countries. So in liberal democracies such as the United States or Canada, services account for as much as two-thirds of GDP and agriculture accounts for only a very small percentage. By contrast, newly industrializing countries are still earning a lot from industry and less from services, whereas the poorest countries in the world have relatively little industry and many of their people still rely on agriculture for a living (see Figure 1).

FIGURE 1

Comparing Economic Structures

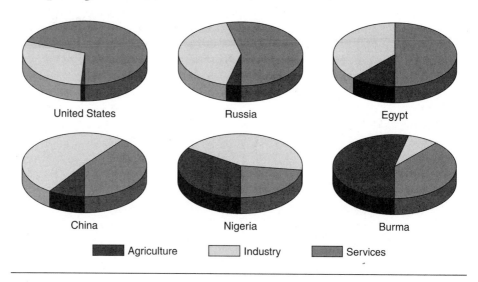

United States   Russia   Egypt

China   Nigeria   Burma

■ Agriculture   □ Industry   ▨ Services

Source: World Bank, World Development Indicators database, 2003, *http://www.worldbank.com*. Figures for 2000–2001.

Finally, we need to look at **economic policies,** because governments approach economic management in different ways. Whereas free-market systems such as the United States, Britain, and Japan have less government control over the economy and less public ownership of industries and services, centrally planned systems such as China have more government regulation and ownership. Meanwhile, emerging Asian and Latin American states have seen their governments adopting increasingly free-market policies, and less successful countries have failed to develop economic stability and are handicapped by problems such as an overvalued national currency, high inflation, an inability to raise taxes efficiently, corruption, inefficiency, and a large black market.

One useful indicator of economic policies is the **Economic Freedom Index** developed by the Fraser Institute, a Canadian nonprofit organization that studies markets and the way they work. Arguing that the key ingredients of economic freedom are personal choice, voluntary exchange, freedom to compete, and protection of individuals and property, the Institute ranks 123 countries according to factors such as the size of government income and spending, how the law protects people and property, monetary policies, and trade policies. It then gives those countries a ranking on a scale of 10 to 1, with 10 being the freest. It finds that Hong Kong and Singapore have the highest ratings (8.8 and 8.6), that most liberal democracies rank 7.5 or better, and that Russia and China rank toward the bottom of the index, among a motley list of Asian and African states (see Table 3).

TABLE 3

Economic Freedom Ratings

	Ranking	Score
Hong Kong	1	8.8
Singapore	2	8.6
United States	3	8.5
Britain	4	8.4
Canada	8	8.0
Japan	24	7.3
Egypt	51	6.7
Mexico	66	6.3
India	73	6.1
China	101	5.3
Nigeria	101	5.3
Russia	116	4.7
Congo, Dem. Republic	123	3.2

Source: Fraser Institute Web site, 2003, *http://www.fraserinstitute.ca*.

Social Variables

We can learn about different political systems by studying institutions and political processes (like voting and party activity), but to better understand the performance of these systems, the best place to look is at the **quality of life** in different countries. What kind of job are they doing in terms of meeting the basic needs of their people, and how do they compare with one another? There are three standard measures of quality of life (see Figure 2):

- *Life expectancy*, or the age to which the average resident of a country can expect to live. This is used as an indicator of the quality of health care, but it can also say something about diet, food and water quality, air quality, and levels of public safety; life expectancy in countries torn by civil war can be significantly reduced. The figures range from a high of about 75–80 in the most successful countries, to about 55–65 in countries with medium levels of development, and a low of 38–50 in the most troubled countries.

- *Infant mortality*, or the number of newborn babies that die within 30 days of birth, expressed as a figure per 1,000 live births. This is another indicator of the quality of health care. Unfortunately, infant mortality is a fact of life, and even in the most medically advanced societies there will be some babies born with severe medical problems or dangerously premature who will die. The figures range from a high of about 4–10 per 1,000 in the most successful countries to a low of as many as 150 per 1,000 in countries with the least advanced health care systems.

FIGURE 2

Comparing Quality of Life

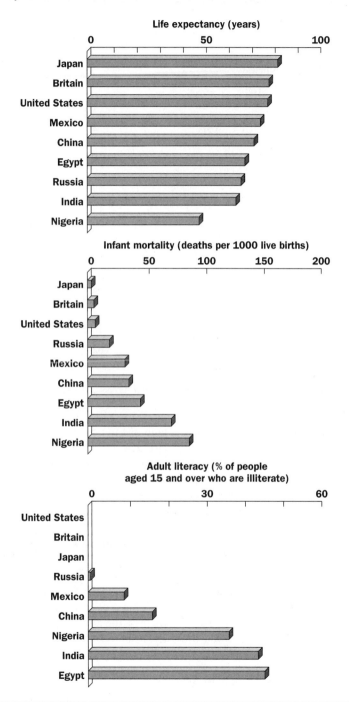

Life expectancy (years)

Infant mortality (deaths per 1000 live births)

Adult literacy (% of people aged 15 and over who are illiterate)

Source: World Bank, World Development Indicators database, 2003, *http://www.worldbank.com.* Figures for 2001.

TABLE 4

Human Development Ratings

	Ranking	Rating
Norway	1	High
Australia	2	High
Canada	3	High
Sweden	4	High
Belgium	5	High
United States	6	High
Japan	9	High
Britain	14	High
Mexico	51	Medium
Russia	55	Medium
China	87	Medium
Egypt	105	Medium
India	115	Medium
Nigeria	136	Low
Sierra Leone	162	Low

Source: United Nations Development Program Web site, *http://hdr.undp.org.*

- *Adult literacy*, or the percentage of the population that can read and write. Unfortunately the definitions of literacy vary from one country to another, and even in countries that claim 100 percent literacy, there are many people who can do no more than read road signs and make only the simplest math calculations. Most industrialized countries claim literacy rates of 100 percent, whereas the rates in poorer countries can be as low as 40 percent.

Several social indicators are used in the **Human Development Index (HDI),** a ranking developed by the UN Development Program. Using life expectancy, adult literacy rates, educational enrollment, and per capita GDP, it rates most of the countries in the world, ranking their human development as high, medium, or low. On the 2001 index, Canada and the United States did well, ranking third and sixth, respectively. Most other rich countries were in the top 30, whereas the poorest countries ranked at the bottom of the table, 127th and lower, with Sierra Leone in last place at 162 (see Table 4).

THE SIX ARENAS

Using these three sets of variables produces six different arenas within which we can classify countries for the purposes of comparison. The boundaries that separate the countries in each arena are debatable; some countries can be classified with more confidence than others, their features are often relative rather than absolute, and membership of the different arenas is transitory. Some countries firmly fit the characteristics of each arena, and some are more peripheral (see Figure 3). Broadly speaking, though, the six arenas work out as follows.

Liberal Democracies

This arena contains 31 mainly European and North American countries with stable and legitimate systems of government; high Freedom House, Economic Freedom, and HDI ratings; wealthy free-market economies based mainly on services; and highly developed and generally efficient social services. If there were some kind of Darwinian scale of political evolution, it could be argued that liberal democracies have advanced further than any others. They are, however, not perfect. Capitalism is criticized for its focus on material wealth, and no one can claim to live in a society in which everyone has equal opportunity regardless of race, gender, religion, sexual preference, educational background, or economic circumstances. But liberal democracies have traveled a long way down the path to that ideal.

The **United States** is used as the first case study because it is obviously an important point of departure for Americans, but also because non-American students will find it important to understand how this powerful and influential system of government works. The American model has also been copied—in whole or in part—in many other countries, so we need to study the U.S. Constitution and American political institutions to understand why and how they have influenced and been adapted by those other countries.

Britain is used as the second case study because it is the home of the parliamentary system and of many of the ideas behind modern capitalism and democracy and because it provides some good contrasts with the United States. We could learn about parliamentary systems by studying Canada or Sweden, but we would always be referring to British precedent. The British political system is also interesting because of the changes that it has undergone since the end of World War II and continues to undergo as it develops a new role for itself as a mid-sized power and a member of the European Union.

Japan is included because of its economic importance in the world, because it shows how liberal democracy can take root outside the West, and because it is a parliamentary democracy with a distinctive political culture and some interesting variations on the parliamentary model. Japan's economic transformation since World War II has been remarkable, but—paradoxically—it finds itself struggling to make reforms aimed at providing lasting political and economic stability. Its record may give us insight into the changes we can expect in Southeast Asian states that are experiencing rapid economic growth.

Communist and Postcommunist (CPC) Countries

This arena contains 29 mainly Eastern European and Asian countries whose modern histories have been dominated by one-party governments claiming to be building communist states and by economic policies driven by central planning and rapid industrialization. None of them are actually communist, nor have they ever been, and most have turned their backs on communism and headed off in several different

FIGURE 3

Overlapping Arenas

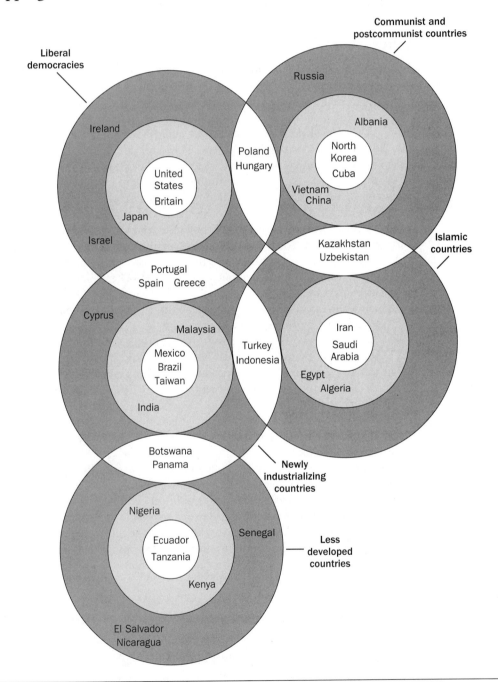

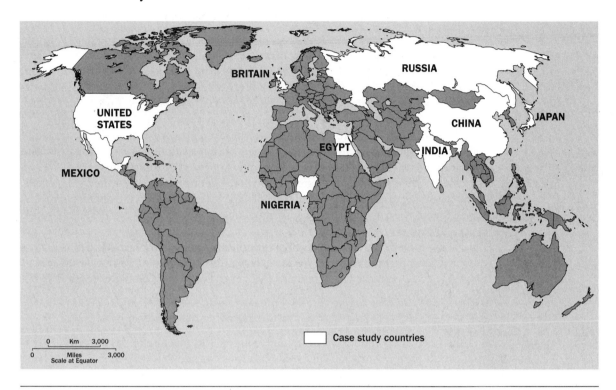

FIGURE 4

The World Today

Case study countries

directions. Some have become liberal democracies, some are moving into the Islamic orbit, and only five (China, Cuba, Laos, North Korea, and Vietnam) still officially subscribe to communism, but not always very convincingly. This group of countries has very different Freedom House, Economic Freedom, and HDI ratings. For now, though, they are still best understood in light of their "communist" past.

Russia is used as the first case study because of its importance to understanding the history of communism, because of its leading role in the former Soviet Union and in the demise of communism, and because of the problems of adjustment it shares with many of its Eastern European neighbors. As the erstwhile competitor to the Western alliance in the cold war, Russia also is a source of continuing fascination for North American and European students. Russia now faces the challenges of building a stable and democratic political system, restructuring its economy, and making related social adjustments.

China was chosen because it is an ancient culture, because it includes one-fifth of the world's population, and because of its rise to global economic power. It also helps bridge the gap between urban-based Soviet-style socialism and peasant-based socialism, showing how Marxism has been adapted to non-European and mainly agrarian societies. In some respects, it could also be approached as a newly industrializing country, but as long as the Communist party holds on to its monopoly on power, China will remain predominantly communist.

Newly Industrializing Countries (NICs)

The label *newly industrializing* has been used by social scientists since the 1970s but has yet to make its way into the mainstream of comparative politics, despite its value to comparative analysis. It is applied in this text to 32 mainly Southeast and South Asian, Caribbean, and Latin American countries undergoing the kind of rapid political, economic, social, and technological change that occurred in Europe and North America in the 18th and 19th centuries. These states are building stable systems of government; have high to medium Freedom House, Economic Freedom, and HDI ratings; enjoy a growing variety of channels of representation and participation; and are experiencing rapid industrialization and export-led economic growth.

Mexico may have a small economy, national debt problems, human rights abuses, and severe disparities in the distribution of wealth and political power, but its industrial base is rapidly expanding and it has seen political continuity since the 1930s. It also has obvious interest for the United States and Canada, given that all three countries are partners in the North American Free Trade Agreement (NAFTA). Mexico is a good point of comparison with the United States given that both countries began from a roughly equal political and economic base, yet evolved very differently. Political stability has helped promote economic growth in Mexico, which has in turn brought democratic reform.

India is used as the second example of a newly industrializing country because it offers fascinating contrasts: It is a huge country with deep religious and ethnic divisions and great poverty and the vast majority of its people earn a living off the land, yet it has a vibrant and democratic political tradition and a record in industrial and technological development that has allowed it to launch its own space and nuclear weapons programs. Rapid population growth could soon make India the world's most populous country, but it needs to ensure that the quality of life for its people continues to improve quickly enough to prevent religious, class, and economic differences from boiling over and undermining the foundations of the Indian state.

Less Developed Countries (LDCs)

This arena consists of 35 mainly African, Central American, and Pacific Island states that have the potential to build political, economic, and social stability but face short-term handicaps. Some are building strong democratic records, some are politically stable but poor, others are overcoming major obstacles to rebuild their political and economic systems, and a few have great economic potential but many social handicaps. Most have elected civilian governments, although political stability is often compromised by corruption, social divisions, poor human rights records, and the intervention of the military. Most have a low per capita GDP, a limited economic base, and poorly developed social services, with medium to low Freedom House, Economic Freedom, and HDI ratings.

Nigeria is used as the case study because it is an ideal laboratory for the study of the problems of state-building in the postcolonial era. It has experimented with different forms of civilian government in an attempt to build stability, but it has suffered from many years of military government. Nigeria also provides insight into the problems of sub-Saharan Africa, an area about which most North Americans know much too little. Its ethnic and religious divisions exemplify problems elsewhere in the continent; they led to civil war in the late 1960s and have undermined Nigeria's experiments with civilian government. The challenges facing Nigeria include building a common national identity and a stable system of government and reducing the role of the military in politics.

Islamic Countries

Where this book breaks most obviously with convention is in approaching Islamic countries as a separate arena. It does this because Islam is the only major monotheistic religion in the world that offers its adherents an entire way of life, including a political system and a body of law. It also does this because Islam is the key political and social force in most of the countries with Muslim majorities. The failure of the West to understand the political nature of Islam is unfortunate, but the growing conflict between Islamic extremists and the West has encouraged us to pay more attention to the nature of Islam, and more political scientists now appreciate its ideological significance. The ongoing tensions between Islam and the West also underline the importance of better understanding these countries.

The arena includes 26 mainly North African and Middle Eastern states where Islam is the religion of the majority and where it plays a significant actual or potential role in politics and government. Although Islamic countries have very different levels of political, economic, and social development, their adherence to Islam is ultimately the most important factor in understanding how they work. However, several countries are excluded because they are better understood (at least for now) in other contexts: The Islamic republics of the former USSR are still influenced by their communist past, Indonesia and Turkey are secular states best approached as NICs, and most sub-Saharan African states with large Islamic populations are better understood as LDCs.

Egypt was chosen as the case study because of its key role in the Islamic world, the Middle East, and the Arab world; because of its strategic importance; because of what its history and political development say about the changing relationship between Islam and the West; and because of the tension in Egypt between religious revivalism and secular modernism, which is common to many Islamic states. Egypt is struggling to build its economy; to stay on good terms with Israel, its Arab neighbors, and the West; and to prevent the activities of Islamic opposition groups from spilling over into revolution. Given Western concern for stability in the oil-rich Persian Gulf, Egypt's welfare is at the forefront of North American and European foreign policy interests.

Marginal Countries

This arena coincides with the UN definition of the poorest countries in the world, which it describes as "least developed countries." However, while the UN factors only per capita GDP, economic structure, and adult literacy into its calculations, marginal states are defined here according to a broader set of political, economic, and social criteria. This group includes 35 mainly sub-Saharan African states with problems that include some or all of the following:

- Political instability, persistent military government, and occasional breakdown into near anarchy and even genocide
- Deep social divisions and sometimes extended civil war
- Poor records on human rights and a very low Freedom House rating
- Few independent or competing sources of political power
- A very limited economic base, with an average per capita GDP of less than $1,500
- Extensive black markets
- A primarily agricultural workforce or few natural resources or exports
- A heavy dependence on foreign aid
- Sometimes serious public health problems and a low ranking on the HDI
- Decaying or minimal infrastructure
- In some cases, deliberate isolation from the international community and disputed legal status

These problems often have different causes, and political scientists are much less ready to agree why these countries are in trouble than they are to agree—for example—why liberal democracies are so successful.

THE CASE STUDIES

Every case study used in the book is structured around the same four questions: Who governs? How do they govern? How do people take part in politics? and With what results? To do this, and to help the process of comparison, each case study is divided into the same four sections:

- **Political development and political culture.** History tells us how political systems have evolved, which is essential to understanding them today. For example, it would be difficult to understand Russian politics without knowing about the influence of Stalin or to understand Indian or Nigerian politics without appreciating the impact of colonialism. Each case study begins with an overview of how government and the state have evolved in that country and then looks at the key features of political culture or the prevailing political values and attitudes of its citizens.
- **The political system.** Understanding how political institutions work is essential for comparison. We need to know how they function, how they relate to each other, from where they derive their authority, the limits that are placed on their powers, and the impact that citizens have on their work. To these ends, this section describes the institutional "rules" of the political system and analyzes and explains the relationships among its elements.

- **Representation and participation.** Government consists of a network of systems and processes, with leaders and citizens relating to each other in a large and complex series of games. This section focuses on the inputs into those systems, or the ways in which people take part (or are prevented from taking part) in politics. They may do this through voting, lobbying, demonstrating, or supporting political parties and interest groups, but they may also do it through bribery, intimidation, violence, and murder.

- **Public policies.** Just as we need to understand institutions and inputs, so we need to understand the outputs of politics: what governments actually do or do not do to meet the needs of their citizens. Although most governments routinely deal with dozens of policy issues, this section in each case covers two of the most important: economic policy and foreign policy. The goal is to use these examples to compare the policy priorities of each country, to understand how agendas evolve, and to see how policies are made and implemented.

KEY TERMS

classification
comparative method
Economic Freedom Index
economic policies
economic structure
Freedom House Index
gross domestic product
(GDP)

gross national product
(GNP)
Human Development
Index (HDI)
new world order
per capita GDP
political culture

purchasing power parity
quality of life
sources of authority
structural-functional
model
Three Worlds system

COMPARATIVE POLITICS ONLINE

Every chapter of this book has a list of recommended Web sites relating to politics in the different countries covered. There are also a growing number of Web sites that offer general information on multiple countries. Among the best are the following:

Political Resources on the Net: *http://www.politicalresources.net*
Offers a wealth of information on every country in the world, including elections, parties, government institutions, and the media.
Elections around the World: *http://www.electionworld.org*
Related to the above site, with all the latest news on elections.
Inter-Parliamentary Union: *http://www.ipu.org*
A site containing useful information and statistics on legislatures around the world.
Library of Congress: *http://lcweb2.loc.gov/frd/cs*
Contains brief studies of countries all over the world, including the nine in this book.
United Nations: *http://www.un.org*
Official Web site of the UN, with links to all its specialized agencies.

BBC News: *http://news.bbc.co.uk*
Probably the best source of truly international news on the Web.

CIA World Factbook: *http://www.odci.gov/cia/publications/factbook/index.html*
Contains basic political, economic, geographical, and demographic information on every country in the world. Updated annually.

Amnesty International Online: *http://www.amnesty.org*
Home page of the respected human rights organization, which includes reports on the human rights situation in nearly 150 countries.

Part I

LIBERAL DEMOCRACIES

Democracy is the worst form of government except all those other forms that have been tried from time to time.

—Winston Churchill, British statesman

By almost every measure, liberal democracies are the most successful societies in the world. They are the freest and most stable, they are the wealthiest and most economically productive, and they have the strongest records on human rights and on providing their citizens with basic social services. They are not perfect by any means and are still troubled by racism, sexism, elitism, exploitation, political corruption, corporate greed, and threats to the environment, but by most measures of human development, they have more fully met the needs of more of their citizens than any other type of political system.

It should be relatively easy to describe and understand their major characteristics, especially given that we all think we know how to define democracy—free elections, freedom of speech, the rule of law, civil rights, government by "the people," and so on. Unfortunately, the reality is not so simple. Liberal democracy is a complex idea surrounded by a fog of philosophical confusion. No political concept has been studied in more detail and yet been so loosely applied that it sometimes seems that almost any society can be described as democratic if the definition is stretched far enough.

Broadly speaking, liberal democracies have six major sets of features that make them distinctive.

Liberalism

One of the most universal of all political concepts, liberalism is also one of the most misunderstood, partly because it has at least three different meanings. An ideological liberal is someone who believes in greater government involvement in people's lives as a way of redistributing wealth, equalizing opportunity, and righting social wrongs. Such a person also supports a managed economy, welfare, higher taxes, and affirmative action. These views are identified in the United States with the Democratic party.

However, ideological liberalism has little to do with the word *liberal* in the term *liberal democracy*, which stems from two other meanings:

- **Classical liberalism** is an arrangement designed to achieve **limited government,** typically through a **social contract,** which is an agreement between government and citizens regarding their obligations to one another and outlining the limits on the powers of government. The broad idea is that government will represent the interests of the people while citizens will respect the law. The embodiment of a social contract is a constitution, which is designed to outline the powers of government, the limits on the powers of government, and the rights of citizens. The majority will prevail, but the rights of minorities are also protected. The extent to which a constitution is respected and applied in practice tells us much about the nature of a system of government.

- **Economic liberalism** (otherwise known as **capitalism**) is an approach to the marketplace based on a belief in private property, a limited government role in the economy, and the promotion of a free market driven by supply and demand. As with most concepts in the social sciences, capitalism is not an absolute, because no market is completely free: Governments influence production and choice through taxes, regulations, and welfare and often own and operate key public services, such as schools and universities, postal services, and transport systems.

For our purposes, a "liberal" democracy is a society that believes in limits on the powers of government, majority rule, minority rights, and free-market economics. This set of objectives is an ideal, however, because governments do not always follow the will of the majority, not all minorities are protected, and there are many disagreements over the definition of the legitimate powers of government and over the appropriate role of government in the economy.

Democracy

Few concepts in political science are more widely and hotly debated than the notion of democracy. In its most basic sense, it means government or rule by the people, and comes from the Greek words *demos* (people) and *kratos* (strength). In its purest form, a **direct democracy** would be one in which everyone who lived under the jurisdiction of a government was asked for his or her opinion every time the government made a decision. Because most societies are too big to be run this way, they opt instead for **representative democracy,** or a system in which citizens elect others to represent their views and interests when decisions are made on law and public policy.

Because the electoral process and the behavior of elected officials are subject to many different pressures and influences, the views of individuals are not equally reflected in the democratic process. This has prompted the development of many different theories about how democracy actually works. Among these is **elite theory,** which argues that most democracies are controlled by a ruling class. The Greek philosopher Plato (c. 428–348 B.C.) was the first to suggest that in every society a minority makes most of the decisions.[1] Many theorists since then have argued that although elected officials rely on individual votes to win office, once in office they

CHECKLIST

LIBERAL DEMOCRACIES
What Are Their Features?

- Representative systems of government based on regular, fair, and secret elections
- Well-defined, consistent, and predictable political institutions and processes
- A high degree of public loyalty to the state
- A variety of institutionalized forms of political participation and representation
- Protection of individual rights under the law
- A belief in human equality
- An active, effective, and protected opposition and respect for freedom of speech

- Postindustrial and free-market economic systems based mainly on services and industry
- High levels of urbanization, with advanced infrastructure
- A relatively high quality of life when measured by the provision of education, health care, and other basic services
- High ratings on the Freedom House, Economic Freedom, and Human Development indexes

Where Are They?

There are 31, and they are mainly in North America, Western Europe, and East Asia/Australasia:

Australia	Iceland	Poland
Austria	Ireland	Portugal
Belgium	Israel	Slovakia
Canada	Italy	Slovenia
Czech Republic	Japan	South Korea
Denmark	Luxembourg	Spain
Finland	Malta	Sweden
France	Netherlands	Switzerland
Germany	New Zealand	United Kingdom
Greece	Norway	United States
Hungary		

often make decisions as a result of the pressures put on them by their networks of supporters.

A second theory is **pluralism,** or group theory, which argues that democracy should be seen not so much in individual terms as in group terms. It has been suggested that instead of the term *democracy* we should use the term **polyarchy** (government by the many).[2] A pluralist society is one in which politics is driven by competition among different groups, with the government supposedly acting as an honest broker. Power is not equally distributed but is manipulated by the groups with the most influence, which may be based on wealth or numbers. These groups may be corporations, special interest groups, labor unions, or regional interests, or they might be based around gender, race, age, religion, or social class.

Whichever theory we apply, the typical features of a democracy include the following: government by elected officials, regular elections at which all eligible voters can make their choices, few (if any) restrictions on the rights of all adults to vote, competing political parties offering a variety of ideological platforms, multiple channels through which citizens can express their views and influence government (such as interest groups and a free press), and a constitution. Perhaps most important, democracies believe in the **rule of law,** meaning that all citizens are equally subject to the same body of laws, which limit the powers of elected officials and protect the rights of citizens. In practice, though, there are many ways people can get around the law, find loopholes, or use their wealth or position to escape prosecution. Equal application of the law is an ideal rather than a reality.

Stable State Systems

One of the advantages enjoyed by liberal democracies is that they all have relatively stable state systems. The notion of the **state** has been debated as long and as intensely as the notion of democracy but—in short—can be defined as a community that lives in a defined territory and comes under the authority of a common and sovereign system of law and government.

A stable state has strong and generally well-respected political institutions and bodies of law, political processes that are mainly consistent and predictable, relatively efficient and professional bureaucracies, and the absence of serious challenges to territorial integrity. Of course, there are exceptions to every rule, and all liberal democracies have economic and social divisions, not all their citizens are always entirely happy with the way they are governed, and several have nationalist or separatist movements (such as the Scots in Britain, the Quebecois in Canada, and the Catalans in Spain), but few of these problems threaten the fabric of the state. The story in less developed countries (see Part IV) is sometimes very different.

Postindustrialism

Liberal democracies have undergone economic and political change that has taken them from feudalism (see later discussion) through an industrial revolution to a postindustrial, service-based economy. Most wealth in liberal democracies is generated by **industry** and **services;** as noted in the Introduction, the former produces tangible goods such as cars, furniture, electrical appliances, and other consumer products, and the latter are intangibles, such as retailing, entertainment, tourism, banking, and insurance. Whereas services account for about two-thirds of national wealth in liberal democracies, agriculture and industry tend to dominate in poorer countries, which usually have a smaller service sector.

Related to the dominance of industry and services, liberal democracies are highly urbanized, with anything from 75 to 95 percent of their people living in towns and cities. In general, the wealthier a country, the smaller its rural population and the fewer the people earning a living directly off the land. Agriculture in most liberal democracies is mechanized, intensive, and highly productive. Liberal democratic economies also produce a wide variety of goods and services and are built on a well-developed and diverse infrastructure with efficient and sophisticated transportation and communication systems.

High Quality of Life

Most people in most liberal democracies have a high standard of living when measured by the availability of jobs, education, health care, consumer choice, and basic services. They can expect to live relatively long and healthy lives, educational levels are high, population growth rates are low, and calorie consumption is at or above minimum needs. Although liberal democracies still experience problems such as illiteracy, poverty, discrimination, crime, pollution, and homelessness, these are all problems that are normally much worse in poorer countries.

Global Influence

Liberal democracies have converted their wealth and stability into political, economic, and military power at both the regional and global levels. Their economic wealth has given them the means to exert influence over trade, currency exchange rates, and the prices paid for goods and services. North American, European, and Japanese banks and corporations have become the world's major sources of investment funds, the poorest countries often rely on aid from liberal democracies, and liberal democracies are the biggest influence on the policies of international lending agencies such as the World Bank. The bigger liberal democracies have converted their economic wealth and technological prowess into military power, making countries such as the United States, Britain, and France among the most powerful in the world.

THE EVOLUTION OF LIBERAL DEMOCRACY

Although the origins of democracy can be traced back to the early city-states of Greece and Rome and to early Chinese and Indian cultures, all of which developed ideas emphasizing the role of the people in government, modern liberal democracy is mainly a product of changes that came to European society between the 13th and 19th centuries. At the heart of those changes was a shift in power away from landowning monarchs and aristocrats to a broader demographic base.

The End of Feudalism (13th to 14th Centuries)

The most common political system in Europe until the Middle Ages was **feudalism,** a rigidly hierarchical class system that allowed little, if any, social or economic mobility. At the bottom of the feudal heap were the peasants, who made up the vast majority of the population, owned nothing, and had virtually no control over their lives. They lived, worked, and died on estates operated by aristocrats, who controlled their movements and settled all legal questions. The aristocracy in turn answered to the monarch, who sat alone at the apex of the system, owned most or all of the land, and granted the aristocrats rights to the estates in return for services (usually military) on the basis of an oath of loyalty. Monarchs could be removed by murder or by defeat in war, but otherwise they ruled by **divine right,** meaning that they claimed to answer to no one but God, and certainly not to the peasants or the aristocrats.

The beginning of the end of European feudalism can be dated to 1215, when King John of England, at the insistence of his barons, signed the Magna Carta. This agreement placed limits on the power of the monarch for the first time, and a long, complex, and often violent process began in which power and rights were gradually transferred to ordinary citizens. This process was taken a stage further in 1265, when the first British parliament was created. Only aristocrats could be members, and they were not elected, but it was the first alternative forum of government to a monarch. The key to democratic change in Europe was the emergence of a balance between the crown and the nobility, allowing the nobility their independence while preventing royal absolutism. Where royal absolutism persisted (as in Russia), democracy did not emerge.[3]

The Reformation and the Enlightenment (16th to 18th Centuries)

Feudalism was underpinned by the Catholic Church, which acted as an international authority exercising most of the real political power in Europe in the Middle Ages and whose authority only finally began to be questioned with the Reformation. The way was led by the German monk Martin Luther (1483–1546), who criticized papal corruption and luxury and argued that individuals should be allowed to worship God directly, rather than through the intermediary of the church. In effect, he was arguing in favor of individual rights and against the powers of the church and the state.

In the 1640s, England went through a civil war, which resulted in the removal for a few years of the monarch. In 1651, as England recovered from the chaos of the war, a book titled *The Leviathan,* written by Thomas Hobbes (1588–1679), was published. In arguing for the restoration of the monarchy, Hobbes suggested that people were selfish and that life without government would be "solitary, poor, nasty, brutish and short." He said that if people were to protect themselves from the unrestrained state of nature and the evil of others, they had to submit themselves to government with absolute power, or a "leviathan" that dominated society. No one had the right to resist or revolt against that power, unless the ruler tried to take the life of a citizen, in which case the contract between ruler and citizen was broken.[4]

One of Hobbes's younger contemporaries was John Locke (1632–1704), who took the opposite view by arguing that humans were rational and self-interested (rather than selfish). He argued that people had "natural rights" to life, liberty, and property and that they entered into a social contract with government to protect these rights. Locke wrote that the only true basis for the power of government was the consent of the governed and that it was the duty of government to protect the rights of citizens. He disputed the divine right of monarchs and argued that men were born equal with rights that no monarch could take away. The transfer of powers from the monarch and the church to the people in England was confirmed in Locke's lifetime with the Bill of Rights, drawn up in 1689 following the restoration of the monarchy to confirm the supremacy of parliament over the monarch.

The spread of liberalism was confirmed in 1776 with the American Declaration of Independence, a radical statement of principles that were taken a stage further in

1787 with the publication of the U.S. Constitution. This was the first written constitution in the world and the kind of social contract proposed by Locke and the French philosopher Jean-Jacques Rousseau (1712–1778) (author of *The Social Contract* and a man often credited with inspiring the French Revolution of 1789). The U.S. Constitution was also based on the principles of limited and representative government outlined by Locke. With the separation of powers (three branches of government and a division of powers between the federal government and the states), it set out to ensure that no one arm of government could accumulate too much power.

The Rise of the Nation-State (17th to 19th Centuries)

During the European feudal era, political allegiance was based on the relationship between monarchs and their vassals. Military control over land, personal agreements, and the exchange of favors and obligations were key components of the system. The relationship between the ruler and the ruled in Europe was gradually formalized and institutionalized, particularly when monarchs began raising money (or imposing taxes) to meet the costs of waging war. This led to the development of more structured and intensified systems of control and the emergence of what eventually became the international state system in which we now live.

Something like the modern frontiers of European states can be seen emerging in the 14th century, but it was not until the 16th and 17th centuries that the earliest European states really began to take shape, beginning with England and France. Until the 19th century, borders in Europe were still loose and people could cross them freely, but the 19th century saw the growth of **nationalism,** as the citizens of different nation-states placed their own interests and values above those of their neighbors or competitors. Borders began to be more jealously protected, the limits of state sovereignty began to be marked out, and the foundations of the state system began to take shape.

The Industrial Revolution (18th to 19th Centuries)

Until the Middle Ages, European economies were based on agriculture. Most people worked on large estates operated by aristocrats and had neither wealth nor power. The balance began to change as agriculture became more productive, more land was tilled, and more efficient methods were developed for growing and harvesting crops and breeding livestock. Farmers became richer, society became more varied and complex, freedom of choice expanded, and a new class of merchants and entrepreneurs emerged. As this class won more political influence, the influence of monarchs, aristocrats, and the church was eroded still further.

The agricultural revolution was followed by an **industrial revolution:** Human energy was replaced by mechanical energy, cheaper and more efficient methods of smelting iron and producing steel were discovered, and technological breakthroughs led to the invention of cotton-spinning machines and the steam engine. Britain was the first country to witness these changes, mainly because its monarch had less control over the economy, the population was growing rapidly (creating a large new market), there was less domestic political discontent than elsewhere in Europe, and feudalism had weakened (creating a less rigid class structure).[5]

Adding momentum to these developments was the work of the Scottish philosopher Adam Smith (1723–1790). In *The Wealth of Nations*, published in 1776, he outlined most of the basic concepts of what we now call capitalism.[6] He criticized the traditional belief that a state's power was based on its wealth and that a state should keep as much wealth as possible within its borders by encouraging exports and limiting imports. He argued instead that supply and demand was the most efficient way of meeting society's needs. He wrote of the power of the "invisible hand" of the marketplace and argued that economies should be supported by a limited form of government that would maintain law and order and guarantee contracts and a stable currency, but little more. In other words, he was supporting a hands-off, free-market approach to economic management.

Early industrialization was made possible by changes in the distribution of political power, and politics was itself now changed by industrialization. The number of people working on the land fell as the urban working class grew. With the rise of a new entrepreneurial capitalist class, aristocrats no longer had a monopoly on economic wealth, and the commercial and industrial classes were much less willing than before to tolerate limits on their freedom of choice.[7] The new urban middle and working classes demanded greater input into the political system, trade unions formed to represent the workers, the vote was extended, towns and cities grew, and the new capitalists used their power to bring about changes in representation. In 1854, the English philosopher John Stuart Mill published his classic *On Liberty*, which argued in favor of civil liberties and minority rights (but against free-market economics, which he believed would bring about exploitation and the virtual enslavement of workers).[8]

Despite all of these new democratic tendencies, the political changes of the postfeudal era were not aimed at giving rights to all citizens but rather only to a privileged few. The American Declaration of Independence says that "all men are created equal," but it might as well have been worded "all white male property and slave owners are created equal." Adam Smith may have praised the free market, but he had little respect for the working class; he believed that the modern industrial worker who spent his whole life performing simple operations "generally becomes as stupid and ignorant as it is possible for a human to become."[9] Even Karl Marx, the alleged champion of the working class, had little respect for workers as a group.

The Spread of Liberal Democracy (17th to 19th Centuries)

With a finite population and domestic market, there was a limit to how far European industry could be supported by the home market. As the need for new markets, new sources of raw materials, and cheap labor became more obvious, Spain, Portugal, Britain, France, the Netherlands, and other European countries set off overseas to explore and conquer. The Spanish were the most active in the 16th and 17th centuries, followed by the French. By the 19th century, Britain had become the dominant imperial power, establishing a presence on every inhabited continent. Some of its colonies (such as Canada and Australia) were created for settlement, whereas others (such as India and most of Britain's African colonies) were created for economic exploitation, particularly of raw materials and labor.[10]

To protect themselves and their trade interests, the Europeans expanded their military power. When Britain won the edge over its French and Dutch rivals, the

WHAT IS A COUNTRY?

Most of us think of ourselves as citizens of one country or another, and scholars approach comparative politics in terms of the differences and similarities among these countries. But—like so many terms in political science—the term *country* is hard to pin down; we think we know countries when we see them but are often hard pressed to describe their major features. In order to understand them, we need to look at their origins.

In feudal Europe, land was tied to monarchs and aristocrats and the peasants who lived on that land were the subjects of the monarchs, with whom they were identified. Over time, people came to be identified with **nations,** or communities distinguished from each other by a common history, culture, and language. Systems of law and government also emerged, and people came under the jurisdiction of states. In some cases, nations coincided with states to produce **nation-states.** Because many of these nation-states were brought together by force, the boundaries of nations and states often did not coincide, so these new entities were often multinational states: territories inhabited by two or more national groups coming together under a common system of law and government.

When Europeans began building empires in the Americas, Asia, and Africa, they often divided territory among themselves on the basis of war and competition, paying little or no attention to cultural realities. The result was that most of the countries in these regions were created not as a result of domestic political developments but as a result of forces and pressures far away in Europe. The international state system entered its most dramatic era of change after World War II, with the breakup of empires and the emergence of newly independent African and Asian states. The changes have continued right up to the recent past and the present: the reunification of Germany; the breakups of the Soviet Union, Czechoslovakia, Yugoslavia, and Ethiopia; and the possibility of the independence of Chechnya, Kosovo, and Palestine.

UN Photo 185522/A. Brizzi (January 1995)

The headquarters of the United Nations in New York. Its members are the basic unit of study in comparative politics, although not all sovereign states are members of the UN and the definition of "country" is open to debate.

So where does this leave us? Generally, a country can be defined as a territory inhabited by people who come under a common system of government and that is politically and legally independent, meaning that it has sole jurisdiction over the manner in which the people and the land are governed (within the confines of international law). Unfortunately, anomalies and exceptions to the rule present difficult-to-answer questions: How do we classify microstates that are part of larger surrounding countries (such as Monaco, San Marino, and Vatican City)? What do we do with countries that are not recognized under international law (such as Taiwan and Western Sahara)?

world entered the **Pax Britannica,** or the peace policed by Britain. One of the results was that many British political values were exported or copied elsewhere, providing a foundation for the spread of liberal democracy. This developed strong roots in countries that were settled by British immigrants (such as the United States, Canada, Australia, and New Zealand) but not in those taken over by force and for economic exploitation.

LIBERAL DEMOCRACY TODAY

The principles of liberal democracy today form the basis of politics and government throughout Western Europe, North America, Japan, and Australasia, although some converts have been relatively recent. Germany and Japan did not begin to emerge as nation-states until the 1860s, and both underwent devastating experiences with failed democracy and dictatorship before finally settling with liberal democracy after World War II. Norway has governed itself only since 1905, Finland was part of the Russian Empire until 1917, and Ireland was under British administration until 1922. Until the mid-1970s, Spain and Portugal were dictatorships, Greece was under a military government from 1967 to 1974, and the Czech Republic, Hungary, Poland, Slovakia, and Slovenia were part of the Soviet bloc until 1991.

Although we call these countries liberal democracies, they are neither purely liberal nor perfectly democratic. Not only is the free market limited by government regulation and public ownership, but civil liberties and rights are often compromised, as they have been in Northern Ireland, prompting extremist groups in some cases to respond with violence. In Japan, political power is concentrated in the hands of bureaucrats and party leaders. In the United States, ethnic minorities do not have the same opportunities as the white majority, and there is still widespread discrimination against homosexuals. In all liberal democracies, women still have less political power and opportunity than men, do not earn as much as men for equal work, and are still prevented from rising to positions of corporate and political power as easily as men.

Despite these problems, liberal democracy has been stable and lasting, and no country with a sustained history of liberal democracy has ever freely or deliberately opted for an alternative form of government. The stability and the development of liberal democratic ideas have been helped by the strong patterns of political and economic cooperation that have emerged among liberal democracies, particularly since World War II (see Figure I.1). Even before the war had ended, representatives of 44 countries met at **Bretton Woods,** New Hampshire, to discuss their plans for the postwar world and agreed to promote global free trade. Out of Bretton Woods came the World Bank, the International Monetary Fund (IMF), and the General Agreement on Tariffs and Trade (GATT, which was replaced by the World Trade Organization, or WTO, in 1995). The World Bank and the IMF have provided financing to encourage economic development and international trade, and the reduction of barriers to global free trade is negotiated under the auspices of the WTO.

Four other organizations have been at the heart of cooperation among liberal democracies:

- **North Atlantic Treaty Organization** (NATO). The end of World War II saw the beginning of the **cold war,** a war of words and ideas between the West and the

FIGURE 1.1

Membership of Liberal Democratic Organizations

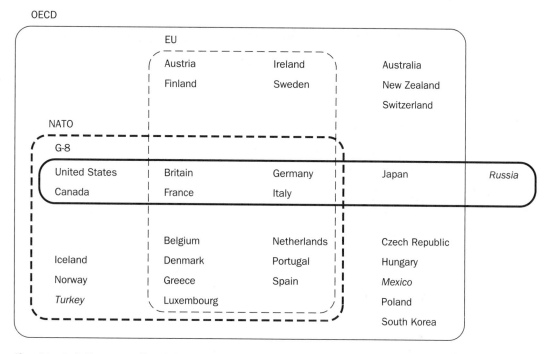

(Countries in italics are not liberal democracies.)

NATO   North Atlantic Treaty Organization

OECD   Organization for Economic Cooperation and Development

G-8   Group of 8

EU   European Union

Soviet bloc, together with a nuclear arms race and competition between the two sides for influence in the rest of the world. Faced with a common enemy, Western Europe and North America created NATO in 1949 to guard against Soviet attack. Since the collapse of the USSR and the end of the cold war in 1991, NATO's task has had to be redefined. In 2002, it was announced that seven Eastern European countries—Bulgaria, Estonia, Latvia, Lithuania, Romania, Slovakia, and Slovenia—had been invited to join NATO. However, following the serious diplomatic fallout in 2002–2003 between the United States and some of its key European allies over the invasion of Iraq, a large question mark hung over the future of NATO.

- **Organization for Economic Cooperation and Development** (OECD). Founded in 1961, and sometimes nicknamed the "Rich Man's Club" because its members include the world's major economic powers, the OECD coordinates and promotes the economic policies of member states, helps expand ties between them and poorer countries, and promotes world trade.

- **G-8 Group**. Beginning in 1975, the leaders of the seven wealthiest members of the OECD (Britain, Canada, France, Germany, Italy, Japan, and the United States) began holding annual summits as the G-7 Group. They initially discussed global economic issues, but with time the agenda broadened to include political issues. Russia has since joined in, pushing membership to eight.

- **European Union** (EU). Although this is exclusively a European organization, it has also developed the strongest ties among its members, has helped poorer European states such as Portugal and Greece develop political and economic stability, and is currently planning to expand to Eastern Europe (see Close-Up View, p. 88). Tracing its roots back to the early 1950s, the original goals of the European Union were to lower the barriers to trade among Western European countries, in part to discourage them from going to war again and in part to help promote the general prosperity of their citizens. Since then, however, its 15 member states have built common laws and policies in areas including transportation, agriculture, consumer protection, and the environment, and in 2002 a common currency—the euro—was adopted by 12 of its members.

Liberal democracy has many attractions, and many of its ideas have taken root in other countries, with varied results. With the end of the Soviet hegemony, for example, Eastern Europeans have turned increasingly to liberal democratic ideas, and countries such as Hungary, Poland, and the Czech Republic have joined the ranks of liberal democracies. Countries in other parts of the world are also developing democratic traditions (for example, India, Mexico, and Costa Rica), and even some sub-Saharan African states (notably Botswana) have recently started moving away from personal and one-party rule toward multiparty democracy. Some analysts have suggested that such trends represent an expansion of liberal democracy, but it is too early to be certain.

KEY TERMS

Bretton Woods	feudalism	pluralism
capitalism	industrial revolution	polyarchy
classical liberalism	industry	postindustrialism
cold war	liberalism	representative democracy
democracy	limited government	rule of law
direct democracy	nation	services
divine right	nation-state	social contract
economic liberalism	nationalism	state
elite theory	Pax Britannica	

KEY PEOPLE

Thomas Hobbes   John Stuart Mill   Jean-Jacques Rousseau
John Locke   Plato   Adam Smith
Martin Luther

STUDY QUESTIONS

1. What are the responsibilities of government?
2. Are individual rights absolute? If not, what limits are acceptable?
3. Which is the most compelling theory of democracy: elitism, pluralism, or a combination of the two?
4. What does *majority rule* mean, and how are minority rights protected?

LIBERAL DEMOCRACIES ONLINE

There are no Web sites for liberal democracies as such, but the sites of the following key international organizations provide useful insight into liberal democratic goals and values:

European Union: *http://europa.eu.int*
North Atlantic Treaty Organization: *http://www.nato.int*
Organization for Economic Cooperation and Development: *http://www. oecd.org*
World Trade Organization: *http://www.wto.org*

FURTHER READING

Almond, Gabriel, and Sidney Verba, *The Civic Culture: Political Attitudes and Democracy in Five Nations* (Princeton, NJ: Princeton University Press, 1963), and *The Civic Culture Revisited* (Newbury Park, CA: Sage Publications, 1989). Classic studies of political ideas in selected liberal democracies.

Dahl, Robert Alan, *On Democracy* (New Haven, CT: Yale University Press, 2000). An accessible introduction to democracy, providing a history of the concept and a discussion of its qualities.

Mandelbaum, Michael, *The Ideas That Conquered the World: Peace, Democracy, and Free Markets in the Twenty-First Century* (New York: Public Affairs, 2002). An analysis of the role of these three concepts in shaping the world.

Parenti, Michael, *Democracy for the Few*, 7th Ed. (Belmont, CA: Wadsworth, 2001). A short and pithy critique of American democracy that raises some challenging and controversial questions about many treasured assumptions.

Tilly, Charles (Ed.), *The Formation of National States in Western Europe* (Princeton, NJ: Princeton University Press, 1975). A good survey of the rise of the nation-state.

UNITED STATES

UNITED STATES: QUICK FACTS

Official name: United States of America

Capital: Washington, D.C.

Area: 3.56 million square miles (9.22 million sq. km)

Languages: Overwhelmingly English, with some minority languages (notably Spanish)

Population: 284 million

Population density: 80 per square mile

Population growth rate: 1.1 percent

POLITICAL INDICATORS

Freedom House rating: Free

Date of state formation: 1776

System type: Republic

Constitution: Written; published 1787

Administration: Federal; 50 states

Executive: President elected for maximum of two 4-year terms

Legislature: Bicameral Congress; Senate (100 members, two from each state, serving 6-year renewable terms), and House of Representatives (435 members, serving 2-year renewable terms)

Party structure: Multiparty, but two dominant parties (Democrats and Republicans)

Judiciary: Separate Supreme Court (nine members appointed for life by president and confirmed by Senate)

Head of state: George W. Bush (2001–)

Head of government: George W. Bush (2001–)

ECONOMIC INDICATORS

GDP (2001): $10,171 billion

Per capita GDP: $34,870

Distribution of GDP: Services 72 percent, industry 26 percent, agriculture 2 percent

Urban population: 77 percent

SOCIAL INDICATORS

HDI ranking: 6

Infant mortality rate: 7 per 1,000 live births

Life expectancy: 77.1 years

Illiteracy: 0 percent of people aged 15 and older

Religions: Predominantly Christian, with many denominations

INTRODUCTION

As the world's biggest economic and military power, and a country with a deeply vested interest and role in global affairs, the United States has been more immediately affected by the changes that have come to the world in the last few decades than any other country. It played the leading role after World War II in helping rebuild Western Europe and Japan and in setting up and defining both the United Nations and the North Atlantic Treaty Organization. As one of the two superpowers during the cold war, the United States led the Western alliance in responding to threats posed by the Soviets and their clients. Today it is the last remaining military superpower, facing growing economic competition from Europe and Southeast Asia, and—since September 2001—playing a controversial role in defining and fighting the war against international terrorism.

The United States is the world's biggest economy in absolute terms, with a GDP of more than $10 trillion, and one of its biggest in per capita terms, at nearly $35,000. It is a large country—the fourth biggest by land area after Russia, Canada, and China—and the third biggest by population after China and India. It has a wealth of natural resources, from land and minerals to fuels, forests, and cropland. The U.S. dollar is the world's strongest and most respected currency, and the United States is the world's biggest importer and exporter, the biggest producer of natural gas and nuclear electric power, and the second biggest producer of crude oil and coal. U.S. corporations feature heavily on the Fortune 100 list of the world's largest industrial corporations, which is topped by Wal-Mart and General Motors. Within their respective fields, General Electric, Texaco, Hewlett-Packard, Citicorp, PepsiCo, Walt Disney, Boeing, Microsoft, and others are major actors.

In social terms, diversity has long been the hallmark of life in the United States. The proportion of white Americans has fallen since 1970 from 87.5 percent of the total to about 75 percent today. Blacks long made up the biggest minority (about 12.3 percent of the population) but have recently been overtaken by Latinos (12.5 percent of the population according to the 2000 census). The proportion of Asian Americans is also growing rapidly (nearly 4 percent of the population). Recent decades have also seen a shift in the balance of population away from the older industrialized states of the Midwest and the Northeast and toward southern and western states such as Florida, Texas, and California, whose role in national politics has grown accordingly.

The population of the United States is also growing older as birth and fertility rates have declined and people live longer. This is a typical feature of a liberal democracy and contrasts with the situation in poorer countries, where the population is growing faster and young people outnumber older people. The median age in the United States has grown from 29.4 years in 1960 to 35.7 years today,[1] and the proportion of the population aged 65 years or older has grown from 9.7 percent to 14.2 percent. This has not only exerted more pressure on the health care system but has also meant a greater burden on social security and has created an increasingly powerful lobbying group in the form of retirees.

In political terms, the United States is unique among liberal democracies in the structure of its government—it is based on three separate branches whose powers are shared, checked, and balanced with one another. This structure has been copied

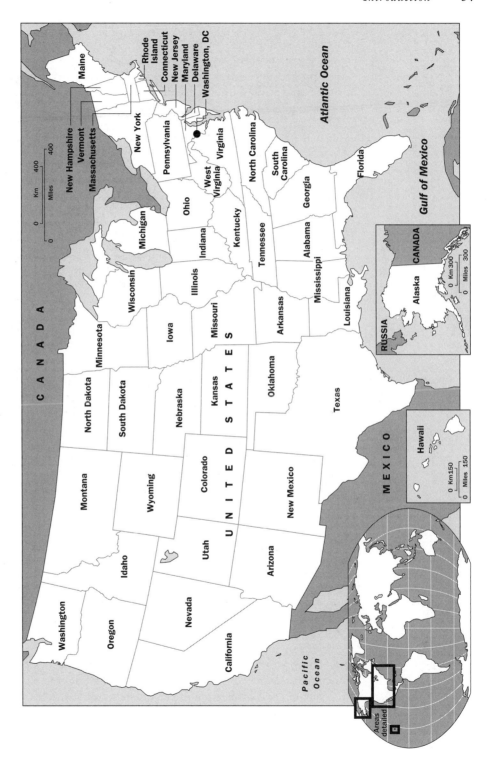

or adapted in several Latin American and African countries, but most other liberal democracies have opted instead for variations on the theme of the British parliamentary system (see Chapter 3). The United States is also unusual in the extent to which power is decentralized, with states and local governments being responsible for much of the day-to-day administration of their communities and a political culture that shies away from **"big government"** (meaning regulation and large government programs). Finally, it is alone among liberal democracies in the monopoly on power held by two political parties and in the relatively weak role these parties play in government.

POLITICAL DEVELOPMENT

The United States is an old country, but most Americans have very little sense of their own history besides a sometimes selective and even idealized version of America's relationship with democratic values. Unlike Europeans, for whom history is important for an understanding of themselves and of their relations with each other, Americans live more in the present and the future and tend to think more in terms of what might be, rather than what once was. Europeans originally immigrated to North America to find new beginnings, and even today Americans like to reinvent themselves, changing homes and jobs more often than almost anyone else, particularly the relatively immobile Japanese.

The peculiar circumstances of the United States in the late 18th century compelled it to develop what were then unique ideas about government, including a written constitution and a political system in which powers were divided horizontally among the institutions of government and vertically between national government and the states. Since then, politics has been driven in large part by debates over the appropriate role of government and the best balance between the institutions of government. There have been problems and failures along the way, and the American model of democracy is far from perfect (see Political Debates, p. 43), but the long-term result has been the creation of a successful and dynamic society whose influence is felt all over the world.

The Colonial Era (1607–1776)

Although the Americas were inhabited by native peoples when Columbus made his first voyage of discovery in 1492, the modern political values of the United States are ultimately the product of European ideas. Although native ideas continue to play a role in Latin American society (see Chapter 6), they have a negligible effect north of the Rio Grande. The United States was settled by Europeans, Europeans continued to arrive in large numbers in the 19th and early 20th centuries, and although emigrants from Latin America and Southeast Asia have changed the social and cultural balance of the United States in the last generation, it is still ultimately a product of the European political and cultural tradition.

The British were the first to settle and develop North America in any great numbers, with the first arrivals coming in the early 1600s and settlement moving into high gear with the Puritan migrations of the 1630s. By the early 1700s, Britain had colonized the entire eastern seaboard, setting up colonies that were governed by appointed governors with substantial powers and by elected bicameral legislatures. British monarchs tightened their control over the colonies, but not to the point where the colonists were encouraged to think about independence. The mood began to change in the 1760s, when new taxes and duties were imposed on the colonies and criticism of British interference in American domestic affairs began to grow. Revolution broke out in April 1775, the colonies declared independence in July 1776, and the creation of the new state was finally confirmed with the surrender of the British at Yorktown in October 1781.

State-Building (1776–1865)

For its first few years, the United States was a loose association governed by the **Articles of Confederation,** under which Congress had the power to make war and peace, conduct foreign affairs, and borrow and print money, but could collect taxes or enforce laws only through the states. A combination of problems—the financial difficulties of fighting the war with the British, the barriers to trade among the states, and the handicap posed by the lack of a single currency—led to the Constitutional Convention in 1787 to address the defects in the Articles of Confederation. The result of these deliberations was a new federal system in which power was divided, checked, and balanced among the states and three major branches of national government: the president, a bicameral Congress representing the states and the people, and a judiciary. Following ratification by nine states, the Constitution came into force in June 1788, and in 1789 George Washington became the first president.

The years following independence saw the United States steadily expanding westward from the original 13 colonies, and by 1787 the western frontier of the United States had reached the Mississippi. With the Louisiana Purchase from France in 1803, the United States doubled in size. Texas was annexed in 1845, the Pacific Northwest was absorbed in 1846, and the Southwest was ceded by Mexico in 1848. Meanwhile, a transportation revolution was underway, which had connected much of the eastern half of the country with roads, canals, and railroads by the middle of the 19th century. The national economy began to diversify, the most notable change being the emergence of the cotton- and slave-based economy of the southern states, whereas northern states were influenced more by the development of cities and industry and by the steady growth of emigration from Europe. By the 1850s, immigrants were arriving at a rate of more than 300,000 per year, and between 1790 and 1860 the population of the United States grew from 4 million to 31 million.

The economic and social divisions between the North and the South spilled over in 1860 with the election as president of Abraham Lincoln, whose Republican party was a northern-based, antislavery party. Secessionist views gathered steam in the South, leading to the declaration in February 1861 of the Confederacy (eventually joined by 11 states) and the outbreak in April of the Civil War. The war lasted 4 years, cost half a million lives, was accompanied by the end of slavery, and forced Americans to make important new choices about their future political, economic, and social development.

TABLE 1.1

Key Dates in U.S. History

1492	Christopher Columbus unwittingly reaches the West Indies
1585	First English colony established at Virginia
1607	First permanent English settlement at Jamestown, Virginia
1620	Arrival of pilgrims aboard the *Mayflower*
1775	Outbreak of the American Revolution
1776	Declaration of Independence
1781	War of Independence ends, Articles of Confederation take effect
1787	Writing of the Constitution (came into effect 1788)
1803	Louisiana Purchase doubles size of United States
1845	Annexation of Texas
1848	Southwest ceded to United States by Mexico
1849	California gold rush
1861–1865	Civil War
1870	Black men given the right to vote
1917	United States enters World War I
1920	Women given the right to vote
1920–1933	Prohibition
1929	(October) Wall Street crash ushers in Great Depression
1941	(December) Japanese attack on Pearl Harbor brings United States into World War II
1945	(May) end of European war; (August) end of Far Eastern war
1950–1953	Korean War
1954	*Brown* v. *Board of Education* decision ends segregation
1961	Alan Shepherd becomes first American in space
1962	(October) Cuban missile crisis
1963	(November) Assassination of President John F. Kennedy
1965–1973	Height of the Vietnam War
1972–1974	Watergate scandal; President Richard Nixon resigns August 1974
1983	(October) Invasion of Grenada
1990	(November) Invasion of Panama
1990–1991	United States leads coalition to respond to Iraqi invasion of Kuwait
1994	(January) Free trade agreement among United States, Canada, and Mexico comes into force; (November) Republicans take control of both houses of Congress for first time in 40 years
1995	(April) Oklahoma City bombing kills 169 people
1998	(December) Impeachment proceedings begin against President Bill Clinton
1999	(February) Senate votes not to convict Clinton; (April) United States leads NATO attack on Yugoslavia; (December) riots break out during meeting of World Trade Organization in Seattle
2000	(December) George W. Bush declared winner in contentious presidential election
2001	(September) terrorist attacks on World Trade Center and Pentagon kill 3,100 people; Bush administration response includes invasion of Afghanistan
2003	(March–April) Controversial U.S.-led invasion of Iraq

Reconstruction and Growth (1865–1945)

Following the **Civil War,** the United States was transformed from a society in which half of all workers had been employed in agriculture to one in which agriculture was increasingly mechanized and industry played the dominating economic role. It was the age of the railroad and the entrepreneur, of technological change, of the growth of monopolies and cities, and of expansion to the West. The influence of political parties began to decline as that of interest groups—representing the new sectors that emerged out of these economic changes—began to rise.

After spending much of its first century focused on internal matters, the United States also began cautiously to become more active in world affairs in the later decades of the 19th century, its main focus being on commerce with eastern Asia and on watching political developments in the Caribbean and Central America. Its new role as a global actor was emphasized by the decision to enter World War I in April 1917 and the involvement of the United States in the peace conference at Versailles in early 1919 and in the creation of the League of Nations.

The near decade of prosperity that followed the war ended with the Wall Street crash of October 1929, which ushered in the **Great Depression.** The unemployment rate soared to 25 percent, prompting the federal government to take a radically different approach to economic and social issues. President Franklin D. Roosevelt took office in 1933 and announced his **New Deal** program aimed at economic recovery, help for the victims of the depression, and new approaches to financial regulation. Notable among the changes of the 1930s were the introduction of social security and the creation of public works programs.

While these developments were taking place at home, problems that had been unresolved—and even created—by the Versailles conference fed into the growth of support for the Nazis in Germany, and Hitler's expansionism sparked World War II in September 1939. The United States initially chose to remain neutral, but the Roosevelt administration gave economic and military assistance to Britain and then entered the war following the Japanese attack on Pearl Harbor in December 1941.

Pax Americana (1945–)

With the end of the war in 1945, the old regime under which world affairs had been dominated by European powers was replaced by a new one in which there were two superpowers: the United States and the Soviet Union. The end of the war saw the beginning of a new kind of global hostility in which the United States played a lead role: the cold war. Instead of direct military conflict, this new competition was marked by a war of words and ideas between the Soviet Union and its allies on one side and the United States and its Western allies on the other. The conflict occasionally broke out into fighting wars between clients of the two sides, as in Korea in 1950–1953, Vietnam in the 1960s and early 1970s, and Afghanistan in 1979–1989. As the dominant military power in the world, the United States became actively involved in promoting its objectives on several different fronts and continents, thus launching the **Pax Americana** (the peace policed by the United States).

At home, the economy began a period of sustained expansion, with mass production and consumerism feeding off each other and growing numbers beginning to live the **American Dream:** a home, a car, a nuclear family, and a wife who stayed at home to raise the children. Behind the façade, however, there was simmering social discontent. Many were denied opportunity or were dissatisfied with their situations, and tension began to brew that took the United States into a period of political and social turbulence. Cold war neuroses brought a Red Scare that reached a trough of absurdity with the anti-Communist witch-hunt organized by Senator Joseph McCarthy in 1950–1954. The civil rights movement used the court system successfully to challenge **segregation,** the continuing problem of racism becoming a key policy concern throughout the late 1950s and early 1960s. At the same time, women began to be more assertive in their demands for political, economic, and social equality.

The assassinations of John F. Kennedy (1963); Martin Luther King, Jr.; and Robert F. Kennedy (both 1968) forced many Americans to think about the violence that ran through their social system. The **Great Society** programs of the Johnson administration—aimed at combating poverty and discrimination—expanded the activities of the federal government in social policy but also served to highlight the gaps between aspirations and realities. Americans were deeply split in the late 1960s and early 1970s over the war in Vietnam, and faith in government leaders sustained a heavy blow with the Watergate scandal. These events, combined with the energy crises and economic problems of the 1970s, brought doubts and disillusionment to replace the optimism of the 1950s.

In 1980 Ronald Reagan was elected president, pulling vital support from a religious right that was in favor of a redefinition of moral values. He moved the United States into conservative positions on economic and social issues, proclaiming that it was "morning in America." **Reaganomics** was based on addressing problems such as double-digit inflation, high interest rates, and unemployment by cutting back on the role of the government in the economy and reducing taxes. At the same time, Reagan moved to restore the U.S. presence in global affairs by rebuilding the military. While the United States came out of recession, and both inflation and unemployment fell, the combination of reduced taxes and increased military spending contributed to a dramatic increase in the federal budget deficit and the national debt, which—during the Reagan years alone—grew from $1 trillion to $3 trillion. (By 2003 it stood at about $5.5 trillion.)

The United States Today

By the 1990s, there was a growing division within American society about the appropriate role of government and about the direction that the United States should be taking on social, economic, and foreign policies. On one hand, conservatives argued that the government was too involved in making choices for citizens, that the economy was stifled by too much regulation, and that most of the country's social problems could be addressed by a return to "traditional" family values. On the other hand, liberals argued that there were still too many people who were denied their share of the rights and opportunities afforded by the American brand of democracy, that social discrimination remained a critical problem, and that government should be more assertive in promoting equality.

Despite strong economic growth during the 1990s, including low unemployment and inflation and high productivity and consumer confidence, there were concerns

HOW HEALTHY IS AMERICAN DEMOCRACY?

Americans and their political leaders often portray the United States as the pinnacle of democracy and as a torch for the values of liberty around the world. Yet the U.S. model of democracy is full of contradictions. A prime example came with the November 2000 presidential election. Not only were there many voting irregularities and technical problems that left many votes uncounted, but the winner of the popular vote— Democrat Al Gore, who won 50,999,897 votes, or 543,895 more than his Republican opponent George W. Bush[2]—did not win the election. Why not? Because the United States uses an **electoral college** in which every state has as many votes as it has seats in Congress, and the winner of the popular vote in a state typically wins *all* the electoral college votes from that state. Thus George W. Bush won 271 electoral college votes to Al Gore's 266. Meanwhile, Green party candidate Ralph Nader won nearly 3 million votes (almost 3 percent of the total) but won no electoral college votes.

The characteristic features of a democracy include the ideas that (1) every voter should be allowed to cast just one vote, (2) every vote should have equal weight, and (3) the candidate with the most votes wins. The U.S. model of democracy failed on all three counts in 2000. Consider some additional problems:

- Voter turnout in presidential election years is about 50 to 55 percent, and in midterm elections is about 35 to 40 percent.[3] This means that the majority of Americans are not being heard at the ballot box, encouraging elected officials to respond only to the interests of those who vote.

- The borders of voting districts are decided in most states not by independent commissions but by the majority political party in each state, which will routinely draw those districts in such a way as to maximize the chances of its members winning congressional seats.

- There is relatively little public funding of elections in the United States, which means that candidates must raise money from private sources. Among these are groups representing a variety of special interests, most notably corporate interests and single-issue interest groups, whose views strongly influence the behavior of elected officials, occasionally running counter to majority public opinion.

Under the circumstances, how can we be sure that the interests of all Americans are in fact being effectively represented in government? Just how healthy is American democracy?

that Americans had become polarized, that politics in the United States was driven less by voting and parties than it was by special interests, and that elected officials in Washington, D.C., had forgotten the needs and interests of their constituents. Polls regularly found low levels of faith and trust in government and elected officials, a view that was not helped by sex scandals and charges of perjury surrounding President Clinton, leading to his impeachment in 1998 by a Congress dominated by Republicans. Paradoxes also continued to color the relationship between government and the people. How could the wealthiest country in the world still have 15 percent of its population living in poverty? How could the country with the best medical technology in the world have rates of infant mortality that are higher and a life expectancy that is lower than those in several other liberal democracies? How could a country built on the sanctity of equality and individual rights still witness as much discrimination as it does against women, ethnic minorities, and gays?

On the morning of September 11, 2001, four domestic airliners flying out of Boston, Newark, and Dulles were hijacked by Middle Eastern terrorists. Two were crashed deliberately into the World Trade Center towers in New York City, which subsequently collapsed; one was crashed into the Pentagon in Washington, D.C.; and the fourth crashed into the Pennsylvania countryside. A total of 3,100 people were killed, including the 19 hijackers and citizens from many different countries. This was the single biggest terrorist attack in history and had a dramatic impact on the lives of Americans and on both domestic and foreign policy. The United States responded by launching a war on Afghanistan, which was charged with harboring the terrorist organization Al-Qaeda and its leader Osama bin Laden. Furious diplomatic activity was targeted at building a broader "war on terrorism" and specifically at isolating Iraq, which was accused of building weapons of mass destruction. At the same time, the biggest reorganization of U.S. government in 50 years took place as many different agencies were brought together under a new Department of Homeland Security.

It is still too early to know what the long-term effects of the 2001 attacks will be on politics, the economy, and the American national psyche. The most fundamental short-term effect was an undermining of the sense of national security—excepting the attack on Pearl Harbor, which took place before Hawaii became a U.S. state, the 2001 attacks were the first by an external enemy on U.S. soil since 1812. They were also launched by an enemy that was difficult to pin down and that was not linked with a single country, making it difficult to decide how to respond. President Bush's response—holding incommunicado suspected terrorists captured in Afghanistan, breaking decades of U.S. policy by launching a preemptive attack on Iraq, and giving the Department of Homeland Security expansive authority to pursue its goals—attracted charges of abuses of presidential power. It also drew complaints from many governments around the world that he had shown a worrying willingness to take unilateral action, that he had not fully grasped the broader causes of terrorism, and that his strategy was therefore fundamentally flawed. Was this a sign that U.S. policy was increasingly at odds with policies in many other liberal democracies, or should the short-term policies of one administration be distinguished from the long-term values of the United States?

POLITICAL CULTURE

Textbooks on American government routinely emphasize the role of individual liberty in American political culture and values such as a belief in political equality, equality of opportunity, equal sharing of the material rewards of democracy, and equal access to the political process. They almost seem to suggest that these are somehow uniquely American values, or at least that they are much more centrally a part of the American political system than is the case in other liberal democracies. However, there are at least two problems with this notion. First, these are all characteristics that are common to all liberal democracies. Second, the gap between aspiration and achievement is as significant in the United States as in other liberal democracies.

To appreciate the features that truly distinguish political culture in the United States, we need to look beyond the ideals and focus our attention elsewhere.

Patriotism and Optimism

The United States is without question the most patriotic of liberal democracies. This is evident in the reverence accorded the icons of national identity, such as the flag, the Constitution, the national anthem, and the military. In no other country has there been the same level of debate as in the United States about flag burning as a form of political expression, and in no other country are military veterans accorded so much respect as public servants. Opinion polls confirm the levels of patriotism: 80 percent of Americans routinely describe themselves as being "proud" or "very proud" of being American. The figures for most European countries are in the range of 40 to 60 percent and for Germany are as low as 20 percent.

Most Americans are also relatively optimistic about the opportunities and choices they face and about the quality of life they enjoy or expect their children to enjoy. Europeans since World War II have seen their lives and their societies undergo considerable change, and many as a result are doubtful about their present circumstances and future options (even though the overall quality of life is far better than it was even a generation ago). Americans, on the other hand, generally have a positive attitude about the condition of their country. Even in the face of persistent problems such as poverty, racism, drugs, and violence, they have a high degree of faith in political institutions and the process of government. Even with the knowledge that domestic conditions are not always perfect and that the motives behind U.S. foreign policy have not always been noble, most still believe that the United States is better, stronger, and freer than any other country.

Individualism and Self-Determination

To a much greater extent than is true of any other liberal democracy, the popular view in the United States is that government should play a limited role in the lives of citizens. It should provide selected public services, uphold the rule of law, and enable individuals to achieve their goals, but it should resist the temptation to make too many decisions on behalf of individuals. This is why socialism is so unpopular (or, actually, misunderstood) in the United States, why it is the only liberal democracy without a national health care system (which many Americans—tellingly—like to call "socialized medicine"), and why large government programs are so often a subject of public discussion. There has always been something of a frontier mentality in American society and a feeling that distance from government is good. This is partly why many immigrants came to the United States from Europe, why the opening up of the western United States in the 19th century was so significant, and why civil liberties—such as freedom of speech—are so much a part of political discourse among Americans.

Aspirational Politics

Most Europeans approach politics from the perspective of the "here and now" and within the confines of what they believe is possible. By contrast, political debate in the United States is peppered with words such as *dream* and *vision*. It is understood that the creation of the ideal society is a work in progress, but the ultimate goal is achievement of the "American Dream." This is rarely defined but is generally associated with ideas of the United States as a land of opportunity where initiative and hard work can bring success, which is usually measured by material wealth and private property. The dream is there, but many Americans are still denied equality of opportunity, and the differences that pervade American society suggest that the sentiment in the second paragraph of the Declaration of Independence—that all men are born equal—remains an aspiration rather than a reality.

A Puritan Streak

More than is the case in almost any other liberal democracy, and despite claims that there is a separation between church and state in the United States, moral issues are high on the agenda of American politics. Ironically, while there have been debates in recent years about whether the Ten Commandments should be posted on public buildings or whether it is appropriate to display "In God We Trust" in courthouses or on banknotes and coins, religious values overlap with public policy on many issues. Most prominent among these has been the abortion debate. Abortion has been legally available in most liberal democracies for decades and is rarely any longer a matter for public debate in Western Europe. The debate has been kept alive here by an active disagreement between pro-life and pro-choice campaigners. The former hope to see a conservative future Supreme Court overturn the 1973 *Roe v. Wade* decision that established a woman's right of access to abortion, and the latter work to protect that decision.

POLITICAL SYSTEM

In addition to the typical features of a democracy (including representative government and a belief in the rule of law), four key principles give the American system of government its distinctive character:

- It is a **republic,** or a political system in which all members of government are either elected or appointed by elected officials. (Britain, Canada, and Japan are not republics, because they all have monarchs, who are not elected.)
- It is a **federation,** or an administrative system in which national and local levels of government have separate and independent powers and responsibilities.
- There is a **separation of powers** at the national level among a legislature responsible for making laws, an executive responsible for overseeing the application of those laws, and a judiciary responsible for checking the constitutionality of the laws and actions of government.

- A system of **checks and balances** divides powers and responsibilities and obliges the key institutions—and the different levels of government—to work together to make and implement policy.

This combination makes the U.S. unusual among liberal democracies. Of the 31 liberal democracies in the world, 12 are monarchies or duchies rather than republics, all but 7 are unitary systems in which most political power is vested in national government, and all but 6 have fused executives and legislatures in the sense that their heads of government are prime ministers who depend for their power on having the support of a majority of members of the national legislature.

THE CONSTITUTION

The Constitution of the United States was the first such document of its kind in the world and has been the model for most of the constitutions that have since been developed by other countries. It is the centerpiece of the American political system, the blueprint by which the United States is governed, and the subject of much debate and analysis among lawyers and scholars.

The Articles of Confederation, under which the newly independent United States was initially governed (1781–1788), formed a very loose association among the founding 13 states. It did not give Congress the power to tax people directly, nor did it make provisions for a single market or a single currency, because states could tax the goods of other states and issue their own currency. A Constitutional Convention met in 1787 to revise the Articles but quickly opted to develop an entirely new system. The new Constitution of the United States was subsequently ratified by the states and took effect in June 1788. It did four things:

- It established the structure of government, which was based around three branches of government within a federal system.
- It distributed powers among the different elements of government, giving Congress the power to coin, raise, and spend money; to regulate commerce with other countries; and to declare war. It also gave the president command of the armed forces, wide authority over foreign policy, the power to make selected appointments, and the power to veto legislative proposals from Congress.
- It distributed powers between the federal government and the states, denying the latter, for example, the right to sign treaties with other countries or to have their own currencies.
- It described limits on the powers of government. Many of these were outlined in the first ten amendments to the Constitution, passed in 1791 and constituting the Bill of Rights. These made sure certain individual rights were preserved, such as freedom of religion, speech, and the press and the right to a speedy public trial.

The U.S. Constitution is not immutable, and one of its great strengths is that it was designed to be changed when necessary to meet changed circumstances. Amending the Constitution is a two-stage process. First, amendments must be proposed, either by two-thirds of both houses of Congress or by two-thirds of state legislatures.

Then the amendments must be ratified by three-quarters of state legislatures, usually within 7 to 10 years. Thousands of amendments have been proposed, but only 33 have won the necessary support in Congress to be considered and only 27 amendments have been ratified. The most recent was in 1992; it forbids members of Congress from giving themselves a midterm pay raise.

The structure of government can also be changed in three other ways. First, the Supreme Court can issue decisions on whether or not laws and the actions of government are constitutional. Second, many of the details of the structure of government are determined by laws passed by Congress. For example, such laws have established the size of the House of Representatives and the Supreme Court and have created all federal courts below the level of the Supreme Court. Finally, the Constitution is affected by custom and tradition, out of which have developed political parties, party leadership, and party conventions.

THE EXECUTIVE: PRESIDENT

The presidency of the United States is often described as one of the strongest government offices in the world. In terms of the resources that presidents have at their disposal, this is true: They are commanders-in-chief of the world's most powerful military force and make decisions affecting one of the world's two biggest economies (the other being the European Union). However, compared directly with the powers of the leaders of other democracies, presidents of the United States are often hamstrung: They are limited by the terms of the Constitution, their options are limited by Congress, and much government activity in the United

TABLE 1.2

Modern Presidents of the United States

Term	Name	Party
1933–1945	Franklin Roosevelt	Democratic
1945–1953	Harry Truman	Democratic
1953–1961	Dwight Eisenhower	Republican
1961–1963	John Kennedy	Democratic
1963–1969	Lyndon Johnson	Democratic
1969–1974	Richard Nixon	Republican
1974–1977	Gerald Ford	Republican
1977–1981	Jimmy Carter	Democratic
1981–1989	Ronald Reagan	Republican
1989–1993	George Bush	Republican
1993–2001	Bill Clinton	Democratic
2001–	George W. Bush	Republican

States goes on *despite* the president. In reality, the power of the office boils down to the abilities of incumbents to persuade and to build coalitions of support inside and outside Congress.

The framers of the Constitution feared anarchy and tyranny in about equal measure and wanted to make sure that the powers of the executive and the legislature checked each other. Throughout the 19th century, Congress was the dominant branch of government and few presidents were able to exert substantial leadership; this is partly why so few early presidents—the exceptions including Washington, Jackson, and Lincoln—made much of a mark. The situation changed with Franklin Delano Roosevelt (1933–1945), the first president to fully exert the powers of the office rather than simply respond to Congress. Since then, the power and influence of the presidency have changed out of all recognition, for five main reasons.

First, as the population of the United States has grown, so have people's needs. Responding to them has demanded a more systematic way of evaluating priorities, so presidents have won more powers to set the policy agenda, which in turn has motivated them to work harder at winning congressional support. Second, the president is better placed to respond quickly to policy needs than Congress, which is big, cumbersome, and divided along party lines. Third, the emergence of the United States as a global superpower has given more influence to the president, who has had a large amount of freedom to set foreign policy. Fourth, presidents are generally more newsworthy than Congress and have exploited this to manipulate the media and public opinion to their advantage. Finally, the presidency itself has grown, making it easier for presidents to respond to a broader set of policy issues. Whereas George Washington had 1 staff member, Lincoln had 4, Roosevelt had 50, and George W. Bush has more than 1,500 people working directly for him.

In terms of the qualifications for the office, the Constitution says that anyone who is a natural-born citizen, is older than 35 years, and has been a U.S. resident for at least 14 years can be president. In practice, however, every president so far has been a white male, and most have English, German, or Scandinavian heritage and come from states with large populations. In terms of experience, elected political background is important, preferably as a state governor or a U.S. senator. Governors used to be prime contenders for the presidency, but this changed in the 1960s and 1970s, when a rash of former senators ran, including the Kennedy brothers, Richard Nixon, and George McGovern. As part of the reaction against Washington "insiders" that followed the Watergate scandal of the early 1970s and as a reaction against big government, the advantage has since shifted to state governors: Jimmy Carter from Georgia, Ronald Reagan from California, Bill Clinton from Arkansas, and George W. Bush from Texas.

The constitutional powers of the president are modest: They include being commander-in-chief (although what this means is not specified) and having the powers to grant pardons, to make treaties (with Senate approval), to appoint ambassadors and Supreme Court judges, and to veto congressional bills. More generally, the powers of the presidency have expanded into at least nine different spheres of responsibility:

- **Head of state.** The president is the symbolic leader of the United States, representing the entire country rather than just the people who voted him into office. In this sense, he carries out many of the duties reserved in other countries to the monarch or to nonexecutive presidents, such as receiving ambassadors and other heads of state, making goodwill tours, providing a unifying influence, and acting as something like a national figure at times of crisis. This can be time-consuming but can also be politically useful—the more that a president can associate himself with popular feelings of patriotism and national unity, the more persuasive he can be at winning support for his policies. George W. Bush showed this clearly with the fallout from the attacks of September 11, 2001, when most of the country rallied around him in his calls for a war on terrorism.

- **Head of government.** The president is also a politician, a representative of his party, and the champion of his particular set of policy objectives. In this role, he needs to keep the support of the voters who elected him into office, the members of Congress on whom he depends to vote his programs into law, the Washington establishment, and the national media.

- **Commander-in-chief.** The president has principal authority over U.S. armed forces and over their involvement in military operations. His powers in this regard declined as a reaction to the role of the presidency in involving the United States in Vietnam and making all the key subsequent decisions on that war. The 1974 **War Powers Act** made it illegal for presidents to commit U.S. troops overseas for more than 60 days without congressional approval. But George W. Bush reasserted his military powers when he was able to convince Congress in 2002 to give him sweeping authority as he made preparations for the 2003 invasion of Iraq.

- **Chief executive.** The president is head of the federal cabinet and of the federal bureaucracy. He uses this power to oversee the process by which laws adopted by Congress are executed.

- **Agenda setter.** The president has considerable influence over setting the national political agenda. He does this in part through the annual State of the Union address, which is presented to both houses of Congress and is an opportunity to outline the issues and problems he considers important. He also tries to set the agenda through his use of the media, which tend to regard almost anything that the president does—from making an important policy speech to buying a new family dog—as newsworthy.

- **Foreign policymaker.** The president has the sole power to negotiate treaties with other countries, to extend diplomatic recognition to foreign governments, and to determine the priorities of U.S. foreign policy. Because this is an area where the president has considerable freedom of movement, it is usually a key item in the assessment of the successes and failures of a particular administration.

- **Economic leader.** Congress alone has powers over fiscal policy (taxing and spending), but the White House must develop the federal budget and presidents can influence the direction taken by economic policy. Indeed, the political fortunes of presidents often rise and fall with the state of the economy, and the president is usually closely identified in the public mind with economic issues, such as the rate of economic growth and inflation.

- **Crisis manager.** Life is often unpredictable, and crises break to which government must respond, such as war and conflict, natural disasters such as hurricanes

GEORGE W. BUSH

© AFP/CORBIS

Born in Connecticut in 1946 but raised in Texas, President George W. Bush was educated at Yale and Harvard, leaving the latter with a business degree. (This set him apart from most other contemporary American politicians, who are products of American law schools.) He joined the National Guard as a pilot, then followed his father into the oil business. He lost a run for the U.S. Congress in 1978 and underwent a personal crisis before changing his life around at the age of 40. He made a number of successful business deals, including becoming part owner of the Texas Rangers baseball team, and then in 1994 he followed his father and grandfather into politics by being elected governor of Texas. He was returned for a second term in 1998. Meanwhile his brother Jeb had been elected governor of Florida.

His presidential campaign of 1999–2000 was notable for having raised more money than any previous presidential campaign. He positioned himself on the moderate right of the Republican party, describing himself as a "compassionate conservative" and campaigning on issues such as poverty, education, and minority concerns. After a close-run race against Democratic challenger Al Gore, in which many voters complained that there was little to differentiate the two, the result was so close that Gore initially conceded defeat on election night. But he then withdrew his concession when it became clear that there had been problems with some of the machines used by voters to cast their votes, notably in Florida. After 4 weeks of legal debates, the case eventually went to the U.S. Supreme Court, which declared Bush the winner in a split vote.

Bush has proved a controversial politician. Although few have questioned his personal charm and integrity, some have questioned his intellectual abilities and the long-term implications of his policies. He initially won high public approval ratings among Americans, but he attracted criticism from overseas for his unilateralist positions on a number of issues, ranging from climate change to the International Criminal Court, antiballistic missile treaties, and free trade. He set out as a domestic president, focusing on dealing with a downturn in the economy, but then had to deal with the fallout from the September 2001 terrorist attacks. After the defeat of the Taliban regime in Afghanistan, he made a point of focusing on the threats posed by the regime of Saddam Hussein in Iraq, a position that was disputed by other national leaders, including key U.S. allies—such as France and Germany. As part of efforts to tighten domestic security, his administration in 2002 undertook the biggest reorganization of the U.S. federal bureaucracy in 50 years. In March 2003, he authorized an attack on the regime of Saddam Hussein in Iraq, a move that deeply divided Americans, U.S. allies, and world public opinion.

and floods, the taking of hostages, and acts of terrorism. As one person, the president is in a much better position to respond quickly to such crises than is Congress, and therefore is expected to provide leadership in such instances.[4]

- **Party leader.** Although American political parties have their own governing committees and chairs, the president becomes de facto leader of his party while in office, and the goals of the party are heavily influenced by his programs.

Against the background of all these roles—and the constitutional powers of the president—the job performance of individual presidents is ultimately tied to other, more informal and often less quantifiable factors. These include the president's ability to communicate his program and message, his capabilities as an organizer and the builder of a governing team, his political skills (how well or how badly he is able to work with others to build support for his program), his sense of direction (or what George Bush, Sr., once famously described as "the vision thing"), and his emotional intelligence: how well he manages anger and stress, how secure he feels in himself, his sense of moral character, and so on.[5]

To carry out their responsibilities, presidents have become dependent on an expanding body of people and institutions that collectively come to represent "the presidency." Most notable among these are the staff within the White House itself, including the chief of staff, the press secretary, congressional liaison staff, and a string of advisors. These are all appointed by the president and help keep him informed, but they also become associated in the public mind with the administration.

The president also governs with the help of the cabinet, which consists of the heads of 15 key government departments, including defense, justice, the treasury, and homeland security. The president appoints cabinet heads, who must then be confirmed by the Senate. They come from a variety of backgrounds—some are academics, others have experience in state or federal government, and some are associates of the president from an earlier time. Cabinets in parliamentary systems are something like governing committees, are deeply involved in making political decisions, and meet as often as once per week; by contrast, the U.S. cabinet tends to be an advisory body which rarely meets as a group.[6]

The president is also assisted by a vice president, whose position is generally considered one of the least important in government. Vice presidents may be "a heartbeat away from the presidency," but they usually spend much of their time in relative obscurity, their role dependent almost entirely on the president. They are normally chosen to give ideological or geographical balance to the presidential ticket during the election, after which they often have very little influence over the work of the new administration.

THE LEGISLATURE: CONGRESS

Despite being the political institution that is closest to the people, Congress is the least popular of the three branches of government.[7] There are several reasons for this: Its work is more visible, it does not have the same aura as the other institutions, and it is most closely involved in the process of lawmaking and so is most deeply involved in the struggles of politics. When Americans complain about big

John McCormick

The Capitol Building, home of the United States Congress in Washington, D.C. Congress was designed to represent the interests of the people and to be the most powerful branch of government, but it has lost both its popularity and its power to the presidency, particularly since the mid-20th century.

government, they are usually talking about Congress, which is ironic given the number of supporters of small government among its members.

The Constitution gave Congress several powers, including the authority to levy taxes, borrow money, coin money, declare war, raise armies, determine the nature of the federal judiciary, and regulate commerce with foreign governments and among states. In practice, however, the powers of Congress rest primarily in four areas:

- It is the arm of government responsible for **making laws.** This is where federal laws are introduced, discussed, and either accepted or rejected.

- Through the **power of oversight,** it checks on the work of the federal bureaucracy, making sure that it carries out the intent of Congress. It does this mainly through controlling the budgets of government departments.

- It has the final say over the **federal budget,** which is developed by the president's Office of Management and Budget but must be approved by Congress.

- The Senate has the power to **check and confirm all key presidential appointees** except those who work directly for the president in the White House.

Congress was intended by the framers of the Constitution to be the most powerful branch of government, and so it was for about 150 years; few presidents were able to challenge congressional power, and most of the key political struggles took place within Congress, rather than between Congress and the president. During the 20th century, however, presidential powers grew and decision making within Congress was decentralized. The result is more of a balance between the two branches, which need each other to govern effectively.

Congress has two chambers with different structures but similar powers.

Senate

The Senate is designed to represent the states in the sense that equal representation is given to them all, regardless of size. Each of the 50 states elects two senators, for a total of 100. They serve 6-year renewable terms, and elections are staggered so that one-third of members stand for reelection every 2 years. This system ensures that smaller states are relatively overrepresented and larger states are relatively underrepresented; hence Wyoming, with barely 500,000 residents, has the same level of representation as California, with a population that is 64 times bigger.

In terms of its powers over introducing, discussing, and voting on legislation, the Senate has equal powers with the House of Representatives. However, it has the unique power of approval over presidential nominations for appointments to the cabinet, the Supreme Court, lower federal courts, key government agencies such as the Federal Reserve Board, and ambassadorial posts.

Sessions of the Senate are overseen by a president, who is—ex officio—the vice president of the United States. This is a largely symbolic position, and the president of the Senate can cast a vote only in the case of a tie; most of the time, the president is represented by a junior senator acting as president pro tempore. Much more significant is the post of **Senate majority leader,** held by a member of the majority party in the Senate. The majority leader schedules debates, assigns bills to committees, coordinates party policy, appoints members of special committees, and generally oversees the functioning of the Senate to suit the purposes of the majority party.

House of Representatives

The House of Representatives is the lower chamber, which is designed to represent the people in the sense that every member is elected from a district of approximately equal size. The House has 435 members elected for renewable 2-year terms, all of whom come up for reelection every 2 years. According to the Constitution, all congressional districts must be reapportioned every 10 years to reflect changes in the population. Because of these changes, southern and western states such as Florida and California have picked up new seats in recent years at the expense mainly of older industrial states such as New York and Pennsylvania.

The leader of the House is the **Speaker,** who is chosen from the ranks of the majority party. In contrast to the Speaker in parliamentary systems, whose main job is to keep order during debates and who is expected to be nonpartisan (see Chapter 2), the Speaker of the House is a partisan leader with considerable powers: He presides over debates, recognizes members who wish to speak, votes in cases of a tie, interprets questions of procedure, and influences the committee system by assigning bills to committees and deciding who sits on special and select committees.

Legislation can be introduced in either of the chambers of Congress (with the exception of revenue bills, which can only be introduced in the House). All bills are immediately sent to the relevant committee, are then sent for debate by the chamber as a whole before being voted on, and are then sent to the other chamber where they go through the same stages. If a bill passes both chambers, it is then sent to the president, who can either sign it into law or exercise his veto. A presidential veto can be overridden in Congress by a vote of more than two-thirds of the members of both chambers.

THE JUDICIARY: SUPREME COURT

The nine-member Supreme Court is responsible for ensuring that the laws and actions of government fit with the letter or the spirit of the Constitution. This is a power known as **judicial review,** which was not contained in the Constitution but was won for itself by the Supreme Court in the *Marbury* v. *Madison* decision of 1803. There is nothing in the Constitution, either, about lower federal courts, but a complex system of district courts and courts of appeal has been developed over time. These lower courts now hear about 10 million cases per year.

Plaintiffs who lose their cases in lower courts can appeal to have them heard by the Supreme Court, which typically receives about 6,000 to 7,000 petitions every year but usually agrees to review only about 90 to 120 cases that it believes have important constitutional implications. Since World War II, the Court has paid particular attention to cases relating to civil liberties, civil rights, and social equality. Among the most famous of its decisions were *Brown* v. *Board of Education* in 1954, which ended racial segregation in schools; *Miranda* v. *Arizona* in 1966, relating to the rights of criminal defendants; and *Roe* v. *Wade* in 1973, which prohibited states from outlawing abortion.

There are about 750 federal court judges in all, who must be nominated by the president and approved by the Senate. Although lower-level appointments are usually fairly routine and noncontroversial, appointments to the nine positions in the Supreme Court are politically charged. This is partly because Supreme Court judges are appointed for life and can be removed only for serious dereliction of duty and partly because the ideological leanings of judges can affect their decisions. One of the nine judges is appointed Chief Justice of the United States, again for a lifetime term.

SUBNATIONAL GOVERNMENT

The United States is a federation, in which powers are divided between the national government in Washington, D.C., and the governments of the 50 states, each of which has its own constitution, elected governor and state legislature, and constitutional court. Within states, power is further subdivided, with separately elected bodies for city and county government. Although the federal government is responsible for most aspects of economic, foreign, and defense policy, state and local governments are responsible for managing most of the welfare system, maintaining state highways, managing land use, executing many federal laws and regulations, and overseeing education and policing.

The United States is far too big and heterogeneous to be governed under a unitary system of administration, which would, at any rate, fly in the face of American political culture and its emphasis on keeping government as close as possible to the people. Although federalism helps deal with the size and diversity of the country, allows different states to adopt different positions on key issues that are more in tune with local opinion, and offers citizens more opportunities for participation in government, it also creates problems. It slows the process of decision making (which can be a good thing or a bad thing, depending on circumstances), it can make people too focused on narrow goals and values rather than looking at the broader national interest, and it can reduce the power of national government to even out economic and social differences within a country.

REPRESENTATION AND PARTICIPATION

There are several ironies about political participation in the United States. First, voters are faced with more elected offices and elections than in any other liberal democracy, yet turnout rates are among the lowest in the world. Second, American political culture places great emphasis on democracy and civic duty, yet as the number of eligible voters has increased, the proportion who actually vote has fallen. Third, the United States has some of the oldest political parties in the world, yet Americans are offered fewer choices in the way of parties with a realistic chance of winning office and those parties tend to play a relatively weak role in politics.

All three of these phenomena are related and are a reflection of declining party identification among American voters. They are also indicative of a number of features of the political system that discourage voters from taking an active role in politics:

- **The parties look very similar.** Compared with parties in other liberal democracies, the differences between the two major U.S. parties—the Democrats and the Republicans—are not very great. If they were more clearly polarized, more voters might be motivated to go to the polls.

- **Parties are not effective at mobilizing voters.** Whereas they once had grassroots organizations with which people identified and which were good at engaging voters and supporters, state party organizations have become more independent.

- **There are too many elections, and they last too long.** This has become a particular problem with presidential elections, for which early candidates may begin campaigning as much as 2 years before the event itself. In the year leading up to the election, media coverage is so intensive that it runs the risk of boring many voters.

- **Registration can be time-consuming.** Almost every other liberal democracy places the burden of registration on local government, which might send registrars door-to-door, mail registration forms to all residents, or register voters automatically when they pay taxes. In the United States, the burden of registration falls largely on voters. Procedures vary from one state to another, but registration must

FIGURE 1.1

Comparing Voter Turnout

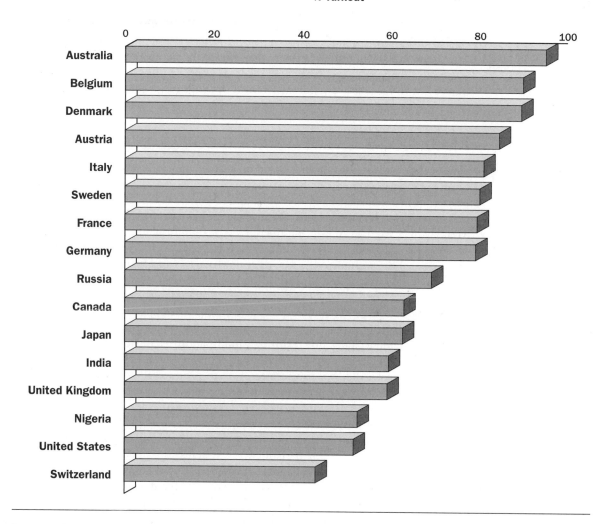

% Turnout

Source: Political Resources on the Net, 2002, *http://www.politicalresources.net*. Figures are for eligible voters, and for the most recent elections in each country. U.S. figure is for 2000 presidential election.

sometimes be completed as much as 25 days before an election. Registration may also qualify voters for jury duty that they can avoid if they remain unregistered.

One of the most distinctive features of U.S. elections is the low voter turnout (see Figure 1.1). European elections usually attract about 75 to 90 percent of eligible voters, but presidential elections in the United States now attract only about 50 to 55 percent of eligible voters (down from 60 to 65 percent in the 1960s), and turnout at midterm congressional elections is as low as 35 percent (down from 45 to 50 percent in the 1960s). It could be argued that low turnout is a reflection of voter satisfaction and that the no-shows believe that the system of government is good enough to continue without their votes. But low turnout reduces the level of legitimacy conferred on government and reduces the accountability of elected officials. It also means that elected officials will tend to look like—and reflect the views of—the people who vote; nonvoters voluntarily cut themselves out of the democratic process. Nonetheless, even though attempts have been made to improve turnout by making registration easier, the absence of so many voters at the polls is not something that seems to concern most Americans very much.

ELECTIONS AND THE ELECTORAL SYSTEM

The American electoral system is based on a timetable under which most elected officials serve an unlimited number of fixed-year terms, the only exceptions being executives (the president, state governors, and city mayors), most of whom serve limited terms. Congressional elections are always held on the first Tuesday after the first Monday in November in even-numbered years, and presidential elections take place on the same day every 4 years. The system is based on the **winner-take-all** rule, meaning that the winning candidate does not have to win a majority (more than half the votes cast) but simply a **plurality** (the largest number of votes).

Elections in the United States are longer, more numerous, and more expensive than in any other liberal democracy. To give citizens the opportunity to have as much say as possible in government, elections are held for offices ranging from the president of the United States down through multiple offices in state and local government. The weakness of political parties has combined with the need for candidates to make themselves known to the electorate to produce a system in which a long process of familiarization is required, resulting in election campaigns that can last several months and can be very expensive.

A notable feature of American elections is the system of **primaries** that are held for most key electoral offices. Rather than parties choosing who will run for office in their name, as is the case in parliamentary systems, the choices are made in the United States by voters casting ballots in primaries. Voters choose from among competing potential candidates, and the winner is then adopted by the party to run in the general election. Primaries are democratic in the sense that they leave it up to voters to choose party candidates, but they also add to the time and expense involved in the electoral process, weaken political parties, and give a few—sometimes unrepresentative—voters considerable impact on the outcome of the nomination process.

The Presidential Election

Without question the dominating event in the American electoral calendar is the race for the presidency, which is the focus of intense national and international media scrutiny and has become a long, drawn-out process. There are four key stages in the process.

The first stage is the informal "preprimary," or exhibition, season, during which the media begin talking about possible candidates and some of the candidates begin forming exploratory committees to look into the possibility of running. The season may begin 2 years or more before the actual election, and in many respects the likely front-runners are determined early according to the amount of attention paid to them in the media. As many as 18 months before the election, the main contenders will start formally to campaign in key states, and some may already have picked up enough sense about the balance of public opinion to have withdrawn. This still often leaves as many as a dozen contenders for the major parties who may start appearing in television debates as much as a year before the election.

The second stage is the formal primary season itself, which begins in the February before the election with votes in New Hampshire and Iowa. It runs until June, peaking on **Super Tuesday** in March, when several states hold their primaries on the same day. The front-runners for the major parties may be decided very early in the process, or the contest may take longer to determine. Either way, the primary season ends in late summer with the holding of national **party conventions.** At one time, it was left to the conventions to finalize the choice of candidate for the major parties, but in recent elections that choice has already been made and the conventions are little more than self-indulgent media events designed to crown the final candidates.

The third stage is the final campaign between the candidates, which by tradition runs from early September until election day in November. At this point, all campaign spending by the major candidates ceases, and their costs are met out of public funds. Media coverage of the candidates intensifies during this period, and it has become usual for the Republican and the Democrat to hold televised debates (although these are not so much one-on-one debates as opportunities for the candidates to outline their programs).

The final stage is the election itself. Even though the candidates for the Republican and Democratic parties are the only ones with a realistic chance of winning, as many as a dozen candidates have run in recent elections, and the 1990s saw the emergence of significant third-party challenges for the first time in decades (see Figure 1.2). Voters do not actually vote directly for the competing candidates, who are instead chosen indirectly through an electoral college. Devised at the time of the writing of the Constitution, this was a compromise between those who wanted Congress to select the president and those who wanted the people to elect the president directly. One of the effects of the college is that candidates are encouraged to focus all their efforts and attention on the larger states; they often bypass smaller states or states they are sure to win or lose. Given that there are 538 electoral votes and that the winner needs only a plurality of those votes to win, a president could theoretically be elected by winning pluralities in just the dozen largest states.

Legislative Elections

Every 2 years, all 435 members of the House of Representatives run for reelection, as do one-third of the members of the U.S. Senate. As with the president, they must all be selected in primaries, but incumbents are rarely seriously challenged and reelection is usually assured. Legislative primaries are subject to much less media and public interest than is the case with their presidential equivalents, but this

FIGURE 1.2

Presidential Electoral Trends in the United States

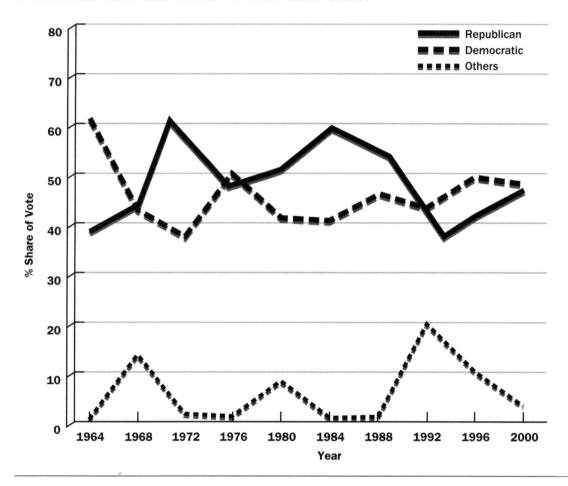

does not mean that candidates do not expend a proportionate amount of effort and money in running for office. This is particularly true of Senate campaigns, for which competition is more intense and in which there is greater public interest. The costs of congressional elections have risen steadily over the last 20 to 30 years, as a result of which campaign funding has become one of the most troubling issues in American politics (see following Close-Up View).

Local Elections

American voters can take part in a wide range of elections at the local level, from those for state governors and legislators to those for mayors, city councilors, chiefs of police, district attorneys, state auditors, library trustees, coroners, town clerks, and

MONEY AND POLITICS

In the country that is the acme of capitalism, it is perhaps only fitting that money has become one of the defining elements of elections. It has always been an issue, notably in the 19th century, when political favors were openly bought by many of the owners of the new corporations then being born in the United States, but it has become a particular bone of contention since the 1970s and changes made to campaign finance laws.

The main problem is the high cost, necessitated mainly by the need for candidates—many of whom may be unknown to voters—to reach a large constituency. In the 2000 congressional elections, the average candidate spent nearly $420,000, with House candidates spending an average of $275,000 and Senate candidates—because they had to cover more ground—spending an average of more than $1.3 million. Total spending on congressional elections has risen from about $200 to $300 million per season in the early 1970s to just over $1 billion in 2000. Presidential campaigns are the most expensive of all, with as little as $2 to $3 million being spent by candidates who dropped out early in 2000, and $150 million being spent by the two final major candidates, Republican George W. Bush and Democrat Al Gore.[8]

Although political culture in the United States places a premium on equality and access to government, the costs of running for office have become so prohibitive that only those with access to large sums of money can now realistically hope to win elected office. Furthermore, changes to the law in 1974 forced candidates to be less reliant on a few large sources of funding and to raise money from a broader constituency. At the same time, a loophole was created by which donors who wanted to give more than they were allowed by federal law could make donations to the national party committees, which could channel the money to state parties faced with less demanding state regulations. This **"soft money"** loophole has become increasingly controversial in recent years, adding to demands for reforms to campaign finance laws.

Another controversial feature of campaign financing is the **political action committee** (PAC). PACs are set up by interest groups to channel money to candidates running for office. A complex body of laws places limits on how much money any one PAC can give to any one candidate directly, but they are also allowed to give money to parties and to spend money promoting particular issues that may help their favored candidates. PACs are controversial because they are a form of institutionalized bribery; they will expect the candidates they support to vote favorably on bills in which their members have an interest.

local school boards. The races for governors and mayors are usually the most hotly contested and draw the most voter interest, with those for local positions being less interesting, if only because most voters know little about the competing candidates.

POLITICAL PARTIES

If you pick up an introductory textbook on American politics and turn to the chapter on parties expecting to see some discussion about what the different parties stand for, you will be disappointed. You will find lengthy histories of party evolution, discussion about party organization, and segments on party conventions and the prospects for third parties, but there will be very little about the differences between the major parties. This reflects the relatively weak role that parties play in American politics.

Only 13 percent of Americans describe themselves as strong Republicans and 19 percent as strong Democrats, whereas the number of independents has risen from 23 percent in the 1950s to about 34 percent today.[9] This suggests that American voters have become disillusioned with the major parties, leading to much discussion in recent years about a realignment of party politics and the declining partisanship of the electorate. American voters will often make their choices at elections on the basis of personalities rather than parties, even to the point of voting for candidates from another party: About 9 to 13 percent of Republicans have routinely voted for Democrats running for the presidency in recent years, and as many as 26 percent of Democrats voted for Republican Ronald Reagan when he ran in 1980 and 1984.

Although there are many political parties in the United States representing a variety of ideological and regional interests, the party system has been monopolized since the 19th century by just two: the Republicans and the Democrats. They have won every presidential election in modern history, and between them they have long held all or most of the seats in the U.S. Congress (see Figure 1.3). The stranglehold of the two parties is based on a variety of factors: They have been able to alter their electoral strategies in such a way as to ensure that breakaway parties or minor parties fail to develop much influence or win seats; they are automatically included on general election ballots, whereas third parties must meet the requirements (such as filing petitions) set by different states; they dominate the middle ground of American politics, which is where most American voters place themselves; and the unpopularity of parties or candidates with strong left-wing or right-wing ideological positions has ensured that the two major parties remain little different from each other.

Republicans

Otherwise known as the GOP (Grand Old Party), the Republicans trace their roots back to the Civil War. During the Civil War, Democrats opposed to slavery broke away to form the new party, which won almost every presidential election for the next 50 years. Republicans alternated with the Democrats in the White House after World War II—being the party of Dwight D. Eisenhower, Richard Nixon, and Ronald Reagan—but they went into opposition in Congress for 40 years, finally winning back a majority in 1994. Most members are moderate conservatives, but the party contains many shades of opinion. Most Republicans today are either traditional conservatives, keen on minimizing the role of government in the economy, or new conservatives, driven by a desire to institutionalize their religious and moral values in the sense of limiting access to legal abortion, promoting prayer in schools, and controlling pornography.[10] The Republicans tend to have the advantage among voters with higher incomes and better education and among voters living in western states such as Arizona, Utah, and Kansas, as well as those living in suburban areas.

FIGURE 1.3

Legislative Electoral Trends in the United States

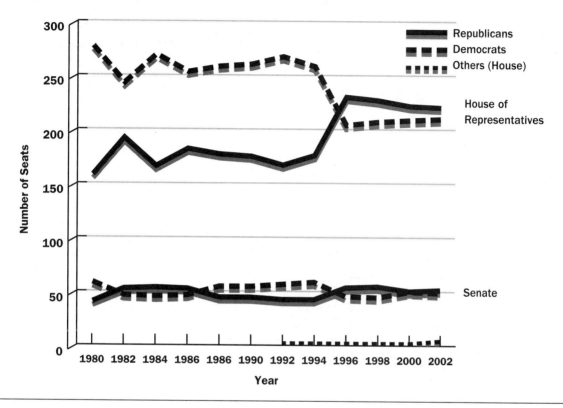

Democrats

The Democratic party traces its roots back to the 1820s and long had its most important base of support in the south. After decades spent mainly in political opposition, the party was swept into office in 1932 on the back of demands that government take a more hands-on approach in dealing with economic and social problems in the wake of the Great Depression. After World War II, it held the White House during the Truman, Kennedy, Johnson, Carter, and Clinton administrations and held a 40-year majority in both houses of Congress. The Democratic party has traditionally been the party of the disadvantaged and continues to be a moderate left-wing party, being in favor of issues such as welfare, regulation of big business, and environmental management. In terms of the sources of its support, it has the advantage among poorer Americans, religious minorities, and the less educated, and it has a very clear advantage among blacks and among voters in southern states and inner-city areas.

Minor Parties

The United States has a long history of minor parties, but the control exerted by the two major parties over the electoral process has combined with the math of the winner-take-all system to prevent any of them from becoming nationally prominent. Among the parties of significance in recent years has been the Reform party, a moderately conservative party which was formed around the presidential bid of Texas billionaire H. Ross Perot in 1992; Perot took away enough votes from Republican George Bush to help Bill Clinton win the presidency that year. It went on to run candidates in several state elections, notably former professional wrestler Jesse Ventura, who won the governorship of Minnesota in 1998. Another national party is the pro-environmental Green party, which ran Ralph Nader as its presidential candidate in 2000 and took enough votes away from the Democrats to help George W. Bush win. Finally, the Libertarian party holds a number of conservative positions but has not yet had an impact on the presidential election. None of these parties has yet won seats in Congress, even though they won more than 15 million votes—or 5.3 percent of the total cast—in the 2000 elections.[11]

INTEREST GROUPS

The United States has a substantial and diverse interest-group community, with organizations representing a variety of interests and occasionally attracting mass memberships. The popularity of groups is, in part, a reflection of the relative weakness of political parties—people who are not particularly interested in politics may be more motivated to become involved in promoting an issue that particularly interests them and therefore more likely to form or join a group that supports that issue. Support tends to be passive for most, however, and there has been evidence of a fall-off in the membership of groups in recent years.[12] Interest groups fall into four major categories:

- **Institutional interests,** or groups that represent other organizations, such as corporations, trade organizations, governments, foundations, and universities. There are literally hundreds of professional organizations based in Washington, D.C., and state capitals that are available for recruitment by individuals or groups wishing to **lobby** government, that is, influence the outcome of public policy. Equally, there are organizations that collectively represent the interests of member bodies; for example, the American Council on Education represents most American colleges and universities, and the U.S. Chamber of Commerce represents thousands of different businesses in multiple areas.

- **Economic interest groups** that are mainly interested in issues relating to wages, prices, and profits. Labor organizations are the most obvious examples and include the AFL-CIO—a federation of unions with a total of 13 million members—and the Teamsters, which represents truck drivers. Like unions everywhere, they campaign for better working conditions and fair wages and also push for the union shop, which would oblige all new employees to join the union representing them.

- **Single- and multiple-issue groups,** which concentrate their efforts on particular issues. The issues they focus on may be as specific as drunk driving (Mothers Against Drunk Driving [MADD], which has been effective at making this problem into a public issue) or as broad as the interests of elderly Americans. One of the most powerful of all multiple-issue groups is the American Association of Retired Persons (AARP), membership of which is open to anyone older than age 50. The group has 33 million members and can mobilize them whenever policies relating to health care, pensions, taxes, or anything that might be of interest to the elderly are under discussion.[13]

- **Public interest groups,** or organizations that do not have a particular set of parochial interests but that try to influence policy in what they define as the public interest. Examples include the Public Interest Research Groups that work in almost every American state, focusing mainly on environmental, consumer, and public health issues.

One of the criticisms leveled at elected officials by many Americans is that government has become less responsive to the needs of citizens as the power and influence of interest groups has grown. Those worried about the health of American democracy point to the existence of **"iron triangles,"** which consist of interest groups, congressional committees, and government agencies. Each needs the other to achieve its goals, and the three elements have developed a symbiotic relationship that ensures that groups have become more influential than individual citizens. (Compare these with the iron triangles in Japan—see Chapter 3.)

THE MEDIA

The United States has one of the most diverse and politically active mass media establishments in the world, with a variety of print and broadcast sources from which to choose and more people linked to the Internet than in any other country. There are four major TV networks (ABC, CBS, NBC, and Fox), dozens of cable networks, many substantial big city newspapers (such as *The New York Times,* the *Los Angeles Times,* and *The Washington Post*), and hundreds of magazines and news radio stations catering to almost every need and taste imaginable.

But although much is made of the role of the media in shaping the views of the electorate and communicating the policies of government, relatively few Americans use the media to help them understand and keep up with politics. On one hand, the media play a critical role in politics in terms of shaping public opinion and helping set the public agenda, and television in particular has become central to every serious election campaign—all candidates for national and key state offices develop TV campaigns, employ media consultants, and spend much of their funding on making and placing commercials. On the other hand, polls indicate that media coverage of issues and campaigns has less impact on voter opinions and choices than once thought. Television coverage of national party conventions has declined, and the once ballyhooed television "debates" between competing candidates have little effect on voter preferences.

Two other important points help explain the reduced impact of the media on American politics:

- With the exceptions of cable television news, nightly public affairs programs on the major terrestrial networks, newspapers such as *The Wall Street Journal*, and National Public Radio (NPR), there is little in the way of a national media establishment in the United States. Most TV and radio stations and newspapers are local, focus on local news, and carry only secondhand national or international news relayed by wire services.

- The amount of hard news coverage has declined as the media compete to attract viewers, listeners, and readers with a view to increasing advertising revenues. This is particularly true of nightly news on the four major networks: In the typical 30-minute broadcast, 9 minutes is given over to commercials, and much of the balance deals less with hard news than with lifestyle stories and "soft news" about developments in medicine, personal finance, education, and related issues.

If the amount of time devoted to hard news has fallen, coverage of international news has all but disappeared (except on NPR, on cable TV channels such as CNN or MSNBC, or in big city newspapers). It is probably now true to say that most Americans look to the media more for entertainment than for news and are more ready to switch on their TVs to watch a football game or a sitcom than to learn about developments in national or global politics.

POLICIES AND POLICYMAKING

Public policy in the United States is driven by a combination of constraints and opportunities that is unique to the American political system. As with all liberal democracies, it has a political system in which many different actors give input to the process, from elected officials to voters, parties, interest groups, the media, and private corporations. At the same time, expectations regarding the role of government are relatively limited. Whereas most Western Europeans are used to large government programs and a relatively high degree of state intervention in social affairs, Americans have traditionally given much weight (in theory at least) to the idea of self-determination. Government is expected to do less than is the case in most other liberal democracies, although in fact it is significantly involved—through regulation, the provision of welfare, subsidies to states, and contracts to private business. The role of government is also influenced by at least five other factors.

First, the government of the United States must respond to the needs of a society that is more diverse than that of any other liberal democracy. As noted earlier, race is a key factor, partly because ethnic minorities make up about 25 percent of the population and partly because racism is still a problem in the United States. In almost every respect—educational opportunities, housing, life expectancy, and so on—there are significant differences between whites, blacks, and Latinos, and Americans are regularly reminded of the implications of these differences. Age is also a factor: As Americans live longer and the population becomes older, more pressure is put on the social security and health care systems.

Second, the freedom of action that the president, Congress, or the courts have on policy is constrained by checks and balances and by the absence of party unity in Congress. Neither the president nor Congress can act alone in making policy or responding to needs and crises. They must constantly reach compromises to ensure that their programs are put into effect, laws are passed, and money is spent. Not only is power divided horizontally, but there is also a vertical division between the federal government in Washington, D.C., and the governments of the states. The latter have a high degree of freedom over policy in a variety of areas—notably education, policing, and criminal justice—whereas federal law and policy usually depend on the cooperation of the states for its successful implementation.

Third, the abilities of the federal government to get anything done are severely constrained by the realities of the budget. The size of the U.S. federal budget has grown to match the expansion of federal government activities: It was $60 billion in 1962, $500 billion in 1982, and $1.88 trillion in 2000. However, most expenditures are made in a limited number of areas. About half goes to payments to individuals in the form of social security, health care, and other benefits; 15 percent goes to grants to state and local governments; 14 percent is spent on defense; 11 percent goes to pay interest on the national debt; and all other operations must be covered by the remaining 5 percent. Furthermore, the federal government does not have much room for maneuver, because about two-thirds of all spending is "mandatory," or committed, and therefore cannot be redirected at will. Finally, the United States has dug itself into a large budgetary hole by building up a large national debt: It stood at about $5.5 trillion in 2002 and promised to become even bigger with the deficit spending and tax refunds of the Bush administration.

Fourth, the options facing the federal government are influenced by the fact that the United States is the world's last remaining military superpower and has obligations as a global leader. Isolationists within the United States argue that it should pull back from these obligations, whereas unilateralists argue that, should the United States remain active in world affairs, it should do so on its own terms rather than working through the United Nations or in concert with allies. But these are minority views, and successive administrations continue to argue that the United States must protect its economic and strategic interests as part of a global community. This has become particularly critical since the launch of the war on terrorism, which has involved the commitment of an even bigger part of the national budget to military spending.

Finally, the United States is a predominantly free-market economic system with some of the largest corporations in the world, so the private sector has considerable influence over the directions taken by policy. The private sector accounts for nearly two-thirds of GDP and 85 percent of employment. Thus, corporations inevitably have a key role to play in issues such as the development of new technology, labor relations, pay scales, the opening of new factories and the closing of old ones, and the revitalization of decaying urban and rural areas.

The effect of all these pressures is that although policies are driven by the president and Congress, they are only two among a variety of actors in the American policy system. The decisions taken by national government in the United States are affected by a complex interplay involving the private sector, government agencies, state legislatures and city councils, governors and mayors, the media, interest groups, the courts, public opinion, foreign governments, and international organizations.[14]

ECONOMIC POLICY

The U.S. economy is the biggest in the world in absolute terms. With a GDP of more than $10 trillion, it has an economy almost as big as those of all 15 members of the European Union combined, and although it has less than 5 percent of the world's population, it accounts for nearly 25 percent of global economic output. Economists have not always agreed on the explanations for the growth and success of the U.S. economy, but it has involved an element of trial and error.

Until the Great Depression of the early 1930s, the United States subscribed to classical economic theories of the kind associated with the writings of Adam Smith, who argued that the market economy was a self-adjusting mechanism that worked best if left alone. Recession would stay away, inflation and unemployment would stay low, and productivity would stay high if the economy was left to the forces of the marketplace. The Great Depression shattered this view: Unemployment jumped to 25 percent and was still at 18 percent in 1936, 7 years after the Wall Street crash of 1929. With questions being asked about the ability of the market to

© B. Roland/The Image Works

The floor of the New York Stock Exchange on Wall Street in New York City. For many, Wall Street represents the heart of global capitalism. The remarkable growth in the U.S. economy in the 1990s was reflected in record trading activity on the floor of the exchange, just as the subsequent economic downturn was reflected in falls in the value of shares and stock indices such as the Dow.

stabilize itself, the theories of British economist John Maynard Keynes began to win support.

Keynes argued that the government should involve itself in economic policy by manipulating demand through the budget. His ideas were reflected in the 1946 Employment Act, which committed the federal government to taxing and spending policies aimed at promoting maximum employment. This worked well during the 1950s and 1960s, but the popularity of Keynesian theory was undermined in the 1970s when the United States experienced stagflation, or inflation and a stagnant economy at the same time. President Reagan described Keynesian economics as "the failed policies of the past," and his administration opted instead for **supply-side economics** (or neoclassical economics). The argument was that taxes penalized hard work, creativity, investments, and savings, so they should be cut, government spending should be held in check, regulations should be minimized, and government should work to stimulate supply rather than demand.

Under Reagan, taxes were lowered, especially for the wealthy. The 1981 Economic Recovery Tax Act cut the top income tax rate from 50 percent to 29 percent, and the average income tax rate fell to 23 percent. The assumption was that this would free up money for investment, encourage people to work, and redistribute wealth and opportunity through a **"trickle-down"** effect. Unfortunately, Reaganomics also reduced federal government income at a time when the Reagan administration was increasing spending on the military from 4.5 percent of GNP to 6.5 percent. Although inflation fell and productivity grew during the Reagan years and unemployment fell from more than 10 percent to 5 percent, the national debt nearly tripled.

By 1991, the United States was in a **recession** (meaning two consecutive quarters of economic decline), a problem that contributed to the defeat of George Bush in the 1992 election. The economy then rallied, and by the end of the decade GDP and industrial production were growing at 3 to 4 percent annually, unemployment was at 4 percent, several regions of the country had labor shortages, and consumer price inflation was running at 2 to 3 percent. The market was so buoyant that President Clinton's popularity rating was at 60 percent or higher even while Congress was holding impeachment hearings against him in the first half of 1999. The United States was meanwhile supporting free trade, pressuring countries that protected their markets (notably China), and signing the North American Free Trade Agreement (NAFTA) with Canada and Mexico in 1993. The national debt continued to grow during the Clinton administration, but agreement was reached between the White House and Congress on the budget, and 1999 saw a budget surplus for the first time since the Nixon administration in the late 1960s.

Not all the news is good, however. After making astonishing profits for entrepreneurs and shareholders, the bottom fell out of the new technology market in 2001–2002, greatly reducing personal savings and pension plans for many. A string of accounting scandals during the same period led to the collapse of major corporations such as Enron and WorldCom, and undermined public faith in corporate America. The U.S. **trade deficit** continues to grow, with imports to the United States in 2000 being 36 percent higher in value than exports. The United States continues to lack a comprehensive energy policy and relies heavily on imported oil, raising the prospect of an energy-price shock to the economy. There has been a steady loss of manufacturing jobs to countries where workers are paid less, and although the shortfall has been met by more jobs in the service sector, many of these are poorly paid. The gap between the rich and the poor has grown to the point where the poorest 40 percent of Americans now make 15 percent of the national income, whereas the richest 40 percent make 67 percent of the national income. Americans save little as a percentage of their income, so there is less money available for investment. At the same time, they borrow a lot, and personal bankruptcies have reached an all-time high.

The U.S. economy is the strongest in the world, but several trends suggest that the United States is facing levels of economic competition that it has not seen since before World War II. In his first 2 years in office, George W. Bush became focused on the war on terrorism, and although this initially won him high public approval ratings, his critics charged that he was not spending enough time addressing the underlying problems that might interfere with long-term economic growth and success.

FOREIGN POLICY

As the world's only remaining military superpower and—with the European Union—one of its two economic superpowers, the United States is a dominant force in international relations. It does not have the world's biggest military—China's is bigger—but it does have the world's biggest military arsenal, the most technologically advanced weapons systems, and the ability to launch quick and devastating attacks almost anywhere in the world with minimal loss of personnel. But there is much debate among Americans at the beginning of the new millennium about just what kind of role the United States should be playing in the world and about how U.S. foreign policy interests should be defined. During the cold war, the overriding objectives were to contain the Soviet Union, to limit the spread of communist influence, and to neutralize the Soviet nuclear threat. With the end of the cold war, however, the world has become a less predictable place. U.S. foreign policy interests were beginning to shift away from defensive and strategic issues toward economic and trade issues, but then came the September 2001 attacks and a new set of issues moved to the top of the agenda.

The worldview held by policymakers in the United States has combined with shifts in public opinion to move U.S. foreign policy in different directions, most of which have been driven by arguments over whether the United States should be isolationist or interventionist. Taking the broad view, foreign policy has gone through three major phases.

Isolationism (1776–1941)

For the first century and a half of its independent existence, the general feeling was that the United States should not become involved in developments outside the Americas. The **Monroe Doctrine** of 1823 (named after President James Monroe) declared that the western hemisphere would be off-limits to colonization or intervention by European states, but the doctrine was little more than symbolic because the United States lacked the military power to back it up. Furthermore, the idea of isolationism should not be taken too literally: There were conflicts and war with Mexico, the United States was active in opening up commercial ties with Japan and Korea in the late 19th century, it became involved in the internal affairs of several Latin American and Caribbean states, and it fought a war with Spain in 1898 over Cuba. On the global stage, however, the Europeans—notably Britain, France, and Germany—held the balance of power, and the United States restricted its foreign policy interests to the western hemisphere.

This began to change with World War I and the U.S. role in the signing of the Treaty of Versailles and the creation of the League of Nations, and it continued to change with World War II. Although the United States was a relative latecomer—the war had already been underway for more than 2 years by the time the Japanese attacked Pearl Harbor in December 1941—there was little public opposition to U.S. involvement, and indeed World War II ultimately became the only really popular war in which the United States has ever been involved. The issues and the goals were relatively clear, the enemy was clear, the Allies were the undisputed victors, and the efforts of the Allies (including the Soviets) made sure that the world was made safe from the threat of fascism.

The Cold War (1945–1990)

World War II had two effects on U.S. foreign policy. First, the European powers emerged from the war economically and militarily drained, and Britain and France were under pressure to dismantle their empires. As the relative influence of these countries declined, the United States and the USSR became the dominating military powers in the world. Second, this new arrangement made it difficult for the United States to revert to isolationism. It has since played an active role in international affairs, backed up by the balance of public opinion, which shifted from the isolationist stance of the prewar years to being in favor of engagement. The wars in Europe and Japan had barely ended before the United States found itself embroiled in a "war" of a very different kind.

The cold war began before the end of World War II, with mutual suspicion between the Western allies on one side and the Soviets, led by Stalin, on the other. Stalin ensured that the peace arrangements would give the Soviet Union control over most of Eastern Europe, and the continent became divided by an **"iron curtain"** of military hardware as both sides staked out their claims to influence and territory. President Truman in 1947 announced the Truman Doctrine, under which assistance would be given to countries threatened with subversion. In the same year, the Marshall Plan was launched to provide Western European states with economic aid aimed at helping their economies rebuild and reducing the likelihood of the spread of communist influence. In 1948, Britain and the United States began airlifting supplies into West Berlin after the institution of a Soviet blockade. In 1949, the United States and ten Western European states formed the North Atlantic Treaty Organization (NATO), designed to send a message to the USSR that an attack on any of its members would be considered an attack on them all.

Thereafter, it became U.S. policy to contain and deter the spread of communism, even if it meant supporting authoritarian regimes, including several in Central America, Southeast Asia, the Middle East, and central Africa. It fought a war in Korea in 1950–1953, and then, driven by President Eisenhower's **"domino theory"** (allowing one state to fall to communism would lead to similar outcomes for neighboring states), became involved in propping up the government of South Vietnam against communist incursions from the north. The war dragged on until the fall of Saigon in April 1975, cost 56,000 American lives, became increasingly unpopular, and raised many questions about the broader motives behind U.S. foreign policy.

The United States also entered a nuclear arms race with the Soviet Union, prompted in part by the 1958 launch by the Soviets of Sputnik (the first global satellite) and in part by the failed Soviet attempt in 1962 to site nuclear warheads in Cuba. President Nixon hoped that confrontation with the Soviets could be replaced with negotiation, to which end the United States and the USSR pursued a policy of **détente** aimed at reducing tensions between the two superpowers. This led to the 1972 Strategic Arms Limitation agreement (SALT I) placing limits on nuclear weapons and antiballistic missile systems. (SALT II—involving further limits—was agreed to in 1979 but never approved by Congress.) During the 1970s and 1980s, the concerns of the United States were focused on a number of regional issues, notably the Arab-Israeli conflict (see Critical Issues, p. 453), the Iranian revolution in 1979, the Iran-Iraq war of 1980–1988, and several disputes in the Caribbean and Central America (Nicaragua, Panama, and Grenada among others). At the same time, the Reagan administration put more pressure on the "evil empire" of the Soviets, increasing spending on the military by more than $100 billion annually and launching research on a Strategic Defense Initiative intended to defend the United States against incoming Soviet missiles.

New World Order (1990–)

The end of the cold war is usually dated from the reunification of Germany in October 1990. In 1991, President George Bush made a speech in which he spoke of a "new world order." He thus gave some identity to the nature of the post–cold war world, even though the meaning of the phrase has never been fully elaborated. The implication is that rather than the balance of power being driven by competition between the United States and its allies on one side and the Soviets and their allies on the other, there are now multiple centers of power in the world and a variety of new issues. The United States is still the dominant military power in the world, with the technology and personnel to carry out military operations almost anywhere it believes U.S. interests are threatened, and it can do so in a matter of days or weeks, with minimal casualties. (Operation Iraqi Freedom in 2003 lasted about 3 weeks and resulted in just over 150 American casualties.)

At the same time, though, the United States is far from omnipotent; because several other countries have nuclear weapons and several have large armies, the United States faces growing economic competition from several quarters, notably Western

THE WAR ON TERRORISM

At least during the last 200 years or so, most of the threats and competition faced by states have come from other states. This has made it relatively easy to identify the source of the problem and to respond. But the September 2001 attacks represented a new kind of threat, one that is more difficult to deal with. Terrorists work in networks broken up into small cells, and destroying the cells—and even killing the leaders—is no guarantee of victory. Unlike states, which launch sustained attacks with troops and military hardware, terrorists strike against different targets at different times, using different methods. And whereas conventional war involves military forces fighting against each other for dominance, and civilians mainly being hurt in the crossfire, terrorism by definition involves attacks on both military and civilian targets with a view to literally terrorizing governments into changing policy.

Terrorism is something to which Western Europeans, Arabs, and Israelis in particular have become quite used to since World War II. Whether it has been over the future of Northern Ireland, independence for the Basques, the Catalans, or the Corsicans, or the struggle for a Palestinian state, terror tactics have often been horribly familiar: car bombs, letter bombs, suicide bombers, threats against mass transit systems, assassinations, hijackings, and so on. They have been used also against mainland American targets, but much less frequently. The first major example of modern times came with the bombing of the World Trade Center in New York in February 1993,

which took six lives but quickly disappeared from the headlines. Then there was the bombing of the federal government building in Oklahoma City in April 1995, which took 169 lives and attracted attention to critics of the federal government.

The attacks of September 2001 were of an altogether different scale and employed entirely unprecedented and audacious methods. They were perpetrated by Islamic extremists, and the Bush administration responded by launching a war against the Taliban regime in Afghanistan, which was harboring the Al-Qaeda organization—accused of being behind the attacks—and its leader Osama bin Laden. President Bush then targeted Iraq, but this time less for its links with terrorism than for allegations that it was producing weapons of mass destruction. Meanwhile, efforts were made to increase domestic security, and American society lost much of the openness for which it was famed.

For several months after the 2001 attacks there was a public debate in the United States about what had driven the extremists, the explanations including criticism of U.S. policy on Israel/Palestine and the presence of the U.S. military in Saudi Arabia, the holy land of Islam. Instead of addressing the complaints, however, the Bush administration chose to orchestrate a program of war and diplomatic pressure on countries it described as threats, leaving its critics to charge that the "war on terrorism" was focusing too much on the effects rather than the causes of the problem.

Europe and Southeast Asia, and there is now the threat posed by international terrorism (see Critical Issues, p. 73). Public and political opinion within the United States is also divided on future policy; at least until September 2001, the majority of Americans wanted the United States to remain a military superpower, but many questioned the amounts spent on defense and asked whether American lives should be risked in such distant locations as Somalia, Kosovo, or East Timor. There are also isolationist elements within Congress, and the average American has very little interest in world affairs, prompted by news media whose coverage of those affairs is often superficial at best.

Whereas foreign policy during the cold war was focused on defense matters, the new world order has raised a much greater variety of issues demanding a much more sophisticated understanding of international relations. Prior to September 2001, polls found that the priorities of policymakers and the public included the following:[15]

- Protecting the jobs of American workers
- Preventing the spread of nuclear, chemical, and biological weapons
- Stopping the flow of illegal drugs and immigrants into the United States
- Securing adequate supplies of energy, mainly oil
- Ensuring economic stability in troubled countries such as Mexico and Russia
- Addressing global environmental problems, such as global warming
- Addressing trade imbalances, notably with China and Japan
- Promoting global free trade
- Ensuring peace in the Middle East
- Playing a constructive role in key international organizations of which the United States is a member, such as the United Nations, the OECD, and NATO
- Responding militarily to regional trouble spots such as the Balkans and Iraq
- Addressing the threat of terrorism, particularly from "pariah" states such as Libya

Since September 2001, the United States has found itself in a new age of foreign policy uncertainty. The goals are not quite as clear as they were during the cold war, the threats and opportunities are coming from a variety of new sources, and questions are raised about the extent to which Americans are prepared to adapt themselves to the new foreign policy priorities. The Bush administration showed itself willing to take a new unilateralist line on foreign policy, preserving what it defined as U.S. interests, with or without the support of its traditional allies. Whether this is just the tactics of a single administration or part of a new long-term trend in U.S. foreign policy remains to be seen.

U.S. POLITICS IN TRANSITION

The 20th century was often described as the American century, a reflection of the extent to which the new-found military and economic power of the United States made it a global leader, notably after World War II. Its population grew and became more affluent, its corporations became world leaders, its economy became the engine of worldwide economic growth, and it led the Western alliance in its opposition to the Soviet bloc during the cold war.

At the same time, the United States went through notable internal political and social change. Women and ethnic minorities became more integrated into the political system, and demographic changes led to a redefinition of the balance of power—the population became older and more ethnically diverse, suburbs expanded at the expense of downtown areas, and southern states grew relative to the old industrial northern states. Cynicism about politics fueled a reaction against politics-as-usual and contributed to declining support for political parties and falling turnout at elections.

At the start of the new millennium, the United States faces new debates about the nature of politics (notably the influence of interest groups and structural problems with campaign funding). It also faces many pressing domestic social needs (notably the persistence of poverty and racism) and must redefine its place in the world now that the Soviet threat has gone and has apparently been replaced by the problem of terrorism. The next few years promise to be an interesting time in American politics as politicians and voters rethink their priorities.

KEY TERMS

American Dream
Articles of Confederation
big government
checks and balances
Civil War
Democrats
détente
domino theory
electoral college
federation
Great Depression
Great Society
iron curtain
iron triangle

isolationism
judicial review
lobby
Monroe Doctrine
New Deal
new world order
party conventions
Pax Americana
plurality
political action
    committee
primaries
Reaganomics
recession

republic
Republicans
segregation
Senate majority leader
separation of powers
soft money
Speaker of the House
Super Tuesday
supply-side economics
trade deficit
trickle-down
War Powers Act
winner-take-all

KEY PEOPLE

George Bush
George W. Bush
Bill Clinton

Richard Nixon
Ronald Reagan

Franklin D. Roosevelt
George Washington

STUDY QUESTIONS

1. Have the goals of the U.S. Constitution kept up with the needs of the American people? What amendments (if any) would you make?

2. Does the president of the United States have too much power, too little, or just the right amount?

3. Does the electoral college any longer serve a useful purpose?

4. Is low voter turnout something that Americans should worry about?

5. Are there too few political parties in the United States?

6. Are there too many elections in the United States?

7. How would you change the law (if at all) to reduce the role of money in politics?

8. What are the causes of the terrorism that the United States has faced since 2001?

9. What are the features of the new world order, and should the United States be taking a unilateral or a multilateral approach to addressing global problems?

THE UNITED STATES ONLINE

White House: *http://www.whitehouse.gov*
Official Web site for the White House, with information on the structure and work of the presidency and the White House staff and advisory bodies.

Library of Congress Web Links:
Contains a host of useful links related to the executive *(http://www.loc.gov/ global/executive/fed.html)* and the judiciary *(http://www.loc.gov/law/guide)*.

Thomas: *http://thomas.loc.gov*
Contains a wealth of information on the workings and activities of Congress.

Elect-USA: *http://www.elect-usa.com/*
All the latest news on elections at every level in the United States, including the most recent polls.

CNN/AllPolitics: *http://www.cnn.com/ALLPOLITICS*
A useful site containing the latest political news from CNN.

FURTHER READING

Barone, Michael, et al., *The Almanac of American Politics* (Washington, DC: National Journal, biannual since 1980). A handbook of information on Congress, with descriptions of members, their districts, and their voting records.

Peters, B. Guy, *American Public Policy: Promise and Performance*, 5th Ed. (Chappaqua, NY: Chatham House Publishers, 1999). An introduction to public policy in the United States, with chapters on the policy process and on seven key policy areas.

Welch, Susan, John Gruhl, John Comer, Susan M. Rigdon, and Jan Vermeer, *Understanding American Government*, 5th Ed. (Belmont, CA: West/Wadsworth, 1999), and Christine Barbour and Gerald Wright, *Keeping the Republic: Power and Citizenship in American Politics* (Boston: Houghton Mifflin, 2001). Two of the dozens of introductory U.S. politics texts on the market.

COMPARATIVE FOCUS

EXECUTIVES

Americans have lived for more than 200 years with the idea that the functions of government should be divided: The legislature makes laws, the executive oversees the application of those laws, and the judiciary ensures that the laws and actions of government fit with the terms of the Constitution. This principle of the separation of powers is usually attributed to the 18th century French philosopher and political theorist Baron de Montesquieu (1689–1755), even though it was implicit in the writings of Aristotle and also addressed by John Locke. Montesquieu believed that the most obvious sign of despotism was when a single leader combined all three powers and that the best way to limit the powers of government was to make sure that the three roles be separated from each other as clearly as possible and balanced against each other.

Although virtually every political system in the world has equivalents of each of these three "branches" of government, power is divided among them very differently, and the role of the executive varies substantially.

- **The parliamentary executive.** This is the most common form of executive, found in Britain and in all those countries that have adopted the British parliamentary system, including almost all Western European states, Canada, Australia, New Zealand, India, Israel, and most Caribbean states. The executive consists of a prime minister and a cabinet, is drawn from the legislature, depends on party numbers in the legislature for its power, and coexists with a symbolic head of state. The prime minister is typically leader of the party with the majority of seats in the legislature or—if there is no majority party—the leader of the biggest party, or of the multiparty coalition that has come together to form the government. He or she governs with the help of a cabinet of ministers drawn from the majority party or coalition. There is no limit to how long a prime minister stays in office, provided he or she calls elections as required, his or her party wins enough seats, and the prime minister keeps the support of enough members of the legislature.

Under this arrangement, the executive and the legislature are fused, because the prime minister is always a member of the legislature and so are most (or all) of the members of the cabinet. They usually all stand for election at the same time as all the other members of the legislature. If members of his or her party vote against the government or drop out of the governing coalition, the prime minister's position is weakened and the executive could even fall if there is a rebellion among members of the governing party or coalition or if the prime minister loses a vote of confidence.

- **The limited presidential executive.** This is the second most common form of executive, found in the United States and in all those countries that have adopted the American political system; they include most Latin American states and several African and Asian states. The executive consists of a president elected separately from the legislature for a limited number of fixed-length terms and who has most of the powers that are divided in the parliamentary system between the head of state and the head of government. Presidents govern with the help of a cabinet of ministers, who are usually nominated by the president and confirmed by one of the chambers of the legislature. Presidents are not formally leaders of their parties, and their position does not depend on them having the support of a majority of members of the legislature; while in office, they can usually only be removed by impeachment.

Under this arrangement, the executive and the legislature are separate, because neither the president nor members of the cabinet can be members of the legislature, and there is a system of checks and balances between the two. Presidents have limits placed on their powers, but they also have independent responsibilities (particularly over foreign policy); it helps if they have a sympathetic legislature, but they can outwit the legislature if they are able strategists, and they usually have the power to veto proposals from the legislature. They do not lose office if there is a rebellion among members of their party in the legislature, and they do not face votes of confidence.

- **The dual executive.** This is a more unusual arrangement, found in Austria, Cyprus, Finland, France, Portugal, Russia, and a few Eastern European states. It involves a mixture of the parliamentary and presidential systems, dividing executive powers between an elected executive president serving fixed (but not always limited) terms and a prime minister and cabinet who head the largest party or coalition in the legislature. The president is head of state but also has considerable powers over policymaking, sharing these with the prime minister in his or her role as head of government. The president and the prime minister do not need to come from the same party; if they do, the prime minister tends to be a functionary of the president, but if they do not, the prime minister can develop more independence.

Under this arrangement, the executive and the legislature are separate, but the president depends on having the cooperation of the prime minister—and preferably the support of a majority of members of the legislature—in order to govern effectively. There is no clear separation of powers, and clever (or devious) presidents can take the credit for successful policies while blaming their prime ministers for failed policies. Presidents do not lose office if there is a rebellion among members of their party in the legislature, and they do not face votes of confidence. But if voters return the opposition to power in a legislative election, the president can find his or her hands tied. However, if no one party has a majority—as has been the case recently in Russia—a clever president can also exploit divisions in the legislature to make policy.

- **The unlimited presidential executive.** This is the kind of system commonly found in African states without military governments. The president coexists with a legislature, but the president's party is usually the dominant party and the president has so many powers that the legislature is little more than a rubber-stamp institution. There may be limits on the length of presidential terms, but there are no limits on the number of terms, and the president is usually assured of reelection. The balance of power lies squarely with the executive, encouraging authoritarian tendencies.

More authoritarian regimes—such as those run by military governments or absolute monarchies—have systems in which all effective power lies in the hands of the executive, and legislatures may have been abolished altogether. Absolutist executives stay in office as long as they can and usually face few limits to the expression of their powers.

CHAPTER 2

BRITAIN

BRITAIN: QUICK FACTS

Official name: United Kingdom of Great Britain and Northern Ireland

Capital: London

Area: 94,249 square miles (244,103 sq. km, about the size of Oregon)

Languages: Overwhelmingly English, with some regional languages (Welsh, Gaelic)

Population: 59.90 million

Population density: 645 per square mile

Population growth rate: 0.3 percent

POLITICAL INDICATORS

Freedom House rating: Free

Date of state formation: Debatable; arguably 1066

System type: Parliamentary democracy with a constitutional monarchy

Constitution: Unwritten

Administration: Unitary

Executive: Prime minister and cabinet

Legislature: Bicameral Houses of Parliament; House of Lords (currently undergoing structural reformation) and House of Commons (659 members). Lords are appointed; MPs are elected to renewable 5-year terms

Party structure: Multiparty, with two dominant parties (Labour and Conservative) and several smaller parties

Judiciary: No separate judiciary; House of Lords is highest court of appeal

Head of state: Queen Elizabeth II (1952–)

Head of government: Tony Blair (1997–)

ECONOMIC INDICATORS

GDP (2001): $1,406 billion

Per capita GDP: $24,230

Distribution of GNP: Services 70 percent, industry 29 percent, agriculture 1 percent

Urban population: 89 percent

SOCIAL INDICATORS

HDI ranking: 14

Infant mortality rate: 6 per 1,000 live births

Life expectancy: 77.3 years

Illiteracy: 0 percent of people aged 15 and older

Religions: Predominantly Anglican, with Catholic and Presbyterian minorities

INTRODUCTION

Britain is routinely included in courses on comparative politics, for several important reasons. First, it was the birthplace of the parliamentary system, elements of which are found in every liberal democracy. Second, it was the birthplace of the industrial revolution and has long had an important influence on economic developments in the rest of the world. Third, it is a leading member of all the key international organizations, notably the North Atlantic Treaty Organization (NATO), the UN Security Council (on which it has veto power), the European Union (EU), and the G-8 group of major economic powers.

Despite Britain's prominence in the world, many of us are still tripped up by its name. The United Kingdom of Great Britain and Northern Ireland (its official title) is actually four countries in one: Great Britain—made up of England, Scotland, and Wales—and Northern Ireland. England predominates because it conquered and assimilated the others; because it is home to more than four out of five Britons; and because London is the wealthiest part of the country and is the political, financial, cultural, and communications capital of Britain. However, Scotland, Wales, and Northern Ireland are also part of the United Kingdom (UK), and it is wrong to call the whole country "England"; it is more correctly known either as Britain or the United Kingdom.

Like all its neighbors, Britain is a small, crowded, and highly urbanized country. With a population of nearly 60 million, it has a population density of 645 people per square mile (compared to about 80 people per square mile in the United States and about 8 per square mile in Canada). The density of the population puts a premium on cooperation and makes it more difficult for the average citizen to move away from the reach of government.

In economic terms, Britain has all the typical features of a postindustrial free-market society. It has a GDP of just over $1.4 trillion, more than two-thirds of which is generated by services. It is one of the world's biggest producers of oil, natural gas, and coal. It exports a variety of manufactured goods and has plenty of prime agricultural land, but it has relatively few other natural resources and must import raw materials such as cotton, wool, rubber, and tin. Its economy is one of the freest in the world and has recently been growing faster than that of almost any other European country, but this latter-day boom has come at the end of several painful decades of economic transition, which has altered the distribution of wealth and political power in Britain.

In social terms, it has several important divisions:

- Regional identity is strong, with cultural and political differences among the English, the Scots, the Welsh, and the Northern Irish. **Devolution**—the shifting of government powers from the central government in London to the regions—has been a continuing issue, prompting the creation in 1998 of regional assemblies for Scotland, Wales, and Northern Ireland. Some nationalists in Scotland and Wales even support the idea of complete independence from England.

- Social class was long a defining characteristic of British society, with a hierarchy in place by which most Britons placed themselves—or were placed—in the upper,

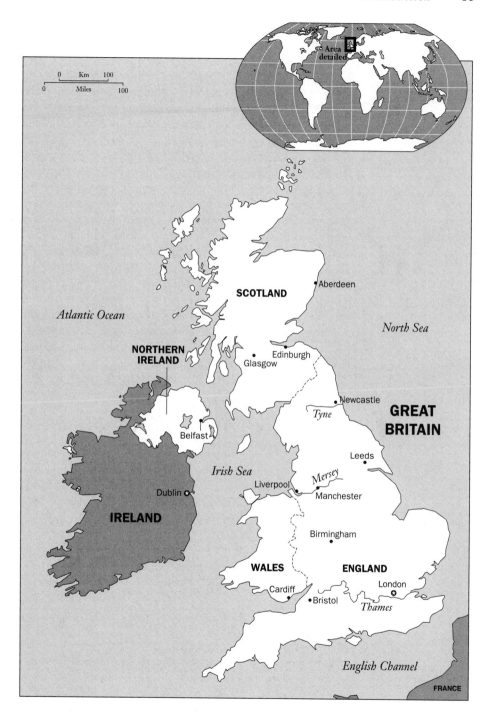

Area detailed

0   Km   100
0   Miles   100

Atlantic Ocean

SCOTLAND

•Aberdeen

North Sea

**NORTHERN
IRELAND**

•Edinburgh
Glasgow

•Newcastle

Tyne

**GREAT
BRITAIN**

Belfast

•Leeds

Irish Sea

Mersey

Liverpool

Dublin

•Manchester

IRELAND

•Birmingham

WALES   **ENGLAND**

Cardiff   London

•Bristol   *Thames*

English Channel

FRANCE

middle, or working class. The class system still exists, but the expansion of the middle class has made the system both less obvious and more complex.

- Race has become a more important issue since the 1950s with the immigration of increased numbers of nonwhites from the Caribbean and the Indian subcontinent. Today about 7 percent of the population is nonwhite, and although ethnic minorities have become more successfully integrated in recent years, racism remains a problem in some of the larger urban areas, notably London.

In political terms, Britain is distinct from most other countries in its record of evolutionary development, driven by what has been described as a "genius for nonviolent progress."[1] There *has* been violence, and Britain's democratic record is far from spotless: Questions are regularly raised about government secrecy, social inequalities, and an electoral system that handicaps smaller political parties, and British governments until recently were often criticized for allowing human rights abuses in Northern Ireland. However, concessions and change have usually come quickly enough to avoid the kinds of political revolutions experienced by other European states.

The evolutionary process continues today. The government of Tony Blair—in power since 1997—has made changes to the constitution of a kind that would be very difficult to engineer in the United States. Political powers have been devolved to the regions, reforms have been made in the electoral system, for the first time in history there is an elected mayor of London, changes have been made to the upper chamber of the British Parliament (the House of Lords), and laws have been changed to ensure greater protection for individual rights.

POLITICAL DEVELOPMENT

Most liberal democracies have at some point experienced a war or a revolution leading to the introduction of a new or substantially altered system of government. For example, Germany had a new system imposed on it after World War II, France adopted a new constitution in 1958, and Spain began a transition to democracy following the end of the Franco dictatorship in 1975. By contrast, Britain has never permanently replaced one system of government with another, instead making changes that have built on the foundations of existing arrangements. For that reason, understanding the British political system means reviewing more than 2,000 years of history.

Early Invasions from the Continent (55 B.C.–A.D. 1066)

Britain's physical detachment from the European continent has helped it evolve differently from its neighbors, but its early history was dominated by repeated invasions by those neighbors. The native people of the British Isles were the Celts, who arrived between 800 and 200 B.C.; they are the ancestors of the Irish, Scots, and Welsh of today. When the Romans invaded in 55 B.C. and occupied what is now England and Wales, the Celts were pushed west and north and England developed a social and political system very different from that of the rest of the British Isles—it had roads, planned towns, and a thriving commercial system. When the Romans left at the beginning of the fifth century, they created a political vacuum into which moved several waves of invaders, notably Germanic tribes such as the Angles and the Saxons (from which come the names England and Anglo-Saxon).

A mission in 597 from the Pope in Rome brought Christianity to Britain, preceding a wave of Viking invasions in the eighth and ninth centuries. These were followed in 1066 by the last invasion of Britain, by William, Duke of Normandy. This brought political stability and centralization to England, but the English and the Celts remained divided ethnically, culturally, and linguistically. Religious differences were added in 1534, when King Henry VIII dissolved England's ties with the Roman Catholic Church and created the Church of England. The Scots today are mainly Catholic and Presbyterian, while the English are mainly Protestant.

The End of Feudalism and the Expansion of the State (1215–1707)

Until about 800 years ago, Britain—like all of Europe—was a feudal society. Sovereign power lay in the hands of monarchs, who ruled by divine right and governed the peasant majority through a land-owning aristocracy. The powers of monarchs and aristocrats began their long and sometimes violent decline in 1215 when King John signed the **Magna Carta,** a document that obliged him to consult with his aristocrats before levying taxes and prevented him from arbitrarily arresting or seizing property from his subjects. It did little more than confirm the privileges of the aristocrats, but it was an important first step in the transfer of power.

A second step was taken in 1265 with the convening of the first British Parliament. It was unelected, met only sporadically, and was dominated by the aristocracy, but monarchs came to rely on it for political support. Tensions between crown and Parliament remained, however, finally boiling over in 1642 with the outbreak of a civil war between monarchists and parliamentarians. This led to the declaration of a brief republic (1649–1660) under the military dictatorship of Oliver Cromwell. When King James II (1685–1688) tried to win back the divine right of monarchs, a Bill of Rights was drawn up which confirmed the supremacy of Parliament over the monarch.

Meanwhile, the dominance of England over the British Isles was expressed in wars and attrition, which led slowly to the incorporation of its Celtic neighbors; a union with Wales was formalized in 1536–1542 and with Scotland in 1707. For its part, Ireland was steadily subjugated and by the late 18th century had to all intents and purposes become part of the British state.

Economic and Political Change (17th–19th Centuries)

Beginning in the late 1600s, Britain underwent wide-ranging economic change, which led in turn to political and social change. New and more efficient processes for smelting iron and making steel were developed, the steam engine was invented, industry was mechanized, and large-scale business enterprises emerged. This in turn brought about improvements in transport, which led to the growth of commerce and markets. Britain was forged into the world's first and most powerful industrial state and by the mid-19th century had become the "workshop of the world," producing two-thirds of the world's coal, half its steel, half its cotton goods, and virtually all its machine tools.

TABLE 2.1

Key Dates in British History

1066	Norman invasion
1215	Magna Carta signed
1265	Parliament founded
1536–1542	Union with Wales
1642–1649	Civil war leads to the deposition of the monarchy
1649–1660	Cromwell's republic ends with restoration of the monarchy
1707	Union with Scotland
1801	Legislative union with Ireland
1914–1918	World War I
1918	Women older than age 30 given the right to vote
1922	Irish independence
1928	All women given the right to vote
1939–1945	World War II
1945	First Labour government elected
1947	Independence of India and Pakistan
1957–1968	Independence of most of Britain's African colonies
1973	Britain joins the European Economic Community
1979	(May) Margaret Thatcher wins first of three elections
1982	War with Argentina over the Falklands/Malvinas
1990	(November) Thatcher resigns as leader of Conservative party and prime minister; replaced by John Major
1991	(January) British forces take part in U.S.-led attack on Iraq
1992	(April) Major leads Conservatives to fourth successive election victory
1994	Opening of English Channel tunnel connecting Britain and France
1996	Controversy breaks out over mad cow disease and sales of British beef in the rest of the European Union
1997	(May) Election of Tony Blair as prime minister ends nearly 18 years of Conservative government; (August) death of Diana, Princess of Wales, poses a challenge to the monarchy to reform; (September) referenda in Scotland and Wales approve idea of regional assemblies
1998	(April) Peace agreement signed in Northern Ireland and approved by public referendum; (December) Britain joins United States in air attacks on Iraq
1999	(January) Creation of single European currency, the euro; (March–April) Britain joins NATO in air attacks on Serbia/Kosovo; (May) first elections to Scottish and Welsh assemblies; (October) hereditary peers sit in the House of Lords for the last time; (November) Northern Ireland regional government meets for the first time
2000	(May) Elections held for first-ever elected mayor of London
2001	(June) Tony Blair elected to a second term; (September) 250 Britons killed in terrorist attacks on New York and Washington, D.C.
2002	(January–February) Britain chooses not to join 12 European neighbors in adopting the new European currency, the euro
2003	(March) Britain joins the United States in invasion of Iraq

Parliament was still dominated by aristocrats representing mainly rural areas, many of which had only a handful of voters and in some of which a seat in Parliament could be bought. The new middle class of industrialists and entrepreneurs found this unacceptable, and pressure for change led to reforms in the 19th and early 20th centuries that eliminated corrupt electoral districts; extended the vote to the wealthy, the upper middle class, and women; introduced secret voting; sparked the growth of mass-membership political parties; created single-member parliamentary districts with roughly equal populations; and took most remaining significant political powers away from the aristocratic House of Lords.

The Imperial Era (18th Century to Early 1960s)

With its industry growing, Britain's priority was to find new markets and sources of raw materials and to build on its competitive advantage over its European rivals, particularly France. Thus began an expansive program of colonization. After losing its 13 American colonies in 1781, Britain colonized Australia, Canada, New Zealand, parts of West Africa, most of southern and eastern Africa, many Caribbean and Pacific islands, the Asian subcontinent, and parts of Southeast Asia. At its height during the late Victorian era, the **British Empire** included about a quarter of the world's population.

The beginning of the end of the imperial era came with World War I, when the cream of a generation of young British men died in one of the most brutal and mismanaged conflicts in the history of warfare. The United States and the Soviet Union began to emerge as economic and military powers, a transition that was finally confirmed by World War II. Britain entered the war in 1939 as the world's biggest creditor nation, and although it played a key role in fighting and winning the war, it emerged 6 years later as one of the world's biggest debtor nations. Its economy was devastated, its political influence diminished, its export earnings and merchant shipping fleet halved, and most of its colonies were agitating for independence.

Postwar Adjustment and the Welfare State (1945–1975)

While its economy prospered in the 1950s and 1960s, Britain found its influence relative to other countries—notably the United States, Japan, and Germany— beginning to decline. The most obvious explanation for this was the dismantling of its empire—India and Pakistan became independent in 1947, and over the next 20 years there was a steady program of decolonization. The decline could also be blamed, however, on the cost of the war, handicaps posed to industrial relations by class divisions, an education system that was prejudiced against business as a career, low levels of mobility within the labor force, inadequate investments in industry and in research and development, and high levels of government involvement in production and employment.[2]

The postwar period saw the completion of a **welfare state** and the shift to a managed economy. Pensions had been introduced in 1908 and national health and unemployment insurance in 1911,[3] but the welfare system was completed only after 1945, when voters wanting a new start swept a socialist Labour government into power. A National Health Service was created that provided free care for almost everyone; there was an expansion of welfare for the unemployed, the ill, and

CLOSE-UP VIEW

THE EUROPEAN UNION

Since 1973, Britain has been a member of the EU. This is an organization that began life as an attempt to develop a common European market and promote economic cooperation among Western European states, but it has taken on many of the features of a new level of government, moving toward the development of a federal Europe. EU membership has redefined Britain's relationship with the rest of Europe and redefined Britain's place in the world.

What is now the EU traces its roots to the creation in 1952 of the European Coal and Steel Community, an experiment in coordinating national policies on these two industries in an attempt—among other things—to remove the seeds of future war in Europe, particularly between Germany and France. Britain refused to join, but by the time the European Economic Community was created in 1958, it had begun to see the merits in taking part. Its first membership applications were vetoed by president Charles de Gaulle of France, but it was eventually allowed to join in 1973.

The refusal of British governments in the 1950s to involve themselves in the discussions that led to the design and launch of the Community heralded a tradition in which Britain has often been out of step with its European partners. Thus, Britain has not always been able to influ-ence the evolution of the EU to its advantage. Membership in the EU has brought economic integration for all its members, EU law has superseded national law in many different areas, the EU has taken increasing responsibility over a variety of policy areas, and growing intra-EU trade has encouraged Britain to build closer economic and political ties with its continental neighbors.

Several European institutions have been created, including a European Commission responsible for proposing and implementing European laws, a directly elected European Parliament, and a European Court of Justice. The EU now has 15 member states, and as many as 10 more Eastern European countries are scheduled to join in 2004. The 15 states have a combined wealth almost as big as that of the United States and together account for more than one-third of all world trade.[4] EU members increasingly speak as one on international trade issues and are working (less successfully) on the agreement of common foreign policies. A major development took place in January–February 2002, when 12 member states (excluding Britain) gave up their national currencies and replaced them with a new European currency, the euro. The Blair government is in favor of adopting the euro, but public opinion in Britain is hostile, so Blair has promised to put the issue to a national referendum.

families with children; and basic services such as railroads and the steel industry were nationalized.

Succeeding Conservative governments agreed to follow roughly the same policies, and—whether the Conservatives or Labour were in power—British politics became driven by a **consensus** on the maintenance of welfare and of managing economic demand so as to sustain full employment. Nonetheless, the British economy, plagued by growing industrial unrest, continued its relative decline through the 1960s and 1970s. In 1976, the Labour government of Harold Wilson was obliged to ask the International Monetary Fund for a loan to help offset a run on the pound and

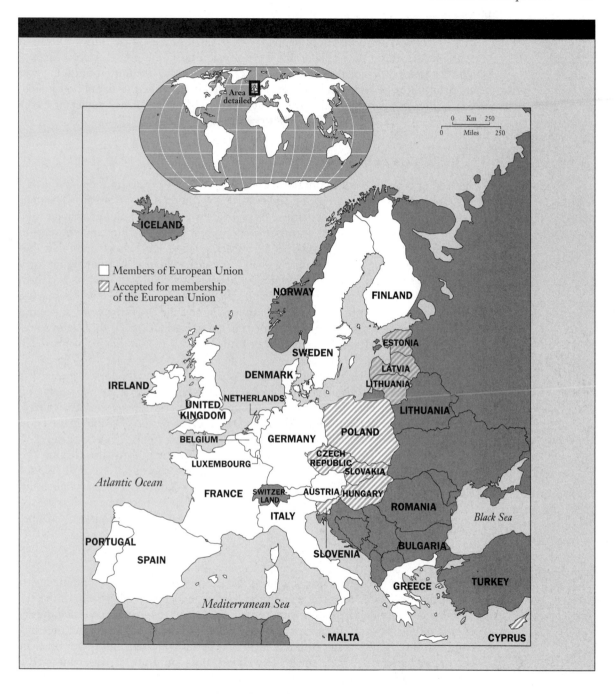

to help Britain service its debts. A new low was reached during the "winter of discontent" in 1978–1979 when public-sector workers went on strike across Britain, almost shutting the country down.

A landmark event took place in 1973, when Britain joined the European Economic Community (EEC). A free-trade agreement among selected Western European states, the Community—created in 1958—was aimed at bringing down the barriers to trade and movement of people, with the goal of creating a unified European market. Dreamers even talked about the possibility of the eventual creation of a United States of Europe. Britain was slow to warm to the Community, arguing that its main interests lay outside Europe, but it quickly changed its mind and joined. Since then, it has developed a (not always deserved) reputation as a reluctant European. (See Close-Up View, pp. 88–89.)

The Thatcher Revolution

Reflecting growing public concern about the state of the economy and about growing international competition, a Conservative government under Margaret Thatcher was elected in 1979 and embarked on a program of wide-ranging change. She claimed to reject the wisdom of consensus politics, arguing that government was too big, there were too many government-owned businesses and services, and that special interests (especially labor unions) had too much influence. Employing her own distinctive brand of "conviction politics," Thatcher launched an assault on socialism and labor unions and worked to create a new "enterprise culture" aimed at making British industry more competitive. **Thatcherism** became the watchword in politics and economics, its most enduring element being **privatization,** or the sale of state-owned services and industries to the private sector, a policy that has since been copied in many other countries.

The impact of Thatcherism on Britain is debatable. Her supporters argue that she spurred the changes needed to reverse Britain's economic decline by freeing up the marketplace, cutting the power of unions, reducing dependence on welfare, and promoting a **stakeholder culture** in which more Britons became involved in creating their own wealth and opportunities. According to her critics, she failed to meet the needs of the underclass, allowed too many people to slip through the safety net of welfare, and widened the gap between the "haves" and the "have nots"; the number of millionaires grew sharply as a result of her tenure, but so did poverty and homelessness, and many believed that Britain became a less caring society. Britain today has a poverty rate of 18 percent, the worst in Western Europe.

Britain Today

Membership in the EEC—now known as the European Union—has combined with the effects of Thatcherism to bring great change to Britain. It is visible in the renewal of cities, in the rise of a new entrepreneurial spirit that has transformed the attitudes of business and industry, and in the growth of the middle class and the consumer society. The average Briton is healthier, better educated, and better off than before, and there is a new spirit of liveliness and optimism, at least among the younger generations. Many even splutter that Britain is being Americanized—not only has its economy rediscovered the competitive culture that made it so strong in the 19th century, but many aspects of politics (notably election campaigns) have taken on a more American character.

The legacy of Thatcherism has been reflected in the policies pursued since May 1997 by the Labour government of Tony Blair. Astonishing political analysts with the scale of its victory, the rejuvenated Labour party swept the internally divided Conservative party out of office after 18 years in power, winning a large majority. Under Tony Blair, "New" Labour has abandoned many of its traditionally socialist ideas and adopted key elements of the Thatcher program. Blair has underlined the importance of the free market but has also emphasized the need to improve education, rebuild the national health care system, and take a tough stance on crime. To date, though, his record on these latter issues has been mixed at best.

There is little question at the beginning of the new millennium that Britain is once again undergoing significant political change. The Blair government wants to see it compete more effectively on the global stage, to have a more constructive relationship with its partners in the EU, to invest more heavily in its human capital, and to build a society that is less dependent on government. Blair has also been outspoken in his opinion that Britain should be "repackaged" as a society that has deep roots in history and culture, but which is forward-looking and economically dynamic.

POLITICAL CULTURE

Tying down the political values of a society is always difficult, especially one with as long a history as Britain. Generally, though, most political scientists agree that the British are pragmatic, have faith in their political system (but not necessarily politicians), and are politically moderate, but that government is not sufficiently transparent, in the sense that people do not have as much access as they might to the workings of government.

Pragmatism

The British tend to keep their feet on the ground when it comes to their expectations of government and their aspirations for their own lives. They take an empirical approach to problem solving, shying away from theory and looking instead at the practical reality of policies. In the United States, argues Vivien Hart, "the emphasis has been on what democracy is and should be, while Britain has been characterized by a more pragmatic and less urgent emphasis on what democracy is and can be."[5]

The two approaches bring out one of the key differences between Americans and Britons: Americans tend to have an optimistic (some would say naive) view of the possibilities for democracy—American political leaders will often sprinkle their speeches with words such as "dream" and "vision"—but Britons tend to be more down-to-earth and to place more faith in what has been tried and tested. This is not to suggest that the British do not dream or that they are opposed to innovation (quite the contrary), but rather that they are less apt to overreach than are Americans or some continental Europeans.

Among older Britons, realism has spilled over into pessimism, making many gloomy about the changes they have seen. The media tend to perpetuate the problem through their fascination with everything from lowered educational performance to the poor record of the national soccer team in international tournaments. While older Americans often talk about making life better for their children, many older Britons grumble that life was better and safer when they were younger. This flies in the face of reality, however, because most of the basic indicators—such as health care, education, economic wealth, individual freedoms, crime rates, and the state of the environment—suggest that life for most Britons has improved significantly in the last 30 years.

Faith in the Political System

Writing about the orientation of individuals toward political systems, Robert Dahl argues that favorable feelings indicate an "allegiant" orientation, neutral feelings reflect apathy and detachment, and unfavorable feelings reflect alienation.[6] Political alienation is often obvious in Italy and France and among disadvantaged Americans who feel cut off from government. Britain, by contrast, is marked by strong feelings of allegiance, reflected in the fact that most people still feel they can influence government.[7] These feelings are tied closely to the long history of political stability and evolutionary change in Britain, which contrasts with the often revolutionary and violent change that has come to political systems in other European states.

Most Britons have a high degree of faith in their political system and are more patriotic and trusting of their fellow citizens than are most of their European neighbors. Faith in the political system was long bound up in strong feelings of political and social deference, to the point where cynics occasionally described Britain as a "Nanny State," or one in which the government acted like the archetypal Victorian nanny in arguing that it knew what was in the best interests of the people.

However, the sense of allegiance is on the decline due to a combination of changes in the class system, a growing respect for succeeding through effort and hard work rather than through privilege, a reduction in individual dependence on the state, a concern that the political system is not as responsive as it should be, and a declining respect for politicians in the wake of a number of headline-making financial and political scandals in the late 1980s and early 1990s. Recent studies suggest that the British are more willing to use unconventional forms of political participation than the citizens of any other democracy: 56 percent are prepared to sign petitions, 35 percent to attend lawful demonstrations, 25 percent to join a boycott, 15 percent to join a wildcat strike, 13 percent to refuse to pay taxes, and 9 percent to block traffic.[8]

Social Liberalism

In contrast to many Americans, most Britons take liberal positions on social and moral issues, and this has an impact on public policy and expectations of government. For example, capital punishment was outlawed in 1965, homosexuality and abortion have been legal since 1967, and British television has nothing like the degree of censorship found in the United States. Perhaps most astonishing to Americans, all handguns were banned in Britain in 1998. The spark for this was a mass killing at a school in 1996, of the kind which is tragically all too common in the United States. The response to such outrages in the United States tends to be hand-wringing about social problems and personal responsibility; the response in Britain was to place the blame squarely on the availability of guns and to tighten the already substantial controls.

Part of the difference between British and American attitudes toward social issues may be rooted in the relative role of religion in the two societies. About two-thirds of Britons still claim to believe in God, but, except in Northern Ireland, church attendance has been steadily declining, and only about 13 percent of the population now actively participates in religious activities,[9] compared with about 43 percent in the United States. Social conservatism in the United States is often tied to religion and to the promotion of "traditional" family values. An attempt by prime minister John Major in 1993–1994 to focus on these same values in Britain won him little public support.

A Closed Society

The British tend to be a private people, hence the often-quoted phrase that an Englishman's home is his castle. Perhaps because Britain is such a crowded country where a premium is placed on personal space, the British can often seem a little standoffish to visitors. This sense of privacy is reflected in the secrecy that often surrounds the functioning of government. Issues of national security are subject to secrecy in every democracy, but government critics charge that state secrets are too narrowly defined in Britain. Those critics say that this has helped increase the power and reduce the accountability of the police, weakened the power of Parliament at the expense of central government, promoted the use of surveillance, reduced the right to personal privacy, and allowed the government to interfere with media freedom.

Such secrecy has become increasingly unacceptable and there has been a movement in recent years for greater freedom of information. Successive governments have promised more open administration, and information has become more freely available, but the most significant changes have come during the Blair administration, which has opened up the bureaucracy and made government departments subject to performance reviews based on their services to the public.

POLITICAL SYSTEM

The structure of the British political system can be summarized in six key principles:

- It is a unitary state in which most significant political powers are concentrated in national government.

- There is a fusion of the executive and the legislature, rather than the separation found in the American system.

- It is a constitutional monarchy in which the monarch has symbolic power, but the prime minister is the true political leader.

- Parliament is sovereign, meaning that it has the ultimate power and right to make or abolish any law it wishes.

- There is a belief in responsible government, meaning that government ministers are responsible to Parliament for the management of their departments.

- Britain is a member of the EU and thus is subject to the common laws and policies of the EU.

At the same time, however, Britain has been undergoing some fundamental political changes in recent decades that have redefined the relative powers of the different institutions of government: Parliament has lost some of its lawmaking authority to the

European Parliament since 1973, and it has lost further authority since 1998 with the creation of regional assemblies in Scotland, Wales, and Northern Ireland. Britain is not a federal state like the United States or Canada, but the national government today has to share authority with European and local levels of government more than ever before.

THE CONSTITUTION

Most democracies have written constitutions in which the powers of government and the rights of the governed are outlined. However, constitutions do not have to be written; they can be abstract, consisting of laws and customs that have the same function as a single written document. Britain has taken the latter course in that it lacks a single, codified document and is governed instead on the basis of constitutional principles. These principles come from five major sources:[10]

- **Common law,** or judgments handed down over time by British courts. Among the more significant are those dealing with freedom of expression and the sovereignty of Parliament.

- **Statute law,** or Acts of Parliament that override common law and have the effect of constitutional law. They include laws that outline the relative powers of the two houses of Parliament.

- **European law,** since Britain is subject to laws adopted by the EU, which override British laws where the two conflict, in those policy areas where the EU has primary authority; these include trade, agriculture, social issues, and the environment.

- **Traditions and conventions** that do not have the force of law but have been followed for so long that they are regarded as binding. For example, there are no laws stating that the prime minister and cabinet should come out of the majority party in Parliament; it has simply become a tradition.

- **Commentaries** written by constitutional experts such as Walter Bagehot and Albert Venn Dicey (author in 1885 of *The Law of the Constitution*).

Where the U.S. Constitution spells out how government works and the Supreme Court has the power to interpret and build upon those rules, the rules of government in Britain are determined "on the basis of what has proved to work rather than on abstract first principles."[11] Supporters of this approach argue that the absence of a codified constitution allows for greater flexibility, but critics argue that there is too much potential for the abuse of powers by a strong prime minister. The result has been growing support for a written constitution, which is now favored by about 80 percent of Britons.

THE MONARCHY

Except for a brief spell between 1649 and 1660, when a republic was proclaimed, Britain since the tenth century has been a monarchy. This literally means "rule by one," but more specifically it means a system governed by someone who typically comes to that position by birth or heredity. British kings and queens once had a virtual monopoly on political power but began giving it up with the Magna Carta, and the monarch is now little more than a ceremonial head of state, expected to be a neutral symbol of history, stability, tradition, and national identity. It is often said that the monarch reigns but does not rule. The present monarch—Queen Elizabeth II—is limited to the following so-called **reserve powers:**

- She has the right to dissolve Parliament and call new elections, although in practice she does this only at the request of the prime minister.
- Just as American presidents must sign all new congressional bills before they become law, the Queen gives the Royal Assent to every piece of new legislation. Theoretically, she has the same right of veto as an American president, but the last time a monarch vetoed a piece of legislation was in 1707.[12]
- She meets with the prime minister at confidential weekly meetings, during which she has the right "to be consulted, the right to encourage, and the right to warn."[13] She also has access to secret government documents.
- If no one party has an absolute majority after an election, the Queen steps in as an arbitrator, and—on the advice of the prime minister—can name the person she thinks is most likely in practical terms to be able to form a government. Queen Elizabeth has had to do this three times since she came to the throne in 1952.
- At the annual State Opening of Parliament, she gives an address in which she outlines the government's program (much like the State of the Union in the United States). However, the address is written by the government, and the Queen simply reads it aloud.
- Above all, the Queen is "a visible symbol of unity"[14] and the symbol of supreme executive authority. She is commander-in-chief, many public duties are carried out in her name, and British postage stamps, coins, and banknotes bear the Queen's image instead of the name of the country. As head of the Commonwealth (see section on Foreign Policy), the Queen also symbolizes Britain's relationship with its former colonies.

For centuries, the monarchy was imbued with an aura of mystery, and little was publicly known about its inner workings; in the words of the 19th-century constitutional authority Walter Bagehot, it was important not to "let in daylight upon magic." This has all changed in the last 15 to 20 years as the private lives of Prince Charles (heir to the throne), Prince Andrew, and their ex-wives and girlfriends have become the focus of intense media coverage. Prince Charles has also caused controversy by being more willing than previous heirs to comment on public issues such as the state of British architecture, education, and the environment.

As an individual, Queen Elizabeth is popular, but opinion polls suggest that public support for the monarchy has slipped since the mid-1980s from 85 to 90 percent to about 70 to 75 percent. The death of Princess Diana, former wife of Prince Charles, in August 1997, sparked a reappraisal aimed at making the monarchy more relevant to public life in Britain. The once unthinkable—that a divorced heir to the throne could become king—has been accepted. Also, attempts have been made to end the ban on the heir marrying a Catholic, to abandon primogeniture (under which a firstborn daughter is overtaken in the line of succession by a younger brother), and to cease expecting the monarch to be head of the Church of England. One of the great strengths of the British monarchy—and the major reason it has lasted so long—is that it has been more adaptable than many of its continental European counterparts. The changes it now faces are just the latest in a long series of adjustments it has had to make to keep up with the times.

THE EXECUTIVE: PRIME MINISTER AND CABINET

The monarch may be British head of state, but the head of government is the prime minister, who provides policy leadership and oversees the implementation of the law through a cabinet of senior ministers. By definition, the prime minister is the leader of the political party or coalition with the most seats in the lower chamber of parliament, the House of Commons. As long as they can keep the support of their party in Parliament, prime ministers have considerable power over deciding which laws will be passed and which policies adopted. In fact, within the scope of their jobs, they have much more power than presidents of the United States, whose decisions are constantly checked and balanced.

As head of government, the prime minister sets the national political agenda, oversees the military, appoints ambassadors, manages crises, leads his or her party, and represents Britain overseas. There are two foundations to the prime minister's authority:

- **The power to call elections to the House of Commons.** These must be held at least once every 5 years, and prime ministers will usually call them when the polls suggest that their party has the best chance of winning. More rarely, they may have to call an election because they have lost a parliamentary vote or the support of their party.
- **The power of appointment.** As well as being party leader, the prime minister decides on the size of the cabinet, calls and chairs cabinet meetings, appoints and removes members of the cabinet and other senior government officials (about 100 people in all), regularly reshuffles the cabinet (bringing in new members and either removing existing members or moving them to new posts), and can even reorganize government departments. By contrast, U.S. presidents need Senate approval for cabinet appointments and the reorganization of departments.

British prime ministers are normally seasoned national politicians who have worked their way up through the ranks of their party and Parliament. They must be members of the House of Commons and usually serve a long apprenticeship before winning the leadership of their parties; John Major and Tony Blair rose to the top relatively quickly, serving as members for 11 years and 14 years, respectively, before becoming prime ministers.

Prime ministers govern with the help of a **cabinet,** which, as in the United States, consists of all the heads of senior government departments (such as the foreign secretary and the defense secretary), numbering about 20 to 24 in all. In the United

TABLE 2.2

Postwar Prime Ministers of Britain

Date	Prime minister	Governing party
July 1945	Clement Attlee	Labour
February 1950	Clement Attlee	Labour
October 1951	Winston Churchill	Conservative
May 1955	Anthony Eden	Conservative
January 1957*	Harold Macmillan	Conservative
October 1959	Harold Macmillan	Conservative
October 1963*	Alec Douglas-Home	Conservative
October 1964	Harold Wilson	Labour
March 1966	Harold Wilson	Labour
June 1970	Edward Heath	Conservative
February 1974	Harold Wilson	Labour
October 1974	Harold Wilson	Labour
April 1976*	James Callaghan	Labour
May 1979	Margaret Thatcher	Conservative
June 1983	Margaret Thatcher	Conservative
June 1987	Margaret Thatcher	Conservative
November 1990*	John Major	Conservative
April 1992	John Major	Conservative
May 1997	Tony Blair	Labour
June 2001	Tony Blair	Labour

*In these years, leadership of the governing party changed—through health, resignation, or loss of political support—without a general election being held.

States, cabinet members cannot be members of Congress and cabinet experience is rarely a launchpad for a presidential bid. In Britain, by contrast, the cabinet is always appointed from within Parliament and is an essential testing ground for anyone with aspirations to becoming prime minister. Senior cabinet members become national figures, and reputations can be made and broken according to their performance in the cabinet.

While U.S. presidents rarely meet with their cabinets, the British cabinet meets frequently and is an important part of the policymaking structure of government: Between them, the prime minister and cabinet constitute **Her Majesty's Government.** Although prime ministers are technically no more than "first among equals"

TONY BLAIR

© Reuters NewMedia Inc./CORBIS

World War II, and the first truly postimperial prime minister.

Exemplifying the potential powers of a strong prime minister, Blair used his 178-seat majority in the House of Commons to bring significant changes to the structure and character of British government. These have included the creation of regional assemblies in Northern Ireland, Scotland, and Wales; proposals to change the electoral system; changes to the structure of the House of Lords; and discussions about a Bill of Rights that could not be overridden by Parliament. At the same time, the Blair government has made greater use of the referendum as a means of putting major issues to a public vote.

In almost every sense, Tony Blair has proved an unusual prime minister and an unusual leader of the Labour party. Born in Scotland in May 1953 of Scottish and Irish parents, he was raised in middle-class comfort in England, attending private schools and studying law at Oxford (where he had his own rock group—called Ugly Rumours—and apparently did a passable impression of Mick Jagger). He practiced as an attorney from 1976 to 1983, specializing in employment and industrial law. In 1980 he married another attorney, Cherie Booth.

Blair was elected to Parliament in 1983 as representative for Sedgefield in northern England in 1983 and was appointed to the shadow cabinet in 1988, holding first the energy portfolio and then the job of shadow home secretary (dealing with issues such as policing). In 1994—at the age of just 40—he was elected leader of the Labour party and moved quickly to abandon some of its more left-wing policies and to bring it closer to the center of the political spectrum. In May 1997, he became the third-youngest prime minister in British history, the first prime minister born after

He easily won reelection in June 2001, his majority reduced by just 12 seats. But there were signs of flagging enthusiasm for his leadership: voter turnout at the 2001 election was down from 71 percent to 59 percent, he drew criticism for continued problems with Britain's public services (notably health care, education, and transport), and he controversially supported President Bush's policies on Iraq in 2002–2003, flying in the face of majority opinion both among the British public and within his own party. However, no other party has been able to put up strong opposition, and—unless something goes terribly wrong for him—he is expected to win the next election, due by June 2006.

(*primus inter pares*), their powers of appointment and agenda setting mean that loyalty to the leader is an essential prerequisite for cabinet members. The cabinet functions on the basis of **collective responsibility,** meaning that once it has made a policy decision, all members are expected to support that decision in public regardless of their personal feelings and to take responsibility for its success or failure. If the government loses an important vote in Parliament, or a vote of confidence, the whole cabinet is expected to resign.[15]

The manner in which prime ministers govern depends on their different management styles.[16] Margaret Thatcher led from the front and was noted for her forcefulness and for stretching the powers of her office almost to their limit. She appointed several weak ministers to the cabinet who could be easily controlled, she reduced the number of cabinet meetings, and she fired 12 ministers in 11 years. By contrast, John Major made more use of his cabinet, allowed a greater variety of opinion, emphasized collegiality and consensus, and intervened less in the affairs of departments.

Tony Blair has developed a reputation for imposing strong discipline on his party and his cabinet, driven by his agenda of changing its ideological tilt. He has delegated discretion to strong ministers prepared to follow the government line, emphasized collegiality in the cabinet, and worked to identify himself in the public mind with populist images, including his personal role in planning Britain's millennium celebrations and his invitations to 10 Downing Street—the London home of the prime minister—of celebrities involved in the arts. His desire to manage—and even to micromanage—has led to charges by his critics that he tries to control too much and that the office of prime minister has become more presidential.

THE LEGISLATURE: PARLIAMENT

The Houses of Parliament are situated in the district of Westminster in central London, which is why the British parliamentary system is called the **Westminster model.** This model dates back more than 700 years and has been adopted (wholly or in part) by virtually every other liberal democracy. Parliament is where laws are introduced, discussed, and either rejected or accepted and where existing laws are amended or abolished. It may seem powerful, but because a prime minister with a good majority can normally count on the loyalty of party members, Parliament usually spends most of its time debating or confirming the program of the government and has much less power in relative terms than the U.S. Congress.

Parliament has two chambers with different structures and powers.

House of Lords

The so-called upper house, the Lords recalls the days when Britain was ruled by aristocrats. Members must be **peers,** which meant—until 1999—that they were either hereditary or were appointed to the House for a life term as a reward for public service or political loyalty. Nearly 1,200 peers had the right to sit in the Lords, although only about 800 ever actually attended, and only about 300 were regular participants—members who attended received no salary, only expenses.

The British Houses of Parliament, on the banks of the River Thames in London. After centuries of struggle with the monarchy, Parliament won supremacy after the English civil war. The British parliamentary model—in which executive and legislature are fused—has since been the basis of systems of government in many other countries.

The Lords was not elected, so it was both unrepresentative and undemocratic, but it had little power. It could introduce its own legislation, and all bills going through Parliament had to be approved by the Lords, but its decisions could be overruled by the Commons and bills on taxation or spending did not need the approval of the Lords. However, it had more time to debate issues than the Commons, it often debated controversial issues, it could force concessions from the Commons, and it was a useful point of access for lobbyists.

During the 1980s, the Labour party threatened to abolish the House altogether if it came to power, but the Blair government took a more moderate position and, after removing the rights of hereditary peers to sit in the House in 1999, appointed a commission to decide what form the new chamber should take. The transitional House of Lords now has four kinds of members:

- A group of 92 **hereditary peers** who have been allowed to stay on pending the next stage in the process of reform.
- **Religious leaders,** consisting of the two archbishops and 24 bishops of the Church of England. (An interesting concept for Americans raised on the idea of a separation of church and state.)
- **The law lords.** These are 28 nominated judges who function as the supreme court of appeal for civil and criminal cases (except in Scotland, which has its own

legal system). They are headed by a Lord Chancellor and hold their positions until the age of 70. They made headline news in 1998, when they upheld the decision of lower courts to detain the former Chilean dictator Augusto Pinochet during a visit to Britain. He was detained at the request of the Spanish government, which wanted to try him for crimes against Spanish citizens living in Chile.

- **Life peers.** Numbering about 600, these are mainly people who have been in public service and are rewarded with a life peerage by the Queen on the recommendation of the prime minister. All former prime ministers are offered a peerage, so Margaret Thatcher, for example, now sits in the Lords as Lady Thatcher. Other people prominent in public life—such as actors, musicians, and entrepreneurs—may also be given a peerage. Many life peerages are political rewards, where favors are returned, or where peerages are given in order to build party numbers in the Lords. (Knights—such as Sir Elton John and Sir Paul McCartney—are not members of the House of Lords.)

House of Commons

The House of Commons is the more powerful chamber of Parliament and the real focus of lawmaking. It consists of 659 **members of Parliament** (MPs) elected by direct universal vote from single-member districts. Debates are presided over by a Speaker, who is elected by the House from among its members and usually comes from the majority party. The last Speaker—Betty Boothroyd—was unusual in at least two respects: She was the first woman appointed to the job, and she came not from the governing Conservatives but from the Labour party when it was still in opposition in 1992. She was replaced in 2000 by Michael Martin. Unlike Speakers in the U.S. House of Representatives, who act as the partisan leaders of their party, the British Speaker is more of an arbiter who keeps order and maintains the flow of business in the House.

To encourage debate, the chamber of the House has been deliberately kept small, with benches rather than seats (see Figure 2.1). The governing party sits on one side, with the prime minister and senior ministers on the front bench. MPs without government office, or with only junior office, sit behind the front bench and are known collectively as **backbenchers.** The next biggest party in Parliament sits across from the governing party and acts as the official opposition. Its leader sits directly opposite the prime minister, beside a shadow cabinet of opposition MPs responsible for keeping up with—and challenging—their counterparts on the government front bench. The **leader of the opposition** and the **shadow cabinet** are formally recognized and salaried positions. If the opposition wins a majority in an election and becomes the government, the leader of the opposition would normally become prime minister and many members of the shadow cabinet would become the real cabinet. In other words, the shadow cabinet is a government in waiting.

Anyone who has seen the Commons in action will wonder how it ever achieves anything. As the news weekly *The Economist* once put it, MPs "snigger and smirk. They sneer and jeer. They murmur and yawn. They gossip salaciously in the bars. They honk and cackle when the Prime Minister or his opposite number is trying to talk. They are like unruly schoolchildren, egged on by the frisson of a chance of being spanked by Madam Speaker but knowing they will usually get away with naugh-

FIGURE 2.1

Floor Plan of the House of Commons

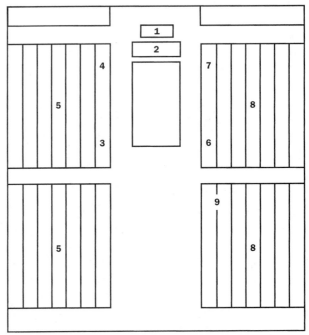

1. Speaker
2. Clerks
3. Prime minister
4. Cabinet
5. Government party
   backbenchers

6. Leader of opposition
7. Shadow cabinet
8. Main opposition party backbenchers
9. MPs of other opposition parties

tiness." In fact, most of the real work of Parliament is done in committees, where specialists go over the details of bills and invite outside experts to give testimony. The chamber of the Commons is normally quiet and sparsely attended, except during controversial debates or **Prime Minister's Question Time,** a half-hour session that is held every Wednesday afternoon during which MPs can ask the prime minister for information on government policy.

Party discipline is much tighter in the British system than in the U.S. Congress, but rumbles of discontent are normal and party revolts have led to 7 of the 11 Conservative leaders since 1900 being unseated by a vote within their own party. This last happened in November 1990, when Margaret Thatcher lost the leadership of her party. Many in her party thought she could not win another election, so a challenge was mounted during the normally routine annual leadership election. She won, but not by a big enough margin to retain her credibility, so she resigned and was replaced as leader—and prime minister—by John Major. A breakdown of party cohesion—usually dubbed a "backbench rebellion" if it is big enough—is normally interpreted as a sign of weakness and can lead to the fall of a government, the resignation of a prime minister, or even the calling of a new general election.

THE JUDICIARY

It is ironic that Britain—home to John Locke (1632–1704), the political theorist whose ideas about a social contract and the separation of powers are at the core of the U.S. Constitution—should have neither a written constitution nor a constitutional court (the former requires the latter). The U.S. Supreme Court has the power to interpret the U.S. Constitution (judicial review), but Britain has no direct equivalent. Instead, judicial review is carried out in a complex system of courts topped by a Court of Appeal and the House of Lords, where law lords will hear final appeals in five-person benches. Appointments to the higher courts are made either by the Lord Chancellor (who is a member of the cabinet) or by the prime minister after consultation with the Lord Chancellor, so they are highly political.

The role of judicial review in the British system is changing with the growing powers of the **European Court of Justice.** One of the key institutions of the EU, the Luxembourg-based Court does not yet have a European constitution to interpret, but it does have a series of treaties and a growing body of European law, whose primacy over national law is established. The European Court is slowly developing the same kind of relationship with the British government as the U.S. Supreme Court has with state governments, and it acts as the final court of appeal on matters of European law.

SUBNATIONAL GOVERNMENT

Federations like the United States and Canada have national and local levels of government with independent powers and distinct rights and responsibilities. Britain, by contrast, is a **unitary state,** where local government units have so little independent power that they can be reformed, restructured, or even abolished by the national government. However, changes made by the Blair administration are altering the balance of power between national and local government.

Scotland and Wales were given their own elected **regional assemblies** in 1998; the first elections for these were held in May 1999. Members of both are elected for fixed 4-year terms and have a variety of powers over local issues such as education, health services, housing, transport, and policing. The 129-member Scottish Parliament also has limited tax-raising powers, but the 60-member National Assembly for Wales does not. The 108-member Northern Ireland Assembly has powers over local issues and also has two councils that address joint policymaking with Ireland and with the British Parliament.

Meanwhile, England does not have a regional assembly but instead has a complex patchwork of unitary and two-tier local authorities, responsible for issues such as education, transport, housing, highways, local services, refuse disposal, and the police. Interestingly, London—which, with its surrounding suburbs, is home to about one-third of the British population—went without an elected city government from 1986 to 2000. It had been governed by a Greater London Council, whose leader was the

Labour politician Ken Livingstone, dubbed "Red Ken" by the tabloid media. He became a thorn in the flesh of the Thatcher government, so—illustrating the powers of national government over local bodies—she abolished the council in 1986. The Blair administration decided that a city the size of London needed its own government, so he created a 25-member elected Greater London Assembly, and Livingstone became London's first-ever directly elected mayor following elections in May 2000.

REPRESENTATION AND PARTICIPATION

As with all liberal democracies, Britain has many institutionalized channels through which its citizens can take part in politics, express their opinions, and have their views reflected in government policy. These include regular elections, political parties representing multiple sets of positions across much of the ideological spectrum, a broad and active interest group community, and one of the most diverse and well-respected media establishments in the world. The options have increased in recent years as the number of elections and parties has grown, the electoral system has diversified, and the number of sources of political news has increased. Only about one in ten Britons has a sustained interest in politics, but most take some periodic, intensive interest in politics (usually in the lead-up to elections), and most are well informed about national and international politics.

ELECTIONS AND THE ELECTORAL SYSTEM

As noted in Chapter 1, the United States is a large country with several levels of government, each with its own elections, each with its own system of primaries, and each with multiple elective offices. These factors combined mean that the United States has more, longer, and more expensive elections than any other liberal democracy. By contrast, Britain is a small country, has a unitary system of administration, offers its voters no primaries, and has relatively few elective offices. Hence the election process is simpler, cheaper, and quicker. Parties choose who will run in their name, elections for the executive and the legislature are combined, and no party has more than one leader. And because these leaders are normally established public figures, they do not need the expensive and lengthy process of public familiarization demanded of candidates in U.S. elections.

While Americans elect 500,000 officeholders at many different levels, British voters are faced with just three sets of elections.

The General Election

Members of the lower chamber of Parliament—the House of Commons—are chosen in the general election, and it is run on the same lines as elections to the U.S. House of Representatives. The UK is divided into 659 constituencies (electoral districts) of roughly equal population size, each represented in the House of Commons by a single member of Parliament. At least once every 5 years, all 659 seats must be contested in a general election, on a date chosen by the prime minister. He must give at least 18 days' notice (excluding weekends and public holidays). Almost everyone older than age 18 can vote, and turnout is normally about 70 to 75 percent, which is about average for Western Europe but considerably higher than the figures in the United States (50 to 55 percent in presidential election years and about 35 percent in midterm elections).

While election campaigns in the United States can last several months (even, it seems, several years), British general election campaigns normally last just 3 to 4 weeks, and voters make a straight choice among the candidates from the different parties standing in their district. The choices are made easier by the fact that parties have strong ideological consistency and there is stronger party identification among voters, who will tend to vote more for parties than for individuals. The differences in emphasis are visible on campaign posters and bumper stickers—in Britain, the name of the party dominates, whereas in the United States, the name of the candidate dominates.

As with the U.S. House of Representatives, the British general election uses the winner-take-all system (sometimes also known as first-past-the-post), under which the winning candidate does not need a majority, but can win with a plurality—in other words, they simply need to win more votes than any other candidate. This system has come under increased scrutiny and criticism in recent years because although it may be quick, cheap, and simple, it is not always fair. It tends to work in the favor of parties that have large blocks of concentrated support around the country but against the interests of parties whose support is more thinly spread; the former tend to win seats, while the latter more often come in second or third. The effects of this were obvious in the 2001 general election, when Labour won 41 percent of the vote but 62 percent of seats in the House of Commons. Meanwhile, the Conservatives won 32 percent of votes and 25 percent of seats (a slightly more equitable result), and the third-placed Liberal Democrats won 18 percent of the vote but just 8 percent of seats.

The Blair administration has investigated the possibility of replacing the winner-take-all method with a form of **proportional representation** (PR) under which parties contesting elections would receive a number of seats in Parliament in proportion to their share of the vote. This system is commonly used elsewhere in Europe and is also used in combination with winner-take-all in Japan and Russia (see Chapters 3 and 4). British voters had their first taste of the system in 1998–1999 with elections to their new regional assemblies and to the European Parliament. The short-term prospects of it being adopted for the general election are slight, though, because of opposition from both the major political parties and a lack of public support.[17]

European Elections

As a member of the EU, Britain has the right every 5 years to elect 87 representatives to the 626-member **European Parliament** (EP) in Strasbourg, France. Direct elections to the EP have been held only since 1979, and many British voters have mixed opinions about the EU, so turnout at European elections in Britain is among the lowest in the EU: After running at about 36 percent (far below even the modest EU average of about 55 percent), it fell to an all-time low of 23 percent in 1999.

HOW UNITED IS THE KINGDOM?

The relationship among the four partners in the United Kingdom has not always been an easy one, with concerns about the cultural, economic, and political dominance of England, and movements to protect and rebuild minority cultural identity. Despite the existence of a "United" Kingdom, regionalism is a factor in national politics and some in Scotland and Wales even support the idea of complete independence.

There are many reminders of the differences among the four: Each has its own flag, culture, "national" sports teams, writers, and artists; Scotland, Wales, and Northern Ireland have their own regional political parties, all of which have seats in both the British Parliament and in the regional assemblies; Scotland and Northern Ireland have legal and educational systems that are separate from those used in England and Wales; and the Church of Scotland is separate from the Church of England.

While talk of the potential break-up of the United Kingdom is exaggerated, there has been pressure since the 1960s for devolution, meaning the transfer of powers from the national government in London to regional governments (hence the creation of regional assemblies in 1998–1999). Supporters of devolution argue that it will reduce demands for independence, particularly in Scotland. However, opinion polls are inconclusive on how far the Scottish independence movement has grown, with recent surveys finding between one-third and one-half in favor.

Regionalism is not simply about national divisions but also about divisions within the four countries. The Scots have different religions, and there are cultural rivalries between highlanders and lowlanders. The Welsh are divided economically between the old industrial centers of the south and the agricultural regions of the north and between those who speak Welsh and those who do not. Northern Ireland suffers a variety of religious, economic, and cultural divisions and is split between those who support continued union with Britain and those who do not. Finally, England has many distinctive regional identities, so the values, attitudes, and priorities of people who live in the economic powerhouse of London and its suburbs are different from those of people who live in the rural and small-town communities near London, in the farmlands and the tourist meccas of the southwest, in the old industrial areas of the midlands and the north, and in the dales of Yorkshire and the mountains and lakes of Cumbria.

These figures are also a reflection of the limited powers of the EP, which can neither introduce nor make the final decision on adopting new laws. Its powers are growing, however, and as they do, more voters may be encouraged to turn out.

Candidates are fielded by the same parties that contest general elections at home. At the 1994 elections, Labour won 63 of the British seats and the more Euro-skeptical Conservatives won just 19. By contrast, the 1999 elections were a major blow for Labour, whose share of seats fell to 30; the Conservatives won 39 seats, and the balance was won by smaller parties, including the Greens. This turnaround was seen as a reflection of a shift throughout Europe to right-wing parties calling for a slowdown in European integration and as a critical comment by British voters on the EU. However, it was also affected by Britain's decision to adopt for the first time the same system of proportional representation used for EP elections in the other 14 EU-member states. Instead of having 87 single-member districts and declaring the candidate in each district with the most votes the winner, Britain was divided into several much larger multimember districts, competing parties put forward lists of candidates, and the seats were divided up among the parties according to the proportion of the vote each received.

Local Government Elections

Because Britain is a unitary state and local authorities have limited power, local elections have traditionally been overlooked by most voters. Members are elected to district, county, city, and town councils on a fixed 4-year cycle, but voters usually make their choices on the basis of national issues and the performance of the national government, they vote along party lines, and turnout rarely exceeds 40 percent. However, the situation may change as the new regional assemblies get off the ground. Because the assemblies have powers over a variety of local government issues, the stakes in the elections have been raised. Turnout at the first elections in 1998–1999 was not inspiring—58 percent in Scotland and 46 percent in Wales—but this may improve with time. Scottish and Welsh assembly elections are based on a combination of winner-take-all and PR, while regional and European elections in Northern Ireland use a variation of PR known as the single transferable vote (STV) (see Comparative Focus, pp. 228–229).

POLITICAL PARTIES

Britain has a substantial range of political parties, covering a broad range of ideological positions. Most have strong internal organization, and voters tend to be loyal to parties, using them to provide the reference points for their political opinions and for the choices they make at elections. Although more than 70 parties contested the 2001 general election and 9 won seats in Parliament, Britain since World War II has been a two-party system dominated by Labour and the Conservatives. Between them, the parties usually take about 75 percent of the vote and about 90 percent of the seats in Parliament (see Figure 2.2). However, this may change as the use of proportional representation in local and European elections allows smaller parties to win seats, build experience, and establish a stronger national reputation.

Labour

The Labour party was founded in 1900 and first came to prominence in the 1920s but only won outright power for the first time in 1945. It immediately set about building a welfare state and a managed economy, nationalizing key industries, and creating the National Health Service, a social security system, and a subsidized education system. It lost power in 1951 but returned in 1964 and again in 1974 under the leadership of Harold Wilson. Labour went into opposition in 1979, losing four straight general elections and undergoing a crisis of confidence before finally regaining power in 1997 under the leadership of Tony Blair.

FIGURE 2.2

Legislative Electoral Trends in Britain

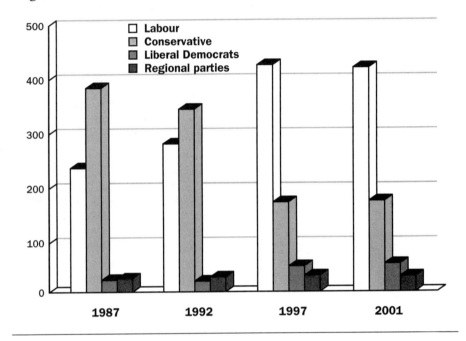

The Labour party's failures in the 1980s were ascribed to a combination of the political shrewdness of Conservative prime minister Margaret Thatcher, a string of "unelectable" party leaders, and the growing unpopularity of many of its more traditional socialist policies, including state ownership of key industries, support of labor unions, and redistributing wealth through taxation. The extent of its internal problems was emphasized in 1981 when a group of moderate Labourites broke away to form the Social Democratic party (SDP). This merged with the Liberal party in 1988 after helping to compel Labour to rethink and moderate its policies. The shift in Labour's philosophy was symbolized by its decision to replace its red flag symbol with a red rose, which sent a much less militant and threatening message to voters.

Tony Blair was elected party leader in May 1994 and made it clear that he was opposed to business as usual. He moved quickly to "modernize" the party and to distance it from its more radical ideas by adopting what he called a new "left-of-center agenda." One of his first priorities was to abandon the controversial Clause Four of the Labour party constitution, which pledged "common ownership of the means of production, distribution and exchange"; in other words, Labour gave up its promise to undo privatization, one of the most successful of Margaret Thatcher's policies. Clause Four was abandoned in 1996, and Labour has since stood for more overtly free-market economic policies of the kind associated with the **"third way"** in politics. While the notion has never been clearly defined, it is taken to mean a philosophy that lies somewhere between the kind of right-wing conservatism and capitalism associated with the Reagan and Thatcher governments and the left-wing liberalism and economic management associated with socialist parties in Western Europe. It has also been described as "capitalism with a conscience" or "market socialism."

The Labour victory in May 1997 was astonishing in almost every sense. Labour was swept back into office with a 179-seat majority, while Conservative representation in the Commons was halved, the party lost all its seats in Scotland and Wales, and even senior members of the cabinet (including several future contenders for the leadership of the party) lost their seats. Debates have since raged about the reasons behind the Labour victory and the Conservative defeat.[18] Britain at the time had rates of unemployment and inflation that were among the lowest in Europe (6 percent and 3 percent, respectively). The Conservatives were also the party of Margaret Thatcher, whose policies of privatization and undermining the powers of labor unions had been popular and effective. However, the turnaround symbolized a widely felt need among Britons for change and a concern that Conservatives had paid too little attention to social problems. Furthermore, there was clearly some tactical voting in the election, with Labour and Liberal Democratic supporters voting for the other party in districts where one of them was in a strong position to challenge the incumbent Conservative.[19] Finally, a new generation of young people who had known nothing but Conservative government was voting for the first time; 52 percent of under 25-year-olds voted Labour, up from 35 percent in 1992. Many analysts also argued that the vote was ultimately less for Labour than against the Conservatives.

Voters were not quite so complimentary to Labour in the 2001 election. Blair was given a second term in office with his majority barely changed, but voter turnout was just 59 percent, one of the lowest levels ever. This was interpreted as criticism of the Blair administration for the continuing problems in Britain's public services and as a lack of enthusiasm for the opposition Conservative party, which was deeply divided on key issues.

The Conservatives

The origins of the Conservatives (also known as the Tories) date back to the late 17th century. They have held power for 36 of the 58 years since the end of World War II but, despite the number of its postwar election victories, have never won more than 42 to 44 percent of the national vote and fell to a new low of 30 to 32 percent in the 1997 and 2001 elections.

Much like U.S. Republicans, the Conservatives are a pro-business, antiregulation, moderate party, with many shades of opinion: Right-wingers in the party emphasize social discipline, authority, continuity, and morals, while moderates emphasize the creation of wealth and efficient economic organization. Until 1975, when Margaret Thatcher became party leader, Conservative policies changed little, irrespective of the leader. Thatcher broke with tradition, and for more than a decade the party developed policies that reflected her values. She supported monetarist economic ideas of the kind favored by Ronald Reagan, such as controls on government spending, reducing the role of government in the marketplace, low taxation, and a free market. Also, she promoted private enterprise and private ownership, believed in a strong global role for Britain and close Anglo-American relations, and was hostile to many aspects of European integration.

Although the Conservatives fought the 1997 election against the background of a strong economy, they faced an electorate that was tired of internal party squabbles; the party had become particularly divided over the issue of Europe, with some of its members arguing in favor of greater support for European integration and some arguing that the process of integration had already gone too far. The Conservatives had also been hurt by a number of financial scandals involving prominent backbenchers (which became known as the "sleaze" factor). John Major was unable to pull the party together, it went into the election 20 percentage points behind Labour in opinion polls, and it sustained its worst election defeat since 1832.

Following his defeat, John Major gracefully resigned the party leadership (although he stayed on as an MP) and was replaced by William Hague (b. 1961), who faced the difficult task of uniting the Conservatives and making them a true party of opposition. The task proved a hard one, however, given the substantial majority enjoyed by Labour and the popularity of Tony Blair and the Labour government. By 1999, the Conservatives were in a state of crisis,[20] and Hague was unable to unite the party, to capitalize on public concerns about the state of health care and education, or to exploit Labour's weaknesses. After the net number of Conservative seats increased by just one at the 2001 election, Hague resigned as party leader and a new leadership election was held. However, instead of picking a moderate who might have been able to bring the party back together, party members chose the conservative and almost unknown Iain Duncan Smith (b. 1954), who was able to do little to improve party fortunes. By 2003, a large question mark hung over his future as leader.

Liberal Democrats

A small, moderate center party, the Liberal Democrats were created in 1988 when members of a Labour party splinter group (the Social Democratic party, or SDP) joined forces with the Liberal party, one of the oldest parties in Britain and for many years the major opposition to the Conservatives. The last Liberal prime minister (David Lloyd George) left office in 1922, and Liberal support declined dramatically. For a while in the 1980s, however, an SDP-Liberal Alliance seemed poised to take over from Labour as the major opposition party. The renamed Liberal Democrats contested their first general election in April 1992, winning nearly 18 percent of the vote but only 20 seats. In the 1997 election they more than doubled their representation in Parliament, winning 46 seats, the best result for a third party since the 1920s. They added six more seats in 2001. Although still very small, new attention has been paid to them by political analysts, especially given that their support and cooperation has been encouraged by the Blair government. They have been led since 1999 by Charles Kennedy (b. 1959).

Other Parties

There are many other smaller parties in Britain, most of which represent regional interests. The Scottish National party campaigns for devolution for Scotland and has undergone a revival in recent years, winning 27 percent of the seats in the Scottish Parliament in 1999. Its then-leader, Alex Salmond, went so far in September 1999 as to predict that Scotland would be completely independent before 2007, the 300th anniversary of the union of England and Scotland. Meanwhile, its Welsh counterpart, Plaid Cymru, won 28 percent of the seats in the Welsh assembly. Both also have a few seats in the House of Commons. There are also nearly a dozen parties that are active only in Northern Ireland; the biggest are the Ulster Unionists, who represent continued union for Northern Ireland with Britain, while the smaller Sinn Fein has campaigned in the past for the reunification of Ireland.

While candidates for the larger parties must go through a rigorous selection procedure, British law allows almost anyone to stand for Parliament under almost any guise, even from prison. The only formal requirement is the payment of a deposit of £500 (about $750), which is returned if the candidate wins more than 5 percent of the vote. Candidates who fail to cross the 5 percent barrier are described as having lost their deposit, the most galling possible result in an election.

INTEREST GROUPS

As with most modern liberal democracies, interest groups play a key political role in Britain. Most British groups are either **sectional interest groups** (existing mainly to represent and provide services to their members, for example, labor unions and professional organizations) or **promotional interest groups** (existing mainly to promote a particular cause). There are thousands of interest groups in Britain, ranging from multimillion-member charities to groups with very limited objectives. Several of Britain's mass movements and interest groups have spread to other countries. For example, the movement against cruelty to animals began in Britain, long famous as a nation of animal lovers. The Royal Society for the Prevention of Cruelty to Animals (RSPCA) was the model for the NSPCA in the United States. Similarly, Save the Children, OXFAM (famine relief), and Amnesty International were founded in Britain and have since become international.

As voters have become disillusioned with political parties in recent years, the membership of interest groups has grown; more than half the adult population is now a member of at least one group, and many people belong to multiple groups.[21] Interest groups have also become more professional, and the methods they use have diversified. Whereas they once focused their efforts on ministers and bureaucrats, they have worked increasingly to mobilize public opinion and have intensified their lobbying of Parliament. The EU has also provided new channels for lobbying, notably giving groups access to the judicial review process through the European Court of Justice.

As in the United States, interest group activity in Britain occasionally adds up to broader movements aimed at bringing political, economic, or social reform. There have been two particularly notable movements in Britain in recent years.

The Labor Movement

Britain has about 300 labor unions, the biggest of which are affiliated to the **Trades Union Congress** (TUC) (roughly equivalent to the AFL-CIO in the United States). Unions were for a long time closely affiliated with the Labour party, having a 40 percent share in the electoral college that elected the leader of the Labour party and sponsoring about 40 percent of Labour candidates in general elections. The

TUC also had arrangements with Labour governments in which it agreed not to make big wage claims or to go on strike, in return for concessions. By the early 1970s, unions had so much power that a general strike was called, which ultimately obliged Edward Heath's Conservative government to call a general election, which it lost.

The failure of the Labour governments of Harold Wilson (1974–1976) and James Callaghan (1976–1979) to reach agreements with the unions on prices and wages led to another near general strike in 1979. This made Labour so unpopular that it lost the 1979 election, ushering in a Thatcher government bent on reducing union power. Laws were passed requiring union leaders to ballot their members before taking strike action, and unemployment reduced union membership from 13 million to 10 million in the 1980s.[22] In addition to a lengthy and divisive strike by coal miners in the mid-1980s, print and journalists' unions also went on strike—all three groups failed in meeting their goals. In recent years, unions have lost much of their support and many of their members, and their political influence has declined further as their influence on the Labour party has weakened.

Business Groups

If the TUC represents workers, then employers are represented by the **Confederation of British Industry** (CBI). Financial institutions are politically important, mainly because of the influence of the financial district of the City of London (the City). This is the biggest market in the world for foreign exchange, gold, international insurance, and international commodities and which also has the world's third largest stock market (after New York and Tokyo) when measured by value. City interests are kept separate from those of industry and there are no formal links between business and the Conservative party (such as those that once existed between unions and the Labour party), but many senior managers in the City and Britain's larger companies had significant influence within the Conservative party during the Major and Thatcher years. They have not been ignored by the Blair government, which has made a point of cultivating contacts with business as part of its philosophy of increasing productivity and promoting British economic influence in the EU.

THE MEDIA

As in most democracies, Britons tend to derive most of their information about politics from the mass media. They generally have a high level of political literacy and interest in national and international affairs, a situation sustained by one of the most active and well-respected mass media establishments in the world, catering to almost every taste and political persuasion. Unlike the United States, where most media tend to be local, Britain—like all European countries—has mainly national or regional media. These create an atmosphere in which people are interested less in local politics than in national or international politics, and the more serious sources tend to provide much more sophisticated analysis of politics than is the case with most U.S. media (with the exception of big-city newspapers such as *The New York Times*, key weekly or monthly journals, and public radio and television).

Until the late 1980s, British television viewers had access to just four terrestrial channels: two government-owned and commercial-free channels run by the British Broadcasting Corporation (BBC) and two independent commercial channels (ITV and Channel Four). (A new commercial channel—Channel Five—was created in the 1990s.) All are editorially independent, are required to give equal air time to the major political parties, and frequently become involved in political controversy. Users pay an annual license fee, which goes to supporting BBC TV and five national BBC radio channels. Despite being government-owned, the BBC has a reputation for being an impartial and dependable source of news both inside and outside Britain. Audience shares for the five channels have been greatly reduced in recent years due to the spread of satellite and digital television offering access to domestic programming (put out mainly by Sky, Carlton, and Granada TV) and even to British versions of U.S. networks such as Discovery, Nickelodeon, and the Disney Channel.

With the exception of major regional dailies (particularly those in Scotland), most newspapers are national morning papers, which between them are read by about 80 percent of the population. There are at least half a dozen serious papers of comment such as *The Times*, *The Guardian*, and *The Independent*, and as many mass-circulation tabloids such as *The Sun* (the biggest-selling newspaper in the world) and *The Daily Mirror*. The latter tend to be blatantly partisan and to present a simplified and exaggerated picture of politics—their popularity has also led to concerns that they allow their owners too much political influence. Particular criticism has been directed at Rupert Murdoch, whose News International Corporation owns Sky Television, three national daily newspapers, and two national Sunday newspapers. Murdoch is an Australian with U.S. citizenship whose papers tend to take strongly anti-EU editorial positions.

POLICIES AND POLICYMAKING

As in most liberal democracies, public policies in Britain are made, implemented, and evaluated through a complex process involving many different actors: the public arena, Parliament, parties, the cabinet, the bureaucracy, the media, and interest groups. While postwar governments had a tendency to bargain, compromise, and build consensus—producing incremental rather than radical change—the changes introduced by the Thatcher and Blair governments have taken policy in Britain in some surprising and notably different new directions.

Britain is technically a constitutional monarchy, but because monarchs have lost all but their symbolic power, control over decision making rests with the government (the prime minister and the cabinet). The government works closely with senior bureaucrats and is accountable to Parliament, which alone has the power to make, amend, and abolish laws, at least in areas where authority has not been transferred to the EU and regional assemblies. Because a solid government majority means that Parliament usually does little more than confirm most government decisions, Parliament's main value is that it provides a point of access for citizens and interest groups, and parliamentary debates and questions help keep the government accountable.

Bureaucrats play an important and often unseen role in government, helped as they are by several advantages over government: They hold long-term appointments, compared with the high turnover among ministers; they have access to the papers of previous ministers, which new ministers do not; and they are powerful traffic police, overseeing the flow of information from ministers to departments and vice versa. Bureaucrats are also closely involved in the development of proposals for new laws, and in negotiations over new policies and regulations.

Outside government, the most important influence on policymaking in Britain is the interplay between public opinion, the media, and interest groups. Prime ministers constantly look at their standing in the polls, calculating the popularity of their decisions and the chances for their parties in the next election. U.S. presidents can shield themselves to some extent from public criticism by exploiting the aura surrounding their office and using checks and balances to spread the blame for failed policies and claim credit for successful policies. By contrast, the unitary structure of Britain means that the prime minister and cabinet are held more directly accountable, so much of what they can and cannot do is tied to their standing in the polls and to their relationship with their party.

ECONOMIC POLICY

The key word in British economic policy after World War II was consensus, a tacit agreement between the Conservatives and Labour that—whichever was in power—they would work to maintain welfare, full employment, a mix of private and public ownership, and the traditional features of the constitution and would agree on policies through compromise involving discussions between government and interest groups, particularly labor unions. Although this approach brought prosperity to Britain in the 1950s, the economy by the 1960s was not growing as quickly as it was in Germany, Japan, or the United States. Conservatives pointed the finger of blame at "creeping socialism," leading to a **British disease** consisting of three main features:

- The growing costs of welfare, which demanded higher taxes and reduced the incentives for entrepreneurs to invest or for workers to improve their productivity. At one time, the wealthiest Britons were subject to a so-called supertax of 95 percent of their earnings, and many became tax exiles as a result.

- The power of labor unions, which intimidated the government by calling frequent strikes and demanding higher wages for reduced working hours. By the 1970s, some of the best-known figures in national politics were union leaders.

- A large public sector. The postwar Labour program of nationalization had resulted in the government taking over large sectors of the economy, including airlines; railroads; and the coal, natural gas, iron, steel, and electricity supply industries. Critics argued that public ownership created inefficient monopolies, leading to reduced quality, inadequate investment, and stagnation.

The skyline of the City of London, with St. Paul's Cathedral on the left and the International Finance Centre on the right. The City gives London a role in the national and international economy unmatched by the capital city of any other country. Some are concerned that the importance of the City might be compromised if Britain continues to stay out of the euro zone.

Liberals questioned the role of creeping socialism. If welfare was to blame, they asked, why did other countries with extensive welfare and high tax rates (such as France and Sweden) not have similar problems? Their explanations focused less on workers and more on management, whom they blamed for failing to compete in the new global market and for failing to invest in new machinery and technology. Allied to this, the class system ensured that entrepreneurial activity and the creation of "new" money were sniffed at by many of those with "old" money, and managers failed to communicate with their workers. Confrontation became more common than cooperation in relations between managers and workers, leading to bitterness, low productivity, and a sense of "us versus them."

Whatever the causes, Britain by 1975 had seen 10 to 15 years of relative economic decline. In that year, Margaret Thatcher became leader of the Conservative party. Accepting most of the standard conservative explanations of the British disease, she argued that major changes were needed if Britain's problems were to be effectively addressed. After winning office in 1979, she pursued several key economic policies.

First, she set about reducing the power of labor unions, refusing to stand down in the face of strikes and union demands. The confrontation peaked in 1984–1985, when the National Union of Mineworkers (NUM) threatened to bring down the Thatcher government by stopping the supply of coal and the generation of electricity. Thatcher had anticipated the confrontation and had given the National Coal Board incentives to produce more coal, thereby building coal stocks. During the strike itself, a breakaway union kept producing coal, so Thatcher was in a position to ignore the demands of the NUM (which she described as "the enemy within"[23]). The strike collapsed, helping bring an end to the era of strong labor unions.

Second, the Thatcher administration lowered taxes. The top rate of income tax was reduced from 83 percent to 40 percent, and the basic rate fixed at 35 percent, the goal being to encourage small entrepreneurs and more private investment. Many new businesses were started, and although many failed, there was an average net increase of 500 new firms every week in Britain in the early 1980s, peaking at nearly 900 per week in 1987. The number of self-employed people grew from 7 percent of the labor force to 11 percent, there was a rise in British overseas investment, and the number of private shareholders tripled between 1979 and 1989.[24]

Third, Thatcher sold off publicly owned companies—so successfully that this policy of privatization was copied in many other countries. Between 1979 and 1989, 40 percent of previously state-owned industries were sold to the private sector, including British Aerospace, Jaguar, British Airways, and Rolls Royce. Profits and productivity in many of these companies improved, but whether as a result of privatization or of a general improvement in the management methods of British industry is unclear.[25] Among the most notable of the privatizations was the sale to their occupants of public housing, greatly expanding private home ownership and improving the quality of housing stock.

Finally, Thatcher encouraged competition. By reducing government subsidies, her administration tried to make basic services more competitive, efficient, and self-supporting. It tried, for example, to encourage universities to rely less on subsidies and to raise funds for themselves. Thatcher also tried to encourage the growth of the private health industry to help make public health care more efficient.

Did Thatcherism address Britain's economic problems? The answer depends on whom you ask. Her supporters argued that she freed Britain from big government and powerful unions and restored an entrepreneurial spirit. However, her critics noted that the poor remained relatively poor, the economic rift between the south and the industrial north persisted, and the number of homeless people increased. Cuts in public spending led to a decrease in the quality of many public services, including education and health care. The high school dropout rate grew, the quality of secondary education declined, and the reduction of university subsidies led to fewer places for students and faculty.

Overall, though, there is little doubt that there has been an aggregate improvement both in British economic health and in the attitudes of business toward customers. The relative decline has been halted, and by the mid-1990s Britain had the fastest-growing economy in the EU; it overtook both Italy and France, and today stands as the fourth biggest economy in the world after the United States, Japan, and Germany. Building and road construction have expanded, there are more private homeowners and shareholders, and the number of luxury cars on the roads has increased. Class distinctions have declined as the middle class has grown, and competition has helped improve the choices available to consumers and the quality of ser-

THE WELFARE STATE

L ike all liberal democracies, Britain is a welfare state, or one in which government makes provision under the law for those in need, particularly the elderly, sick, poor, disabled, and indigent. Elements of a welfare system have been in place since the 16th century, but the foundations of the current system were laid in 1906 with the creation of state schools and the provision of state pensions, free school meals for children, and unemployment benefits. After World War II, a social security system was created to help the unemployed, widows, and the retired, and a National Health Service was founded that provides mainly free medical services to anyone not already covered by other programs.

The social security system is now the biggest item on the national government budget, accounting for about 28 percent of government spending in 2001. The second biggest item (15 percent of spending) is the National Health Service (NHS), which—with a total workforce of about one million people—is the single biggest employer in Western Europe. Public opinion on the NHS is divided. Few question the principle of universal free medical care and there is much pride in the concept of the NHS, but there have been complaints about poor standards, low pay and long hours for doctors and nurses, the amount of time it sometimes takes for a patient to see a doctor, and the waiting time in accident and emergency departments in hospitals.

Most critics have argued that the best response is to spend more money, and the Blair administration has responded accordingly. Spending on the NHS is increasing at an annual rate of 6.4 percent in 1999–2004. Other critics argue that the shortfall of staff is the real problem. Some of the methods used to address this issue—such as launching overseas recruitment drives for doctors and nurses or sending patients to other European countries for treatment—have created their own controversies.

Despite its problems, the effects of health care have improved significantly in Britain: Life expectancy is now 75 years for men and nearly 80 years for women, putting Britain above countries that spend more on health care, such as Germany and the United States. Meanwhile, death rates from cancer and coronary heart disease have fallen, and the number of people smoking has been nearly halved since the mid-1970s. Unfortunately, the trends in two other areas are negative: Britain has the worst drug problem in Western Europe, with nearly five deaths per 100,000 people in 1999, compared with about two in Italy and Germany, and less than one in France; and Britain is seeing rising numbers of people who are overweight or obese. In 1980, just 7 percent of Britons were classified as obese, but by 1999 the number had increased to 20 percent.

vice provided by retailers. By early 2003, the unemployment rate was one of the lowest in Europe (5.3 percent), the inflation rate was a very healthy 2.1 percent, and GDP was growing faster than that of France, Germany, or Japan. As one observer put it in late 2002, "For more than a decade now there has been something seriously right with the British economy."[26]

The free-market philosophy has been so enthusiastically rediscovered that when Tony Blair became leader of the Labour party in 1994 he set about "modernizing" the party and committing it to the maintenance of some of the more popular aspects of Thatcherism, most notably privatization. Indeed, many of the elements of the Labour manifesto as it went into the 1997 election sounded more conservative than socialist. They included a balanced budget, greater independence for the Bank of England, efforts to reduce welfare dependency, promotion of the work ethic, close ties to business, and a rejection of special deals for labor unions. At the same time, however, the Blair government emphasized the need to deal with the problems of the underclass and to pay greater attention to improving education and health care.

Although substantial changes have come to the priorities of domestic economic policy in the last 20 years, the biggest overall influence on that policy today is the EU. Britain now does about 55 percent of its trade with its EU partners, compared with about 15 percent with the United States and 3 percent with Japan. There has also been a substantial flow of foreign investment into Britain, most coming from other EU states, but much also coming from the United States and Southeast Asian corporations that see Britain as a useful base from which to make inroads into the European market.

One of the most troubling issues facing the Blair government at the turn of the millennium is whether Britain should take part in the single European currency, the **euro.** Several EU-member states have hopes that the euro will compete with the U.S. dollar as the most influential unit of international exchange, but the idea of a single currency has proved controversial in Britain, which was not among the 12 countries that adopted the euro in early 2002. The Blair government had launched a program in 1999 aimed at promoting greater awareness of the benefits of joining and promised to put the idea to a national referendum following the 2001 general election, but public opinion against the euro hardened in 2002–2003, encouraged by the growing strength of the pound and economic problems in continental Europe.

FOREIGN POLICY

As the world's policeman and major imperial power during the 18th, 19th, and early 20th centuries, Britain once traded with almost every part of the world, had its troops stationed on every continent, and had a navy that controlled the world's oceans. It is now only a middle-ranking economic and military power, but it is still a significant actor in world affairs: It is one of the five countries with veto powers on the UN Security Council, it is a member of the Group of Eight industrialized countries, it is a nuclear power, and it still has a significant (and efficient) military. However, Britain's aspirations are much more modest than they once were, and it has narrowed its foreign policy interests to focus today on three main arenas: the EU, its relationship with NATO and the United States, and its role in the Commonwealth.

Britain and the European Union

When Europeans began building ties of economic cooperation among themselves in the 1950s and 1960s, they concentrated on reducing the barriers to trade and on building a common European market, with free movement of money, goods, services, and people. European integration has since broadened and deepened significantly. There are now very few remaining barriers to internal trade, and EU residents can live and work in any of the member states (and citizens can even vote in local elections in some of them). Intra-European investment and corporate mergers have grown, and internal transport networks are expanding. The European flag—a circle of twelve gold stars on a blue background—is an increasingly common sight throughout the EU; the member states have brought domestic laws into line with European law; and the EU has a growing network of administrative and lawmaking bodies, headquartered mainly in Brussels and Luxembourg.

The British have always been reluctant Europeans, but since joining the European Economic Community—precursor to the EU—in 1973 they have had to rethink their attitudes toward their neighbors. British economic dependence on the EU was forcefully illustrated in 1996 by a crisis surrounding suspicions that a disease afflicting British cattle (bovine spongiform encephalopathy, or mad cow disease) could be spread to humans. Britain's EU partners boycotted British meat and insisted on drastic remedial action, leading to a political standoff that took several years to resolve.

Some Britons remain hostile to what they see as the federalist tendencies of the EU, but increasing numbers (particularly professionals and those in their 20s and 30s) are now arguing the benefits of membership. Ironically, Britain has one of the best records in the Union on changing its national law to fit with EU law on issues as diverse as trade, agriculture, the environment, public health, transportation, and employment. Perhaps nothing better symbolized Britain's new ties to its neighbors than the completion in 1994—after many false starts—of a rail tunnel under the Channel between England and France. Despite its financial troubles, the tunnel is a key element in the high-speed rail network that is slowly linking all the major cities and regions of the EU.

One area in which the EU has made only mixed progress has been the development of a common foreign policy. Backed by the vast size of the European market—which now accounts for 28 percent of global GNP—the 15 member states have largely worked as one on global trade issues. However, they lack the political unity to work together on security and defense issues. Several member states (such as Finland and Ireland) are neutral, Germany is not allowed by international law to commit its troops outside the NATO area, and the two major military powers—Britain and France—often have different policy priorities. Britain is a supporter of the NATO alliance and U.S. leadership, but Germany and France tend toward a more independent European stance on security issues. The divisions became particularly clear in 2002–2003, when Britain, Spain, and Italy supported plans by the Bush administration to attack Iraq, whereas France and Germany were both actively critical. Many hurdles still must be crossed before the EU has a common foreign policy.

The Atlantic Alliance

Along with Canada, the United States, and most other Western European countries, Britain has been committed since 1949 to the common defense policies of the North Atlantic Treaty Organization (NATO). NATO was founded to counterbalance the feared expansionist threats of the Soviet Union, and Britain subsequently relied heavily on U.S. missiles and personnel to back up its own defenses. Britain has been an active participant in NATO activities; for example, it took a leading role in Operation Allied Force, the NATO attack on Serbia in March–April 1999 that came in response to the ethnic cleansing visited on the predominantly Albanian province of Kosovo. Tony Blair became one of the most vocal spokesmen in favor of the attack, and Britain committed air, sea, and ground forces to the operation. With the end of hostilities, the British military played a dominating role in reconstruction, making up one-third of the peacekeeping force sent in to Kosovo. With the cold war long over, however, questions are now being asked about NATO's role in the world, about the U.S. role in European defense, and about Britain's own defense priorities.

Britain and the United States have long had a **special relationship,** which the United States has often used as a conduit for its relations with the rest of Western Europe. The relationship was closest during the Roosevelt-Churchill years and again during the Reagan-Thatcher years, cooled somewhat during the first Clinton administration, but then warmed considerably with the election of Tony Blair. Although Britain joined most (but certainly not all) of its EU partners in the U.S.-led coalition against Iraq following its invasion of Kuwait in 1990, it was alone in providing political and military support for U.S. efforts to pressure Iraq into removing obstacles to UN arms inspectors during 1998. Britain also split with its EU partners in 2002–2003 when it backed the United States in building up pressure on Iraq to come clean on its stocks of weapons of mass destruction. In March–April 2003, nearly one-quarter of all Britain's military personnel fought alongside U.S. troops in the attack on Iraq. While the French in particular are wary of U.S. influence in European foreign and security policy, Britain has long been a supporter of **Atlanticism,** promoting the idea of working with the United States and encouraging the United States to maintain a military presence in Western Europe.

Britain and the Commonwealth

The third—and least politically important—of the arenas of British foreign policy is the **Commonwealth.** An outgrowth of the British Empire, and known until 1949 as the British Commonwealth, this is an organization that consists of 54 countries, most of which were once British colonies and dominions. Members include Australia, Canada, New Zealand, many Caribbean states, India, Nigeria, and most eastern and southern African countries (such as Kenya, South Africa, and Zambia). Based originally around white dominions such as Australia and Canada, the Commonwealth grew and became increasingly multiracial in the 1950s and 1960s as Britain's former colonies won their independence. It now includes 27 percent of the world's population and has recently even brought in countries that were not British colonies: Namibia joined in 1990 and Mozambique in 1995.

Less a political alliance than an economic and cultural alliance, the Commonwealth remains a significant commitment for Britain, not least because the Queen is head of the Commonwealth and *de jure* head of state in 14 Commonwealth countries (including Australia, Canada, and several Caribbean states such as Grenada and Jamaica, where the Queen is represented by a governor-general). The wealthier Commonwealth countries have provided economic assistance to poorer members, and the ties offered by the Commonwealth have proved useful as a means of promoting diplomatic relations among the members. The Commonwealth has also occasionally taken on a more overtly political role, as when South Africa was expelled in 1961 because of its policies of apartheid (it rejoined in 1994), and when

Nigeria was suspended in 1994 and Zimbabwe in 2002 because of the authoritarian policies of their governments.

The Commonwealth today has a mainly cultural role, thanks in part to its use of English as the sole official language. Among its political and economic objectives are the promotion of democracy, good government, human rights, the rule of law, and sustainable economic development and the development of regional investment funds to promote trade across and within the Commonwealth.

BRITISH POLITICS IN TRANSITION

Britain is distinguished from almost every other country in the world by its long and evolutionary history of political development. Relative peace and prosperity allowed it to build enduring political institutions and to be home to many influential political and economic thinkers. Stability also provided the foundations for an industrial revolution and for the creation of a huge empire.

However, the contribution of two world wars; the end of empire; and the rise of the United States, Japan, and Germany as economic powers forced Britain to undergo a process of political and economic change that has not yet ended. It began by restructuring its economy, building a welfare system, and rethinking both its military role in the world and its attitude toward its European neighbors. Changes of this magnitude inevitably lead to introspection, but after a long period of pessimism there are signs that Britain's political and economic readjustment has begun to develop some long-term stability.

In economic terms, the most significant change has come out of a redefinition of public and political attitudes toward the role of the state. Institutionalized dependency has been replaced by the idea that individuals must take more responsibility for their own opportunities. Membership in the EU has brought many changes, but the most significant changes that are coming to Britain at the turn of the millennium are constitutional. The monarchy is reforming itself in light of demands that it become more relevant, power is being devolved to the regions in response to demands for greater self-determination, and a reappraisal of the structure of government is underway as the Blair administration considers reform of the electoral system and of the House of Lords.

KEY TERMS

Atlanticism
backbenchers
British disease
British Empire
cabinet
collective responsibility
Commonwealth
Confederation of British
  Industry
consensus

Conservative party
devolution
euro
European Court of
  Justice
European Parliament
European Union
general election
Her Majesty's
  Government

Labour party
law lords
leader of the opposition
Magna Carta
member of Parliament
  (MP)
monarchy
Parliament
peers
prime minister

Prime Minister's
    Question Time
privatization
promotional interest
    groups
proportional
    representation

regional assemblies
reserve powers
sectional interest groups
shadow cabinet
special relationship
stakeholder culture
Thatcherism

third way
Trades Union Congress
unitary state
welfare state
Westminster model

KEY PEOPLE

Tony Blair
Winston Churchill

John Major
Queen Elizabeth II

Iain Duncan Smith
Margaret Thatcher

STUDY QUESTIONS

1. What determines social class in the United States, and is it as much of a factor in politics as it is in Britain?

2. Who has the more realistic expectations of government: Americans or Britons?

3. Will Britain be better off now that more political power has been devolved to Scotland and Wales? Could the British learn anything from the United States or Canada about relations between national and local government?

4. Is a written constitution necessary?

5. Which is a more efficient and democratic way of governing a society: a republic or a monarchy?

6. Would a President's Question Time be a useful addition to the way the United States is governed? What difference might it make?

7. Who most deserves the title "revolutionary": Margaret Thatcher or Tony Blair?

8. What are the costs and benefits of having an identifiable opposition party and leader?

9. Are political parties important to the functioning of a democracy?

BRITAIN ONLINE

10 Downing Street: *http://www.pm.gov.uk*
Houses of Parliament: *http://www.parliament.uk*
Official home pages for the office of the prime minister, the House of Commons, and the House of Lords, with links to other useful sources of information.
British Monarchy: *http://www.royal.gov.uk*
Web site for the monarchy, with news and information on activities of the Royal Family.
BBC News: *http://news.bbc.co.uk*
Electronic Telegraph: *http://www.telegraph.co.uk*
Times of London: *http://www.timesonline.co.uk*
Some of the best Web sites for news on politics in Britain.

Europa: *http://europa.eu.int*
Official Web site of the European Union.

FURTHER READING

Clarke, Peter, *Hope and Glory: Britain 1900–1990* (London: Penguin, 1996). A good general history of Britain during the 20th Century.

Hennessy, Peter, *The Prime Minister: The Office and its Holders Since 1945* (Baskingstoke: Palgrave, 2000). A detailed study of the nature of the office and the characters of the officeholders, from Attlee to Blair.

Kavanagh, Dennis, *British Politics: Continuities and Change*, 4th Ed. (Oxford: Oxford University Press, 2000); Dunleavy, Patrick, Andrew Gamble, and Richard Heffernan Peele (Eds.), *Developments in British Politics* 7 (Basingstoke: Palgrave, 2003). Two useful introductions to British politics.

Paxman, Jeremy, *The English: A Portrait of a People* (London: Penguin, 1999). A best-selling analysis of what makes the English distinctive, written by a BBC journalist.

Young, Hugo, *One of Us* (London: Pan Books, 1990). One of the best biographies of Margaret Thatcher.

HEADS OF STATE

In the Comparative Focus for the United States, we looked at executives, or the people responsible for overseeing the execution of policy and law. If that was all they did, they would be nothing more than glorified bureaucrats—what makes them different is that they also provide leadership, doing what they can to have government adopt their policies and their views about society's needs, and generally setting the agenda for government. *Leadership* is a difficult term to define, but when it comes to managing countries, leaders are expected not just to be administrators but to inspire as well. In other words, we are looking for people not only to run the government but to represent the interests of the state. What is the difference between the two roles?

A head of government is usually an elected leader with a particular set of values and goals who appeals to the people who voted him or her into office. Heads of government have specific agendas driven by particular biases, which may be ideological, economic, religious, regional, or nationalistic. They report to their parties and the supporters of their parties, and they tend to be concerned mainly with the immediate agenda and interests of their government and with the views of the people who paid their campaign expenses or voted them into office, generally paying less attention to the interests and wishes of the opposition. Once in office, they appoint all or most of the other senior members of government, who then become part of their administration.

A head of state is someone who may or may not be elected but who uses his or her office to represent the interests, goals, and values of everyone living within the jurisdiction. The head of state is expected to be politically neutral, to rise above partisan politics, to look beyond the immediate interests of the incumbent government, to be symbols of the country and its people, and to be the primary nonpolitical representative of the country in dealings with other countries. Those who hold this position will usually have a few political powers, but only enough to support their roles as arbiters (for example, stepping in to nominate a head of government in the event that no one party or coalition wins a majority of seats in the legislature). They will have few, if any, powers of appointment to political office.

In terms of how they go about allocating the responsibilities of the head of state, most countries have opted for one of two different models:

- **Nonexecutive Heads of State.** A number of countries have chosen to separate the functions of head of state and head of government, placing them in the hands of two different people.

  Several countries have monarchs as heads of state. In the case of liberal democracies, kings and queens (or emperors in Japan) have lost all their significant and direct political powers, play only a marginal role in government, and have been reduced to being symbolic heads of state. Monarchs attain their positions by birth or heredity, being the eldest sons or daughters of the previous monarch, usually keeping the job for life and—upon their death or abdication—passing the title on to their eldest son or daughter, or closest living heir. Despite the argument by their critics that they are elitist and undemocratic, monarchies are still surprisingly common: They can be found in several Western European states (including Britain, Spain, Belgium, Denmark, and Norway), several Arab states (including Jordan, Morocco, and Saudi Arabia), and many countries that were once British colonies still recognize the British monarch as their head of state (including Canada, Australia, New Zealand, Jamaica, and the Bahamas).

Several countries—including a few that once had monarchies—have opted for nonexecutive presidents as their heads of state, giving most of the duties of monarchs to people elected as president for fixed terms of office. Presidents may be former politicians, but once they have become president they are expected to be neutral and symbolic figureheads and to show no political or ideological biases in their dealings with the government, their citizens, or other countries. How they come to office, and how long they serve, varies from one country to another. Some presidents are elected directly by the people (for example, Austria, Iceland, and Ireland), while others are elected by members of the national or local legislatures or a combination of both (for example, Germany, Greece, India, Italy, and Turkey). Terms in office vary between 4 and 7 years.

■ **Executive Heads of State.** Other countries have opted to give their heads of state executive powers, blurring the line between the roles of head of state and head of government.

In France, Russia, Finland, and Portugal—among others—the president is an elected politician, usually with a party identification and an ideological bias, and is expected to be head of state while sharing executive responsibilities with an elected head of government. In the French case, the president is elected for renewable 7-year terms and once in office makes all the key appointments to government. However, the prime minister and council of ministers must have the support of the legislature. If the legislature is dominated by the president's party, then the prime minister will tend to be a functionary of the president, who will dominate the political system. But if the prime minister comes from a different party, he or she will have much more independence and the president will be more a head of state than a head of government.

In the United States, most Latin American countries, and several Middle Eastern and African states, the president is the chief executive and has the combined roles of head of state and head of government. In other words, one person is expected to be both the neutral figurehead of the country *and* the political leader of government. The line separating the two roles almost disappears, which can work to the advantage of the president; a president who runs into political trouble can try to rise above politics by taking on the persona of a statesperson, leaving it to the legislature to become mired in the day-to-day politics of administration. On the other hand, presidents also have to do a convincing job of making the people believe that they have not become too partisan and too focused on the interests of their voters and party.

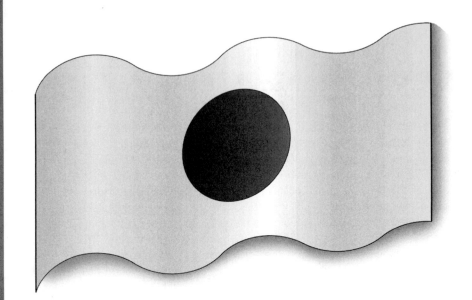

CHAPTER 3

JAPAN

JAPAN: QUICK FACTS

Official name: Japan (Nippon)

Capital: Tokyo

Area: 144,807 square miles (375,050 sq. km, slightly smaller than California)

Languages: Japanese

Population: 127.1 million

Population density: 905 per square mile

Population growth rate: 0.4 percent

POLITICAL INDICATORS

Freedom House rating: Free

Date of state formation: Fifth century (approximately)

System type: Parliamentary democracy with a constitutional monarchy

Constitution: Published 1947

Administration: Unitary

Executive: Prime minister and cabinet

Legislature: Bicameral Diet; House of Councillors (247 members), and House of Representatives (480 members). Councillors are elected for renewable 6-year terms, representatives for renewable 4-year terms

Party structure: Multiparty, undergoing substantial change

Judiciary: Independent 15-member Supreme Court modeled on U.S. Supreme Court

Head of state: Emperor Akihito (1989–)

Head of government: Junichiro Koizumi (2001–)

ECONOMIC INDICATORS

GDP (2001): $4,245 billion

Per capita GDP: $35,990

Distribution of GDP: Services 59 percent, industry 39 percent, agriculture 2 percent

Urban population: 79 percent

SOCIAL INDICATORS

HDI ranking: 9

Infant mortality rate: 4 per 1,000 live births

Life expectancy: 80.7 years

Illiteracy: 0 percent of people aged 15 and older

Religions: 85 percent Shinto and Buddhists

INTRODUCTION

Of the world's 31 liberal democracies, 29 are either European or come out of the European tradition. The two exceptions are Japan and South Korea, where Western ideas of liberal democracy have been grafted onto societies that remain distinctly Asian. It is often argued that Japan is modern but not Western and that its experience proves that it is possible for a society to advance economically and technologically without losing sight of its cultural and social identity. The most obvious signs of its modernity can be found in its economic and technological development, which has become the stuff of legend. Meanwhile, the traditional values are most obvious in the unique features of its political system, where Western ideas about democracy have intermingled with Japanese ideas about faction, obligation, and group identity.

In absolute terms, Japan has the world's second wealthiest economy after the United States, with a GDP of more than $4.2 trillion. In per capita terms, it ranks in the top five at nearly $36,000, compared with $35,000 in the United States and $24,000 in Britain. Its biggest handicaps are that it has few natural resources, few minerals, and limited farmland and must import most of its iron and energy needs and nearly one-third of its food needs. However, it has turned adversity into opportunity by developing a manufacturing sector that leads the world in engineering, machinery, road vehicles, and electronic products and protecting its domestic market with formal and informal barriers. This helped make Japan rich during the 1960s, 1970s, and 1980s, but a combination of problems—including a troubled banking system, corporate difficulties, bad investment choices, a too-powerful bureaucracy, and a political system that seems to be immune to reform—brought an economic downturn in the 1990s. Japan's economy contracted, with GDP falling by nearly one-fifth between 1995 and 2001.

Like Britain, Japan is a small, crowded country, with a population density nearly 12 times greater than that of the United States. About 27 million people (more than 20 percent of Japan's population) live in and around Tokyo, the world's largest and most expensive city. History and geography have combined to create a society that puts a premium on consensus, conformity, and compromise and in which people allow the state to intervene in their lives to a greater degree than in the United States. Its physical and historical isolation have also ensured that Japan is relatively homogeneous: There are no major national minorities or regional languages, most of its people are Shinto or Buddhist, and although Japan has a strong social hierarchy, it is rarely seriously questioned. Minorities make up just 2 percent of the population and include about 2 million *burakumin* (or "village people," whose position is much like that of India's untouchables) and about 700,000 descendants of Koreans brought to Japan as forced labor before and during World War II.

In political terms, Japan is a relative newcomer to liberal democracy. Feudalism predominated until 1868, when the country embarked on a short-lived experiment in parliamentary democracy, followed by a brief imperialist era when Japan conquered large parts of the neighboring east Asian mainland and went to war with the United States and its allies. Parliamentary democracy was forced on Japan during the U.S. occupation after World War II and has generally worked well, although

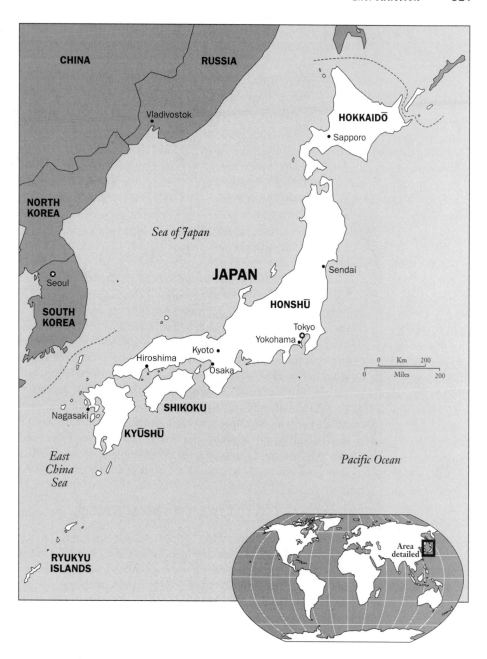

there are several important differences between the Japanese and British parliamentary models:

- Where Britain tends toward pluralism, Japanese politics tends to be paternalistic, elitist, and factional.
- Where British prime ministers lead and become dominating figures in politics, Japanese prime ministers tend to be party functionaries and do not stay in office long.
- Where Britain is dominated by two political parties, one party had a monopoly on the office of prime minister in Japan from 1955 to 1993, and recent talk of the emergence of a two-party system has so far come to nothing.
- Where Britain is governed by a prime minister and cabinet, Japan is governed by an iron triangle consisting of big business, senior bureaucrats, and senior members of the governing party.

For a modern society and an economic superpower, Japan has seen a surprisingly high incidence of political corruption. Much is the result of an electoral system that long encouraged factionalism and forced members of the same party to run against each other. Matters are made worse by a bureaucracy that is powerful, is elitist, and has too close a relationship with big business. Recent prime ministers have tried to reform the system so that government becomes more accountable and politics moves away from deal making among politicians and bureaucrats out into the public arena. After many failed attempts, changes were finally agreed to the electoral system in 1994, setting off a confusing game of musical chairs among Japan's political parties. The stability that was supposed to emerge from these changes has not yet taken root, and the web of obligations in which political leaders and civil servants are often caught has undermined attempts to stop Japan's economic decline. Critics argue that reform is impossible because the problems are built in to the entire structure of government.[1]

POLITICAL DEVELOPMENT

Britain's physical separation from the European continent long helped isolate it from the political and social upheavals that affected its mainland neighbors. The same has been true of Japan, whose physical isolation has helped create a strong sense of identity that has allowed the Japanese to adhere to their own political and social values while copying the best that others have to offer.

The Early Japanese State

The ancestors of the Japanese came from the Asian mainland, most likely by way of Korea. Society was originally based around clans using a system of heredity, and the practice of adopting foreign models began in the sixth century, when Buddhism, Confucianism, and Chinese script were introduced from China. Traditional beliefs in nature worship were nonetheless preserved and distinguished from Buddhism by the name **Shinto** (or "way of the gods"), which officially remains the major religion of Japan.

Also on the Chinese model, a permanent imperial capital was founded in the eighth century near Kyoto and a centralized administrative structure created. Emperors ruled Japan, but their power declined as they rewarded members of their families with grants of land, thereby reducing their revenues and influence. The power shift was confirmed in 1192, when following a series of brutal civil wars, Japan was united under a military dictatorship. Yoritomo Minamoto was appointed by the emperor as *shogun* (or general) and had enough independent power to found a separate capital at Kamakura. The title of shogun became hereditary, and for nearly 700 years the shoguns were the major force in Japanese government.

The Shoguns (1192–1868)

While Japanese emperors were kept powerless and often in poverty at the imperial capital in Kyoto and peasants and merchants were kept at the lower end of the political structure, the shoguns ruled through a complex hierarchy of territorial lords (*daimyo*) and warriors (*samurai*). The *samurai* lived by the *bushido*, a code of conduct based on loyalty, obligation, and self-discipline.

By the beginning of the 17th century, power had shifted to the Tokugawa shogunate, which ruled Japan from its new capital at Edo, dividing the rest of Japan into semiautonomous feudal domains ruled by *daimyo* and their subordinate *samurai*. In the 1630s, the Tokugawas closed Japan off from the outside world, creating *sakoku*, or "the **closed country**." Christianity was forbidden; no one was allowed to leave; and the Dutch were the only Westerners allowed to trade with Japan, but only from a strictly controlled island enclave in Nagasaki harbor.

Japan now entered 250 years of peace and isolation, during which Edo became the largest city in the world. The country came under centralized and authoritarian bureaucratic rule, with a well-established system of law and order and flourishing free enterprise. Although the shoguns were supposedly in charge, real power was wielded by a council of four or five advisors, establishing a tradition of collective leadership that still persists today. By the 19th century, however, it had become clear that the system was unable to keep pace with the social changes brought by economic development or to resist the demands of Western countries impatient to trade with Japan.

The end of Japanese isolationism came in July 1853, when U.S. naval commodore Matthew Perry sailed into Tokyo Bay with a demand from President Millard Fillmore that Japan open its doors to trade. The Tokugawas no longer had the power to resist, and a treaty was signed with the United States in 1854, granting limited trading concessions. Agreements with European powers followed. Ironically, this fulfilled the worst fears of Japanese rulers about destabilizing foreign influences. The shogunate lost prestige, the last Tokugawa shogun abdicated in 1867, and the emperor Meiji was restored to power in 1868. Japan now entered a period of radical change.

Limited Democracy and Imperialism (1868–1945)

The **Meiji restoration** of 1868 marked the watershed between the old regime and the new era of modernization. The new emperor symbolically moved to Edo, which was renamed Tokyo (or Eastern Capital). After much debate, it was decided in 1871 to abolish the feudal system and to create a new system of government that could lead

TABLE 3.1

Key Dates in Japanese History

1192	Beginning of the shogun era
1274, 1281	Attempted Mongol invasions of Japan
1500–1600	Civil war
1603	Beginning of the Tokugawa shogunate
1639	Japan cuts its links with the Western world
1853	Commodore Perry sails into Tokyo Bay
1868	Meiji Restoration
1889	New constitution established, followed by legislative elections in 1890
1894–1895	War with China, occupation of Formosa (now Taiwan)
1904–1905	War with Russia, occupation of Korea
1923	Earthquake in Tokyo region kills more than 100,000 people
1929–1931	Great Depression
1932	Japanese establish state of Manchukuo in Manchuria
1937	War breaks out between China and Japan
1941	Japan attacks Pearl Harbor; declaration of war by the United States
1945	Atom bombs dropped on Hiroshima (August 6) and Nagasaki (August 9); USSR declares war on Japan (August 8); Japan surrenders (August 15)
1945–1952	U.S. military occupation
1947	New constitution comes into force; Japan renounces war
1951	Peace Treaty and Mutual Security Treaty signed with United States
1955	Liberal Democratic party takes power for the first time
1956	Japan joins United Nations
1960	Renegotiation of the Mutual Security Treaty with the United States
1973	Global oil crisis inflicts economic shock on Japan
1988	News breaks of the Recruit scandal
1993	Elections result in the end of a 38-year monopoly on power by the Liberal Democrats
1994	New electoral laws bring major changes in the makeup of the Japanese party system; (June) Tomiichi Murayama becomes the first socialist prime minister since 1948
1995	(January) Earthquake in Kobe leaves 6,000 dead; (March) nerve gas attack on Tokyo subway leaves 12 dead and thousands hurt
1996	The Liberal Democrats return to power in a minority government
1997	Asian financial crisis affects Japanese economy
2001	(April) Junichiro Koizumi becomes prime minister
2002	(September) Koizumi visits North Korea

Note: The Japanese normally give the family name first, followed by the given name (hence Koizumi Junichiro rather than Junichiro Koizumi). This textbook goes with the normal Western practice of placing the given name first.

Japan into the Western-dominated state system. Realizing that it would be impossible to expel the "barbarian," Japan's leaders decided instead to copy foreign models. An imperial declaration in 1868 included the ruling that "knowledge shall be sought throughout the world in order to strengthen the foundations of the Imperial rule."[2]

Shopping around for what they defined as the best of everything, Japanese leaders copied the British parliamentary system (although they included a powerful executive along Prussian lines), French local government, the Prussian (German) civil service, the American system of currency, the Belgian banking system, and the Prussian and French military. They also systematically studied European constitutions before drawing up and adopting the 1889 Meiji Constitution, based mainly on the Prussian model.

Eagerness to learn from other countries, coupled with Japanese self-discipline, led to rapid industrialization, the building of a powerful new military, a new sense of national consciousness, and a doubling of the population between 1867 and 1913. The changes helped Japan win two wars against formidable enemies: China (1894–1895) and Russia (1904–1905). Taiwan (then Formosa) was ceded to Japan after the Sino-Japanese war, Korea and much of Manchuria (in what is now northern China) were occupied after the Russo-Japanese war, and an Anglo-Japanese alliance was formed in 1902 in the face of concerns about Russia. Japan was now established as a regional power.

Although Japan had based its new political system on the parliamentary model, it practiced only a limited form of democracy. The 1889 constitution created a cabinet and a bicameral Diet (parliament), but the emperor still ruled by divine right and appointed the prime minister and cabinet. Competing political parties nevertheless emerged, and in 1918 a commoner became prime minister for the first time. The powers of the emperor were preserved, but the Diet won more power and there was a shift toward multiparty parliamentary democracy.

Japan's leaders hoped that democracy and economic progress could be underwritten by peaceful trade with the rest of the world, but several obstacles prevented this from happening: a tendency toward factionalism, secret deal making, corruption (which undermined the credibility of the political system), and the Great Depression in the 1930s. The depression not only hurt the economy, leading to reduced export earnings and unemployment, but also worsened rural poverty, and—because many members of the military came from rural areas—fed into the dissatisfaction of the military with the civilian government.

Among junior army officers and right-wing intellectuals at the time of the depression there was a feeling that Japan's economic ills could be blamed on politicians and capitalism. There were calls for a restoration of imperial rule, a new social order, and a policy of imperialist expansion, generating several attempted coups and the assassinations of ministers, industrialists, military leaders, and in 1932, the prime minister. With the civilian central government losing control to the military, Japan in 1932 formalized its occupation of Manchuria by establishing the puppet state of Manchukuo under the heir to the Chinese throne. Its actions broke international law, and Japan withdrew from the League of Nations. In 1937, Japan invaded China, capturing the Chinese capital of Nanjing and slaughtering tens of thousands of civilians. Japan then allied itself with Germany and Italy in 1940, signed a nonaggression pact with the Soviet Union in 1941, and invaded Indo-China.

On December 7, 1941, Japan attacked Pearl Harbor in Hawaii, bringing a declaration of war by the United States and Britain. The Japanese attacked the British and the Dutch in Southeast Asia; seized Burma, Malaya, the Philippines, and Singapore in

1942; and seemed poised to attack Australia and India. An Allied counterattack halted the Japanese advance between May and August 1942 in the Coral Sea and at Midway and Guadalcanal islands. American forces then island-hopped across the western Pacific while Chinese, British, and Australian forces attacked from the south and west. American forces landed in Japan at Iwo Jima in February 1945, and the United States delivered the final blow in August with the dropping of atomic bombs on Hiroshima and Nagasaki. Shortly after a declaration of war by the Soviet Union, Japan surrendered.

Whereas Germany and Italy had identifiable leaders during the war, the Japanese tradition of collectivism had persisted, frustrating Western attempts to apportion blame. The prime minister in 1941–1944 had been Hideki Tojo, but he was little more than the representative of the army. Emperor Hirohito ultimately accepted responsibility, but because of debates about the exact powers of the emperor, he was never seen in quite the same light as Hitler or Mussolini and remained on the throne until his death in 1989. Tojo and other military officers, on the other hand, were tried and executed as war criminals.

The Occupation (1945–1952)

Japan emerged from World War II with its economy in ruins, with its social and political systems fragile and confused, and under foreign occupation for the first time in its history. U.S. General Douglas MacArthur was appointed the **Supreme Commander for the Allied Powers (SCAP)** and was charged with disarming, democratizing, and permanently demilitarizing Japan.[3] He oversaw the creation of a political and social system that combined elements of the prewar system with elements of Western-style democracy and also arranged for the writing of a new constitution, which was approved by the Japanese legislature and went into force in May 1947.

Once agreement had been reached on the constitution, there was little reason for the occupying forces to remain, except that some formula was needed to deal with the emerging postwar Soviet threat. Under the new constitution, Japan renounced war as a sovereign right, so an arrangement was made by which the occupation would end in April 1952 and Japan would have its sovereignty restored, but it would also "invite" the United States to station forces in Japan. The Soviets opposed this plan, as did Japanese pacifists, but attention was diverted in 1950 by the outbreak of the Korean War and the plan went ahead. The Japanese Peace Treaty was formally signed in September 1951, becoming effective in April 1952 and returning Japan to its pre-1854 borders. Japan and the United States also signed the **Mutual Security Treaty,** under which U.S. forces continued to be stationed in Japan, bringing it firmly into the Western sphere of influence.

The Rise of the New Japan

When the U.S. occupation ended, Japan began applying its new political system. The 1946 elections had been contested by no fewer than 267 "parties," although most of these were either local parties or the personal organizations of individual politicians.[4] Over the next 10 years, coalitions and attrition reduced the number, and by the late 1950s the Liberal Democratic party had emerged as the dominant force in politics. A pattern of consensus government was also reestablished, in which power was exercised by the bureaucracy with the support, encouragement, and sometimes influence of the Liberal Democrats.

Building on a base of political stability, Japan since 1947 has developed strong trading ties all over the world and has invested heavily in other countries. Within barely a generation, isolationism and feudalism had given way to a new system of democratic government that helped Japan become one of the world's major economic powers and made household names of corporations such as Canon, Fujitsu, Honda, Mitsubishi, Sony, Toshiba, and Toyota. Japan became the world's biggest creditor nation, its stock market one of the most influential, its currency (the yen) one of the strongest, and its banks among the world's largest. Japan established its place as a world leader in the development of new technology and the application of that technology to efficient and dependable manufactured goods.

Underneath the impressive figures, though, there have long been concerns that Japan's political modernization has not kept pace with its economic growth, leading some to question whether the political system met the needs of an economic superpower. Public faith in government was particularly shaken by a string of political and financial scandals. News of one of the biggest broke in 1988, when it was revealed that political donations had been given in 1985–1986 to leading politicians and senior government officials in the form of shares in the **Recruit Corporation,** an information and property conglomerate. When Recruit shares were offered publicly in late 1986, the new shareholders reaped instant and large profits. News of the scandal led to the resignation of 42 politicians and bureaucrats, including finance minister Kiichi Miyazawa and—eventually—prime minister Noboru Takeshita. He was replaced by Sosuke Uno, but he resigned within weeks after news broke that he had once kept a mistress. (After 13 years of hearings and court cases, Recruit chairman Hiromasa Ezoe was finally given a suspended jail term in March 2003.)

Subsequent scandals revealed bureaucratic corruption in the ministry of health that allowed 2,000 hemophiliacs to contract AIDS through transfusions of tainted blood, incompetence in a government response to a devastating 1995 earthquake in the southern city of Kobe that left more than 6,000 people dead, and questions about public safety following a 1995 nerve gas attack on a Tokyo subway by a religious cult called Aum Shinrikyo that left 12 people dead and more than 5,500 hurt.

Critics of the status quo began calling in the early 1990s for a "third opening," which, like the trade openings of 1853–1854 and the SCAP occupation of 1945–1952, would bring the kinds of changes to government, education, and economic and foreign policy Japan needed to become a true superpower. The monopoly of the Liberal Democratic party was finally broken in 1993–1994, but this proved to be only a temporary break, because the party came back in a minority government in 1996 and has been a member of the coalitions that have since ruled Japan.

Japan Today

In the 1980s, *Japan* was a watchword for economic power. Today, it is in danger of becoming a watchword for the inability of a political and economic system to keep up with new opportunities and pressures for change. Although the increasing number of Japanese cars and electronic goods in the United States was once seen as symbolic of the economic threats posed by Japan, it has slowly come to matter less. Japan is still an economic powerhouse, but it entered its longest postwar recession in the mid-1990s, and its GDP fell by 17 percent between 1995 and 2001 (U.S. GDP grew over the same period by 47 percent). While industrial production continued to grow, retail sales and consumer confidence fell, unemployment in 2003 was running at more than 5 percent (about the same rate as in the United States), the Tokyo stock market was down a remarkable 77 percent from its highest level, and Japan was the only major liberal democracy to experience deflation.

On the political front, Japan remains a difficult country both to understand (at least for outsiders) and to reform. It needs leadership, but the idea of leadership—or at least of individuals rising above the pack—runs counter to political culture (see later discussion). So instead of "transparency" (an open political system) and accountability, there is obfuscation and a tendency to hide behind the protective barrier of the group. Prime ministers who are appointed to office on a promise of reform typically end up being cautious and/or conservative, and business as usual continues. Change is occurring, though, regardless of the policies pursued by Japanese leaders: The electoral system has been reformed, government ministries have been reorganized, younger Japanese are rebelling against formality and conformity, and the number of independents elected to the Diet has grown.[5] The problem lies in the relatively slow pace of change and the political and economic effects this could have on Japan in light of the much greater pace of change witnessed by other liberal democracies.

POLITICAL CULTURE

Japan may be a liberal democracy, but the changes it has seen in the last century have come so rapidly that many traditional aspects of Japanese political culture remain intact. Several of these have come under increasing criticism for acting as a brake on Japan's political modernization and for contributing to instability in the leadership of the world's second biggest economy.

Social Conformity and Group Identity

Although almost every society has some kind of social hierarchy, it is particularly obvious in Japan, where people are divided into groups that are not only ranked in relation to each other but also internally. Where politics in most liberal democracies is driven by majoritarian democracy and by winners and losers, decisions in Japan tend to be made by consensus, there is little room for individualism, and emphasis is placed on the group. This is particularly visible in the role of teamwork in Japanese companies.

Japanese political leaders occupy their positions not necessarily because they are good leaders but because of their seniority, their acceptability to the group, their paternalistic concerns for the people, and their ability to build consensus rather than impose their preferences on others. The emphasis on group leadership is one reason few outsiders can name Japanese politicians—few rise above the pack, rock the boat, or threaten the political status quo. Conformity is visible in the way so many Japanese dress alike, and group solidarity is reflected in the way many of the most successful politicians come from families with a tradition in politics. For example, prime minister Junichiro Koizumi's father and grandfather were members of the Japanese legislature.

The collective society also encourages the Japanese to think of themselves as unique,[6] to assume that Japanese culture cannot be adopted by foreigners, and to

CRITICAL ISSUES

WOMEN IN POLITICS

The role of women in politics has improved in most liberal democracies in recent years, but their access to elected office and to the highest levels of government varies from one country to another. The roll call of female prime ministers has grown—including Margaret Thatcher in Britain, Edith Cresson in France, Jenny Shipley and Helen Clark in New Zealand, and Gro Harlem Brundtland in Norway—but a more telling measure of their changing status in government is reflected in the numbers of women being elected to legislative office (see Figure 3.1).

- The record in Japan, with its traditional paternalism, is relatively poor: Less than 5 percent of members of the House of Representatives were women in 1999, a decrease from 1946, when the figure was 8.4 percent. By 2000 the figure was up slightly to 7.3 percent, still far less than in any other liberal democracy except its near-neighbor South Korea.
- The U.S. Congress has seen growing numbers of women members but still does not have a strong record. Only 14 percent of members of the House of Representatives were women in 2002–2004 and only 13 percent of senators, yet women make up just over half the population of the United States. Proportionately, ethnic minorities are better represented.

- The 1997 election in Britain saw the proportion of women elected to Parliament double, from 9 percent to more than 18 percent. A total of 120 women were elected, all but 9 of whom represented the Labour party, which had made a particular effort to field women candidates. In 2001 the figures were almost unchanged.

- Britain and the United States compare well to Italy and France (both about 11 to 12 percent), but every country pales by comparison to the Scandinavians and the Dutch, all of whom are in the range of 36 to 45 percent.

Although there is nothing to suggest that different sexes, races, or religions are necessarily better represented by their own members, the diversity of the membership of legislatures is a strong indicator of how far a society has gone in removing discrimination and barriers to professional achievement. The preceding figures suggest that—for women at least—Japan still lags far behind most other countries.

have a poor record of assimilating non-Japanese. For example, the descendants of the Koreans who were brought to Japan as laborers during World War II are still denied jobs in the bureaucracy, cannot vote, and are generally treated as second-class citizens. Similarly, Japanese-owned companies outside Japan rarely involve non-Japanese managers in high-level decision making.

Loyalty and Obligation

Group identity is further reflected in Japanese ideas of loyalty and obligation, which tend to be based on emotion rather than formal legal contracts.[7] Political power is based on a web of social and financial ties that bind a small political elite and promote nepotism and factionalism. These values help explain the Japanese support for militarism and imperialism in the 1930s, promoted by military leaders under the

FIGURE 3.1

Comparing the Membership of Women in Legislatures

% of total membership

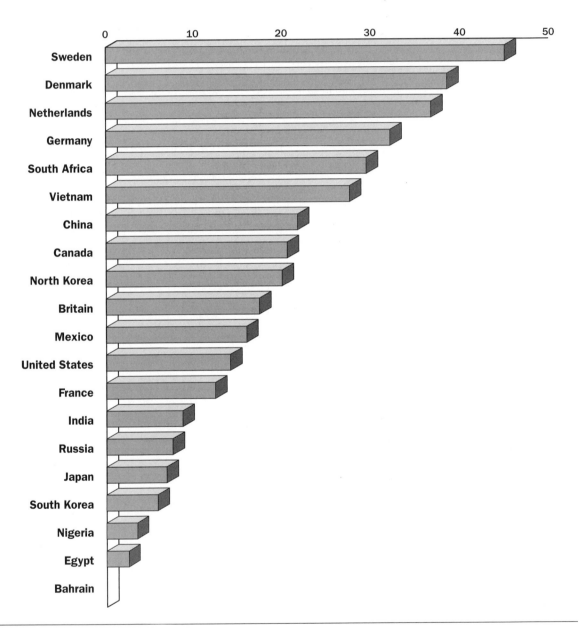

Source: Inter-Parliamentary Union Web site, 2003, *http://www.ipu.org*. Figures are for 1999–2003, for lower chambers of national legislatures.

guise of loyalty to the emperor. Loyalty is reflected today in the way workers tend to stay with one company all their lives, and obligation is reflected in the frequency of influence peddling in politics.

Allied to the notion of group identity and loyalty is the achievement ethic. As the performance of Japanese business and industry shows, the Japanese are goal-oriented, but their goals are driven less by personal ambition than by collective achievement.

A Male-Dominated Society

While Europe and Japan both have a feudal past, most European countries have left that past behind. In Japan, however, paternalism is still a feature of social and political relations, and in no other liberal democracy is the gender gap so obvious or the feminist movement so weak. Women earn just over half as much as men, and the number of women in politics has actually fallen since World War II (see Critical Issues, p. 137). The underlying reason (or excuse) for this paternalism is tradition and the social order. Despite this, Japanese women have a close sense of group identity, in contrast to women in other liberal democracies, and their social position has improved since the prewar era, when they were regarded by men as little more than chattels. Women were given the vote in 1945 (mainly because General MacArthur insisted) and the 1947 constitution gave them equal legal status with men for the first time. The divorce rate has increased at least partly because more women demand more from life than being housewives and mothers, and the number of women college graduates has grown. However, opportunities for women in business, politics, and the professions are still limited.

POLITICAL SYSTEM

Japan is a liberal democracy, with many of the same political institutions, values, and processes as the United States, Canada, or Britain. In all these countries, democracy is influenced by the activities of groups representing economic, social, and special interests, and policy decisions are often reached through a process in which these groups bargain with elected officials. Japan is most obviously different in the extent to which group politics is institutionalized. Consensus is the ultimate goal of the Japanese political process, and the methods used to achieve it include personalism, factionalism, the exchange of political favors, and an almost constant process of bargaining within and among big business, political parties, and the senior levels of the bureaucracy. For these reasons, Japan is often called a **patron-client democracy**.

The pressure and desire to break with this tradition has grown in recent years, driven by cynicism toward government among voters and prompted in particular by political scandal, which has been a problem for decades but seems to have become worse. Changes were made to the structure of the political system in 1994–1996; most important, an electoral system that forced members of the same party to run against each other and resulted in many small parties winning seats was replaced by a mixed system of winner-take-all and proportional representation (PR). This helped make the party system more stable, but not enough for critics of group politics—calls are still being made today for additional reforms, including a reduction in the number of members of the legislature elected by PR.

THE CONSTITUTION

Like Britain, Japan was governed for most of its history without a written constitution, relying instead on custom and tradition. But while Britain still has no written constitution (in the sense of there being a single, codified document), Japan has had two in modern times.

The first of these was the Meiji Constitution, adopted in 1889, partly to convince Western countries that Japan should be taken seriously and treated equally and partly to lay down rules on the distribution of power, promoting social discipline and national unity so that Japan could deal with the economic and security challenges posed by the West. The Meiji Constitution was authoritarian and was based on the ideas that government was omnipotent and benevolent and gave rights and liberties to citizens as gifts. The constitution itself was portrayed as a gift to the people from the emperor, who alone had the right to amend it (although he never did). Despite its limitations, the constitution provided a bridge for Japan's transition from a feudal to a modern society. It also gave rise to a tradition of party politics and electoral competition, resulting in power being devolved to a new generation of leaders.

The second constitution—and the one in force today—was published in 1947. Symbolizing the extent to which World War II was a watershed in Japanese history, the new document did not come out of Japanese political tradition, nor was it even written by the Japanese themselves. Seeing the disagreement among Japanese leaders about the future course of their country, General MacArthur instructed his Government Section to write the constitution, which it did in just 6 days in 1946. Had the Japanese themselves done the job, it might have been less liberal and more paternalistic. The fact that it was written by foreigners—in less than a week—is remarkable. That it was accepted by the Japanese, even though it includes many principles alien to Japanese political culture, is even more remarkable. That it is still working more than 55 years later is most remarkable of all.

The new constitution created a parliamentary system similar to the one that had existed until the late 1920s and replaced the emperor-based state with the doctrine of popular sovereignty. It guaranteed basic human rights, renounced war and the maintenance of military forces, abolished the aristocracy, severely limited the powers of the emperor (who had to renounce his divinity), and created a new supreme court. In short, it replaced the prewar system, in which civilian and military groups had been allowed to exercise the powers of the emperor, with a new system in which authority was clearly centered in the new legislature (the Diet), which was controlled by a popular vote. Where the prewar distribution of power and responsibility had been unclear, the new constitution clearly defined the lines of responsibility. Although conservatives disliked the limits placed on the military and the emperor and wanted him instead to be declared head of state, the constitution has remained in effect, essentially unchanged, to this day.

THE EMPEROR

Both Britain and Japan are constitutional monarchies, meaning that their governments are headed by hereditary leaders who have almost no real political power but whose job is to act as the symbolic leader of the country. One technical difference between the two jobs is that whereas the British monarch is head of state, the Japanese emperor is only the "symbol of the state." The distinction stands as a reminder of the new role of the emperor, who was an important element in the political system until much more recently than the British monarch.

The job has been held since 1989 by Emperor Akihito, the 125th descendant of the first emperor of Japan and the son of Emperor Hirohito (1902–1989), who holds a controversial place in Japanese history because of questions about his part in Japan's role in World War II. Much like the British king or queen, Akihito (b. 1933) presides over openings of the Diet, his seal is needed for important state documents, and he confirms the person chosen to be prime minister by the Diet. He is also a living embodiment of the history and culture of Japan, even more so than most other monarchs—although Japan has used the Gregorian calendar since 1873, the numbering of years is still based on the reign of the emperor. So 2003 was Heisei 14, or the 14th year of the reign of the Heisei emperor Akihito. He will be succeeded in due course by Crown Prince Naruhito and his wife Masako, who give birth to a daughter in December 2001.

Despite being members of the oldest dynasty in the world, with a continuous line said to go back 2,600 years, Japanese emperors have rarely personally ruled the country. From 1192 until 1868, they were kept in isolation at Kyoto while the shoguns ruled Japan from Kamakura and then Edo. When the rule of the shoguns ended in 1868, real power fell into the hands of coalitions of elites surrounding the throne.

Until World War II, emperors were surrounded by an aura of near-divinity that contrasted sharply with the way most European monarchs were seen by their subjects. For example, Hirohito was treated with such reverence that in his early years his court tailors were not allowed to measure him for his clothes, because this would have meant touching him. His status misled many people into thinking that he had more power than he actually had, but because the power structure in prewar Japan was unclear, it was difficult for the Allies to decide what role Hirohito had played in World War II. But Japan's defeat in the war made the emperor seem less god-like, and the 1947 constitution finally stripped the emperor and surrounding institutions of all direct political power. The reduced role of the emperor was symbolized in 1958, when Crown Prince Akihito was allowed to marry a commoner, Michiko Shoda.

THE EXECUTIVE: PRIME MINISTER AND CABINET

In the British system, the parliamentary agenda is driven by the prime minister—he governs with the help of the cabinet, but cabinet members play only a supporting role. By contrast, Japanese prime ministers have few opportunities to show or exert much leadership and are among the weakest heads of government of any liberal democracy.[8] The Japanese prime minister is more like the keeper of the helm than the captain of the ship, and few leave a lasting personal stamp on government. Turnover in recent years has been so rapid that Japan is sometimes jokingly called a *karaoke* democracy: While the United States had two presidents and Britain had two prime ministers between 1992 and 2003, Japan had eight prime ministers, serving average terms of 17 months each.

Limits are placed on prime ministerial power by the bureaucracy, factions within political parties, party leaders, and the consensus style of Japanese politics. Their standing in the polls is only marginally important to their power base, some may not even have policies of their own, and few succeed in making substantial changes in government policy. Nevertheless, they are not completely powerless: They can hire and fire members of the cabinet, and they do not face the same checks and balances as U.S. presidents. Even so, prime ministers are usually less important than the policies of the governments they lead.

Technically, the Diet chooses the prime minister from among its members. Because the lower House of Representatives has more power than the House of Councillors and because political parties tend to vote together, what in effect happens is that the prime minister comes out of the majority party (or coalition) in the House of Representatives. But unlike in Britain, where the leader of the biggest party or coalition becomes prime minister, in Japan it is the person who wins the most political support who takes over the top job.

From 1955 to 1993, Japan was ruled by a single party, the Liberal Democratic party (LDP). Although supposedly a united political party, the LDP is actually made up of several factions, each with a different leader (see Close-Up View, p. 155).

During this period, the prime minister was not necessarily the leader of the LDP, nor even the leader of the biggest faction, nor even the leader of any faction, but rather the person who won enough support among the competing factions to form a government. Just to make things more interesting, LDP prime ministers were rarely changed at elections, nor did their positions depend on how popular they were with voters; they were usually changed in midstream as a result of several weeks (sometimes even months) of negotiation within the party. There is a dictum that power and popularity are not synonymous in Japanese politics. It is well illustrated by the recent history of the office of prime minister:

- August 1993 saw the first non-LDP government in 38 years taking power. It was a seven-party coalition headed by ***Morihiro Hosokawa,*** and it had political reform and economic deregulation at the top of its agenda. Although he was popular, Hosokawa's grip on power was weakened by stories about skeletons in his political closet, including financial indiscretions, and by disruptive infighting within the coalition. It finally collapsed in April 1994, when Hosokawa resigned, upset by public criticism of his past performance, and a key coalition partner—the Social Democrats (SDPJ)—pulled out.

- A new coalition led by ***Tsutomu Hata*** was formed but lasted just 2 months before the SDPJ once again pulled out of the government, this time concerned that there was a conspiracy to marginalize them.

- To almost universal astonishment, the SDPJ then struck a deal to form a coalition with their old enemies the LDP, and in June 1994 SDPJ chairman ***Tomiichi Murayama*** became the first Socialist in 46 years to hold the office of prime minister. Murayama was leader of the far left of the SDPJ and a well-known parliamentarian, beloved of cartoonists for his distinctive long gray eyebrows. Under his leadership, the SDPJ abandoned its opposition to the existence of a Japanese military and came out in favor of including Japanese troops in UN peacekeeping operations and of the security alliance with the United States. But Murayama proved an unimaginative leader and was widely held responsible for the slow government response to the 1995 Kobe earthquake and the nerve gas attack on the Tokyo subway. He finally resigned in January 1996, leading to rumors that he had

TABLE 3.2

Postwar Prime Ministers of Japan

Date	Prime minister	Party
April 1945	Kantaro Suzuki	
August 1945	Naruhiko Higashikuni	
October 1945	Kijuro Shidehara	Progressive
May 1946	Shigeru Yoshida	Liberal
May 1947	Tetsu Katayama	Socialist
March 1948	Hitoshi Ashida	Democrat
October 1948	Shigeru Yoshida	Democratic Liberal
October 1952	Shigeru Yoshida	Liberal
December 1954	Ichiro Hatoyama	Democrat
November 1955	Ichiro Hatoyama	Liberal Democrat
December 1956	Tanzan Ishibashi	Liberal Democrat
February 1957	Nobusuke Kishi	Liberal Democrat
July 1960	Hayato Ikeda	Liberal Democrat
November 1964	Eisaku Sato	Liberal Democrat
July 1972	Kakuei Tanaka	Liberal Democrat
December 1974	Takeo Miki	Liberal Democrat
December 1976	Takeo Fukuda	Liberal Democrat
December 1978	Masayoshi Ohira	Liberal Democrat
July 1980	Zenko Suzuki	Liberal Democrat
November 1982	Yasuhiro Nakasone	Liberal Democrat
November 1987	Noboru Takeshita	Liberal Democrat
June 1989	Sousuke Uno	Liberal Democrat
August 1989	Toshiki Kaifu	Liberal Democrat
November 1991	Kiichi Miyazawa	Liberal Democrat
August 1993	Morihiro Hosokawa	Coalition
April 1994	Tsutomu Hata	LDP-Coalition
June 1994	Tomiichi Murayama	LDP-Coalition
January 1996	Ryutaro Hashimoto	LDP-Coalition
July 1998	Keizo Obuchi	LDP-Coalition
March 2000	Yoshiro Mori	LDP-Coalition
April 2001	Junichiro Koizumi	LDP-Coalition

done so in return for a promise from the LDP that it would help the SDPJ boost its declining support among voters before the next election.

- Murayama was replaced by LDP president ***Ryutaro Hashimoto.*** Arrogant, quick-tempered, and colorful, Hashimoto made it clear that he wanted to give the office of prime minister a more assertive role in government. He called early elections in October 1996, the first held under new reforms to the electoral laws and the first in many years to be contested by two major party groups led by two distinctive candidates: Hashimoto himself and Ichiro Ozawa of the New Frontier party. The LDP failed to win a majority, but won enough seats to form a minority government headed by Hashimoto. Dashing hopes yet again of some stability in the office of prime minister, Hashimoto resigned in July 1998 following LDP losses in elections to the upper chamber of the Diet—the House of Councillors—for which he accepted responsibility. However, he kept his position as leader of the LDP's biggest faction in the Diet.

- Former foreign minister ***Keizo Obuchi*** was appointed to see out the remainder of Hashimoto's term. Thought of as a caretaker and nicknamed "Mr. Ordinary," Obuchi surprised everyone by taking control of the office and winning strong public approval ratings. But he failed to carry out more electoral reforms, drawing criticism from his coalition partners. In July 1999, a newly formed left-wing party—New Komeito—joined the coalition, giving it a majority in the House of Councillors for the first time. This was intended to strengthen Obuchi's hand but was seen by voters as a cynical bid to strengthen the LDP by making a deal with its political enemies. Public support for Obuchi was beginning to slip when—in March 2000—he suffered a stroke and died.

- The prime ministership was now taken over by ***Yoshiro Mori,*** a politician who had been tainted by scandal and who was unpopular from the outset of his term in office. Nevertheless, he led the LDP into the June 2000 general election, and although turnout was low (just 62 percent) and the LDP lost 10 percent of its seats in the Diet, Mori was able to form a new government. He was a lame duck prime minister, however, and by early 2001 was so reviled that some polls had his approval rating as low as 9 percent, making him one of the most unpopular prime ministers in Japan's postwar history.

- In April 2001, ***Junichiro Koizumi*** became Japan's 29th postwar prime minister, at the head of an LDP-led coalition. The leadership of the LDP had wanted to return Ryutaro Hashimoto to office, but the membership of the party—which had had no say in picking Yoshiro Mori—had demanded a vote, and gave overwhelming support to Koizumi; Koizumi won just 51 percent of the vote among the LDP's members in the Diet, but 87 percent of local political leaders voted for him. The results were interpreted as a clear message that voters were tired of mainstream politics.[9]

Although prime ministerial politics in Japan and Britain are very different, the two jobs have similar powers, and the relationship between executive and legislature in both countries is similar. The Japanese prime minister has the same powers over policy, the power to call elections, and the power of appointment. One key difference lies in the role of the cabinet, which by law can have no more than 20 members. Whereas the British cabinet is an important power base for the prime minister and a core part

PEOPLE IN POLITICS

JUNICHIRO KOIZUMI

© AFP/CORBIS

Taking over the helm of Japanese politics in April 2001, Junichiro Koizumi—like a number of his predecessors—was hailed as someone who could bring badly needed change to Japanese politics and economic policy. He came from a political family, both his father and grandfather having served as representatives and as cabinet ministers, and Koizumi himself had spent 28 years in the House, part of it also as a minister. He was a supporter of reform, was a critic of the Japanese faction system, and came over well in the media, helped by his distinctive wavy black hair, his willingness to break with tradition, and his fondness for both opera and heavy metal rock music. So unusual was he that one of his ministers once described him as "weird."

Initially, the prospects were strong. He had a public approval rating in the range of 80 to 90 percent, he led the LDP to impressive gains in elections to the House of Councillors in July 2001, he appointed cabinet ministers on the basis of merit rather than their membership of factions, and 5 of his 17 ministers were women. He then announced an ambitious reform program, including the privatization of government-owned businesses, a new tax system, an overhaul of the banking system, and spending cuts aimed at reducing the budget deficit. He even came close to achieving pop celebrity, running his own email magazine in which he proclaimed, "I am Koizumi the lionheart."

However, doubts quickly arose about how far he was prepared to go with reform, particularly when he intervened to save several large and inefficient businesses from bankruptcy. He then fired his popular foreign minister, Makiko Tanaka, who had developed a reputation as someone prepared to stand up to the bureaucrats in her department. In a controversial move, he visited Yasukuni, a shrine in Tokyo to Japan's 2.5 million war dead, which happens to include a small number of war criminals. Despite the outcry from his first visit in August 2001 and criticism from China, South Korea, and other Asian countries, he made a second visit in 2002. Then senior members of his party became involved in corruption scandals, and his party did poorly in local elections.

Koizumi had been elected prime minister by a vote involving the entire membership of the LDP, rather than just party leaders, who had wanted to appoint one of their own. In Japanese terms, his victory was revolutionary, and—to use that tired phrase—a mandate for change. But Koizumi quickly showed that he was willing to use factionalism to get his own way, a philosophy that combined with his cautious approach to Japan's economic problems and his slowness to institute political reforms to reduce his base of support. By April 2002, his opinion poll ratings were down to 56 percent.

Courtesy of Japanese Embassy, Washington, DC

The National Diet building in Tokyo. It was opened for use in 1936, replacing temporary wooden structures that had been burned down twice. The completion of the new permanent building confirmed Japan's transition from an imperial to a parliamentary system of government.

of the government of Britain, the Japanese cabinet is little more than an executive committee of the Diet. British ministers make policy and take collective responsibility for their decisions, but Japanese ministers look out for their departmental interests first and place the interests of the government second. Ministers are usually given their posts as political favors, and turnover is normally high.[10]

THE LEGISLATURE: THE DIET

The name of the Japanese legislature is usually translated into English with the anachronistic term *Diet*, even though the most accurate translation of the Japanese name *(Kokkai)* is National Assembly. It has all the typical lawmaking powers of a legislature, and—like the British Parliament—it has powers over the budget, can unseat the prime minister and cabinet through a vote of no confidence, holds a question time for members of the cabinet, and has a range of specialist committees. There is one key difference, though: While the British Parliament defers to the power of the prime minister and cabinet, the Japanese Diet defers to the power of the governing party or coalition and to the bureaucracy.

Like most liberal democratic legislatures, the Diet has two chambers.

House of Councillors

The House of Councillors is the upper house, consisting of 247 members. Of these, 149 are elected from 47 local government units known as prefectures, and the remaining 98 are elected using proportional representation; hence they represent the whole country, not individual districts. Councillors serve fixed 6-year terms, with half coming up for reelection every 3 years. The House is presided over by a president chosen from among its members.

The House of Councillors replaced the prewar House of Peers, an almost direct copy of the old British House of Lords. Members of the House of Peers included the imperial family, hereditary aristocrats, army representatives, and government appointees. The U.S. occupation authorities after World War II argued that Japan did not need an upper house because it was a unitary state and did not have local government units that needed separate representation at the national level. The Japanese, on the other hand, argued that a second chamber was needed to check the popularly elected lower chamber. In any event, an upper house was created, but with no clear idea about what it should do, beyond giving the prefectures some representation. It can reject bills from the lower house, but treaties and budgetary matters do not need its agreement. Its most important role in recent years has been in allowing voters to comment on the record of the government between elections to the House of Representatives.

House of Representatives

The House of Representatives is the lower—and more powerful—of the two houses of the Diet. Until 1994, it had 511 members elected using a complex system based on multimember districts, but electoral reforms replaced this with the present system, which has 480 members elected using a combination of 300 single-member districts and 180 seats filled by proportional representation. Elections must be held within 4 years of each other, but as with the British House of Commons, the House of Representatives rarely sees out a full term. The lower house chooses the prime minister, passes laws, passes the budget, makes treaties, and can override an upper house veto with a two-thirds majority. It is presided over by a speaker, along British and American lines.

The weakness of the Diet relative to the bureaucracy is symbolized by the fact that the Diet meets for only 5 months per year, 2 months of which are usually tied up over the annual budget debate. By contrast, the British Parliament meets for 7 months, and the U.S. Congress for 8 months. Further weaknesses are added by the large number of political parties represented in the House (typically six to seven in recent years), the divisions within the major parties created by factions, and the tradition of consensus politics that makes most members disinclined to disagree with the executive.

THE JUDICIARY: SUPREME COURT

One of the legacies of the U.S. role in designing the postwar Japanese political system is the existence of a separate Supreme Court with the power of judicial review. Separation of the judiciary from the executive was motivated by American plans to decentralize Japanese government. The allied occupation force under SCAP transferred authority over the courts from the Ministry of Justice to a new Supreme Court, giving it powers as the guardian of civil rights and liberties written into the new constitution. Although similar in their general goals, the U.S. and Japanese courts are different in their details:

- While the U.S. Supreme Court has 9 justices appointed by the president and confirmed by the Senate, the Japanese court has 15 judges, 14 of whom are chosen by the cabinet from lists submitted by the court itself. The chief justice is appointed by the emperor on the recommendation of the cabinet.

- While U.S. Supreme Court justices have jobs for life, new members of the Japanese court must be confirmed by a popular vote at the next general election and again at the next general election following 10 years of service. Partly because of their lack of activism, Japanese Supreme Court justices remain little-known public figures and are regularly reconfirmed.

- Much of the justification for setting up the U.S. Supreme Court came from the need to have an authority that would rule in disputes between the states and the federal government. As a unitary state, Japan does not have such disputes, so the Japanese court has less to do.

- While the United States is one of the most litigious societies in the world, in which people often go to court as a first resort rather than a last resort, the Japanese predilection for consensus encourages them to attach less importance to formal rules and regulations than they do to custom. Most Japanese assume that disputes can be worked out through informal discussion and compromise; falling back on laws and rules is often seen as an admission of failure. One consequence of this is that Supreme Court decisions in Japan impact a narrower range of policy issues than is the case with the U.S. Supreme Court.

Probably the most important difference between the U.S. and Japanese courts is their relative roles in politics. The U.S. Supreme Court is supposed to be a neutral arbiter that simply rules on the constitutionality of government laws and actions. However, it has often been activist and thus has had a key role in influencing public policy. For example, it addressed the core issue of racial segregation in its 1954 decision *Brown* v. *Board of Education*, and it addressed abortion in its 1973 decision *Roe* v. *Wade*. By contrast, the Japanese Supreme Court tends to avoid using its powers of judicial review and becoming involved in controversial public issues. It is also inclined to support the government, rather than acting as a check on the powers of the executive or the legislature.

SUBNATIONAL GOVERNMENT

With its small size, heavy population density, social homogeneity, and consensual political culture, Japan is a ready candidate for a centralized system of government. No surprise, then, that it is a unitary state.

During the American occupation, SCAP policy was to make sure that a clearly identifiable source of political authority was created. At the same time, SCAP believed that elected local government was a vital element in grassroots democracy.[11] General MacArthur was particularly keen to encourage small independent farmers, and SCAP also gave powers over education and the police to local government. It has been argued that SCAP was motivated by the American experience of the "frontier" and independent-minded citizens, an approach that was inappropriate in a Japan that had long been used to centralization. One result was that decentralizing reforms instituted by SCAP were reversed by the Japanese once the occupation had ended.[12]

Japan today is highly centralized, and local government is correspondingly less important. There are two main levels of local government: the 47 **prefectures,** which in turn coordinate the activities of the municipalities, which may be cities, towns, or villages, depending on the distribution of population. Just as in Britain, but unlike the United States or Canada, local units of government have no independent powers; they can be created, abolished, or reorganized by central government. But while Britain has seen regular disputes between central and local government, Japanese local government generally operates as a willing and efficient channel for the implementation of central government policies. Local governments are allowed to collect only 30 percent of their own revenue needs, depending for the rest on grants from central government.

Given its size, Tokyo—home to one in five Japanese—plays a substantial role in national politics. It is the political, economic, social, and communications hub of Japan, and it wields major influence over the entire country. The April 1999 election for governor of Tokyo was particularly important because the incumbent—a former television comedian named Yukio Aoshima—had decided not to run again, having been overwhelmed by the city's economic, social, and environmental problems. The race was won by Shintaro Ishihara, an outspoken former LDP politician who ran as an independent. Ishihara had come to national prominence in the late 1980s by coauthoring a best-selling book titled *A Japan That Can Say No*; in the book he argued that Japan should stop falling in with U.S. demands on foreign policy and should revise the constitutional principle renouncing war.

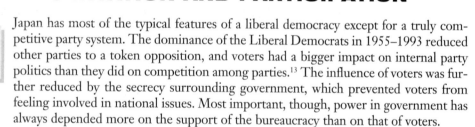

REPRESENTATION AND PARTICIPATION

Japan has most of the typical features of a liberal democracy except for a truly competitive party system. The dominance of the Liberal Democrats in 1955–1993 reduced other parties to a token opposition, and voters had a bigger impact on internal party politics than they did on competition among parties.[13] The influence of voters was further reduced by the secrecy surrounding government, which prevented voters from feeling involved in national issues. Most important, though, power in government has always depended more on the support of the bureaucracy than on that of voters.

It became clear in the late 1980s and early 1990s that voters—especially younger ones—were becoming tired of political corruption, of the factions that divided the parties, and of the role of special interests. Changes were made to the election laws in 1994, but opinion polls in 1996 revealed that about half of all voters still did not identify with any of the parties on offer. They were proving their point by voting with their feet: Turnout at elections fell from 70 percent during the 1980s to 67 percent in 1993 and just 59 percent in 1996, rising slightly in 2000 to 63 percent. The 1994 election laws were aimed at making elections less expensive and thus less prone to bribery and corruption. Combined with recent changes in the lineup of political parties, however, all they did was make the party system more fluid and make clear the need for further reforms.

The frustrations continue today, with the gap between the priorities of leaders and voters symbolized by the rebellion that took place within the LDP in 2001—the party rank-and-file elected Junichiro Koizumi as prime minister in place of Ryutaro Hashimoto, the preferred candidate of the party leadership. If voters were tired of corruption and mainstream politics ten years ago, they are even more tired of it today.

The problem, though, is that the political leaders who must make the needed changes benefit too much from the current system, and they anyway face a powerful bureaucracy that is deeply hostile to change.

ELECTIONS AND THE ELECTORAL SYSTEM

There are no primaries in Japan, and official election campaigns are restricted by law to a maximum of 30 days. The result is that Japanese elections are as short as those in Britain, but they are not always as cheap or as simple.

Legislative Elections

Japan uses a combination voting system for elections to the Diet. Of the 247 members of the House of Councillors, 149 are elected using the single-member system and 98 are elected by the country as a whole using multimember districts and proportional representation (PR). Members of the House serve fixed 6-year renewable terms and elections are staggered, with half the members coming up for reelection every 3 years. At the election, each party publishes a list of at least ten candidates, ranked in order of priority. Voters choose one of the competing lists, and when the votes are totaled, the seats are divided in proportion to the votes cast.

In the House of Representatives until 1994, all 511 members were elected using the single nontransferable vote (SNTV) system. There were 129 districts, each represented by between two and six members. Every voter in each district voted for one candidate only, and when the votes were totaled, the two to six candidates with the most votes were declared elected, even if they all came from the same party. Although this system provided a fairer reflection of voter preferences than a single-member system, it also created a number of problems:

- It led to a large number of parties winning seats in the Diet.
- It weakened interparty competition and strengthened intraparty competition by forcing candidates from the same party to run against one another. Because they had no substantial policy differences, they had to use other methods to win, including using personal appeal, building networks of supporters, and buying political support. The system also encouraged the formation of factions within parties as candidates sought whatever advantages they could over their competitors.[14]
- Although electoral districts were supposed to be regularly reapportioned to take account of demographic changes, this did not happen often enough to keep pace with the shift of the population from rural to urban districts. The result was that some members of the Diet represented as many as six times more voters than other members. The LDP was unwilling to change the system for fear that it would lose seats, but a reapportionment was forced on them in 1986 by the Supreme Court, and the LDP ended up losing fewer seats than it had anticipated.

In 1993, the coalition government of Morihiro Hosokawa argued in favor of reducing the number of seats in the House of Representatives to 500, increasing the number of urban districts to catch up with demographic changes, banning corporate contributions to individual politicians, and using public funds to subsidize election campaigns. With members of the same party prevented from running against one another, campaigns would hinge on policy differences rather than money.

Revisions to the Public Offices Election Law passed since 1994 have given the House of Representatives the same system used in the House of Councillors: It now has 480 seats, of which 180 are elected by PR and 300 by the single-member system, for renewable terms of a maximum of 4 years. Voters cast two ballots: one for a candidate and one for a party. There are 11 PR districts, which overlap the single-member districts, and candidates can run in both. Thus, if they lose in a single-member district, they might still win enough votes to be elected under PR. Ironically, this system favors the LDP and works against smaller parties, which became clear when it was tried for the first time at the October 1996 elections and several smaller parties lost many of their seats.

Electioneering in Japan is controlled by the strongest restrictions found in any liberal democracy. This is a legacy of campaign rules passed in 1924, when the government assumed that voters were not sophisticated enough to understand the differences among parties and so might be an easy target for the growing socialist movement. Even today, door-to-door canvassing, signature drives, mass meetings, polling, unscheduled speeches, parades, and literature produced by candidates are either illegal or strictly regulated. Candidates are instead limited to a small number of government-sanctioned mailings, newspaper advertisements, and radio and TV announcements.

Local Government Elections

In addition to the Diet elections, Japanese voters take part in a variety of local elections. Mayors and members of the assemblies of villages, towns, and cities are elected, as are governors and assembly members of Japan's 47 prefectures. As in all unitary systems, however, the significance of local government elections is relatively minor.

POLITICAL PARTIES

Japan does not have a long history of party politics. Several parties were formed after the Meiji restoration, but they were not constitutionally recognized, and any potential for the development of a multiparty system was halted in the 1930s with the Great Depression and the rise of Japanese militarism. The party system was reborn after 1945 and has since gone through considerable and often confusing change.

From 1955 to 1993, every government was formed and led by the LDP, which dominated both houses of parliament until 1989, when the party lost its majority in the House of Councillors for the first time. Changes in the party system took another dramatic turn in the 1993 elections to the House of Representatives, when defections from the LDP resulted in big losses and the emergence of three new parties. A new multiparty coalition government was formed under Prime Minister Morihiro Hosokawa, and the LDP went into opposition for the first time since 1955. Hosokawa was to remain in office for barely 8 months, however, and realignments in the late 1990s brought rapid turnover in the office of the prime minister. There were predictions that a two-party system might emerge, with the LDP on the right and the New Frontier party (NFP) on the left, but this idea died in late 1997 with the collapse of the NFP.

Running from left to right on the political spectrum, the five main parties active in politics today are as follows.

The Japan Communist Party (JCP) *(Nihon Kyosanto)*

Founded in 1922 with Soviet support, the Japan Communist party was not legalized until 1945. It won 10 percent of the vote in 1946, but it became increasingly militant and was torn by an internal battle between pro-Soviet and pro-Chinese factions. It purged these factions in the 1960s and softened its stance. As it became wealthier and more respectable, radicals charged that it had become too close to the establishment, and many switched their allegiance to the Socialists. With the collapse of Soviet-style communism, the party lost 10 of its 26 seats in the House of Representatives, but it regained them all in 1996 as left-wing voters abandoned the discredited Socialist party and disenchanted LDP supporters cast protest votes for the JCP.

Social Democratic Party (SDP) *(Shakai Minshuto)*

The Japan Socialist party (JSP) was long Japan's main opposition party. It was part of a short-lived coalition government with the Democratic party in 1947, and its support grew quickly enough to alarm Japanese conservatives into forming the LDP, which took power in 1955. The Socialists won 33 percent of the vote in 1958 but subsequently lost support because of their more militant policies: arguing that the maintenance of a military was unconstitutional (which was true), supporting unilateral conventional disarmament and "unarmed neutrality," criticizing the U.S.-Japanese relationship, and opposing nuclear power.

In 1986, leadership of the party fell to Takako Doi, a former law professor notable for being Japan's first female party leader. She rapidly established herself as a popular and outspoken figure, began moderating Socialist policies, and exploited the scandals then rife in the ruling LDP to help the party win a large block of seats in the upper house in 1989 (although this was as much a protest against the LDP as a sign of growing support for the JSP). Reflecting the schizophrenia that haunted the party, the JSP changed its English name to the Social Democratic party (SDP), but initially kept the same Japanese name. In the interests of forming a coalition with the LDP in 1994, it abandoned almost all its traditional policy positions, disgusting many of its supporters. Despite reappointing Takako Doi leader, the party became a shadow of its former self, and in 2000 won just 19 seats in the House of Representatives.

Clean Government Party (CGP) *(Komeito)*

New Komeito was created in 1998 on the center-left of the political spectrum as a result of a string of changes dating back to the early 1990s, when the cumulative effect of scandals, political arrogance, unfulfilled promises of political reform, and a growing feeling of voter powerlessness was beginning to prove too much for the LDP. Groups of disaffected LDP members of parliament broke away during 1992–1993 to form three new parties: the Japan New party, the Japan Renewal party, and the New Harbinger party. These then joined forces with four other small parties—including Komeito (founded in 1964) and the Social Democrats—to form the multiparty coalition that finally broke the LDP's 38-year grip on power in 1993. Morihiro Hosokawa, leader of the 35-member Japan New party, became prime

TABLE 3.3

Legislative Electoral Trends in Japan

House of Representatives

	1990	1993	1996	2000
Liberal Democrats	275	223	239	233
Democratic party	—	—	52	127
New Komeito—CGP	45	51	—	31
Liberal party	—	—	—	22
Japan Communists	16	15	26	20
Social Democrats	136	70	—	19
New Frontier party*	—	—	156	—
Democratic Socialists—DSP	14	15	15	—
Japan New party—JNP	—	35	—	—
Japan Renewal party—JRP	—	56	—	—
Independents and others	26	47	12	28
Total	**512**	**512**	**500**	**480**

House of Councillors

	1992	1995	1998	2001
Liberal Democrats	108	112	102	110
Democratic party	—	—	47	59
New Komeito	—	—	22	23
Japan Communists	11	4	23	20
Social Democrats	69	38	13	8
Liberal party	—	—	12	8
New Frontier party	—	56	—	—
Independents and others	33	32	33	19
Total	**252**	**252**	**252**	**247**

*CGP, DSP, JNP, JRP.

minister, but he had barely begun his program of economic and political reform when the Social Democrats pulled out of the coalition in April 1994.

A reorganization of opposition forces had by then taken place, leading to the launch in December 1994 of the New Frontier party (NFP), which united no fewer than nine opposition groups. The leader of the new party was Ichiro Ozawa, an aggressive and ambitious opposition politician who was behind the rebellion among LDP members that led to the loss of its majority in 1993. Almost all its support came from blue-collar labor unions, and despite its name, the party became more conservative, overlapping with the liberal wing of the LDP. The NFP proved to be a formidable force, winning more votes than the LDP in elections to the House of Councillors in July 1995 and winning 31 percent of the seats in the House of Representatives in October 1996.

However, its failure to win a majority caused grumbles of dissent within the party. To remove some of his critics, Ozawa disbanded the NFP in December 1997. Instead of joining a new Ozawa-led party, however, most NFP members went their own way, and in November 1998 they agreed to create New Komeito. Where Ozawa had controlled 173 members of the Diet, he was left in charge of a new right-wing Liberal party with 54 members,[15] which joined a new coalition with the LDP. This increasingly unhappy partnership was strengthened in July 1999, when it was joined by New Komeito.

Democratic Party (DP) *(Minshuto)*

Among the parties that broke away from the Liberal Democrats in 1992–1993 was the small, moderately left-wing New Harbinger party *(Shinto Sakigake)*. Although it had as many as 23 seats in the House of Representatives, it was not as actively pro-reform as it claimed and quickly lost support. In August 1996 it finally broke apart, with defectors forming the centrist Democratic party under the joint leadership of a popular former health minister, Naoto Kan, and Yukio Hatoyama, a member of a wealthy family often compared to the Kennedys because of its long lineage in politics (Hatoyama's grandfather was a prime minister and his father was a foreign minister). More defections pushed DP numbers in the House up to 52, and the emergence of the Democratic party as the major opposition to the LDP-Liberal government was confirmed at the June 2000 elections when it won 127 seats.

Liberal Democratic Party (LDP) *(Jiyuminshuto)*

The LDP can trace its roots back to the 1870s, but it was reformed in 1955 when the two main conservative parties (the Liberals and the Democrats) joined forces to prevent the Socialists from winning power. It then became the dominating influence in Japanese politics, regularly winning more than 50 percent of the vote. However, a string of scandals and mounting criticism of the electoral system steadily drove away its supporters, and it suffered its heaviest blow in 1993 when many of its members defected. After winning only 44 percent of the vote in the general election, it went into opposition. It regained some of its lost ground in 1994, forming a minority government with the support of the Socialists and the New Harbinger party. It has been in government ever since, but always in coalition with other parties.

The LDP is a classic example of Japanese consensus politics. It is a mainstream, pro-business party, but it is less a party than a coalition of factions; hence the common jibe that the LDP is neither liberal, nor democratic, nor even a party. Each faction is headed by a senior party figure, every LDP member of parliament is associated with one of these factions—of which there are usually five to seven but as many as ten—and party leadership is decided by interfactional bargaining. So strong was the LDP in 1955–1993, and so important the role of faction, that the real struggles for political power in Japan took place within the LDP rather than among the different parties.

CLOSE-UP VIEW

FACTIONALISM IN JAPANESE POLITICS

Understanding all the changes that have come to the Japanese party system in the last few years is challenging enough by itself, but the existence within many of these parties of factions tied to competing political leaders adds an additional layer of complexity. The word *faction* is the nearest English translation of the Japanese word *habatsu*. Unlike the common Western notion of factions as ephemeral and self-seeking, Japanese factions are usually permanent and well organized, and it has been argued that it may be more accurate to think of Japanese political parties as coalitions of self-standing and independent-minded *habatsu*.[16]

Factionalism was encouraged by the pre-1994 electoral system, which obliged candidates from the same party to compete against each other in multimember districts. The LDP has been particularly famous for its factions, which have their own leaders, policies, and political funds and run their own campaigns. Although they were officially disbanded several years ago, they are still part of LDP politics and have become so pervasive that they could be more accurately described as "parties" and the opposition parties as "quasi parties."[17] There are factions too in opposition parties (such as the Social Democrats), in government ministries, businesses, higher education, and even

schools of sumo wrestling. Wherever they are found, they serve the same basic purposes: providing group identity and personal connections and encouraging individual and group advancement.

Factions may help prevent too much centralization of power and allow different policies to be discussed within one party, but the problems they cause are legion. They weaken the power and authority of party leaders, encourage elitism and nepotism, and contribute to the prominent role of money in Japanese politics; the factions provide the money and contacts to help with election campaigns, and the bigger factions regularly raise more money for their candidates than the parties raise as a whole.

The factions do not provide real policy alternatives so much as they promote their leaders to positions of power. Party leaders find it more important to win the support of other members of the party than to win the support of voters. Factionalism in the LDP prevented the party from responding to the changing place of Japan in the world while it was in power, and it threatens to leave Japan in a position of stalemate when its major trading partners demand less protectionism and a greater Japanese contribution to global security issues.

There were several explanations for the longtime dominance of the LDP:

- It presided over the economic boom that began in the 1950s, so it was able to argue that it was the party of experience and could meet popular expectations for stability and economic prosperity.

- Opposition parties were unable to cooperate long enough to form a government, and the major opposition party—the Socialists—differed significantly with the LDP only on foreign policy issues, thus failing to offer a distinct ideological alternative.

- The LDP has an impressive network of grassroots supporter groups *(koenkai),* consisting of friends and supporters with personal (rather than political) ties to Diet members; the *koenkai* are less concerned about party policies than about ensuring the reelection of their representatives.[18]

- Japanese voters tended to be conservative, preferring continuity and consensus. They regularly showed signs that they might be about to drop the LDP, periodically voting against the government in by-elections and local elections and giving the Socialists a majority in the House of Councillors in 1989. At general elections, however, they always went back to the LDP. Even the Recruit scandal was not enough to remove the LDP from power: At the height of the scandal in 1989, the popularity of the Takeshita government fell to a dismal 3.9 percent, yet the LDP won more than 50 percent of the vote at the February 1990 elections.

- The LDP is a chameleon party, adapting its policies to meet the changing tastes and needs of voters. Ostensibly conservative, it has members whose positions cover points from the left to the right of the political spectrum, leading its critics to charge that it has no ideology at all.

- With its extensive contacts in business and the bureaucracy, the party has long been able to raise more money than its opponents and has also had much more power of patronage at its disposal. Although usually an advantage, this also paved the way for repeated cases of bribery and political scandal.

Although it lost its majority in the House of Representatives in 1993, the LDP has remained the biggest party in the Diet by far. It came back into government as part of a coalition in 1994 and retained its preeminence after the 2000 general election. But Japanese voters are not as conservative or as tolerant as they once were, and many are tired of politics as usual. They are looking for leaders who are prepared to try to change the status quo, although whether the status quo *can* be changed is another matter.

INTEREST GROUPS

Given its predilection for group activity, Japan would seem to be a natural habitat for interest groups. There are many such groups, which have combined to produce several substantial movements, but there is a fundamental difference between groups in Japan and those in other liberal democracies: They all use external pressure tactics, such as lobbying, campaign contributions, and generating public awareness, but Japanese groups try to influence the political system from inside as well. They will often try to have their members elected to public office, blurring the line between an interest group and a political party.

There is a particularly close relationship between business and government, and the LDP has regularly been a target of attempts by business to influence economic policy. Trade associations and Japan's biggest companies come together under the umbrella of Keidanren (the Federation of Economic Organizations), which was set up by the MacArthur administration in 1946. It works to maintain a market economy and to present a united front on behalf of its members to the government. Keidanran was once so powerful that its chairman liked to be known as "the prime minister of business." It is also a significant source of funding for the LDP, channeling about $100 million per year to the party through the National Association for Politics, which is run jointly by the LDP and Keidanran.[19] Close ties exist between industrialists and pro-business conservative parties in other liberal democracies, but they are not nearly as close as those between Japanese business and the LDP.

By contrast, organized labor has relatively little influence over government in Japan. While the British labor movement was relatively strong and influential until the advent of Margaret Thatcher, Japanese unions were excluded (often violently) from access to government before World War II, and their position has changed little since. Unions are weak in part because they are organized along company lines rather than craft lines and in part because of their close identity with the minority opposition parties, particularly the Social Democrats. Only one in four Japanese workers is a member of a union (about half the proportion of 1948), there are few industry-wide unions, and Japan's labor federations are relatively weak.[20]

One issue that has generated much public interest and the development of an important mass movement is the state of the environment. The speed of Japan's postwar economic development brought severe environmental problems, the effects of which have been exacerbated by the density of Japan's population and the shortage of land. Tokyo by the late 1960s had become one of the most polluted cities in the world, its air quality reduced to the extent that it had become—and remains—a major health hazard. Uncontrolled effluent discharge into the sea not only hurt the fishing industry but also led to human health problems, creating a watchword for the global environmental movement of the 1970s: **Minamata.**

Chemical production dating back to the 1930s had resulted in an accumulation of mercury wastes in Minamata Bay, opposite Nagasaki. By 1956, neurological disorders had begun to be noticed among fishing families. Concentrations of mercury were discovered in fish caught in the bay and in the tissues of local people who had died of what came to be known as "Minamata disease." The chemical company involved denied any relationship between mercury and the disease, but between 1961 and 1964 it paid out small compensations to disease victims, finally agreeing in 1973 to pay damages to victims. (The remaining legal questions were only finally resolved in 1996.)

Because of its links with business and its interest in economic development, the LDP was relatively slow in recognizing the urgency of environmental protection. The strengthening of environmental laws in 1970 and the creation of a new government environmental agency in 1971 led to an improvement in the domestic situation, but Japan is still regularly criticized for its apparent lack of concern about global issues: Fisheries are overused, Japanese demand for timber threatens tropical forests, and the country has refused to end whaling despite an international moratorium.

THE MEDIA

Like all liberal democracies, Japan has an extensive free press. About four out of five Japanese read a newspaper ever day, choosing (like the British, but unlike Americans) from a wide range of national papers, such as *Asahi Shimbun, Yomiuri Shimbun,* and *Mainichi,* and even from a selection of small-circulation English-language papers such as *The Japan Times.* Japan has a technologically advanced and vibrant broadcasting system with a choice of five national terrestrial television channels: the giant public television network NHK, TV Asahi, Fuji TV, Nippon TV, and Tokyo Broadcasting System. It also has a rapidly growing cable and satellite TV sector and has been a world leader in the provision of high-definition TV (HDTV). Imported television programs do not go down well, but the Japanese are creative at developing homegrown versions. There are also several national radio networks, including the one operated by NHK.

In keeping with the consensual nature of Japanese society, newspapers in particular differ little in terms of their content, do not take strong political positions, and generally avoid investigative reporting. Unlike Britain or the United States, where the media are used to convey political messages and where there is regular political debate, Japanese media focus more on providing information and raising public awareness about policy issues. Where American politicians usually have substantial media budgets and make heavy use of television in campaigning, Japanese candidates are required to devote most of their budgets to cultivating direct personal links with the electorate.

Japanese press freedom is conditional. To interview politicians or civil servants, journalists must submit their questions in advance. Direct access to government is also restricted by the existence of *kisha kurabu*, or press clubs. Each news outlet (such as the office of the prime minister, LDP headquarters, the finance ministry) has its own *kisha kurabu*. In return for an exclusive news franchise offered to the journalists in each club, those journalists are expected to abide by rules that critics charge amount to a surrender of their editorial independence and that contribute to the homogeneous character of Japanese journalism.[21]

POLICIES AND POLICYMAKING

Elected officials in most liberal democracies feel at least a little responsible to the voters and keep a wary eye on opinion polls, but elected officials in Japan are less concerned about public opinion than about personal ties to voters in their districts and their relationship with party leaders, faction leaders, and senior bureaucrats. As the central actor in politics and policymaking, the LDP has been able to rely on the Japanese preference for pragmatism and consensus. The result is that policy initiatives in the party arena have been driven mainly by developments within the LDP and driven more by internal competition than by the competition offered by other parties.

Policymaking in Japan is also heavily influenced by the special place of the bureaucracy in the power structure. Bureaucrats, by definition, are supposed to implement rather than make policy, but Japanese bureaucrats have several features that distinguish them from their counterparts in most other liberal democracies:

- The bureaucracy is efficient and, as such, has contributed to Japan's postwar economic and political success. Japan is one of the few countries (France being another) where being a bureaucrat is a high-status occupation, subject to demanding entrance exams. The higher levels are dominated by the top graduates of the best law schools, notably those at the universities of Tokyo and Kyoto.

- Bureaucrats are government leaders. Japan is governed by a class of administrators who first run government ministries, then retire to become corporate executives or to sit in the Diet.[22] This practice of the "revolving door" is common in the United States as well, and is criticized in both countries. In Japan it is described as ***amakudari,*** or "descent from heaven."

■ More than in any other liberal democracy, policy decisions are made out of public view and mostly within government ministries. This process has reached the point where there is a standing joke that the Diet passes a law, and the bureaucrats then write it. Put another way, "the politicians reign and the bureaucrats rule."[23]

In short, public policy in Japan is made not so much as a result of all the activities we normally associate with pluralism, such as electoral competition, interest-group pressure, public debate, and political parties reflecting the views of voters, but rather as a result of what has unhappily come to be called **Japan Inc.:** bargaining within an iron triangle involving the higher levels of the governing political party (or coalition), the bureaucracy, and big business.[24]

ECONOMIC POLICY

It is rare these days to read or hear any reports about the Japanese economy without coming across the word *crisis*. After its remarkable growth during the 1970s and 1980s, when Japan was routinely described as an emerging economic superpower, there has been little but bad news over the past decade: falling GDP, record unemployment, declining share prices, a falling trade surplus, record numbers of bankruptcies, a growing national debt, and a banking system in trouble. These and many other problems are illustrative of a system in trouble, leaving analysts undecided as to where the blame lies, or whether Japan can recover. One administration after another has tried to address the problem, but so far with little success.

Japan's economic record after World War II was remarkable. Barely two generations ago, Japan was a militaristic and predominantly agrarian society. As recently as the mid-1960s, more Japanese worked on farms than in factories, and the label *Made in Japan* was synonymous with inferior and rapidly disposable products. But the Japanese economy grew at an average annual rate of 10 percent (three times the U.S. rate), laying the foundations for Japan's emergence in the 1970s and 1980s as an economic powerhouse.

The country's economic success was based on importing raw materials (it has little coal, oil, or steel of its own) and turning them into superbly designed consumer and industrial products that are still synonymous with quality, reliability, and durability; Japanese road vehicles, machinery, and consumer goods swept both the home and the export markets. Almost every North American and European owns at least one Japanese consumer product. Japan became by far the world's largest source of surplus wealth for international investment, and parallels were drawn between Japan's record and those of other Southeast Asian states, with the implication that countries such as South Korea, Taiwan, Malaysia, and Indonesia could be the Japans of the future. (See Part III.)

At the same time, Japan was economically vulnerable because of its need to import so much. This encouraged it to protect its industry from foreign competition by im-

Mark Henley/Panos Pictures

Rapid economic growth has brought new wealth and influence to Japan since the 1960s, but it has also compromised the quality of life for many urban Japanese. Tokyo is crowded and polluted and has the highest cost of living of any city in the world.

posing formal and informal barriers on imported manufactured and consumer goods, making them expensive to Japanese consumers and making it difficult for Europeans and North Americans to break into the Japanese market. In 1982, manufactured goods accounted for just 25 percent of Japan's import bill. That figure is now nearly 60 percent, but even that is still short of comparable figures for Germany, Britain, or the United States, where manufactured goods account for 70 to 80 percent of the import bill. Protectionism has also helped Japan build a large trade imbalance with most of its trading partners: In 2001, its imports totaled just over $350 billion in value, but its exports were worth nearly $405 billion, leaving it with a healthy $55 billion trade surplus. By contrast, the United States was importing goods with a value of $1.18 trillion, but exporting goods with a value of just $730 billion, leaving it with a trade deficit of $450 billion (up from $245 billion in 1998). (See Figure 3.2.)

Explanations for Japan's remarkable economic record included the national character of the Japanese, the effort put by Japanese industry into product design and development, and the unfair trade practices employed by Japan. Initially, Japan was helped by a global economic system that encouraged exports by keeping the

FIGURE 3.2

Comparing Trade Balances

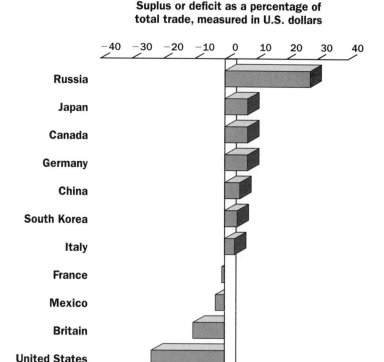

Suplus or deficit as a percentage of total trade, measured in U.S. dollars

Source: Based on figures in World Bank Web site, 2003, *http://www.worldbank.org.* Figures are for 2001.

yen cheap against other currencies. It also invested heavily in new plant and equipment during the 1950s, laying the foundation for later economic growth. The energy crisis of the early 1970s slowed that growth, but it encouraged Japan to conserve energy and develop new fuel- and labor-efficient technology, which in turn lowered the break-even points of Japanese industry.

Other key factors in Japan's economic success include the following:

- A close relationship between government and business, which allowed Japanese companies to borrow much more than their American counterparts and protected established industry from competition while encouraging the growth of new industries.

- A close relationship between government, business, and labor unions, which meant that the number of days lost through strikes is among the lowest in the liberal democratic world, and workers are not only highly productive, but they tend to put the good of the company before their own personal welfare.

- Major investments in new technology and research and development, where the emphasis has been on greater automation.

- High levels of household savings. While most Americans (like their political leaders) like to spend money and live on credit and fail to achieve even the modest suggested goal of saving 10 percent of their income, the Japanese save a remarkable 23 percent of their income, much of which is invested, thus helping economic development.

Along with the economic successes, the value accorded to discipline, conformity, and group behavior has created a prosperous and successful society. The streets are clean, there are few drug problems, there is an efficient transport system, the crime rate is one of the lowest in the world, the primary and secondary education system is one of the best in the world (Japanese pupils spend longer at school than American pupils, devote more time to homework, follow a compulsory national curriculum, and are subject to stricter discipline), and the Japanese live longer than almost anyone else, including nearly 4 years longer than Americans.

Unfortunately, economic growth has come at the expense of quality of life. Remarkably little has been invested in environmental protection, welfare, and basic services, and the Japanese work long hours, driven partly by the high cost of living but mainly by notions of loyalty and obligation toward their employers. This has led to *karoshi* (death from overwork) and to the filing of court cases against companies by the families of workers who have died relatively young from heart attacks or strokes; labor laws have recently been changed to limit companies with more than 30 employees to a 40-hour working week. Despite their work ethic, the Japanese have less purchasing power than Europeans or North Americans. Not only are consumer goods relatively expensive, but land and real estate prices are among the highest in the world. Cities are crowded, housing is in short supply, homes are small, and commuters often have to travel up to 2 hours a day each way between home and work.

To these problems has now been added the specter of an economy in decline. Just what has happened is a puzzle, mainly because of the difficulty of differentiating business and politics.[25] The problem of Japan Inc.—and the heavy dependence of the government, the bureaucracy, and big business on one another—has made it difficult for each to make independent judgments. One result is that the government subsidizes inefficient businesses to keep unemployment low or builds public works projects (such as airports and bridges) that no one needs simply to keep their networks of supporters happy. In return, many of the companies pay off the politicians or bureaucrats, and voters routinely make sure their representatives are returned to office. The most infamous relationship between the bureaucracy and business is the so-called *amakudari* ("descent from heaven"), whereby retired bureaucrats are given jobs in the industries that they once were supposed to regulate. More generally, there is so much secrecy within the political system, and so little accountability, that it is difficult to apportion blame, and the people who should be responsible for making the changes have no motivation to take action. Under the circumstances, it is difficult to see how Japan can reform itself.

CAN JAPAN CHANGE ITS WAYS?

Japan is a society full of interesting contradictions. On one hand, opinion polls suggest that the Japanese are happier than the citizens of most liberal democracies, and the data reveal a society that is more socially and economically equal, with a bigger middle class and smaller income disparities than in the United States or almost any Western European country. On the other hand, there are elements of the Japanese way that are causing social and economic difficulties:[26]

- It is an unusually homogeneous society, but it is also one in which anything foreign is kept at a distance. For a city of its size, Tokyo is notable for its lack of racial diversity, and unlike many other economically successful countries, Japan has kept out immigrants who might have helped fuel economic growth. It has also kept out ideas and practices that might help it solve its economic problems. The record of liberal democracies suggests that one of the keys to political and economic success is openness and transparency, commodities that are undersupplied in Japan.

- As the Japanese live longer, the population is growing older. At the same time, younger Japanese are marrying later—or not at all—and having fewer children. These trends are typical of liberal democracies, but there are some interesting differences in the Japanese case.

Where more Europeans and Americans are having children outside marriage (62 percent of all births in Iceland, 40 percent in Britain, and 33 percent in the United States[27]), this is still frowned upon in Japan, where just 1 percent of children are born outside marriage. Also, there is a tradition in Japan that the wife of an eldest son will take care of her parents-in-law when they grow older. With more Japanese women pursuing careers, this is an increasingly unwelcome prospect, so more are delaying marriage.

- The number of Japanese in their 20s is falling, which is already having an impact on the labor market; it is placing a greater burden on the young to look after the elderly and to meet the bill for social security and health care, and it places greater pressure on older Japanese to work longer. Furthermore, an older society tends to be more conservative and more resistant to change.

There is little question that although Japan still reflects many traditional social values, it is also undergoing fundamental change. But it is debatable whether these changes can help it address the core contradictions in its political and economic systems: a belief in democracy and capitalism, yet an inability to make either of them work in the same way as most other liberal democracies.

FOREIGN POLICY

Japanese foreign policy since World War II has been influenced by three short sentences contained in Chapter II, Article 9, of the 1947 constitution:

> Aspiring sincerely to an international peace based on justice and order, the Japanese people renounce war as a sovereign right of the nation and the threat to use force as a means of settling international disputes.
>
> In order to accomplish the aim of the preceding paragraph, land, sea and air forces, as well as other war potential, will never be maintained. The right of belligerency of the state will not be recognized.

Just as the Allied powers restricted the rearming of Germany after World War II, so this clause was included in the Japanese constitution to prevent the reemergence of Japanese militarism. Although it may have kept the Allies happy, it has provoked much controversy within Japan, has not been strictly followed, and has complicated Japan's relations with the United States and with its immediate neighbors.

Japan and the United States

The rise of economic powers such as France and Britain was accompanied by a parallel growth in their military power. By contrast, Japan and postwar Germany were prevented from using their economic power to become threats to regional security. Japan was restricted to being little more than a regional representative of U.S. foreign policy, a role underpinned by the U.S.-Japanese Mutual Security Treaty of 1954, by which it agreed to the stationing of U.S. troops on its soil. Japan has also maintained the **Self-Defense Force** (SDF), whose job during the cold war was to provide the United States with intelligence, serve the interests of the Western alliance in the western Pacific, be prepared to repel an invader, and keep open the sea lanes supplying Japan. To underpin this policy, the United States stations about 47,000 military personnel and 190 aircraft in Japan at an annual cost of $6 billion, half of which is paid by Japan.

Although this arrangement has generally worked well, it has occasionally shown signs of strain. U.S. and Japanese economic and defense interests are linked together closely, but the two countries are economic rivals. There has been particular concern in the United States (less so today than 5 to 10 years ago) about the inroads made into the U.S. automobile and appliance markets by Japanese products and about Japanese investment. When Japanese companies purchased Rockefeller Center in New York and Columbia Pictures, news headlines decried the sale of U.S. "landmarks" to Japan. (Interestingly, the sale of such "landmarks" as Pillsbury, Burger King, and Holiday Inn to British companies elicited almost no response at all.)

Meanwhile, dissident voices in Japan argue that Americans have lost the ability to compete, that Japanese dependence on the U.S. military is wrong, and that Japan's economic power gives it the right to a stronger voice in world affairs and that it should not necessarily defer to the United States. The 1990–1991 Gulf War heightened tensions. Because Japan imports about 70 percent of its oil from the Middle East, many in the United States felt that it was obliged to help in the war effort. Japanese public opinion was opposed to the war but in favor of helping the allies, if only to avoid U.S. criticism. Japan eventually agreed to pay $13 billion toward the cost of the war effort, but not without controversy that ultimately threatened the tenure of prime minister Toshiki Kaifu. Japan remained remarkably quiet as tensions in the Gulf built again prior to the second Iraqi war in 2003.

Japanese-U.S. relations were strained in 1995 when three U.S. servicemen abducted and raped a 12-year-old girl on the island of Okinawa. Okinawa, one of a chain of islands south of the Japanese mainland, is home to about 29,000 U.S. military personnel. Against a background of growing doubts about the U.S. presence, the incident set off mass protests and led to a September 1996 referendum in which 90 percent of Okinawans supported a cutback in U.S. presence. The Japanese government essentially ignored the result, raising questions about the gaps between public policy and public opinion.

The visits made by prime minister Junichiro Koizumi to the Yasukuni shrine for Japan's war dead were interpreted by some as symbolic of his desire—shared by an increasing number of Japanese—to see Japan play a more assertive role in world affairs, to cease hiding the Japanese military behind the label "Self-Defense Force," to develop a more active role for Japan's military in alliance with the United States, and to at least reinterpret—if not revise altogether—Article 9.[28] Achieving the change will be difficult though, because of opposition within Japan to anything that even hints at militarism, and concerns from Japan's neighbors, particularly China and South Korea, who still remember with disquiet their unhappy experiences at the hands of the Japanese.

Japan and Its Neighbors

Japan officially spends only 1 percent of its GNP on defense, not as much as most European nations (2 to 3 percent) or the United States (nearly 4 percent). In fact, creative accounting hides the fact that it probably spends closer to 2 percent of GNP. This means that it has the third largest military budget in the world, amounting to almost as much as Britain and France combined. Even this is too small to provide Japan with more than a token defense capability, however. In 1994, it had 440 combat aircraft, compared with 4,970 in China and nearly 2,150 operated by Russia. It had 237,000 troops, compared with Russia's 1.25 million and China's 2.93 million.

Despite its vulnerability, Japan has tried to limit its global activities and has kept a low profile in international disputes. Its main priority has been to stay friendly with everyone and to build trade, but this has brought criticism that it is taking a free ride at the expense of the United States and not giving the United States a fair deal on trade in return. Japan is now torn between continuing to be a regional arm of U.S. foreign policy and building closer relations with Russia, China, and other Asian nations.

The debate over Japanese policy on the two Iraqi crises seemed to reflect the lack of direction in Japanese foreign policy, but it is not only the Japanese who are confused. For all the criticism that was leveled at Japan by the United States and others at the time of the 1990–1991 Gulf War, it is unlikely that anyone (even the Japanese themselves) would look favorably on an expansion of the Japanese military. Japan now finds itself torn between military self-sufficiency, meeting the responsibilities and expectations that come with economic wealth, and meeting the goal of nonbelligerence required by its U.S.-written constitution.

In recent years, Japan has become interested in spreading its influence to poorer countries. For example, it has by far the biggest foreign aid budget in the world, has cut tariffs on the import of tropical products from poorer countries, has taken steps to help reduce the debt burden of these countries, and has increased its investments in Southeast Asian countries. Given its dependence on imported raw materials and trade, Japanese planners want to encourage economic development in countries such as India and China, with their potentially huge consumer markets, and in newly industrializing countries such as Indonesia and Malaysia.

JAPANESE POLITICS IN TRANSITION

Japan has seen a dramatic transformation in the last 60 years. Defeated in war and economically devastated, it was faced in 1945 with the challenge of adopting a new political system imposed on it by the terms of the peace settlement, becoming more fully a part of the international community, and building economic independence against a background of limited natural resources.

There are no questions about its economic success. In 1946, it had a GDP of just $1.3 billion, and more than half its workforce was employed in agriculture. Its GDP today is nearly 3,300 times bigger, its industries and services have grown in leaps and bounds, and barely one in ten Japanese now works in agriculture. Japanese products, sold all over the world, have become synonymous with quality and durability.

However, although Japan has become wealthy, many argue that its political system has not modernized as quickly or as effectively as its economy. Vested interests, factionalism, and deal making have dominated the policymaking process, self-interest on the part of party leaders has helped perpetuate a corrupt electoral system, and Japan has been left with a strangely archaic way of governing itself. It now faces the challenges of opening its markets to its trading partners, finding a new role for itself at the heart of an Asia filled with rapidly growing economies, and reforming its political system in a way that takes government out of smoke-filled rooms and moves it more fully into the public arena.

KEY TERMS

amakudari	Liberal Democratic party	Self-Defense Force
closed country	Meiji restoration	Shinto
Diet	Minamata	shogun
emperor	Mutual Security Treaty	Supreme Commander for
factionalism	patron-client democracy	the Allied Powers
Japan Inc.	prefectures	(SCAP)
koenkai	Recruit Corporation	1947 constitution

KEY PEOPLE

Emperor Akihito	Douglas MacArthur	Keizo Obuchi
Junichiro Koizumi	Yasuhiro Nakasone	Ichiro Ozawa

STUDY QUESTIONS

1. What is the difference (if any) between modernization and Westernization?
2. What evidence is there of social hierarchies in the United States and Britain, and how do their political consequences compare with those of Japanese social hierarchy?
3. What are the costs and benefits of a single-party-dominant system like that of Japan?

4. It is often said that Japanese prime ministers are caretakers or functionaries, rather than leaders. To what extent could the same be said of U.S. presidents and British prime ministers?

5. Which is best for government and the people: regular or slow turnover in the office of the executive?

6. To what extent is factionalism a part of politics in other liberal democracies? Is it something peculiarly Japanese?

7. Compare and contrast the power and role of political parties in Japan and the United States.

8. Should Japan be allowed to take care of its own defense?

9. What reforms are needed to bring stability to the Japanese political system?

JAPAN ONLINE

Government and Politics: *http://jin.jcic.or.jp/navi/category_2.html*
Provides links to the Diet, the Supreme Court, government departments, and political parties.

Kantei Home Page: *http://www.kantei.go.jp/foreign/index-e.html*
Home page of the office of the prime minister, which includes links to other government institutions.

House of Representatives: *http://www.shugin.go.jp/itdb_main.nsf/html/index_e.htm*
Home page of the Japanese House of Representatives.

Liberal Democratic Party: *http://www.jimin.jp/jimin/english/index.html*
Home page for Japan's dominant political party.

Asahi Shimbun: *http://www.asahi.com/english/english.html*

Japan Times: *http://www.japantimes.co.jp*
News in English from two of Japan's major daily newspapers.

FURTHER READING

Curtis, Gerald L., *The Logic of Japanese Politics: Leaders, Institutions and the Limits of Change* (New York: Columbia University Press, 2000). A survey of the current state of Japanese politics, with predictions on how matters are likely to evolve.

Johnson, Chalmers, *Japan: Who Governs? The Rise of the Developmental State* (New York: W. W. Norton, 1995). A series of essays by a longtime observer of Japan, focusing on government and on economic and foreign policy.

Kerbo, Harold R., and John A. McKinstry, *Who Rules Japan? The Inner Circles of Economic and Political Power* (Boulder, CO: Prager, 1995). A study of the elites who rule Japan, their methods and motives, and their role in Japan's postwar economic growth.

Schlesinger, Jacob M., *Shadow Shoguns: The Rise and Fall of Japan's Postwar Political Machine* (Stanford, CA: Stanford University Press, 1999). An assessment of the link between economic wealth and political corruption in Japan, by a former member of the *Wall Street Journal*'s Tokyo bureau.

Stockwin, J. A. A., *Governing Japan: Divided Politics in a Major Economy*, 3rd Ed. (Oxford: Blackwell, 1998) and Timothy Hoye, *Japanese Politics: Fixed and Floating Worlds* (Upper Saddle River, NJ: Prentice Hall, 1999). Introductions to Japanese political institutions, processes, and culture.

LEGISLATURES

Legislatures are the institutions within political systems that are responsible for making laws. The legislative process normally involves the introduction of proposals (or bills), discussion and amendment, and the acceptance or rejection of those proposals. The effect of these duties is to give legislatures at least four major roles in the political system: They legitimize government policies, represent the views of the people, act as a national debating chamber in which views are exchanged about government policies, and oversee and supervise the work of the executive and the bureaucracy.

Legislatures come in a variety of forms. The key differences among them are based on their relationship with the executive, the nature of the representation they provide, the terms of office of their members, and their organizational structure.

■ **Relationship with the executive.** The vast majority of legislatures are deliberative bodies that tend to follow the lead of the executive rather than having any real independence or the ability to set the policy agenda. Particularly in parliamentary systems such as Britain, Japan, and Canada, where the prime minister and most members of the cabinet are also members of the legislature and where their ability to lead depends on tight party discipline within the legislature, the powers of legislatures relative to the executive have tended to decline. Hence they have become more a source of votes and support for the goals of the executive than a source of key policy initiatives or places where important decisions are taken. This is particularly true in more authoritarian systems, such as Egypt, where the legislature is little more than a rubber stamp for the policies of the leadership, which uses it as a means to legitimize power

The only exceptions to these supportive legislatures can be found in the United States and systems that have adopted the U.S. model. Where there is a true separation of powers and a system of checks and balances, legislatures become important sources of policy initiatives, and executives must often work hard to win the support of legislators to see their pet programs voted into law. Whereas a failure to win an important vote in a parliamentary system could result in the fall of the government and the resignation of the prime minister, it is not unusual for a vote in the U.S. Congress to go against the plans of the president.

■ **The nature of representation.** Legislatures are the embodiment of the idea of representative democracy, meaning that voters elect into office legislators who are then supposed to represent their views when policies are debated and bills are voted upon. In authoritarian systems, where elections are manipulated and executives wield most of the power, this process is usually a sham. Nowhere is this more obvious, for example, than in China, where only the Chinese Communist party is allowed to field candidates at elections, where the National People's Congress meets once annually for sessions of 2 to 3 weeks, and where "representatives" do little more than discuss and endorse decisions already made by the party.

Even in liberal democracies, there are questions about how far legislators really represent the views of voters. They may be influenced by much narrower agendas, for several reasons. First, because they are members of parties with different ideologies and have been elected by voters who support those parties, legislators may have an ideological bias that means they represent only the opinions and values of that particular group of voters. Second, some may decide to be delegates, in the sense that they are driven by majority opinion among their constituents, regardless of their party affiliation. Third, some may see themselves as trustees, being driven by what they feel is in the best interests of their constituents. Finally, some will be influenced by special interests that have bought their support by being key sources of campaign funding.

In parliamentary systems, where party discipline is tight and members of the same party are expected to vote as a group, legislators will be led from above rather than from below. This means that they will tend to vote as their party leaders instruct rather than being influenced by the views of their constituents or of special interests. For Japanese legislators, they have the added complication of being responsible to their different factions and may make their decisions out of a sense of obligation to faction leaders rather than being influenced by the party leadership or their constituents.

■ **Terms of office.** Legislators in democratic systems are usually elected directly by voters and most commonly for terms of 4 to 5 years. This is enough time to allow them to make their mark on government and to allow voters to assess their impact, but it is also a short enough time to allow voters to review their performance at elections. The United States has gone to two extremes, using a fixed 2-year election cycle for members of the House of Representatives, which forces members into almost constant campaigning and fund-raising, and a fixed 6-year cycle for the Senate, which produces relatively little turnover.

The United States has opted for fixed terms for its legislators, but parliamentary systems usually have maximum terms, allowing their executives to call new elections at any time within those terms. The method used can have a significant impact on the nature of politics: With fixed terms, legislators are assured of a particular period of time in which to reach their goals and can time their actions accordingly; with maximum terms, legislators can never be sure when the next election will come and are much more subject to manipulation by the executive as a result.

■ **Internal structure.** Legislatures are structured in many different ways, depending on how they are elected and what kind of representation they are expected to provide. The United States, Canada, Britain, and Japan all have bicameral legislatures, but these are relatively rare—about two-thirds of the world's national legislatures have just a single chamber. Two chambers are normally found only in large or diverse countries and are designed to give two different kinds of representation. In federal systems such as the United States, Germany, and Australia, the upper chambers normally provide equal representation for states, regardless of how big or small they are, while lower chambers give equal representation to the people. Legislation may have to go through the same stages in both chambers—as is the case in the U.S. Congress—but upper chambers will often be weaker than lower chambers and may only have the power of delay.

For their part, lower chambers tend to be designed to represent the people in the sense that members come from districts of equal size. In most parliamentary systems, the executive—the prime minister and cabinet—comes from the lower chamber, giving it more political significance.

Part II

COMMUNIST AND
POSTCOMMUNIST COUNTRIES

Liberty is precious—so precious that it must be rationed.

—Vladimir Lenin, Soviet political leader

The cold war was the most important driving force in global politics after the Second World War. A struggle of ideas and wits between the United States and the Soviet Union and their respective allies, it made the world a dangerous place in which to live, mainly because of the build-up on both sides of nuclear weapons. But—if anything good can be said for it—at least the struggle for a balance of power provided the world with an element of predictability. With the collapse of the Soviet Union in 1991, the cold war came to an end, and the bipolar world of the cold war era was replaced with the more uncertain and unpredictable multipolar world of today.

During the cold war, communist states included all those that officially subscribed to the political, economic, and social theories of Karl Marx and his key followers, notably Vladimir Lenin in the Soviet Union and Mao Zedong in China. For some countries, such as the USSR, China, and Cuba, communism had arrived through revolution; for Eastern Europe, it came with the expansion of a postwar Soviet hegemony. Since the breakup of the Soviet Union, the communist world has undergone some dramatic changes:

- The USSR itself broke up into 15 independent countries. Some of them, such as Russia and the Ukraine, have moved unsteadily toward a democratic and free-market future but are still keeping their distance from the West. The three Baltic republics—Estonia, Latvia, and Lithuania—are moving more rapidly into the Western orbit and are in line to join both the European Union and NATO. Muslim republics such as Kazakhstan, Turkmenistan, and Uzbekistan are headed in a more uncertain direction that may take them into the Islamic orbit.

- Most of the Eastern European states have moved quickly to shake off the heritage of Soviet-style one-party government and central planning. They are becoming liberal democracies, and they have either already joined—or will soon join—the OECD, the European Union, and NATO.

- Yugoslavia (now Serbia and Montenegro) broke up into five newly independent states, almost all of which are also moving into the liberal democratic orbit.

- Only five countries still officially claim to be communist: China, Cuba, Laos, North Korea, and Vietnam. But the claims are much stronger than the hard evidence. Cuban communism is already wilting and may not last much longer than Fidel Castro, and China and Vietnam have made so many free-market reforms that they are further than ever from becoming communist. The only country that still comes close to old-style communism is North Korea, where the administration of Kim Jong Il runs the only remaining Stalinist dictatorship in the world.

Of course, no country has ever been truly communist, and to describe the USSR or China as such was never correct. For most socialist thinkers, communism has always been an ideal that would follow the creation of a socialist state. This, at least, was the official claim of the USSR (the Union of Soviet *Socialist* Republics), whose 1977 constitution argued that a developed socialist society was "a necessary stage on the road to communism" and that the goal of the Soviet state was to lay the foundations of "a classless communist society in which there will be public, communist self-government."[1] In fact, the USSR by the 1980s was very far from achieving that goal. For their part, Chinese leaders still claimed in 1989 that their country was headed toward the achievement of "genuine" socialism at some distant and unknown time. By 1995, public enthusiasm for socialism and political appeals to socialist goals were hard to find.[2]

As theories for understanding society, Marxism, Leninism, Maoism, and all their related ideologies still have some uses, but as a model for studying comparative politics, communism is fast losing its value. The old "communist" world as we once knew it is fast fading away, which is why this text now classifies the Czech Republic, Hungary, Poland, Slovakia, and Slovenia as liberal democracies. But the legacy of the past in much of the former USSR, Eastern Europe, and Southeast Asia remains strong enough that these communist and postcommunist (CPC) countries are still—at least for the time being—best studied with that legacy in mind.

Before looking at the features of CPC countries, it is important to be clear about the differences among three fundamental concepts:

1. **Socialism.** This philosophy is based on the argument that the best way to remove social inequalities is through government ownership of key industries and services and through the redistribution of wealth and resources by taxing the wealthy and providing extensive welfare. Elements of socialism can be found in most liberal democracies—even the United States—in the form of progressive income taxes (the more you earn, the more you pay), social security, public health care and subsidized education, and the regulation of economic activity.

2. **State socialism.** This takes socialist ideas much further and is based on large-scale state intervention in the economy, the centralization of political authority, government by a single political party supported by a large bureaucracy, state ownership of property, and the virtual elimination of the free market. The most extreme form of state socialism was the **totalitarianism** associated with Joseph

CHECKLIST

COMMUNIST AND POSTCOMMUNIST COUNTRIES
What Are Their Features?

- Almost all are undergoing significant political, economic, and social change.

- One-party government in some, the lingering effects of one-party rule in others.

- Political institutions and processes where links between the governing party, the bureaucracy, and opposition groups are either strong or are still being redefined.

- A growing variety of forms of political participation and representation in most, all channels controlled by the governing party in a few.

- Authoritarianism in some, the lingering effects of a heritage of authoritarianism in others.

- The development of an active opposition and increased respect for freedom of speech in some, little or no opposition tolerated in others.

- Official claims of a deep respect for human equality, but a record on human rights ranging from indifferent to poor.

- Increasingly free-market policies in most, but heavy state control in some, and economic difficulties (including inefficiency, incompetence, and corruption) arising out of the heritage of central control in almost all.

- A mixed record on the provision of public services, ranging from excellent in some areas to poor in others.

- Varied Freedom House, Economic Freedom, and Human Development Index rankings.

Where Are They?

There are 29, and they are mainly in Eastern Europe and Asia:

Albania	Estonia	North Korea
Armenia	Georgia	Romania
Azerbaijan	Kazakhstan	Russia
Belarus	Kyrgyzstan	Serbia and Montenegro
Bosnia and Herzegovina	Laos	Tajikistan
Bulgaria	Latvia	Turkmenistan
Cambodia	Lithuania	Ukraine
China	Macedonia	Uzbekistan
Croatia	Moldova	Vietnam
Cuba	Mongolia	

Stalin in the Soviet Union between 1928 and 1953: complete government control of the political system, the economy, and the private lives of citizens.

3. **Communism.** This is an end state, which has been described in theory but has never been achieved in practice on a large scale. Theoretically, communism would involve the elimination of the state system and private property and the creation of a classless, nonexploitive, and self-governing society in which there would be no political institutions, wages, or prices. The USSR came nowhere

close to achieving these goals and actually eradicated many of the essential prerequisites for real communism, such as a strong **civil society**—a community of individuals and groups capable of acting separately from the state on the basis of pluralism, tolerance, civility, and mutually acceptable rules.

None of the countries in this group are truly communist, but instead they have practiced variations on the theme of socialism and state socialism. Most are now moving away from state control and are undergoing three levels of transformation: political, economic, and social.

Political Transition

In theory, communism is the most purely democratic of all political systems because it is based on a governing structure in which everyone plays a part and has an equal role. The late Chinese leader Deng Xiaoping once claimed that Chinese democracy was "the broadest democracy that has ever existed in history" and was superior to Western-style "bourgeois democracy."

In practice, the principles of communism were so distorted and abused by leaders with their own narrow agendas that most communist states became the antithesis of individual and social freedom, denying their citizens most of the political rights and liberties associated with liberal democracy. Communism included severe abuses of human rights, systematic repression, the elimination of opposition, controls on freedom of speech and movement, and the construction of a **police state**—one in which power is distributed and stability maintained by force and intimidation and in which civil liberties are routinely abused. The critics of communism would argue that these problems were inevitable; supporters would counter that the ideals of Marx and Lenin were never properly applied and that Soviet-style communism was an aberration.

Most communist states developed a centralized system of government, where power was in the hands of a small elite and supposedly directed at mobilizing the masses in the interests of building socialism. This usually produced four kinds of political institutions:

1. A single political party, which went well beyond political parties in liberal democracies in its attempts to make and implement policy and to control and direct government, the bureaucracy, and even the private lives of citizens.
2. A hierarchical government structure that was supposedly separate from the party but was still heavily controlled by the party.
3. A large and usually inefficient bureaucracy, which was subordinated to the party and used to implement the party's political, economic, and social goals.
4. A complex network of "social organizations." Many of these looked like liberal democratic interest groups and even (in some cases) alternative parties but were actually used by the party to gather information and impose additional social control, usually by mobilizing and socializing workers on behalf of the party.

Postcommunist states have abandoned these structures and are now building the institutions and systems we associate with liberal democracy. These new institutions are often still weak, and the boundaries between the responsibilities of the state and the individual are not yet clear. But competitive multiparty systems are on the rise, the structures of government and the bureaucracy have been reorganized, and citizens have many more channels for the expression of their views. Communist and socialist parties are still active and prominent in a few CPC countries, but their influence has been reduced substantially.

Meanwhile, the record on human rights in most CPC countries has improved. This has been particularly true in Eastern Europe, where most governments have abandoned the vestiges of the old totalitarian methods of conducting political business. It is less true in some of the former Soviet republics and in China and Cuba, both of which still have a poor record on human rights. It is least true in North Korea, which grimly hangs on to its old Stalinist ways.

Economic Transition

Because communism emerged mainly in economically underdeveloped countries, its leaders emphasized modernization and industrialization, moving beyond economic growth to include wider social change.[3] Communist governments became heavily involved in running industry and in regulating the economy. In most cases, this meant the virtual elimination of the free market and competition. It also meant the creation of state-owned monopolies and a centrally planned **command economy** in which huge government departments used quotas, price controls, subsidies, and 5-year plans to decide what would be produced, where and when it would be produced, how it would be distributed, and at what prices it would be sold.

Virtually all CPC states are now cutting back on the role of government in the economy and are switching to free-market methods. Most have sold off state-owned monopolies to private owners and shareholders; have allowed the development of competition; and are letting the marketplace determine supply, demand, and prices. Russia and the other former Soviet republics are finding this a painful process, but China and Vietnam are making a more orderly transition, slowly allowing the private sector to expand and compete with state-owned industries and services.

Social Transition

Centralized political and economic control in the old communist regimes meant that individual citizens came to rely heavily on the state: It was the only significant employer, it ran all the basic services (such as transport, health care, and education), and it made all the decisions about the supply and the cost of goods and services. Centralized control also meant restrictions on the movement of people; international travel was allowed only for a privileged few (almost always ranking party members), and even domestic travel was often controlled through internal passports. At the same time, communist economies were often geared more toward the development of a strong military or toward the rapid development of industry, and governments were proportionately less interested in the welfare of individuals and the needs of consumers.

In the postcommunist era, the citizens of these countries are having to learn to look after themselves and to make more of their own decisions about their lives and about the choices they make. They are allowed virtually free movement, although many cannot afford to exploit the new opportunities available to them. Governments have switched their economic focus away from the military and toward the provision of basic services, but in terms of access to education and health care, postcommunist states lag far behind liberal democracies. Most CPC countries have only a Medium ranking on the Human Development Index, infant mortality is about two to three times the rate in liberal democracies, and their citizens have a life expectancy that is typically 5 to 10 years shorter.

THE EVOLUTION OF SOCIALISM AND COMMUNISM

Socialism and communism—much like democracy and capitalism—have undergone a convoluted evolutionary process that has resulted in the development of many variations on several central themes, most of them based on the ideas of Karl Marx. However, if he had been able to see how his ideas were adapted to the different situations in Russia, China, and Latin America, he probably would have been shocked.

Marx and Marxism

Modern socialism was a response to the rise of European industry in the early 19th century. Industrialization produced a class system in which wealth was unequally distributed, voting rights were limited, and unemployment, poverty, child labor, and malnutrition were rife. The **utopian socialists**—such as Claude Henri Comte de Saint-Simon and Pierre Joseph Proudhon—believed that change was best achieved through a patient reform of existing institutions. One person who tried to put such reforms into practice was Robert Owen (1771–1858), who rose from being a child laborer to becoming part owner of the largest steel mills in Scotland. In 1824 he came to the United States and created a communal society at New Harmony, Indiana. When his experiment failed, Owen returned to Britain to continue his reforming efforts and later became one of the founders of British socialism.

Karl Marx was much less patient. He built on the emerging ideas of socialism and ultimately provided the foundation for all modern communist and socialist thinking. Marx argued that all history was a tale of class antagonism and that this was particularly clear in the social divisions and exploitation emerging out of the industrial way of life in Western Europe. He identified two classes—the **proletariat** (the workers) and the **bourgeoisie** (the middle- and upper-class employers and owners of production)—and argued that the state represented the interests only of the bourgeoisie. Because workers were paid so poorly, their purchasing power was kept at a minimum, causing overproduction and underconsumption and leading to periodic economic crises.

Marx warned that it was only a matter of time before workers organized themselves and overthrew the ruling class. But, he said, the historical conditions would have to be right before this happened. Revolutions were most likely to come to advanced industrial societies with a large proletariat, such as the United States, Britain, Germany, or France, where capital was concentrated in the hands of a few. The transition was likely to come peacefully in the United States and Britain, but he believed that it would be more violent in more authoritarian states such as Germany and France.

MARX AND LENIN

They never met each other, but Karl Marx (1818–1883) and Vladimir Lenin (1870–1924) will probably always be spoken of in the same breath as the most influential thinkers in the evolution of socialist ideas. Marx was mainly a theorist. Lenin was both a thinker and an organizer; he took Marxist ideas and applied them to the particular circumstances of Russia at the beginning of the 20th century.

Marx was born in Trier, Prussia (in what is now Germany). After studying at the Universities of Berlin, Bonn, and Jena, he began a lifelong collaboration with Friedrich Engels (1820–1895), and between them they developed much of the theoretical foundation of socialism and communism. Marx's writings on economic and social issues made him so unpopular with the authorities that he moved to Paris, then to Brussels, and in 1849 to London, where he spent the rest of his life, living mainly on financial support from Engels and from relatives. Among his many writings, *The Communist Manifesto* and *Das Kapital* stand out as the most influential. Although both men argued against the idea of communists forming themselves into parties, Marx took part in the International Working Men's Association, or the First International, founded in London in 1864. He died in 1883, having outlived his wife Jenny and five of their seven children. At his funeral, Engels described Marx as "the best hated and most calumniated man of his time."

Lenin was born Vladimir Ilyich Ulyanov in Simbirsk, Russia. His opposition to the tsarist regime was sparked by the execution in 1887 of his brother Alexander, implicated in an attempt to assassinate Tsar Alexander III. After finishing his law studies, Ulyanov traveled abroad, where he came into contact with many leading exiled socialists. Returning to Russia, he was arrested in 1895 and banished to Siberia from 1897 to 1900. Upon release, and to make it more difficult for the Russian police to keep track of his movements, he renamed himself Lenin, after the River Lena in Siberia.

During the 1890s he studied the prospects for revolution in Russia from a Marxist perspective and concluded that Russian workers would not develop a revolutionary consciousness spontaneously. He argued instead that the key to success was a small party of dedicated professional revolutionaries, who could force the revolution without losing sight of Marx's basic ideas and theories. Following the failure of the 1905 revolution, Lenin went back into exile in Europe, helping to set up the newspaper *Pravda* in 1912. He returned to Russia after the March 1917 overthrow of the tsar and led the coup of November 1917. Lenin survived an assassination attempt in 1918 and the civil war of 1918–1922, but in May 1922 he suffered a stroke from which he never fully recovered. After two more strokes, he died in January 1924 at age 53. His body was embalmed and subsequently lay in state in a mausoleum built in Red Square next to the Kremlin walls.

For Marx, who lived in poverty most of his life, private property was at the root of all key social problems; he criticized it for creating social divisions and antagonism and for alienating humans from one another, and he argued that people would have their dignity and freedom restored only when it was abolished. He predicted that revolution would bring about a **dictatorship of the proletariat.** This would lead to the end of the class system, the withering away of the state, and the creation of a classless, nonexploitive communist society in which everyone would have equal opportunities, would work for the common good, and would take back from society what they needed: "From each according to his abilities, to each according to his needs," as he put it.

For a while in 1848 it seemed as though Marx's predictions might come true because there was a surge of revolutionary activity in several continental European countries, during which Marx himself was forced to escape to Britain. The surge died down, however, and Europe never again came so close to revolution, partly because workers and labor unions won concessions on working conditions and voting rights. Marx died long before any of his ideas were applied, but after his death, Marxist parties sprang up across Europe and even in the United States. The American Socialist party was founded in 1901, won nearly 1,200 local offices in its heyday, and ran Eugene V. Debs as its presidential candidate. Debs won nearly 6 percent of the vote in the 1912 election, one of the best results ever for a minor party in the United States.

Lenin and Leninism

Among those influenced by Marxist philosophy was the Russian Vladimir Ilyich Ulyanov, otherwise known as Lenin. He argued that the chances of a revolution in Europe were diminishing with the emergence of a small class of relatively wealthy workers and that Marxism had to be adapted to fit new circumstances. Marx had argued that revolutionary socialism would come to industrialized countries through the efforts of the workers; Lenin believed it could also come to less industrialized countries such as Russia if the peasants, ethnic minorities, and other aggrieved groups were mobilized. His adaptation of Marx added several original ideas to socialism:

1. He argued that a dedicated and professional **vanguard party** would have to foment and guide the revolution on behalf of the proletariat, promoting revolutionary consciousness among the workers using agitation and propaganda (or *agitprop*).[4] Other European Marxists believed that Russia had to advance much further industrially before it would be ready for revolution and criticized Lenin for trying to force the process. They also argued that his vanguard party would simply replace the old elite with a new elite and that this would undermine the possibility of a socialist workers' revolution. They were proved right when the vanguard party become a permanent and elitist feature of the Soviet system.

2. For the vanguard party to succeed, Lenin argued, it could accept only devoted revolutionaries as members and it had to be carefully organized. He outlined the idea of **democratic centralism,** or free political discussion and free elections within one strictly hierarchical party, in which all power would be concentrated. Every level of the party would elect the next highest, and decisions would be passed down through the ranks. The party would in turn control every other organization and social unit, from the family to the school to the factory. This principle is often blamed for paving the way for the totalitarian rule of Stalin.

3. Lenin talked of the need for a worldwide struggle against capitalism and tried to explain why revolution had not occurred in Western countries, as Marx had predicted. He described imperialism as "the highest stage of capitalism," arguing that the profits of colonialism allowed capitalists to pacify their workers by paying them better, thereby postponing the revolution.[5] At the same time, imperialism was mak-

Andy Johnstone/Panos Pictures

The image of Lenin—along with those of Marx and Engels—was present throughout the Soviet Union in the form of posters, murals, and statues. Here a group of Soviet soldiers wait to take part in the annual May Day parade in Moscow in 1990 and are reminded of Lenin's impact on their lives by a much larger-than-life mural of the former Soviet leader towering over Red Square.

ing class exploitation and polarization a global phenomenon. Lenin predicted that the colonies would accept only so much exploitation before eventually fighting for their independence. The struggle against capitalism would then spread back to Europe when workers lost the concessions bought from the profits of colonialism.

4. In 1919, 2 years after the Russian revolution, Lenin formed the Third Communist International (or **Comintern**), a network of 35 national communist parties. Until it was disbanded in 1943, Comintern coordinated the activities of communist parties, giving them advice and helping them build a local following in their own countries. Probably the most successful product of Comintern was the Chinese Communist party.

Unlike Marx, Lenin was able to apply his revolutionary ideas, and he and Leon Trotsky (1879–1940) became the driving forces behind the Russian revolution of November 1917. But before he could oversee the building of his new proletarian utopia, he unexpectedly died in 1924. This set off several years of infighting within the Soviet communist party, the leadership ultimately going to Joseph Stalin. Lenin's legacy was summed up in the term **Marxism-Leninism,** coined in the USSR after his death to describe a combination of Marx's theoretical analysis of capitalism and Lenin's doctrine of revolutionary action.

Mao and Maoism

Marx had focused on a worker revolution and argued that peasants had no role to play. Lenin cultivated the peasants, but support for the Russian revolution came mainly from urban workers. By contrast, the Chinese revolution (when it came) was spearheaded by a peasant army raised and trained by Mao Zedong (1893–1976). Few countries were as far from Marx's idea of an industrial-capitalist society as China, but Mao nonetheless helped spark a revolution affecting one-fifth of humanity.

Mao's major contribution to socialist theory was to rethink Marxism-Leninism to suit rural and agricultural societies and to develop a populist and antielitist form of Marxism with some uniquely Chinese influences. For example, China had long regarded foreigners as barbarians, an idea that Mao perpetuated by encouraging resentment against imperialism and anyone who had profited from dealing with foreigners. He argued that authority should be questioned and criticized by the people, and he worked to make communism less reliant on the kind of bureaucratic elite that was emerging in the USSR under Stalin. He stressed communalism, small-scale social and economic units, and a rejection of elitism.[6] Mao also emphasized thought reform and indoctrination, building on Chinese ideas of the state as the supreme educator. To discourage elitism, for example, he ordered that students, professionals, and other urban residents be sent off occasionally to work on farms and in factories.

Maoism was more radical than Marxism and, because it applied Marxism to rural societies, was also attractive to nationalist movements in less industrialized Asian, Latin American, and sub-Saharan African states. Mao had argued in the 1920s that "political power grows out of the barrel of a gun," and he used a peasant army and revolutionary guerrilla warfare to take power in China. His methods inspired nationalist movements such as those led by Fidel Castro in Cuba, Ernesto "Che" Guevara in Bolivia, and Ho Chi Minh in Vietnam.

Other Varieties of Socialism

Lenin and Mao developed the major variations on the theories of Marx, but Marxism was adapted in so many ways in other parts of the world that a new word was added to the Marxist lexicon in 1956: **polycentrism,** or independent models or centers of communism. Polycentrism began in earnest when the Soviets and the Yugoslavs fell out; Yugoslavia under Josip Broz Tito (1892–1980) took a neutral line independent of either the USSR or China and allowed a limited free market.

Three subvariations of socialism are worth mentioning:

1. **Revisionism.** A number of socialist thinkers argued that change was best achieved by working through existing political and economic systems rather than through revolution. The oldest and perhaps most lasting variation on this theme is **social democracy.** It dates back to the late 19th century, when Eduard Bernstein (1850–1932), a leader of the German Socialist party, argued—like Lenin—that Marxism needed to be revised to reflect changing conditions in Europe. He be-

lieved that the best way to create a more just and equal society was to do it through gradual democratic change, or through evolution rather than revolution.[7] Since World War II, almost every country in Western Europe—including Britain, France, Germany, and Sweden—has been governed by a social democratic party.

Another revision emerged in the 1970s and 1980s, when European communist parties (especially those in Italy, France, and Spain) adopted a liberal democratic form of socialism known as **Eurocommunism.** They argued that the only way to work toward the ultimate communist state was not by revolutionary activity but through parliamentary democracy, or "the ballot rather than the bullet." Support for Eurocommunism peaked in the 1970s, when French communists regularly won 20 to 22 percent of the vote and Italian communists as much as 30 percent of the vote. Their following later collapsed.

2. **Nationalist movements.** In their attempts to become independent, several African, Asian, and Latin American colonies turned to socialism for inspiration and to the USSR or China for help. This led some U.S. foreign policymakers to equate nationalism with communism, so they withdrew support from nationalists and instead supported oppressive right-wing regimes because they were anti-communist. The best known example of this came in Vietnam; the United States and its allies refused to help the newly independent North Vietnam in 1954, mainly because its leader, Ho Chi Minh, was a communist. The United States went further by supporting the government of South Vietnam, becoming involved in one of the most tragic and costly wars in U.S. history.

3. **Neo-Marxism.** This term describes a diverse set of 20th century writings by theorists who have tried to elaborate on the many (often conflicting) ideas generated by Marx, ranging from studies of human consciousness and alienation to calls for a return to **utopianism** (a society without violence, property, or oppression). Neo-Marxist ideas continue to be used today as the basis for trying to understand a broad variety of political, economic, and social conditions.

COMMUNISM TODAY

Communism is dead in most countries and is on life support in a few others, although some of the more optimistic Marxists insist that it has simply reached the end of its first epoch. Its critics argue that it was always structurally flawed, strongest in its critique of capitalism and weakest in its lack of blueprints for change. Its supporters argue that it was never applied in the way Marx predicted; was abused by Lenin, Stalin, and Mao; and has been unfairly discredited. Wherever the truth lies, most former strongholds of communism have abandoned the Soviet model of government and perhaps communism as an ideology altogether.

The changes arguably began in China in the 1980s with the reformist policies of Deng Xiaoping, who combined limited free-market policies with Chinese socialism. The watershed in the collapse of communism, however, came during the administration of Mikhail Gorbachev in the USSR (1985–1991). Gorbachev came to office determined to undo the abuses of Stalinism and the lethargy of the Brezhnev years and to make the Soviet model of socialism more efficient and more democratic. He had no intention of presiding over the end of communism, but the changes he launched took on a life of their own. After giving up Soviet control over Eastern Europe, he lost power, the Soviet Union broke up in 1991, and the former Soviet republics abandoned state socialism.

The long-term prognosis remains unclear. In Russia, the government struggled throughout the 1990s to liberalize the economy and to democratize the political system, using legal and illegal means. Pro-reformists have had to fight a rearguard action against communist and nationalist hard-liners opposed to reform and have had to keep the lid on simmering separatist problems on Russia's southern border. The 1993 constitution created a new and more democratic political system, but democratic ideals have not yet taken firm root in Russian society and economic conditions have been dire. Much depends on how much longer it will take for the benefits of democracy and capitalism to be broadly felt and on how far the patience of the Russian people can be stretched.

The Islamic republics of central Asia (such as Kazakhstan, Uzbekistan, and Turkmenistan) may find themselves being pulled increasingly into the orbit of Islam. The Caucasian republics (Georgia, Armenia, and Azerbaijan) have either broken down in civil war or have fought one another. As economic difficulties bring increasing hardships, the Slavic peoples of Ukraine and the troubled state of Belarus may find an economic union with Russia appealing; an early step was taken in this direction with the establishment of an economic community between Russia and Belarus in 1996. Reform in all these countries involves finding a balance between the demands of liberal reformers, communist hard-liners, and nationalists concerned about economic and social decline.

The future for the Eastern European states that were once under Soviet control is much more certain, because most are moving quickly toward the liberal democratic camp. Most have relatively strong national identities, especially now that most of the ethnic minorities who lived in the former Yugoslavia have their own independent states. Seven countries (Bulgaria, Romania, Slovakia, Slovenia, and the three Baltic states) have been invited to join NATO, eight countries (Bulgaria, Hungary, Poland, Slovakia, Slovenia, and the three Baltic states) have been accepted for membership in the European Union (EU), and three countries (the Czech Republic, Hungary, and Poland) have joined the Organization for Economic Cooperation and Development (OECD). The EU has meanwhile sent investment and development aid to Eastern Europe, helping underpin the switch to free-market economic policies and the building of democratic, multiparty political systems.

KEY TERMS

bourgeoisie
civil society
Comintern
command economy
communism
democratic centralism
dictatorship of the
    proletariat
Eurocommunism

Leninism
Maoism
Marxism
Marxism-Leninism
neo-Marxism
police state
polycentrism
proletariat
revisionism

social democracy
socialism
state socialism
totalitarianism
utopian socialists
utopianism
vanguard party

KEY PEOPLE

Eduard Bernstein	Vladimir Lenin	Leon Trotsky
Fidel Castro	Karl Marx	Deng Xiaoping
Friedrich Engels	Ho Chi Minh	Mao Zedong
Mikhail Gorbachev	Josip Broz Tito	

STUDY QUESTIONS

1. Is communism still a useful analytical tool for comparative politics?
2. How well do the values of communism fit with human nature?
3. Is the Marxist analysis still relevant to an understanding of modern society?
4. Where would you look to find socialism or social democracy practiced in liberal democracies today?

COMMUNISM AND SOCIALISM ONLINE

Marxists Internet Archive: *http://www.marxists.org/txtindex.htm*
Provides information on the works of Karl Marx and key Marxists.
Marxism Page: *http://www.anu.edu.au/polsci/marx/marx.html*
A site maintained by the Australian National University, which includes introductory material on Marxism and the text of *The Communist Manifesto*.
Socialist International: *http://www.socialistinternational.org*
The home page of the London-based Socialist International, with links to many socialist parties.

FURTHER READING

Drakulic, Slavenka, *How We Survived Communism and Even Laughed* (New York: Harper Perennial, 1993) and *Café Europa: Life After Communism* (New York: Penguin USA, 1999). Two books written by a Croatian journalist, reflecting on life under communism and how Eastern Europe has changed since.

Muravchik, Joshua, *Heaven on Earth: The Rise and Fall of Socialism* (San Francisco: Encounter Books, 2002). The fortunes of socialism, told through the lives of its major thinkers and practitioners.

Schram, Stuart, *The Thought of Mao TseTung* (Cambridge, MA: Cambridge University Press, 1989). A commentary on the principles of Maoism.

Tucker, Robert C. (Ed.), *The Marx–Engels Reader* (New York: W. W. Norton, 1978). A comprehensive introduction to the lives and works of Marx and Engels.

Wolff, Jonathan, *Why Read Marx Today?* (New York: Oxford University Press, 2002). An analysis of the continuing relevance of Marxism to an understanding of current society.

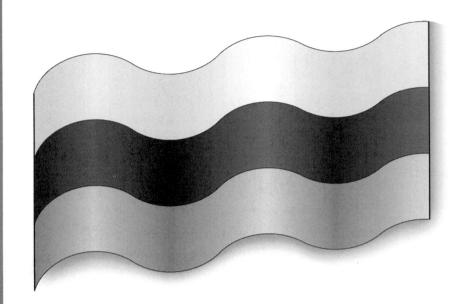

CHAPTER 4

RUSSIA

RUSSIA: QUICK FACTS

Name: Russian Federation

Capital: Moscow

Area: 6,592,800 square miles (17,075,400 sq. km)

Languages: 82 percent of the population speaks Russian

Population: 147.2 million

Population density: 22 per square mile

Population growth rate: 0.2 percent

POLITICAL INDICATORS

Freedom House rating: Partly Free

Date of state formation: June 12, 1991

System type: Federal republic with dual executive

Constitution: 1993

Administration: Federal

Executive: Executive president elected by direct popular vote for maximum of two 4-year terms

Legislature: Bicameral Federal Assembly, with upper Federation Council (178 members appointed by the president) and lower State Duma (450 elected members)

Party structure: More than 30 parties are currently active, of which 5 have developed a broad following, but a stable multiparty system has not yet emerged

Judiciary: Constitutional Court (19 members appointed for 12-year terms by the president and confirmed by the Federation Council)

Head of state: Vladimir Putin (1999–)

Head of government: Mikhail Kasyanov (2000–)

ECONOMIC INDICATORS

GDP (2001): $310 billion

Per capita GDP: $1,750

Distribution of GDP: Services 55 percent, industry 38 percent, agriculture 7 percent

Urban population: 73 percent

SOCIAL INDICATORS

HDI ranking: 55

Infant mortality rate: 16 per 1,000 live births

Life expectancy: 65.3 years

Literacy: 99% of people aged 15 and older

Religions: Predominantly Russian Orthodox, with significant Muslim, Buddhist, and Jewish minorities

INTRODUCTION

Russia has undergone such revolutionary changes since 1985 that Russians and non-Russians alike have had to rethink their perceptions of the country, its government, and its national identity. For nearly 70 years, Russia was the dominant partner in the Union of Soviet Socialist Republics (USSR), a country that most Westerners feared or distrusted and largely misunderstood. The USSR was a communist country, governed by a single political party, which controlled the state, the economy, and society and whose leaders often used totalitarian methods of control. The Soviet Union broke up in 1991, and Russia became an independent country that has moved toward democracy and free-market economics, but with mixed results. Is it on its way to a stable and successful liberal democratic future, or will it have trouble leaving behind its authoritarian past and surviving its social divisions?

At nearly 6.6 million square miles, Russia is the largest country in the world; it stretches across 11 time zones and is nearly twice the size of the United States. Using a straight conversion against the U.S. dollar, Russia is a poor country: It has a GDP of about $310 billion, which works out to $1,750 per capita, or about one-twentieth the figure for the United States. Using purchasing power parity, however, Russian GDP rises to more than $1.2 trillion, or more than $8,000 per capita, suggesting that the Russian economy is actually more substantial than it at first appears. But Russia is still far from a postindustrial, service-based economy.

Russia's main economic challenge is making the transition from an economy that was centrally planned and geared toward the military to a free-market system geared toward the consumer. It has a wealth of natural resources, including land, minerals, oil, natural gas, timber, gold, coal, and iron, but it lacks the capital and technical expertise to fully exploit these resources, most of which are in **Siberia,** the huge and sparsely populated eastern expanse of the country. It also has the potential to build successful businesses, but few are yet in the position to withstand foreign competition. When the western United States was being opened up in the 19th century, it was helped by capital investment from Europe; Russia's best hope may also lie in foreign investment, but this will not be forthcoming without greater economic and fiscal stability, more efficient government, and more open markets.

Economic reforms have so far proved difficult to apply, leading to hardships for many Russians. They could once rely on the state to provide jobs and to subsidize food and basic services, but they now face shortages, lost jobs, falling wages, rising prices, and a transition to a free-market system with which they have little familiarity. Industrial output, agricultural output, and GDP have all grown, but they have not always met their potential; inflation has fluctuated wildly from a high of 350 percent to a low of 15 percent; and the presence of the black market and organized crime have undermined attempts to build economic stability. Although these problems are serious, Russians have long been a fatalistic people, used to hard times and sacrifice. There have been regular predictions of social unrest, rebellion, and violence, but most Russians continue to survive, as they have done many times before.

In social terms, Russia is remarkably varied. From a nucleus in the state of Muscovy, successive Russian leaders steadily conquered and subjugated neighboring peoples, and the Russian empire that emerged between the mid-15th century and the 19th century incorporated many different ethnic groups. Even in the new

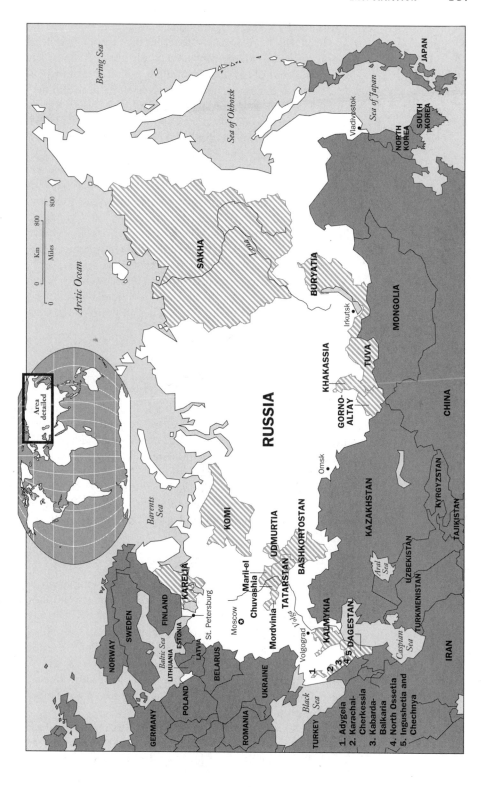

Bering Sea

Sea of Okhotsk

JAPAN

Vladivostok

NORTH KOREA

SOUTH KOREA

Sea of Japan

SAKHA

Lena

BURYATIA

MONGOLIA

800

800

Km

Miles

0

0

Irkutsk

KHAKASSIA

TUVA

Arctic Ocean

GORNO-ALTAY

CHINA

RUSSIA

Omsk

KAZAKHSTAN

Area detailed

KYRGYZSTAN

Barents Sea

KOMI

UDMURTIA

BASHKORTOSTAN

TAJIKISTAN

Aral Sea

UZBEKISTAN

KARELIA

Marii-el

Chuvashia

TATARSTAN

Moscow

Volga

Mordvinia

TURKMENISTAN

FINLAND

St. Petersburg

Baltic Sea

ESTONIA

KALMYKIA

DAGESTAN

Caspian Sea

NORWAY

SWEDEN

LATVIA

LITHUANIA

BELARUS

UKRAINE

Volgograd

4 5

2 3

1

IRAN

POLAND

GERMANY

ROMANIA

TURKEY

Black Sea

1. Adygeia
2. Karachai-Cherkessia
3. Kabarda-Balkaria
4. North Ossetia
5. Ingushetia and Chechnya

Russia 60 to 90 national minorities still exist, including Tatars, Ukrainians, Bashkirs, and even 840,000 Germans—together they account for nearly 20 percent of the population. Several of these groups, especially in the volatile Caucasus region, resent being under the control of Moscow and are agitating for independence. To further complicate matters, as many as 25 million Russians still live in neighboring former republics of the USSR, posing a problem for relations between Russia and those republics.

In political terms, the key challenge facing Russia is that of building a multiparty democracy in a country that has known only monarchy, one-party rule, totalitarianism, or oligarchy. The Communist Party of the Soviet Union (CPSU) had a monopoly on power from 1917 to 1991, and although the changes that have taken place since then have had democratic tendencies, Russia's new leaders have never lost sight of the Soviet tradition of strong and centralized executive authority and they still find it hard to tolerate criticism and opposition. On paper, the Russian political system now looks much like that of France, with an executive president, a separately elected legislature, and a prime minister nominated by the president and confirmed by the legislature. In practice, the new Russia has seen a divisive battle for power between an executive armed with considerable powers, a legislature in which no one party has yet been able to win a majority, and a cluster of often rowdy regional governors. Against this background, Russian politics remain volatile and the prognosis for the future uncertain.

POLITICAL DEVELOPMENT

For hundreds of years, Russia was a feudal empire, with most of its citizens bypassed by political and economic developments in nearby Europe. In the last 90 years, however, Russians have seen dramatic change. The revolutions of 1917 removed a centuries-old and autocratic monarchy but led ultimately to several decades of brutal repression under the Stalin administration. Then came the tensions of the cold war and the Gorbachev "revolution" of the late 1980s, which ended decades of central planning and one-party government. Finally, the breakup of the Soviet Union created an independent Russia, which has had to redefine itself and its place in the world.

The Russian Empire (15th Century to 1917)

For most of its history, Russia was more an imperial power than a nation-state. From humble beginnings in the 9th century, it was liberated in the 15th century from more than 200 years of Mongol control by Ivan the Great (1440–1505), who set up his capital at Moscow. Under Ivan the Terrible (1533–1584), Russia expanded into Kazan, Astrakhan, and Siberia. Peter the Great (1682–1725) laid the basis for the country's military and industrial growth; Russia became a European power, the nobility adopted European culture and values, the army and bureaucracy were based on European models, and the new capital—St. Petersburg—was overtly a European city.

Through all these changes, however, Russia remained a feudal system, in which the vast majority of Russians remained powerless peasants (or serfs), a small aristocracy controlled virtually all national wealth, there were no free elections or free speech, most people lived in abject poverty, land was often arbitrarily seized and redistributed, and the tsars violently suppressed opposition. Despite efforts at reform during the 19th century and the emancipation of the serfs in 1861, Russia remained rigidly divided into classes, with the tsar and the nobility jealously guarding their rights.

Unlike other more pragmatic European monarchs, the last tsar, Nicholas II (1894–1917), failed to respond to the pressures for change. Popular opposition was led by the Social Revolutionary party and the smaller Russian Social Democratic Labor Party (RSDLP), a Marxist party founded in 1898. At its Second Congress in London in 1903, the RSDLP split into two factions: the Mensheviks (or "minority"), who advocated a mass membership party, and the more elitist **Bolsheviks** (or "majority"). Led by Lenin, the Bolsheviks subscribed to his idea of a vanguard party and developed a tight and disciplined structure with Lenin's authority at the core. Russia came close to revolution in 1905, when it was defeated in a war with Japan, but the tsar survived with the help of the military. A new parliamentary assembly (the Duma) was convened in 1906, but Nicholas II was never able to fully accept the idea of a constitutional monarchy.

Lenin and the 1917 Revolutions

The 1917 revolutions grew out of three interconnected factors: the huge losses suffered by Russia in World War I; the theories of Karl Marx and the related ideas of Russian thinkers; and the leadership skills of Lenin and Trotsky, who were able to identify themselves with peace and the redistribution of land and bread, both popular issues. The opportunity for the revolutionaries came with World War I, when the Russian army suffered humiliating defeats. When worker demonstrations and food riots in March 1917 turned into a revolution against him, Tsar Nicholas abdicated and was replaced by a provisional government, which made the fatal error of continuing the war.

In April, Lenin returned from exile in Europe and began campaigning for an end to the war and the creation of a socialist state. In November, he and his followers staged a second "revolution" (actually a coup rather than a popular uprising),[1] took over the government, and established a one-party socialist state. He changed the name of his party to the Communist party, abolished the class system, and created the Red Army. In March 1918 Lenin negotiated a peace treaty with Germany at Brest-Litovsk, which he was able to repudiate when Germany was defeated. In July 1918, the tsar and his family were shot to death on the orders of the Bolsheviks.

Lenin's new state was almost immediately split by a civil war between the Red Army and White Armies led by former tsarist generals intent on overthrowing the Bolsheviks. The Whites were defeated in 1922, but Soviet Russia found itself the only socialist revolutionary state in the world, cut off by a Western economic blockade. Faced with a war-ravaged economy, falling industrial and agricultural output, and public discontent, Lenin decided in 1921 to compromise on his principles by launching a **New Economic Policy,** based partly on free enterprise policies designed to encourage peasants and small businessmen. Before he could press these reforms, however, he died.

A succession struggle followed, with the most obvious successor—Leon Trotsky—being pushed aside by a trio of party leaders, one of whom was Joseph Stalin. Stalin

T A B L E   4 . 1

Key Dates in Soviet/Russian History

1147	Founding of Moscow
1812	Napoleon invades Russia, advancing as far as Moscow
1861	Emancipation of the serfs
1914	Outbreak of World War I
1917	(March) Revolution ousts Tsar Nicholas II; (April) Lenin returns from exile; (November) a coup brings Bolsheviks to power under Lenin
1918–1922	Russian civil war; establishment of USSR (December 1922)
1924	Death of Lenin
1929–1933	Collectivization of agriculture and resultant famine
1941	Hitler attacks the USSR
1945	The end of World War II leaves the USSR with a hegemony over much of Eastern Europe
1953	Death of Stalin
1957	*Sputnik* becomes first satellite in space
1961	Yuri Gagarin first human in space
1962	Cuban missile crisis
1979	Soviet invasion of Afghanistan
1985	Gorbachev becomes general secretary of the CPSU
1991	(June) Boris Yeltsin elected president of Russia; (August) attempted coup by communist hard-liners fails to win support; (December) Gorbachev resigns and the USSR officially ceases to exist
1992	Price controls are lifted in Russia; Russia takes over the UN Security Council seat formerly occupied by the USSR and joins the International Monetary Fund
1993	(September–October) Hard-line deputies occupy the Russian Congress in an attempt to set off an uprising against Yeltsin, who responds with force; (December) new Russian constitution approved, new legislature elected
1994	(December) Yeltsin sends troops into Chechnya to quell uprising
1995–1996	Legislative and presidential elections indicate a resurgence of support for the Communists
1996	(July) Yeltsin reelected president; (August) cease-fire declared in Chechnya; (November) Yeltsin undergoes major heart surgery
1998	Yeltsin causes alarm by hiring and firing three prime ministers
1999	(August) Hostilities break out again in Chechnya; (August–September) bombs explode in Moscow, killing more than 300 people; (December) pro-reform parties make gains in State Duma elections; Boris Yeltsin suddenly resigns as president
2000	(March) New presidential elections result in victory for Vladimir Putin; (August) nuclear submarine *Kursk* sinks with loss of 118 lives
2002	(June) The EU and the United States announce that they consider Russia a market economy
2003	Putin administration highly critical of U.S.-led invasion of Iraq

JOSEPH STALIN

The man ultimately responsible for shaping Soviet government and bureaucracy was Joseph Stalin (1879–1953). So influential was his administration that—in structural terms at least—the USSR by 1985 was more Stalinist than Marxist-Leninist, although Lenin arguably laid the groundwork for Stalin's policies.

Born Joseph Vissarionovich Dzhugashvili in Georgia, he trained for the priesthood before being expelled from his seminary and joining the political underground in 1900. He took part in bank robberies aimed at raising funds for the Bolsheviks and in 1912 changed his name to Stalin ("man of steel"). Arrested several times, he was exiled to Siberia in 1913 but returned to Petrograd (formerly St. Petersburg) in 1917. In 1922 he became first secretary of the Communist party, a position he held until his death.

Stalin outmaneuvered his rivals following Lenin's death so that by 1928–1929 he had become the undisputed ruler of the USSR. His main rival, Leon Trotsky, was exiled in 1929 and murdered by Stalin's secret police in Mexico in 1940. Other rivals—such as Georgy Zinoviev, Lev Kamenev, and Nikolai Bukharin—were murdered, executed, or exiled. Pursuing mass control through mass terror,[2] Stalin launched a program aimed at making the USSR a world power, using systematic oppression to enforce his reforms. In the process, perhaps as many as 20 million people died from famine, execution, or war. Many millions more were purged, or exiled to concentration camps (or *gulags*) in Siberia. To support his policies, he even began a project in the late 1930s to rewrite Soviet history.

In June 1941, Hitler invaded the USSR, precipitating what the Soviets called the Great Patriotic War. Following the siege of Leningrad, the Soviet army advanced deep into Eastern Europe, allowing Stalin to expand Soviet control over neighboring countries to the west. Europe was divided into eastern and western blocs, laying the basis for the cold war.

Stalin died from a brain hemorrhage in March 1953. His cult of personality had been so effective that prisoners in Siberian *gulags* wept at the news and more than 400 people died in the crush to see his embalmed body lying in state beside that of Lenin. As part of Khrushchev's campaign of de-Stalinization, Stalin's body was removed in 1961 and buried in a modest grave between the Lenin Mausoleum and the Kremlin walls.

organized and manipulated the party bureaucracy to establish personal control over the party and to confirm the party's control over the country.[3] After a brief collective leadership, Stalin had by 1928–1929 made his office of first secretary of the CPSU the most important in the party hierarchy, and he won uncontested control over both the party and the country. Over the next 25 years, Stalin stamped his personal mark on the USSR, creating the system that was to persist until the late 1980s.

The Stalin Era (1928–1953)

Under Stalin, the USSR moved further away from Marxist principles and toward a totalitarian style of government that was distinctive enough to earn its own label in the dictionary of political science. **Stalinism** is an absolutist, inflexible, and highly undemocratic version of communism that demands unquestioning support for the state and a belief in the unchallenged authority of the party and its leaders. Abandoning Lenin's idea of promoting global revolution, Stalin's priority was to build **"socialism in one country"** and make the Soviet Union a political, industrial, agricultural, and military model for others. Thus driven, Stalin created a society based on the systematic use of terror, the elimination of human rights, and a cult of personality (providing the model for Big Brother in George Orwell's novel *1984*).

Stalin also established a centrally planned economy in which all activity was determined by the state. The bureaucracy became increasingly powerful, monolithic, and inefficient. The economic planning agency **Gosplan** decided what should be produced, when it should be produced, where it should be delivered, and at what prices it should be sold. A series of **5-year plans** set production figures with the goal of increasing industrial production by 100 percent. Stalin forced millions of farmers into huge new collective farms, eliminating an entire social class (the *kulaks*, or wealthy peasants) and causing a famine that claimed several million lives. He also closed down all small shops, arranged for the state to take over all services, and promoted one-party rule. The CPSU infiltrated every part of Soviet life, creating a new class of privileged political leaders and dashing any real hope of achieving Marx's goal of a classless society.

The Cold War (1945–1990)

Stalin was succeeded as Soviet leader by Nikita Khrushchev, whose priority was to end the years of terror. In February 1956 he electrified the Twentieth Party Congress of the CPSU with a "secret speech" denouncing the excesses of Stalin and extolling the virtues of collective leadership. The speech was not made public in the USSR until 1989, but it set the tone for Khrushchev's reformism, which influenced a new generation of party members, including Mikhail Gorbachev and Boris Yeltsin, both then in their mid-20s.

Khrushchev continued the attempts to build industry and agriculture, with limited success. To prove Soviet technological prowess, he launched a space program that sent the first satellite *(Sputnik)* into space in 1957 and the first human (Yuri Gagarin) in 1961. The Khrushchev years also saw the perpetuation (in fits and starts) of the cold war. Tensions between the two superpowers peaked in 1962 with the Cuban missile crisis, when U.S. President John F. Kennedy had a battle of wills with Khrushchev over the stationing of Soviet nuclear warheads in Cuba. The warheads were withdrawn, but for a few weeks in late 1962 the world stood on the brink of nuclear war.

With his popularity falling in the wake of repeated policy failures and because of concerns about his erratic style of leadership, Khrushchev was ousted by the CPSU in 1964 and replaced by the more conservative Leonid Brezhnev. The bold reforms ceased, and the USSR's leaders became older, less imaginative, and more concerned with the maintenance of the status quo. There was a major military buildup that led to near parity with the United States, and the Soviet Union helped several nationalist movements in Africa and Asia. The Brezhnev era culminated in the ultimately disastrous decision by the Soviets in 1979 to invade Afghanistan, which led to a costly and unpopular war.

Brezhnev died in office in November 1982, to be followed by two transitional figures, the reformist Yuri Andropov (1982–1984) and the conservative Konstantin Chernenko (1984–1985). Both were elderly and in poor health, and both died in office. Chernenko was succeeded by Mikhail Gorbachev, the man who, in his words, now set about launching the second Russian revolution.

Gorbachev and Yeltsin (1985–1999)

Gorbachev denounced the stagnation of the Brezhnev era and set out to make many of the reforms envisioned by Khrushchev and Andropov. There were initially two core planks to his program: ***perestroika,*** or the "restructuring" of the Soviet economic and political system, and ***glasnost,*** or "openness," meaning a willingness to encourage more public discussion of key issues and a greater frankness in admitting mistakes. A third plank—*demokratizatsiia,* or democratization—had been added by 1988. Gorbachev's goal was not to dismantle the socialist system but to make it more efficient and more democratic and to reduce the role of central planning. However, his position was ultimately undermined by several problems:

- He lacked legitimacy. He preached democratic accountability, yet was never popularly elected to office and insisted on maintaining the CPSU monopoly long after other groups had demanded equal rights.

- He found himself caught between liberals who thought his reforms were too timid and conservatives who thought they had gone too far. Partly because of the entrenched power of the Soviet bureaucracy to sabotage and delay his changes and partly because of his own caution, Gorbachev lost control.

- His reforms brought into the open the underlying tensions among the Soviet republics, prompting nationalist sentiments and secessionist movements. As these grew, it was doubtful that anyone could have kept the USSR together.

In August 1991, on the eve of the signing of a new union treaty that would have redefined the relationship among the Soviet republics, a group of communists staged an attempted coup in Moscow. Although it quickly failed, Gorbachev's credibility was fatally undermined, and it became only a matter of time before he had no office to hold and no nation to govern. He resigned as president of the USSR on December 25, 1991, and the following day the Soviet Union ceased to exist. Where there had once been a superpower, there were now 15 independent countries. The biggest and most influential was Russia, which just 6 months before had elected Boris Yeltsin as its president.

Yeltsin found himself plagued by the same problems as Gorbachev: balancing the demands of reformers and hard-liners, trying to promote greater political and economic liberalism, and trying to negotiate a new federal treaty that would keep Russia from civil war. The problems were underlined by attempts made during 1993 to unseat Yeltsin, which peaked in September when he dissolved the Russian legislature, the Congress of People's Deputies. A small group of conservatives barricaded themselves inside the Congress building and gave the acting presidency to Yeltsin's biggest critic— his own vice president, Alexander Rutskoi. Yeltsin responded with military force, the attempted coup failed, and Rutskoi and many of his supporters were briefly jailed.

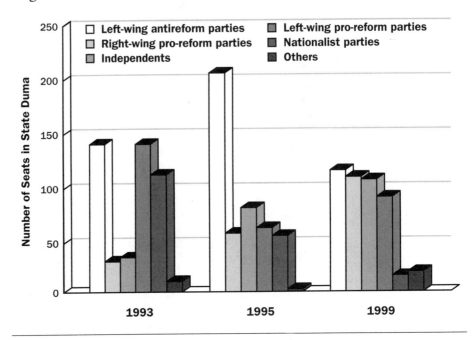

FIGURE 4.1

Legislative Electoral Trends in Russia

Number of Seats in State Duma

□ Left-wing antireform parties   ▨ Left-wing pro-reform parties
▨ Right-wing pro-reform parties   ■ Nationalist parties
▨ Independents   ■ Others

1993   1995   1999

Throughout 1992 and 1993, Russian politics was diverted by a conflict between conservatives and reformers anxious to stake their claims before the new political system was committed to paper with a new constitution. The constitution was "approved" in a hurried public referendum in December 1993, and a new legislature was elected. But questions remained about Russia's stability. Despite threats from communists on the left and nationalists on the right, a civil war in the southern republic of **Chechnya** (see Critical Issues, p. 222), and his own severe health problems, Yeltsin managed to be elected to a second term as president in July 1996. But trust in government fell to an all-time low, the legislature failed to be an effective source of policy ideas or of opposition to the president, nationalist problems in the south boiled over into renewed war and urban terrorism, wealth and power continued to accumulate in the hands of a new elite, the value of the ruble fell as inflation grew, confidence in the banking system declined, and unemployment grew. Then, in December 1999, Yeltsin suddenly resigned.

Russia Today

Yeltsin was succeeded by Vladimir Putin, whose reformist political party Unity had been given a confidence boost by its gains in the December 1999 legislative elections (see Figure 4.1). However, Putin faced the same daunting challenges as his predecessor.

His rise to power was based on overseeing a bloody government response to an uprising in Chechnya, an event that did not augur well for those concerned about the tradition of authoritarianism in Russian politics. Putin continued to show a worryingly heavy hand in his management of Russia, whether through his low tolerance of criticism in the media, through the increased powers he has given to the security services, or through the way he has exerted his powers over regional governments.

Russia has undergone considerable change since 1991, and the general trends have been toward greater democracy, a freer market place, and a more cooperative stand on issues of foreign policy. Many questions remain, however. Will the democratic changes be lasting, and how quickly can they be consolidated in a society that has known nothing but authoritarian rule? Can Russians learn how the free market works? Can Russia define a new place for itself in the world that keeps citizens and outsiders happy? Superficially, the signs seem positive, but significant problems still need to be overcome.[4] The economy is growing, but there is too little foreign investment. The structure of government is still "top down" rather than "bottom up," and government is still in the mode of providing leadership rather than listening to what the people want. There is still considerable aversion and resistance to change, both among Russians and among old-style bureaucrats. Infrastructure is in an advanced state of decay. The quality of life for most Russians is poor: The population is unhealthy, relatively poorly educated, ageing quickly, and shrinking in size. And Russia is still struggling to come to terms with its new status as a former superpower.

POLITICAL CULTURE

One of the consequences of the collapse of communism and the breakup of the USSR has been to allow political scientists to open the hood, examine the engine of traditional Russian political culture, and study the effects of communism. Recent events suggest a strong continuity between public attitudes toward politics and government from the pre-Soviet era through to the present, although there are signs of increasing openness, tolerance, and support for individual rights.

An Authoritarian Tradition

Russians have known little but authoritarian government. The tsars clung to autocracy long after most other European monarchs had given up their powers to popularly elected assemblies, and government during the tsarist era was centralized, bureaucratic, authoritarian, and intrusive.[5] The Soviet experience after 1917 was little different because tsarist autocracy was replaced by Leninist elitism, which was followed by Stalinist totalitarianism. Russia since 1991 has seen more democracy than the country has ever had, but democracy is having trouble taking root, in large part because Russians have had to learn how it works, in part because of the unwillingness of presidents Yeltsin and Putin to entirely abandon authoritarian methods, and in part because many Russians look back nostalgically on the authority and unity of the past.

Strong Leadership

Russians tend to like strong leaders, and public opinion surveys have found that people are more concerned with the state providing order than they are with it ensuring their civil liberties.[6] Many older Russians in particular still admire Stalin as someone who provided a stable and tightly regulated social order and whose use of force is often excused as being "necessary for the time." Views such as these have been both a cause and an effect of a tradition of Russian political **patrimonialism:** a sense of leaders as father figures. Boris Yeltsin's attempts in 1992 to circumvent the legislature and use his powers of decree to bring about his own ideas of change appeared to be consistent with this tradition, although his actions were sharply criticized by some. The tradition also helps explain the emergence of something close to a cult of personality surrounding Vladimir Putin. Although strong leadership has its place, no political system that relies on the fortunes and methods of one person can hope to develop stability.

Closed Politics

Liberal democracies have a tradition of relatively open politics, where most political decisions are publicly discussed and citizens can express their opinions. In Russia, by contrast, most decisions traditionally have been made behind the scenes with little (if any) public discussion. **Closed politics** was described as "the basic identifying characteristic" of the Soviet political system in the 1970s. It left most Soviet citizens feeling that there was little they could do to influence government, and many were disinclined to express their political opinions or bring their influence to bear on the decisions of government.[7]

The relative openness of the post-Soviet era has given Russians an unaccustomed level of freedom to express their opinions, although polling in Russia is still in its infancy and many Russians are still loathe to share their views. The vestiges of secrecy remain; it was often difficult to be sure, for example, about the seriousness of Boris Yeltsin's heart problems during 1996, when his handlers at first said he was suffering from fatigue, a cold, or laryngitis, and he all but disappeared from public view for weeks. A liberal democratic leader in similar circumstances would find it nearly impossible to keep such illness a secret.

The Collective Society

While liberal democracies place great value on individualism and self-determination, Russian society traditionally has been group-oriented. Even after the emancipation of the serfs in 1861, they owned land not individually but collectively. Opinion polls during the Soviet era showed a high level of support for state planning and ownership of the economy, for state ownership of transport and communications, for collectivist public welfare in the fields of education and health care, and for living in a welfare state. There was also wide support for the idea that the state should not only look after the material welfare of its citizens but their spiritual welfare as well. The Soviet era is gone, but big government is still widely supported. It has been argued that the key to understanding Russian political culture is *sobornost*, meaning an attachment to **collectivism** and an opposition to individualism.[8]

Fear of Chaos

Liking order and fearing chaos, Russians historically have leaned toward conservatism.[9] They have been preoccupied with national security and fear of foreign invasion, particularly from the west, where the land is flat and difficult to defend. Russian **nationalism** is partly a reaction to these fears, and many Russians place a heavy reliance on the state to maintain order and security. Given the extent of the changes the Russian people have experienced in the last few years, many believe that their country is headed toward "the abyss." These traditions make it difficult to build democracy, given that democracy by definition involves a high degree of uncertainty.

POLITICAL SYSTEM

"The most dangerous time," wrote the French historian Alexis de Tocqueville, "is when a bad government begins to reform itself." Seldom has this been more true than in Russia since the breakup of the Soviet Union. Nearly 150 million people have had to rethink their old assumptions as a society once founded on one-party rule and central economic planning has struggled to adopt an open, competitive political and economic system. The transition has not been easy, torn as Russia has been between those who want the status quo and those who want change and by arguments about how best to achieve the change.

Although the Soviets claimed that their political system was democratic, all real power was focused in the Communist Party of the Soviet Union (CPSU), to which all other institutions answered, either directly or indirectly. The CPSU was run by an elite that made all policy, which was implemented in turn by a bureaucracy directed by the party. Mikhail Gorbachev set out to make the system more democratic and efficient, but he had barely warmed to the task before he lost control. He left his successors with the challenge of building a new system while having to be careful about how quickly they abandoned the old system, for fear of leaving Russia without direction or generating a backlash among disgruntled Russians longing for the predictability of the old days.

With the breakup of the USSR, Russia became an independent country, and its newly elected president, Boris Yeltsin, found himself leader of a society burdened with severe political, economic, and social problems. The 1993 constitution provided some direction, giving Russia a political system much like that of France or Egypt: In what is known as a **dual executive,** it has both a directly elected president and a prime minister who is appointed by the president and confirmed by the legislature. The challenge of making this new system work was undermined by an attempted coup (1993), by the unpredictable behavior of Boris Yeltsin, by civil war and unrest in the southern provinces of Chechnya and Dagestan, by doubts about the political agenda of Vladimir Putin, and by qualified faith in political institutions.

The system has persisted nonetheless, and for every year that goes by, its chances for success increase.

THE CONSTITUTION

One of the measures of the effectiveness of a constitution is its longevity. Bad constitutions sometimes last a long time, so the measure has to be treated with some caution, but repeated rewriting of constitutions is usually a sure sign that they have no roots in society and that they are being used as a tool of manipulation by political leaders. This was certainly the case with the USSR, which had four constitutions in 59 years: 1918, 1924, 1936, and 1977. The 1936 version described the USSR as "a true democracy" in which "all power" belonged to the people, included a bill of rights, and created a directly elected legislature. However, it also said that the rights and freedoms of citizens should not be expressed to the detriment of "the interests of society or the state," left power in the hands of the party leaders, and underwrote the hegemony of the CPSU.

With the collapse of the USSR, Russia inherited the 1978 constitution of the Russian republic, which was modeled on the 1977 Soviet constitution. This was amended so many times during 1990–1991 that work was begun on drafting an entirely new document, a job complicated by the fact that no previous constitution had ever clearly spelled out the relative powers of executive and legislature. Concern grew within the legislature (the Congress of People's Deputies) that Boris Yeltsin was using the hiatus to consolidate presidential power before the relationship between executive and legislature was committed to paper.[10] The dispute finally broke into open hostility with the attempted coup of September–October 1993.

In December 1993, elections were held to the reformed Russian legislature (now renamed the Federal Assembly), and the new constitution was put to a public referendum. Voter turnout was just under 55 percent, and just 58 percent of those who voted (32 percent of all eligible voters) expressed their approval. In other words, 68 percent of eligible voters either voted against the constitution or did not vote at all. This was hardly a popular mandate and augured poorly for the development of a democratic system of government. Nonetheless, the constitution went immediately into force.

The constitution had been deliberately written to avoid the political stalemates of 1992–1993 and to reverse the trend toward the devolution of power to regional and local government. It has created a federal republic in which power is shared between an elected and powerful executive president, the Russian government (consisting of a prime minister and federal ministers), a bicameral Federal Assembly, a complex high court system, and 89 local government units. The legacy of the Soviet era encouraged the framers to open the constitution with a lengthy bill of rights (Articles 17–64) that not only established the personal freedoms normally associated with a democracy but went into even further detail; it includes the right to a private life, nationality, artistic expression, ideological diversity, and even protection from being subjected to medical experiments without consent.

Amendments to the constitution can be proposed by the president, either chamber of the Federal Assembly, and even by a group of at least 20 percent of the deputies of either chamber of the Assembly. Most amendments must be approved by a three-quarters majority in the Federation Council (the upper chamber of the Federal Assembly), a two-thirds majority in the State Duma (the lower chamber of the Federal Assembly), and a straight majority in two-thirds of local legislatures.

THE EXECUTIVE: PRESIDENT AND PRIME MINISTER

Executive power in the USSR was theoretically vested in a prime minister and Council of Ministers, operating alongside a figurehead president. However, all real power lay with the CPSU, so the de facto leader of the USSR was the general secretary of the CPSU, the post to which Gorbachev was elected in 1985. In March 1990, Gorbachev was hastily elected by the reformed Soviet legislature to a new post of executive president, for a 5-year term. The creation of this office shifted authority from the party to the government and was the first step toward making the executive more accountable to the people. But it was too little too late, and the office was eliminated with the collapse of the USSR in 1991.

While still part of the USSR, Russia had copied the model of the new Soviet presidency, and Boris Yeltsin was elected to that post by a popular vote in June 1991, 6 months before the collapse of the USSR. Elected for a 5-year term, he was less an executive in the American sense than an overseer responsible for maintaining political and economic stability.[11] Because most Russians believed that the Soviet Union would continue to exist in one form or another, Yeltsin had to fight hard to define and build the status of his new office. He was helped by the lack of a unified legislative opposition and by his own unwillingness to ally himself with any one political party. Just 6 months into his term, the USSR collapsed and Yeltsin was transformed into the leader of a newly independent Russia. He struggled to establish the new office between 1991 and 1993, finally winning a legal base with the passage of the 1993 constitution. He was reelected in 1996 and resigned on December 31, 1999. As required by the constitution, his prime minister Vladimir Putin stepped in as acting president and was confirmed in the post at the March 2000 presidential elections.

With his headquarters in the Kremlin in central Moscow, the president is elected for a maximum of two 4-year terms; serves as head of state, commander-in-chief, and overseer of foreign policy; and has considerable tools of power at his disposal:

- He can issue **edicts** that have the force of law unless and until the legislature passes laws that supersede them (although they must not contravene the constitution or federal law). Yeltsin used this power extensively, notably in areas such as the privatization of state-owned industries, reform of the banking system, and fighting organized crime. Among the edicts issued by Putin have been those reestablishing mandatory training for military reservists, censoring news from the war-torn province of Chechnya, and allowing the 15-year old *Mir* space station to be destroyed by crashing back to earth. The president can also introduce draft laws to the State Duma and even bypass it altogether with a referendum.

- He can appoint and dismiss the prime minister and federal ministers, move ministers from one job to another, and even influence the appointment of senior ministerial staff. The State Duma must approve all key appointments, but if it turns down the president's nominee for prime minister three times in a row, then new elections are called for the Duma. Because most members of the Duma would not want to bring forward the date of the election, it is unlikely they would push a president that far; they would be more likely instead to pass a vote of no confidence in the government. In the event of such a vote, the president can either dismiss the prime minister or ignore the vote, but—if it was passed again within 3 months—he would either have to replace the prime minister or dissolve the Duma and call a new election.

- With the approval of the State Duma, the president can appoint the heads of all major government agencies, such as the Russian Central Bank. He also nominates justices to the Constitutional Court, who must win approval by the Federation Council, and he can appoint and dismiss military commanders and ambassadors at will.

- He can dissolve the State Duma and call new elections. To prevent the president from arbitrarily dissolving the Duma and holding repeated elections until he gets a result he likes, he cannot dissolve the house if it is considering impeaching him, during a state of national emergency or martial law, or within a year of a vote of no confidence.

- All bills must be signed by the president before they become law, and he can veto bills adopted by the Duma, although they can overturn the veto with a two-thirds majority.

- If he perceives the threat of aggression against Russia, he can introduce martial law (under which he can use the military to control and govern using direct force) or declare a state of emergency (under which normal legislative and judicial powers may be suspended). He must have the approval of the Federation Council to do either.

Although some of these powers border on dictatorial, they are not unlimited. Not only must the president win support from the Duma for his appointments and policies, but he can also be impeached by the Federation Council for treason or a serious crime. Much like the "high crimes and misdemeanors" clause in the U.S. Constitution, this is an ambiguous notion that is open to wide interpretation. A successful impeachment is also difficult to actually achieve: It must be brought by one-third of the members of the Duma, its grounds must be confirmed by the Constitutional Court and the Supreme Court, and it must then be confirmed by a two-thirds majority in both chambers of the Federal Assembly.

As in the United States, the presidency in Russia is much more than the individual who holds the office. Both presidents have a supporting network of offices and institutions that play a key role in determining the character of an administration; for the Russian president these include the State Council (a consultative forum created by Putin in 2000 and made up of Russia's 89 regional leaders),[12] the Executive Office (with representatives from nearly 40 government agencies), and the Security Council (which provides advice on national security). However, the reach of the

TABLE 4.2

Postwar Leaders of Russia

CPSU party leaders	Prime ministers
(1922) Joseph Stalin	(1941) Joseph Stalin
1953 Georgy Malenkov	1953 Georgy Malenkov
1953 Nikita Khrushchev	
	1955 Nikolai Bulganin
	1958 Nikita Khrushchev
1964 Leonid Brezhnev	1964 Alexei Kosygin
	1980 Nikolai Tikhonov
1982 Yuri Andropov	
1984 Konstantin Chernenko	
1985 Mikhail Gorbachev	1985 Nikolai Ryzhkov (Acting)
	1991 Valentin Pavlov

Presidents	
1991 Boris Yeltsin	1991 Boris Yeltsin
	1992 Yegor Gaidar (Acting)
	1992 Viktor Chernomyrdin
	1998 (April) Sergei Kiriyenko
	(Aug) Viktor Chernomyrdin (Acting)
	(Sept) Yevgeny Primakov
	1999 (May) Sergei Stepashin
	(Aug) Vladimir Putin
1999 Vladimir Putin (Acting)	
2000 Vladimir Putin	2000 (May) Mikhail Kasyanov

Russian president goes much further than that of his U.S. counterpart. The job has even been described as a **superpresidency,** and comparisons have been made between the way Yeltsin and Putin have run their presidencies and the way the old tsarist imperial court was structured. Yeltsin grouped around himself a number of advisors and confidantes, known collectively as "the family"; among them were his daughter, Tatyana Dyachenko, and the businessman Boris Berezovsky. For his part, Putin relies heavily on the advice of his prime minister, Mikhail Kasyanov; the head of the domestic security service, Nikolai Patrushev; and a small group of economic advisors.[13]

The president governs with the help of the Government of the Russian Federation, consisting of the prime minister, as many as nine deputy prime ministers, and

PEOPLE IN POLITICS

VLADIMIR PUTIN

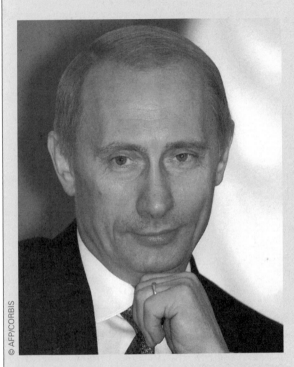

© AFP/CORBIS

After several years of uncertainty under the increasingly unpredictable leadership of Boris Yeltsin, the helm was passed to a new generation of leaders in December 1999 when Yeltsin resigned and the acting presidency of Russia fell to the relatively unknown Vladimir Putin. Putin's tenure was confirmed in March 2000, when he convincingly won Russia's second presidential election. His age, vigorous good health (he is a judo expert), and decisive leadership stood in stark contrast to that of the ailing Yeltsin.

Vladimir Vladimirovich Putin was born in 1952, and after graduating from Leningrad University in 1975, he joined the KGB, the Soviet intelligence organization. Exactly what he did in the KGB has been the subject of much speculation, but he is not thought to have had a stellar career and spent 10 years working in what was then East Germany. In 1989 he returned to Leningrad University as an administrator, subsequently working for reformist St. Petersburg mayor Anatoly Sobchak. He was then brought to Moscow to work for deputy prime minister Anatoly Chubais. Putin was little known in national politics until Boris Yeltsin named him prime minister in August 1999.

As prime minister, Putin attracted considerable support within Russia—but much criticism from abroad—by pursuing an aggressive campaign against the rebellion in Chechnya. His rhetoric about the restoration of Russia's status as a great power led to concerns both at home and abroad that he might prove to be an authoritarian leader. However, he claimed to be a pro-Western modernizer who was a particular admirer of former British prime minister Margaret Thatcher. Putin won the March 2000 presidential election convincingly: With a voter turnout of nearly 70 percent, he won more than 52 percent of the vote, pushing the communist Gennady Zyuganov into a distant second place and avoiding a second-round runoff.

As president, Putin has focused heavily on the economic reconstruction of Russia, has moderated his position on Chechnya, has shown less opposition to the expansion of NATO than was once feared, has built strong relations with the Bush administration (although he was critical of the 2003 U.S.-led invasion of Iraq), and has invested much effort in building close ties with the European Union. Opinions about him are still divided, however. He has strong public approval within Russia and is confidently expected to win the next presidential election, due in 2004. His supporters see him as a decisive modernizer, a democrat, and a supporter of free-market policies. But his critics point to his occasionally authoritarian methods and the emergence of a cult of personality, and they wonder whether he has a hidden agenda. Many of those who remember the cold war still find it hard to trust Russia or Putin, but he once said that "anyone who doesn't regret the passing of the Soviet Union has no heart, but anyone who wants it restored has no brains."

about two dozen federal ministers, the most influential of which are the four "power ministers": foreign, interior, intelligence, and defense. The main jobs of the government are to draft the federal budget, oversee economic policy, and oversee the implementation of law and policy by the bureaucracy. Neither the prime minister nor the ministers need come from the largest party or coalition in the Federal Assembly; they simply need to win the approval of the State Duma. If and when one party wins a majority in the Duma, however, these posts will almost certainly be filled by members of that party.

The office of prime minister is both subsidiary and—given that the holder is caught between executive and legislature—thankless. The president sets the broad direction of government policy, but the job of the prime minister—who is a member of the State Duma—is to take care of the details and work to get the president's program through the Duma. He helps select ministers, advises the president on policy, and—because there is no vice presidency—is next in line to become president if the incumbent dies, resigns, or becomes permanently incapable of governing. The prime minister takes power as acting president, but new presidential elections must be held within 3 months. When Yeltsin resigned in December 1999, he was replaced by Vladimir Putin and new elections were held in March 2000.

Yeltsin's prime minister from 1992 to 1998 was Viktor Chernomyrdin, a moderate liberal on economic issues and the former chairman of Russia's state-owned natural gas monopoly, Gazprom. He profited so much from its privatization that when he became leader of a new party called Our Home Is Russia in 1995 wits quickly dubbed it Our Home is Gazprom. Chernomyrdin proved both loyal and a good manager, with a style that was so understated as to be dull. This may have been his greatest strength, however, giving him an aura of solid reliability and honesty against a background of political turmoil.

After several years of stability in the office of prime minister, Yeltsin caused much consternation during his second term by suddenly appointing and dismissing a string of prime ministers, going through five in less than 18 months (1998–1999). This was interpreted by some as a sign that he wanted to prevent any one prime minister from becoming too powerful or popular[14] and by others that he was out of control. Yet others suggested that he may have made the changes to create contenders for the presidential election in 2000. Strategically, nothing could have made it more difficult for the communists to win the election.

Putin's choice for prime minister was Mikhail Kasyanov (b. 1957), a technocrat and free-market economist with an 8-year career in the Ministry of Finance, mainly as Russia's chief debt negotiator but including several months as Russia's finance minister. Kasyanov confounded those who predicted that he would not last long and quickly became a close Putin confidante. He oversaw a vigorous legislative program that included major new laws dealing with tax reform, money laundering, changes to the judicial system, a new pension scheme, and a reduction in the amount of bureaucratic paperwork demanded of Russian business.

Just as the real power of the president of the United States took decades to evolve, so it will take time before the balance of power between the different arms of the Russian system is settled.[15] In much the same way as the parameters of the U.S. presidency were determined by the personality of George Washington, so Boris Yeltsin stamped his own mark on the office in the way he used his actual or implied powers. For now, the evolution of the presidency lies in the hands of Vladimir Putin and how

The Kremlin in central Moscow, home of the office of the president. The Kremlin was a well-known symbol of Soviet power during the cold war and remains a potent symbol today of the authority of the presidency in the new Russian political system.

he uses the office to deal with the other arms of government and with Russia's political, economic, and social problems. Critics argue that the executive has too much power relative to the legislature, but that is mainly because the legislature is still in a state of flux.

THE LEGISLATURE: FEDERAL ASSEMBLY

The Soviet legislature was the 1,500-member bicameral Supreme Soviet. Its lower chamber was elected from districts with roughly equal populations across the country, and its upper chamber was elected from the 15 republics. They met only twice each year for sessions of 3 to 5 days each and did little more than rubber-stamp party decisions. At other times, legislative power was held by a 39-member Presidium, whose members were appointed by the party leadership and which could take any action that was constitutional, provided that it was ratified by the Supreme Soviet. In his attempts to turn the Soviet Union from a "party-governed" state into a "law-governed" state, Gorbachev created a tricameral Congress of

People's Deputies and a smaller and more powerful Supreme Soviet, which sat for two sessions of 4 months each year. (Compare these with China's legislative bodies— see pp. 246–250.)

With the breakup of the USSR, Russia ceased to come under the authority of Soviet law, and its own republican parliament became the supreme legislative body. This was virtually a mirror image of the Gorbachev model, with a Congress of People's Deputies elected for 5-year terms, a smaller and more powerful bicameral Supreme Soviet, and a prime minister and Council of Ministers. Elements of this system worked their way into the 1993 constitution, but the powers of the executive and legislature were more clearly defined and the old system was replaced with a Federal Assembly consisting of two chambers.

The Federation Council

The less powerful upper chamber, the Federation Council—much like the U.S. Senate—is designed to represent the regions. It initially consisted of two representatives elected from each of the 89 "subjects" (regions and republics), for a total membership of 178. They were replaced in 1995 by the chief executives and the chairs of local legislatures in each of the subjects. In other words, its members were not directly elected to the Council but became members by virtue of holding office in local government. The most recent change came in 2000, when—in an attempt to limit the powers of Russia's regional leaders, who in his view had accumulated too much influence over national politics—Vladimir Putin steered a new law through the State Duma that stripped the local leaders of their rights to sit in the Council, replacing them with 178 full-time representatives appointed by local legislatures and their executives.

The Council has jurisdiction over relations between the federal government and the regions and republics and can examine all laws passed by the Duma, but its approval is needed only for laws involving economic or defense issues (although the State Duma can override a Council veto with a two-thirds majority). It confirms presidential nominations to the Constitutional Court and Supreme Court, must approve changes to the internal borders of Russian local government units, must approve decisions by the president to declare martial law or a state of emergency, schedules presidential elections, and has the sole power to initiate impeachment proceedings against the president.

The State Duma

The **State Duma** is Russia's major lawmaking body and the focus of real political power in the Federal Assembly. It has 450 members elected for maximum 4-year terms, half by proportional representation and half on a winner-take-all basis. None of the elections held since 1993 has given any one party a majority in the Duma, so it has been neither a predictable source of support nor a source of opposition to the president, and multipartisanship has been the norm to date. The Duma is overseen by a chairman who would normally be appointed from the majority party, but because no one party has had a majority, chairs so far have been compromise appointees with relatively little political influence.

As well as being the primary actor in the lawmaking process, the State Duma must confirm the president's choice for prime minister and must approve all government ministers except defense, foreign affairs, and internal affairs. It can also introduce motions of no confidence in the government. If these are passed by a majority, the president can either ignore them or dismiss the prime minister, but if they are repeated within 3 months, the prime minister must be dismissed and replaced. Given the current balance among the parties in the Duma, there is no prospect of a vote of no confidence succeeding without multiparty support. An example came in March 2001 when the communists—accusing Putin of "suicidal" policies and talking of a decade wasted on so-called "democratic reforms"—called for a vote. They were initially supported by the Unity party, which backed the proposal because it hoped it could win more seats in the subsequent election. But when Unity withdrew, the motion was soundly defeated.

The new Russian lawmaking process has two notable differences from that of the U.S. Congress:

- The Federal Assembly can discuss and adopt both federal laws and constitutional laws (which change or clarify the constitution).

- Proposals for new laws can be submitted by many different people and groups, including the president, the government, either house of the Federal Assembly, legislatures of local units of government, or even the Constitutional Court and Supreme Court. Of the more than 3,300 bills that went through the Duma in 1996–1999, nearly half came from the Duma itself, but 20 percent came from the government, 16 percent from regional assemblies, 9 percent from the Federation Council, and 5 percent from the president.[16]

Once passed by the State Duma, federal laws must go within 5 days to the Federation Council, which has just 2 weeks to vote in favor or against. A rejection can be overruled by a two-thirds majority in the Duma, or else the law is sent to a conciliation committee to settle the differences. Once a law has been adopted by the Assembly, it must be submitted to the president within 5 days and he has 2 weeks to sign it or reject it. A presidential veto can be overruled by a two-thirds majority of both houses of the Assembly.

The Assembly remains relatively weak in relation to the president, handicapped as it has been by the absence of a majority party (which would give it more direction and more power to contest presidential policy), by the president's powers to issue edicts and decrees, and by ongoing questions about the balance of power between the executive and the legislature. As did Yeltsin before him, Putin has taken advantage of the situation by manipulating the Assembly to his own ends.

THE JUDICIARY: CONSTITUTIONAL COURT

At the apex of the Russian judicial system is the Constitutional Court, which—like most such courts—has the task of protecting and interpreting the constitution. It does this by resolving disputes over political jurisdiction (including disputes between federal government departments) and ensuring that the legislative and executive branches abide by the constitution. It has 19 members nominated for 12-year terms by the president and confirmed by the Federation Council. Marat Baglai was elected chairman of the Court in February 1997.

The job of the Court was limited at first by the fact that it had no constitution to defend or interpret (other than the discredited 1977 version), so its members were unable to define a place for the Court within the new Russian system[17] or to act as neutral arbiters as Yeltsin and the legislature bickered. The passage of the 1993 constitution provided the legal foundation for the Court's powers, but its structure was only finally settled with the passage of a 1994 law. The Court has since faced four major challenges: building legitimacy for the constitution, providing more definition to the principles and objectives of the constitution, establishing a tradition of judicial review, and promoting public respect for the rule of law in a society in which both the law and the constitution were discredited by being manipulated to suit the ends of the CPSU.

Russia also has a Supreme Court, which is the highest court of appeal for civil, criminal, and administrative cases and has the power of oversight over the activities of lower courts. Meanwhile, a Supreme Arbitration Court deals with economic and business matters, and the constitution also provides for a single, centralized system of prosecution, headed by a prosecutor-general.

SUBNATIONAL GOVERNMENT

The USSR was legally a federation, but in practice it was governed more like a unitary state. It consisted of 15 republics, which varied in size and power from the sprawling Russian Soviet Federated Socialist Republic (RSFSR), which covered 76 percent of the land area of the USSR, to the three Baltic republics (Estonia, Latvia, and Lithuania), which among them covered just 0.8 percent of the land area of the USSR. Elections provided the same illusion of democracy as those at the federal level, but the heads of local government bodies were appointed by the general secretary of the CPSU and were accountable to no one but the higher levels of the party.

Throughout the Soviet period, ethnic and cultural differences were minimized or understated because Marxism-Leninism stipulated that such differences would disappear under communism. Official policy was to promote Russian language and culture and even to encourage non-Russians to identify themselves as Russian. Few realized the levels of resentment many non-Russians felt toward these policies until Gorbachev came to power, and his reforms released pent-up demand for change. Every Soviet republic declared sovereignty during 1990–1991, Russia included. In an attempt to save the union, Gorbachev announced plans in early 1990 to draw up a union treaty that would give the republics greater powers, but he was too late. The proposed signing of the treaty on August 20, 1991, sparked the attempted coup of August 19 by hard-liners opposed to the more liberal terms of the treaty. Ironically, this ended any real possibility of the Soviet Union remaining intact, and it was formally dissolved 4 months later.

Under the 1993 constitution, Russia now consists of 89 equal "subjects," or components: 21 republics, 6 krays (territories), 49 oblasts (provinces), 2 "cities of federal significance" (Moscow and St. Petersburg), and 11 autonomous okrugs, all of which have their own legislative and executive organs of government and their own systems of law. Each republic elects a president and is based around a non-Russian national-ity or ethnicity, whereas krays and oblasts have governors, who were appointed by the president of Russia until 1996 but are now elected. A number of the regional leaders have developed strong independence and have proved a thorn in the flesh to the Putin administration—thus the change of law in 2000 by which they were replaced in the Federation Council with appointed representatives.

REPRESENTATION AND PARTICIPATION

One of the biggest challenges faced by the new Russia has been to break with the legacy of a system in which political power was centralized and representation was token and to build in its place a system that allows citizens to take part in democratic decision mak-ing in such a way that government actually responds to their opinions and concerns. Given that Russians have little experience with democracy, this has not been easy.

During the Soviet era, all significant policy decisions were made by the **Commu-nist Party of the Soviet Union (CPSU).** Voters were offered no real choice at the polls, all interest groups were overseen by the party, and the media were controlled and censored. Gorbachev began the transition to a more open society, but he neither lifted all controls on the media nor allowed the completely free expression of opposi-tion sentiment, inside or outside government. In 1993 Russian voters—for the first time—were offered real choices at the polls. By March 2000, they had cast their votes at two presidential elections, three sets of legislative elections, and multiple local elec-tions. Although they are becoming used to the idea of choice, the evolution of a sta-ble democratic system is still compromised by the strength of the presidency, the weakness of the legislature, the instability of the party system, and limits on the abil-ity of the media to act as a channel for the free expression of opposing political views.

ELECTIONS AND THE ELECTORAL SYSTEM

The USSR was governed on the Leninist principle of **democratic centralism,** mean-ing that limited democracy existed within a single legal party, the CPSU. In theory, every level in the party delegated its authority to the next highest level through the electoral process. All decisions passed down by the higher levels were to be followed by the lower levels, but the higher levels were also supposedly accountable to the lower levels. In reality, rank-and-file party members had little impact on party policy, all electoral nominations were controlled by the CPSU, and because the CPSU claimed to represent the public interest, only one CPSU-approved candidate was slated for each seat. The CPSU decided the dates of elections, made all the arrange-ments, counted the ballots, and even organized light entertainment to keep voters amused. According to official statistics, turnout was never less than 99 percent.

The March 1989 elections to the Soviet Congress of People's Deputies marked a significant departure from previous practice. The CPSU was still the only legal party and the elections were still organized by the party, but anyone could be nominated to run for office and nearly 75 percent of districts were contested. The result was that several high-ranking party officials were defeated, and a number of reformers and government critics won office. Among these was Boris Yeltsin, who survived an attempt by the CPSU to discredit him and won 89 percent of the vote in his Moscow district, defeating the official CPSU candidate.

In March 1990, new elections were held for the Russian Congress of People's Deputies, still under the control of the CPSU. When the USSR ceased to exist in 1991, Congress became the supreme legislative body of Russia and its hard-line communist deputies persisted in blocking Yeltsin's reforms. He finally suspended the legislature in September 1993 and called new elections. This sparked the September occupation of the Congress building and the attempt to overthrow Yeltsin. With the end of the siege in October, the way was cleared for new elections in December 1993, the first under the new constitution and the first contested by multiple parties.

In Russia today, voters can elect representatives to a number of government offices, from the national level to the local.

The Presidential Election

Russian presidential elections are much shorter and cheaper than their U.S. counterparts, mainly because they do not include primaries. Anyone can run, provided that they register and collect 1 million signatures to qualify for inclusion on the ballot. Voter turnout has been healthy and consistent, running at about 69 to 70 percent. Once the votes are counted, a candidate who wins more than 50 percent of the vote is declared elected. If no one crosses the 50 percent barrier, however, the top two finishers must run off against each other in a second round held within 15 days. In 1996 Boris Yeltsin won the biggest share of the vote in the first round with 35.3 percent of the total, followed by the Communist candidate, Gennady Zyuganov, with 32 percent. In the runoff between these two, Yeltsin was elected with nearly 54 percent of the vote. Significantly, nearly 4 million voters—about 5 percent of the voters who turned out—made a political statement in the second round by voting for "none of the above" (see Table 4.3).

The March 2000 election was significantly different both in its character and its outcome. A change of leadership was inevitable (because Yeltsin could not run again), and 11 candidates contested the election. The clear front-runner was former prime minister and incumbent acting president Vladimir Putin, whose lead in opinion polls was never seriously challenged. Putin won the first round with more than 52 percent of the vote, ensuring that a runoff was unnecessary. Gennady Zyuganov came in second with a slightly smaller share of the vote (down from 32 percent in the first round in 1996 to just under 30 percent), and all the remaining candidates were in the single-figure range.

Legislative Elections

Although elections to the Federation Council were held in December 1993, these were intended only to provide it with a temporary membership pending clarification of the role of the Council. With subsequent changes in the law, the Council is no longer elected but is made up instead of representatives appointed by the local government.

TABLE 4.3

Results of Presidential Elections in Russia

	Candidate	% share		Ideology/party
1991*	Boris Yeltsin	57.30		None
	Nikolai Ryzhkov	16.85		Communist
	Vladimir Zhirinovsky	7.81		Liberal Democrat
	Others	10.93		

Turnout: 69.2%

	Candidate	First round	Second round	Ideology/party
1996	Boris Yeltsin	35.28	53.82	None
	Gennady Zyuganov	32.03	40.31	Communist
	Alexander Lebed	14.52	—	Russian Communities
	Grigory Yavlinsky	7.34	—	Yabloko
	Vladimir Zhirinovsky	5.70	—	Liberal Democrat
	Others	2.16	—	
	None of the above	2.97	4.83	
	Invalid ballots	1.42	1.04	

Turnout: 69.8% in first round; 68.9% in second round

	Candidate	% share		Ideology/party
2000†	Vladimir Putin	52.52		None
	Gennady Zyuganov	29.44		Communist
	Grigory Yavlinksy	5.85		Yabloko
	Aman Tuleyev	3.04		None
	Vladimir Zhirinovsky	2.72		Liberal Democrat
	Others	6.44		
	None of the above	1.90		

Turnout: 68.8%

*Russia in June 1991 was still a Soviet republic, so this was a regional rather than a national election.
†No second round was needed because Putin won more than 50% of the vote in the first round.

The most important legislative elections are those to the State Duma. Following the lead of several Western European states, Russia adopted a mixed voting system for the lower house, in which voters cast two votes. Half the 450 members are elected using the same winner-take-all, single-member district system used in the U.S. House of Representatives, with the candidate who wins the most votes in each of the 225 districts winning the seat, irrespective of whether they have a majority. The remaining 225 seats are filled using a system of proportional representation (PR) based on party lists. Voters cast a second vote, but this time for a party rather than an individual. The seats are then filled by parties in proportion to the number of votes they receive, provided only that they win at least 5 percent of the national vote. Only the biggest parties with the broadest base of support win seats under the PR element.

Local Elections

Russians also go to the polls to elect officials to local government, including presidents (in republics), governors, and local legislators. So far, these elections have not been held at the same time as the presidential elections, as many of them are in the United States. A series of gubernatorial elections held in the last 4 months of 1996 allowed voters to confirm or reject leaders previously appointed by Yeltsin, thereby extending democracy to local government. But with Putin's efforts to rein in unruly and sometimes corrupt provincial leaders, local elections have lost much of their significance.

POLITICAL PARTIES

Parties in liberal democracies may be the lifeblood of politics, but they are ultimately subservient to the state; governments change with elections, but the state persists. By contrast, the Soviet government was simply the administrative arm of the CPSU, which controlled all other institutions. Lenin claimed that the CPSU was a temporary vanguard, in place until a classless communist society was created, but under Stalin the party became a permanent part of the Soviet political system and membership became the ultimate accolade for the privileged few. Not only was party membership essential for anyone wanting to take an active role in the party itself, but it was also a basic condition of promotion to any position of leadership, whether this was managing a factory, a college, or a trade union. The benefits for top party leaders included special schools for their children, special medical services, official cars, access to state-owned dachas (country homes), and overseas travel.

Party organization was strictly hierarchical, beginning at the grassroots with more than 440,000 primary party organizations (PPOs), to which every party member belonged, and moving up through local, provincial, and republican levels to the national level, where the CPSU was dominated by three main institutions:

- **The Party Congress.** With more than 5,000 members, this was where policies were discussed and the leadership usually announced major policy changes. However, it met only once every 4 to 5 years and did little more than rubber-stamp party decisions and delegate authority to higher levels.
- **The Central Committee.** This consisted of 470 of the most senior party, government, and military leaders, and it directed the party between meetings of the Congress. Between its biannual meetings, the party was managed by a Secretariat, which met weekly, was overseen by the general secretary of the party, and ran the party bureaucracy.

■ **The Politburo.** The core of real power in the USSR lay in this body, which functioned much like a cabinet, was elected by the Central Committee, and usually met weekly. Its members included the president, the prime minister, the foreign and defense ministers, the head of the KGB security agency, and senior military officers. The senior member of the Politburo was the general secretary of the CPSU, who—despite the principle of collective leadership—became the de facto leader of the USSR. This was the job held by Stalin, Khrushchev, Brezhnev, Gorbachev, and other Soviet leaders.

Since 1991, Russians have had to become used to competing political parties that offer different views about Russia's problems and priorities and different ideas about how the country should be governed. The challenge before the voters has been complicated by the creation of dozens of political parties with a bewildering variety of platforms. So many parties have come and gone, and their membership has been so unstable and changeable, that they were once jokingly called "taxicab" parties because they seemed to go around in circles, stopping occasionally to let old members jump out and new members climb aboard. Some were so small that they were dismissed as "divan" parties (all their members could fit on a single couch). The prospects for a more orderly system were improved in 2001 when the State Duma passed a law limiting the number of small political parties that could take part in elections. No party can now compete unless it has at least 10,000 members and branches in at least half of Russia's 89 provinces.

The first elections to the State Duma in December 1993 were contested by 13 parties, all but one of which won seats. More musical chairs followed, however, and more than 250 parties registered before the 1995 elections, among the more colorful of which were the Muslim Movement, Cedar (a green party), the Association of Lawyers of Russia, the Union of Municipal Workers, and the Beer Lovers party. Just over 40 parties eventually ran, and 23 won seats (although 10 won just one seat each). By the time of the 1999 elections, many smaller parties had fallen by the wayside, and two major new parties—the pro-government Unity party and the centrist Fatherland-All Russia coalition—had appeared on the scene.

Mainstream Russian parties now fall broadly into four major groups.

Left-Wing Antireform Parties

The dominant party on the left of Russian politics is the reformed **Communist party** of the Russian Federation (KPRF), which—not surprisingly—has been the most actively antireformist. Led by Gennady Zyuganov, the Communists represent the remains of the old CPSU, and although they have gone to some pains to reassure foreign investors and Russian entrepreneurs that a communist government would not restore state ownership and a planned economy, few have been convinced. Zyuganov has been an apologist for Stalin (blaming his worst excesses on Stalin's acolytes), and he has hopes for a voluntary future reunification of the former Soviet republics. He also has written of his concerns about Jewish influence in the world, often criticizes capitalism, and blames the West for the fall of the USSR.

The Communists won only 11 percent of State Duma seats in 1993, but then surprised many by winning nearly a quarter of the vote in 1995 and the biggest block of seats in the Duma (up from 48 to 157). Zyuganov used this as a launchpad for his bid for the presidency in 1996, promising to restore order to Russia and briefly being described as a possible winner—until Yeltsin was able to snatch victory from the jaws of defeat. The fact that Zyuganov attracted 40 percent of the vote in the second round of the presidential election was a reflection of the extent to which communism still appealed to many Russian voters. The party was attracting voters who felt worse off because of economic reforms, notably blue-collar workers and retirees. The Communist share of the vote held steady in the December 1999 elections, and although the momentum of the late 1990s had trailed off, the Communists remained the biggest party in the State Duma (with 114 seats) and controlled about 40 percent of Russia's regions.

Communism is steadily losing its allure to Russians. The Communist party attracts little support among younger Russians, there have been struggles over ideology within the party, and although Zyuganov held on to the leadership while more militant communists moved to more radical parties on the left, if it is to remain the major political force on the left of Russian politics, it will need to move further away from its pre-Russian roots. In time, the party will almost inevitably adopt the mantle of socialism, leaving substantially reduced numbers of old-style communists to jab away at the government from small parties on the far left.

Left-Wing Pro-Reform Parties

The major ally of the Communists in 1993–1995 was the Agrarian party (APR), which represents the interests of Soviet-era collective farms and the agricultural sector. Its leader, Ivan Rybkin, was elected first chairman of the State Duma in January 1994 but—exemplifying the fluidity of Russian politics—subsequently became a Yeltsin loyalist and was appointed national security advisor in 1996. The party subsequently moved toward the center and became part of the new **Fatherland-All Russia** coalition set up by Moscow mayor Yuri Luzhkov, former Russian prime minister Yevgeny Primakov, and several regional governors. The members of this coalition are united by the view that Russia should become a market economy but that there should be a high degree of state intervention and regulation.

Also on the moderate left is Yabloko, whose name is an acronym derived from the names of its founders: Grigory Yavlinsky, Yuri Boldyrev, and Vladimir Lukin (a former ambassador to the United States). Founded in 1993, the party won the fourth biggest block of seats in the 1995 Duma elections (a modest 45), and Yavlinsky subsequently emerged as one of the major contenders for the 1996 and 2000 presidential elections. Relatively young and liberal, he is a Harvard-trained economist and former advisor to presidents Gorbachev and Yeltsin, favors a gentler transition to a market economy, and warns of the dangers of public monopolies being replaced with private ones. Yabloko won just 22 seats in the 1999 elections.

Right-Wing Pro-Reform Parties

At the 1993 State Duma elections, the main party in this group was Russia's Choice, which was led by first deputy prime minister Yegor Gaidar and strongly supported Yeltsin's economic policies. It won the biggest block of seats in the Duma (70) and

POLITICAL DEBATES

ARE THE OLIGARCHS TOO POWERFUL?

An important phenomenon in Russian national life—during both the Yeltsin and the Putin administrations—has been the role of **oligarchs.** These are entrepreneurs who exploited privatization and changes in economic policy to build massive business empires, particularly in energy and banking, and used their new power to build influence with government. Several of the most prominent played an important role in helping Boris Yeltsin win reelection in 1996 and then committed enormous financial resources to helping Yeltsin stay in power. In the run-up to the 2000 election, they used their media influence to attack two of the contenders for the presidency, Moscow mayor Yuri Luzhkov and former prime minister Yevgeny Primakov.[18]

Among the best known are the following:

- Boris Berezovsky started out as a car dealer and then moved into the oil business and the mass media, buying stakes in the state television channel ORT and taking control of the Russian airline Aeroflot. His influence with Boris Yeltsin allowed him to be appointed to various government positions, and in 1999 he won election to the State Duma. By 2001 he was living in exile in Paris.

- Vladimir Gusinsky was head of the Media-Most conglomerate, which owned NTV, the second largest Russian television station, as well as the radio station Ekho Moskvi. He was a champion of Western ideas and used his media outlets to support Yeltsin's policies. But he was hurt by Russia's financial problems and became increasingly critical of government policies, particularly in Chechnya, prompting a raid in May 2000 of his offices by masked and armed tax police. In 2001, in a move that was seen as symptomatic of Vladimir Putin's limited tolerance for press freedom, NTV was taken over by the state gas company Gazprom. Gusinsky by then was living in exile in Spain and was fighting attempts to have him extradited back to Russia to face charges of fraud.

Their influence has fallen during the Putin administration, in large part because of financial problems they have faced, which—among other things—have allowed the government to take over media once owned by the oligarchs. However, they continue to have strong links with government officials, there are questions about Putin's willingness to address those links, and there are concerns that he has simply used their misfortunes to win stronger control—particularly over the media—for the government.

ran in 1995 as Russia's Democratic Choice, but the party suffered from residual ill feelings among voters about the economic "shock therapy" program Gaidar promoted in 1992 (see section on Economic Policy). The reformist banner was taken up instead by Our Home Is Russia, a coalition of parties led by Viktor Chernomyrdin, describing itself as the "party of the establishment" and supporting the current market reforms. It won the second biggest block of seats in the Duma (55) and—

although Boris Yeltsin as president was not allowed to ally himself with any one party—tended to be most closely in tune with his policies.

This segment of the party spectrum changed out of all recognition during 1999 with the rise of **Unity,** created just 3 months before the December 1999 State Duma elections and designed to be a platform for then–prime minister Vladimir Putin, to be a counterweight to Fatherland-All Russia, and to support free market reformist policies. It won the second biggest block of seats in the 1999 elections but was formed so quickly and had so few strong leaders that it spent its first few years in a state of some confusion. Further to the right was the Union of Right-Wing Forces, a coalition of conservative pro-reform parties that included Russia's Choice, headed by Anatoly Chubais, the former deputy prime minister responsible for Russia's privatization program.

Nationalist Parties

The nationalist parties are united mainly by their concerns about Russia's place in the world, but they take different positions on economic reform. In 1995 they included the Congress of Russian Communities (KRO), founded to promote the interests of the 25 million ethnic Russians living in neighboring former republics of the USSR. One of the leaders of KRO was Alexander Lebed, an Afghan war veteran who became one of the most trusted figures in Russian political life and came third in the first round of the 1996 presidential election. Within days he had been appointed national security advisor by Boris Yeltsin, ensuring that many of his supporters would vote for Yeltsin in the second round (which they did). After winning kudos by brokering a cease-fire in Chechnya in August 1996, he was fired by Yeltsin in October, probably because his usefulness to the president had expired. He was subsequently elected governor of Krasnoyarsk, a key industrial region in Siberia, before dying in a helicopter crash in 2002.

The most notorious of the nationalist parties is the Liberal Democratic party (LDPR). Despite its name, this is a neofascist party that surprised many in the West by winning 23 percent of the vote in the 1993 State Duma elections and the second largest block of seats. Many LDPR supporters felt that Russia's loss of empire and international prestige were the fault of reformers such as Yeltsin, resented the influence of the West, and believed that an alternative to capitalism could be developed. The founder and leader of the LDPR is Vladimir Zhirinovsky, whose popularity in the early 1990s attracted comparisons with the rise of Hitler in Germany in 1933. Zhirinovsky threatened to launch nuclear attacks on Japan and Germany, spoke of taking Alaska back from the United States, and promised to respond to Russian feminism by finding husbands for all unmarried women. Zhirinovsky's poor showing in the 1996 presidential election (he won just under 6 percent) started a decline that was confirmed in the 1999 State Duma elections. The LDPR was disqualified because of problems with income declarations by many of its members, so Zhirinovsky ran with two smaller nationalist parties as the Zhirinovsky Block, which won barely 6 percent of the vote and just 17 seats.

INTEREST GROUPS

One of the hallmarks of a liberal democracy is a pluralistic society that offers its citizens a variety of channels through which they can influence government. There were interest groups in the USSR, but they were incorporated into the system and carefully controlled by the CPSU[19] and were less a forum through which people could influence public policy than an additional means by which the CPSU could control society, gather information, and implement policies. Among the biggest of these groups were the membership associations or "public organizations," such as the 40-million-member Komsomol (the Communist Youth League) and the labor unions, which among them had a membership of 131 million.

Among the prerequisites for a meaningful interest group community is a government that groups can lobby and influence and an ability and desire among citizens to build voluntary organizations around common interests. Many older Russians are still influenced by the contradictory messages they were sent under the Soviet regime about the role they were to play in society. They were supposed to provide the government with feedback, yet they were allowed neither to be critical nor to oppose the basic principles and structures of the regime. Participation was a form of "organized enthusiasm" in which the population was mobilized to support party policies. There was little room for voluntary political commitment, political activism tended to be a social duty, participation was underpinned by a fear of social spontaneity, and there was an unwillingness to tolerate any political activity that was not closely managed by the party.[20]

Democratization since the era of *glasnost* has seen the emergence of thousands of politically active interest groups. Initially, so-called "informals" emerged spontaneously as Russians took advantage of the idea that they could now express competing opinions. Some evolved into political parties, and others grew around more narrow interests. Changes in the law combined with the opening up of the market in the early 1990s to encourage the creation of commercial lobbies and groups representing particular sectors of the economy, such as banking, farming, and the energy industry.[21] Today there is a large and active community of interest groups, likely to become even more active in light of changes in the law that place a minimum limit on the size of groups competing as parties in elections.

THE MEDIA

Just as political institutions in the USSR gave the superficial impression of democracy, so the media provided the superficial impression of variety and choice. Although more than 8,000 newspapers were published in the USSR, they were all ultimately controlled by the party and subject to universal and stringent censorship. Comprehensive official guidelines prevented them from publishing or broadcasting military information or anything that would reflect poorly on the USSR, including information about earthquakes, train or plane crashes, the salaries of government and party workers, figures on the Soviet cost of living, or reports of food shortages.

At the national level, the major newspapers included the party organ *Pravda* (Truth), the government paper *Izvestiya* (News), and the military paper *Krasnaya zvezda* (Red Star). Uniformity of news was perpetuated by the monopoly enjoyed by the government news agency TASS and the "nongovernmental" Novosti news service. Radio and TV broadcasting were controlled by a state monopoly, and the Soviet government went to great lengths to jam broadcasts of foreign radio services, such as the Voice of America and the BBC World Service. Under these circumstances, many Soviets relied for news on the underground press or on a thriving rumor mill, which was often so successful that the official media felt obliged to occasionally deny the more popular rumors.

Russia today has greater press freedom than ever before, but there are troubling signs that it is under attack, both from government policy and from the bad habits of journalists themselves. Television has been a particular object of concern. The government owns 51 percent of Public Russian Television (ORT) and fully owns Russian Television and Radio (RTR), so both take pro-Kremlin lines. The third major national channel, NTV, was independent until 2001, when, having incurred large debts, it was taken over by Gazprom, the natural gas monopoly in which the state is the major shareholder. This left only a few local stations—such as TV6 and TNT—taking an independent line, but even they became the target of Gazprom takeovers, and TV6 was closed down in 2002. Furthermore, the state runs the major national radio stations and the two news agencies (now known as ITAR-TASS and RIA-Novosti). For its part, much of the press is owned by a few large business empires, and the Putin administration charges that they have too much influence over national affairs.

The Russian media had their greatest levels of freedom just after the collapse of the Soviet Union, but since then they have fallen prey to the concentration of political and economic power in the hands of government and big business. Unlike politicians, who have become used to democratizing tendencies, journalists have not yet broken away from the habits developed during Soviet times and have not yet learned the importance of objectivity. Financial problems have also left them vulnerable to bribery and pressure from political groups, and advertising revenues in Russia are not big enough yet to let media develop financial—and thus editorial—freedom.[22] The result is that Russians have to work harder to find independent or competing sources of news and information.

POLICIES AND POLICYMAKING

Identifying the sources of power in Russia during the Soviet era was relatively simple; policy was made by the leadership of the Communist party and implemented by the state bureaucracy under CPSU supervision, and the average citizen was barely consulted. With the demise of the USSR, however, the Russian state entered a new era of uncertainty in which the hierarchy of power became fluid and changeable. The 1978 constitution was amended so often that it had lost much of its meaning by 1993, and a power struggle broke out between executive and legislature, prompted by questions over the lack of clear rules.

The 1993 constitution provided more focus, but doubts about the nature of Russian democracy remain even today, confused by ongoing struggles over authority, by party divisions within the State Duma, by the concentration of power in the hands of the presidency, and by a debate over the direction Russia should be taking on economic and foreign policy. In both spheres, the priorities of nearly 150 million people have had to be redefined: Russians have had to give up the (false) security of an economic system in which all key decisions were made for them and the supply of basic needs was guaranteed, and they have had to rethink their relationship with a world in which they once had considerable influence. The transition has not been easy.

ECONOMIC POLICY

In liberal democracies, production and consumption are driven by the supply of goods and resources and by the demands of consumers; the role of the government tends to be limited to regulation, taxes, welfare, and subsidies. By contrast, the USSR maintained a **command economy** in which government decided supply, distribution, and prices. No private enterprise was allowed, so everyone with a job worked for the state, all property was owned by the state, and all key services were provided by the state. At the core of the system was Gosplan, the State Planning Committee, which drew up 5-year plans listing targets for economic production. This was an enormously complex task that meant coordinating the operations of more than 60 economic ministries and more than 130 million employees.

Central planning brought rapid industrialization and impressive economic growth, helping the Soviet Union build a powerful military machine and become a nuclear superpower. Beneath the veneer of achievement, however, the system was inefficient and irrational, and although the standard of living improved, it remained inferior to that of the West and probably lingered well below its true potential. The emphasis on military spending drew investment away from the civilian sector, and there was too little investment in infrastructure or in the rural economy.

Mikhail Gorbachev was not the first to attempt to reform the system (Nikita Khrushchev had tried and failed before him), and he provided neither a new diagnosis of Soviet economic problems nor even a new set of prescriptions. Where he differed was in his willingness to actually make changes. He began cautiously, easing restrictions on farms and factories, promoting small private businesses, allowing farmers to lease land and workers to lease businesses from the state, and allowing the managers of state enterprises to make more of their own decisions and sell some of their produce directly to consumers. Then in September 1990 Gorbachev launched a 500-day program aimed at nothing less than turning the Soviet Union into a free-market system. He accepted the principle of private property, gave ownership of industrial assets to the republics, decentralized the tax system, and outlined a timetable during which state-owned industrial enterprises and trading firms would be sold, the federal budget deficit cut, and subsidies to state enterprises ended. But it was all too late; he failed to alter the structure and attitude of the CPSU, and his policies meant few positive changes for Soviet citizens, who saw worsening shortages and a visible decline in the short-term quality of their lives.

Andy Johnstone/Panos Pictures

A staff member of a foreign exchange business in the Arbat district of Moscow makes adjustments to a sign listing the value of the Russian ruble against the U.S. dollar. Fluctuations in the relative value of the two currencies have been symptomatic of the rapid changes in the state of the Russian economy in recent years.

Boris Yeltsin built on the changes begun by Gorbachev, but he faced the same obstacles. He opted for **"shock therapy,"** taking his first revolutionary step in January 1992 when he lifted price controls on selected consumer goods, services, machinery, and equipment. He also agreed to a stringent budget aimed at reducing Russia's deficit and cutting military spending. Finally, he launched a privatization scheme, building on changes begun under Gorbachev. At the same time, he made it clear that he wanted to keep state ownership of strategic resources such as water and forests and to carefully control the sale of property and businesses to foreign investors.

Against a background of falling real wages, worsening inflation, declining exports, and growing imports, Yeltsin sought loans and financial aid from other countries and from lending institutions such as the International Monetary Fund (IMF), which Russia joined in March 1992. In 1993 the G-7 countries agreed to provide more than $30 billion in aid to Russia, and in 1996 the IMF agreed to a $10.1 billion 3-year loan, conditional upon more economic reforms, reduced inflation, and a reduced national budget deficit. In mid-2002, the European Union and the United States both declared that they considered Russia a market economy, and indeed it had probably never been so stable, productive, or prosperous. However, Putin had inherited a long list of problems from his predecessor:

- **Controlling inflation.** From its peak of 350 percent in 1992, inflation fell but was still running at about 15 percent in early 2003. The ruble had lost much of its value, falling from 30 rubles to the dollar in 1991 to an astonishing 5,800 rubles by mid-1997. A new ruble was introduced in mid-1997, with a rate of five to the U.S. dollar, but by early 2003 this too had fallen, to 32 to the dollar. One of the consequences of inflation has been a worrisome flight of capital as assets are moved abroad rather than being invested locally.

- **Improving industrial output.** After falling by nearly 10 percent in 1997–1998, output grew by 12 percent in 1998–1999, but it had fallen back to 4 percent in 2002. Furthermore, the figures failed to show that the quality of production remained variable. Much of the problem stems from the obsolescence or decay of much of the physical plant in Russian factories. So poor has been the quality of Russian aircraft manufacture, for example, that staff members of the Russian civil aviation authority refuse to fly anywhere—even within Russia—on Russian-made planes.

- **Making Russia more self-sufficient and competitive in the global market.** After falling for several years, GDP has been growing since 1999 at rates of between 4 and 9 percent annually. However, some of the growth was due to increases in the international price of oil (of which Russia is a major producer), and the Russian consumer goods industry has so far failed to rise to the challenge posed by imports of superior Western products. Also, Russia needs to export more and to reduce its heavy reliance on exports of raw materials.

- **Making the benefits of economic growth more widely felt.** According to official estimates, more than one-third of Russians were living below the subsistence level of $480 per year in mid-1999. (Contrast this with the government definition of poverty in the United States: $16,530 for a family of four.) So big is the wealth gap between the cities and the rural areas that in 1997 Moscow alone was generating nearly half the entire Russian federal budget.[23]

- **Dealing with decaying infrastructure.** So much of the USSR's limited economic wealth was invested in the military that the private sector was often overlooked. Buildings, roads, and bridges were poorly designed and constructed, and industrial machinery and equipment were inadequately maintained. The result is that much of Russia's infrastructure today is severely outdated and in a poor state of repair. There have been improvements in industry because of increasing private ownership and investment, but public services have declined.[24] Most Russians make do, but the absence of infrastructure handicaps attempts to rebuild the economy.

- **Reducing unemployment and closing the income gap.** Successful liberal democratic systems are founded on a substantial and secure middle class. There is an emerging middle class in Russia, but unemployment is high (believed to be in the range of 7 to 10 percent, although official figures are not available). New wealth has come to a few Russian entrepreneurs, and it is becoming increasingly common to hear *biznesmeni* discussing corporate *imidzh* over a meal in Moscow restaurants, but many more Russians have yet to benefit from economic change, and homelessness is widespread.

- **Generating investment.** Much is already coming from outside Russia, but this tends to fan the flames of nationalism and does not help Russians themselves learn the pitfalls and possibilities of capitalism. To make matters worse, Russia needs investment and loans from abroad to help fuel its economic recovery, but its national debt in 2001 stood at nearly $155 billion, and it has several times defaulted on its debts, making lenders disinclined either to lend it more or to cancel its debts.

- **Addressing the crisis in the banking system.** Among the sectors most urgently in need of reform is banking. Banks have faced financial problems, the government has not had enough money to bail them out, and several have gone bankrupt. Ordinary Russians have so little faith in private banks that they make few long-term deposits. Concern and embarrassment has been added by the involvement (usually unwitting) of local and foreign banks in money laundering—by which money acquired criminally in Russia is made "respectable"—and in capital flight as Russians with money move it overseas to keep it safe. A large part of the problem stemmed from the persistence of Soviet-era attitudes, notably in the person of the president of the central bank, Viktor Gerashchenko. Once described as "the worst central banker in history,"[25] he maintained time-consuming bureaucratic procedures, employed too many staff, and refused to make public key pieces of information, such as the size of the bank's reserves. He resigned in March 2002.

- **Dealing with crime.** Russia still has a substantial black market. Although bartering is the purest form of capitalism and helps people learn the value of goods and services, it reduces the ability of a government to raise taxes and plays into the hands of organized crime. It is estimated that crime bosses may control as many as 4 out of every 10 businesses in Russia and 60 percent of state-owned businesses. They have also been involved in the murders of businesspeople, journalists, and politicians, such as the shooting death in November 1998 of Galina Starovoitova, a leading reformist politician. Such incidents are symptomatic of a broader problem within the justice system, which is notoriously incompetent and whose failings have allowed crime to grow: Russia now has the second highest per capita homicide rate in the world after South Africa.

- **Curbing corruption.** Putin has reduced the influence on politics of the oligarchs who were so prominent during the Yeltsin years, the amount of bureaucratic paperwork demanded of businesses has fallen, and a government Audit Chamber has been investigating the financial practices of state-run agencies. However, the links between government, the bureaucracy, and business are still close, and Transparency International ranked Russia 71st out of 102 countries on its 2002 Corruption Perceptions Index.[26]

Russia is a country with considerable human capital and a wealth of natural resources, but it is still a long way from being in the position to exploit its potential to its fullest. The Putin administration has shown that it is impatient for change, its most critical challenge being to capitalize on that potential before economic

CRITICAL ISSUES

THE CHECHNYAN PROBLEM

Russia is home to about 60 to 90 national minorities,[27] many of whom live on the periphery of the country and several of whom want greater self-determination and even full independence. The most serious effects of nationalism have been felt in the semi-independent republic of Chechnya. Since being conquered by Russia in 1858, Chechens—who are Muslims—have resented Russian control and, like many national minorities, saw the breakup of the USSR as an opportunity to win independence.

- A September 1991 coup brought former Soviet air force general Dzhokhar Dudayev to power. Tensions mounted under his leadership, leading to the launch of a Russian attack in December 1994. Vicious fighting over the next 20 months claimed the lives of several thousand Russian troops and as many as 100,000 Chechens—about one-tenth of the total population of Chechnya. Dudayev himself was killed in a missile attack in April 1996, and in May a cease-fire was negotiated that left Russia without any authority in the republic.

- In early 1999 the Chechen government announced plans to phase in Islamic *sharia* law, and in August Chechen-led Islamic rebels began to invade from neighboring Dagestan as part of a campaign to set up an independent Islamic republic in the north Caucasus. The government claimed that Chechens were behind bomb attacks in Moscow in August that

left more than 300 people dead, and the Putin government responded with force but, instead of relying on recruits and conscripts as in 1994–1996, used professional soldiers and worked to win public support both inside and outside Russia. Facing international criticism but backed by domestic public opinion, Russia launched an air and land attack on Chechnya, razing the capital of Grozny and prompting an estimated 200,000 refugees to flee to neighboring republics. Direct control from Moscow was instituted in May 2000.

- During 2001, human rights groups expressed concern about violations in Chechnya, citing allegations of torture and widespread detentions. A mass grave filled with mutilated bodies was found.

- In October 2002, Chechen rebels took 800 people hostage in a Moscow theater. Most of the rebels and 120 hostages were killed when Russian troops stormed the building. The following December, a suicide bomb attack on the government headquarters in Grozny killed more than 50 people.

Chechen rebels describe the conflict as a war of liberation, but Vladimir Putin calls it an antiterrorist operation. The problem continues to test the multinational identity of Russia and the administrative abilities of its government, while acting as another flashpoint on the borders of the deeply troubled Middle East.

and social decay go too far. One of the administration's priorities is to see Russia given membership in the World Trade Organization (WTO). Under the WTO's rules, applicants must convince all existing members of their genuine commitment to a market economy. With China's accession at the end of 2001, Russia now believes that it too should be allowed to join but faces opposition from its largest trading partner, the European Union (EU). The EU must be persuaded that Russia has made the changes needed to provide its trading partners and investors with access to all key sectors of the Russian economy and that it is dealing effectively with corruption. A number of Russian executives are also opposed, fearing that membership would mean direct competition from efficient Western multinational corporations.

FOREIGN POLICY

Between 1945 and the late 1980s, Soviet foreign policy was driven by strategic competition with the United States and its allies. For the latter, it often seemed that the enormous Soviet military machine posed a constant threat to peace and security, that the USSR took an aggressive posture, and that the West should respond in kind. Yet much Soviet foreign policy during the cold war was based on a long tradition of insecurity stemming from the difficulties of defending the largest country in the world. "Russia is always stronger, and weaker, than it looks," went the adage.

Its insecurities were behind the creation of an East European buffer zone after World War II, in which economic ties were formalized in 1949 with the creation of the Council of Mutual Economic Assistance (Comecon) and military ties in 1955 with the Eastern European Mutual Assistance Treaty (the **Warsaw Pact**), the Soviet counter to the North Atlantic Treaty Organization (NATO). Subsequent events in Eastern Europe reflected the extent to which Soviet policy was aimed at ensuring the "cooperation" of its satellite states: the suppression of reform movements in Hungary in 1956 and Czechoslovakia in 1968, the building of the Berlin Wall in 1961, and the crackdown on the Solidarity labor union in Poland in the early 1980s. Meanwhile, the USSR gave support to Cuba and to nationalist movements in Angola, Ethiopia, and Somalia, although this was no different in principle from the aid given by the United States and its allies to their client states in Africa and Asia.

Not all was hostility. Progress was made on the control of nuclear weapons, beginning with the signing in 1968 of the Non-Proliferation Treaty between the United States, the USSR, and Britain. In 1972 the Strategic Arms Limitation Treaty (SALT I) was signed, in 1975 the 35-nation European Security Conference was convened, and discussions on SALT II might have resulted in a second arms reduction treaty but for the December 1979 Soviet invasion of Afghanistan. The Brezhnev administration sent troops in to prop up a pro-Soviet government and quickly found itself bogged down in a war that proved unwinnable, largely because of the resistance put up by Afghan guerrillas supported by the West. By the time Soviet forces were withdrawn by the Gorbachev administration in February 1989, the war had cost more than 15,000 Russian lives. In terms of damage to national pride, it had been the Soviet Vietnam.

Gorbachev introduced a philosophy of "New Thinking" based on the argument that Soviet security depended on a political, rather than a military, relationship with the West. He entered into negotiations with the United States aimed at making substantial cutbacks in nuclear weapons and conventional weapons, paving the way for reductions in the Soviet military presence in Europe. In Eastern Europe, he made a notable change of policy in his refusal to intervene militarily as communism began to collapse and the Soviet hegemony dissolved. The symbolic end to that hegemony came with the dismantling of the Berlin Wall in 1989 and the reunification of Germany in October 1990.

Russia during the Yeltsin years became more introverted, its leaders too focused on domestic problems to take an active role in foreign affairs and disappointed by the lukewarm response of the West to its economic and social needs. Russia inherited the Soviet seat on the UN Security Council but opted to pursue a **"Russia First"** policy driven in large part by its traditional mistrust of the West.[28] Yeltsin and U.S. President Bill Clinton developed a warm personal relationship, and they met more times than all their postwar predecessors combined, but Yeltsin's few overseas visits were aimed mainly at attracting economic support and at building ties with Russia's neighbors. The only major international disputes in which Russia's name was raised were the crises in the former Yugoslavia, where Western countries were slow to take an overtly anti-Serbian stance in part because of Russia's traditional links with the Serbs.

A key item on the military policy agenda is Russia's relationship with NATO, the "winner" of the cold war. In 1994 NATO introduced a Partnership for Peace program aimed at promoting military cooperation and strengthening ties between NATO members and Eastern Europe. Signatories had to declare their commitment to democracy and the principles of international law. Russia joined in May 1994 and, by the end of 1996, 26 countries had joined, including all 15 former Soviet republics except Tajikistan. However, NATO remained unpopular in Russia, as shown by the public and political outcry against the NATO-led attack on Yugoslavia in 1999.

More recently, the controversial issue has been the expansion of full NATO membership to Eastern Europe. It has not been welcomed by Russia, but plans have proceeded regardless: Poland, Hungary, and the Czech Republic joined in 1999, and in 2002 an invitation was extended to seven more Eastern European countries: Bulgaria, Romania, Slovakia, Slovenia, and—more significantly—the former Soviet republics Estonia, Latvia, and Lithuania. The Putin administration continues to oppose expansion but realizes that there is little it can do to stop it, and there is even a minority within Russia that sees eventual Russian membership as inevitable. Meanwhile, there has been a reappraisal of NATO's role, which is increasingly focused on building political links among its members and their allies, providing political support for security operations, and redefining "the enemy," with much talk of the need for a common approach to terrorism.

Following the attacks of September 11, 2001, there were signs of warming relations between the West and Russia, with the Putin administration supporting the U.S. war in Afghanistan and even backing down on its initial opposition to plans by the Bush administration to develop a ballistic missile defense system and to withdraw from the 1972 Anti-Ballistic Missile treaty. Putin made a number of successful visits to Western Europe and made it clear that he wanted to better understand the goals of NATO and the EU. He also stressed that Russia's earlier implied criticism of American global leadership and its talk of the importance of strong relations with China and North Korea were in the past. Putin may have been motivated by two key philosophies: his own war against Islamic insurgency in Chechnya and his belief that building a strong and modern Russia needs investment and encouragement from the West.[29]

Meanwhile, the state of the Russian military remains a cause for concern. Once a formidable fighting force, which protected the USSR against the Nazi invasion in 1941 and then pushed Hitler's war machine back into the heart of Germany, the Russian military today is a shadow of its former self. It is still large, although no one knows exactly how large because many commanders exaggerate numbers to collect more pay, rations, and equipment, and it still has nuclear missiles and other advanced weapons. However, it is top-heavy and badly paid; morale is low following failures in Chechnya; its equipment is old; and alcoholism, drug addiction, and suicide are common among its youngest conscripts. Putin has plans to reduce troop numbers and build a smaller and more professional military by 2007, but he faces many bureaucratic hurdles.

The future for Russian foreign policy depends in large part on how economic reforms go at home. Many older Russians still hark back to the "good old days" when the USSR was a superpower, and they are wary of any attempts to compromise Russian economic independence or to encircle Russia. This is partly why nationalist political parties have struck a chord with many Russians. The challenge for Russia, for Eastern Europe, and for the Western liberal democracies is to ensure that Russia is able to redefine its position in the world without feeling that its interests are compromised. It will be no easy task.

RUSSIAN POLITICS IN TRANSITION

In 1991 the world's last great empire broke up. Out of the collapse of the Soviet Union came 15 sovereign states that have had to redefine themselves, both domestically and internationally. The biggest, Russia, is simultaneously undergoing a transition on at least three fronts: from empire to nation-state, from one-party state socialism to liberal democracy, and from a command economy to a free-market system. The magnitude of these changes—and their impact both on Russia and on the rest of the world—is enormous. Without help, the right political and economic choices, and plain good luck, Russia will not become the liberal democracy that the West would like to see.

Russians themselves have shown only mixed levels of support for the values and beliefs that support such a system. At the very least, they must organize and participate and must learn an entirely new set of rules about their place in the system relative to one another and to their government. Equally as important, economic decline must be reversed and social discontent must be addressed. Russian nationalism is partly a reflection of widespread dissatisfaction with the old system, the change brought about by the new system, and the uncertainty inherent in transition. Russia's challenges in the 1990s were complicated by the lack of a stable government or opposition within the State Duma. Since then, the office of president has won more definition, the party system is settling down, and the Duma is slowly becoming a more effective policymaking body. Worrisome elements of the tradition of Russian authoritarianism remain, however, and Russia still has some way to go before it meets the definition of working free-market democracy.

KEY TERMS

Bolsheviks
Chechnya
closed politics
collectivism
command economy
Communist party
Communist Party of the
    Soviet Union (CPSU)
Constitutional Court
dual executive
edicts

Fatherland-All Russia
Federation Council
5-year plans
glasnost
Gosplan
nationalism
New Economic Policy
oligarchs
patrimonialism
perestroika
politburo

Russia First
Siberia
shock therapy
socialism in one country
Stalinism
State Duma
superpresidency
Unity
Warsaw Pact

KEY PEOPLE

Boris Berezovsky
Leonid Brezhnev
Viktor Chernomyrdin
Mikhail Gorbachev

Mikhail Kasyanov
Nikita Khrushchev
Vladimir Putin
Joseph Stalin

Leon Trotsky
Boris Yeltsin
Gennady Zyuganov

STUDY QUESTIONS

1. By the time Gorbachev took power in 1985, was the USSR predominantly a Marxist, a Leninist, or a Stalinist state?

2. Is Russia under Putin headed toward becoming a liberal democracy?

3. Does the dual executive help or hinder the prospects for political change in Russia?

4. How does the structure of federalism in the United States and Russia compare?

5. What signs are there—if any—that the authoritarian tradition is still a factor in Russia today?

6. Has Russia become the "party-governed" state for which Mikhail Gorbachev hoped?

7. If adopted in the United States, would a two-round presidential election improve or detract from the quality of American democracy?

8. What impact has the mixed winner-take-all/proportional representation electoral system had on the way Russia is governed?

9. What is the significance of the Chechnyan problem for Russia's stability?

RUSSIA ONLINE

There are Web sites for the Russian government (*http://www.gov.ru*), the presidency (*http://president.kremlin.ru*), and the State Duma (*http://www.duma.ru*), but they are all in Russian. Among the most useful English-language sites are the following:

Russia on the Net: *http://www.ru/eng/index.html*
Russia on the Web: *http://members.valley.net/transnat*
Two sites that provide links to a variety of other sites on news, politics, and business.
Russia Today: *http://www.einnews.com/russia*
Radio Free Europe/Radio Liberty: *http://www.rferl.org*
Pravda: *http://english.pravda.ru*
The Russia Journal: *http://www.russiajournal.com/index/shtml*
A variety of sources of news on Russia, *Pravda* ("Truth") being the former CPSU party paper and *The Russia Journal* being a Moscow-based weekly.

FURTHER READING

Hosking, Geoffrey, *Russia and the Russians* (Cambridge, MA: Harvard University Press, 2001). A general history of Russia that raises important questions about the viability and purpose of the Russian state.

Kelley, Donald R., *Politics in Russia and the Successor States* (Fort Worth, TX: Harcourt, 1999). An introductory survey, with chapters on the constitution, political culture, institutions, parties, and policies.

Remington, Thomas F., *Politics in Russia* (New York: Longman, 1999) and Sakwa, Richard, *Russian Politics and Society* (London and New York: Routledge, 2002). Two general surveys of Russian politics, covering political culture, institutions, process, and policies.

White, Stephen, Alex Pravda, and Zvi Gitelman (Eds.), *Developments in Russian Politics 5* (Durham, NC: Duke University Press, 2001). The Russian volume in the excellent Palgrave/Duke series, with chapters on the presidency, parties, policies, and the non-Russian former Soviet republics.

ELECTORAL SYSTEMS

One of the hallmarks of a democracy is an electoral system in which every citizen can take part in regular, free, and fair elections. However, elections are truly fair only if every vote cast has equal weight and if seats are divided among candidates competing for office in a way that reflects the balance of opinion in the electorate. Ideally, electoral systems should also produce stable governments, where a single party is in charge or a workable coalition of two or more parties can be agreed. Unfortunately, these ideals are difficult to achieve, because the math of most electoral systems means that some votes are worth more than others. In an effort to achieve a more balanced system, several different electoral systems have been developed, which fall into one of four categories: plurality, majority, proportional representation, and combination systems.

- **The plurality system.** Otherwise known as winner-take-all or first-past-the-post, this is used for elections to the lower chamber in most English-speaking democracies, including the United States, Canada, and Britain. The country is divided into districts with roughly equal population size, and each district is contested by candidates representing different parties. Every voter casts a single vote, and the candidate who wins the most votes wins the seat, regardless of whether the candidate wins a majority.

    The system is simple, usually inexpensive (except in the United States), does not require much thought from voters, and gives each district a single representative. However, because it works in favor of parties that have solid blocks of support around the country (they win seats) and against parties whose support is more widely and thinly spread (they more often come second

or third), it often leads to victorious parties winning a much bigger percentage of seats than votes. It also provides no representation for voters who vote against the winner.

- **The majority system.** This is used in countries such as Australia and France and is set up in such a way as to ensure that the successful candidate must win a majority of the votes. Like the plurality system, it is based on single-member districts, but the similarities end there. Australia uses a system known as **alternative vote,** which requires that voters—instead of casting a single vote—must rank all the candidates running in their district. The candidate with the highest overall score wins. This means that every candidate is voted on by every voter, so the one with the highest average wins. The system demands more thought by voters, who have to develop an opinion about every candidate, and it can also lead to even more disproportionate results than the plurality system.

    Another variant is the **dual ballot,** used for presidential elections in Austria, Finland, France, Portugal, and Russia, and for legislative elections in France. Under this system, multiple candidates compete against one another in the first ballot, and a winner is declared if he or she wins more than half the vote. If no one wins more than half the vote, a second ballot is held that usually involves just the two highest-placed candidates in the first round. The second round is usually preceded by bargaining among parties as the two final candidates try to encourage voters from other parties to support them.

- **Proportional representation (PR).** This is widely used among continental European liberal democracies but has so far been adopted by neither the United States nor Canada. Political parties win seats in proportion to the number of votes they receive, but PR comes in many different forms, none of which produces an exact reflection of the popular vote.

The most basic form is the **party list system.** This divides a country into districts with roughly equal population size that are much bigger than the districts used in the plurality system and that are represented not by a single member but by multiple members. Each of the contesting parties publishes a list of candidates, ranked in order of preference. Voters then choose among the parties, and the seats are divided up among the parties in proportion to the vote they receive. So, in a ten-member district, if Party A wins 50 percent of the vote, the first five people on its list are elected. If Party B wins 30 percent of the vote, the first three people on its list are elected, and so on. A threshold is also usually used so that no party wins any seats unless it wins at least 5 percent of the vote.

A more complex form of PR is the **single transferable vote (STV).** Voters must choose at least one candidate and then declare their preference for as many other candidates as they like, writing *1* next to the name of their favorite, *2* next to their second choice, and so on. To be elected, a candidate must win a minimum number of votes (or a quota), which is worked out by dividing the number of valid voting papers cast by the number of seats to be filled plus one. So if the number of votes cast in a district is 500,000, and there are five seats to fill, the quota would be $500,000/5 + 1 = 83,000$. First preference votes are then counted, and any candidate winning more than 83,000 votes is elected. All the surplus votes for winning candidates are then transferred to other candidates. So if Joe Smith wins 100,000 first preference votes, his surplus is 17,000. All 100,000 of his first-preference votes are examined again to establish the distribution of second-preference votes among the other candidates. If Ann Jones receives 80,000 of the second-preference votes cast by Joe Smith supporters, then in addition to the 70,000 first-preference votes she has received (not enough to get her elected), she receives $17,000/100,000 = 0.17$ of an additional vote for each second preference, or $80,000 \times 0.17 = 13,600$ votes. This puts her above the 83,000 minimum, and she is elected.

Although this is an achingly complex system as far as the electoral officials are concerned, it gives voters much more control over how their votes are used than is the case with the party list system. It also ensures that no votes are wasted, because voters know that all their preferences will be taken into account. It was used in the United Kingdom for the first time in the Northern Ireland assembly elections in 1998.

- **Combination systems.** These use plurality and PR together, with some seats being decided with one system and others with the second system. The main advantage is that voters end up being tied to individual representatives and smaller parties are able to win seats. Combinations are used for legislative elections in Japan and Russia and have also been used for elections to the Scottish and Welsh regional assemblies in Britain. For example, Scotland has 129 seats in its assembly, 73 of which are decided by the plurality system, and the remaining 56 of which are divided among 8 parliamentary regions, each represented by seven members. Voters cast two ballots: one for their constituency member and one for a party. Constituency winners are determined by a plurality, and the regional seats are divided among the parties according to the proportion of the seats they win. The plurality system usually works in favor of bigger parties, whereas the regional system works in favor of smaller parties, which tend to win no seats under the plurality system.

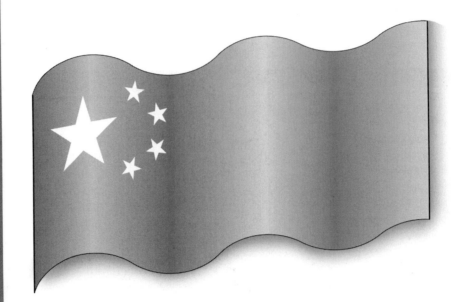

CHAPTER 5

CHINA

CHINA: QUICK FACTS

Official name: People's Republic of China (Zhonghua Renmin Gonghe Guo)

Capital: Beijing

Area: 3,695,000 square miles (9,571,300 sq. km) (slightly larger than the United States)

Languages: Predominantly standard or Mandarin Chinese, with many dialects and several minority languages

Population: 1,272 million

Population density: 351 per square mile

Population growth rate: 1.3 percent

POLITICAL INDICATORS

Freedom House rating: Not Free

Date of state formation: 1949

System type: Socialist republic

Constitution: Published 1982

Administration: Unitary

Executive: Premier and State Council

Legislature: Unicameral National People's Congress of nearly 3,000 members, with Standing Committee of 20 members; members of Congress serve 5-year terms

Party structure: Dominated by the Chinese Communist party (CCP)

Judiciary: No separate judiciary

Head of state: President Hu Jintao (2003–)

Head of government: Premier Wen Jiabao (2003–)

ECONOMIC INDICATORS

GDP (2001): $1.16 trillion

Per capita GDP: $890

Distribution of GDP: Services 34 percent, industry 51 percent, agriculture 15 percent

Urban population: 32 percent

SOCIAL INDICATORS

HDI ranking: 87

Infant mortality rate: 32 per 1,000 live births

Life expectancy: 70.3 years

Literacy: 84 percent of people aged 15 and older

Religions: None officially sanctioned, but Confucianism, Taoism, and Buddhism were traditionally prevalent

A note on spelling: There are two systems for the Romanized spelling of Chinese words and names: the 19th-century Wade-Giles system and the Hanyu Pinyin system preferred by China today. This text uses Hanyu Pinyin, but gives Wade-Giles equivalents where they are more familiar.

INTRODUCTION

The West has had to rethink its views of Russia in the last few years, but this could just be a prelude to the dramatically different role China may be about to play in the world. Recent recalculations of economic data suggest that China has the world's second biggest economy, a discovery that has led to a spate of predictions that it could become the world's next economic superpower. This depends, though, on three major factors: Will the free-market tendencies that China has seen in the last decade persist? Will political liberalization keep pace? And will Chinese leaders be able to control the speed of change and avoid the shock therapy that Russians have had to endure?

Although China's economic potential has been clear to China watchers for a long time, it became headline news in 1994 when the World Bank—using questionable official statistics and the purchasing power parity (PPP) method—announced that the Chinese economy was much bigger than previously thought. The news encouraged the major liberal democracies to take a new interest in the Chinese market. The figures have since grown further, and in 2001 China had a GDP of $5.5 trillion in PPP terms, placing it second only to the United States. But the figure should be treated with caution; conventional calculations of GDP put the figure at just $1.16 trillion, making it the sixth biggest in the world. And in relative terms it is still a poor country because its per capita GDP is just $890 (or $4,260 using PPP calculations).

The most notable feature of the People's Republic of China (PRC) is its sheer size. It has about the same land area as the United States, but it has nearly five times the population—with nearly 1.3 billion people, it is by far the most populous country in the world. That population is relatively young and, because most of China is uncultivable mountain or desert, is concentrated along the east coast, where 90 percent of the population lives on 17 percent of the land. No surprise, then, that some of the biggest and most crowded cities in the world are in China, including Shanghai (13.5 million) and the capital, Beijing (11.3 million).

Despite the positive economic growth figures, an estimated one-third of all Chinese live in poverty, and two-thirds live in the rural areas and make a living off the land. More than half of China's wealth is generated by industry, with services making a relatively modest contribution of 34 percent of GDP. China is the world's biggest coal producer and has rich deposits of iron ore, but it lacks mining and distribution capacity. Self-sufficient in oil until the mid-1990s, it now has to import more of its energy needs. All of China's postrevolutionary leaders have agreed on the need for industrialization and modernization, but they have disagreed on the means of achieving those ends. In the 1950s and 1960s, Mao Zedong occasionally used draconian measures to build the national economy through mass mobilization and Stalinist 5-year plans. In the 1980s, his successors liberalized the economy, encouraging a limited free market, consumerism, and an open-door policy toward the West that continues today.

In social terms, China is relatively homogeneous. The vast majority of its people are ethnic Han Chinese, and only about 7 percent belong to an ethnic minority (of which there are about 55 to 60). But given the sheer size of China, some of those minorities are big enough to make up the population of a medium-sized country: There are about 17 million Thais, 6 million Mongols, and 5 million Tibetans. Many

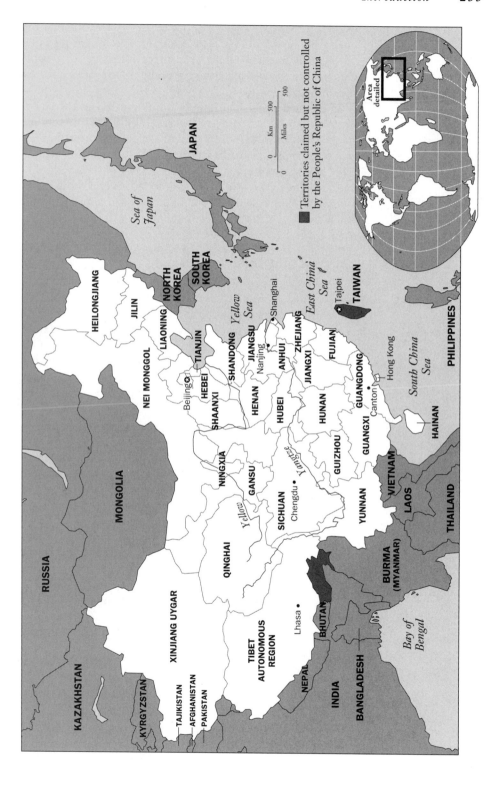

of these groups live in areas thought to have rich mineral resources, and others live on the borders of China, close enough to related groups in other countries to pose a potential threat to China's territorial integrity. To complicate matters, the Han Chinese tend to see aliens as culturally inferior and have had a poor record of assimilating minorities.

In political terms, China underwent dramatic and often confusing changes during the 20th century that pulled it in several different directions. For centuries it sat in splendid isolation, but the arrival of European traders in the 19th century paved the way for changes in the first half of the 20th century that left China struggling to build a new identity and a viable system of government. These changes included a nationalist revolution in 1911 that ended several thousand years of imperial rule, a second revolution in 1927–1928 that brought a decade of quasi-fascist nationalism, and a civil war that launched China in 1949 on a course of socialism that was confused by the often idiosyncratic ideas of Mao Zedong.

Chinese politics since the revolution has been commonly described with words such as *corporatism*, *obedience*, and *bureaucracy*, rather than *individualism* or *democracy*,[1] and policy has been heavily influenced by the personalities of leaders such as Mao and his most prominent successor, Deng Xiaoping. China today is more stable and peaceful than it has been for decades, and a new generation of pragmatic and technocratic leaders has brought economic liberalization. However, it still has a poor record on human rights, the Chinese Communist party still has a monopoly on government, and power is determined by struggles within the ruling elite rather than by the wishes of the citizens.

POLITICAL DEVELOPMENT

China has the longest recorded history of any country in the world, dating back more than 3,600 years. For most of that time, the Chinese lived under an imperial system of government, relatively untouched by the outside world. China called itself Zhongguo (Middle Kingdom), thought of itself almost literally as the center of the world, and regarded all other cultures as peripheral. Chinese culture was rich and sophisticated, making great strides in the arts and the sciences and developing an intricate political system and social structure. However, the old imperial China is not the modern socialist China, which is mainly a product of events that have taken place in the last 90 years, including three revolutions (1911, 1927–1928, and 1949), periods of near anarchy, and lengthy debates about the goals of political, economic, and social development.

The Imperial Era (1766 B.C.–A.D. 1911)

Prerevolutionary China was based on an agrarian economy and governed by the ideas of Confucius (551–479 B.C.), a philosopher who lived during the late Zhou dynasty. **Confucianism** was a secular and ethical system of moral rules and principles, but although it was akin to a religion, it had no institutionalized church and was more tolerant toward other systems of thought than Christianity. Officially denounced in the 1970s as the root of all China's evils, it is now being taken more seriously again.

Confucian theory taught the importance of obeying the authority of the emperor, but it also promoted "government by goodness," arguing that the emperor (the Son of Heaven) had the right to govern (the Mandate of Heaven) only so long as he ruled with honor and virtue. If rulers set a good example, they would not have to use coercion to rule; if they did not, the right to rule could be withdrawn. The government of goodness also depended on all citizens knowing their roles, so Confucianism provided a social code governing interpersonal relationships, emphasizing (like Japan) conformity and self-discipline and discouraging individualism. Emperors ruled through senior government officials, or mandarins, who won appointment through an examination system that was theoretically open to anyone but that was based largely on a test of their "morality" and knowledge of Confucian ethics. The mandarins formed a small but powerful ruling elite, running a sprawling and hierarchical bureaucracy.

The decline and fall of the last of China's 24 imperial dynasties—the Qing Manchus (1644–1911)—began in the early 19th century when the dynasty was unable to respond to the needs of a growing population for land and food. Imperial credibility was further weakened by the opium war with Britain in 1839–1842, which resulted in China being forced to open its doors to traders and missionaries from the outside world and to cede harbors (such as Hong Kong and Shanghai) to European powers. Growing resentment sparked the Taiping Rebellion of 1850–1864, led by the failed Confucian scholar Hong Xiuquan, who believed he was Jesus Christ's younger brother and responsible for bringing Christian morality to China. The rebellion cost an estimated 20 to 40 million lives before being put down with Western help. Financially and politically drained, the Manchus suffered a final blow when China was ignominiously defeated by Japan in the war of 1894–1895.

Nationalism and Chaos (1911–1949)

With pressures for revolutionary change mounting, Sun Yat-sen (1866–1925), an expatriate Chinese physician, founded a secret society among Chinese living abroad in 1894. From headquarters in Tokyo and Hanoi, Sun's followers launched a number of attacks on the Manchu regime, finally succeeding (on their 11th attempt) in October 1911. However, Sun's government relied on the military for its authority, was undermined by continuing Western inroads into China, understood little about how Western democracy worked, and was unable to win the allegiance of the people; it soon lost control and China fell into chaos.

Between 1916 and 1926, China was torn apart by warlords fighting among themselves for power. Sun was nominally leader, but he had no real power or credibility. In 1922, having failed to win help from the West, Sun signed an agreement with the Soviet Comintern through which he received help to transform his Nationalist party (the **Guomindang**) and to provide arms and training for the Chinese army. In the interests of national reunification, he also entered a brief and acrimonious coalition with the new Chinese Communist party (CCP), which had been founded in 1921.

When Sun died in 1925, he was replaced by his senior military commander, Chiang Kai-shek (1886–1975), who abhorred communism and set about defeating the warlords and uniting China. In an attempt to unify the Nationalists, Chiang launched a lightning strike against the CCP in June 1927 (the "Shanghai Massacre")

TABLE 5.1

Key Dates in Chinese History

1815	First British envoys arrive in China
1839–1842	Opium wars with Britain; Britain gains Hong Kong
1850–1864	Taiping rebellion
1894–1895	Sino-Japanese war
1911	Nationalist revolution
1916–1926	Era of the warlords
1921	Founding of the Chinese Communist party
1925	Death of Sun Yat-sen
1927	Shanghai massacre
1927–1937	China under Guomindang rule
1934–1935	Long March
1937–1945	Sino-Japanese war
1945–1949	Chinese civil war
1949	Proclamation of People's Republic of China and of the Republic of China (Taiwan)
1949–1953	Land redistribution program and execution of 2 to 4 million owners of large estates
1951	China invades Tibet
1950–1953	Korean War
1953	First 5-year plan
1954	First constitution of China published
1958–1960	Great Leap Forward
1964	China detonates its first atom bomb
1966–1969	Great Proletarian Cultural Revolution
1971	China admitted to UN; Taiwan expelled
1972	Meeting of Mao Zedong and Richard Nixon
1975	Death of Chiang Kai-shek
1976	(January) Death of Zhou Enlai and (September) Mao Zedong
1979	(February–March) Chinese invasion of Vietnam
1982	New constitution brings an end to Maoism
1986	China applies for GATT membership
1989	(June 4) Tiananmen Square massacre; Dalai Lama wins Nobel prize for peace
1992	CCP declares establishment of a market economy an official goal
1995	(February) China's population reaches 1.2 billion
1997	(February) death of Deng Xiaoping; (July) Hong Kong returned to China after 155 years of British rule
1999	(May) NATO bombing of Chinese Embassy in Belgrade; (December) Macau returned to China after 442 years of Portuguese rule
2001	(December) China joins the World Trade Organization
2002	Jiang Zemin retires as CCP general secretary and is replaced by Hu Jintao

and expelled Soviet advisors. He then set up his own right-wing nationalist government in Nanjing, which was widely recognized in the West as the legitimate government of China. Although he improved the administrative and educational systems and built a modern German-trained army, Chiang made the fatal mistake of doing nothing about land reform, leaving the peasants poor and unhappy.

Some Chinese now began seeing the solution to their problems in the work of the CCP. Outlawed by Chiang in 1927, it was forced to survive as underground groups in cities and as small experimental councils in the rural areas. It came under the influence of Mao Zedong, who built a base of support in Jiangxi province, to which the party headquarters was moved in 1931. Three years later, a Guomindang campaign forced Mao to uproot his 150,000 followers and move them west and then north on the 6,000-mile **Long March.** The migration lasted a year, and the party lost almost 90 percent of its number to disease, starvation, and nationalist attacks, but Mao was now beyond the reach of the nationalists and he was able to strengthen his control over the CCP.

In 1936 Chiang was obliged to agree to a second alliance with the CCP to stave off the Japanese, who had invaded Manchuria in 1931 and begun moving southward. Mao's Red Army suffered repeated military defeats but nevertheless expanded its membership; by 1945, when Japan surrendered and civil war broke out in China between the Guomindang and the Red Army, Mao was in a strong position. Attempts by the United States to mediate failed, and in 1949 Chiang fled with his followers to Taiwan, an island off the coast of mainland China. On October 1, 1949, the People's Republic of China was proclaimed in Beijing.

The Communist Era (1949–)

China under communism has been relatively united and relatively immune from outside interference. Within its borders, however, there has been enormous social upheaval, considerable violence, disruptive political change, and a vocal debate about how best to achieve the goals of socialism. The **shifting lines** of the debate saw radicals wanting to force the process by pursuing an ideological commitment to Marxism-Leninism-Maoism and pragmatists arguing that change needed more than an ideological commitment.

Mao clearly played a central role in the creation of the PRC and the restoration of China's independence, but his leadership was flawed, especially after 1957; his goals of combating bureaucracy, improving health care and education, and encouraging popular participation and self-reliance were laudable, but the methods he used were often self-defeating.[2] He saw his first priority as the redistribution of land, which was still in the hands of a privileged few; the majority of Chinese were tenant farmers. In 1950, 300 million landless peasants were given their own plots, but it soon became obvious that many of these plots were too small to support a family, so the government set up new and bigger cooperatives, borrowing from Stalin's program of collectivization.

Mao's second priority was to build industry. He initially followed the Stalinist model of long-term centralized planning based on 5-year plans. These produced impressive growth rates, but they relied too heavily on professionals and bureaucrats, ignoring millions of peasants. To promote debate on how the party should relate to the people, to reduce the urban-rural divide, and to diffuse the growing criticism of his policies, Mao in 1957 allowed public discussion of China's problems, declaring that he would "let one hundred flowers bloom, let one hundred schools of thought contend." Alarmed at the extent to which his critics took up his invitation, he then decided to decentralize industry and agriculture and—by substituting capital (of which China had little) with manpower—encourage the Chinese to use their own resources to launch the **Great Leap Forward** (1958–1960).

Vowing that China would progress "20 years in a day," Mao mobilized the peasant masses, put the unemployed to work, forced the employed to work harder under almost military discipline, and launched a systematic program of indoctrination to create a new breed of "complete communists" and a classless society. The Great Leap Forward ended in failure, in part because peasants received little reward for their labor. Matters were made worse by a fallout between China and the USSR, the withdrawal of Soviet technical aid, and floods and famines in 1959–1961 that led to an estimated 15 to 20 million deaths. Agriculture was set back by nearly a decade, and Mao, heavily criticized for being arrogant and impatient, came close to losing power. The new president of China, Liu Shaoqi, effectively became the leader of the country and quickly moved to reintroduce private farming plots and markets.

In an attempt to regain his lost influence, Mao turned his attention to ideological reform and in 1966 launched a program of mass criticism known as the **Great Proletarian Cultural Revolution.** Supposedly a debate on the nature of the revolution, it was actually a scheme to neutralize Mao's opponents by attacking bureaucrats, "intellectuals," Confucianism, and those accused of wanting to follow the "capitalist road," such as Liu Shaoqi and Deng Xiaoping (then CCP general secretary). Radical students known as Red Guards ran criticism sessions, and tens of millions of leaders and "intellectuals" (anyone with a high school education) were sent to the rural areas to work on the land and to discuss Maoist thought, as contained in the famous *Little Red Book* (see People in History, p. 239). Public education and government came to a virtual standstill, Deng Xiaoping was disgraced, and Liu Shaoqi was dismissed in 1968. (He died in prison in 1969 but was later hailed as a hero.)

The period 1966–1976 is now described as the Ten Catastrophic Years. The early 1970s saw an aging Mao withdraw from public life, and China increasingly came under the steadying influence of premier Zhou Enlai, one of the most widely respected of all China's modern leaders. Zhou began rebuilding the economy and the bureaucracy and established a collective leadership for the party. The deaths of both Zhou and Mao in 1976 intensified a power struggle that had been brewing since 1973 between radicals and pragmatists. Mao's widow, Jiang Qing, and three other radicals formed a **"Gang of Four,"** which worked to continue Maoist ideas. They were quickly arrested by Mao's designated successor, Hua Guofeng; put on trial; and later jailed for life.

Hua was never able to build a solid base of support, and through most of the 1980s, China was under a collective leadership: The party was run by general secretary Hu Yaobang and the government by premier Zhao Ziyang, while Deng Xiaoping (who had been rehabilitated in 1974) functioned as the power behind the throne. Deng implemented a policy of Four Modernizations: industry, agriculture, national defense, and science and technology. Where Mao had looked for a Chinese road to socialism, Deng spoke of "socialism with Chinese characteristics." He also oversaw the

MAO ZEDONG

The towering influence in the history of China during the 20th century was Mao Zedong (1893–1976), instigator of the 1949 communist revolution; leader of China for 27 years; and a man of exceptional personal power, prestige, and ruthlessness.

Mao was born in rural Hunan province in south-central China. In 1918 he was hired as an assistant at Beijing National University by Li Dazhao, a professor of history, economics, and political science. Influenced by Li and by the writings of Marx and Lenin, Mao joined the CCP and in 1928 organized a series of uprisings in Hunan; when these failed he was dismissed from his posts in the CCP. The party split and Mao left for the mountains of Jiangxi province, where he established the Chinese Soviet Republic and became leader of the CCP. In 1931 Chiang Kai-shek launched a series of campaigns against Jiangxi aimed at eliminating the communists, finally forcing Mao to leave with his followers on the Long March. Thousands died on the march (including Mao's first wife), but it established him as a legendary figure and convinced millions that he offered China the best hope for peace.

From a new base in Shaanxi, Mao rebuilt the Red Army, and while China was at war with Japan (1937–1945), he extended his control. The civil war of 1945–1949 ended in victory for the Communists, and Mao became first chairman of the People's Republic of China. His tenure saw the introduction of policies aimed at establishing and cementing a distinctly Chinese revolutionary ideal (the "Chinese Road to Socialism"), which brought many social improvements, but which also brought famine, civil disorder, and economic ruin; Maoism was ultimately responsible for the loss of millions of lives. Despite his failures, he became the focus of a cult of personality and was acclaimed the Great Helmsman (although his second wife, Jiang Qing, became increasingly powerful as Mao grew older and more unsteady). He died in September 1976, at age 82.

The Maoist cult was sustained by the publication of the *Little Red Book* of quotations from Mao.[3] Although many dealt with themes such as public service, personal responsibility, and moral virtue, the more militant have been longer remembered:

- Political power grows out of the barrel of a gun.
- Politics is war without bloodshed, while war is politics with bloodshed.
- All reactionaries are paper tigers.
- People of the world, unite and defeat the U.S. aggressors and all their running dogs!

drafting in 1978 of a new constitution that established liberalizing tendencies, leading some to call democracy the **Fifth Modernization.**

Deng's economic reforms went well beyond anything envisaged in the USSR by Mikhail Gorbachev. Mao had argued that elements of capitalism could be used as a means to the end of achieving true socialism; Deng developed this idea by running the economy on a mixture of capitalism and socialism, allowing factories and farms to produce for market demand as long as they filled their basic state quotas and to buy raw materials through the market rather than depending on central allocation; he also allowed more prices to be set by supply and demand. Whether China has adopted capitalism or has merely changed the way in which it plans and manages socialism is a topic of debate inside China and abroad. Deng himself said in the early 1960s that he supported private farming, arguing: "It doesn't matter if the cat is black or white as long as it catches mice." Whatever the truth is, economic liberalization has led to rapid growth and a consumer boom that at times has threatened to run out of control.

Although Deng Xiaoping was able during the early 1980s to replace conservatives at the head of the party and the government, he was unable to take complete control. The party elected the conservative Li Peng to the post of premier in 1987, dismaying members of the growing Chinese pro-democracy movement. In the autumn of 1988, Li launched an austerity program in an attempt to control inflation. In April 1989 the death of the reformist general secretary of the CCP, Hu Yaobang, encouraged students to put up posters and hold meetings, ostensibly as a memorial to Hu, but actually to draw wider attention to their demands for democracy and freedom. By late April, peaceful pro-democracy demonstrations had begun to grow in several major towns and cities. More than a million students occupied **Tiananmen Square** in Beijing, demanding greater democracy and an end to corruption[4] and planning to occupy the square until the June 20 meeting of the Chinese legislature, the National People's Congress.

When a number of party leaders (most notably Zhao Ziyang, the new CCP general secretary) appeared willing to talk to the students and to support political reform, the way was cleared for the opening of the most serious battle within the CCP since the Cultural Revolution. Conservatives such as Premier Li Peng and President Yang Shangkun were pitted against reformers such as Zhao, presenting the party with a crisis of credibility.

Fears that the demonstrations would spread led to a clampdown on June 3–4, when the army was sent in to break them up, a move endorsed by Deng Xiaoping. No one knows how many died in and around the square; the government claimed about 200 (most of whom were soldiers), but Western media estimates went as high as 7,000. The most generally accepted figures are now in the range of 1,000 to 1,500, a toll that included soldiers from the Beijing garrison, which apparently rebelled and took the side of the students. The massacre proved a victory for the conservatives, who strengthened their position when Zhao was removed from all his party posts at the end of June and replaced as general secretary by Jiang Zemin. The West, which had begun to warm to China during the 1980s, was suddenly reminded once again of the repressive nature of Chinese government. At the same time, it also became clear that a generation gap was emerging and that many younger Chinese no longer shared the political views of their elders.

China Today

China since Mao has been described as a "consultative authoritarian" regime, meaning that the Communist party has increasingly recognized the need to gauge public opinion and win public support but still suppresses dissent and retains ultimate political power.[5] Deng began working in the mid-1980s to raise a "third generation" of leaders who would continue building on his economic and political reforms, but he became increasingly frail and reclusive and it was clear that his reforms were still not complete when he died in February 1997. An intensified struggle for power followed and was resolved in September when Jiang Zemin, Deng's hand-picked successor, was reelected as general secretary of the CCP. Questions surfaced about his hold on power, and there were concerns abroad that he may have had plans for a newly assertive foreign policy, but—except for an aggressive posture toward Taiwan—China under Jiang was relatively quiet and continued to build links with its Asian neighbors and its major trading partners.

In 2001 China's place in the global economic system underwent a fundamental change when it joined the World Trade Organization (WTO). Membership means that China must open up its markets to foreign investors and importers, and it also means that there is more pressure for China's economic policies to be coordinated with those of other WTO members. The economy is growing rapidly, and Chinese products are working their way into consumer markets all over the world; it is virtually impossible, for example, to buy children's toys in the United States that are not made in China. But there are important economic concerns, such as underdeveloped industrial infrastructure, growing unemployment, and pressure for the government to create as many as 9 million jobs annually just to keep up.

Meanwhile, political change continues. In 2002–2003, China underwent its most substantial change of leadership since the 1970s, bringing in a so-called **"fourth generation."** It began in November 2002 when Jiang Zemin was replaced as party leader by Hu Jintao. (See People in Politics, p. 247) Formerly vice president of China, Hu had been identified 10 years before as Jiang's successor by Deng Xiaoping.[6] Hu's hold on the leadership was strengthened in March 2003 when he also became China's president. Although this is a job with more symbolic power than real power, it nonetheless ended Jiang's formal leadership role. Meanwhile, Wen Jiabao replaced Zhu Rongji as premier of China in March 2003, and Wu Bangguo replaced Li Peng as chairman of the Standing Committee of the National People's Congress. In short, in the space of just 4 months, the entire leadership of China had been replaced; in the process, the average age of the leaders dropped from 74 years to about 62.

POLITICAL CULTURE

Several thousand years of political continuity gave imperial China a political culture that was both stable and sophisticated. The imperial system was bound together by Confucian ideals that emphasized morality and authoritarianism and by social and political systems that were both elitist and hierarchical. The 1949 revolution had a disruptive effect on political values and norms, but it did not completely clean the slate; many elements of traditional political culture remain intact, although many new values and norms have emerged.

Kinship and Communalism

Like Japan, China has traditionally been a collective society marked by group orientation. Individual well-being, economic security, and the definition of political functions were traditionally based around kinship and the family unit, outside of which few social organizations existed. The head of the family was held responsible for the behavior of members of the group, who could bring collective honor or shame to the family. Recourse to the law or to the intervention of government officials was rare, because most disputes were settled locally and family heads were responsible for punishing wrongdoers. In short, everyone became his brother's keeper.[7] A good example of the emphasis on the group is the strategy known as "creating your own society," under which a group takes care of itself. For example, if a construction unit is employed on a major new project, it will provide its own housing, education, and health facilities rather than relying on government agencies.[8]

The Importance of Consensus

It may sometimes seem as though China since 1949 has lurched back and forth between rule by conservatives and rule by reformers. In fact, radical change has consistently been rejected, delayed, or watered down in the interest of reaching a consensus.[9] Allied to this has been a traditional preference for gradual and cautious change. A good example was the issue of restoring ranks to the Chinese military; the idea was first proposed in 1980, and the army received new uniforms in 1984, but because of disagreements between retired and active officers over whether the retired officers should receive formal ranks, the ranks were not actually restored until October 1988.[10] The emphasis on consensus and gradualism may also explain why China has achieved many of the same reforms as those once proposed by Mikhail Gorbachev for the USSR, but over a longer period of time and without the same explosive consequences.

The Dominance of the State

Although the legal system may impinge little upon the life of the average Chinese citizen, politics impinges upon their lives almost daily. Even the most minimal political activity means regular exposure to propaganda, attendance at meetings, and the regular expression of support for government policy. China since 1949 has witnessed massive and pervasive political education and indoctrination and a system of government whose policy decisions have reached into the home, the school, the workplace, and every other sphere of human existence to a greater extent than in almost any other society (including Stalinist Russia). This has created a society that emphasizes the state, the party, and the idea of mass cooperation at the expense of individualism and competition. At the same time, though, Chinese political culture is not opposed to political liberalization, and one of the challenges that continues to face the CCP is correctly gauging the pressures for democratic change. Its grip on society has loosened in recent years and with it the dominance of the state.

POLITICAL SYSTEM

One school of thought in political science questions whether it is worth studying formal political institutions, on the grounds that they do not tell the real story about how government and politics works. About few societies is this question more often asked than China. Institutions are a façade for a complex and changeable political process where everything is not as it seems, and understanding how decisions are made involves reading between the lines. The gap that exists between formal structures and informal realities can be summarized in four key principles:

- China is a **unitary state** in which all significant power is centralized in the national government. Although it officially subscribes to Leninist democratic centralism, local government has little independence. The sheer size of China suggests that a federal system might be more suitable, and although there has been a continuing debate about how much power should be delegated to local government, this enormous country is still governed by a small group of people based at the apex of government in the capital city of Beijing.

- All real power lies with the **Chinese Communist party.** As in the former USSR, China has an intricate governmental structure, with a cabinet, a legislature, and a network of supporting agencies and mass organizations. But they do little more than legitimize the decisions already taken by the party leadership and subscribe to the authority of that leadership.[11] The relationship between party and government has been described as one between a principal and an agent: The party has formal political authority (based mainly on its power to appoint and promote government officials), while the government does the actual work of running the country.[12]

- Deciding who actually runs China can be difficult because **titles are not always what they seem** and there is a mismatch between power and rank.[13] China has had periods of collective leadership; holding formal office is not a requirement for leadership; and identifying the source of real power is less a question of understanding the political hierarchy and the powers of officeholders than of understanding links across institutions, personal networks, and the standing of key figures in the system. For example, Deng Xiaoping, "paramount leader" of China from 1978, never held any of the highest offices in government and formally retired in 1987, yet he remained de facto leader of China by virtue of his personal power and influence until his death in 1997. Even though Jiang Zemin left most of his offices in 2002–2003, it seemed that he too wished to pull strings from behind the scenes.

- There has long been **an important supporting role for the military in politics.** During the Cultural Revolution, when government broke down, the military became the dominant political institution. In recent years, as power has shifted from a generation of leaders who were veterans of the Long March and the sustained guerrilla war of the 1930s and 1940s, the power and influence of the military has declined. However, it was still strong enough to cause sleepless nights for China's leaders during the Tiananmen Square demonstrations in 1989, when some units of the People's Liberation Army (PLA) took the side of the demonstrators.

THE CONSTITUTION

In liberal democracies, constitutions usually focus on the structure of government and the rights of individuals, and the political parties play an independent and separate role in government. By contrast, the Chinese constitution describes the system of government *and* spells out the programs and policies of the CCP. These programs and policies are further elaborated in the constitution of the CCP itself, which in many ways is more politically significant than the state constitution, is more regularly revised, and offers important indicators of new policy directions being taken by China's government.

████ **T A B L E 5 . 2** ████

Political Institutions in China

Party	Government	Bureaucracy
	President: Hu Jintao, 2003–	
General Secretary Hu Jintao, 2002–	**Chairman** Wu Bangguo, 2003–	**Premier** Wen Jiabao, 2003–
Standing Committee 6–8 members. Apex of the Chinese political system. Meets regularly.	**Standing Committee** About 135 members. Meets bimonthly	**Standing Committee** About 15 members: premier, vice premiers, senior counselors. Meets twice weekly.
Politburo 18–28 members elected by Central Committee. Meets monthly.		
Central Committee About 200 senior party members. Meets annually for varying periods.		**State Council** About 60–70 members; premier, vice premiers, heads of ministries and commissions. Meets monthly.
National Party Congress About 2,000 delegates; meets once every 5 years for 1–2 weeks to confirm party policy.	**National People's Congress** Unicameral, with 2,970 members elected by provincial congresses. Meets once per year for 2–3 weeks.	
Local party groups Provincial, county, and primary party organizations.	**Local, county and** **provincial congresses**	**Government ministries**

There have been four state constitutions since 1949. The first, published in 1954 after several years of debate, was replaced by new versions in 1975, 1978, and 1982. Together with their various amendments, each provides a good indication of the changed thinking of new leaders. For example, the 1954 constitution reflected Mao's ideas on government and society, and although these themes can be traced through the 1975 and 1978 versions, the 1982 constitution finally deleted lavish praise for Mao. Each of the revisions also steadily shifted powers from the state to the party, and recent amendments have shown growing acceptance of the role of the non-state sector of the economy, which has moved from being "a complement to the socialist public economy" to being "an important component of the socialist market economy."[14]

The 1982 state constitution took 2 years to draft and was reportedly read and debated at several million meetings held across the country before being adopted by the National People's Congress in December 1982. With 138 articles, it is one of the longest constitutions in the world. It describes China as "a socialist state under the people's democratic dictatorship led by the working class and based on the alliance of workers and peasants." It emphasizes the importance of continuing "socialist modernization" and argues that it is China's fundamental goal to follow the socialist road and "step by step to turn China into a socialist country." Although it vests all power in the people, it also emphasizes that China is led by the CCP, functioning as the vanguard of the people under the guidance of Marxism-Leninism-Mao Zedong Thought.

Articles 33–65 contain an impressive list of the rights and duties of citizens, including freedom of speech, the press, assembly, association, demonstration, and religion and the right to criticize any state organ or functionary. However, Article 51 says that the exercise of personal rights may not infringe upon the interests of the state or society, or upon the freedoms and rights of other citizens, and Article 54 prohibits acts "detrimental to the security, honor and interests" of China. These clauses clearly allow the party or the government to neutralize any dissent regarded as being against the national interest and to limit the civil rights and liberties listed in the constitution.

THE EXECUTIVE: STATE COUNCIL

The highest executive office in the Chinese state system is the State Council, the nearest functional equivalent to a cabinet. Normally meeting once per month, the Council is elected by the National People's Congress and consists of the premier of China, as many as a dozen vice premiers, and the heads (and their deputies) of ministries and government departments. Membership of the Council has occasionally been as low as 30 but currently runs at about 60 to 70.

Until the late 1980s, when it began to develop some independence, the Council was little more than the executive arm of the party, responsible for making sure party policies were implemented by government ministers. Membership of the Council overlapped with that of the Central Committee and Politburo of the party, where most policy decisions were made, leaving the Council with little more than executive responsibilities. The Council has begun to reassert itself in recent years, though, particularly as the former military heads of ministries have been replaced by a new generation of civilian technocrats.

Because meetings of the full Council are too large to function efficiently, the key decisions are made by a small inner cabinet consisting of a **premier** and a group of vice premiers (about 15 people in all). The premier, the nearest equivalent to a prime minister in a parliamentary system, is arguably the second most powerful person in China after the leader of the party. The dominating personality in the history of Chinese executive politics was Zhou Enlai, premier from 1949 until his death in 1976. Thanks to Zhou's close relationship with Mao, membership of the Council remained stable during the Cultural Revolution and the Council was a pool of relative calm during the upheaval of the revolution.[15]

Zhou, a moderate, had groomed Deng Xiaoping to be his successor as premier, but Deng was purged in January 1976 following Zhou's death. Zhou was followed by Hua Guofeng and the pragmatist Zhao Ziyang, a linchpin of the collective leadership that governed China through the mid-1980s. In 1982 a decision was made to limit premiers to two consecutive 5-year terms. In 1987 the office went to Li Peng, foster son of Zhou Enlai and one of the key figures in the suppression of the 1989 democracy movement. Despite his public unpopularity and regular predictions in the early 1990s that his downfall was imminent, he began a second term as premier in 1992. He was succeeded in 1998 by Zhu Rongji, architect of China's recent economic reforms.

Zhu retired in 2003 after just one term and was replaced by Wen Jiabao. Trained as a geologist and with a good reputation as a communicator, Wen was one of the most popular members of the party leadership, serving as vice premier before being promoted to the top job in government. As premier, he is charged with overseeing China's economic policy.

THE LEGISLATURE: NATIONAL PEOPLE'S CONGRESS

Theoretically the "highest organ of state power," the unicameral **National People's Congress** (NPC) is the nearest equivalent China has to a legislature. Its members are elected for 5-year terms, although these can be shortened or lengthened. The Congress normally meets once per year, but during the Cultural Revolution it met only once in 10 years. On paper, it represents the people of China and has the power to make and enforce laws, to amend the constitution, to designate and remove the premier and the State Council, and to elect the president of the Supreme People's Court. In reality, its powers are limited in several ways:

- It is huge and unwieldy. Its membership began at 1,226 members in 1954, peaked at a staggering 3,459 members in 1978, and was down to just under 3,000 in the Tenth NPC (2003–2008).

- Although the NPC has the power to discuss, pass, and oversee the execution of laws, it is allowed to do little more than discuss and endorse decisions already made by the party.

- Delegates are only indirectly elected by the people. Voters elect local congresses, which elect county congresses, which elect provincial congresses, which finally elect the NPC. Membership is structured so that workers, peasants, intellectuals, and soldiers have occupational representation, and delegates tend to be appointed as a reward for exemplary work and public service rather than because they have particular administrative abilities. This has raised questions about the quality of delegates and their ability to understand the issues discussed by the Congress.

- Congresses meet only briefly, for one session of 2 to 3 weeks every year (usually in March or April). Even then they rarely meet in full plenary session, spending most of the time in group sessions. During meetings, delegates can question senior government ministers, submit motions, make suggestions, and raise questions about government policy, but there is obviously a limit to what can be achieved.

PEOPLE IN POLITICS

JIANG ZEMIN AND HU JINTAO

In 2002 the world's biggest country had a change of leadership. Yet the event barely made a dent in international news headlines, and the incoming leader was wrapped in a veil of anonymity. His name was Hu Jintao (shown on the right in the photograph), and his accession to the leadership of China was the result not of a popular vote, nor a party vote, nor even of the wishes of his predecessor, but had been arranged years before by a now-dead former leader of China. Questions were immediately asked about just how much power he really had.

The dominating figures in revolutionary Chinese politics have been Mao Zedong and Deng Xiaoping. Just as Deng eventually won control over China following Mao's death in 1976, so it was reasonable to suppose that Deng would be succeeded by a third dominating figure following his death in 1997. The man recruited in 1989 as his successor was Jiang Zemin (shown on the left in the photograph), who was dismissed as a lightweight and was not expected to last long. However, Jiang quickly stepped out from beneath the shadow of Deng, removing his major opponents in the Central Committee and winning control of the CCP, attracting the loyalty of the military, chairing a Politburo that appeared to be in agreement with his policies, deepening the process of economic reform begun by Deng, and developing a strong record on foreign affairs. He made the office his own, but he never developed the charisma or international public recognition of Mao or Deng.

Just as Jiang had been little known internationally upon coming to power, so too was Hu Jintao. Born in 1942, he trained as an engineer and in 1988 became CCP leader in Guizhou province. From 1988 to 1992, Hu was CCP leader in Tibet, where he developed some notoriety for his crackdown on antigovernment protesters. He was promoted to the Politburo in 1992, a sign that he had been informally chosen by Deng Xiaoping as eventual successor to Jiang. He was introduced to the outside world in late 2001 when he undertook a tour of Russia and Europe (but not the United States). He became vice president of China in 1998, CCP general-secretary in November 2002, and president of China in March 2003.

Hu now has the same challenge as Jiang had before him: making the leadership his own. The challenge is complicated by the fact that Jiang had not nominated Hu as his successor and by the fact that Jiang remains active in the background, refusing to give up the chairmanship of the Central Military Commission, thus remaining commander-in-chief of China's vast armed forces.

TABLE 5.3

Postrevolutionary Leaders of China

Party Leader*	Premier	Chairman of Standing Committee of NPC	President of Republic People's of China†
1949 Mao Zedong	1949 Zhou Enlai	1949 Mao Zedong	1949 Mao Zedong
		1959 Liu Shaoqi	1959 Liu Shaoqi
			1966–1982 vacant
		1966 Dong Biwu (acting)	
		1975 Zhu De	
1976 Hua Guofeng	1976 Hua Guofeng	1976–1978 Sung Qingling (acting)	
		1978 Ye Jianying	
	1980 Zhao Ziyang		
1981 Hu Yaobang			
			1982 Li Xiannian
		1983 Peng Zhen	
1987 Zhao Ziyang	1987 Li Peng		
		1988 Wan Li	1988 Yang Shangkun
1989 Jiang Zemin			
		1992 Qiao Shi	
			1993 Jiang Zemin
	1998 Zhu Rongji	1998 Li Peng	
2002 Hu Jintao	2003 Wen Jiabao	2003 Wu Bangguo	2003 Hu Jintao

*Chairman, 1949–1982, then general secretary.
†Chairman of Chinese People's Political Consultative Conference (1949–1954), Chairman of the PRC (1954–1966), and president of China from 1982.
Note: In 1978–1997, the "paramount leader" of China was Deng Xiaoping, who held none of the positions listed above.

- Unlike liberal democratic legislatures, where most of the real work is done in specialist committees, the NPC has no committees. This denies delegates the opportunity to become specialists or to spend time working through the details of legislative proposals and party policy.

Its huge size, short sessions, and lack of real power suggest that the NPC is simply a rubber stamp for the party, but it has not always accepted the party line; it has been known occasionally to criticize the party leadership and, particularly since the

© CORBIS

The National People's Congress in session in the Great Hall of the People, Beijing. The sheer size of China's legislature—coupled with its short meetings—means that it is able to achieve little beyond confirming policy decisions that have already been reached by the Chinese Communist party.

mid-1980s, has not always been unanimous on votes. The NPC certainly has more real powers than the old Supreme Soviet of the USSR.

Standing Committee of the NPC

When the NPC is in recess, its work is carried out by a Standing Committee, which is roughly equivalent to the Presidium of the Supreme Soviet in the former USSR. Elected by the NPC, the Committee meets twice per month and consists of a chairman, several vice chairs, and senior members of Congress. Although membership has run as high as 175, it has settled down in recent years to about 135. The powers of the Committee have changed over time, but they now include the right to declare and enforce martial law, oversee NPC elections, supervise the work of the State Council and Supreme People's Court, appoint and remove members of the State Council on the recommendation of the premier when the NPC is not in session, and serve as the interim NPC when Congress is not in session. It also runs a series of specialist committees dealing with issues such as foreign affairs, finance, and education.

The Chinese Head of State

China has a presidency (and a vice presidency), but the significance of the post has waxed and waned depending on the other positions held by the incumbent. The presidency was usually held by a semiretired former leader of China, but in the 1990s

Jiang Zemin held both the presidency and the job of general secretary of the communist party, as does Hu Jintao today. This combination has made both men more like the president of the United States in the sense that they have both carried out political and nonpolitical jobs at the same time.

The office of president traces its roots back to the 1954 constitution, which provided for the election by the NPC of a chairman and vice chairman of the People's Republic. The chairman effectively became the head of state, with all the ceremonial duties this entailed, but he also had significant political powers: For example, he could hire and fire the premier, vice premiers, and other members of the State Council. Mao was elected first chairman in 1954 but did not stand for reelection in 1959 and so was replaced by Liu Shaoqi. Mao, however, remained chairman of the CCP Central Committee, so Liu was unable to use his position to challenge Mao's leadership and fell from grace in 1966. After several years in abeyance, the powers of chairman and vice chairman were revived by the 1982 constitution when new posts of president and vice president of China were created. Both positions are filled for a maximum of two 5-year terms by a vote of the Standing Committee of the NPC.

The Cadres

Although not exclusively a part of the legislative system, nor of the party system, **cadres** are a defining part of the Chinese system of government. China has the world's biggest bureaucracy and a long history of bureaucratic government. Chinese leaders since 1949 have expanded the bureaucracy, while trying to limit its powers by keeping its structure simple and efficient and making sure that it remains responsive to party pressure. Central to this policy has been the role of the cadre, usually defined simply as a party worker but actually a figure of authority within the party or state bureaucracy, who may or may not be a party member. Cadres include the leaders of production units, officials in public institutions (such as schools or hospitals), members of the PLA, or anyone in a position of leadership.[16]

Mao saw the cadres as revolutionaries who were essential to the promotion of the party line and to the achievement of the goals of the revolution. They are chosen less as a result of educational achievement than because of their ideological correctness, loyalty, hard work, and administrative ability. At the lower levels, they are the primary link between the people and the party and government, and the success or failure of government policies has often depended on the competence and abilities of cadres. For example, they became the focus of both public and party criticism during the Cultural Revolution.

THE JUDICIARY: SUPREME PEOPLE'S COURT

China does not have an independent constitutional court like the United States, Japan, or Russia. Instead, it has a dual judicial system consisting of local people's courts answering to a Supreme People's Court and to a Supreme People's Procuratorate.

The judiciary and law enforcement agencies exist less to protect individual rights than to enforce party and state policies and regulations.[17] Justice is administered through a system of more than 3,000 people's courts at the district, county, municipal, and provincial levels. All these answer to the Supreme People's Court, which is accountable in turn to the NPC. The president of the Supreme Court is elected by the NPC, and its other members are appointed by the NPC Standing Committee. Members of lower-level courts are elected or appointed by the corresponding state organ at each level. For its part, the Procuratorate traces its roots to Chinese imperial days and to the Napoleonic civil code, which also influenced the Soviet legal system. A procurator is a monitor who reviews the work of government bodies, making sure they observe the constitution and deciding whether cases should be brought to trial.

Chinese courts developed a reputation for independence during the 1950s, a reputation that came under attack during the Cultural Revolution, when the formal court system was regularly bypassed. The 1982 constitution restored their independence, although questions remain about the extent to which this is respected in practice. Law enforcement in China relies less on a formal legal system than on ideological control. Whereas the rule of law dominates liberal democracies, the party dominates in China. Class enemies (however that concept is defined) were long treated as different from—and unequal to—class allies, especially during the Cultural Revolution, when the administration of law was taken out of the hands of the formal legal system and placed in the hands of mass groups, notably the Red Guards.

SUBNATIONAL GOVERNMENT

Because it is a unitary state, all effective political power in China rests with the national government and the leadership of the party. Although China subscribes in theory to the principle of democratic centralism, local government has little if any real power or independence.

The most important local government units are the provinces, or *sheng* (22 in all), four major municipalities (Beijing, Chongqing, Shanghai, and Tianjin), two Special Administrative Regions (Hong Kong and Macao), and five "autonomous" regions for ethnic minorities. Provincial government in China is roughly equivalent to state government in the United States, except that all provincial leaders are appointed by central government. Another feature unique to Chinese local government is the military region, of which there are 11. The significance of these regions is heightened by the political role of the military, which—as noted later—has been particularly important during times of civil unrest.

Below the provinces are 210 prefectures *(diqu)*, 2,080 rural counties *(xian)*, and nearly 290 municipal districts and townships *(shi)*. The lowest level of government was once the commune, introduced in 1958 and consisting typically of about 10,000 people. The original intention was that communes would become the focus for almost all political, social, and economic activity and that the government could use them as the front line for the modernization of China. However, most were either too small or too large for the job, and they were finally wound up during the early 1980s. The township has since largely replaced the commune, with powers over the administration of law, education, public health, and family planning. In the rural areas, local administration is overseen by nearly 1 million village committees.

China is a multinational state, although ethnic minorities make up only about 7 percent of the population. Among the minority groups are the Zhuangs, Tibetans,

Mongols, and Koreans. Although small in number, they are spread out so thinly in the more hostile regions of China that they inhabit nearly 60 percent of Chinese territory. More important, most of this territory is on China's borders, raising the constant danger of minority grievances spilling over into border disputes involving related ethnic groups in neighboring countries. The most serious of these problems, and the one that has attracted most world attention, concerns the autonomous region of **Tibet.** Annexed by China in 1951, Chinese troops were sent into Tibet in 1959 to put down a rebellion, and the Dalai Lama, spiritual and political leader of the Tibetan theocracy, went into exile. He has since been joined by more than 10,000 Tibetan refugees and has posed a constant embarrassment to the Chinese government, drawing attention to Chinese repression, agitating for the creation of an autonomous Tibet, and winning the 1989 Nobel prize for peace for his efforts.

THE PEOPLE'S LIBERATION ARMY

Most brief surveys of the politics of different countries pay little attention to the military, except when the military plays an active role in politics (see Chapter 8). One of the exceptions to the rule is China, where the **People's Liberation Army** (PLA) has regularly played a critical political role.

Established in 1927–1928 as the Red Army, its first political officer was Mao Zedong, and its members were at the core of the Long March. During World War II the army perfected its guerrilla warfare techniques, motivated by the strategic ideas that people were more important than weapons and that winning the hearts and minds of the people could overcome even the most sophisticated military hardware (a principle convincingly illustrated in Vietnam in the 1960s and 1970s). The PLA has been involved in few foreign military excursions, being used instead as a means of extending and consolidating internal political control. In many ways, it has been the third major arm of the political structure, working as an extension of the party and the government.

The PLA is not only an army, air force, and navy in the conventional sense, but it also recruits for the party, educates and informs people, and was used by Mao to act as an example to the people. Members of the PLA were encouraged to work on farms and in factories, and the PLA even went so far as to abolish ranks in 1965 in order to stand as an example of egalitarianism. (The ranks were reestablished in the mid-1980s.) During the Cultural Revolution—when regular government effectively broke down and many government posts went unfilled—the PLA took over various administrative duties, kept the Chinese economy functioning, and essentially held the country together. In any other country, it might have used the opportunity to stage a coup; instead, it helped neutralize the Red Guards and restore the party to power.[18]

The PLA came directly under Mao's command and played a vital role in helping Deng Xiaoping win power upon Mao's death in 1976. Since then, the party leadership has tried to reduce the influence of the army by delegating powers of internal security to other agencies, reducing the number of military men in the Politburo, cutting the size of the PLA, and playing down the army's role as the guardian of socialist ideological purity. The tension between the party and the military remains, however. It became particularly obvious during the Tiananmen Square demonstrations just how much the party still relied on the PLA to control dissent and how nervous the party leadership had become about the possibility of an army revolt. That the army would back Deng was not certain; several military regions made it clear they had divided loyalties, and many soldiers were reportedly killed in fighting between rival units. Ultimately, the massacre was spearheaded by the 27th PLA, which helped restore the political power of conservatives within the CCP.

China's armed forces today (at just under 3 million members) are the world's largest. Chinese arms sales are also growing, and China is now the world's fourth largest arms exporter after the United States, Russia, and Germany.

REPRESENTATION AND PARTICIPATION

Voting is a small and relatively insignificant part of political participation in China. Voters elect only the members of their local people's congresses, the schedule of elections is regularly changed, and the party system is dominated by the CCP. How this has affected turnout is difficult to say; official figures have not been released since the 1956 elections, when 86 percent of voters turned out. Because elections are so marginal to an understanding of the Chinese political process, most studies of Chinese politics refer to them only in passing,[19] and more emphasis is placed on other channels through which citizens can take part in the political process, most of which have a more direct effect on party policies. These include mass organizations, mass campaigns, wall posters, and small study groups.

ELECTIONS AND THE ELECTORAL SYSTEM

Chinese voters (the legal voting age is 18) take part directly in only one election, that of delegates to county and district congresses. Every other election above the local level is indirect; members of county or district congresses elect delegates to provincial congresses for 5-year terms. These delegates in turn elect delegates to the NPC for 5-year terms. Although the 1982 constitution fixed the terms of local congressional delegates at 3 years, elections in postrevolutionary China have been sporadic, with as few as 2 years and as many as 13 years between them. The 1982 constitution even stipulates that the term of the NPC can be extended if necessary.

The entire electoral process is overseen by the CCP, which controls the election committees that draw up the approved slates of candidates for every elective office. Until 1980, only one candidate was put forward for each office, so the party effectively determined the outcome of every election. In this sense, elections were little more than exercises in building consensus, with agreement on candidates being decided in advance by the party and the election itself functioning simply as a rubber stamp. Public and media debate in 1978–1979 about the fairness of this system led to changes in electoral laws from 1980; these changes allowed multiple candidates in elections, a more open nomination process, and the use of secret ballots. Little is known in detail about how subsequent local elections have fared; although the party has been known to interfere in the outcome of elections by actively supporting its preferred candidates, unpopular local party officials have occasionally lost reelection.

POLITICAL PARTIES

Political parties in liberal democracies exist to put forward different sets of policy options and leaders, allowing voters to choose the direction in which they want their country to move. Parties are subservient to the state and can be removed or kept in office by voters casting ballots at regular elections. (For more on this, see Comparative Focus, pp. 272–273.)

In China, there is only one significant political party—the Chinese Communist party—and it is the source of all political power, controls all other political organizations, plays a key role in deciding the outcome of elections, and dominates both state and government. Policy changes come not through a change of party at an election or a meaningful public debate, but rather through changes in the balance of power within the leadership of the party. The dominant role of the party is symbolized by the Chinese flag, which consists of one large gold star and four small stars on a red background; the four smaller stars represent the four major classes (peasants, workers, petty bourgeoisie, and owners of enterprises), and the large star represents the party.

(Strictly speaking, China is a multiparty system because there are eight other sanctioned "democratic parties and groups" with alternative policy platforms, including the Democratic League and the National Construction Association. However, they have very few members—numbered in the tens of thousands—and are really little more than professional associations, although they could one day become the nuclei of alternative parties. One of the few direct challenges to CCP rule came in 1998 with the launch of the China Democracy party, which was quickly closed down by the government and its members arrested or harassed.[20])

The CCP in 2003 had a membership of 64 million, making it bigger than many large countries and the largest party political organization in history. Despite this, it remains elitist, since only about 7 percent of the adult population are members. As with the old Communist Party of the Soviet Union (CPSU), membership provides status, career opportunities, and personal influence. Application is a convoluted process, requiring careful screening. Once admitted, a member is expected to perform tasks set by the party; study the works of Marx, Lenin, and Mao; reject factionalism or personal gain; be loyal; undertake self-criticism; and generally set a good example. The Gang of Four apparently launched a "crash admittance" program aimed at boosting party numbers in the mid-1970s; attempts have since been made to weed out "unfit or unqualified" members, with the goal of improving the professionalism and competence of party members in support of China's modernization plans.[21]

Although party membership is growing, the balance of that membership is changing. The drop in the number of urban Chinese employed by state-owned businesses has also meant a fall in the number of party branches that were once so much a part of their lives, and—at least in towns and cities—the party is increasingly associated with government departments and institutions, rather than the economic sector.[22] And where the Chinese would once accept and follow the dictates of the party (at least in public), it is now coming under increased criticism for China's fast-growing crime problems, the steady emergence of an economic class system that has led to the growth of an underclass, and economic changes that are causing social unrest and unemployment.

Party strategy and policies constitute the **"party line,"** a concept that is often difficult to pin down but is nevertheless regularly quoted as the principal guide to the direction of Chinese politics. Despite the official criticism of faction, party politics is ultimately driven by factionalism, clientelism, and the establishment of personal ties and networks.[23] Leaders rise and fall according to their abilities to make (and keep) friends and allies in the right places and to identify and control, sideline, or eliminate their opponents. In that sense, the CCP is not so different from a conventional liberal democratic political party.

The structure and role of the CCP follows almost exactly the hierarchical model of the old CPSU. At the lowest level are about 3.5 million **primary party organizations** (PPOs), formed wherever there is a minimum of three full party members. They can be formed in the workplace or local neighborhoods or within units of the People's Liberation Army, and each has a committee elected for 3-year terms. Primary party organizations, the major point of contact between the party and the masses, are overseen in turn by provincial and county-level party organizations. These have committees elected for 5-year terms, have considerable power over economic activities, and have responsibility for convening provincial and county party congresses. Despite this show of concern for the input of the people, however, real power is focused at the national level, and the party is ultimately a closed institution on which outsiders have no significant influence.

Organizationally, the national party consists of five major bodies.

National Party Congress

In theory at least, the National Party Congress (not to be confused with the National People's Congress) is the highest organ in the party hierarchy. It meets once every 5 years, although it did not meet at all between 1945 and 1956, nor between 1958 and 1969, thanks in part to the upheavals created by Mao's policies. The 1982 party constitution still allows meetings to be convened early or postponed "under extraordinary circumstances." Congresses are usually convened in Beijing, are attended by more than 2,000 delegates, and meet for no more than 2 weeks (although the Ninth Congress in April 1969 met for 24 days, presumably to clear up some of the backlog of work that had accumulated since 1956). Given their size and the rarity of their meetings, they have time to do little more than rubber-stamp party policies and decisions. The most recent Congress met in 2002.

In theory, delegates are selected at lower party levels; in practice, allocations are engineered by the party leadership to ensure representation of the military and the central party, often at the cost of seats for representatives from the provinces. Normally, the National Party Congress does little more than hear a report by the chairman of the party, hear another report on changes to the constitution, and—more significantly—"elect" members to the Central Committee, although all it really does is confirm a list already drawn up by the party leaders. Nonetheless, balloting and politicking have occasionally produced changes in the list and there are now more candidates than there are posts for party positions, so even influential figures have been known to fail to be voted into the Central Committee. Generally, however, the Congress has little significant power.

Central Committee

As in the former Soviet system, the Central Committee is the major governing body of the party. Although it rarely initiates or introduces policies, it must approve the policies of the leadership. As with most Chinese political institutions, size is again a determining factor in the powers of the Committee; as membership of the CCP grew, and as appointment to the Central Committee was used increasingly as a means of rewarding service to the party, so Committee membership grew from just over 40 members in the mid-1950s to almost 350 members in 1982, settling down to about 200 today. The Committee usually meets annually for varying periods, during which time it elects members of the Politburo and of the Standing Committee of the Politburo.

Central Secretariat

Working as an adjunct to the Politburo, the Secretariat has up to a dozen members; meets twice weekly; provides administrative backup; plays a key role in developing policies; and evaluates the choices for appointments to senior party, state, and military positions. It is appointed by the Standing Committee of the Politburo.

Political Bureau (Politburo)

Ultimate party power in China (and therefore ultimate political power) lies in the Politburo of the CCP and most notably in the Standing Committee of the Politburo. The Politburo, which meets about once a month to initiate and discuss party policy, takes collective responsibility for its decisions. It is within this small group of about 18 to 28 people that power—and the leadership of China—is negotiated, given, and taken away.

Although the Central Committee technically elects the members of the Politburo, this has not always been the case. Until 1975, membership was determined entirely by Mao and merely confirmed by the Central Committee. Mao's choices were determined by seniority, loyalty, and usefulness to Mao and by contributions made to his rise to power.[24] The result was that there was relatively little change in membership, most Politburo members came from the military, and the average age of members climbed to well over 70, leading some to describe China as a gerontocracy. Deaths and replacements brought the average age by the mid-1980s down to just over 60, and the military members had been replaced by younger and more professional members. The membership stays relatively young today under the leadership of Hu Jintao.

Standing Committee of the Politburo

When the Politburo is not in session, the party is run by a Standing Committee of six or seven members. This meets about twice per week and constitutes the most powerful and senior group of individuals in the entire Chinese political system. At the head of this group sits the general secretary of the party (or chairman until 1982). After the changes of 2002–2003, this group included Hu Jintao (general secretary), Wen Jiabao (premier), and Wu Bangguo (chairman of the NPC Standing Committee).

POLITICAL LEADERSHIP

The government of communist countries such as China and the former Soviet Union can seem enormously complex, especially when all is not as it seems, when labels and titles do not always accurately identify the people and institutions with the real power, and when the formal flowcharts do not really capture the essence of the decision-making system.[25] Studies of Chinese leadership are peppered with words such as fluid, ambiguous, shadowy, and flexible. The key feature of that leadership has been the dominant role of a single individual: first Mao, then Deng, then Jiang, and next—if tradition continues—Hu. Mao and Deng owed their power and influence mainly to their political abilities and charisma, while Jiang owed his mainly to his positions as party leader, president, and commander in chief. Try as he might, Jiang never had—nor, in retirement, is he likely to have—the status or authority of Mao or Deng. Indeed, given the increasingly technocratic nature of Chinese government, the unwillingness of the Chinese people to be manipulated as blatantly as they were by Mao, and China's increasing integration into the global system, it is unlikely that old-style paramount leaders will ever be seen again in China.

Normally, the de facto leader of China is the general secretary of the CCP, but even this is not a fixed rule. After 1978, Deng Xiaoping was effectively the "paramount leader" of China, but the most senior posts he ever held were party vice chairman and chairman of the party's Military Commission (a post from which he retired in 1989). By 1993, the only position of any kind that Deng held was the presidency of China's bridge association. Technically, General Secretary Jiang Zemin was the leader of the party, and thus of China, but it was always clear that Deng was in charge. Much the same was expected of Jiang Zemin following his 2002 retirement; Jiang retained the important position of chairman of the Military Commission, and many of the members of the Politburo were his acolytes.

The key to making sense of all this is to appreciate three key points:

- Personal relationships (or *guanxi*) are a more important indicator of who has power in China than formal titles.
- Leadership and the distribution of power depend on political maneuvers among a small group of people at the apex of the party (mainly the Standing Committee of the Politburo).
- The driving force behind Chinese politics in recent decades has been the struggle between reformists and conservatives. (There are close parallels on all these points between China and the former USSR, and more than a fleeting similarity with elements of politics in Mexico and Egypt.)

Much like in Japan, power in China is based around factions, which are based less on ideological differences than on personal relationships. Power is also based on the particular leadership skills of perhaps no more than two or three people and on the

CLOSE-UP VIEW

THE FALUN GONG: A THREAT TO THE PARTY?

The Chinese Communist party has always been good at identifying potential sources of competition for power and has usually moved quickly to ensure that they have never developed into a significant threat. One such potential threat on which attention began to focus in 1999 was the Falun Gong, a movement variously described as a sect, cult, or religion. Its members practice a combination of breathing exercises (*qigong*), Buddhism, Taoism, martial arts, and faith healing.

Although it claims to have its origins in pre-historic culture, Falun Gong has only begun to attract wider interest since 1992, when its self-proclaimed leader Li Hongzhi set up a study center in Beijing. It now claims to have a following of more than 100 million worldwide, of which 70 million live in China. If that claim is true, then the group has a larger number of members than the CCP, a statistic that is enough to give party leaders pause for thought. It also claims to be apolitical and argues that it is neither a religion nor a cult. However, between 10,000 and 20,000 adherents staged a demonstration in April 1999 outside the compound in Beijing where China's senior leaders live. This not only frightened the leadership and caused it much embarrassment but also indicated that the movement was well organized.

Reflecting the extent to which the CCP regarded the Falun Gong as a threat, Jiang Zemin used the opportunity of the June 1999 anniversary of the founding of the CCP to make a speech denouncing "feudal, superstitious, or other negative practices." His comment came in the midst of his attempts to restore the moral authority of the party in light of a growing number of instances of corruption and against a background of growing debates about a spiritual vacuum that many felt was afflicting China. Critics of the CCP argued that although it had provided political and economic direction, it did not meet all the needs of the Chinese people. Not only has religion been dismissed by Marxists as the "opium of the people," but—more immediately—party leaders believed that a movement such as Falun Gong could quickly compete with the party for the attentions of the people.

abilities of these leaders to keep control, a process that involves regular purges of rivals and opponents. For example, Mao held on to power for decades, but only because he regularly dismissed or shuffled his lieutenants. Around him he built what has been described as a "first generation" (or echelon) of supporters, most of whom were veterans of the Long March.[26] Among those shuffled during these changes was Deng Xiaoping, who was purged from the highest levels of the party no fewer than three times.

With Mao's death in 1976 and the arrest of the Gang of Four, at least two major factions emerged within the party leadership: the "Whatever" group of Mao loyalists led by premier Hua Guofeng and including veteran economists and technocrats and a group of reformists led by Deng Xiaoping and including veteran party and military leaders.[27] Beginning in 1978, Deng and his reform-minded supporters wrested power for themselves, forming a second generation of leaders. Deng used many of the same methods as Mao to retain power, carrying out purges of his own and using a mix of "cajolery, compromise, and threat" to keep his faction together.[28] He arranged in 1981 for the reformist Hu Yaobang to replace Hua Guofeng as CCP general secretary, but Deng had to remove him in 1987, apparently to placate conservatives within his faction. His successor, Zhao Ziyang, was in turn removed from power in 1989 for being too unwilling to crack down on the Tiananmen Square demonstrations.

Realizing that many of the members of the second echelon were old and ailing, Deng developed a third generation of leaders who would build on the economic reforms he had begun. This group, which steadily rose to a new prominence in the Politburo, was both younger and more technocratic than its predecessors. By the early 1990s, the most prominent of the reformists was Jiang Zemin. Conservatives were represented by premier Li Peng (often described after Tiananmen Square as "the most hated man in China"). Li forged his own alliance with President Yang Shangkun (whose power base rested with the military) and Chen Yun, another member of the Standing Committee of the Politburo and an advocate of central planning.[29] With the retirement of Yang in 1993 and the death of Chen in 1995, Li's star appeared to be on the wane and Jiang's position strengthened. Jiang's hold on power was confirmed in September 1997 when the Central Committee reelected him to a new term as general secretary. Li, meanwhile, had to be content with the relatively weak post of chairmanship of the National People's Congress.

In 2002–2003, the leadership of China passed to a new fourth generation of leaders, headed by Hu Jintao. There was every indication that they would continue to develop and promote the reformist policies of the Jiang generation. The China they inherited was quite different from that ruled by the first generation, and significantly different even from the China of the third generation. Hu was in charge of an economy from which the state was steadily retreating, a political system in which the future of the CCP was in question, and a society that was beginning to show the first cracks coming from policies that were not keeping up with needs.

MASS ORGANIZATIONS

In theory, China subscribes to the Leninist principle of democratic centralism (every level of government elects the next highest level and is in turn accountable to the level below) and to the idea of the **"mass line"** (whereby the masses are allowed to present their ideas to the party and to oversee the implementation of policy with a view to keeping leaders in touch with their followers). In practice, government is heavily centralized, and the mass line is used as much as a method of control as of keeping in touch with public opinion. Collective participation in Chinese politics is selective and heavily controlled, so except for membership of the CCP (which is very selective), mass organizations are really the only channel through which government and people can interrelate.

Although mass organizations superficially look much like interest groups in liberal democracies, they serve a more direct role in the process of political education in China. As in the former USSR, they are based around democratic centralism and are exploited by the party as **"transmission belts"** for party policy, or in other words, as a means of mobilizing the masses to win support for party policies. Most are national in scale, and their sheer size ensures that millions take part in politics by "discussing" and learning about party policies.

One example is the All-China Youth Federation, which—like the old Soviet Komsomol—acts as the main recruitment vehicle for future leaders of the party. It has a membership of 57 million, but this is still only 25 percent of eligible members, and there have been signs in recent years that membership is becoming unattractive, offering fewer opportunities for upward mobility.[30] Other important mass organizations include the All-China Federation of Trade Unions (102 million members) and the All-China Women's Federation. Most of these organizations were dissolved in 1966–1969 during the Cultural Revolution, when the Red Guards became the only significant mass organization in China. By the late 1970s, all the major organizations had regrouped, and many went on to increase their membership. Some also moved beyond mobilizing support for the party and dealt more centrally with issues related to their membership; the Women's Federation, for example, has become increasingly active in gender-related issues (although they have not been able to increase pressure for an improvement in the social and economic position of women).[31]

THE MEDIA

As in most authoritarian political systems, the media in China are controlled by the party in the interests of supporting the basic party line. However, Mao really imposed draconian control over the media only after 1966, when they became part of a well-oiled propaganda machine and when hundreds of newspapers and journals were suspended or shut down. As the party line moderated under Deng, so the media became more open and critical. This does not mean that China has a free press, but political changes resulted in 1988 in an event of dramatic significance: After years of leading the way in guiding the Chinese press, the *Red Flag* (the official journal of the CCP) ceased publication. Reformists in the party have also been given greater freedom to express their views in the media, and journalists joined students in the 1989 pro-democracy demonstrations.

The linchpin in the system has traditionally been the Xinhua (New China) News Agency, which is directly controlled by the CCP Central Committee and acts as the primary domestic news gatherer and gatekeeper for news leaving and coming into China. The official organ of the CCP Central Committee is the *People's Daily*, but even this has been known to send mixed messages and not always toe the party line. The English-language *China Daily* (founded in 1981) has achieved a substantial circulation and is used as an important source of information by the educated elite and China watchers. Particular groups in society are serviced by other newspapers such as the *China Youth Daily*, the *Workers' Daily*, and the *Peasants' Daily*, all controlled to some extent by the party.

The dominance of the official organs is declining as Chinese publishers respond to growing public demand for more variety; between 1978 and 1996, the number of newspapers grew from 186 to 2,200, and the number of magazines rose from

930 to 8,100.[32] There are also signs of more competition emerging in the newspaper sector, with publishers increasingly trying to appeal to their readers by providing a choice of editorial approaches. This has been forced on them to some extent by the end of government subsidies in the 1990s that forced papers to earn more from advertising revenue.

The Central Broadcasting Administration oversees the operation of radio and television, although management of broadcast stations is slowly being decentralized. The 1980s saw massive growth in TV ownership as China launched several communications satellites and built relay stations in order to make television more widely available. Oddly enough for a so-called communist country, television advertising has become more common, and new program varieties have been introduced to meet consumer demand. Despite the existence of one of the world's largest mass-media establishments, perhaps the most active source of news for most people in China remains *xiao-dao xioaxi* (back-alley news, or the rumor mill). Given doubts about the accuracy of official news, many people turn instead to word-of-mouth. Economic liberalization has also increased access to faxes and personal computers in China, which the 1989 democracy movement used to keep in touch with supporters inside and outside the country.

Meanwhile, the Internet is affecting communications in China, as it is almost everywhere. There are relatively few Internet sites in China and relatively few users, but access is growing and cyberspace is proving to be an interesting new channel for gauging public opinion. For example, much of the traffic following the terrorist attacks of September 11, 2001, was favorable to the terrorists, a reflection of the extent to which nationalism is alive and well in China.

POLICIES AND POLICYMAKING

Pinning down the processes, individuals, and principles involved in policymaking in China is difficult, and foreign political scientists have developed different models over the last 30 years in attempts to better understand the system. Some have focused on particular policy areas (such as education and agriculture) and some on the struggles within the top levels of Chinese leadership. One study of Chinese policymaking[33] argues that three key principles are involved:

- There is a fragmented bureaucratic structure of authority, involving 25 to 35 top leaders, senior bureaucrats, and government ministries.
- Consensus building is central to the process, mainly because of the cooperation needed from the lower levels of government.
- Decision making is a lengthy, disjointed, and incremental process.

Another study concludes that because Mao fashioned the political institutions of China on those of Stalinist central planning, he brought to China some of the critical flaws of the Stalinist system. These included the creation of a heavily centralized and chronically overloaded decision-making system. The system compelled policymakers in China to maintain dysfunctional policies for long periods and to rely on simplistic performance indicators. It also discouraged party subordinates from drawing attention to policy problems, preferring to wait until the failure was acknowledged by the party itself.[34]

The Chinese leadership claims to believe in the value of ensuring that public policy is openly debated within the party system and down through the many levels of government. There is an element of truth in this claim, as reflected in the way that policies have occasionally been changed or abandoned as a result of public debate, officially permitted or not. China is not a democracy in the Western sense, but the views of the Chinese public, and the outbreak of occasional civil disorder, have not always passed unnoticed by the leadership. Public opinion also plays a role in influencing the balance of power at the apex of the party; for example, Premier Li Peng may have kept his post following Tiananmen Square, but his policies were unpopular, and he apparently softened his hard-line position. Recent changes in the direction of Chinese economic and foreign policies also suggest a softening of the official party line and reduced state and party control over people's lives.

ECONOMIC POLICY

Until Mao's death, China was a poor country that subscribed to central economic management, relying on a series of 5-year plans to map out its development goals. It initially enjoyed rapid agricultural and industrial growth, but this was followed by several years of stagnation during the Great Leap Forward and the Cultural Revolution, when there was little order and not enough investment in the agricultural sector, which survived nonetheless, growing almost every year and being hurt as much by weather as by politics.

Over the last decade, the West has had to reassess its image of China as new economic figures have revealed a dynamic society that, despite widespread poverty and high unemployment, has the makings of an economic giant. The first step in its transformation was the proclamation in 1978 of an open-door policy aimed at expanding trade, opening up production to factors of supply and demand, reducing the role of central planning, and introducing what some have described as **"Market-Leninism."** Incentives for workers and peasant farmers that had been removed during the Cultural Revolution—including promotions, bonuses, and wage increases—were reintroduced. Greater emphasis was placed on light industry over heavy industry and on the expansion of production in consumer goods. Finally, greater support was given to domestic research and development, and China proved more open to the idea of importing foreign technology. This in turn meant that it needed more foreign exchange, which led to a decision to boost the tourist industry, to expand exports, and to encourage foreign companies to invest in China.

During the 1980s, further changes were made, including a decision to introduce "household contracts" for farmers. Under this system, a household was allocated a piece of land (for use but not for sale) and was required to meet state quotas, but it was allowed to sell whatever it produced over the quotas and keep the profit. Collective agriculture ceased to exist, and rural residents saw increases in both income

The rapid growth in the Chinese economy in recent years and its increased absorption into the global capitalist system, are symbolized by this view of the Pudong financial district in Shanghai, seen from an outdoor restaurant on the other side of the Huangpu River.

and consumption. In urban areas, the state gave up its monopoly on services and—largely to deal with high unemployment—allowed the creation of small businesses and collectives.[35]

The middle class grew, overall unemployment fell, public ownership of land declined, the Chinese economy grew at more than 9 percent annually, and exports grew at 15 percent annually. However, planners wrestled with trying to combine the new market economy with the vestiges of the old centrally planned system, and foreign investor confidence stumbled following Tiananmen Square, which was itself brought on at least in part by growing public complaints about a fall in the standard of living.

During the 1980s, China set up a number of special economic zones aimed at attracting foreign investment, a program that was given new significance in 1997 when Hong Kong reverted to China after 155 years of British rule. The enclave had already been used as a conduit for Chinese trade and investment connections with the rest of the world and as a source of foreign exchange, investment, trade, and expertise. Now a Special Administrative Region, it continues in the same role and is helping bring significant changes throughout the Chinese economy.

FIGURE 5.1

Sources of Industrial Output in China

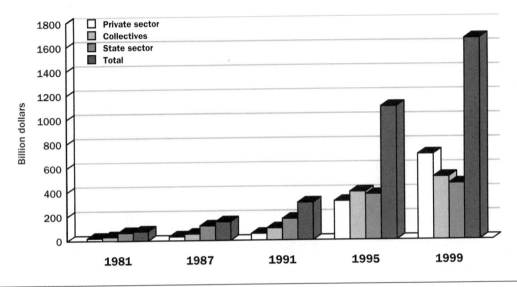

Source: Based on figures from J. P. Morgan Chase, reproduced in *The Economist*, June 30, 2001, p. 22.

Figure 5.1 shows how quickly industrial production has grown in recent years and how China is relying less on state production and more on the private and collective sectors. Trade between China and the rest of the world is growing, foreign investors are finding China more attractive than Russia (investing $45 billion in China in 1998 alone), and capitalism is no longer officially condemned in China (not even by the *People's Daily*, which has run editorials in favor of more open markets). Perhaps nothing symbolized the new era as much as the opening in 1993 of a Ferrari dealership in China.

Problems remain, however, not least of them being environmental pollution, worsening crime rates, and corruption among party and government officials, who have been implicated in everything from running smuggling rings to extorting illegal taxes from peasants. Another problem is population growth. Improvements in health care have helped more babies to survive and more people to live longer, so China now has nearly 1.3 billion people, most of whom are concentrated in arable coastal areas and several huge cities. Population growth fell from 1.5 percent in 1990 to 0.9 percent in 2000, but it is back up to 1.3 percent today; this means more than 16 million more Chinese every year, straining and even defeating attempts by economic planners to keep up with demand. Deciding that drastic measures were needed, the government introduced a **one-child policy** in 1979, limiting every family to no more than one child. Not only did this lead to widespread resentment, but because boys were more useful in economic and labor terms to poor families, it also promoted infanticide, with firstborn girls often being murdered.

A related problem is the lag between supply and demand in education. One of the reasons several Southeast Asian countries have seen rapid economic growth in recent years is that they have improved their schools; adult male literacy in many of these countries runs at 90 percent or more, and there have been notable increases in the provision of secondary education. In China, 16 percent of adults are still illiterate, and postsecondary education is the privilege of a small minority (less than 2 percent, compared with about 30 percent in the United States). To make matters worse, there is the "lost generation": As many as 30 million Chinese were forced to drop out of school during the Cultural Revolution and had no formal education at all. Many are now in their 40s and 50s, and instead of playing a central role in society, they are on the periphery. Students today who see little future in China—among them the best and brightest of the new generation—try to go abroad for their university education, and very few return.

An important economic breakthrough came in December 2001, when—after 15 years of diplomatic pressure and negotiation—China joined the World Trade Organization (WTO). Membership obliges China to open its markets to other countries (notably its banking, insurance, telecommunications, and agricultural sectors), increases pressure on China to make capitalist reforms, and over the long term may encourage greater openness and accountability in government. On the other hand, it could open China to a level of economic competition that it may not be prepared to face, which could worsen unemployment and promote financial instability.[36] Like the United States, China also has a worryingly high level of reliance on imported oil, which will increasingly hold its economy ransom to changes in the world oil price.

China is not yet a market economy, and it has structural weaknesses that could complicate, or even undermine, the reforms that it has made and continues to make: In particular, industry suffers from poor quality output, low productivity, and a shortage of skilled workers. Economic problems have led to growing dissatisfaction, as has the corruption that continues within the CCP and the continued existence of an elitist party system. The structural problems of the Chinese system were emphasized in March–April 2003 by the slowness of the government response to the outbreak of severe acute respiratory syndrome (SARS). It showed that the Chinese government was poorly equipped to handle crises, even those that threatened to undermine China's economic progress. But whatever happens, changes in the nature of the global marketplace are combining with a shift of power to a new technocracy to make it difficult for the CCP to resist demands for democratization.

FOREIGN POLICY

The United States and China in the 19th century both preferred not to be involved in world affairs, but the 20th century saw both being much influenced by their place in the world, with very different results. While the United States abandoned isolationism and actively tried to determine the outcome of external events, China spent more time reacting to those events and trying to understand its place in the global system. From the isolation of the imperial era, China switched to the unwilling dependence of the nationalist era, went through the shifting coalitions of the communist era (being initially pro-Soviet and then falling out with the USSR), and finished the century with attitudes that indicated growing accommodation with the rest of the world, although neither side really knew what to think of the other.

Throughout the imperial era, China had little to do with the outside world and considered all other cultures inferior. Outsiders were known as *yang guizi* ("foreign devils"), anything from abroad (goods, people, or ideas) was described as *yang* (foreign), and anti-Western feelings ran so high that wild rumors spread among the more superstitious peasants, including one that Westerners ate their children.[37] Then China was violently and unwillingly drawn into closer relations with the outside world, a process that contributed to the collapse of the imperial order. Britain began the process by forcing concessions in the 1830s on trade in opium and winning a foothold in Hong Kong. France, Portugal, the United States, Japan, and other countries subsequently wrested similar agreements out of the Chinese, so by the turn of the century China had given up much of its economic and political independence. The arrival of Western ideas, and the inability of China to oppose them, encouraged many Chinese to rethink the nature of Chinese society, led many to resent the influence of the West, and sowed the seeds of nationalism.

Chinese resentment toward the West deepened after World War II, when Mao—who had led China's fight against the Japanese—was not invited to the conferences convened to plan the postwar world. When the West then supported Taiwan and refused to recognize the PRC, Mao—driven by his overarching interest in rebuilding China—decided to "lean to one side" in foreign policy. He portrayed the United States as the archenemy of the Chinese people, formed an ideological alliance with the USSR in the struggle against capitalism, and for much of the 1950s followed the Soviet model of economic development. He also promoted China as a champion of decolonization, sending Zhou Enlai to the Bandung conference in 1955 (see the Introduction to Part III), and winning new friends in Southeast Asia and sub-Saharan Africa. To limit Western influence in Southeast Asia, China helped North Korea and North Vietnam, and worked to isolate Taiwan (see Political Debates, p. 267).

By the late 1950s, ideological differences had emerged between China and the USSR, not least over the role of the peasants (whom Mao respected but the Soviets did not) and attempts by Soviet leader Nikita Khrushchev to improve relations with the United States. Unprepared to accept any cooperation with the West, Mao cut ties with the USSR in 1960–1961, and the Sino-Soviet split developed into a bitter war of words and ideology, along with active disputes over their joint border. By the late 1960s, China was beginning to see the United States as less of a threat than the USSR. Following the 1968 Soviet invasion of Czechoslovakia and Sino-Soviet border clashes in 1969, Sino-U.S. relations took a new turn in 1971 as secret talks began between Zhou Enlai and Henry Kissinger, the national security advisor to U.S. President Richard Nixon. China was admitted to the United Nations in October 1971 at the expense of Taiwan, and the new friendship was confirmed in February 1972 with Nixon's remarkable visit to China and meeting with Mao, encouraged by the desire of both nations to form a strategic partnership against the USSR.[38] In 1978, the United States agreed to recognize the People's

POLITICAL DEBATES

ONE CHINA OR TWO?

Ever since its creation in 1949, China has been variously dogged, embarrassed, irritated, and annoyed by the status of the other China that was created that same year: the Republic of China, otherwise known as Taiwan. Taiwan has been an international outcast since the 1970s, but its economic success and military power have ensured that it cannot be ignored, and tensions between the two Chinas have grown in recent years as Taiwan has decided to become more assertive of its rights.

A Japanese colony from 1895 until 1945, Taiwan was returned to Chinese sovereignty just in time to be taken over by the Nationalists, under the leadership of Chiang Kai-shek, as they retreated from Mao's Red Army. Violently suppressing his opponents and winning the support of a U.S. government alarmed at the spread of communism, Chiang claimed that his government was the legitimate government of all China and made the recovery of the mainland one of his primary goals.

While Mao's China experienced political and economic turbulence during the 1950s and 1960s, Taiwan developed its agricultural and industrial base with the help of foreign investment and by the early 1970s had all the hallmarks of a newly industrializing country. However, as part of the strengthening of relations between the United States and China, China's seat in the United Nations was taken away from Taiwan in 1971 and given to the PRC, beginning a process by which Taiwan was steadily pushed out of the international community. Chiang died in 1975, and in 1979 the United States withdrew its diplomatic recognition of Taiwan.

A political outcast it may be, but Taiwan's economy has flourished and its political system has liberalized. It held its first competitive presidential elections in 1996 and today has a per capita GDP about six times that of mainland China and a substantially better record on almost every social indicator, from infant mortality to education. Opinion has been divided in recent years about whether Taiwan should continue to seek reunification with China or should declare itself an independent state.

Tensions between the two Chinas began to heat up again in 1995 following attempts by Taiwan to strengthen its international status by, among other things, being readmitted to the United Nations. The PRC responded by holding military "exercises" in the straits of Taiwan. The restoration of Hong Kong and Macao to China, in 1997 and 1999, respectively, was accompanied by talk of a **"one country, two systems"** policy that may one day encourage reunification. But in 1999, Taiwan insisted on opening talks with the PRC on a "state-to-state" basis, further angering the Chinese government. While the United States has continued to refuse to recognize Taiwan, there is considerable support for it within the U.S. Congress, Taiwan remains an important market for U.S. arms sales, and the Bush administration has upset China with its pro-Taiwan position.

Republic of China as the sole legitimate government of China, and in 1979 Deng made the first visit by a Chinese leader to the United States. Trade and cooperation between China and the United States, and between China and Japan, has since grown steadily.

China's relations with its near neighbors have not always been close, leading many to question the sincerity of the claim in the preamble to the 1982 constitution that

China supports "mutual respect for sovereignty and territorial integrity...non-interference in each other's internal affairs...and peaceful coexistence." China was strongly critical of the Soviet invasion of Afghanistan in 1979 and of aggressive Soviet posturing on the Chinese border, but it has occupied Tibet since 1951 and shows no inclination to withdraw. China was also worried about the close ties that had developed between the USSR and Vietnam in the 1970s and about the Vietnamese invasion of Cambodia in 1978. Vowing to teach Vietnam a lesson, China launched a limited and inconclusive invasion in February–March 1979; instead of humiliating Vietnam, the PLA lost more than 30,000 men.

Under Deng Xiaoping, China became more extroverted, opening itself to investment from—and trade with—the outside world, abandoning the Stalinist and Maoist models of economic development, and making itself almost overnight into a newly industrializing country in the character of Taiwan and South Korea.[39] At the same time, it followed "an independent foreign policy," a phrase thought to mean that it would not align itself with either superpower or that it may simply have been trying to work out some consistency in its relations with its Asian neighbors.[40]

The Tiananmen Square massacre brought widespread revulsion, provided a reminder of the authoritarian nature of Chinese government, and caused a shift in Chinese relations with the rest of the world. Since 1989, China has restored its tarnished image to some extent through its constructive role in encouraging peace in Cambodia and through supporting—or at least not opposing—allied action against Iraq in the aftermath of the August 1990 invasion of Kuwait.[41] As a potential economic superpower, however, China needs (and probably wants) to be taken more seriously and is taking an increasingly assertive role on the world stage. It has had several disagreements with the United States over trade (the Clinton administration briefly tried to make an issue of Chinese commercial piracy in 1994–1995), has renewed its aggressive posture toward Taiwan, and has taken a more assertive stance on ownership of the Paracel and Spratly Islands in the South China Sea; the seabed around them is thought to contain oil, natural gas, and other valuable mineral resources.

China has the world's biggest military, but it poses only a limited threat to any but its nearest neighbors. This may be changing, however. It is a nuclear power and has been building up and modernizing both its short-range ballistic missiles and its long-range strategic missiles. It is also expanding its navy, although it is still very small. China poses nothing like the threat once posed by the Soviet Union, but its growing economic power may give it the wealth over the longer term to back up its political values with hard military capacity.

An uneasy peace currently prevails in China's foreign relations. In recent years it has moved to strengthen ties with its Asian neighbors, continues to ensure the isolation of Taiwan, and has joined the WTO. Relations with the United States have generally been warm, although Taiwan remains a potential point of dispute. China has also continued to talk about the dangers of a U.S. "hegemony," has systematically stolen nuclear secrets from the United States for more than 20 years, and saw an outpouring of nationalist rage following the NATO bombing of the Chinese Embassy in Belgrade in May 1999 during the Kosovo military action. There is a growing consensus that China has an important role to play as a regional power in Southeast Asia, but questions remain about the implications of changes in economic policy for China's status as one of the last officially "communist" nations in the world.

CHINESE POLITICS IN TRANSITION

China is undergoing economic changes of a kind that promise to make it one of the major powers of the 21st century. However, its search for a political form and for answers to its economic needs since 1948 has brought social upheaval, economic experimentation, and human tragedy on a huge scale. The question now is whether it can continue to make the changes at a pace needed to keep up with the demands of its huge and growing population. A strong China could present opportunities for trade and the promotion of democratic values to one-fifth of the human population, but that strength could also pose a threat if the nationalism that often colors the words of Chinese leaders and the actions of the Chinese people is channeled in the wrong direction. At the same time, the world faces the real danger of a weak China with internal divisions, social problems, rising crime, and unemployment, where leaders might try to divert attention away from internal problems by being more aggressive on foreign policy, notably toward Taiwan and other near neighbors.

The economic and political changes begun by Deng and developed by Jiang remain incomplete, and it will be some time before we can really see the extent to which reform has taken root in Chinese society. The steady rise of the Chinese consumer and entrepreneur will continue to place growing pressure on the leadership for democratic change. In 2002–2003 China underwent its most substantial change in leadership for a generation. We will have to wait and watch to see what impact that change will have on China, and on its place in the world.

KEY TERMS

cadres
Chinese Communist party
Confucianism
Fifth Modernization
fourth generation
Gang of Four
Great Leap Forward
Great Proletarian Cultural Revolution
Guomindang

Long March
Market-Leninism
mass line
mass organizations
National People's Congress
one-child policy
one country, two systems
party line
People's Liberation Army
Politburo

premier
primary party organizations
shifting lines
standing committees
transmission belts
Taiwan
Tiananmen Square
Tibet

KEY PEOPLE

Chiang Kai-shek
Confucius
Deng Xiaoping

Hu Jintao
Jiang Zemin
Mao Zedong

Sun Yat-sen
Wen Jiabao
Zhou Enlai

STUDY QUESTIONS

1. What changes did Mao make to Marxism and Leninism to make them more appropriate to the Chinese setting?
2. Does China have a Marxist-Leninist system?
3. Is it still appropriate to think of China as a "communist" country?
4. Is China a newly industrializing country?
5. The relationship between party and government in China has been described as one between a principal and an agent. To what extent can the same be said of the relationship between parties and government in liberal democracies?
6. Who governs China?
7. How does leadership change in China, and how does the process compare with changes of leadership in liberal democracies?
8. What will China look like in 20 years?
9. What differences are there between the methods used by Chinese leaders to win control and the methods used by politicians in liberal democracies?

CHINA ONLINE

ChinaSite.com: *http://chinasite.com*
China Today: *http://www.chinatoday.com*
Megasites with links to sites on Chinese news, government, politics, the economy and social issues.
Consulate-General of the PRC in New York: *http://www.nyconsulate.prchina.org/eng/index.html*
A source of official government information on everything from government to history, culture, and the economy.
South China Morning Post: *http://www.scmp.com*
Asiaweek: *http://www.pathfinder.com/Asiaweek*
China Daily: *http://www.chinadaily.com.cn*
Good sources of news on Chinese and Asian affairs; the first two are a Hong Kong–based daily newspaper and a weekly magazine, the third is the online version of the major English-language Chinese daily newspaper.

FURTHER READING

Benewick, Robert, and Paul Wingrove (Eds.), *China in the 1990s* (Basingstoke, UK: Macmillan, 1999). An edited collection of chapters on Chinese politics, economics, social issues, and public policies.

Dreyer, June Teufel, *China's Political System: Modernization and Tradition*, 3rd. Ed. (New York: Longman, 2000). An introduction to the Chinese political system, with chapters on history, the economy, education, and foreign policy.

Kristof, Nicholas, and Sheryl WuDunn, *China Awakes: The Struggle for the Soul of a Rising Power* (New York: Times Books, 1995). A personal narrative of recent changes in China, written by a husband-and-wife team from the *New York Times*.

Saich, Tony, *Governance and Politics of China* (New York: Palgrave, 2001). Another good survey of Chinese politics, including chapters on economic, social, and foreign policy.

Wang, James C. E., *Contemporary Chinese Politics:. An Introduction*, 6th Ed. (Upper Saddle River, NJ: Prentice Hall, 1999). One of the standard introductions to Chinese politics, society, and culture.

COMPARATIVE FOCUS

POLITICAL PARTIES

A political party is an organization that brings together people with similar views about how to govern societies and tries to pursue its goals by getting its members elected into political office. Parties normally have six major functions: (1) developing a series of goals behind which voters can unite to influence policy, (2) recruiting members and supporters to help promote the party platform, (3) mobilizing voters and raising funds to promote the campaigns of their candidates, (4) providing the reference points that help voters make sense of the policy options before them, (5) giving candidates and elected officials a label by which voters can tell them apart from opponents, and (6) encouraging elected officials to work together to support or oppose bills working their way through legislatures.

Parties usually organize around ideological differences, but they can also be based around social class, economic status, religion, or regional differences. They use varied methods, they often relate in different ways to voters and to the institutions of government, and although some are the servants of the political system, others sit at the very core of that system. Their impact depends in large part on how much competition they have.

- **One-party systems.** These are found mainly in dictatorships or communist systems. As was the case in the USSR—and as is the case in China today—monopoly parties do not offer voters choices but instead work to extend the reach of government and to ensure uniformity of purpose among voters. They often try to give the impression of democracy without actually giving voters the opportunity to have much impact on policy, which is made by the party leadership, using elections as a means of giving its decisions an aura of legitimacy.

- **One-party-dominant systems.** These are fairly rare and are usually found in authoritarian regimes, such as Mexico (until recently, anyway), Egypt, and several African states. One political party not only holds the executive and a majority of seats in the legislature but also controls the electoral commission and so is able to determine the outcome of elections. In Mexico, the Institutional Revolutionary Party (PRI) was able to dominate politics between 1929 and 2000 by reaching out to all the elites and interest groups it needed to win power, by bargaining with the groups it needed and pursuing policies that those groups favored, and by manipulating the electoral system. As Mexicans became better educated and more affluent, however, they became less easy to manipulate.

Single parties can also dominate in democracies. In India until the 1990s, the Congress party was consistently either the governing party or the biggest party, its power underpinned by a combination of the charisma of the Nehru-Gandhi dynasty and a divided opposition. Similarly, Japan was dominated until 1993 by the Liberal Democratic Party, which was flexible and clever enough to outwit the opposition and ultimately became associated in the minds of voters with Japan's postwar economic success.

- **Two-party-dominant systems.** These are fairly common and are mainly the product of the winner-take-all electoral system, which helps parties with large blocks of support to turn votes into seats; smaller parties with more thinly spread support more often come in second or third. It is not unusual for one or the other of the two parties to lose support and be supplanted by another party, but the two-party dominance is maintained by the electoral system. Britain is an example, having been dominated by the Liberals and the Conservatives, now by Labour and the Conservatives.

   The United States is another example, where there is little likelihood of a third party being able to compete effectively with the Republicans or the Democrats. They are both moderate parties that contain many shades of opinion, party discipline tends to be loose (members of Congress from one party often cross over to vote with the other), they run elections in most states and can manipulate electoral districts to increase their chances of winning seats, and while voters tend to vote for candidates rather than for parties, the majority also look for candidates who are associated with either the Republicans or the Democrats.

- **Multiple-party systems.** In several European countries (notably Germany, France, and Italy), there are so many political parties that few ever win a majority, governments are routinely formed by coalitions of two or more parties, the coalition partners usually have to make more effort to reach compromises, and governments can be fragile. This has not affected political stability in Germany, but Italian coalitions can often depend on parties with fewer than a dozen members who can hold all the others to ransom and exert an influence out of all proportion to their size and following. Coalitions collapse so often that in the period 1945–2003, Italy had more than 55 governments.

   Electoral systems that are based on proportional representation contribute to multiple-party systems by making it easier for small parties to win seats and harder for large parties to win clear majorities. A government based around multiple parties will be obliged to take note of a much broader selection of political values and policy ideas, but it will also be less able to provide leadership and consistent policies.

Interest groups are related to political parties, the main difference being that they do not nominate members to run for office under the name of the group, working instead to influence government from outside. They can do this by raising funds and channeling them to parties or candidates, giving candidates or elected officials seals of approval or disapproval or encouraging their members to vote for particular parties or candidates. Whereas parties try to build mass followings and win as many votes as possible from members and nonmembers alike, interest groups are usually more focused in terms of their goals, values, and policies. Whereas parties mainly look for the support of their members and supporters only at election time, interest groups may attract more sustained involvement from most of their members. So while there may be a few dozen serious political parties at most in any one country, there may be tens of thousands of interest groups, varying greatly in their size, goals, methods, and relationship to the political system.

Part III

NEWLY INDUSTRIALIZING COUNTRIES

What can we do? We can do much! We can inject the voice of reason into world affairs. We can mobilize all the spiritual, all the moral, all the political strength of Asia and Africa on the side of peace . . . we can mobilize what I have called the "Moral Violence of Nations" in favor of peace.

—President Sukarno of Indonesia, launching the Non-Aligned Movement, 1955

There was a time in the 1950s and 1960s when the label *Third World* almost made sense. Most of the countries of Asia, Latin America, and non-Soviet Asia had been colonized at one time or another, had comparable records of development, and saw themselves affected by cold war tensions that were mainly beyond their control. They were far from identical in terms of their political features, economic values, and social aspirations, but enough connections could be made among them to give the idea of the Third World some semblance of consistency.

This is no longer true. Since the end of the cold war, it has become clear that the differences among the countries of the Third World far outweigh the similarities. Their political systems come in many different forms, they have very different levels of economic development, they play very different roles in the global economic system, and they have had different experiences with social development. Nothing so vividly illustrates the inconsistencies in the concept of the Third World as the emergence since the 1970s of a group of newly dynamic countries with improving democratic records, increasingly productive economies, and social conditions that are improving to keep pace. Known by several different terms, including emerging economies, newly industrializing economies, and newly industrializing countries (NICs, pronounced "nicks"), these countries have long been recognized as a subgroup on the margins of comparative politics. Yet many Western political scientists still cling doggedly to the idea of the Third World, failing to acknowledge that NICs have left behind the heritage of authoritarianism and poverty.

NICs are commonly described according to their economic features, distinguished by measures such as per capita income, manufacturing rates, gross domestic product (GDP), and the contribution of manufacturing to GDP.[1] However, we need to begin seeing them in terms of their political and social features as well to better understand why they have progressed while many of their neighbors have not.

Most NICs have seven major features in common.

Emerging Democracy

NICs have improving democratic records, revolving around increasingly fair and competitive elections that offer the real possibility of changes of leadership. On the Freedom House scale, they are all described as Free or Partly Free, and most have ratings of 1 to 3.5. Their citizens have a choice of political parties with ideological variety, an increasingly free press, a variety of channels for political representation and participation, and legal systems that better protect their civil rights and civil liberties. Put another way, NICs have moved away from the kinds of erratic, corrupt, and personalized systems of government that were once the hallmarks of the Third World and have developed more structured, legalized, and predictable systems of decision making.

Democracy is qualified in some NICs (such as Indonesia and Malaysia), political violence still afflicts others (notably Colombia and India), and the leaders of NICs such as Singapore and Venezuela still use occasionally authoritarian methods to exert control, but the underlying trend in NICs is toward greater public accountability, greater respect for the rule of law, and greater political choice.

Some NICs also suffer internal divisions, but these divisions do not threaten their underlying stability. A good contrast is offered by India (a NIC) and Nigeria (a less developed country, or LDC). Both have almost every kind of religious, ethnic, regional, and economic division known to humanity; but, while Indian democracy weathers the storms they generate and is bolstered by a growing sense of an Indian national identity, Nigerian government is undermined by corruption and by ethnic and religious divisions, which regularly degenerate to the point where the military feels that it needs to step in to keep order.

Export-Led Growth

A stroll around the average North American home will reveal one of the clues to the success of NICs. The clothes many of us own may bear Western corporate trademarks, but they are probably made in countries such as Costa Rica, India, Indonesia, and Thailand. The same is true of the televisions, VCRs, DVD players, phones, computers, refrigerators, and ovens we own; unless they are Japanese, they are probably made (for Western corporations) in countries such as Brazil, Malaysia, and Mexico.

One of the keys to the growth of NIC economies has been a change in export policy. Instead of exporting low-profit primary products that can be converted into high-profit manufactured goods in the rich industrialized countries, NICs have made these goods themselves. They once protected domestic economies from imports and subsidized local producers, but they have increasingly opened up their markets and taken part in international negotiations on free trade. As well as giving tax breaks to exporters and setting export targets, they have also developed the urban labor pools needed to attract foreign investment. Japan and South Korea were once the source of cheap and expendable consumer goods, but they combined qual-

CHECKLIST

NEWLY INDUSTRIALIZING COUNTRIES
What Are Their Features?

- Generally improving records of representative government and regular, fair, and competitive elections.
- Increasingly well-defined, consistent, and predictable political institutions and processes.
- Improving levels of public loyalty to the state.
- A variety of institutionalized forms of political participation and representation.
- Improving records on the protection of individual rights under the law.
- A belief in human equality, if sometimes imperfectly implemented.

- An active, effective, and protected opposition, and respect for freedom of speech.
- Postindustrial and free-market economic systems based mainly on services and industry, and driven by a vigorous export market.
- Rapid urbanization and improvements in the quality of infrastructure.
- A relatively high quality of life when measured by the provision of education, health care, and other basic services.
- High to medium ratings on the Freedom House, Economic Freedom, and Human Development indexes.

Where Are They?

There are 33 NICs, and they are mainly in Latin America, Southeast Asia, and the Caribbean:

Antigua and Barbuda	India	St. Vincent and the Grenadines
Argentina	Indonesia	South Africa
Bahamas	Jamaica	Sri Lanka
Barbados	Malaysia	Taiwan
Brazil	Mauritius	Thailand
Chile	Mexico	Trinidad and Tobago
Colombia	Panama	Turkey
Costa Rica	Peru	Uruguay
Cyprus	Philippines	Venezuela
Dominica	Singapore	Hungary
El Salvador	St. Kitts and Nevis	
Grenada	St. Lucia	

ity with quantity to overcome the disadvantages of being resource-poor and became export-led economic powers. The same is happening now in Chile, Indonesia, Singapore, and the other NICs, some of which may be the Japans or the South Koreas of the future.

The growth of their manufacturing sectors has helped NICs to return some of the fastest economic growth rates in the world, with annual increases in GDP and industrial production as much as 5 to 15 times higher than rates in liberal democracies (see Figure III.1). They have adopted liberal trade policies, they are building diverse economies and producing a variety of goods and services, they are replacing low-profit

Jeremy Horner/Panos Pictures

Heavy traffic backed up around the World Trade Center in downtown Bangkok, Thailand. Newly industrializing countries like Thailand are witnessing rapid economic, commercial, and urban growth, built on a foundation of free-market principles and political stability.

agricultural exports with high-profit manufactured exports, and their governments have had good records in controlling inflation. Industry and services are making a growing contribution to their national wealth: Services usually account for 45 to 65 percent of GDP, industry 25 to 40 percent, and agriculture less than 15 percent. Most NICs now have a per capita GDP in the range of $2,000 to 9,000, which is low compared to liberal democracies ($20,000 to 35,000) but high compared to LDCs ($1,000 or less).

Urbanization

Not only are NICs becoming wealthier, but the shift of the workforce from agriculture to industry has brought in its wake a movement of people from the rural areas to the cities. The result is that NICs now have some of the world's biggest and fastest growing cities, so big that they have been elevated to the status of **megacities;** they include Mexico City, Mumbai (formerly Bombay) and Sao Paulo (18 million people each), Buenos Aires (13 million), and Jakarta (10 million).

The growth of the urban population has contributed to expansion of the middle class and the development of large new consumer markets, which has fed in to the economic growth of NICs. Urbanization has also changed the balance of political power: Compared to rural dwellers, city dwellers tend to be better

FIGURE III.1

Comparing Levels of Economic Growth

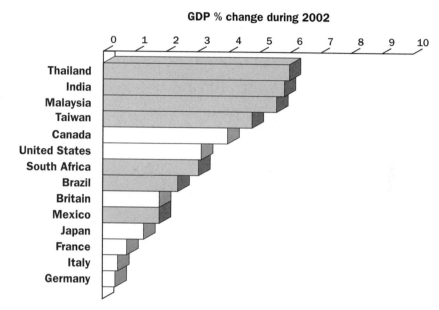

GDP % change during 2002

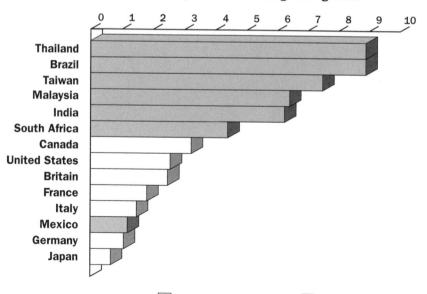

Industrial production % change during 2002

☐ **Liberal democracies**　☐ **NICs**

Source: *The Economist*, January 2003.

educated, more likely to organize for political change, and more inclined to make demands for democratic change. At the same time, though, the growth of urban populations has often outpaced the availability of jobs, and city governments have been unable to keep up with the demand for services. This has meant more urban slum dwellers, inadequate public transport, traffic congestion, worsening crime, problems with water and energy supply, and often severe air and water pollution.

New Levels of Foreign Investment

Just as the United States economy grew with the help of large infusions of foreign investment during the 19th century, so the growth of NICs has been underpinned by foreign investment aimed at building export capacity. Keen to exploit cheap labor and the growing consumer markets of NICs, corporations from Japan, Western Europe, and North America have invested heavily in Southeast Asia and Latin America. This has meant job losses in manufacturing in the liberal democracies, but it has brought new wealth and opportunities to NICs and has made the products we buy in our stores much cheaper. Unfortunately, it has also brought exploitation of workers, common instances of child labor, and the operation of **sweatshops** where men, women, and children work long hours for very little pay. In many ways, NICs are experiencing the same labor conditions as today's liberal democracies saw when they were undergoing their industrial development in the 19th and 20th centuries.

Foreign investment has also meant a surrender of control for emerging economies. Although foreign **multinational corporations** (MNCs) probably control less than 5 percent of U.S. assets, they control 25 percent of all the assets and 40 percent of all the sales in Brazilian industry, and 60 percent of output and 36 percent of employment in Singapore. By controlling the flow of investment and profits in NICs, MNCs have considerable influence over domestic economic policies. At the same time, though, they provide the kind of investment needed to help NICs build industrial economies and expand their manufactured exports.

An Efficient Bureaucracy

A key factor in the success of liberal democracies has been the development of efficient, responsive, and professional bureaucracies. Governments can pass all the laws and regulations they want, but they mean nothing unless they are implemented. Effective implementation depends on having bureaucrats who are motivated, educated, well paid, and well trained and whose career advancement is based more on merit than on nepotism. Whereas LDCs such as Ecuador and Zimbabwe are handicapped by bureaucratic corruption and incompetence, NICs such as Chile and Indonesia have become more like liberal democracies in the sense that government departments and agencies have a stronger record on overseeing the implementation of laws and regulations.

CRITICAL ISSUES

MEASURING NATIONAL WEALTH

The standard measure of national wealth is gross domestic product (GDP), defined as the total value of all goods and services produced by a country within its territory in 1 year. It tells us the absolute size of economies, but to make it useful for comparison, we need to divide it by population to give us a per capita figure. This reveals that Luxembourg and Switzerland are the most productive countries in the world, with a per capita GDP of $37,000 to 42,000; the United States ranks fifth with nearly $35,000; and Ethiopia is the least productive, at just $100 per person per year. The world average is about $5,200.

GDP is a useful measure, but it presents several problems. First, production may not always be the best measure of human welfare. Certainly, a strong economy contributes centrally to a successful society, but material wealth is not the only measure of the relative ability of societies to meet the basic needs of their members.

Second, it is often mistakenly interpreted as a measure of income or personal wealth, but all it measures is the value of production. The average Swiss citizen does not have an income of $37,000, but rather produces goods and services worth $37,000. In fact, the average Swiss citizen has a personal income of about $28,000, which is about the same as the figure for the average American;

given the high cost of living in Switzerland, however, the average American is better off.

Third, it may not give an accurate picture of the relative wealth of different societies. Poorer societies may have considerable wealth in the form of minerals, land, water, forests, or ecological variety, which has not yet been exploited but which signifies that they are resource-rich and therefore wealthy, at least potentially.

Finally, GDP totals are usually calculated on the basis of a straight conversion from local currencies into U.S. dollars at the official exchange rate. But currencies in poorer countries may have an inflated value, and costs of living vary from one country to another. To give us a more accurate idea of the relative wealth of countries, some economists have started using a calculation known as **purchasing power parity** (PPP), which is based on comparing the value of goods using the purchasing power of each national currency. The result has been a dramatic recalculation of the relative size of national economies. For example, China's economy leaps from $1.2 trillion to $5.5 trillion, and India's from $480 billion to $2.6 trillion. These recalculations have given comparativists food for thought as they consider how to measure economic wealth, and have further emphasized the significance of NICs in the global economy.

Social Development

Many NICs have religious, ethnic, and regional problems; many of their citizens lack steady jobs and access to basic public services; and poverty is still a critical problem. However, they are investing much more capital in their people than are neighboring LDCs and are building better hospitals, schools, and roads. The overall quality of life is also improving, as reflected in the statistics: While the citizens of most African LDCs can expect to live an average of 54 years, those of

NICs can expect to live an average of 66 to 69 years. Similarly, while infant mortality rates in African LDCs are as high as 80 to 90 per 1,000 live births, the rates in NICs are about 40 to 60 per 1,000 live births. On the Human Development Index, most NICs sit just below liberal democracies with a ranking of High or Medium.

NICs also differ from their poorer neighbors in the extent to which they have invested in infrastructure: they have built strong transportation systems, provided commercial energy and other utilities to a growing number of their people, and developed modern communication systems. Taking advantage of improvements in technology, some NICs have actually leapfrogged over liberal democracies, building new transport and telecommunications systems that are technologically superior to the often much older systems in Western Europe or North America. Improvements in infrastructure have underpinned economic growth, provided social stability, and reinforced political stability.

New Regional and Global Influence

The new economic wealth and political stability of NICs has given them stronger voices regionally and globally, leading to one suggestion that the acronym NIC could as easily stand for Newly *Influential* Countries.[2] The Southeast Asian "tiger" economies are becoming magnets for workers from poorer neighboring states and are being taken more seriously as trading partners by North Americans and Europeans. Many NICs are also strengthening their regional influence through cooperative groups such as the ten-member Association of South East Asian Nations (ASEAN) and Mercosur, which has four South American members.

The power of NICs is reflected in their increasingly effective and aggressive role in international negotiations. Jeffrey Garten, an undersecretary for commerce in the Clinton administration, recalls his experiences during global trade negotiations in Geneva in 1994. The Europeans wielded considerable power, as he expected, but what surprised him was the skill and energy of negotiators from Asia and Latin America: "These men and women had a superb grip on the trading rules and how to negotiate them. They also had a strategic concept of how they wanted to shape the new World Trade Organization...and what they wanted the new body to accomplish."[3] The significance of NICs lies mainly in their new role in global manufacturing and in the extent to which the rich industrialized countries now rely on them as a source of cheap manufactured goods.

THE EVOLUTION OF NICs

Why has a select group of NICs left the Third World behind? How have they built democratic traditions and expanding economies when many other countries with very similar backgrounds have not? To find the answer to these questions, we first need to look at the legacy of **colonialism** (the one experience that almost all Third World states had in common) and at the postcolonial experience of these countries. We will then look at some of the explanations for the emergence of NICs and—in Part IV—look at why other countries have remained poorer and less stable.

The Colonial Era (1450–1950)

A colony is a settlement established in a territory by citizens of a foreign state. The settlement may be small and temporary or large and permanent; either way, its inhabitants answer wholly or partly to the authority of the mother state, with their social and economic life sustained in the colony.

By this definition, almost every country in the world has been colonized at one time or another. However, the most significant and sustained program of colonization was launched by the Europeans in the 15th century and affected every region of the world, directly or indirectly. In chronological order, the major colonial powers were Portugal, Spain, Britain, France, and Russia, with the Dutch, the Germans, the Italians, and the Belgians making up a second and later wave. Their motives varied by time and place:

- **Settlement.** In some cases (such as the Americas, Australia, New Zealand, and southern Africa), people left the mother country with the idea of permanent settlement, displacing or subjugating native populations.

- **Extraction.** In some cases, imperial powers (or private companies from those powers) were simply looking to exploit raw materials and discouraged settlement. The Dutch, for example, established trading posts in the East Indies (now Indonesia) in the 17th and 18th centuries but prohibited permanent settlement. They more or less succeeded there, but failed in South Africa, where the descendants of the earliest Dutch settlers, the Afrikaners, still live today.

- **Strategic advantage.** Competition was behind almost all colonization, but some colonies were created primarily for strategic reasons. For example, Gibraltar was ceded to Britain by Spain in 1713 and maintained as a garrison defending the western entrance to the Mediterranean; Hong Kong was ceded to Britain by China in 1842 and acted as the gateway for trade between China and the world.

The first phase of colonialism began with the Portuguese, who reached the west coast of Africa in 1444, southern Africa in 1487, India in 1498, Brazil in 1500, and China in 1517. Spanish interest dated from 1492, when Columbus crossed the Atlantic, reaching what by 1494 was being called the New World. The Spanish and Portuguese went on to colonize most of what is now Latin America, developing an economy based on plantations and mining, and eventually destroying native civilizations and replacing them with a *mestizo* (mixed-race) society.

The second phase of colonialism came in the 17th century with Dutch interest in the eastern spice trade and the first British and French settlements in North America. Britain and France began a bitter colonial rivalry, competing in the Caribbean, southern Asia, and North America. By the mid-18th century, Britain had won the upper hand, colonizing most of Canada, the American colonies, Australasia (where the main motive was settlement), and India (where the main motive was first trade, then strategic advantage over the French and the Dutch).

With the independence of the United States in 1776 and of most of South America in 1810–1830, a third phase of colonialism began in the 19th century when the Europeans trained their sights on Africa and on trade in slaves, gold, and ivory. Their priorities were clearly reflected in the names they gave to stretches of the West African coast: the Slave Coast (now Nigeria), Grain Coast (Liberia), Ivory Coast, and Gold Coast (Ghana). As trade grew, Europeans created permanent settlements, protected their interests, competed for strategic gain, and moved inland. The competition accelerated with the "Scramble for Africa," when European states raced to stake their claims to Africa. The division of the spoils was confirmed at the Berlin Conference in 1884–1885, which left almost no part of Africa untouched. Only Liberia, created as a haven for freed American slaves in 1847, was never formally colonized, and Ethiopia was only briefly occupied by Italy in 1936–1945. The rest was divided between Britain, France, Portugal, Belgium, Germany, Italy, and Spain.

The final phase of colonialism began in the early 20th century when the Europeans turned their attention to the Middle East. Here the main competitors were again Britain and France, and the main motive was strategic advantage. The Suez Canal, for example, was built to promote trade with India, but it later took on major strategic value (see Chapter 9).

Nationalism and Independence (1920–1970)

By the beginning of the 20th century, there were about two dozen independent nation-states in Europe and the Americas and several dozen colonies in Africa and Asia. Most of South America was independent, as were China and Japan, but global political and economic power lay firmly in the hands of the Europeans and North Americans. Despite this, the first signs of a desire for self-determination and independence began to emerge in the colonies. Pressure for **decolonization** began to grow in the Middle East, where Egypt was given sovereignty in 1922, and Iraq and Lebanon in 1932 and 1944, respectively. The pressures intensified after World War II, from which the European colonial powers emerged on the brink of economic collapse. Unable any longer to justify or support colonialism, they began to withdraw from Asia and Africa.

The independence of India and Pakistan in 1947 marked the beginning of the most intensive period of new state formation in history, with independence given to 95 new countries in just 40 years (see Figure III.2). In 1957, Ghana became the first African state to win independence. France withdrew virtually overnight from 14 of its colonies in 1960, Britain had granted independence to most of its colonies by 1968, and Portuguese dictators grimly put down guerrilla wars in Angola, Mozambique, and Guinea-Bissau until being overthrown by a military coup in 1974.

Developing an Identity (1955–)

Prospects for the newly independent countries of Asia and Africa were not good. Because most had been used as sources of cheap raw materials and labor, little investment had been made in them or their people. Since their frontiers had been set not by competition among the inhabitants of those regions (as was the case in Europe)

FIGURE III.2

The Progress of State Formation

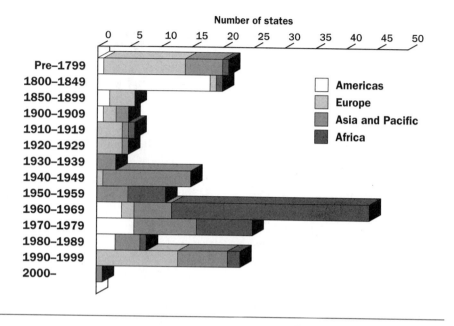

Note: This table includes those countries internationally recognized as sovereign independent states in January 2003.

but by colonial powers competing with one another, many were also artificial creations, with almost every social division known to humanity. Recognizing their weaknesses, the more ambitious Third World leaders began investigating ways of developing a common front, promoting economic and political solidarity, and building common foreign policies.

The first such attempt came with the creation of the Nonaligned Movement in 1955, when 29 countries met in Bandung, Indonesia, to establish positions that would allow them to avoid taking sides in the cold war. The United Nations at that time had only 59 member states, so the creation of a bloc of 29 nonaligned countries seemed to augur well for the future influence of the Third World. **Nonalignment** was based on a set of principles, including the importance of national sovereignty, the equality of nations, and noninterference in the internal affairs of other states. Members agreed not to join military pacts dominated by the superpowers, but this goal was undermined from the start when some aligned themselves with the communist bloc (for example, North Vietnam and Cuba), and others with the Western alliance (for example, Pakistan and the Philippines).[4]

The Nonaligned Movement today has 114 members, representing about half the world's population, and has held regular summit conferences over the last 40 years:

Belgrade (1961), Cairo (1964), Lusaka (1970), Algiers (1973), Colombo (1976), Havana (1979), New Delhi (1983), Harare (1986), Belgrade (1989), Jakarta (1992), Cartagena (1995), Durban (1998), and Kuala Lumpur (2003). But although it has been a symbolic rallying point for Asian and African diplomacy, it has amounted to little more than a gesture, undermined by political and economic divisions among its members. Since the end of the cold war, the concept of nonalignment has been weakened and the movement has switched its focus to issues such as reform of the United Nations, a new system of international relations, solidarity among its members, and an end to nuclear proliferation.

The United Nations has been a more important forum for the expression of the views of African, Asian, and Latin American states; the governments of these countries make up two-thirds of UN membership. None of them has the power of veto in the Security Council enjoyed by the United States, Britain, France, Russia, and China, and the bargaining power of poorer states has been undermined by the dependence of many of them on UN assistance and by the declining credibility of the United Nations. Even so, African, Asian, and Latin American delegates have used their numbers to place their concerns on the UN agenda.

They have also tried to renegotiate the terms of the global economic system. The first step in this process was the creation of the **United Nations Conference on Trade and Development** (UNCTAD) in 1964. Headquartered in Geneva, UNCTAD works to maximize trade, investment, and development opportunities for poorer countries, its work revolving around quadrennial meetings among its member states, which include almost every country in the world. UNCTAD also became the foundation for the creation of the **Group of 77** (G-77), which originally consisted of the 77 countries that took part in the first UNCTAD conference, but which now (confusingly) has 133 members.

G-77 used its voting powers in the UN General Assembly to campaign for the creation of the **New International Economic Order** (NIEO). A response to the liberal economic order dominated by rich industrialized countries and geared toward the promotion of free trade, the idea of the NIEO was launched in 1974. The goal was to reform the global trading and financial system so that it was not weighted against poorer countries, mainly by negotiating new trade agreements that would allow these countries to make greater profits out of their exports of raw materials. The NIEO was based on general principles, and made no suggestions for specific action or for ways of achieving its own goals, and it offered no explanation of what poorer countries could offer richer countries in return for the concessions they demanded.[5]

In 1989, G-77 shifted the focus back to itself, and after asking what its members could do to help themselves, agreed on a Global System of Trade Preferences (GSTP). Much like the General Agreement on Tariffs and Trade, this was designed to promote and sustain trade and economic cooperation among its members by reducing barriers to trade. Two rounds of negotiations have been completed so far, and a third is planned. The problem, though, is that most G-77 countries export more in the way of low-profit raw material and agricultural products than high-profit manufactured goods, and even where they export the latter, it is often only wealthy liberal democracies that can afford to import them in significant quantities.

NEWLY INDUSTRIALIZING COUNTRIES TODAY

The defining characteristics of NICs include improved democratic records, export-led growth, and social investment, but trying to explain the effects of the links among the three has left social scientists scratching their heads. Many have tried to develop theoretical explanations for the postcolonial record of African, Asian, and Latin American countries to explain why some have become rich while others have not, but few of their explanations have been widely accepted.

During the 1950s and 1960s, it was often argued that several preconditions were needed for the emergence of a stable democracy, including a minimum level of wealth (so a country could provide its people with basic needs and services, reducing the tensions that led to political conflict), a social consensus on the value of democracy, and a sense of national identity. The argument was made that greater wealth would improve the chances of democracy emerging.[6] However, political change in Latin America and sub-Saharan Africa in the 1980s and 1990s seemed to undermine these arguments. How, for example, did they explain the fact that Indonesia and Mexico were increasingly wealthy NICs, yet their politics remained authoritarian? Similarly, why was democracy emerging in poor countries such as Tanzania and Zambia?

The contradictions led some scholars to the conclusion that there was probably no one precondition for the emergence of democracy and that rather than paving the way for democracy, growing economic wealth and improvements in the quality of life may instead be a consequence of democratization.[7] Which came first—the chicken or the egg—remains a matter of debate. All that can be said with any certainty is that economic growth is difficult (but not impossible) without political stability, and economic growth can lead to political stability (but not inevitably). Investment in infrastructure—such as education, health care, and transportation—is also critical.

Although many poorer countries have tried to renegotiate the terms of the global economic system to suit themselves and to provide them with greater opportunities, NICs have emerged from the pack by taking on the rich industrialized countries at their own game. They have exploited their two greatest resources—plentiful cheap labor and often substantial natural resources—to undercut labor markets in the liberal democracies and attract new investment. This has been used to invest in infrastructure and to shift their economies away from a reliance on agriculture to a much heavier reliance instead on industry and services. As people have become healthier, wealthier, and better educated, they have demanded political change. Indeed, democratization has been a critical element in the process by which economic development has proceeded.

It is often said that the 19th century was the British century and that the 20th century was the American century. All the key indicators suggest that the 21st century will belong to Asia or Latin America. These are the two regions of the world where we will have to look for the next great economic powers—and with economic power comes political influence. Already, four of the world's biggest economies are NICs (India, Brazil, Mexico, and Indonesia), and—although it is not classified as a NIC in this text because of its poor record on democratization—it is only a matter of time before China, already the biggest emerging economy in the world, joins the ranks of the NICs.

KEY TERMS

colonialism
decolonization
export-led growth
Group of 77
megacities

multinational corporations
New International
    Economic Order
nonalignment
purchasing power parity

sweatshops
United Nations
    Conference on Trade
    and Development
    (UNCTAD)

STUDY QUESTIONS

1. Is there anything that the experience of liberal democracies in the 19th century can tell us about the political and economic changes being witnessed by NICs today?

2. Is there anything in the Japanese experience to suggest that some NICs may be the Japans of the future?

3. Is political stability possible without economic growth? Is economic growth possible without political stability?

4. There is an old saying that if you cannot bite, you should not show your teeth. What would it take to give NICs the ability to "bite" in their relationship with rich industrialized countries?

NICs ONLINE

Group of 77: *http://www.g77.org*
Web site of the Group of 77, with information on its goals and programs.
UNCTAD: *http://www.unctad.org*
Web site of the UN body that has played a key role in the economic development of poorer countries.
Nonaligned Movement: *http://www.nam.gov.za*
Web site of the nonaligned movement, containing information on its meetings and objectives.
South Movement: *http://southmovement.alphalink.com.au*
An unofficial guide to the Nonaligned Movement, from Australia.

FURTHER READING

Garten, Jeffrey, *The Big Ten: The Big Emerging Markets and How They Will Change Our Lives* (New York: Basic Books, 1997). A study of the political and economic potential of ten Third World states, including India, Mexico, Brazil and Argentina.

Harris, Nigel, *The End of the Third World* (London: Penguin, 1990). Although now dated, still an interesting study of the reasons why NICs emerged and why the concept of the Third World is misleading.

Marber, Peter, *From Third World to World Class: The Future of Emerging Markets in the Global Economy* (Cambridge, MA: Perseus Publishing, 1999). A New York investment manager argues that free trade is good for the United States and for emerging economies.

Weatherby, Joseph N., et al., *The Other World: Issues and Politics of the Developing World*, 4th Ed. (New York: Longman, 2000). A general introduction to the politics, policies, and problems of the non-Western world.

MEXICO

MEXICO: QUICK FACTS

Official name: United Mexican States

Capital: Mexico City

Area: 737,000 square miles (1,908,000 sq. km) (almost three times the size of Texas)

Languages: Predominantly Spanish, with several indigenous languages

Population: 98 million

Population density: 133 per square mile (51 per sq. km.)

Population growth rate: 1.4 percent

POLITICAL INDICATORS

Freedom House rating: Partly Free

Date of state formation: 1821

System type: Presidential republic

Constitution: Published 1917

Administration: Federal, with 31 states and the Federal District of Mexico City

Executive: President, elected for a single 6-year term

Legislature: Bicameral National Congress: Senate (128 members elected for 6-year terms) and Chamber of Deputies (500 members elected for 3-year terms). Members may not serve consecutive terms

Party structure: Multiparty

Judiciary: Supreme Court (11 members appointed for life and confirmed by Senate)

Head of state: Vicente Fox Quesada (2000–)

Head of government: Vicente Fox Quesada (2000–)

ECONOMIC INDICATORS

GDP (2001): $617.8 billion

Per capita GDP: $5,540

Distribution of GDP: Services 69 percent, industry 27 percent, agriculture 4 percent

Urban population: 74 percent

SOCIAL INDICATORS

HDI ranking: 51

Infant mortality rate: 29 per 1,000 live births

Life expectancy: 73 years

Literacy: 90% of people aged 15 and older

Religions: Predominantly Catholic

INTRODUCTION

Mexico is not a country that often appears in international news headlines, yet the changes that have taken place there since the late 1970s have been revolutionary and have affected all of the Americas, including the United States. A program of democratization has been so successful that the Institutional Revolutionary party—in power without a break since 1929—lost the presidency in 2000. Almost equally significant has been Mexico's program of economic reform, which has brought greater freedom to a market with 98 million consumers and has broadened the base of the world's ninth biggest economy and eighth biggest producer of oil.

All of this has been happening right on the doorstep of the United States, yet although the two countries share a 2,000-mile border and a nearly 500-year history, most Americans show a remarkable lack of interest in Mexico. Most of those who travel there head for border towns like Tijuana or resorts like Cancun and make little effort to experience or understand Mexico on its own terms. Popular perceptions among Americans have long been driven by concerns about drugs, illegal immigration, and the loss of manufacturing jobs to low-paid workers south of the Rio Grande.

But all this is changing. Latinos are now the biggest ethnic minority in the United States (more than 12 percent of the population), and Mexican Americans make up about 58 percent of those Latinos; in parts of southern Texas and California, Latinos are in a majority (see Close-Up View, p. 299). The United States, Canada, and Mexico have also been partners since 1994 in the **North American Free Trade Agreement** (NAFTA), which has meant an increased overlap of U.S. and Mexican interests on issues as varied as immigration, trade, tourism, labor, water supply, drugs, and the environment. The importance of stability south of the border was graphically emphasized by the collapse of the peso in late 1994 and the speed with which the United States led a multinational rescue mission. The health of the Mexican economy is of direct interest to all Americans.

Mexico is still large and relatively poor, but it has many of the classic features of a newly industrializing country, including steady democratization, export-led growth, a service-based economy, a rapidly developing industrial base, and often startling economic and social paradoxes. It is common to hear talk of two Mexicos: one wealthy, urban, and modern and the other poor, rural, and traditional. One in ten Mexicans is illiterate, yet one in six goes on to higher education (a figure comparable to that of many European countries). Mexico City is a nightmare of congestion, yet it has an extensive subway that carries more passengers every day than the New York City subway. Within sight of urban slums with open sewers you might see smartly dressed investment brokers driving to work in air-conditioned luxury cars, using cell phones to close a deal or make a restaurant reservation.

In social terms, Mexico has few serious religious or ethnic problems. More than 90 percent of the population is Catholic and *mestizo* (of mixed Spanish and native American blood). About 5 percent of the population is pure native American, descendants of the Mayas, Zapotecs, Tarascans, and Aztecs. They may be few, but they have had a greater impact on Mexican society and politics than their northern cousins have had on U.S. society. Because the term *Indian* has cultural rather than racial connotations, it is possible to move across cultures,[1] and there is less direct racism or discrimination in

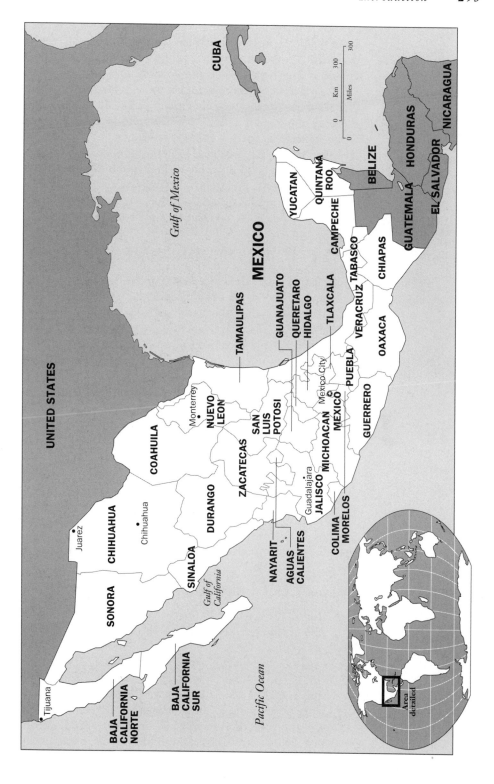

Mexico than in the United States. However, native Americans are often poorer and more politically marginalized than *mestizos*. Their problems have been exemplified by outbreaks of violence in several poor southern states, which have also emphasized the economic gaps between rich and poor in Mexico.

The Mexican political system has some similarities with the U.S. system: It is a federal republic with a separately elected president and legislature. In practice, though, there are important differences. Mexican presidents have much more power than their U.S. counterparts, there is limited press freedom, and despite the existence of a federal structure, the political system is heavily centralized. This has left political scientists undecided about how to describe Mexico. Some call it authoritarian; others use words such as *bureaucratic*, *elitist*, and *patrimonial* when trying to describe it. But reforms to the electoral system have made Mexico more democratic, and the old assumptions about the nature of the political system are now under active review.

POLITICAL DEVELOPMENT

Unlike either the United States or Canada—which come mainly out of the European tradition and where the early colonists did not try to integrate with natives but destroyed them or pushed them aside and seized their land—Mexico is a product both of its European and its native American heritage. It is, as the late Mexican Nobel laureate Octavio Paz put it, a "land of superimposed pasts"[2] and continues today to be a melding of European and native American ideas about law, government, and society.

The Precolonial Era

Until the 15th century, native peoples such as the Mayas and the Aztecs inhabited most of what is now Mexico. The Aztecs arrived in central Mexico from the arid north in the 12th century, building their capital at Tenochtitlán (now Mexico City). Subduing their enemies, they built an empire with its own local governments, a centralized tax and court system, and ruling castes of religious and military leaders. In many ways, modern Mexican politics reflects the centralized and hierarchical Aztec system, but despite the sophistication and reach of native society and despite the remaining native American cultural influence in Mexico, modern Mexican politics is mainly a product of changes that have taken place since the arrival of the Europeans.

Spanish Occupation (16th Century to 1821)

The Spanish arrived in 1519 under the command of Hernán Cortés, subjugating the Aztecs relatively easily. Not only did the Spaniards have better weapons but they also had horses (which the Aztecs had never seen before), and they were helped by Aztec religious beliefs that "white gods" would one day arrive in the region and by the resentment of tribes under Aztec rule who took the opportunity to rebel.

By the middle of the 16th century, the whole of what is now Mexico (along with large parts of what is now the southwestern United States) had been conquered and occupied by Spain. Mexican gold and silver were sent home to feed the Spanish economy, and Christianity was brought to Mexico, becoming the linchpin of a new and authoritarian political system. The Spanish also brought diseases to which the natives had no immunity, such as measles and smallpox. In the more than 300 years of Spanish occupation, the native population fell from 11 million to 6 million; nearly 3 million natives died in epidemics of one unidentified disease in the mid-16th century alone.

At least partly inspired by the American Revolution, Mexican revolutionaries began agitating for independence in the early 19th century. The struggle became one between Spanish administrators (the *peninsulares*) on one hand and Mexicans of Spanish descent *(criollos)* and *mestizos* on the other. In contrast to the claims made by its U.S. counterpart, however, the Mexican independence movement was aimed not so much at promoting liberalism and equality as at preserving privilege and elitism. In fact, Spain had introduced a new constitution in 1812 that was more liberal than the new Mexican version was to be.

Independence and War (1821–1848)

After a long struggle (1810–1821), Mexico finally won its independence in 1821 and then tried to build its own empire in central America. However, its economy was weak; it lacked the stability needed to attract foreign investment; and doubts about the kind of society Mexicans wanted to build led to a power struggle between liberals espousing a democratic, federal system of government and conservatives favoring a more centralized system.[3] Politics broke down in revolution, rigged elections, and rapid changes in leadership; in the first 50 years of independence alone, there were 30 presidents.

Mexico's development was also affected by conflicts with the United States. In 1825 Mexico invited Americans to settle in and develop Texas, which was then part of Mexico. By 1830, about 20,000 settlers had arrived, alarming Mexico into banning further immigration and trying to tighten its control over the new immigrants in 1835. The immigrants responded in 1836 by declaring their independence and requesting U.S. annexation. Although General Antonio López de Santa Anna defeated the defenders of the Alamo mission in San Antonio, he was beaten at the battle of San Jacinto and forced to agree to Texan independence. In 1845 the United States annexed Texas over Mexican protests, precipitating the war of 1846. This war ended in 1848 with the Treaty of Guadalupe-Hidalgo, which ceded half the land area of Mexico (including California, New Mexico, Arizona, and part of what is now Texas) to the United States.

Mexico saw further threats to its independence when France, Britain, and Spain demanded reparations for losses suffered during the war. Napoleon III of France took advantage of Mexico's internal weaknesses in 1864 by declaring a French-dependent Mexican empire with Archduke Maximilian of Austria as emperor. A resistance movement overthrew and executed Maximilian in 1867, and Benito Juárez became president. This introduced many political changes, including stronger civil liberties, regular elections, reductions in the powers of the church, and expanded public education. These changes did not amount to a new liberal order, however, and in 1877 the military government of José de la Cruz Porfirio Díaz came to power.

The *Porfiriato* (1877–1910)

Díaz dominated Mexican politics for 35 years, serving as president for all but one 4-year term (1880–1884). During the era that came to be known as the *porfiriato*, Mexico enjoyed political stability and economic expansion; national income, foreign investment,

Key Dates in Mexican History

1519	Spanish occupation begins
1810–1821	War of independence
1821	Independence of Mexico
1836	Independence of Texas
1846–1848	War with the United States
1848	Loss of New Mexico and California to the United States
1864–1867	Rule of Archduke Maximilian of Austria
1877–1911	*Porfiriato*
1910	Outbreak of the Revolution
1913–1917	Civil war
1917	Publication of the Mexican constitution
1929	Creation of National Revolutionary party, precursor to PRI
1938	Creation of Pemex
1953	Women given the right to vote
1968	Mexico City Olympic games; massacre of student demonstrators
1977	Electoral law changed to add 100 seats elected by proportional representation to the Chamber of Deputies
1982	Debt crisis
1985	Mexico City earthquakes kill 20,000
1986	Mexico joins the General Agreement on Tariffs and Trade (GATT) and signs a loan agreement with the International Monetary Fund (IMF); number of seats in Chamber of Deputies elected by proportional representation increased to 200
1992	Mexico signs the North American Free Trade Agreement
1994	(January) Mexico joins NAFTA, and insurrection breaks out in southern state of Chiapas; Mexico joins the OECD; (December) Ernesto Zedillo takes office, promising to govern with respect for the rule of law; loss of foreign investor confidence leads to devaluation of peso
1995	(January) President Clinton bypasses Congress to authorize economic rescue package for Mexico
1996	(August) Political reform package unanimously passed by both houses of Congress
1997	(June) PRI loses its majority in the Chamber of Deputies for the first time
1999	(November) First ever primary to choose PRI presidential candidate
2000	(July) National elections; PRI loses the presidency for the first time in 71 years, and loses its majority in the Senate; (December) Vicente Fox takes office as president
2001	(February) George W. Bush chooses Mexico for the first foreign trip of his presidency

and trade all grew; the railroads were expanded; and vast new tracts of land were opened to settlers. However, economic development came at the cost of political freedom. Díaz ended free elections, curtailed freedom of speech and the press, put down dissent in the rural areas, ignored the separation of powers and states' rights, and tried to suppress native American culture. Elections were held, but the results were rigged. Large landholders became wealthy, but peasants lost their land and were forced to become laborers, and the majority of Mexicans remained illiterate. The middle classes were unhappy about being excluded from power and demanded greater democracy. When Díaz announced that he would step down in 1910 and then changed his mind, a rebellion broke out. His forces quickly defeated, Díaz resigned and went into exile in 1911.

Revolution and Civil War (1910–1917)

Much like the 1917 Russian Revolution, the **Mexican Revolution** came out of the middle and upper classes. Unlike their Russian counterparts, however, who claimed that they wanted to end the inequalities of the tsarist regime and to spread political and social justice, Mexican revolutionaries were mainly interested in opening up opportunities for themselves and in reducing the power and influence of foreign capitalists.

The first of the post-*porfiriato* leaders was Francisco Madero, leader of the revolution and member of a wealthy landowning family. Although he restored freedom of the press and individual property rights, he let too many officials from the Díaz era stay in office and failed to make the kind of reforms that would have won him the support of the peasants. In 1913 he was murdered in a U.S.-sponsored coup led by the brutal and corrupt Victoriano Huerta. A brief and violent civil war broke out, with three competing groups ranged against Huerta: a peasant army led by Emiliano Zapata, an army of workers and cattlemen led by Francisco "Pancho" Villa, and a group of ranchers and businessmen led by Venustiano Carranza. More than a million people died in the war, Carranza was in control by 1915, and Villa and Zapata were both later assassinated.

In 1917 a new constitution was drawn up that has been the basis of Mexican government ever since. Radical and progressive, it included many of the same basic ideas as the U.S. Constitution (including separation of powers, federalism, and a Bill of Rights), but Mexico's constitution differed in giving the state control over all natural resources, the federal government the right to redistribute land, and workers greater rights than they had in the United States.

The Mexican Revolution is often described as one of the first great social revolutions of the 20th century, predating both the Russian and Chinese revolutions. Revolutions supposedly involve major political and social change, but although Mexico may have enjoyed more freedom of expression, more tolerance of opposition, and more open criticism of government, its political system still shows signs of authoritarianism. One in four Mexicans still live in poverty, women are still politically and economically marginalized, land is still unequally distributed, and concerns about Mexican economic independence remain an important public issue. This is why many Mexicans argue that the goals of the revolution have not yet been met and that the revolution is continuing.

Stabilizing the Revolution (1924–1940)

Of the early postrevolutionary presidents, two in particular made key contributions to Mexico's political development. The first was Plutarco Elías Calles (1924–1928), who in 1929 created the National Revolutionary party as a way of perpetuating his political influence. The party went on to govern Mexico for the rest of the century. (Its name was changed in 1945 to the *Institutional Revolutionary party,* or PRI, pronounced "pree.") Even more influential was Lázaro Cárdenas (1934–1940), the most left-wing of Mexico's presidents. He redistributed more land than his seven predecessors combined, supported labor unions, and—most important—launched a program of nationalization. Concerned at the extent to which Mexican companies were controlled by foreigners, he brought several industries under state control and in 1938 created the state oil corporation, today called Petróleos Mexicanos *(Pemex).* This so upset the United States and other countries that they began a boycott of Mexican oil. For all these changes—aimed at economic and political equality and stability, and at asserting Mexican independence—Cárdenas remains the most revered of Mexico's 20th century presidents.

Portillo and the Oil Crisis (1976–1982)

After Cárdenas, Mexico's economic and political development paved the way for steady economic growth in the 1960s and 1970s, but signs of underlying structural problems began to emerge. Falling agricultural exports indicated a loss of competitiveness, leading in turn to middle-class discontent. This was reflected in the events of the summer of 1968, when students used the media spotlight provided by the Mexico City Olympics to demand political liberalization. A government crackdown resulted in as many as 500 students being killed by the army, leading in turn to a crisis of political legitimacy. To make matters worse, Mexico's economy was in trouble.

Taking advantage of new profits from oil price increases in the 1970s, the Echeverría regime (1970–1976) launched an expensive oil exploration program that found vast new oil resources. This encouraged José López Portillo (1976–1982) to follow a more liberal line in domestic politics and economic policy, making him popular with investors and the upper and middle classes and moving toward greater independence from the United States in foreign policy. Heavy investments were made in transport, industry, communications, health care, and education, and hundreds of thousands of jobs were created. However, the high spending brought inflation and encouraged more imports and fewer exports. When the price of oil began to fall, Mexico borrowed to cover its spending, building a large national debt. In 1982 Mexico came close to defaulting on its debt, prompting talk of a "Third World debt crisis." Chastened, the Mexican government began a shift away from centralized economic management to a more open and competitive free-market system.

In 1986 Mexico joined the General Agreement on Tariffs and Trade (GATT), in 1994 it became a member both of NAFTA and of the Organization for Economic Cooperation and Development (OECD), and recent governments have pursued a policy of privatization—all signs of a more liberal line on the economy. However, the

CLOSE-UP VIEW

THE RISE OF THE MEXICAN DIASPORA

The term *diaspora* refers to the broad community of a group of people, transcending national borders. In the case of Mexicans, it refers to everyone of Mexican origin living both inside and outside the country. The latter group has been growing: According to U.S. Census data for 2000, there are now 18 to 21 million people of Mexican origin living in the United States. The majority are U.S. citizens, but about 9 million are Mexican-born and mainly still citizens of Mexico, and about 3 to 4 million are illegal residents. Another 300,000 arrive each year to settle permanently in the United States, and an estimated 1 to 3 million arrive every year to work in seasonal agriculture.

The expansion of the diaspora has implications for both Mexico and the United States. It is significant for Mexico because so many of its skilled and unskilled workers have left for better-paying jobs in the United States, taking away an important part of Mexico's labor pool but also providing an important source of foreign income; it has been estimated that Mexicans living in the United States send an estimated $5 to $10 billion annually back to their families at home. It is also significant because of the large numbers of Mexican voters who now live in the United States; so

many, in fact, that during the 2000 Mexican presidential election, the major candidates visited the United States to campaign among expatriate Mexicans.

The expansion of the diaspora is significant for the United States for several reasons. Most obviously, Mexican workers—both legal and illegal—play an increasingly important role in the American economy, providing a growing proportion of the unskilled labor force, for example, especially in seasonal agriculture. There are concerns about the quality of life for many of these workers, who are exploited in a way that would not be tolerated if American workers were involved. There are also concerns about the impact of illegal immigration from Mexico on national security and the war on terrorism because of the increased demand for false identity documents. Finally, immigration is changing the social, cultural, and political makeup of the United States. This is particularly true in border states such as Texas, New Mexico, Arizona, and California, where the population of Mexican origin makes up 20 to 25 percent of the total. In several American border towns, such as Yuma, Nogales, Douglas, El Paso, Laredo, and Brownsville, there are Latino majorities in the range of 75 to 95 percent.

fragility of Mexico's economic development was emphasized by the collapse of the peso in late 1994, to which the Clinton administration responded with a $50 billion international rescue package of loan guarantees to again help Mexico avoid defaulting on its debt. Drug trafficking has also grown alarmingly and has been made more difficult to control because of widespread police and political corruption, harming U.S.-Mexican relations.

At the same time, the fragility of Mexico's political development was emphasized by unrest in the poor southern states of **Chiapas,** Oaxaca, and Guerrero. Complaining about being cheated out of their land and being denied basic services, and feeling the effects of falling coffee prices, peasants in Chiapas rebelled in January 1994. Led by the charismatic Subcomandante Marcos, their masked and pipe-smoking leader, several hundred members of the Zapatista National Liberation Army (named after Emiliano Zapata) seized several towns and denounced NAFTA as a "death sentence" on Mexico's natives. Hundreds of troops were sent in to put down the rebellion, resulting in more than 150 deaths. The Zapatists stopped fighting almost immediately, and a peace agreement was eventually signed, but troops stayed on in Chiapas.

Meanwhile, a series of electoral reforms encouraged the rise of opposition parties and gave them more seats in the national Congress. The share of the PRI vote fell steadily as the governing party lost the support of unions and of a middle class hurt by Mexico's worsening economic problems. In 1997 PRI lost its majority in the Chamber of Deputies for the first time, and in 2000 lost its majority in the Senate and—most remarkable of all—lost the presidency of Mexico. The new president, Vicente Fox, came to office on a platform promising fiscal reform, sustainable economic growth, more social spending, political decentralization, and a more assertive foreign policy.

Mexico Today

Just in the last decade, Mexico has undergone a major transformation:

- It has begun to transform into a healthy multiparty democracy, and the Fox administration has been unable to manipulate government like its predecessors, instead having to work to build multiparty support for its policies.

- The state has retreated from the marketplace in the wake of an extensive program of privatization, under which inefficient state-owned monopolies have been replaced by more competitive privately owned businesses better placed to take on international competition.

- Mexico now has a bigger GDP than that of Spain, India, South Korea, or Russia, and its new economic status was confirmed in 1994 when it joined OECD. Until then, OECD had been a club for the world's liberal democracies; Mexico's accession was confirmation that it could finally sit alongside the world's richest and most democratic countries.

- A tenuous peace has been achieved in Chiapas, symbolized in 2001 when Subcomandante Marcos (still wearing his famous mask) marched with his followers to Mexico City. However, rebels still control much of the state.

- Mexico's foreign policy—long hidden under the shadow of the United States—has become more assertive and independent. The Fox administration has worked hard to improve ties with the United States and to influence U.S. policy, and Mexico has strengthened its ties with other Latin American countries and developed a reputation as a champion of free trade.

Despite all of these changes, Mexico is not yet a liberal democracy. Its political institutions have not developed the necessary consistency and predictability, power is still too heavily focused in the hands of the presidency, there is still much to be done to improve the quality of life for its people (especially those living in rural areas), corruption is still a major problem in government and public services, and Mexico's record on human rights still needs improvement. But in almost every respect, the trends are positive.

POLITICAL CULTURE

There is a tension in Mexican society between democracy and authoritarianism. It has been said that while North American political culture is driven by the values of John Locke and liberalism, Latin American political culture is "elitist, hierarchical, authoritarian, corporatist, and patrimonialist."[4] Economic pressures and calculated changes to the system of government have begun to challenge these traditions in Mexico, promising to fundamentally rearrange the relationship between government and people. Put another way, economic modernization has increased the demand for political modernization.[5] For now at least, Mexican political culture has six main features.

The Continuing Revolution

While Americans tend to focus on the future, Mexicans hark back to the past, to missed opportunities and unfulfilled dreams. Most have faith and pride in the 1917 constitution, agree with the goals of the Revolution, and support their political institutions. Revolutionary principles and national aspirations are perpetuated by the myths built around heroes as varied as Cuauhtémoc (nephew of the Aztec emperor Moctezuma and leader of the opposition to the Spanish conquistadors), Pancho Villa, and Emiliano Zapata. The Institutional Revolutionary party exploited these symbols by associating itself with them and portraying itself as the standard-bearer for revolutionary ideals.

At the same time, Mexicans recognize that the constitution is a work in progress and that it contains many goals that have not yet been met. Its supporters argue that Mexico is democratizing but that there are still many handicaps to the final achievement of democracy. For example, a strong presidency was seen as essential to helping Mexico restore order and build strong political institutions after the Revolution, but first there had to be economic growth. Now that Mexico is richer and has a growing middle class, there are greater opportunities for political modernization.

Nationalism

For many Mexicans, the history of their country has followed a pattern in which they have repeatedly had to defend themselves against more powerful foreigners. In some cases, the threats have taken the form of direct military confrontation, such as those between Mexico and Spain in the early 19th century, between the United States and Mexico in 1846–1848, and between Mexico and France in the 1860s. In other cases, the threats have been economic, such as the foreign investment that took place during the *porfiriato*. Debates over NAFTA and the 1995 bailout of the peso once again raised the issue of economic dominance by the United States.

Hierarchy and Elitism

Like many of its Latin American neighbors, Mexico has many of the hierarchical features of the Catholic Church and the elitism of native American society. Spanish Catholicism was based on the idea that political authority emanated from God, and all lower levels of society had progressively less power and status. Mexican society is still class-based, with people and groups ranked within the political system and real power held by an elite whose attitudes are both paternalistic and authoritarian. The elite was once made up almost exclusively of the military; today it consists mainly of technocrats (technical experts) and of the entrepreneurs who have benefited most from privatization.

The Corporatist State

Mexico offers a good example of a phenomenon most often found in Latin American societies: **corporatism.** A corporatist state is one in which groups representing the major social and economic interests are incorporated by government. The groups are given privileged official positions, access to government, and permission to bargain with the government on public policies; in return, group members respect and support the policies agreed on. This tends to create a system that is top-down and elitist, is based heavily on patronage, and works against political or economic liberalism. In the Mexican case, the most important groups are workers, peasants, and the "popular" sector (mainly the middle classes, small businesspeople, government employees, and the professions).

The signs of corporatism in Mexico are becoming harder to find. Democratic changes have coupled with improved education to make workers and peasants more difficult to manipulate and have also taken power away from the governing elite and distributed it to a broader, popular base. Meanwhile, economic changes have opened up the Mexican marketplace. The result has been a move away from the corporatist traditions of the last 70 years and toward the pluralist ideas associated with liberal democracy.[6]

Centralism and Corruption

Mexico may be a federal republic, but power traditionally has been centralized in the ruling political party, and political power often revolves around groups of supporters and confidantes known as *camarillas,* each of which has a single leader at its core. In such systems, personalities become more important than ideology or policies in determining political behavior, and power revolves around patron-client relationships, with followers providing support in return for political favors. Political careers often depend heavily on "old-boy networks," which contribute to the corruption that is a common feature of Mexican politics.

Machismo

Although many of the ideas in the Mexican constitution reflect those in liberal democratic constitutions, not all have been put into practice, in part because *machismo* (assertive masculinity) is still a central characteristic of Mexican political culture. *Machismo* expresses itself in the political marginalization of women, who won the right to vote only in 1953 and still rarely move into positions of authority within government. It can also be seen in political violence, such as demonstrations, riots, kidnappings, political assassinations, and even guerrilla warfare. Government occasionally responds with its own kind of violence, which may take the form of direct repression or human rights abuses. Recourse to violence may also be a symptom of the feeling among more frustrated Mexicans that nonviolent participation is futile.

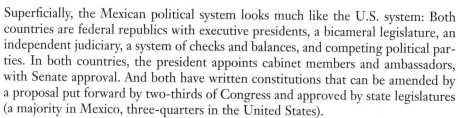

POLITICAL SYSTEM

Superficially, the Mexican political system looks much like the U.S. system: Both countries are federal republics with executive presidents, a bicameral legislature, an independent judiciary, a system of checks and balances, and competing political parties. In both countries, the president appoints cabinet members and ambassadors, with Senate approval. And both have written constitutions that can be amended by a proposal put forward by two-thirds of Congress and approved by state legislatures (a majority in Mexico, three-quarters in the United States).

Appearances deceive, however, because there are at least two critical differences between the United States and Mexico:

- Power in Mexico is centralized in the presidency, with Congress and the judiciary playing supporting roles and the constitution giving the federal government many powers to intervene in the affairs of Mexico's 31 states. The president has wide-ranging control over appointments to key positions in government, can issue decrees and declare states of emergency (like his Russian counterpart), has substantial powers of patronage at his disposal, and—at least until recently—has played a major role in deciding who will win the nomination to be his successor.

- Mexico has been dominated since 1929 by one party, the Institutional Revolutionary party (PRI). By agreeing to pacts with the major economic and social groups in Mexican society and even with opposition political parties, PRI for many years had little trouble having its programs passed by the Mexican Congress. Its longtime control of the electoral process—sometimes even altering the results when necessary—also ensured that it routinely won elections at every level of government. At the same time, opposition parties were given enough concessions to keep them cooperative.

This has all now begun to change. Elections are more honest and competitive, PRI has been pushed into opposition, the checks and balances between president and legislature now finally mean something, and power is being redistributed to a broader, popular base.

THE CONSTITUTION

Drawn up in 1917, the Mexican constitution is one of the oldest in Latin America, the major legacy of the Revolution, and the blueprint by which progress in meeting the goals of the Revolution is measured. Nineteenth century Mexican constitutions drew heavily on the U.S. Constitution and were seen less as blueprints for government than as outlines of goals to which Mexico aspired. The 1917 constitution was different in that it was grounded more firmly in the realities of Mexico, and as such had characteristics that made it different from its U.S. counterpart.

First, **economic nationalism** is at the core of its principles. As Mexican revolutionaries wrote the constitution, they cast worried glances over their shoulders at the looming economic power of the United States. To protect Mexican interests, they included limits on foreign investment and foreign ownership of land and other natural resources, denied anyone but Mexicans the right to own land or water resources, and—in the controversial Article 27—vested ownership of all minerals and other underground resources in the state. Ideas like this have become increasingly difficult to defend as Mexico opens up its market under the terms of NAFTA and the other free-trade agreements of which it is a part, and have posed a barrier to President Fox's attempts to open up the Mexican energy market.

Second, while the gap between church and state in the United States is sometimes ambiguous and often hotly contested, there have—until recently—been few such ambiguities in Mexico. Until reforms to the constitution in 1992, the church had no legal standing, which meant that priests could not vote (although many did), and it was prohibited from owning property or taking part in politics. This has not stopped church leaders from campaigning for social justice, however; priests have been active in defending the rights of native Mexicans, in criticizing electoral fraud, and in speaking out about the problems of poverty. During the PRI era, Mexicans frustrated with the weakness of opposition parties often turned to the church as a vehicle to express their political demands.[7] Among his other mold-breaking characteristics, Vicente Fox became the first openly practicing Catholic president since the Revolution, and he promised to allow the church a greater role in public and political life.

Finally, to prevent anyone from accumulating too much power, the Mexican constitution places limits on the number of terms that can be served by elected officials. The Mexican president is limited to a single 6-year term, and no members of Congress or of state and local governments can be elected to the same public office for consecutive terms.

The constitution is relatively easy to change, with amendments needing the support of only two-thirds of the members of Congress. In the United States, making amendments to the constitution is both controversial and time-consuming, which is why it has been amended only 27 times in 215 years. American politicians rely on changes in the law to bring about changes in the structure of government. By contrast, Mexican leaders will frequently propose constitutional amendments, even for trivial matters. For example, while he was still a local politician in 1994, Vicente Fox successfully petitioned for an amendment that would allow him—the son of a Spanish mother—to run for the presidency. More broadly, presidents have often used the constitution to legitimize controversial policy issues. The result is that the Mexican constitution has been amended nearly 350 times in 85 years. A package of electoral reforms in August 1996 alone involved 18 amendments, and President Fox was quick to propose more amendments when he came to office. All these changes have led its critics to ask whether the constitution still reflects the goals and principles of the Revolution.

THE EXECUTIVE: PRESIDENT

Presidents dominate the Mexican political system: All real political power flows from—and revolves around—the president, who decides the policies and character of Mexican government. This was particularly true between 1929 and 2000, when PRI had a monopoly on the presidency, but it would probably have been true whichever party was in government, simply because of the powers that come with the job. So powerful is the office that the term *presidencialismo,* or **presidentialism,** has been coined to describe the phenomenon; it means that most power lies in the hands of the president and that all policy, whether good or bad, stems personally from the president.[8] During the PRI years, no Mexican president ever had his legislation turned down by Congress.

Like his U.S. counterpart, the Mexican president has both formal (explicit) and informal (implicit) powers. The formal powers include the power of appointment, which goes well beyond the equivalent powers of the U.S. president: Mexican presidents can appoint and dismiss cabinet members, control party nominations for Congress and state governors, appoint the leadership of Congress, and appoint the heads of state-owned banks and industrial enterprises. In addition

- Through the power of decree (the *reglamento*), the president can decide how a law passed by Congress is enforced.
- He has the power to use the armed forces for external and internal security, to declare a "state of siege," and to assume emergency powers.
- He also has a host of other powers, from the substantial (the power to control and regulate foreign investment in Mexico), to the potentially substantial (the powers to control the supply of newsprint to the press and to give concessions for radio and TV channels), to the relatively trivial (the power to oversee the writing and updating of primary school textbooks).[9]

Informally, the power of appointment allows presidents to build a system of patron-client relationships, dispensing power and influence in return for loyalty. Central to the process is the network of *camarillas,* or cliques of politicians bound to a president or cabinet minister. Mexican cabinets have 18 to 22 members and routinely include the heads of government departments but also include the director of Pemex (the state oil company), the director of the Central Bank, the governor of the Federal District, and the mayor of Mexico City.

Mexican presidents can also exploit the aura of their office for political ends. As heads of state, U.S. and Mexican presidents often attract the kind of respect reserved in parliamentary systems for monarchs or nonexecutive presidents. This is carried to the extreme in Mexico, where care has been taken in the past to immunize the president from criticism and to hold cabinet ministers or others in government responsible for policy failures.[10] U.S. presidents are not so different, often blaming Congress for their own policy failures.

Mexican presidents serve a single 6-year term, or *sexenio.* In theory, they are directly elected by the people. In practice, the popular vote was all but meaningless until 2000, because the PRI candidate always won, and he was chosen as candidate not through a democratic primary process but through a secret selection process within

TABLE 6.2

Postrevolutionary Presidents of Mexico

Date	President	Party
1917–1920	Venustiano Carranza	PNR
1920	Adolfo de la Huerta	PNR
1920–1924	Alvaro Obregón	PNR
1924–1928	Plutarco Elías Calles	PNR
1928–1930	Emilio Portes Gil	PNR
1930–1932	Pascual Ortiz Rubio	PNR
1932–1934	Abelardo Rodríguez	PNR
1934–1940	Lázaro Cárdenas	PNR
1940–1946	Manuel Avila Camacho	PRM
1946–1952	Miguel Alemán Valdés	PRI*
1952–1958	Adolfo Ruiz Cortines	PRI
1958–1964	Adolfo López Mateos	PRI
1964–1970	Gustavo Díaz Ordaz	PRI
1970–1976	Luis Echeverría Alvarez	PRI
1976–1982	José López Portillo y Pacheco	PRI
1982–1988	Miguel de la Madrid Hurtado	PRI
1988–1994	Carlos Salinas de Gortari	PRI
1994–2000	Ernesto Zedillo Ponce de León	PRI
2000–	Vicente Fox Quesada	PAN

*PRI began life as the National Revolutionary party (PNR). It was reorganized in 1938 by President Cárdenas and renamed the Mexican Revolutionary party (PRM), and in 1945 was renamed the Institutional Revolutionary party (PRI).

PRI known as *dedazo,* or pointing the finger. Typically, the process would consist of the following steps:[11]

■ By about 4 years into his term, the incumbent would have finalized the membership of his cabinet. By this time, it was understood that the new president would come from that cabinet lineup.

■ At the end of his fifth year, the incumbent might replace the party chair with someone sure to be sympathetic to his choice of successor. After conferring widely with former presidents, party leaders, and leaders of the military, the labor movement, and the business community, he would give the party chair a list of "precandidates" from which his successor would be chosen. The list was then

PEOPLE IN POLITICS

VICENTE FOX

AP/Wide World Photos

The 2000 presidential election was a landmark event in Mexican political history. For the first time in 71 years, the candidate of the Institutional Revolutionary party lost and Mexico saw a change at the helm with the victory of Vicente Fox, the candidate of the National Action party, the main right-wing opposition party. The incumbent governor of the rural central Mexican state of Guanajuato at the time, Fox's arrival meant not only a change of party, but a new governing style and a change of direction for Mexico.

Born in Mexico City in 1942, Fox was raised in Guanajuato. He studied business at the Ibero-American University in Mexico City and earned a diploma from the Harvard School of Business.

He joined Coca-Cola in Mexico in 1964 as a supervisor, and by 1979 had worked his way up to becoming president of the company's operations in Mexico and Central America. He was elected to the Mexican Congress in 1988 and lost the fraudulent race for the governorship of Guanajuato in 1991 before winning at his second attempt in 1995. Along the way Fox was married, and he and his wife adopted four children, but by the time he ran for the presidency he was divorced.

His record as governor was good, with unemployment in Guanajuato down, exports growing, increased federal funds for schools and farmers, and a balanced budget. On the campaign trail Fox became known for his cowboy image and brash style; he rarely wore suits, instead dressing his 6-foot-5-inch frame in open-necked shirts or T-shirts and often wearing a belt with a large buckle bearing his name. Running on a moderately conservative platform, his policy priorities included championing the rights of Mexico's indigenous population, resolving the conflict in Chiapas, reforming the bureaucracy, and making changes to the constitution (including a requirement that cabinet appointments be approved by Congress and that Mexicans overseas be allowed to vote in elections). He initially won high approval ratings and won unanimous support for his first budget, but his tax reform proposals were unpopular, and critics charged him with being too cautious in pursuing his promises for change. His popularity was also affected by the economic downturn that affected both the United States and Mexico in 2002–2003.

He has had a close friendship with George W. Bush, who made his first foreign journey as president in 2001 to meet with Fox. However, he was unable to convince Bush to agree to give a blanket amnesty to the estimated 3 to 4 million Mexicans living illegally in the United States. In July 2001, Fox ended months of gossip and speculation by marrying his press secretary, Martha Sahagun.

made public, supposedly to gauge public opinion and encourage public debate. At this point, the successor was popularly known as *el tapado* (the "hidden one" or the "hooded one").

- After about 2 months of "debate," the name of the successor was made public, and a party convention ratified the choice. The successor then launched a national campaign to build public recognition and held meetings with local party leaders.

- The election was held the following July, the winner would then begin assembling his new cabinet team, and he would be inaugurated in December.

How incumbents chose their successors was thought to depend on the kind of person the outgoing president thought Mexico needed in the following *sexenio*, how the potential successor performed under the outgoing administration, how well he was regarded by key political and economic interest groups in the country, and the kind of personal and political relationships the outgoing president had developed. Personal links were also important, because they increased the likelihood of ex-presidents being able to influence their successors.

An attempt was made in 1988 to make the nomination process more democratic, with a dissident group within PRI demanding greater openness in selecting a successor for Miguel de la Madrid. When it failed, one of its leaders—Cuauhtémoc Cárdenas—broke away from PRI and ran against Salinas, the anointed PRI candidate. Heading a coalition of parties on the left, Cárdenas officially won 31 percent of the vote, while the right-wing National Action party (PAN) candidate (Manuel Clouthier) won nearly 17 percent. Although most independent estimates suggest that Cárdenas probably won, Salinas was declared the winner, but with the slimmest margin of any PRI candidate for president (50.7 percent) and only after a lengthy delay in announcing the results, blamed on a "breakdown" in the computers counting the votes.

The most revolutionary change to the selection process came in 1999, when the *dedazo* system was replaced by an open primary. Fulfilling a promise made soon after coming to office, President Ernesto Zedillo had ordered a review of the selection process, the results of which were published in May 1999. They showed that 70 percent of PRI party members were in favor of a primary, in which all registered voters would be allowed to take part. Under a 1996 law, no one was allowed to run in the primary without experience in elected office, but all contenders were required to resign any such office by June 15, and campaigning was not allowed to begin until August 1. The winner would not have to win a straight majority but rather would have to win a majority in more of the 300 electoral districts for the Chamber of Deputies than his competitors. Four candidates put their names forward, the primary was held in November 1999, and Francisco Labastida was declared the official PRI candidate for the July 2000 presidential election.

All presidents so far have been men, they have come mainly from politically prominent, urban, upper-middle-class families, and—particularly in recent years—they have served apprenticeships not as **políticos** (elected officials) but as **técnicos** (government bureaucrats). Until Fox they had all been graduates of the National Autonomous University (UNAM) in Mexico City, and several (including de la Madrid,

Salinas, Zedillo, and Fox himself) attended graduate school in the United States. Fox has broken the mold in several ways, having been raised in a rural part of Mexico and having been elected as a state governor before running for the presidency.

THE LEGISLATURE: CONGRESS

The Mexican Congress looks much like its U.S. counterpart in the way it is structured and managed, but it has traditionally had much less power, prestige, or influence over the president and, until recently, did little more than legitimize the actions of the president and rubber-stamp the policies of PRI. Its real significance tended to be found in its informal functions: PRI used it as a safety valve for opposition parties, and seats in Congress were used as rewards for party workers or as a means of recognizing second-level leaders within PRI.

This all began to change in the late 1970s as PRI changed the electoral system to give opposition parties more seats in Congress. As opposition numbers grew, and as PRI's share of the vote fell, Congress became more openly critical of the president and won more real power. It became a major political actor as a result of the 1997 elections, when PRI lost its majority in the lower Chamber of Deputies for the first time. Although opposition parties were divided among themselves, PRI could no longer rely on deputies to support the program of the president, whose grip on power began to loosen. With Vicente Fox's victory in 2000, the role of Congress changed completely. Instead of rubber-stamping the president's policies, it became the chief source of opposition.

The Mexican Congress has two chambers.

Senate

Like its U.S. counterpart, the Senate represents the states. It has 128 members, with four coming from each of the 31 states and four from the Federal District of Mexico City. Senators serve 6-year terms, and all run for reelection at the same time as the president (a system of staggered elections was introduced in 1991 but suspended in 1993). PRI had a monopoly of Senate seats until 1976, when the Popular Socialist party was given a seat in return for keeping quiet about fraud in a state election in another part of the country. In 1988 the opposition Cárdenas Front won four Senate seats, and in 1993, electoral reforms not only increased the number of seats in the Senate from 64 to 128 but also changed the electoral process so that the biggest party in every state won three seats, and the second biggest won the fourth. Hence, the 1994 elections saw 32 opposition senators elected, the 1997 elections saw 51 elected, and the 2000 elections saw 68 elected and PRI losing its majority for the first time.

Chamber of Deputies

Like the U.S. House of Representatives, the Chamber of Deputies represents the people rather than the states. Its 500 members are elected for 3-year terms through a direct universal vote. As with the Senate, PRI once had a lock on the chamber, which until 1977 had 320 members—300 elected from single-member districts that PRI was virtually guaranteed to win and 20 elected from party lists

The Mexican Chamber of Deputies in session. Long exploited by the governing Institutional Revolutionary party to prove its "democratic" credentials, the Chamber has recently won more powers relative to the presidency and is increasingly becoming a meaningful source of policy ideas and political opposition.

by proportional representation, giving opposition parties a few seats in Congress. To give those parties greater representation, PRI increased the number of party list seats to 100 in 1977 and then to 200 in 1988, where it now stands. In the 1988 elections, opposition parties won few of the single-member seats, but won almost all the party list seats. This gave them 48 percent of the seats in the Chamber, enough to at least temporarily meet their demands for government influence and to deny PRI the two-thirds majority needed to amend the constitution. Their share of seats fell in 1991, but they won majorities in 1997 and 2000, obliging PRI to reach more accommodations with the opposition parties in order to move business along.

There are several important differences in the structures of the U.S. and Mexican Congresses:

- Since a Mexican constitutional amendment in 1928, consecutive terms in either chamber have been forbidden, so senators and deputies must skip a term before being eligible for reelection. Members of Congress who cannot get enough of politics have been known to move alternately from one chamber to the other, and even to have spells in state or local government.

- While the U.S. Congress—particularly the Senate—is often used as a platform for a bid for the presidency, the preference among presidents from PRI for appointing technocrats as their successors minimized the importance of experience in Congress. President Fox broke the mold with his background as an elected state governor, and PRI has changed its own party rules to require that anyone seeking nomination as its presidential candidate should have experience in elective office.

- The U.S. Congress has powerful committees and an extensive body of staff that can generate information, but Mexican members of Congress have only a few staff each and must still rely heavily on the executive branch for information and policy ideas.[12]

The new independence and importance of Congress was underlined in late 2001 by a fight over a tax reform program submitted by President Fox. To increase tax revenues and thereby reduce government dependence on fluctuating oil income, Fox proposed a number of changes, including raising taxes on food and medicine. Critics charged that the plan would place an excessive burden on the poor, and after 9 months of haggling, even the president's own party dropped its support. Congress proposed an alternative plan that would shift the burden more to business and the wealthy, mainly by taxing a selection of luxury items, including cell phones and computers. The debate gave Congress a new sense of purpose and—after more than 70 years as a supporting actor in government—emphasized its newly assertive role in politics. It also showed that the president could no longer make any assumptions about the support he would receive from Congress but instead had to negotiate and appeal to public opinion.[13]

THE JUDICIARY: SUPREME COURT

Although theoretically equivalent to the U.S. judicial system (and very similar in structure), the Mexican judiciary has traditionally played only a supporting role in government and has been more apolitical than its U.S. counterpart. It has occasionally—and usually reluctantly—passed down decisions against the executive, but it has done little to limit executive power or control electoral fraud and has generally protected the interests of political and economic elites. President Zedillo set out to change its role by replacing all its members in 1995, introducing the power of judicial review, and appointing a member of the opposition party PAN as attorney-general.

The Supreme Court has 11 members, including a chief justice, each appointed for 15-year terms. As in the United States, members are nominated by the president and confirmed by the Senate, but unlike the United States, where only Congress can impeach a justice of the Supreme Court, the Mexican president has the power (with the approval of Congress) to remove a justice. Below the Supreme Court there is a system of circuit courts of appeal and district courts of first instance. The Supreme Court appoints circuit and district judges for renewable 4-year terms (their U.S. equivalents are appointed for life by the president, subject to Senate confirmation).

Whereas most English-speaking countries base their legal systems on English common law, Mexico uses the Roman civil law tradition. The former is unwritten, tends to be adversarial or accusatorial (rather than inquisitorial), and relies heavily on precedent (the principle of *stare decisis*, or standing by previous decisions); the latter is based on written codes and the written opinions of legal scholars, and does not recognize precedent.[14] One of the most important types of cases heard by Mexican federal courts is an *amparo* suit, a concept unique to Mexico for which there is no direct equivalent in the United States. *Amparo*, which literally means favor or protection, can be used in several ways: as a defense of individual rights, as protection against unconstitutional laws, or to force examination of the legality of judicial decisions.[15]

SUBNATIONAL GOVERNMENT

In theory, Mexico has a federal system of administration, with the country divided into 31 states and the Federal District of Mexico City. The states each have a governor elected for a 6-year term, a small unicameral Chamber of Deputies whose members are elected for 3-year terms, and a number of *municipios*, which may be towns, counties, or consolidated city-county governments. As at the federal level, local government officials cannot serve consecutive terms.

In practice, there are two differences between the U.S./Canadian and Mexican models of federalism. First, although Mexican state governments have independent powers, it has been unusual in the past for a state government to contradict or defy a federal government decision or ruling. Even local or state PRI organizations have been all but powerless and obliged to refer back to headquarters in Mexico City on all decisions.[16]

Second, the federal Senate has the power to remove an elected governor, whose successor may be nominated by the president and confirmed by the Senate. Because each state has its own electoral cycle, and because the *sexenios* of governors do not necessarily coincide with those of presidents, incoming presidents always inherit incumbent governors, over whom they may not have as much control as they would like. Even so, governors are dismissed much less rarely today than they were during the turbulent 1920s and 1930s. On the whole, state governments have a larger measure of autonomy over their routine functions, and the federal government usually intervenes only in cases of extreme corruption or abuse of power.

As in other federal systems, Mexican states differ in their ranking and political importance. In political, commercial, and demographic terms, the dominance of Mexico City gives it a level of power and influence over national affairs that far outstrips that of any urban area in the United States or Canada. The Federal District itself is home to 9 million people, and the surrounding state of Mexico to a further 12 million. One of the effects of its size has been to create inequalities in the distribution of public investment and in access to public services. Mexico City has only 22 percent of Mexico's population, but it is the source of more than half of all federal government revenues and receives more than half of all spending on education, health, and public housing. Mexico City is also home to many in the political elite; about 40 percent of all federal government officials are born in Mexico City. Its preeminence also has the effect of making the position of mayor of Mexico City the second most important and powerful job in Mexican politics.

REPRESENTATION AND PARTICIPATION

The meaning of representation and participation in Mexico has changed out of all recognition in recent years. PRI once manipulated the system to ensure continued control, meddled with the results of elections, engineered the electoral system to give opposition parties enough seats in Congress to keep them cooperative but to deny them power, and was careful to incorporate any groups that might pose a threat to the status quo. In short, key political decisions were made more as a result of competition within PRI than of competition among different parties and interest groups. Elections were used less to determine who would govern than to mobilize support for those who already governed; that is, they were used to legitimize power rather than to distribute power.[17]

However, reforms to the electoral system have allowed opposition parties to win more power. With majorities in both chambers of the legislature, and their victory in the 2000 presidential elections, those parties have now become a more important force in government, and politics has moved outside PRI to a broader public constituency.

ELECTIONS AND THE ELECTORAL SYSTEM

The process of electoral reform first moved into high gear in 1977–1978, when the number of legal political parties grew from four to seven, a mixed single-member and proportional representation electoral system was introduced, and a quarter of the seats in the Chamber of Deputies were effectively reserved for opposition parties (provided that they ran candidates in at least one-third of the electoral districts). Subsequent changes included adding another 180 PR seats in the Chamber of Deputies, doubling the number of Senate seats (from 64 to 128), creating an independent Federal Electoral Institute, introducing tamperproof photo ID cards for voters, and broaching the idea of allowing expatriate Mexicans (there may be as many as 10 million) to vote in presidential elections. Most significantly, elections are now subject to such close domestic and foreign scrutiny that it has become difficult for parties to manipulate the outcome.

A number of political scientists have theorized that the motive underlying all these changes was to build a bipartisan system in which PRI and its main conservative opposition, PAN, became the permanent parties of government, leaving the left-wing Party of the Democratic Revolution (PRD) marginalized.[18] However, PAN proved much less willing to cooperate than PRI had hoped, and the PRD has done much better in elections, creating a fluid situation. The PRI hegemony is gone, Mexican elections are fairer than they have ever been, and voter interest has been piqued.

Mexicans take part in three main sets of elections.

The Presidential Election

The presidential election is held every 6 years. Each of the major parties fields a single candidate, and there is a straight winner-take-all contest among those candidates. Although PRI once routinely won with an 85 to 95 percent share of the vote, that share has steadily fallen, and in 1994 Ernesto Zedillo became the first PRI candidate to win with less than 50 percent of the vote (see Table 6.3). In the landmark 2000

```
T A B L E   6 . 3
```

Results of Recent Presidential Elections in Mexico

	Candidate	Party*	Number of votes	% share of vote
1994	Ernesto Zedillo Ponce de León	PRI	16,825,607	48.70
	Diego Fernandez de Cavallos	PAN	8,962,141	25.94
	Cuauhtémoc Cárdenas Solórzano	PRD	5,735,217	16.60
	Cecilia Soto Gonzalez	PT	946,656	2.74
	Others		2,079,880	6.02
2000	Vicente Fox Quesada	PAN	15,104,164	43.78
	Francisco Labastida Ochoa	PRI	12,654,930	36.68
	Cuauhtémoc Cárdenas Solórzano	PRD	5,842,589	16.94
	Gilberto Rincón Gallardo	PDS	563,839	1.64
	Others		332,243	0.96

*PRI, Institutional Revolutionary party; PAN, National Action party; PDS, Social Democratic party; PRD, Party of the Democratic Revolution; PT, Workers party.

election, the PRI share of the vote fell to 36.7 percent as Vicente Fox of PAN won the presidency. Turnout at presidential elections has fluctuated from a low of 52 percent (1958) to a high of 77 percent (1994).[19]

The election itself is held in July, but the president does not formally take office until the following December. This gives Mexican presidents one of the longest lame duck periods in the world. In parliamentary systems, new prime ministers typically take office within hours of winning an election; in the United States there is a period of 2 months between the election and the inaugural. Five months may have suited presidents during the PRI era, giving incumbents plenty of time to work with successors on ensuring policy continuity and giving PRI officials plenty of time to learn about their new leader. It may also have helped Vicente Fox in 2000 as PAN prepared to take office for the first time in its history. But whether such a long transition continues to work in a newly democratic Mexico remains to be seen.

Federal Congressional Elections

Elections to the Senate are held every 6 years, at the same time as the presidential election. All Senate seats are contested at the same time; changes introduced in 1993 reserved three seats in every state for the majority party and ensured that the fourth was won by the second-placed party.

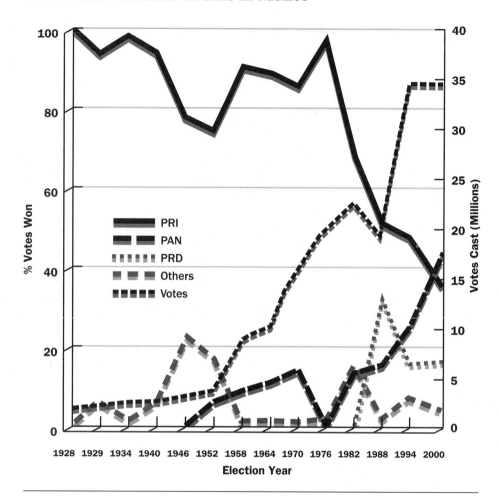

FIGURE 6.1

Presidential Electoral Trends in Mexico

Elections to the Chamber of Deputies are held every 3 years. All 500 seats are contested at the same time, but a mixed electoral system is used: 300 seats are contested on the basis of winner-take-all single-member districts, and 200 are determined by proportional representation (PR). For the PR seats, each party fields a list of candidates, and seats are assigned by a complex formula based on the percentage of the vote won by each party. Voters cast two votes: one for the "uninominal" member for their district and one for a party list of "plurinominal" candidates running at large in the local electoral region, who represent their parties rather than a geographical area. The country is divided into five such regions, and the formula is designed so that no party can win more than two-thirds of the seats altogether. Voter turnout at congressional elections has ranged in recent years between 42 percent (1979) and 77 percent (1994) but was back down to 64 percent in 2000.

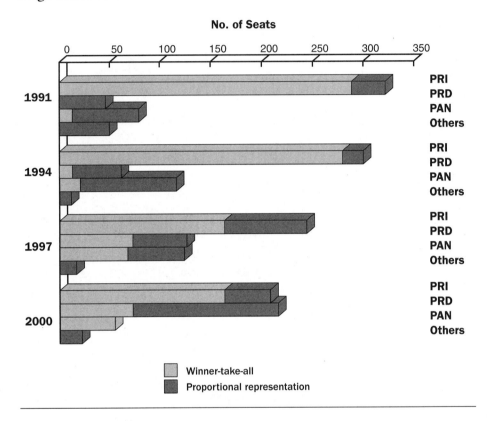

FIGURE 6.2

Legislative Electoral Trends in Mexico

No. of Seats

Winner-take-all
Proportional representation

State and Local Elections

Mexican states operate on their own electoral cycles, which rarely coincide with national cycles. Elections are held for municipal governments (a mayor and council), the single-chamber state assemblies, and state governors (there are no lieutenant governors).

POLITICAL PARTIES

Mexico has been a multiparty system since 1929, but PRI held a majority in both houses of Congress until 1997, won every presidential election until 2000, and until recently controlled almost every state government. However, five parties won seats in Congress in 1997, and with the PRI stranglehold weakening, the significance of parties has changed. In recent years, three major parties have dominated Mexican politics, with smaller parties playing a supporting role.

Institutional Revolutionary Party (*Partido Revolucionario Institucional*, PRI)

The role of PRI in Mexican politics has changed dramatically in the last few years. Although it once had a monopoly on the presidency, had a constant majority in Congress, and was so dominant that Mexico was a one-party system almost in the same vein as the old Soviet Union, PRI has been in a state of retreat and confusion since it lost its majority in Congress in 1997.

During its heyday, PRI was not a political party in the liberal democratic sense because it was created less to compete for power than to decide how power would be shared; it was not so much a channel for political participation as a means for political control.[20] It kept its grip on power by being a source of patronage, by incorporating the major social and economic sectors in Mexico, by co-opting rival elites, and by mobilizing voters during elections and overseeing the electoral process. In many ways like a Leninist vanguard party, PRI was more a formal part of the state system than an independent arena of political competition. It even identified itself with revolutionary mythology and the symbols of the Mexican state and continues to have the same official colors (red, white, and green) as those in the Mexican national flag.

There were two particular features that gave PRI its distinctiveness:

- It had no obvious ideology, but instead shifted with the political breeze and with the changing priorities of its leaders. The **pendulum theory** of Mexican politics described the way that its presidents swung back and forth between conservative and progressive policies.[21] So while Echeverría was progressive, Portillo moved to the right, de la Madrid was a conservative, and Salinas and Zedillo moved back toward the center. Politics in Mexico was not so much about competition among different parties as it was about competition among different factions within PRI—in this sense it was much like the Japanese Liberal Democratic party. Strands of thought ranged from the conservative antireformism of the so-called **"dinosaurs"** to the pro-reformism of democrats who wanted more open government.

- Given PRI's dominance, and the power of the executive branch, Mexico was governed by **political centralism.** Paralleling Leninist democratic centralism, this was a phenomenon by which each level of government was weaker and less autonomous than the one above it, and all key policy decisions were made within PRI, as were all choices about who would run for office. Incoming presidents appointed leaders of Congress, PRI, the military, and state-owned industries; they could veto appointments to lower-level offices; and they could also confirm state governors from PRI, who in turn influenced the appointment of members of courts and state assemblies. Everyone running for office in the name of PRI was chosen by higher levels in the party, and PRI used local political bosses to mobilize peasants and urban workers, encouraging them to vote for PRI.

The signs of PRI's declining role can be found as far back as the 1970s, when turnout at elections fell and PRI could no longer argue that people had faith in the system. One of the motives behind subsequent electoral reforms was to encourage greater turnout, but although turnout improved, more people were voting for opposition parties. At the same time, Mexicans were becoming better educated, more affluent, and more worried about Mexico's economic problems, and because PRI had governed for so long, it could not avoid taking the blame. Labor union support for PRI fell, and the number of independent unions grew. The most powerful unions had long been affiliated to PRI and had earned privileges (such as higher wages) in return for their support. But economic problems meant that workers saw their real incomes falling, they became less pliant and more demanding, and an important part of the base of PRI support deteriorated.

The cumulative effect of these changes began to emerge in 1989 when PRI lost its first state election. They became more significant at the June 1997 elections to the Chamber of Deputies, when PRI lost its majority for the first time in its history. It was still the biggest party, with 239 seats, but the opposition parties among them had 261 seats, which forced PRI to negotiate, bargain, and ultimately compromise, something that it had never really had to do before. At the 2000 congressional elections its share fell yet further, to 209 seats, and it lost the jewel in the crown of Mexican politics, the presidency. Since then, PRI has had a crisis of confidence, once again torn between dinosaurs and democrats and failing to stake out a clear place on the political spectrum between PAN on the moderate right and the PRD on the left.[22]

As part of its program to reinvent itself, PRI has tried to appeal to younger voters, who had given most of their votes to PAN in 2000. In the run-up to the 2003 congressional elections, PRI decided that at least 30 percent of its candidates would be younger than 30 years old and at least half would be women. In the minds of many voters, though, PRI is still associated with corruption. Voters were reminded of this in 2002 when one of the dinosaurs—Roberto Madrazo, a contender for the PRI presidential nomination in 2000—was elected chairman of the party. Madrazo had won the governorship of the state of Tabasco in 1994 in a highly questionable election.[23]

National Action Party (*Partido de Acción Nacional*, PAN)

A moderate right-wing party, PAN was founded in 1939 and until the early 1990s played the role of loyal opposition. Its policies were pro-clerical, pro-American, and pro-business, favoring a limited government role in the economy and the promotion of private land ownership rather than communal ownership, and generally opposing collectivist ideas. It was strongest in the urban areas of the wealthier northern and central states but was long seen as the party of the wealthy and drew little support from rural or working-class voters. This began to change in the late 1980s when a new and younger generation of pro-business members joined the party, promoting new policies and irking the old-style party members known as *panistas* who had dominated its leadership until then.

In 1989 PAN took control of the government of Baja California Norte, becoming the first opposition party officially to win a state election since the Revolution. It went on to take the state governments of Guanajuato in 1991, Chihuahua in 1992, and Jalisco in 1995. In 1994 PAN candidate Diego Fernandez came in second in the

HOW CORRUPT IS MEXICO?

Corruption is a problem in every country, even in liberal democracies such as the United States, Britain, and Canada, where bribes, kickbacks, misuse of public funds, and nepotism are not unknown. In political systems where power is more concentrated, the opportunities for corruption are greater, so the problem is deeper. In Mexico, *camarillas*, elitism, and political centralization continue to provide tempting opportunities for personal profit, even as the Fox administration tries to reform the system. The extent of the problem is difficult to measure because it usually involves influence peddling and the trading of favors rather than open bribery or embezzlement, but it persists in government, the bureaucracy, labor unions, and the police, hampering Mexico's efforts to become a successful democracy.

The most infamous recent example of corruption at the highest levels came during the administration of President Carlos Salinas (1988–1994). Once hailed as a world statesman and the leader of a new breed of modernizing Mexican politicians, Salinas has since come to symbolize continuing doubts about the abilities of the Mexican leopard to change its political spots. The first blemish on his record came in March 1994 when his anointed successor, Luis Donaldo Colosio, was assassinated. Then in September 1994 PRI secretary-general José Francisco Ruiz Massieu was assassinated. In February 1995 the former president's brother Raul was arrested on suspicion of complicity in the Massieu murder. Then it was found that Raul Salinas had opened Swiss bank accounts into which millions of dollars had been deposited.

Rumors circulated that Carlos Salinas had been involved in a conspiracy either to murder—or to cover up the truth behind the murder of—Colosio, whose independence and public popularity had begun to make PRI hard-liners nervous. It was also clear that a select group of entrepreneurs in Mexico had profited substantially from privatization and had become major sources of funding for PRI. Salinas fled into exile in Ireland, Raul Salinas was found guilty in January 1999 of complicity in the murder of Massieu, and when Carlos Salinas returned briefly to Mexico in June 1999 for a 48-hour visit, he was greeted by so much hostility that he quickly left.

Most of the corruption in Mexico is much more routine and small-scale. The complexity of regulations and laws combines with the inefficiency of bureaucracy to make people conclude that it is cheaper to bribe than to be honest; police and junior officials make matters worse by often demanding *una mordida* (a bite) to take care of business.[24] The Fox administration has launched initiatives to address the problem—including sting operations and audits of public bodies—but critics charge that the underlying problems remain. Transparency International, a nonprofit organization based in London and Berlin that studies corruption around the world, ranks Mexico 57th out of 102 countries in terms of how much corruption is perceived to exist among public officials and political leaders.[25] Clearly President Fox still has a long road ahead of him.

presidential election with nearly 26 percent of the vote, and PAN won the second biggest block of seats in the Chamber of Deputies. Its steady rise to power was capped by its victory in the 2000 presidential election and its gains in Congress, where it became the biggest party. Although PAN remains an essentially conservative party, Vicente Fox has adopted policies more toward the center, putting him at odds with some of his party colleagues.

Party of the Democratic Revolution (*Partido de la Revolución Democrática*, PRD)

Founded in 1988, PRD is the major opposition party on the left of Mexican politics. It grew out of mergers involving small left-wing parties, including the Mexican Communist party (PCM) and the Mexican Worker's party (PMT), and defectors from PRI. In 1988 the PRD joined with three smaller parties and the *corriente democrática* group of PRI dissidents to form the National Democratic Front (*Frente Democrática Nacional*, FDN), which provided a platform for the presidential candidacy of Cuauhtémoc Cárdenas and contested that year's congressional elections. Cárdenas had high name recognition, being the son of President Lazaro Cárdenas, the hero of the oil nationalization of the 1930s. Officially, Cárdenas won 31 percent of the vote (the best result ever for an opposition candidate), but he may in fact have won the election, losing only because of fraud. The FDN also won four Senate seats and more than tripled its representation in the Chamber of Deputies.

The 1997 electoral season saw PRD's numbers in the Chamber of Deputies nearly double, from 71 to 124, but Cárdenas came in a disappointing third in the 2000 presidential election, and the party lost more than half its seats in the Chamber of Deputies. It subsequently broke down in factional fighting. One bright spot was the election of Lázaro Cárdenas—grandson of the president and son of the presidential candidate—as state governor of Michoacan in 2001. The office of mayor of Mexico City—generally regarded as the second most powerful job in Mexican politics—has also been held by PRD since 1997, first by Cuauhtémoc Cárdenas and then by Andres Lopez Obrador.

Other Parties

Mexico has long had a cluster of smaller parties, none of which has yet been able to build substantial national support, and some of which have hovered on the brink of extinction. They include the Worker's party (*Partido del Trabajo*, PT), whose candidate Cecilia Soto Gonzalez in 1994 became the first woman ever to make a showing in a Mexican presidential election, winning nearly 3 percent of the vote. The Popular Socialist party (*Partido Popular Socialista*, PPS), founded in 1948, was for many years the main opposition party on the left, walking a fine line between collaborating with PRI and following instructions from Moscow that Communist parties should not form coalitions with other parties. The Mexican Ecological Green party (PVEM), founded in 1986, surprised almost everyone by winning nine congressional seats in 1997 and finally establishing a national presence. It ran with PAN in an Alliance for Change in 2000 but lost five of its seats. Several smaller parties—notably the Democratic Center party (CD) and Social Democracy (DS)—were expected to be spoilers in 2000 by drawing votes away from the PRD and PAN, but they ended up having little impact.

INTEREST GROUPS

Every democratic political system—and even, sometimes, their undemocratic cousins—has to deal with a variety of political interests operating outside the party arena. In Mexico, the corporatist tradition has formalized the links between selected groups and the government, creating a community of quasi-governmental interests alongside the more usual body of independent interest groups.[26] Among the most important of these interests are the peasants, labor unions, big business, and the military.

The Peasants *(Campesinos)*

The peasants emerged from the Revolution as a major source of support for the government; they could always be relied on to vote PRI and believed strongly in the ideals of the Revolution, particularly concerning redistribution of land. The National Peasant Confederation (CNC) was formed in 1938 and became a formal part of the PRI structure. Being less educated and having less access to independent resources, peasants have usually been the easiest sector for PRI to manipulate.[27]

The relationship between *campesinos* and PRI has weakened in recent years, for several reasons: Land ownership is now less important than the creation of nonagricultural jobs and the provision of basic services such as electricity and piped water; the *campesinos* are becoming more middle class and competing for resources with the urban sector; Mexico's debt problems have made the government less interested in small farmers and more interested in large-scale agriculture; and the growth in Mexico's urban population has meant that peasants have had correspondingly less power and influence in electoral terms.

Labor Unions

Controlling public sector labor unions was always essential to the power base of PRI. Not only did members of affiliated unions pay annual dues to PRI, but by regulating wages and strikes, the official labor movement helped PRI argue that Mexico was a stable market for investors. Most unions were linked with PRI through the Confederation of Mexican Workers (CTM), which has 14,000 affiliates representing 5 million workers. One of the most powerful men in Mexico for many years was Fidel Velázquez (1900–1997), secretary-general of the CTM for more than 40 years. It was largely thanks to him and his powers of patronage that militancy in the Mexican labor movement was contained; Velázquez had woven such a web of personal loyalties that strikes never had much effect, and one political scientist has argued that Velázquez deserved credit for doing more to preserve Mexican stability than all 10 of the presidents with whom he worked.[28] However, unrest is growing among PRI-affiliated unions, and new independent unions—such as the National Workers Union, founded shortly after the death of Velázquez in 1997 to counter the influence of CTM—are gaining power. The pro-business Fox administration has been less willing to compromise over labor matters than were most of its predecessors.

The Private Sector

Despite the historical tradition of state ownership of basic services and natural resources and the existence until recently of a large public sector, Mexico is predominantly a capitalist society and has several large business confederations through which the private sector can influence government. Among these are the National Confederation of Chambers of Commerce (Concanaco), the National Confederation of

Chambers of Industry (Concamin), and the National Chamber of Industries of Transformation (Canacintra). All were set up by the government, but all have suffered financial problems since a 1996 Supreme Court ruling against obligatory membership. There is also a growing number of **grupos,** or large private companies, that have developed something like the kind of influence with government that large U.S. companies have with their government. The biggest of the *grupos* include Alfa (petrochemicals, steel, food processing), Carso (telecommunications, auto parts, retail), Cydsa (chemicals, packaging), and Maseca (the world's largest tortilla maker).

The Military

Latin American politics was once synonymous with military dictatorship, but although the military dominated postindependence politics in Mexico, the last military president of Mexico, Manuel Avila Camacho, left office in 1946, having dissolved the military sector of PRI in 1940 and thus ending the tradition of having a bloc of military representatives in Congress. The role of the military was further reduced by the frequent rotation of commanders (so none could build up a personal following), the provision of generous economic incentives for officers to stay out of politics, and a policy of requiring officers who wanted to be active in politics to do so as civilians rather than as representatives of the military. Lacking any major external threats to its security, Mexico has also dramatically decreased its defense budget, from 17 percent of the federal budget in 1940 to as little as 1 to 3 percent today.

The military, now 145,000 strong, is occasionally used to put down internal dissension (including counterinsurgency campaigns against rural guerrillas, such as the uprising in Chiapas) or as a means of heading off potential protests against electoral corruption. The political role of the military has strengthened as a result of U.S. pressure on Mexico to crack down on drug traffickers, but the chances of the military reentering politics are slim, especially given the evolution of other channels for political participation and the growing internationalization of the Mexican economy.

THE MEDIA

Mexico boasts a large and varied media community, with Mexico City alone serviced by at least 20 news dailies (including *Novedades, El Heraldo, El Economista, Excélsior,* and *El Sol de México*), many minor papers and journals, and many TV and radio channels. Most media are privately owned, in contrast to the kind of extensive government media ownership found in many less developed countries.

Despite the apparent choice, the Mexican media have only conditional freedom, the level fluctuating according to the wishes of successive administrations. Recent trends are toward greater freedom, but just as PRI controlled opposition party representation in order to defuse criticism, so the media were controlled to the same ends. Until 1986, when Mexico joined GATT, the government exerted control over the printed press through its monopoly on the supply of newsprint. The government could penalize a particular newspaper or journal by cutting newsprint deliveries, forcing the paper to buy it at a higher price on the open market. Similarly, the government could reward a paper by oversupplying it with newsprint, which the paper could sell at a profit. Since most newspapers relied on government advertising for most of their revenues, the government had significant powers of persuasion, and most newspapers remained loyal to PRI policy.

Even though many radio and TV channels are privately owned, the government still controls them through licensing and regulation. Mexican television is dominated by the major privately owned commercial television network, Televisa. Created in 1973 on the condition that it produce high-quality public and educational programming, Televisa has become one of the world's largest producers and exporters of television programs. In return for its continued commercial freedom, Televisa took positions that supported the status quo, rarely questioning or criticizing government policy. Under Fox it has enjoyed greater editorial independence, but it has also been facing competition from the new private networks Multivision and TV Azteca (the latter now has nearly one-fourth of the viewing market). The market for cable and satellite television is exploding, and greater choice of new sources is also offered in the northern states by the availability of news about Mexico from U.S. radio and TV stations on the border. This is not only expanding U.S. cultural penetration of Mexico, but it is also growing as the influence of NAFTA spreads, impacting Mexican politics.

POLICIES AND POLICYMAKING

Understanding how public policies are made and implemented is often less a question of knowing the formal rules of government than of appreciating how power is informally manipulated among and within government institutions. In few countries is this more true than Mexico. Policy is supposedly made as a result of the interplay between the federal government, the state governments, and competing political parties, taking into account public opinion. In reality, policy has long been made by a small political elite, through a process that—at least until recently—has been authoritarian, bureaucratic, and corporatist.

Policymaking under PRI could be compared with the workings of an orchestra, with the president as the conductor. Using his formal and informal powers, he worked through his *camarilla* to compel key individuals and institutions to support his program. In large part, his success or failure in determining the tempo of the orchestra depended on his control of the bureaucracy, the party, and the media. At the same time, the president was not a dictator, and political realities demanded that he gauge opinion and consult others within the ruling elite before implementing his program. The tempo of the music depended on the abilities and sensibilities of the lead musicians and the extent to which they followed their conductor.

Much has changed since PRI lost the 2000 presidential election. The Fox administration has reached out to a broader constituency for policy advice, and because no one party has a majority in Congress, it has not been able to have its own way. For the first time, a Mexican president has had to amend his policy proposals and objectives to reach a compromise with the opposition. It is too soon for the old ways to have gone altogether, but the policy process in Mexico has moved several steps closer to the broad-based model of negotiation found in liberal democracies.

ECONOMIC POLICY

Mexican economic policy after the Revolution was driven by two underlying goals:

- Mexico worked to reduce the influence of foreign investors and its dependence on imports of manufactured goods. Along with other Latin American countries, it supported the **Calvo Doctrine** (a trade principle named for a 19th century Argentinean diplomat). This doctrine argues that foreigners involved in economic activities should place themselves on the same footing as the nationals of the country in which they do business, agreeing to abide by its laws, using local courts, and refraining from appealing to their home governments to intervene in disputes.[29]

- Mexico worked to achieve sustained economic growth and low inflation. A mixed economy was created, with the government owning and operating key economic sectors (mainly energy production and communications) but also promoting development of the private sector.

Between 1940 and 1970, these policies worked so well that it was common to hear talk of a Mexican economic miracle. By the mid-1970s, Mexico had the most successful economy and society of any country where Iberian languages (Spanish and Portuguese) were spoken. It was not very democratic, but it was relatively stable and peaceful, and its economy was growing at a healthy rate. However, poor choices in the wake of the discovery of new oil reserves in the 1960s brought economic problems whose effects are still being felt today. Mexico slipped down the league of Iberian countries, the national debt grew, the purchasing power of the average worker declined, and economic growth in the 1980s was providing less than half the 900,000 new jobs needed every year to keep pace with population growth. Despite an annual growth in GDP of 6 to 7 percent, by the mid-1990s the word crisis had begun to appear with alarming frequency in discussions about Mexico's economy.

Over the last decade, the direction of economic policy has shifted significantly.[30] Most notably, a program of privatization has transformed the economy from one of the most state-dominated and protectionist in Latin America to one of the freest. Mexico is now a vigorous exporter, stability has replaced the economic crises of the 1970s and 1980s, and the government has both created new institutions—such as a competition agency—and given existing institutions (such as the central bank) greater independence. Unfortunately, the benefits of the changes have not yet trickled down to everyone. Poverty is widespread, and there is a significant income gap between the north of the country—where per capita GDP is $5,000 or more—and the southern and central regions of Mexico—where per capita GDP is $3,000 or less.

The Era of Growth (1940–1970)

Building on the political stability that emerged following the Revolution, Mexico saw sustained economic growth supported by government subsidies to business; protectionism; and the building of basic infrastructure such as roads, irrigation systems, hospitals, and schools.[31] Along with many of its Latin American neighbors, Mexico pursued **import-substitution industrialization.** This strategy involved the use of tariffs, quotas, and other methods to protect domestic industries from the competition posed by imports; the replacement of consumer imports with locally manufactured alternatives; and encouragement by the government to export manufactured goods rather than primary products. This policy brought an average annual economic growth rate of 6 percent, increased the contribution of industry to GDP, and attracted rural people to the cities. The major catalyst in this process was the public sector, which had expanded in the 1930s when the government nationalized the railroads and created Pemex, the state oil company. At the same time, the government provided support for the private sector, giving local entrepreneurs incentives that included subsidies, tariffs on imports, and low tax rates.

Despite the positive changes, Mexico by the late 1960s had painted itself into a corner. By building a large public sector and lowering taxes to promote private investment, the government left itself financially strapped and unable to provide many basic services to the people. Although unemployment was not high, underemployment was widespread, the income gap between the poor and the wealthy grew, and urban areas attracted a disproportionate share of wealth and investment. To make up some of the shortfall, Mexico began borrowing, and the public debt grew from $810 million in 1960 to more than $6 billion in 1970. By the end of the Echeverría *sexenio* (1970–1976), the debt stood at nearly $20 billion. Inflation grew to 20 to 25 percent, and the peso was overvalued, making Mexican goods expensive abroad.

The Oil Crisis (1978–1985)

Oil was known to the Aztecs and Mayas, but commercial production did not begin in Mexico until the late 19th century. With the help of American and British investors, Mexico by the 1920s had become the largest oil producer in the world, accounting for 25 percent of global production. The role of foreign oil companies was seen as a threat to national independence, however, which encouraged President Lázaro Cárdenas to nationalize the oil industry in 1938, creating Pemex and making himself a national hero.

When massive new oil and natural gas reserves were discovered in the Gulf of Mexico in the late 1960s and early 1970s, Mexico was transformed almost overnight into an oil production giant, more than tripling its output and becoming the fourth biggest producer in the world. Unfortunately, Mexico's national debt rose as the government overspent in an effort both to curb unemployment and support the private sector. To make matters worse, domestic political problems combined with the leftward-leaning, anticapitalist postures of the Echeverría regime to lead to a flight of foreign investment. The oil price increases forced by OPEC in the 1970s seemed to offer Mexico a way out of its economic problems, but as Nigeria was also to find to its cost (see Chapter 8), oil is not always the boon it seems. Against the promise of increased profits, the government borrowed heavily from abroad and launched a program of reckless development spending. During the Portillo *sexenio* alone (1976–1982), Mexico borrowed $60 billion.

Western industrialized nations had by then begun to respond to the oil crisis by cutting consumption and investing in alternative energy sources. As a result, oil prices began to fall on the world market, Mexican oil revenues fell, and by

1981 Mexico could not even afford to pay the interest on its debt, which had by then reached $73 billion. Unemployment and inflation grew in tandem, and Mexico's despair was symbolically underlined in 1985 by earthquakes in Mexico City, which not only killed 20,000 people, but also revealed that corruption and kickbacks had led to government buildings being poorly built. This in turn reduced confidence in PRI and added to the support being given to opposition political parties.

Postcrisis Adjustment (1982–)

Hoping to force Mexican companies to become more competitive and to reduce Mexican dependence on oil by promoting nonoil exports, Miguel de la Madrid opened Mexico to greater foreign investment. In the short term, at least, the policy seemed to work. Oil and minerals accounted for 78 percent of the dollar value of Mexico's exports in 1982; by 2001 they accounted for just 8 percent of exports, and manufactured goods accounted for 90 percent of exports.

At the heart of this shift was a program launched in 1965 under which factories were built in northern Mexico to make goods for export. Known as *maquiladoras*, these factories allowed foreign corporations to take advantage of cheap Mexican labor and loose environmental standards to make consumer goods for export to the United States (and since 2001 for sale inside Mexico as well). They initially focused on textiles and small electrical appliances, then graduated to more expensive consumer products, including electronic goods, computers, and vehicles parts. Key components were imported duty-free into Mexico, where they were assembled for export. By 2001 the *maquiladoras* employed about 1.2 million people, had helped make Mexico the world's 13th biggest exporter, were providing Mexico with a new source of foreign investment capital, and were exporting nearly $80 billion-worth of goods per year, nearly half of Mexico's total merchandise exports.

Growth in the *maquiladoras* has fallen off in recent years, however, thanks in part to the withdrawal of their duty-free status in 2001, which made imported components more expensive, and in part to the economic downturn in the United States.[32] They have also been controversial because of a combination of poor working conditions, the blatant exploitation of cheap labor, the environmental problems they have caused, and the fact that too few of the profits made by corporations have been reinvested back into local communities in the form of improved housing, roads, and services. And although *maquiladoras* may have helped boost Mexico's industrial sector, they have exacerbated one of the primary worries in Mexican economic policy: the influence of the United States. Consider the following statistics:

- Virtually all of Mexico's national debt—which stood at $155 billion in 2001—is owed to U.S. banks.
- Nearly 90 percent of Mexico's exports go to the United States, and 75 percent of its imports come from the United States.
- U.S. companies account for about 70 percent of all the foreign capital invested in Mexico, and their subsidiaries account for half the manufactured goods exported by Mexico.

MEXICO AND FREE TRADE

Inspired in part by the example of the European Union (EU), North Americans for the last decade have been building a free-trade area that—with a population of 410 million and a combined GDP in 2001 of nearly $11.5 trillion—is bigger than the EU. The North American Free Trade Agreement (NAFTA) is not so much a free-trade agreement as one espousing *freer* trade; it is aimed at allowing companies to do business more easily throughout the continent, providing more goods at lower prices, phasing out duties on farm products, making it easier for professionals to live and work in any of the three countries, making companies in the three countries more competitive, and giving each country greater access to each others' markets.

The agreement traces its origins to 1988, when Canada and the United States signed the Canada-U.S. Free Trade Agreement. This was expanded to include Mexico from January 1, 1994, a move that raised many concerns in the United States about loss of jobs, illegal immigration, drug trafficking, and environmental quality. However, NAFTA has raised even more fundamental questions for Mexico:

- It has meant more competition for Mexican companies as Mexico has opened up its markets, and an increased trade deficit because its imports from the United States have grown more quickly than its exports. Membership in NAFTA immediately removed tariffs from nearly half of Mexico's imports from the United States, and by 2009 all U.S.-Mexican trade is scheduled to be tariff-free. At the same time, there are opportunities for Mexican companies if they can rise to the challenge: They have more access to the U.S. and Canadian markets, more foreign investment is flowing into Mexico, and more jobs are being created in Mexico as U.S. and Canadian companies take advantage of cheap Mexican labor.

- The investment and trade offered by NAFTA may have improved the quality of life for the average Mexican worker, but it has not done so quickly enough to reduce illegal immigration to the United States over the short term.

- NAFTA has meant political and social changes for Mexico because of the links between economic liberalization and democratization. A free-trade partnership with two liberal democracies has brought with it greater pressure for democratic reform. Just as membership in the EU has helped Spain, Portugal, and Greece build stable democracies, so NAFTA brings Mexico economic benefits that have underpinned its efforts at democratization.

One of the key problems with NAFTA is that it has deepened Mexican dependence on the United States, and thus the health of Mexico's economy is driven by the health of the U.S. economy. No surprise, then, that the Fox administration has championed the cause of a free-trade area covering all of North and South America.

One of the effects of Mexican economic dependence on the United States is that the wealthiest states in Mexico are in the north and the poorest in the south. This is partly because workers from northern states are crossing into the United States and bringing their wages back, partly because American tourists visit Mexican border towns in large numbers (700,000 people visit Tijuana from San Diego alone every year), and partly because of the influence of the *maquiladoras*.

Economic reforms over the last decade have had mixed results. A major program of privatization since 1983 has led to the sale or closure of more than 80 percent of the nearly 1,200 businesses once owned by the state, including the two airlines Mexicana and AeroMéxico, the telephone company Telmex, as well as banks and shipyards. The sales have raised $21 billion for the government, but they have also led to the loss of 400,000 jobs, and critics charge that privatization has simply replaced public monopolies with private ones. A prime example is offered by the case of Telmex. Although it was privatized in 1990, it had a monopoly on the long-distance phone market until 1997 and even today dominates the telephone industry. Its controlling shareholder, Carlos Slim, is the richest man in Latin America and has considerable political influence.

Meanwhile, inflation rates have fluctuated from 160 percent in 1987 to just 7 percent in 1994, back up to 17 percent in late 1999, and down again to 6 percent in early 2003. The peso has lost value, falling against the U.S. dollar from 1 peso in 1986 to nearly 11 pesos in 2003. Major investments are needed in infrastructure, Mexicans had less disposable income in 1996 than in 1980, only 55 percent of Mexicans complete their high school education, industrial production fell in the 1990s, and the gap between the rich and the poor has worsened: 37 million Mexicans are still classified as poor or extremely poor (yet Mexico has several U.S. dollar billionaires, most of whom have made their money out of buying newly privatized companies).

The Fox administration has continued to free up the market and promote exports, but has been too timid for its critics. One of its priorities is to reduce government control over the energy sector, which will not be easy. The 1938 nationalization of the oil industry is still regarded as a landmark event; state ownership of oil and gas, as well as state control over electricity generation and supply, are written into the constitution; and any attempts to privatize the energy industry typically result in a public outcry. However, critics charge that the private sector is better placed to provide the investment so badly needed by the energy industry. The Fox administration has made reforms that allow for more such private investment, but they are only halting steps toward the level of privatization that many think is needed.[33]

FOREIGN POLICY

Mexican foreign policy has traditionally been driven by three major principles: a belief in **universalism,** support for leftist movements in other parts of Latin America, and nonalignment.[34] Universalism can be roughly defined as a willingness to recognize other countries regardless of their ideological leanings. The Estrada Doctrine of 1930 stated that Mexico would grant diplomatic recognition to all governments rather than being judgmental about the way they chose to govern themselves. This philosophy long encouraged PRI governments to take a hands-off approach to events around the world.

All three principles pale into insignificance, however, when measured against the single biggest influence on Mexican foreign policy: the United States. Any discussion about the relationship between the two usually begins with the famous quote by Porfirio Díaz: "Poor Mexico. So far from God and so near to the United States." For many Mexicans, the core goal of foreign policy for decades has been to move out from under the shadow of the United States. As long as the two have been so closely bound in economic terms, however, this has been difficult, and the love-hate relationship has given much of Mexican policy a split personality.

Take, for example, the case of Cuba. While the United States has obsessively tried to outwit and undermine the Castro regime since it came to power in 1959, Mexico remained a strong supporter of Cuba throughout the cold war. It was the only Latin American country not to break diplomatic ties with Cuba following the Castro revolution, it opposed the U.S. embargo of Cuba, it criticized the 1961 Bay of Pigs invasion, and it helped persuade the Organization of American States (OAS) to lift sanctions against Cuba in 1975. Vicente Fox even made a point of visiting Cuba soon after taking office. At the same time, while refusing to go along with U.S. attempts to isolate Castro, it has helped the CIA track the movements of Cubans in Mexico.

Relations between Mexico and its northern neighbor have been anything but steady. Although both embarked on independence from roughly similar demographic and territorial bases, the United States quickly established its superiority. The two countries came into direct conflict over Texas in 1846–1848, resulting in a devastating loss of land for Mexico. Most Americans today know little about the war beyond the myths that have built up around the defense of the Alamo, but Mexicans still carry resentment over "the war of the North American invasion."[35] Mexico's loss gave birth to a strong tradition of nationalism, and concerns about U.S. "imperialism" live on to this day. There is still a strong element of anti-Americanism in Mexico (particularly among elites), and the United States is often used as a scapegoat for many of Mexico's problems. For example, attempting to deflect attention away from the failure of his economic policies in 1982, President Echeverría argued that Mexico could not "work and be organized only to have its life blood drained off by the gravitational pull of the colossus to the north."[36]

However, the relationship is not as unbalanced as it is often portrayed. There has, for example, been a strong historical dependence by the United States on Mexican labor. Mexican workers were first recruited to work on U.S. farms, railroads, and mines in the 1880s. Although Mexico subsequently tried to reduce its dependence on the United States, it never succeeded. Exports of labor even became institutionalized through the *bracero* program; between 1942 and 1964, 4 million Mexicans were brought to the United States to work in seasonal agriculture. The program ended in 1964 at U.S. insistence, but large numbers of immigrants still cross the border today, most of them illegally. Controlling the flow has always been complicated by the fact that Mexico and the United States share a 2,000-mile (3,220-km) border that is difficult to police.

Controlling what happens on that border has become the key issue that ties the two countries today. Immigration—legal and illegal—has made the border less distinct, and the drug trade has made Mexican stability a critical issue not just for border states but for the entire country. Meanwhile, the cultural balance of the United States is changing thanks to the presence of as many as 21 million Americans of Mexican ancestry (more than 7 percent of the population). The importance to the U.S. of Mexican economic stability was illustrated by U.S.-led bailouts of Mexico in 1982 and again in 1995. Economic problems in Mexico could hurt U.S. corporations

Clive Shirley/Panos Pictures

Shanty housing in Tijuana nestles up alongside a fence marking the Mexican border with the United States. The border has become more porous in recent decades with the movement of increasing numbers of Mexicans—legally and illegally—into the United States and the growing integration of the economies of the two countries.

and investors, promote civil unrest, and encourage more emigrants to leave for the United States.

The war on terrorism has given Mexico new significance in U.S. policy, and President Fox—rather than trying to keep the Americans at arm's length—has tried to forge a new relationship. He must have been buoyed by the famous utterance by George W. Bush just before the September 2001 terrorist attacks that "The United States has no more important relationship in the world than our relationship with Mexico." With 300 million border crossings between the two countries every year and many places where illegal workers cross into the United States literally within view of border patrols, policing the U.S.-Mexican border is a key element in protecting the American homeland. Vicente Fox lobbied after the attacks for the extension of police, immigration, and customs cooperation among the three members of NAFTA, hoping to reassure the U.S. government that Mexico was not an easy back door into the United States for terrorists. He has also been pushing for an amnesty for illegal immigrants in the U.S., in return for which he has suggested that he will reduce the flow of new immigrants by developing poor regions and by more actively policing the border.[37] However, Mexico has so far played no more than a peripheral role in the Bush administration's war on terror.

Beyond its relationship with the United States, Mexico has been taking a more active role in foreign policy under the Fox administration. It has helped Colombia in its search for peace by putting pressure on rebels involved in an insurrection, it has been promoting a multinational regional development plan for Central America, and it has been active in its criticism of human rights abuses around the world.

MEXICAN POLITICS IN TRANSITION

Mexico's political development has been driven in recent years by the tensions arising out of two competing sets of forces: the need for economic liberalization against a background of fragile economic growth and the need for political liberalization against a background of changes in the expectations of Mexican consumers and voters. Mexico seemed to be riding the crest of a wave of modernization and democratic reform in early 1994, but its confidence was shaken by the Chiapas rebellion, the Colosio assassination, and the peso crisis. These all emphasized just how much political and economic change was out of synchronization and brought new attention to the importance of the reforms being made to the electoral process, which resulted in PRI losing the presidency in 2000.

The overwhelming presence of the United States has had mixed results for Mexico in the past, but the growth of NAFTA raises the possibility of new economic opportunities for Mexico that will increase the pressures for democratization and economic liberalization. Mexico, which has long had many of the classic features of a newly industrializing country, has the potential to move closer to the realms of liberal democracy if it can balance economic growth, political reform, and the needs of its growing population. It is a substantial regional power, and its membership in NAFTA and the OECD shows just how far it has traveled in its journey away from the old image of the Third World and into the ranks of newly industrializing countries.

KEY TERMS

Calvo Doctrine
camarilla
campesinos
Chamber of Deputies
Chiapas
corporatism
dedazo
dinosaurs
economic nationalism
grupos
import-substitution
    industrialization

Institutional
    Revolutionary party
machismo
maquiladoras
Mexican diaspora
Mexican Revolution
mestizo
North American Free
    Trade Agreement
    (NAFTA)
National Action party
Pemex

pendulum theory
political centralism
políticos
porfiriato
presidentialism
sexenio
técnicos
universalism

KEY PEOPLE

Cuauhtémoc Cárdenas
Lázaro Cárdenas
Porfirio Díaz

Luis Echeverría
Vicente Fox
Subcomandante Marcos

Carlos Salinas
Ernesto Zedillo

STUDY QUESTIONS

1. To what extent are the elitist and hierarchical tendencies of Mexican politics found in liberal democracies?

2. Is democratization in Mexico more a result of decisions made by PRI or a result of pressures arising out of domestic and international economic change?

3. Is there an element of *machismo* in politics in liberal democracies?

4. Compare and contrast the costs and benefits of a single 6-year term for a president with two 4-year terms.

5. Compare and contrast the handicaps that face the Congress of Mexico with those that face legislatures in countries like the United States and Russia in their relations with their respective executives.

6. How does the role of PRI in the Mexican political system compare to the role of the Communist party in the former Soviet Union and in China?

7. To what extent does corporatism apply to liberal democracies such as the United States or Canada?

8. Was bringing Mexico into a free-trade agreement with the United States and Canada a good idea or a bad idea for the three countries? Why?

9. What would it take for Mexico to become a liberal democracy?

MEXICO ONLINE

Presidency of the Republic: *http://www.presidencia.gob.mx*
Senate of the Republic: *http://www.senado.gob.mx*
Web sites for the presidency and the federal Senate, both available in English. The Web site for the Chamber of Deputies (*http://www.cddhcu.gob.mx*) is available in Spanish only.
Mexican Political Parties: *http://www.georgetown.edu/pdba/Parties/Resumen/Mexico/ desc.html*
Links to the Web sites of Mexico's major political parties, most of which are in Spanish.
Consulate General of Mexico in New York: *http://www.consulmexny.org*
Offers links to official news and information on the government, the economy, and Mexican culture.
Latin American Network Information Center: *http://lanic.utexas.edu/la/Mexico*
Mexico Channel: *http://www.trace-sc.com*
Both offer links to a wide variety of sites on government, the economy, and the media.
The News: *http://www.thenewsmexico.com*
Web site of an English-language Mexican daily newspaper.

FURTHER READING

Camp, Roderic A., *Politics in Mexico: The Democratic Transformation*, 4th Ed. (New York: Oxford University Press, 2002), and Needler, Martin C., *Mexican Politics: The Containment of*

Conflict, 3rd Ed. (New York: Praeger, 1995). Two general introductions to politics and economics in Mexico.

Cornelius, Wayne A., *Mexican Politics in Transition: The Breakdown of a One-Party Dominant Regime* (San Diego: Center for U.S.-Mexican Studies, 1996). A short study of the nature and implications of recent political reforms in Mexico.

Fuentes, Carlos, *A New Time for Mexico* (New York: Farrar, Straus & Giroux, 1996). A personal view of Mexico's past and current problems, with a focus on events leading up to the 1994 peso crisis.

Levy, Daniel C., with Emilio Zebadua, *Mexico: The Struggle for Democratic Development* (Berkeley, CA: University of California Press, 2001). A guide to the political, economic, and social changes taking place in Mexico today.

Oppenheimer, Andres, *Bordering on Chaos: Guerrillas, Stockbrokers, Politicians, and Mexico's Road to Prosperity* (Boston: Little, Brown, 1996). A controversial study of events surrounding Chiapas and the Colosio murder, written by a Pulitzer Prize–winning journalist with the *Miami Herald*.

COMPARATIVE FOCUS

CONSTITUTIONS

One of the key ideas in Mexican politics is that of the "continuing" revolution. This stems from the argument that the Mexican constitution is a work in progress and that many of its core principles still have not been fully applied. Was this simply an excuse used by PRI to explain away its abuses of power, or is it a genuine explanation of the problems that continue to complicate Mexico's progress toward becoming a liberal democracy? In this Comparative Focus we will look at constitutions and their record in different societies.

A constitution is a set of rules that typically does at least four things: sets out the general principles by which a country is governed, outlines the structure of government, establishes the procedures used in the political process (such as elections), and outlines the powers of government and the rights of citizens. Most countries have a written or codified constitution, with notable exceptions being Britain and Israel. In other words, the constitution usually takes the form of a structured physical document.

Constitutions do not contain all the rules of government and in fact are usually rife with generalities and ambiguities. They also must be adapted to meet the changing needs of the societies to which they apply, so they are usually supplemented with amendments, laws, and judicial interpretations. Much of what government does also comes down simply to unwritten understandings about acceptable and unacceptable behavior, and political activity is often driven by customs and traditions, few (if any) of which are actually committed to paper. There is nothing in the U.S. Constitution, for exam-

ple, about political parties or interest groups, yet it is understood that they are a normal and acceptable part of the political process.

There are three key performance indicators for all constitutions: How old are they? How many times have they been amended? and How big is the gap between the principles they espouse and the way government and politics function in reality?

- **Liberal democracies.** Most do well on all three measures. The U.S. Constitution probably does best of all, given that it was the first written constitution in the world (dating back to 1788) and that the U.S. Supreme Court routinely provides dozens of interpretations every year on the meaning of its articles and principles. Not everyone always agrees with these interpretations, but universal agreement is impossible: There will always be disagreement, for example, on the meaning of freedom of "speech," on whether some of the rights listed in the constitution are relevant any longer (such as the "right" to bear arms, which may or may not be dependent on the existence of militias), and on whether or not some of the procedural rules of government should be changed, such as placing limits on the terms of elected officials.

  Longevity by itself is not a measure of performance; several liberal democracies have undergone relatively recent changes that have led them to rewrite their constitutions. Germany had a new constitution forced on it by the occupying powers after World War II, and France developed an entirely new political system in 1958, adopting its 17th constitution since the 1789 revolution. However, there is nothing to suggest that either the German or the French constitutions are in danger of collapsing, and in fact they may well be the best constitutions that either country has ever had. The same is true of Greece, Portugal, and Spain, all three of which threw off authoritarian regimes in the mid-1970s, adopted new constitutions, and have since enjoyed unprecedented levels of political stability.

- **Communist states.** These did relatively poorly on all three measures. The Soviet Union, for example, had four constitutions in 59 years, they were routinely manipulated by rulers such as Stalin as a means of achieving political and ideological goals, and the gap between their principles and political reality was substantial. China has had four constitutions since 1949, and each has also been changed to reflect the different thinking of new leaders. Both countries included impressive lists of individual rights in their constitutions but also inserted loopholes that made it possible to justify infringements on those rights.

- **Poorer states.** The role and performance of constitutions in poorer or less stable countries varies dramatically. On one hand, the record in NICs has improved: Although many of them have relatively young constitutions, the trends suggest that they are unlikely to collapse or to be rewritten any time soon. In terms of longevity, Mexico is one of the leaders in this group—or actually in any group—with a constitution that is now more than 85 years old, but it has also been amended so often as to raise questions about the extent to which the original constitution really applies any more. On the other hand, several Latin American states that have experienced persistent political instability have also experienced many short-lived constitutions: The Dominican Republic has had 25, Haiti has had more than 20, El Salvador has had 16, and Honduras has had 12.

The most important performance indicator of a constitution is the gap between theory and reality. Many constitutions include noble principles and objectives, but they mean little unless they are respected and actually applied. The U.S. Constitution, for example, opens by talking of the need to "establish Justice, ensure domestic Tranquility,…promote the general Welfare, and secure the Blessings of Liberty," but it was written by a group of white men, several of whom owned slaves, and black men were denied the right to vote for nearly 90 years after its ratification, and women for more than 120 years. And despite all the claims made about liberty, freedom, and democracy in the United States, the American model of democracy has important imperfections (see Political Debates, p. 43). However, the principles of the constitution are promoted and defended (if not always perfectly) by an independent constitutional court that is subject to relatively little political interference. This cannot be said about more authoritarian regimes in other parts of the world, where governments often interfere with the work of courts, intimidate their members, and try to force through amendments that would strengthen their powers relative to their citizens.

CHAPTER 7

INDIA

INDIA: QUICK FACTS

Official name: Republic of India (Bharat Janarajya)

Capital: New Delhi

Area: 1,230,540 square miles (3,174,800 sq. km) (just over one-third the size of the United States)

Languages: Hindi (spoken by 31 percent) and English are the official languages, but there are 16 major languages and 1,400 local dialects

Population: 1,033 million

Population density: 888 per square mile

Population growth rate: 2.0 percent

POLITICAL INDICATORS

Freedom House rating: Free

Date of state formation: August 15, 1947

System type: Federal republic

Constitution: Published 1950

Administration: Federal; 25 states with a large degree of self-government and 7 union territories

Executive: Prime minister and cabinet

Legislature: Bicameral: Rajya Sabha (250 members, mostly elected for fixed 6-year terms by state legislatures) and Lok Sabha (545 members, elected for maximum 5-year terms by all eligible voters)

Party structure: Multiparty

Judiciary: Supreme Court (26 members appointed by president after consultation with courts)

Head of state: A. P. J. Abdul Kalam (2002–)

Head of government: Atal Behari Vajpayee (1998–)

ECONOMIC INDICATORS

GDP (2001): $477 billion

Per capita GDP: $460

Distribution of GNP: Services 48 percent, industry 27 percent, agriculture 25 percent

Urban population: 28 percent

SOCIAL INDICATORS

HDI ranking: 115

Infant mortality rate: 69 per 1,000

Life expectancy: 62.8 years

Literacy: 57 percent of people aged 15 and older

Religions: Hinduism (83 percent), Islam (11 percent), Christianity (2 percent), and Sikhism (2 percent)

INTRODUCTION

India is a land of dramatic contrasts. It has one of the world's oldest cultures, yet it has been an independent nation-state only since 1947. It is the world's largest democracy, yet it has so many social divisions that it seems constantly to hover on the brink of disintegration. It is a nuclear power with its own space program, yet most of its people still live a simple village life. Such apparent contradictions help explain why the West has been fascinated by India for more than 400 years. It was this fascination that led Britain to colonize India and then describe it as the "jewel in the crown" of the British Empire, and this fascination has continued since independence with the charisma and tragedy surrounding the Nehru-Gandhi dynasty and with India's growing importance in the world.

The common Western image of India as crowded and poor is only partly true. It is certainly crowded, with more than 1 billion people living in an area one-third the size of the United States. And it is certainly poor, with a per capita GDP of less than $500. Three-fourths of its people live off agriculture, many of them mired in abject poverty. At the same time, though, India is a multiparty democracy, with a growing middle class and an expanding economy. It not only feeds itself but also is a net food exporter. It has a bigger consumer market than any European country, and economic liberalization has led to accelerating industrial growth. Like China, India has the potential to become one of the economic superpowers of the 21st century, but to do that it must first build political stability.

In social terms, India is home to almost every division known to humanity:

- **Urban-rural.** India is a predominantly rural society in which 72 percent of the people live in villages. New agricultural technology has reached many of the rural areas, and so have television and consumer products, but life for many villagers remains tied to the villages in which they live. At the same time, India has some of the biggest and most crowded cities in the world, such as Mumbai (formerly Bombay), Calcutta, Delhi, Chennai (formerly Madras), and Bangalore. Indian cities cannot keep up with the demand for housing, sanitation, and transport, making life miserable for the poor and frustrating for the middle class.

- **Cultural.** Nowhere else has colonialism forced so many cultures to live together. There are three racial strains (Aryan, Dravidian, and proto-Australoid), 16 major languages, 30 additional languages each with 1 million speakers or more, and many different scripts. There are two official languages: English and Hindi—the latter is spoken by 31 percent of the population, mainly in the north. Disputes over state and religious boundaries have been common since independence, leading to secessionist movements and insurrections.

- **Religious.** Despite an official separation of religion and the state, religious conflict regularly spills over into politics. More than 80 percent of Indians are Hindu, but India also has a large Muslim community (11 percent of the population) and a vocal Sikh minority (2 percent). Religious disputes were behind the assassinations of Mahatma Gandhi, the champion of Indian independence, in 1948 and of Prime Minister Indira Gandhi in 1984, and they have been behind continuing tensions between India and Pakistan over the disputed territory of Kashmir. The

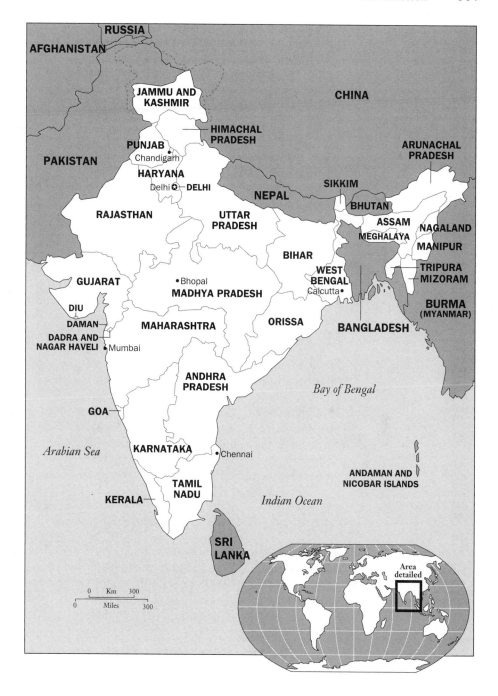

significance of religion has come to the fore in recent years with growing support for the Hindu nationalist Bharatiya Janata party.

- **Social class.** The most important of India's social divisions is **caste.** A complex Hindu hierarchy, caste was originally based on family and occupation and went on to become a form of social apartheid, with the behavior of castes restricted and controlled, no intermarriage allowed across castes, and different jobs carried out by particular castes. The more than 3,000 castes and subcastes can be generally aggregated into four broad categories: the *Brahmins* (who produce most of India's political leaders), the *Kshatriyas* (warriors), the *Vaisyas* (traders and merchants), and the *Sudras* (menial laborers).[1]

  At the bottom of the heap are India's 150 million *Dalits* (formerly called **untouchables**), who were once regarded as almost subhuman and who performed service jobs such as laundry, scavenging, sewage disposal, and removal of the dead. Their touch, and sometimes even their shadow, was considered polluting to high-caste Hindus. In an attempt to improve the position of untouchables, Mahatma Gandhi called them *harijans*, or children of God. The status of untouchable was formally abolished with the 1950 constitution, but a controversial affirmative action policy has reserved jobs, scholarships, government positions, and even seats in parliament for the so-called "scheduled castes."

Despite these divisions and the regular threats they pose to national stability, India is politically vibrant. It has a written constitution that is generally respected, has had 13 free elections and 12 prime ministers since 1947, and has more than half a dozen significant national political parties and many more regional and local parties. Party competition is keen, voter turnout is high, and there is an extensive free press. Unfortunately, the number of political parties has prevented any one from winning a majority in recent years, which has led to the creation of unstable coalitions and threatens to undermine India's continuing economic success.

POLITICAL DEVELOPMENT

India has been an independent nation-state only since 1947, but its culture is one of the oldest, most complex, and most sophisticated on Earth, with a history that goes back more than 5,000 years. Unlike many other former colonies, where precolonial political values were largely subsumed to those of the new imperial power, many of the links between the traditional and the modern can still be found in Indian politics today.

The Hindu Heritage

Before the arrival of Europeans, the Indian subcontinent was made up of numerous principalities, kingdoms, and empires. A civilization that paralleled that of Egypt in importance emerged in the Indus River Valley between about 4000 and 2500 B.C. Beginning in about 1500 B.C., waves of nomadic Indo-Aryans began arriving in the northern and central plains from the Caucasus, pushing the native Dravidians further south. The fusion of Aryan and Dravidian culture produced a philosophical system known as the Vedanta; although this is based on a belief in an all-pervasive cosmic system and the unity of all forms of life, the Aryans also imposed a hierarchical structure on Indian society in the form of the caste system.[2] These beliefs formed the foundation of **Hinduism,** now the world's third largest religion after Christianity and Islam.

A second religious and social influence came in the fifth century B.C. with the teachings of Siddhartha Gautama (c. 563–483 B.C.), better known as Buddha. He spent much of his life wandering through northern India teaching his philosophy, which included a rejection of the caste system. By about 250 B.C., what is now India was mainly Buddhist,[3] but Hindu priests countered the influence of Buddhism by arguing that it was subservient to—and part of—Hindu belief. Much of India was unified between 321 and 184 B.C. by the emperor Ashoka and later reunited by the Gupta dynasty (A.D. 300–500).

The most significant alien influence began in about 1000, when Muslims invaded the area. By the early 16th century, most of the northern half of India had come under the control of the Moguls, one of the subdivisions of Islam, created by descendants of Genghis Khan. The caste system was strengthened as a defense against Muslim influence, and Hindus refused to cooperate with Muslim invaders, a policy that was to be paralleled by Mahatma Gandhi's strategy of civil disobedience in the 20th century.[4] Throughout these changes, India remained a village society, divided into competing kingdoms and principalities but with central authority barely affecting the life of the average villager. Villages were self-sufficient and run by councils of elders, or *panchayat*. Communal self-sufficiency was another idea that Gandhi tried to revive during the drive for independence.

The British Raj (18th Century to 1947)

By the beginning of the 18th century, Mogul power in India had all but disintegrated, undermined by internal divisions and new invasions from the north. Unlike Japan, which had been united under a strong central authority and so was able to resist European traders, India had a power vacuum into which the Europeans moved relatively easily. Attracted by the prospects of trade, Britain, Portugal, France, and Holland competed for influence in the region, but it was the British who emerged as the dominant power; this was confirmed with the defeat of a Bengali army at Plassey in 1757 by Robert Clive, remembered by history as Clive of India.

From their base in Bengal in the east, the British eventually moved into most of what are now India, Pakistan, Bangladesh, Sri Lanka, and Burma. In some cases they used direct control, and in others they allowed existing leaders to keep power. By setting rulers and religious groups against one another and establishing military dominance, Britain had brought the entire subcontinent under its direct or indirect control by the early 1850s. The creation of the **British Raj** (Hindi for reign) was achieved with a remarkably small number of people. At no time in the 19th century were there more than 65,000 British troops or 500 administrators in India, and less than 60 percent of India came under direct British control. Until 1857, India was not even directly ruled by the British government but was administered (and in a sense "owned") by the 1,700 shareholders of the East India Company, founded in 1599.

TABLE 7.1

Key Dates in Indian History

1599	Establishment of the British East India Company
1757	Battle of Plassey
1857–1858	Indian Mutiny
1858	Britain assumes direct control over India from the East India Company
1885	Indian National Congress founded
1919	Amritsar massacre
1935	Government of India Act
1942	Launch of the "Quit India" campaign
1947	Independence and partition of India and Pakistan
1948	Mahatma Gandhi assassinated; independence of Burma and Ceylon (the latter renamed Sri Lanka in 1972); dispute with Pakistan over Kashmir
1950	New constitution comes into force; India becomes a republic
1952	Launch of the first 5-year plan
1962	Border conflict with China
1965	War with Pakistan over Kashmir
1971	Pakistan civil war, India-Pakistan war, and creation of Bangladesh
1974	India explodes underground nuclear device
1975–1977	State of emergency
1984	Indira Gandhi assassinated
1989	Congress loses more than half its seats in general election, and BJP increases its representation from 2 seats to 86
1991	Rajiv Gandhi assassinated
1992	(December) Destruction of mosque at Ayodhya leads to widespread rioting
1996	(January) Charges are brought against politicians involved in one of India's biggest ever bribery scandals; (May) voters looking for change inflict major losses on the Congress party in general election; a BJP-led government soon falls and is replaced by a leftist-regionalist United Front coalition led by Deve Gowda
1997	(April) United Front government collapses, and Gowda replaced as prime minister by Inder Kumar Gujral
1998	(March) General election brings BJP-led coalition to power; (May) India carries out five nuclear tests, Pakistan responds with six
1999	(April) BJP-led government falls and becomes caretaker; (May–July) fighting between India and Pakistan over Kashmir; (October) general election returns BJP-led government to power; military coup in Pakistan
2000	(May) Indian population officially reaches 1 billion
2001	(January) An estimated 25,000 people die in earthquake in northwestern India; (December) police and gunmen killed in suicide attack on Indian Parliament
2002	(February) More than 800 people killed in Hindu-Muslim violence

Under the British Raj, India was united for the first time and social reforms were made, leading to the abolition of traditions such as *suttee* (the burning of widows on the funeral pyres of their husbands) and *thagi* (institutionalized robbery and murder, from which the English word *thug* is derived). Western education, science, and technology were introduced; English was introduced as the lingua franca; a railroad and communications network was developed; and investments were made in industry and agriculture.

The beginning of the end of the Raj can perhaps be dated to 1857 and the outbreak of the Indian Mutiny. British rule relied heavily on a huge army of Indian soldiers (or *sepoys*), many of whom were devoted Hindus or Muslims. Already concerned about the spread of Christian influence, the *sepoys* were even more alarmed in 1857 when they were issued new rifles that used cartridges wrongly rumored to be greased with a mixture of cow fat (which offended Hindus) and pig fat (which offended Muslims). The refusal of some troops to accept the cartridges led to the outbreak of the Indian Mutiny, which lasted 18 months, cost several thousand deaths, and saw appalling savagery on both sides. Although Britain now took over direct administration of India from the East India Company and Queen Victoria was declared empress of India in 1877, the cracks in the edifice of the Raj had begun to show.

The emerging Indian middle class was particularly unwilling to accept foreign domination. In 1885 the Indian National Congress was founded, not so much to campaign for independence as to win greater self-determination and the integration of India into the British Empire on more equal terms. Indians, like Americans before them, did not want to be treated as second-class citizens. The Congress was initially moderate and even had a member elected to the British House of Commons, but as Britain rejected its demands for equality, it became more militant.

A symbolic turning point came in April 1919, when Indian troops under British command fired on demonstrators defying a ban on public meetings in the city of Amritsar. According to the official count, nearly 380 were killed and 1,200 wounded. Duly outraged, the Congress—inspired by Mahatma Gandhi—began campaigning for independence, using nonviolent civil disobedience, or noncooperation. This strategy cut to the heart of the British administrative system, which was based on ruling India mainly through Indians themselves.

India was given a large measure of self-government in 1935 with the Government of India Act. In 1937 elections were held and a new constitution was published, but these changes came too late for the nationalists, who began calling for full independence. Their plans were complicated, however, by divisions between India's Hindus and Muslims. Gandhi and his main associate, Jawaharlal Nehru, hoped that the Congress could represent all Indians and achieve a united, independent India, but Muslims were doubtful about living in a Hindu-dominated state. Their cause was represented by Muhammed Ali Jinnah (1876–1948), leader of the Muslim League. Gandhi had refused to recognize the League's claims to represent Muslims, but Jinnah argued that the Muslims were a nation and refused to cooperate with the "Quit India" movement launched by Gandhi against the British in 1942.

MAHATMA GANDHI

One of the greatest political figures of the 20th century, Mohandas Karamchand Gandhi (1869–1948) was also one of the few leaders of modern independence movements never to have held elective office. Popularly known as the Mahatma (or "great soul"), he was the spiritual leader of India during its struggle for independence.

Born in 1869, Gandhi was trained as a lawyer in Britain. In 1893 he was invited to South Africa to represent South African Indians against discriminatory laws; in that cause, he began experimenting with a brand of nonviolent and passive resistance he described as *satyagraha* (roughly translated as "soul force" or "truth force").

He returned to India in 1915 and by 1920 had emerged as the undisputed leader of the Indian nationalists. Recognizing the administrative and military power of the British, he agitated for Indian independence by using *satyagraha*. Through resistance, noncooperation, hunger strikes, and other symbolic acts for which he was repeatedly imprisoned, he drew attention to the injustices of British rule and focused the attention of a mass movement on achieving independence.

Gandhi also advocated social change among Indians themselves but found himself having to walk a careful line between campaigning for independence and trying to encourage Hindus and Muslims to live together. Before and after independence, violence broke out between Hindus and Muslims, prompting Gandhi to go on hunger strikes until the violence ended. He campaigned for an improvement in the status of untouchables (to the consternation of his caste-ridden Hindu following) and advocated personal simplicity and national self-sufficiency. Clothed in his trademark loincloth and shawl, he would spend at least 30 minutes every day making homespun cloth. The spinning wheel became his symbol and later became part of the national flag of independent India.

India finally won its independence in August 1947, but Gandhi felt this was a hollow victory given partition and the religious and social divisions of India. Five months later, a militant Hindu, disgusted at Gandhi's attempts to maintain peace between Hindus and Muslims, shot the 79-year-old Mahatma to death. India's first prime minister, Jawaharlal Nehru, declared: "The light has gone out of our lives and there is darkness everywhere."

Britain was now faced with two conflicting demands: one from Jinnah that India be partitioned into Hindu and Muslim states and then given independence and one from Gandhi that India be given independence and be allowed to settle the religious problem itself. Against a background of mounting violence between Hindus and Muslims, Britain concluded that the only option was partition, and so on August 15, 1947, the separate states of India and Pakistan achieved their independence. Partition gave rise to one of the biggest human migrations in history, with Muslims moving to Pakistan and Hindus to India, and the two groups occasionally coming to blows with each other. Altogether, more than 12 million people migrated, and as many as 1 million died in the process.

Nonetheless, 20 million Hindus remained in Pakistan and 40 million Muslims in India, which still has the second biggest Muslim population of any country in the world (surpassed only by Indonesia). Pakistan was faced with the additional problem of forging a new nation out of two separate pieces of territory: West Pakistan, with 34 million people, and East Pakistan, with 46 million people living in an area one-fifth the size of West Pakistan. To complicate the issue, India and Pakistan disagreed over the future of Kashmir, which had a Hindu leader but a predominantly Muslim population.

Independent India (1947–Present)

India entered independence torn by religious turmoil and facing the challenge of forging a nation out of many hundreds of princely states. For the first 2 years of its independence, it was supervised by a British governor-general while a new constitution was written. This was completed in 1950, when India became a republic. The princes were made to give up their political powers, the old British provinces were abolished, and a federal system was introduced.

India's priorities since independence have been self-reliance, economic development, political stability, and stabilizing relations with its neighbors, especially Pakistan. The Nehru administration (1947–1964) followed a moderately socialist economic line, with a limited land reform program and a series of 5-year plans that emphasized the growth of heavy industry. An agricultural program was also launched, which eventually made India self-sufficient in food. But these achievements were offset by India's population growth, its religious and social divisions, and conflicts with its neighbors. India has fought three wars with Pakistan over territorial issues; became involved in the Pakistan civil war in 1971; has faced continuing conflict over Kashmir; has seen border disputes with China, which claims part of northern India; has become involved in Sri Lanka's internal problems, which led to Indian troops occupying part of Sri Lanka in 1987; has faced domestic conflict between Hindus, Muslims, and Sikhs; and has had to wrestle with the bigger issue of defining a place for itself in the global system.

India's government was also dominated for more than 40 years by the **Congress party,** which was itself dominated by a family dynasty: Jawaharlal Nehru was prime minister for nearly 17 years (1946–1964), and his daughter Indira Gandhi (no relation to the Mahatma) was the major character in national politics for the next 20 years (nearly 10 of which she spent as prime minister). She was grooming her son Sanjay to replace her, but when he was killed in a 1980 plane crash, she recruited her son Rajiv to replace her. Following her 1984 assassination, Rajiv took over as prime minister. With his assassination in May 1991, the influence of the family briefly declined, but Congress eventually recruited Rajiv's Italian-born widow, Sonia, as its leader.

Many of the cracks in the political edifice began to show in early 1996, when the reforming government of Prime Minister Narasimha Rao was found to be riddled with scandal and when national elections left the Indian parliament divided among nearly 30 political parties. A 5-party coalition government fell in just 12 days and was replaced by a 13-party coalition in which communist and regionalist parties had much influence. It collapsed after 10 months, showing that national government was critically divided at a time when India needed firm leadership, political stability, and economic reform.

The most notable recent developments in Indian politics have been the rise of the Hindu nationalist **Bharatiya Janata party** (BJP) and the fragmentation of the party system. Where Congress was once dominant and there were a few much smaller parties in opposition, 39 parties were elected to the Indian parliament in 1999, and 24 of them became part of the BJP-led government. Party politics has since settled down into three competing blocs: Congress and its allies, the BJP and its allies, and parties of the left. But all three blocs depend on regional parties intent on putting local interests above those of the general national interest.

Under its leader Atal Behari Vajpayee, the BJP has moderated its policy positions, and the talk of militant Hindu nationalism that circulated in the early 1990s has all but disappeared. This is not to say that India has not taken an assertive role in foreign policy, however: An invasion of Kashmir in May 1999 by Pakistani and Afghan irregulars led to a brief skirmish, with a death toll estimated to be in the hundreds. Although Kashmir continues to be a flashpoint in Indo-Pakistani relations, much more worrisome has been the development of nuclear weapons by both countries. When India carried out five nuclear tests in May 1998, Pakistan responded with six, and both countries were heavily criticized by world leaders. Among the many regional disputes that have come to the fore in the post–cold war world, the persistent disagreement between India and Pakistan ranks among the most potentially dangerous.

India Today

There is no question about India's potential, but there are many questions about how long it will take for that potential to be fulfilled. It has most of the trappings of an emergent democracy, but it also has many substantial problems. These include religious and class conflict, widespread poverty, too many political parties, persistent political corruption, a bureaucracy that is often slow and cumbersome, and a government that is heavily involved in the economy.

The divisions were emphasized in the structure of the government of Atal Behari Vajpayee, a multiparty coalition whose member-parties had so many different platforms and priorities that the work of government was routinely interrupted by internal squabbles. Instead of making progress on badly needed economic reforms, the government found itself torn by small parties driven by vested interests. The opposition Congress party used the opportunity to make its own attempts to undermine the authority of the BJP-led administration. At the same time, the government was able to make little headway on its most critical foreign policy challenge—the ongoing dispute with Pakistan over the province of Kashmir (see Political Debates, p. 374).

Underlying the immediate political problems of India has been the question of the role of Hindu nationalism. The BJP is identified with the Hindu cause, and Vajpayee was once regarded as one of its leading proponents, but he has come to be seen as a relative moderate in recent years, his positions standing in contrast to those of his leading rival, L. K. Advani. A member of the Vajpayee government— holding the portfolio of home minister, in charge of many domestic administrative matters—Advani first came to national prominence in 1992 when he led the movement that demolished the Muslim Babri Masjid mosque at Ayodhya in northern India; subsequent violence led to the deaths of 1,700 people and the injuries of 5,500 others. Seen as the most likely successor to Vajpayee, Advani could inject a worrisome element of Hindu nationalism into Indian politics at a time when relations among India's many religious and regional groups—and India's relations with its Muslim neighbor Pakistan—are balanced on a knife edge.

POLITICAL CULTURE

Political culture is easiest to define when a political system has settled features and values. Even after more than 55 years of independence, however, politics in India are unpredictable. Not only do social divisions threaten the viability of the state, but the party system has seen constant change, a modern urban society coexists with a traditional village society, and the role of Hinduism in politics has still not been fully settled. Despite the uncertainties, there are several distinct facets to Indian political culture.

A Dominant State

The most prominent feature of Indian political culture in recent years has been the emergence of a dominant state system, which has come to affect every sphere of Indian life and has promoted a pan-Indian middle-class consciousness at the expense of traditional culture.[5] One of the consequences has been a tendency toward homogenization and away from recognizing the variety and pluralism of Indian society. This has led to a political system based increasingly around popularity contests and American-style elections that have become quasi-presidential. Nowhere was personality more obviously an issue than in the dominance of the Nehru-Gandhi dynasty until 1991; the strength of the dynasty suggested that personality was more important than ideology or administrative ability.

A Village Society

All societies have their traditional elements, which have varying degrees of influence on politics. Despite the dominance of the modern Indian state and central government, most Indians still live a simple village life that is largely bypassed by national politics, except during elections, when candidates fleetingly become interested in the village vote. Television and satellite dishes may have reached nearly every village, but life for the average villager still extends no more than a few miles from the village. The caste system has a strong hold, limiting opportunities for villagers, and traditional local community values still play an important role in Indian politics.

A Society of Violence

Political, social, and religious conflicts regularly lead to physical violence. Perhaps more pervasive and intrusive, though, is the more generalized problem of **structural violence.** Originating in neo-Marxism, this term is used to describe intangible forms of oppression, or the "violence" concealed within a social and political system.

Hence the oppression of women is a form of structural violence perpetrated by male-dominated political systems, and extreme poverty is a form of violence perpetrated by one part of society on another. Structural violence in India refers to the invisible effects of poverty, inequality, and caste oppression, which have a psychological impact on the way Indians relate to their political system.

Rising Frustrations

Many people find that the more they have, the more they want, and as their lives improve, they find it harder to compromise. As urban India has modernized and as the middle-class consumer society has grown, so the expectations of Indians (especially urban Indians) have grown and their frustrations risen. Gaps have grown between aspiration and achievement, and the government has been unable to keep up with the demands of new groups entering politics.[6] In particular, the middle classes have become impatient with India's poverty and with what they see as the limits placed on social change by the traditional sector. The gap between expectations and performance goes to the heart of the argument posed by the political scientist Samuel Huntington, who suggests that "the primary problem of politics is the lag in the development of political institutions behind social and economic change."[7] This is certainly true of India.

POLITICAL SYSTEM

India is a federal republic with a parliamentary system of government. It is also a democracy, if democracy is measured by the existence of free political parties, competitive elections, different forms of participation and representation, the stability and continuity of political institutions, and the protection of individual rights and freedoms. But it is far from being a liberal democracy, because there are too many gaps between theory and practice:

- There may be regular elections, but they are often accompanied by violence and fraud; in some cases (such as in the Punjab during the 1980s) elections have been suspended because of violence.

- Indian prime ministers have more potentially dictatorial powers than their liberal democratic counterparts, although their abilities to abuse these powers have become more limited as communications have been modernized and leaders have had to rely on fragile multiparty coalitions as the base of their support.

- India may be federal in theory, but in practice the central government wields so much power over the states that state governments have little real independence. This has been changing, though, with the rise of regional political parties.

- The rights of individuals may be constitutionally protected, but many minorities still rail against the authority of central government and the caste system still exists.

- Despite recent economic growth and liberalization, the vast majority of Indians live a preindustrial lifestyle, many live in crushing poverty, and India is still a poor country.

For now, India is best seen as a newly industrializing country that is working to develop the political and economic form best suited to the needs of its people. It has the potential to become a stable, influential, and wealthy state, but many handicaps must first be removed.

THE CONSTITUTION

The constitution of India created a federal republic based on a parliamentary system of government with guaranteed civil rights and liberties and a separate Supreme Court with the power of judicial review. The constitution is one of the longest in the world, with 395 articles, 8 schedules, and more than 40 amendments. The wording occasionally sounds like parts of the U.S. Declaration of Independence, but the principles come out of the Westminster system of government; nearly 250 articles are taken almost verbatim from the 1935 Government of India Act.

The constitution was drawn up by a Constituent Assembly indirectly elected in 1946 by India's provincial assemblies. The Assembly became the provisional government following independence and oversaw the drafting of the constitution in 1948–1950. Among its priorities were the following: to establish a democratic, sovereign, and independent republic; to ensure the unity of India; to offset the potential for violence and disorder; to set up a secular state; and to establish economic independence and self-sufficiency.[8] Despite the discussions that followed, the dominance of the Assembly by the Congress party meant that a handful of Congress leaders—including Nehru—set the course for the debate and influenced the final form of the constitution, which went into effect on January 26, 1950.

During the debates, some argued that India should be set up as a decentralized state based on village *panchayat*, and some even said that *satyagraha* should be a fundamental right of the people.[9] Others argued that India had long experience with representative parliamentary government and that the unity of India could be ensured only through a strong, centralized authority. At the same time, the need to recognize India's cultural diversity and to keep the princely states happy led to the decision to create a federal system.

The most controversial element of the constitution was the power it gave to the president (on the advice of the prime minister) to suspend or abrogate freedoms during a "grave emergency," that is, when the security of India or its territory were threatened by "external aggression or internal disturbance." Emergencies were declared in 1962 and 1971 during conflicts with China and Pakistan, but emergency powers were given their loosest interpretation by Prime Minister Indira Gandhi in June 1975, when she "advised" the president to declare an emergency in response to an alleged threat to internal security from her political opposition. After she lost the 1977 election, the constitution was quickly changed so that emergency powers could be declared only in the event of external aggression or armed rebellion.

THE PRESIDENT

India's decision to keep the parliamentary system of government after independence was unusual; almost all other former European colonies (except Australia, Canada, and New Zealand) opted for a presidential system with American undertones. Some

TABLE 7.2

Presidents and Vice Presidents of India

Date	President	Vice president
1950	Rajendra Prasad	—
1952	Rajendra Prasad	Sarvapalli Radhakrishnan
1957	Rajendra Prasad	Sarvapalli Radhakrishnan
1962	Sarvapalli Radhakrishnan	Zakir Hussain
1967	Zakir Hussain*	V. V. Giri
1969	V. V. Giri	G. S. Pathak
1974	Fakhruddin Ali Ahmed*	B. D. Jatti
1977	Neelam Sanjiva Reddy	—
1979		Mohammed Hidayatullah
1982	Gaini Zail Singh	—
1984		Ramaswamy Venkataraman
1987	Ramaswamy Venkataraman	Shankar Dayal Sharma
1992	Shankar Dayal Sharma	K. R. Narayanan
1997	K. R. Narayanan	Krishan Kant
2002	A. P. J. Abdul Kalam	Bhairon Singh Sekhawat

*Died while in office.

Indians have called for the creation of a presidential system along French or Russian lines, and Indira Gandhi centralized powers to the point where her administration became quasi-presidential, but the parliamentary system persists and includes a president with about the same (mainly symbolic) powers as the British monarch or Japanese emperor.

The president of India is elected for a renewable 5-year term by an electoral college made up of members of both houses of Parliament and of the state legislatures. A vice president is also elected for 5-year terms by an electoral college made up of both houses of Parliament, and several have gone on to become president. All presidents to date have been men, and given the long dominance of the Congress party in Indian politics, most have been the handpicked choices of the party. The presidential candidate of the Congress (I) (for Indira) party in 1987, Ramaswamy Venkataraman, was so assured of confirmation that he did not even bother to campaign. President K. R. Narayanan, elected in 1997, was notable for being the first Dalit to become president. The current president—A. J. P. Abdul Kalam—is a retired scientist who was architect of India's missile program, for which he earned the nickname "Missile Man." He is India's third Muslim president.

The president technically "appoints" the prime minister and members of the Council of Ministers, although—like the British monarch—all he really does is confirm as prime minister the leader of the largest party or coalition. The president also has several other constitutional powers, but these are exercised on the advice of the Council of Ministers, which is dominated by the prime minister. These powers include the ability to dissolve Parliament, declare a state of emergency, declare an emergency in a state and rule that state by decree, veto parliamentary bills, and promulgate ordinances that have the same power and effect as acts of Parliament. The president is also the commander-in-chief and appoints state governors and Supreme Court justices. The vice president takes over temporarily if the president dies, resigns, or cannot carry out the duties of office, and (like the U.S. vice president) is ex officio chairman of the upper house of the legislature.

Despite having to make almost all their decisions on the advice of the prime minister, presidents have several times had to step in to arbitrate following indecisive elections. For example, after the collapse of the Janata government in 1979, President Sanjiva Reddy asked Charan Singh (leader of a Janata splinter party) to be prime minister. Singh was unable to form a workable government and resigned within 3 weeks. Reddy then asked Singh to oversee a caretaker government, which held power until the January 1980 elections returned Indira Gandhi to power. Similarly, President Shankar Dayal Sharma had to step in several times during 1996–1997 to identify the politicians in the best position to form a government during the confusion that followed the 1996 national elections. In both cases, the president played an important role as an arbiter and guide during power vacuums.

THE EXECUTIVE: PRIME MINISTER AND COUNCIL OF MINISTERS

In theory, Indian prime ministers are the leaders of the majority party or coalition in Parliament. However, the fluidity of party politics in recent years has meant that—in the interests of building a stable coalition—parties may bypass the leadership and look elsewhere. For example, Deve Gowda, who was appointed prime minister in May 1996, was not the leader of any of the parties in the United Front coalition but was chief minister of the southern state of Karnataka. He was recruited by other chief ministers who wanted someone sympathetic to the cause of local government.

Prime ministers appoint and oversee the Council of Ministers (although the appointments are technically made by the president on the recommendation of the prime minister). Like the British cabinet, this council consists of the heads and deputy heads of government departments. Ministers either must be members of parliament (either house) or within 6 months of their appointment must become members by nomination or by winning a by-election. Unlike the British cabinet, the council is too big (about 45 members) to work effectively as a body and never meets collectively. A tradition has instead evolved of convening a smaller cabinet of the 15 to 20 most important government ministers, which meets weekly, takes collective responsibility, and generally works more like the British cabinet.

Indira and Rajiv Gandhi went further by creating "inner cabinets" of close advisors (something like the traditional Indian *durbar*, an inner circle of advisors to the ruler). During the emergency years of 1975–1977, Indira Gandhi created a six-member "kitchen cabinet" called the Political Affairs Committee, which included her son

TABLE 7.3

Prime Ministers of India

Date	Prime minister	Governing party or coalition
September 1947	Jawaharlal Nehru	Congress
May 1952*	Jawaharlal Nehru	Congress
March l957*	Jawaharlal Nehru	Congress
January 1962*	Jawaharlal Nehru†	Congress
June 1964	Lal Bahadur Shastri†	Congress
January 1966	Indira Gandhi	Congress
March 1967*	Indira Gandhi	Congress
March 1971*	Indira Gandhi	Congress (R)
March 1977*	Morarji Desai	Janata Front
July 1979	Charan Singh (caretaker from August 22)	Janata (S)
January 1980*	Indira Gandhi†	Congress (I)
October 1984	Rajiv Gandhi	Congress (I)
December 1984*	Rajiv Gandhi	Congress (I)
December 1989*	V. P. Singh	Janata Dal–led coalition
November 1990	Chandra Shekar	Janata Dal (S)
June 1991*	P. V. Narasimha Rao	Congress (I)
May 1996*	Atal Behari Vajpayee	BJP-led coalition
May 1996	Deve Gowda	United Front coalition
April 1997	Inder Kumar Gujral	United Front coalition
March 1998*	Atal Behari Vajpayee	BJP-led coalition
October 1999*	Atal Behari Vajpayee	BJP-led coalition

*General elections.
†Died while in office.

Sanjay. When Rajiv Gandhi became prime minister, he too had a small coterie of associates, known widely as the "Doon clique" after the name of the private school he had attended.

A notable feature of the Indian prime ministership for many years was the dominant role of personality. Liberal democratic prime ministers do not usually stamp strong personal influence on their office, but India was ruled for all but 4 of its first 42 years of independence by the **Nehru-Gandhi dynasty.** This worried many Indians, for several reasons. First, personal leadership is fragile, as emphasized by the traumatic effects of the assassinations of Indira and Rajiv Gandhi, which showed just how far India had come to depend on individuals rather than institutions. Second, leaders who come to power through inheritance need to show little in the way of character or past performance,[10] which means that they may not be battle-hardened by the time they come to power. Finally, dynasties can tend toward authoritarianism, as exemplified by the performance of Indira Gandhi.

Nehru was never formally selected as party leader by the Congress party but became leader and prime minister as the political successor to Mahatma Gandhi[11] and held office for nearly 17 years. The impact of personality on government was consolidated during the first administration of Indira Gandhi, who in 1966 became the world's first female prime minister. She had so personalized and centralized government by the early 1970s that her administration verged on authoritarian. Gandhi's tactics ultimately backfired when she was held personally responsible for food shortages and inflation in 1973–1974, leading her to take her powers to a new extreme by declaring a state of emergency.

The role of personality government was further emphasized during the administration of Rajiv Gandhi, who came into politics only because he was recruited by his mother following the death in a 1980 plane crash of his elder brother Sanjay, who had been groomed to replace her. Rajiv was transformed in just 4 years from a commercial airline pilot into a prime minister. After just more than 5 years in office, he lost the 1989 election, but the inability of the opposition to form a workable government contributed to a revival of the Gandhi mystique. Rajiv seemed to be on the brink of being returned to office when he was assassinated in May 1991.

Recent events suggest that the power of the office may be on the decline and that parties have become (at least temporarily) the chief centers of power. Narasimha Rao surprised many observers by holding on to office for a full term (1991–1996), making popular policy decisions, and reducing the influence of personality in Indian politics. However, 27 parties won seats in Parliament after the 1996 elections, the traditional power of Congress was gone (although it remained a key power broker), and confusion reigned as India was ruled by a series of multiparty coalitions. Deals were vigorously pursued behind the scenes, bringing three prime ministers to office in the space of a year, including one (Atal Behari Vajpayee) who was in office for just 12 days. His two successors held office for 10 months and 11 months, respectively, before Vajpayee came back as prime minister in March 1998. The ghosts of the Nehru-Gandhi dynasty still hover in the background, however, because Congress was led into the 1999 elections by Sonia Gandhi, the Italian-born widow of Rajiv.

THE LEGISLATURE: PARLIAMENT

As in Britain, the prime minister and the cabinet in India are collectively responsible to Parliament and must keep its confidence to stay in power. When the Congress party was dominant, Parliament took a subsidiary role in the relationship between executive and legislature, with members of Parliament tying their political careers to the fortunes of the prime minister. On several occasions, though, the support of members of Parliament (MPs) has been critical to the continued power of the government. This has become clear in recent years as governments have been based on coalitions of multiple parties. Following the October 1999 elections, for example, the Vajpayee government was made up of an astonishing 24 political parties.

ATAL BEHARI VAJPAYEE

© CORBIS

One of the defining political developments of recent years in India has been the growing role of Hindu nationalism, which has been behind the successes of the Bharatiya Janata party (BJP) and its leader Atal Behari Vajpayee.

The precursor to the BJP was the Jana Sangh, founded in 1951 with the goal of building a modern Hindu society, removing foreign influences, and "nationalizing" non-Hindus. For its part, the BJP campaigns for **Hindutva,** or Hinduness, a philosophy that includes the reintroduction of basic Hindu beliefs and values, such as the caste system. It initially won millions of supporters by

championing Hindu pride but alienated millions more with the militancy that peaked with the December 1992 destruction of a mosque in the northern town of Ayodhya. It has since moderated its policies under the leadership of Vajpayee.

Born in Gwalior in the central Indian state of Madhya Pradesh in 1926, Vajpayee entered politics in 1952, became a member of Parliament in 1957, and eventually became chief spokesman for Jana Sangh, earning a reputation as a moderate. He was Indian foreign minister during the 1977–1979 Janata-led coalition government and, with the breakup of that administration, pulled together former members of the Jana Sangh to form the BJP. The new party got off to an inauspicious start when it won just two seats in the 1984 elections, and Vajpayee lost his seat. He lost the presidency of the party in 1985, being replaced by L. K. Advani who moved the BJP back to its more overtly nationalist roots. Its representation in the Lok Sabha grew dramatically (85 seats in 1989 and 119 in 1991), but there was a limit to how far it could exploit militant Hindu nationalism, and when Vajpayee was restored as leader and moderated its position, it won enough seats in 1996 to briefly form a coalition government.[12] Vajpayee became prime minister in 1998 and was reconfirmed in office with the elections of October 1999. (Despite Vajpayee's increasingly prominent role in Indian politics, then-U.S. presidential candidate George W. Bush could not remember his name when quizzed during an interview.)

A poet in his spare time, Vajpayee is known as a good speaker, has a strong reputation for personal integrity, and continues to be seen as the moderate voice of Hindu nationalism, refusing to support the anti-Islamic and anti-Western stance of more militant Hindus. Under his leadership, the BJP has become—for now at least—the dominating element in Indian party politics.

The Indian Parliament building in New Delhi. Although it shows the classic style of much British colonial architecture, its role in government is significantly different from that of its British counterpart. The recent dominance of coalition governments has reduced the powers of the prime minister and moved many of the key struggles in Indian politics away from the prime minister's office and into the parliamentary chamber.

Parliament consists of two houses, which have the same powers over legislation but are elected differently.

Rajya Sabha (House of States)

The Rajya Sabha is the upper house, designed to represent the states. It has 250 members, of which 12 are appointed by the president to represent the professions, the sciences, and the arts and the rest are elected for 6-year terms by the state legislatures. The number of members from each state is decided on the basis of population. Unlike the lower house, the Rajya Sabha has fixed terms, so it cannot be dissolved by the president. Like the U.S. Senate, its elections are staggered, so one-third of its members stand for reelection every 2 years. Following the March 1998 elections, Congress held 81 of the elected seats and the BJP held 41.

Lok Sabha (House of the People)

Like many lower houses in bicameral legislatures, the Lok Sabha is the more powerful of the two chambers. It has 545 members, elected from single-member districts by universal suffrage for maximum 5-year terms: 525 are elected by voters in the

FIGURE 7.1

Comparing Levels of Representation

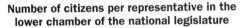

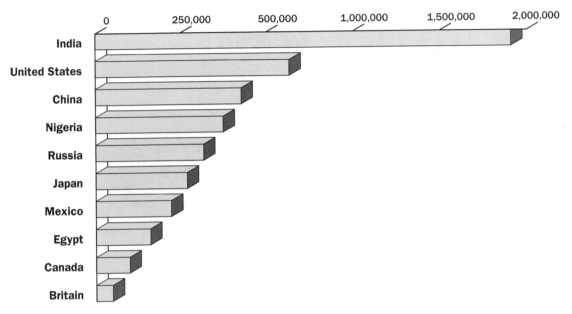

Number of citizens per representative in the lower chamber of the national legislature

states, 18 are elected by voters in the union territories, and 2 seats are reserved for Anglo-Indians. The seats are allocated among the states and territories on the basis of population, with each district roughly the same size in terms of population. A notable feature of Indian politics is the relative underrepresentation of citizens at the national level: Whereas the average British MP represents 91,000 people and the average member of the U.S. House represents 650,000 people, the average Indian MP comes from a district of 1.9 million people (see Figure 7.1). For Indians to have the same level as representation as Americans, the Lok Sabha would need to have nearly 1,600 members.

The Lok Sabha must meet at least twice per year, with no more than 6 months between sessions. Like the British House of Commons, it is essentially a debating chamber that provides support and opposition to the government. It has most of the trappings of the Westminster model, such as a neutral speaker elected from among the members of the house, parliamentary committees, and government question time, but—thanks to the forcefulness of many Indian prime ministers and to the high turnover among members after elections—it was for a long time less powerful in real terms than the House of Commons. With the advent of the multiparty coalitions of the 1990s, it took on a much more significant role in government.

The legislative process in India is similar to those used in the British Parliament and the U.S. Congress. Any bill other than a money bill can be introduced in either house, but most are introduced in the Lok Sabha, where they go through the same process of readings, debates, and consideration by committee as used in the House of Commons. Once passed in the lower house, a bill goes to the Rajya Sabha, where it goes through the same stages. Disagreements between the two chambers are debated, and if they are not resolved, the president can call for a joint meeting of Parliament. Once both houses have passed the bill in the same form, it goes to the president for assent. He can refuse to give it assent and can send it back to Parliament, but if it is passed again, the president must give his assent. Most parliamentary debates take place in English or Hindi.

THE JUDICIARY: SUPREME COURT

India has a Supreme Court responsible for interpreting the constitution and arbitrating in the case of disputes between the states or between the Union (federal) government and the states. The Court originally had eight justices, but the number has been increased to 26. Justices are appointed by the president after consultation with members of the Court and the state courts. Turnover is higher than in the U.S. Supreme Court, because members can hold office only until age 65. Normally, the most senior justice automatically becomes chief justice when the incumbent retires, although Indira Gandhi broke this precedent by promoting her own candidates over senior justices, leading to protests from the legal profession about political interference.

The Court has the power of judicial review, but the Indian constitution is so detailed that the Court has less latitude than its U.S. counterpart. Just as the U.S. Supreme Court spent its early years defining its powers in relation to Congress and the presidency (finally winning the power of judicial review with *Marbury* v. *Madison* in 1803), so the Indian court had a running battle for many years with Parliament, particularly over the issue of the Fundamental Rights contained in Articles 12–35 of the constitution. Several amendments have been passed redefining the relative powers of the Court and Parliament. The 24th Amendment, passed in 1971, gave Parliament the power to amend any part of the constitution, but the Court decision *Keshavananda Bharati* v. *State of Kerala* in 1973 declared that any amendments that attacked the "basic structure" of the constitution would be invalid.

The Supreme Court played a critical role in uncovering and pursuing the scandal that proved to be one of the final straws that broke public support for the Congress party in 1996. In 1991 police discovered evidence that a business family, the Jains, had been bribing senior members of the government. When four citizens filed a public interest suit with the Supreme Court, its judges took the opportunity to order an investigation. It was finally revealed in January 1996 that 65 politicians and bureaucrats—including perhaps Prime Minister Narasimha Rao himself—had received more than $18 million in bribes.

SUBNATIONAL GOVERNMENT

India is a federal republic, with the Union government at the center and powers over many local issues devolved to the governments of the 25 states and seven union territories. Several of the states are big enough to be countries in their own right: In terms of population, Uttar Pradesh is as big as Russia, Maharashtra is as big as Germany, and Tamil Nadu is as big as Britain.

Every state has its own government, which almost exactly mirrors the structure of the Union government. Each has a figurehead governor appointed by the president of India for 5-year terms. To discourage parochialism and encourage objectivity, the governor is usually from another state and is someone who is both politically neutral and acceptable to the state government. Governors appoint the chief ministers, although all they actually do is confirm the leader of the biggest party or coalition in the state assembly. Chief ministers are members of the state assembly, are directly elected by all eligible voters in the state, and rule with the help of a Council of Ministers. Most states have a unicameral Legislative Assembly (Vidhan Sabha), but five of the larger states also have an upper Legislative Council (Vidhan Parishad). The assemblies consist of between 60 and 500 members, depending on the size of the state, and serve 5-year terms. (Union territories are ruled by lieutenant governors or administrators appointed by the president of India.)

The Union government once had so many powers that, in 1951, India was described as "quasi-federal."[13] Some observers once denied that India was federal at all,[14] and others spoke instead of a kind of "cooperative federalism." The balance has begun to change in recent years, though, with the rise of regional political parties, some of which have become big enough to be nationally important. Although there were only about 15 to 20 recognized state parties active until the early 1990s, that number has more than doubled in the last decade, leading to the fragmentation of party politics in India.

The southern state of Tamil Nadu has been a notable hotbed of regional politics, with two parties promoting Tamil self-determination: the Dravida Munnetra Kazhagam (DMK) and the Tamil Maanila Congress (TMC). In 1967 the DMK became the first opposition party to win a clear majority in a state assembly. In 1972 a splinter party (the AIADMK) split off from the DMK, claiming that the latter had lost sight of its roots and basic goals. Led by the popular film star M. G. Ramachandran, the AIADMK went on to win a majority in the Tamil Nadu state assembly. After Ramachandran's death in 1987, the party split into factions, one led by his widow and the other by his former leading actress, Jayaram Jayalalitha. The latter swept to victory in the 1991 state elections and Jayalalitha became chief minister of Tamil Nadu. Her party also won 18 seats in the Lok Sabha, became part of the BJP-led government in 1998, then brought the government down by withdrawing its support in April 1999.[15]

The issue of who has the real power in the relationship between the center and the states in India is debatable. In many respects, the balance lies with the Union government: It has control over defense policy, foreign affairs, and income tax; in a conflict between the Union and the states, Union law always prevails; the Union government has the power to change the boundaries of states, create new states, and even abolish existing states; the president of India, on the "advice" of a state governor, can declare an emergency and transfer powers over the state to the Indian Parliament; an emergency can be declared if a state fails to comply with a law passed by parliament, thereby effectively forcing that state to comply; the Union government has the power of the purse and can decide how to share national revenues out among the states; and finally, a strong prime minister can manipulate and limit state powers, as did Indira Gandhi when she centralized decision making in the Congress party at the national level and took steps to break the power of state party leaders.

Despite their relative weakness, however, the states cannot be ignored. The Union government relies on state governments to implement policy in several key areas, the performance of national parties at the state level affects the overall strength of those parties, opposition to national parties running in state elections can be turned into opposition at the national level, and recent coalitions at the national level have depended on key regional parties for their support.

REPRESENTATION AND PARTICIPATION

India has generally free and fair elections. It also has one of the most complex party systems in the world, a free press, and a variety of interest groups. Political corruption is a problem, with voter intimidation and occasional vote rigging, but national election results generally reflect the preferences of voters, whose political awareness makes them difficult to manipulate. Political activity and literacy is particularly high among the urban middle classes, and turnout at elections is generally high, even in rural districts. The party system is more fluid than in many liberal democracies, with parties and coalitions coming and going. Party politics was long dominated by the Indian National Congress, which was in turn dominated until the late 1980s by the Nehru-Gandhi dynasty. Congress has now become the main party of opposition, because recent governments have been controlled by the Hindu BJP and its coalition partners.

ELECTIONS AND THE ELECTORAL SYSTEM

With some notable differences, the Indian electoral system looks much like the British model. Elections to the Lok Sabha and the state assemblies must be held at least once every 5 years, and all eligible voters take part. Until 1971, elections to the Lok Sabha and the state assemblies were held at the same time. In that year, Indira Gandhi called a general election without calling for state elections. Although her motive was short-term political gain—she was trying to capitalize on her national popularity to neutralize her opponents in the Congress party and in the states—it has been common since then to hold national and state elections separately.[16]

Despite electoral fraud and regular outbreaks of violence (nearly 300 people died during the 1991 elections), Indian elections are mostly free and fair. Everyone older than 21 years of age can vote, and voter turnout has increased from nearly 47 percent in 1952 to an average of 60 to 65 percent today (although it fell to 53 percent in the troubled 1991 elections, raising questions about public faith in the system). By every measure, Indian elections are the biggest in the world: At the 1999 general election, there were about 620 million eligible voters, of whom about 372 million turned out to vote at 800,000 polling stations manned by 4 million officials. From a time in the 1950s when elections were held over a period of 4 months, improvements in communications and counting methods helped bring the process down to just a few days in 1999.

The General Election

Like Britain and the United States, India uses single-member districts in elections to the lower house (the Lok Sabha), and a plurality on the first ballot is enough to return the winner. The low level of literacy in rural India means that ballots have to be printed with the name of the party and an easily recognizable symbol (see Figure 7.2). Election campaigns are short (3 weeks), meaning that rural candidates have to undertake a

FIGURE 7.2

Election Symbols of Indian Political Parties

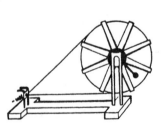

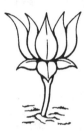

Janata Party

Bharatiya
Janata Party

Communist Party
of India

Indian National
Congress (I)

Communist Party
of India (M)

Indian National
Congress (S)

Lok Dal

grueling campaign, visiting as many as 600 villages in a single district, often traveling nearly impassable roads. Although most villages now have televisions and there is increased access to the Internet, most candidates still try to reach people through leaflets, speeches, and personal influence. Appeals will often be made on the basis of class, community, caste, faction loyalty, and charisma,[17] but issues are not forgotten. Campaigns have been known to become "waves" or landslides, such as the Indira wave in 1971 and the wave of sympathy that led to the election of Rajiv Gandhi in 1984 in the wake of his mother's assassination. The label *wave* should not be taken too literally, though, because no one party has ever won a majority of votes.

State Elections

In addition to national elections, Indian voters also take part in regular state assembly elections. These are held at 5-year intervals and contested by both national and regional parties. The outcome of state elections often has national implications, particularly given the strength of the bigger regional parties.

POLITICAL PARTIES

The Indian party system has become extraordinarily complex of late. From a time when it was a stable, one-party-dominant system, it has become increasingly unstable, erratic, and fragmented, with new parties coming and going and national parties losing ground to an increasingly messy community of regional parties. The effects of the atomization of the party system were only too clear after the 1999 general election, when 39 parties were represented in Parliament and the government was a coalition of 24 parties. The number of parties has never been constant, nor does it matter so much as the coalitions they form. Hence, the best way of trying to understand the Indian party system is not to look at each party in turn, but to follow the different phases in the relationship among the major national parties and the many competing smaller parties.[18]

Congress Dominant (1947–1967)

The first phase of Indian party politics revolved around the Indian National Congress, which was the major force in the independence movement, and—until 1967—routinely won four times as many votes as any other party. Like the Japanese Liberal Democrats, it consisted of several factions bound by a consensus, was flexible enough to absorb policies from other parties, and ran a political machine based on patronage and political favors. Virtually all significant Indian politics took place within Congress, which—thanks to the charisma and ability of Jawaharlal Nehru—had a cohesion and sense of direction that the weak and fragmented opposition lacked.

The centralization of Congress had already begun to break down when Nehru suffered a stroke in January 1964. By the time he died in May, the glue was gone and factional differences had emerged based on personality rather than ideology. The Syndicate, a group of five powerful Congress party leaders from the states, named Lal Bahadur Shastri prime minister. When Shastri died suddenly in January 1966, a vote was held on the party leadership for the first time, resulting in victory for

Indira Gandhi. The end of the unified Congress system was confirmed in the 1967 state and national elections, when Indira Gandhi was returned as prime minister, but Congress lost control of six state governments and had a reduced majority in the Lok Sabha.

Congress Divided (1967–1977)

With Congress now weakened by defections, Gandhi moved to reassert her control of the party, so upsetting the Syndicate that Congress split in two: a group of 226 MPs that supported Gandhi and a rump of 65 that supported the Syndicate. To win a mandate for her wing of Congress, Gandhi called a general election in 1971, which resulted in a landslide for her newly renamed Congress (R) (for Requisitioned, and then for Ruling). Meanwhile, the Syndicate's faction, Congress (O) (for Opposition or Organization), saw its share of seats fall from 65 to 16. Almost immediately, Gandhi found herself caught up in Pakistan's civil war and capitalized on the triumph of the Indian military by calling state elections in March 1972. These resulted in a landslide for Congress (R), which became virtually her personal fiefdom. Whereas Congress had once been a national party that reached through every level of Indian society, Gandhi centralized decision-making power by making senior appointments on the basis of personal loyalty and by regularly reshuffling the cabinet to make sure no one could build a strong opposing base. She even renamed her party Congress (I) (for Indira).

As criticism of her autocratic methods grew, she "advised" the president to declare a national emergency and went on nationwide radio to warn that "a widespread conspiracy" had been growing against her and that the armed forces had been incited to mutiny and the police to rebel. The 1976 general election was postponed, direct rule by New Delhi was imposed on the states, opposition organizations were banned, the bill of rights was effectively abrogated, the press was heavily censored, 110,000 people were arrested and detained without trial, and some of the detainees were tortured and murdered in jail. A new amendment to the constitution was even passed, denying the Supreme Court the power of judicial review. Likening herself to Joan of Arc, Indira Gandhi tried to paint herself as the savior of Indian democracy rather than its enemy.

In March 1977, convinced that Congress (I) could win, Gandhi called a general election. Although taken by surprise, the opposition quickly formed a new coalition, the Janata Front, and campaigned on a manifesto that argued that voters were faced with a choice between "freedom and slavery; between democracy and dictatorship." Janata and its allies won a majority, Gandhi lost her Lok Sabha seat, and her faction of Congress was reduced to 154 seats. She was forced to admit defeat, which to many was vindication that Indian democracy was strong enough to withstand abuses of power.

The Janata Coalition (1977–1980)

The 81-year-old Morarji Desai became prime minister, but despite its mandate, his Janata coalition rapidly fell apart, largely because of a lack of direction, personality clashes, and a series of unpopular policy decisions. Janata leaders also made the mistake of launching personal attacks on Gandhi and even occasionally placing her under house arrest, making her a martyr in the eyes of many. In July 1979 Desai resigned and was replaced by Charan Singh. However, Singh's coalition too was torn by internal dissension, and within a month he had resigned, although he stayed on as head of a caretaker government.

Meanwhile, after briefly considering retirement, Gandhi had rebuilt both her political reputation and her faction of Congress. In November 1978 she won re-election to the Lok Sabha but faced criminal prosecution on charges of misconduct and abuse of authority. After refusing to testify before a parliamentary inquiry into the activities of Maruti, an automobile company founded by her younger son, Sanjay, she was held in contempt and jailed for a week. Before the government could prosecute Gandhi, the Janata government had fallen and new elections were called for in January 1980. Gandhi portrayed herself as the only person capable of forming a strong government, campaigned tirelessly, and was returned to office with a strong majority.

The Gandhis Return (1980–1989)

Gandhi's moment of triumph was short-lived. She had been grooming Sanjay to succeed her, but he was killed in a plane crash in June 1980, forcing her to rethink her plans. She persuaded her elder son, Rajiv, to enter politics, and in a June 1981 by-election he won the Lok Sabha seat left vacant by Sanjay.

In October 1984, in the wake of her attempts to put down an insurrection by Sikh extremists, Indira Gandhi was assassinated by her Sikh bodyguards, leaving Congress (I) without a leader. Rajiv was immediately drafted to replace his mother, automatically becoming prime minister. Two months later, seeking his own mandate, he called a new general election and was returned with a landslide. Rajiv was young and charming, portrayed himself as spokesman for a younger generation, and vowed to end government corruption and prepare India for the 21st century. He won the prime ministership partly because of sympathy over the assassination of his mother but also because of the inability of the opposition to offer a credible alternative. His lack of a political past also helped him portray himself as a figure of renewal and change and of stability and continuity.[19]

Despite his 1984 mandate, Rajiv became increasingly arrogant, centralizing power in his office and in the hands of a small group of advisors, and regularly reshuffling his cabinet.[20] An anticorruption program he had promised was run by the new finance minister, V. P. Singh, who pursued his new task with such vigor that many powerful business leaders with close connections to Rajiv Gandhi were investigated. In 1987 Singh was shifted from finance to defense but continued his anticorruption drive with such persistence that he made many enemies and was forced to resign. Then news of the Bofors scandal broke.

In 1986 the Indian government had signed a contract with the Swedish arms manufacturer Bofors for $1.3 billion worth of 155-mm howitzers. In 1987 Swedish radio reported that Bofors had paid Indian middlemen nearly $40 million in "commissions" to make sure that Bofors won the contract. There were even charges (never proved) that the bribes had reached the highest levels of government, possibly including Rajiv Gandhi himself. To add to his problems, Rajiv was unable to reduce India's religious tensions, and the conflict and violence between Hindus and Muslims worsened. A united opposition was now able to grow around Rajiv's weaknesses. With his removal from the cabinet in 1987, V. P. Singh created a centrist coalition, called the National Front, consisting of Singh's own Janata Dal, Congress (S), and several local parties. In November 1989, with his 5-year term up, Rajiv called a new election.

Congress in Opposition (1989–1991)

India's ninth free election was significant in that—unlike all eight previous elections—the outcome was not a foregone conclusion. For the first time, Indian voters were offered a straight choice between two leaders who were truly being compared as alternatives: Rajiv Gandhi and V. P. Singh. There was no particular crisis, and there were plenty of strong political issues. Singh and his coalition partners ran a coordinated campaign, agreeing not to run against each other in most constituencies.

The election resulted in huge losses for Congress and also saw the rise of the Bharatiya Janata party (BJP), which increased its support from 1 percent to 16 percent, leading some to predict the beginning of a new Hindu nationalist trend in Indian politics. V. P. Singh formed a government with the help of the BJP and communist parties, but his coalition rapidly fell apart. In November 1990 the BJP pulled out of the coalition, and another group of MPs led by the socialist Chandra Shekar broke away. Rajiv Gandhi was invited to form a new government but opted instead to support Shekar. India now witnessed the peculiar sight of a government run by Shekar and his 54 Janata Dal (S) MPs, backed by the 213 Congress MPs and their allies. Shekar was patently a Congress puppet and was unable even to pass a budget.

In March 1991, when Rajiv Gandhi withdrew his support, Chandra Shekar's 117-day government fell, and a new election was called for May—the second in 18 months. On May 21, while campaigning in the southern state of Tamil Nadu and apparently headed for victory, Rajiv Gandhi was killed when a suicide bomber blew herself up only feet away from him. Rajiv's Italian-born wife, Sonia, was asked to take over Congress and to run for prime minister but she refused, and Congress went into the remainder of the election with a new president—the 70-year-old P. V. Narasimha Rao—and several contenders for the post of prime minister. When Congress won, Rao became prime minister.

The Emergence of the BJP (1991–)

Following Rajiv's death, India (or Congress at least) seemed obsessed with identifying someone who could take up the Gandhi mantle. No one was found, however, and Narasimha Rao surprised many observers with his abilities as a political tactician and with his popularity, helped in large part by his economic liberalization policies. He quickly ran into problems, however, beginning in December 1992 with the destruction of the mosque at Ayodhya. Rao moved too slowly to control the communal riots that broke out as a result, and the gloss continued to fade as defections weakened his coalition; then news broke in early 1996 of a corruption scandal involving senior politicians and bureaucrats, including Rao himself and seven cabinet ministers.

In the May 1996 elections, Congress was routed, the BJP increased its representation by one-third to become the biggest party in the Lok Sabha for the first time, and parties representing regional interests and the lower castes made notable gains. No one party won more than 30 percent of the seats, however, leaving a leadership vacuum. A BJP-led government collapsed after just 12 days and was replaced by a left-leaning 13-party coalition that lasted just 10 months before collapsing. Its successor fell apart after 11 months, and the March 1998 election resulted in a new government

FIGURE 7.3

Legislative Electoral Trends in India

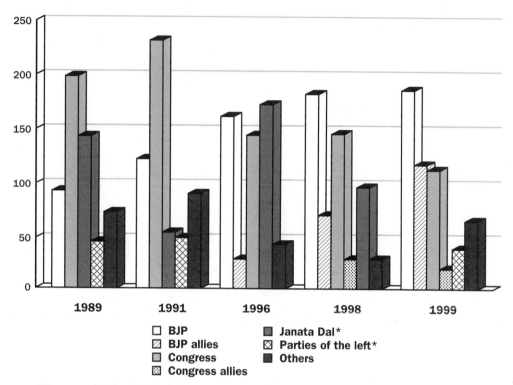

*These parties fought the 1996 and 1998 elections as the United Front.

Legend:
- □ BJP
- ▨ BJP allies
- ▦ Congress
- ▩ Congress allies
- ■ Janata Dal*
- ⊠ Parties of the left*
- ■ Others

headed again by the BJP and its leader, Atal Behari Vajpayee. Meanwhile, Sonia Gandhi had broken a long silence and taken over the leadership of Congress.

The fragility of India's coalition governments is well illustrated by the events of April 1999. One of the partners in the Vajpayee government was the AIADMK, the regional Tamil party led by former actress Jayaram Jayalalitha. She had apparently entered into an agreement with the defense minister, George Fernandes, that if she supported the BJP he would try to weaken charges of corruption made against her during her term as chief minister of Tamil Nadu in 1991–1996. Dissatisfied with the action taken, she demanded that Fernandes be fired, but Vajpayee refused. Jayalalitha responded by withdrawing the support of her 18 MPs, reducing the BJP government to a minority.[21] The government then lost a vote of confidence by a single vote but stayed on as caretaker until a new general election (the third in 3 years) was held in September–October.

The economic record of the Vajpayee government was poor, but it faced a divided opposition, it had a popular leader, and it profited from a wave of patriotic sentiment with its handling of tensions in the Kashmir in May–July. The outcome of the new

CLOSE-UP VIEW

PARTIES CONTESTING THE 1999 GENERAL ELECTION

Bharatiya Janata party (BJP) (Indian People's party). A Hindu nationalist party that traces its roots back to 1951 and whose precursor (Jana Sangh) was a partner in the 1977–1980 Janata coalition, the BJP advocated economic nationalism and a return to Hindu values. Its representation in the Lok Sabha grew from two seats in 1984 to 161 in 1996, when its leader Atal Behari Vajpayee formed a short-lived coalition government. He returned to power in 1998, and the BJP won 182 seats in the 1999 election. It built its power on a wave of Hindu nationalism in the early 1990s but has since moderated its position, leaving the more hard-line policies to one of its coalition partners, **Shiv Sena.** The biggest of the BJP allies in 1999 (with 29 seats) was **Telugu Desam,** a party based in the southern state of Andhra Pradesh and led by N. T. Rama Rao, a former movie star. Other BJP allies included **Dravida Munnetra Kazhagam** from Tamil Nadu, the **Akali Dal** of the Punjab (promoting Sikh interests), and the West Bengal–based **Trinamool Congress.**

Congress. Congress went into the election lacking unity and ideological coherence. After 42 years under the leadership of the Nehru-Gandhi dynasty, it lost ground during the 1990s to regional and religious parties and saw its membership in the Lok Sabha more than halved. It went into the 1999 election under the leadership of Sonia Gandhi, who was born and raised in Italy and whose main claim to leadership was her relationship to the party's former leaders. Many

within Congress believed that her leadership did not pose a handicap to the party but others did, including those who formed the National Congress party in May 1999. The election saw the Congress share of seats in the Lok Sabha fall to an all-time low; from a peak of 415 seats in 1984, it was down to just 112.

Communist parties of India. India has several communist parties, including the once pro-Moscow **Communist Party of India** (CPI) and the once pro-Beijing **Communist Party of India (Marxist).** India had the distinction of having the world's first democratically elected communist governments, when the CPI (M) won the states of Kerala and West Bengal in 1977. The CPI and CPI (M) between them won 44 seats in the Lok Sabha in 1996 and entered government for the first time as part of the United Front coalition led by Deve Gowda.

Regional parties. Indian governments have found themselves relying increasingly on regional and state parties, which have not only won significant blocks of seats in the Lok Sabha but also have taken power in several state governments. Notable among them is the **Samajwadi party,** which derives most of its support from lower-caste Indians and has its main base of support in Uttar Pradesh, India's biggest state. Eight regional parties won 70 seats in the 1996 Lok Sabha; by 1999 there were nearly twice as many regional parties with nearly 120 seats. Voters were sending a strong message to national government about their concerns and aspirations.

election was hardly a BJP wave (the party won only three more seats), but Sonia Gandhi's Congress fell to a new low of 112 seats and Vajpayee was able to form a new government, becoming the first prime minister since 1971 to win consecutive elections. The continued rise of the BJP left India at the start of the new millennium with a party system in which the old dominance of Congress had gone, and the membership of the Lok Sabha had become highly fragmented. Following the 1999 election, the BJP held just 33 percent of the seats, Congress held 20 percent, and the remaining 47 percent were divided among a remarkable 37 parties. Of these, 22 operated mainly or exclusively in a single state, 13 had just one seat each in the house, and 11 had between two and five.

INTEREST GROUPS

As Indian society has become more politicized, more people have been drawn into the political process and the variety of their needs and demands has increased. Interest groups have been formed in response, but they are weaker than their North American or European counterparts. India's political leaders tend to see them as disruptive and too narrowly focused; some of the groups have responded with demonstrations, strikes, and civil disobedience. Political leaders are particularly alarmed by groups representing class, religious, or regional issues, seeing them as a threat to national unity. Yet the groups may actually offer the best hope of crossing India's social divisions, providing links between the masses and the elite, between the traditional and modern sectors, and between different castes and religions. If their demands are met, their members may come to see government as more responsive to their needs.

Hindus and Muslims alike have communal groups representing their interests, such as the Hindu Rashtriya Swayamsevak Sangh (RSS), which has moderated its anti-Muslim stance in recent years, and the Muslim Jamaat-e-Islami. In terms of numbers, one of the biggest of all Indian mass movements has been that representing the Dalits, who have their own political party, the Bahujan Samaj party. Other groups have been formed around economic issues, with labor unions, business federations, and groups representing landless agricultural laborers, who make up more than 25 percent of the workforce. Many work in near-feudal conditions, tied for life to one master, living in wretched conditions, and being paid a pittance. Most are too unorganized to offer resistance, but occasional revolts break out and a network of Gandhian organizations work to improve educational opportunities, win higher wages, and provide legal and medical aid for workers.[22] Agricultural laborers have also been helped by India's communist and socialist political parties.

One example of grassroots mobilization that has affected not only national government but interest groups outside India as well concerns local people fighting to protect natural resources such as forests. Forest dwellers, who for centuries have used trees as a source of fuel, shelter, and food and who have maintained those forests, have launched spontaneous local campaigns to prevent overcutting. In some cases this has brought them into violent confrontation with local police. Among the best known of these local movements is Chipko Andolan, or the "movement to hug trees." Beginning in the early 1970s, villagers in the northern state of Uttar Pradesh began using civil disobedience to prevent contractors from cutting down forests. Their methods inspired similar movements in other parts of the world.

THE MEDIA

The strength of Indian democracy is underscored by its media establishment, one of the most active and well respected in the world. India has about 1,250 independent and government-owned daily newspapers, about 18,000 magazines, and an extensive network of radio and TV stations, and the government has plans to reach 70 percent of Indians within the next few years using satellite television systems. India also has the most productive film industry in the world, making more films every year than the United States, Britain, and Australia combined.

Given the high levels of illiteracy in India (38 percent among men and 66 percent among women), radio and television have a wider reach than the printed press, so the central government has kept them under careful control. State governments have several times tried to gain control of the electronic media but without success. The availability of new alternative channels—such as CNN and MTV (broadcast out of Hong Kong)—have made it more difficult for Indian leaders to dominate the airwaves.

Freedom of the press has been threatened several times but it has survived. For example, when Indira Gandhi tried to stifle press criticism during the 1975–1977 state of emergency, several opinion journals opted to cease publication rather than accept censorship. Others published critical stories regardless. The independence of the press was further exemplified in 1987 when *The Indian Express*, the country's largest English-language newspaper, published Swedish radio reports of the Bofors scandal, and a Madras-based newspaper, *The Hindi*, investigated the scandal.

POLICIES AND POLICYMAKING

In theory, India is a federal parliamentary republic with a symbolic head of state, an elected prime minister, a council of ministers (all of whom are members of Parliament), a bicameral legislature, a written constitution, a separate supreme court, and elected state governments with separate powers. In practice, political power was so heavily centralized in the prime minister's office until recently that India has often looked more like a unitary than a federal system. Past prime ministers—through the president—have limited or suspended the powers of state governments. The role and power of the center was also intensified by the long dominance of the Nehru-Gandhi dynasty and its Congress party machine and by the inability of other parties to provide sustained and united opposition. This encouraged Indira Gandhi to accumulate so much power at the center that she took her country to the brink of dictatorship.

As memories of the dynasty fade, the balance of power has begun changing. Recent coalition governments have had to depend for their power on regional political parties, which has shifted the balance of power more toward the states. Furthermore, politics is increasingly driven by competition among class, religious, ethnic, and economic groups. Supporters of centralization say it is the only short-term option if India is to stay united, but critics counter that greater self-determination for the states is the best guarantee for the future of the whole. The challenge is to balance the needs of the parts with the common good of the whole.

ECONOMIC POLICY

India has enormous human resources, some sectors of its economy are growing rapidly, and it has a big consumer market—yet it is still ultimately a poor country. It has a GDP of just under $500 billion, but if the PPP method is used, that figure rises to $2.5 trillion, making India the world's fourth largest economy in absolute terms.

However, it has a population of 1 billion, and—using the World Bank definition of a poor person as someone with a daily income of less than a dollar—about two in every five poor people in the world are Indians (a staggering 450 million people).

All is not doom and gloom, however. Given the growth in India's population, the fact that the proportion of poor people has stayed about the same for the last century is a major achievement in itself. Life expectancy for Indians has risen since independence from 32 years to nearly 63, the number of children ages 6 to 11 in school has doubled, the number in higher grades has quadrupled, and the literacy rate for men is up from 15 to 62 percent, although women still languish at 34 percent, a sign of their disadvantaged position. The economy has grown 200-fold since independence; the value of exports more than quintupled between 1981 and 2001; and India is now self-sufficient in food, many consumer goods, and basic commodities like steel and cement. It is 90 percent self-sufficient in energy needs, and its factories build ships, locomotives, trucks, cars, and electronic equipment.

At the same time, India's economy has been strangely staid in comparison with those of neighboring NICs. It often puzzles political scientists and economists that many Indian entrepreneurs living outside their own country can work hard and make themselves rich while many of their compatriots at home remain so poor. Part of the answer lies in the long reliance of India after independence on a series of Soviet-style 5-year plans, which set goals for economic development while extending state control over industry. The plans grew in part out of socialist ideas picked up by Congress leaders during visits to pre–World War II Britain, and their aim was to transform India from an agricultural to an industrial economy. The Nehru administration nationalized 17 of India's biggest industries, severely restricted private entrepreneurial activity, set price controls on key commodities such as steel and chemicals, and strictly limited imports. This system brought steady economic growth, but it also created a public sector that was overmanned, uncompetitive, and inefficient.

Indira Gandhi initially pursued hands-on economic policies similar to those of her father, but during her second term she opted for a limited policy of liberalization. Rajiv Gandhi maintained this policy, cutting income tax and corporation tax, abolishing death duties, relaxing industrial licensing laws and antitrust regulations, and abolishing or lowering quotas and tariffs on many imports. He also set about modernizing the textile industry with the goal of increasing exports and competing with Hong Kong, Taiwan, and South Korea. The Rao government (1991–1996) announced further liberalization, twice devalued the rupee, and cut government spending to qualify for a new loan from the International Monetary Fund. During its administration, India began to transform itself into a market economy.

In many ways, these policies have succeeded. The contribution of industry to GDP has grown from 5 percent in 1950 to nearly 27 percent today, and India has an industrial base that is bigger than that of several European countries. Foreign investment has flowed into the country, inflation in early 2003 stood at 3.4 percent (a low rate for a poor country), and GDP and industrial production grew in 2002–2003 at a rate of about 6 percent.

Because most of the world's biggest multinational companies (MNCs) are based in Europe, Japan, and North America, westerners often overlook the possibility of multinationals emerging out of poorer countries. India has several MNCs, however, including Tata Sons, a company on a par with some of the biggest in the West. Founded in 1868, Tata Sons now presides over an industrial empire with annual sales of $8.5 billion. In a cooperative agreement with Mercedes-Benz of Germany, Tata Sons builds 80 percent of India's commercial road vehicles. It also runs India's biggest steelworks and has interests in everything from iron to chemicals, electricity generation, and computers. One of its subsidiaries owns and runs hotels in London, New York, Paris, and Los Angeles.

India also stands out from many other poorer countries by virtue of its growing middle class and consumer market. The number of televisions in Indian homes grew from 500,000 in 1976 to nearly 60 million in 2001, the number of home computers and private cars has grown rapidly, Indian vehicle production more than quintupled between 1970 and 1997, and there has been a parallel growth in consumer credit.

Perhaps the greatest challenge faced by India's economic planners lies in bringing its population growth under control—or at least keeping up with the demands of a growing population. With slightly more than 1 billion people, India is the second most populous country in the world after China and is home to about one in six of all the humans on Earth. Its population is growing at about 2 percent annually, and although this is not a high growth rate when compared with many poorer Asian and African states (the average for the latter is 2.6 percent), it still means that India must meet the needs of an additional 20 million people per year (equivalent to a new Australia every year). The United Nations projects that India will overtake China in about 2045, when both countries will have populations of 1.5 billion.

Much of the evidence from population studies suggests that there is an inverse relationship between population growth rates and economic development. For the world's poor, children are a key form of welfare, providing families with labor and security against illness, old age, and unemployment. Thus, in agricultural societies with high infant mortality rates, women tend to have more children in the belief that the more they have, the more will survive to provide for their families. (The absence of contraception contributes to the high fertility rate.) As access to health care improves and infant mortality rates decline, population begins to grow, not because women are having more children, but because more of those children are surviving.

As societies become wealthier and more urbanized, government provides more in the way of social security, women marry and have children later in life, children become more expensive to raise and educate, and parents are able to make choices about the number of children they have. Thus, population growth rates fall to the levels found in liberal democracies: typically in the range of 0.1 to 0.5 percent. Although better education and family planning programs have contributed to bringing population growth under control in many parts of the world, the critical element is an improvement in the quality of life. The downward trend in the population growth rate in India has been one of the effects of its rapid industrialization and of the improvements made in education and health care, but the trend needs to continue if the government is to make progress in its attempts to meet the needs of its people.

Economic changes have brought social and political changes. With the rise of the middle class, the hold of the caste system has been weakened and new groups have entered politics, forcing political parties to appeal to a broader constituency and reducing the influence of the urban elite. At the same time, the benefits of India's economic growth have not been equally spread. The middle class has moved from a "revolution of rising expectations" to a "revolution of rising frustrations." The gap between rich and poor also continues to grow. On one hand, India now feeds itself,

Typical of the dramatic contrasts in poverty and wealth that characterize many newly industrializing countries, this view of Mumbai (formerly Bombay) shows families living in extreme poverty, in view of the affluent high-rise suburb of Bandra in the distance.

and the days when India was a net food importer and famines could leave thousands dead are over. India is now a net food exporter, and bad harvest years are not as serious as they once were. This improvement is thanks in large measure to the **"green revolution"** of the 1960s, which brought agricultural change to much of Asia, based on improvements in irrigation and seed quality and on the greater use of fertilizers. The result was that output grew while the area of land under crops stayed the same. Growth in the agricultural sector has also brought more investment in villages, which has created new wealth and jobs.

On the other hand, the poorest of India's rural people have been bypassed by economic development, encouraging many of them to seek jobs in cities such as Mumbai (formerly Bombay) and Calcutta. The cities cannot meet the growing need for housing and basic services, further dissatisfying the newly affluent middle class. While urban economic growth has accelerated, real farm incomes have stagnated over the past 30 years. In few places are the effects of rural poverty more marked than in the northeastern state of Bihar, where illiteracy runs at 75 percent, annual per capita income is just over $100, corruption is endemic, hundreds are killed every year in clashes between radical peasant militias and feudal landlords, and most people have never voted.

Even the wealthier parts of India have their problems, though. This was tragically emphasized in January 2001 when the northwestern state of Gujarat was hit by the most destructive earthquake in India's postindependence history. An estimated 25,000 people were killed, and property-damage costs ran to nearly $6 billion. Gujarat is one of India's most prosperous states, yet the earthquake revealed that buildings were badly constructed, that inspections and building codes were not enforced, that urban disaster planning is inadequate, and that coordination among emergency agencies was almost nonexistent.

One of India's economic priorities since the early 1990s has been a program of privatization aimed at selling off hundreds of government-owned businesses, which among them make up nearly half of India's capital stock. Analysts suggest that India's relatively low productivity can be blamed in large part on too much government involvement in the economy; the benefits of privatization are already being felt as more competition opens up markets and helps consumers with lower prices and better services.

FOREIGN POLICY

By virtue of its size and location, India is a major regional power, yet there is little question that it operates below its potential in terms of its influence on world affairs. Its population is almost as big as that of China's, and it is much more democratic than China, yet its voice is heard less often in international relations than that of China. Much of the difference can be ascribed to economic policies; while India has been limited by the long-time role of government in the economy, China has been slowly building a large private sector that is exporting all over the world. India is only slowly catching up.

If India's economic voice is not yet heard as loudly as it might be, there is no question about its diplomatic and military influence. It pursued a semiautonomous foreign policy for at least 30 years before independence, and at the time of independence there were calls to have India completely sever its ties with Britain. Nehru, however, took over the foreign policy portfolio, secured India's entry into the Commonwealth, and made India an influential member of the wider Afro-Asian bloc. He used India's influence in the United Nations to promote the cause of decolonization, and Indian troops took part in UN peacekeeping operations in Korea, the Congo, and Cyprus. Nehru argued that India should not align itself with any other power, and in 1955 India became a founding member of the Non-Aligned Movement. For India, nonalignment meant independent action; although refusing to commit itself to any other country or bloc of countries, it reserved the right to take action to protect its security interests whenever necessary.

During the cold war, the United States had a closer relationship with Pakistan than with India, regarding the former as a bulwark against Soviet expansionism and the latter both as an enemy of Pakistan and a friend of the USSR. Certainly the USSR was an important arms and oil supplier and trading partner for India. With the end of the cold war, however, both India and the United States began rethinking their policies in the region. India has intervened militarily in the affairs of all its smaller neighbors, maintains the world's second largest army (with nearly 1.2 million men and women under arms), and in 1974 exploded a nuclear device. Already saddled with secessionist movements within its borders, India has also had to deal with border disputes with its neighbors. For example, it has been at odds with China since the late 1950s over Kashmir and the Indian state of Arunachal Pradesh. The most serious conflict between the two countries came in 1962, when China invaded northern India and advanced 150 miles before halting. The dispute, which remains unresolved, threatened to become a problem once again in the late 1980s with a buildup of troops on the Chinese side of the border.

Central to India's regional policy has been its relationship with Pakistan. Ever since the 1947 partition of India and Pakistan, relations between the two neighbors have been precarious, a key source of tension being the province of Kashmir (see Political Debates, p. 374). The two countries fought over Kashmir in 1947 and again in 1965 when China—which had its own border disputes with India—took the side of Pakistan, leading to concerns about the broader potential impact of the conflict. The Soviet Union, hoping to check Chinese influence in the region and strengthen ties with both India and Pakistan, stepped in as mediator, and a peace agreement was signed in Tashkent in the central USSR in 1966.

The worst outbreak of fighting between the two countries came in 1971, when India became involved in the Pakistan civil war. The relationship between East and West Pakistan had been uncertain and unequal from the beginning. Divided by 1,000 miles of Indian territory, the wealthier and mainly Urdu-speaking West dominated the poorer, overcrowded, and mainly Bengali-speaking East. The East provided not only cheap labor but also natural resources such as cotton and jute, earnings from which kept the federal budget balanced. With 55 percent of the total population of the two Pakistans, the East was given only 36 percent of development spending.

In March 1971 the East declared its independence as Bangladesh. The Pakistani army immediately clamped down, heralding 9 months of civil war and repression during which untold thousands of East Pakistanis were killed (claims range from tens of thousands to 3.5 million) and 10 million refugees (mainly Hindus) crossed into India. Concerned about the possibility of communal rioting in India, the government of Indira Gandhi began taking a more active interest in the war, and when Pakistan launched a series of air strikes against India on December 3, the Indian response was immediate. On December 6, 1971, India recognized the government of Bangladesh, and just 10 days later its troops entered Dacca and accepted the surrender of Pakistan. India's troops were withdrawn 3 months later, and Bangladesh was recognized as an independent, sovereign state.

India's role in the war established it as the undisputed power in the subcontinent, a fact that was reemphasized in 1974 when India exploded a nuclear device and became only the sixth country to openly acknowledge a nuclear capability. The explosion was an unmistakable signal to India's neighbors, but it also had global implications, raising concerns in the United States about a nuclear arms race between India and Pakistan. India has been developing missiles—the Agni 1 and the Agni 2—which can carry nuclear and conventional warheads; the latter has a range of 1,375 miles, putting all of Pakistan and much of China in range.

In the 1980s, India accused Pakistan of supplying weapons to Sikh terrorists in the Punjab, and relations between the two countries became so jittery that in 1987, when both countries held military exercises near their joint border, tensions escalated to the point where 340,000 troops were massed on the border in a state of high alert. Problems arose again in May 1999 when Pakistani soldiers infiltrated Indian-held Kashmir. India launched an attack that cost the lives of several hundred soldiers before Pakistani-held positions were recaptured in July.

The most worrisome element of the relationship between the two countries is that they are both now nuclear powers, and the United States in particular fears that a conventional war between them could quickly escalate into a nuclear war. In 1993 the director of the U.S. Central Intelligence Agency was quoted as saying that "the

THE MOST DANGEROUS PLACE IN THE WORLD?

In March 2000 U.S. President Bill Clinton described south Asia as "the most dangerous place in the world." He was referring to a potentially lethal combination: two archenemies living next door to each other, both armed with nuclear weapons, and both at odds over a large piece of disputed territory. That territory is **Kashmir,** claimed by both India and Pakistan, over which the two countries have already twice gone to war (in 1947 and 1965), and which has recently become embroiled in the "war on terrorism."

The dispute dates back to independence and the partition of the two countries in 1947. The Hindu maharajah of Kashmir announced that it would become part of India, a decision Pakistan refused to accept because of the large Muslim population in the province. Fighting then broke out between Hindu and Muslim residents, as a result of which both Pakistan and India moved in troops. A UN cease-fire line was accepted by both sides in 1949, leaving one-third of the state under Pakistani control, but India refused to have an arbitrator appointed to review the problem for fear that this would lead to a plebiscite that would favor Pakistan.

In 1965 tensions increased and the two countries went to war again, Pakistan taking a beating from Indian forces. Since then there has been a deeply troubled peace in Kashmir. The Muslims who make up 60 percent of the population of Indian Kashmir oppose rule by India, militant anti-Indian groups have attracted growing support, and Pakistani leaders have been pressured by right-wing Islamists to support the cause of Kashmir's militants. India has continued to insist on claiming all of Kashmir, and there has been a steady buildup of India's military presence in the region and regular exchanges of fire between Indian and Pakistani troops. A new dimension was added to the problem in 1998 when India and Pakistan formally confirmed that they were nuclear powers (something that had been known informally for many years).

In February 1999 Indian prime minister Vajpayee traveled to Pakistan to meet with Pakistani leader Nawaz Sharif, and the two promised to resolve their differences peacefully. But when Pakistani troops captured territory inside Indian Kashmir, India responded with force. The problem took on a new significance September 11, 2001, because Vajpayee subsequently portrayed himself as the leader of a democracy in a struggle against terrorists. There have been a number of terrorist attacks, including the October 2001 car bomb attack on the legislature of Indian Kashmir. In December 2001, terrorists allegedly trained in Pakistan attacked India's Parliament while it was in session; none of the legislators were hurt, but all six terrorists and five security officers were killed. International attention was subsequently drawn away from Kashmir by problems in Iraq and North Korea, but the problems of this very troubled area of the world remain.

arms race between India and Pakistan poses perhaps the most probable prospect for future use of weapons of mass destruction, including nuclear weapons."[23] The dangers were given graphic illustration in May 1998 when India carried out five nuclear tests and Pakistan responded with six tests of its own. The actions of both governments were universally condemned by other countries.

Indian foreign policy has also included a strong peacekeeping element, as when India sent troops to the Maldives in 1988 to prevent a coup from taking place, and stationed troops in Sri Lanka through most of the 1980s, supposedly helping underwrite

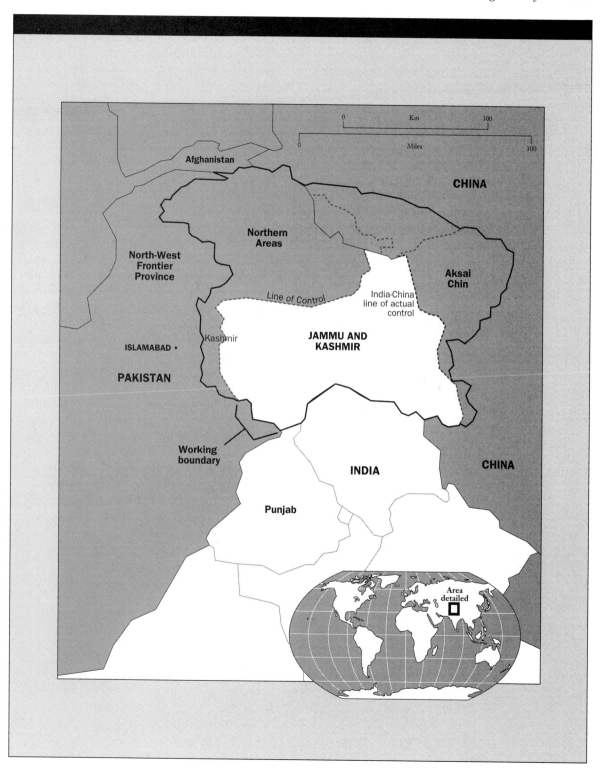

a peace agreement aimed at ending Sri Lanka's civil war. Conflict between the Sinhalese majority and the Tamil minority worsened during the 1970s, leading in 1976 to the creation of a political coalition demanding the creation of an independent Tamil state. The activities of separatist Tamil Tiger guerrillas led to a state of emergency in Sri Lanka in 1983, along with the dispatch of the Indian peacekeeping force (whose numbers grew from 7,000 to 50,000, eliciting charges of Indian imperialism from Tamil separatists). It was a Tamil Tiger who was implicated in the 1991 assassination of Rajiv Gandhi, supposedly over resentment at how the arrival of the Indian peacekeeping force in Sri Lanka had forced the Tigers back on the defensive.

INDIAN POLITICS IN TRANSITION

Questions have been regularly raised since India's independence in 1947 about the country's governability and political stability. Several times it has seemed that India has been on the brink of breaking down in religious, social, and economic chaos, yet it has survived. It has come through territorial wars with its neighbors, secessionist struggles by religious minorities, frequent communal violence, a dangerous reliance for leadership on a single family, and attempts by some of its leaders to subvert the democratic process. It still has religious tensions, its population growth is outpacing its ability to meet basic needs for most of its people, and its economy still suffers from the burden of a long history of state intervention. That intervention helped India feed itself and develop an extensive industrial base, but the signs are that it now needs to accelerate the process of economic liberalization and allow its entrepreneurs to create the same opportunities at home as those who have left India have created abroad.

The Rao government began quickening the process of economic liberalization in 1991, and India's economy has since grown ever faster. If the benefits of economic reform are spread widely enough, then social tensions may be eased and political stability improved, but the fragmentation of party politics reduces the prospects for the latter. India has the potential to become one of the wealthiest and most prosperous countries in the world, but it must first balance its political, economic, and social reforms.

KEY TERMS

Bharatiya Janata party	Hinduism	Rajya Sabha
British Raj	Hindutva	*satyagraha*
caste	Kashmir	structural violence
Congress party	Lok Sabha	untouchables
green revolution	Nehru-Gandhi dynasty	

KEY PEOPLE

L. K. Advani	Rajiv Gandhi	Jawaharlal Nehru
Indira Gandhi	Sonia Gandhi	Atal Behari Vajpayee
Mahatma Gandhi	Muhammed Ali Jinnah	

STUDY QUESTIONS

1. Is the concept of structural violence helpful to an understanding of social problems outside India?

2. Compare and contrast the effects of colonialism on the United States, Mexico, and India.

3. How were Japan and China able to avoid colonization, while India was not?

4. What are the implications of "emergency" powers for democracy in countries such as Russia and India?

5. Which is more appropriate to the needs of a divided society such as India: coalition governments or strong leaders with legislative majorities?

6. Compare and contrast the roles of the prime minister in Britain, Japan, and India.

7. Do dynastic traditions help or hinder the development of emergent states such as India?

8. What reforms (if any) would you make to the Indian electoral system to produce stronger governments?

9. Is there anything wrong with the idea of Sonia Gandhi as prime minister of India?

INDIA ONLINE

Prime Minister's Office: *http://pmindia.nic.in*
Official home page of the Prime Minister of India.
The Indian Parliament: *http://parliamentofindia.nic.in*
Official home page of the Indian legislature, with links to information on the membership, committees, debates, and the budget.
Government of India Directory: *http://goidirectory.nic.in*
India Image: *http://indiaimage.nic.in*
Two sites offering an extensive selection of links on government and politics in India.
The Hindu: *http://www.hinduonline.com*
The Times of India: *http://timesofindia.indiatimes.com*
Online versions of two respected daily Indian newspapers.

FURTHER READING

Brass, Paul, *The Politics of India Since Independence*, 2nd Ed. (New York: Cambridge University Press, 1994). A comprehensive study of India's postcolonial development.

Hardgrave, Robert L., and Stanley A. Kochanek, *India: Government and Politics in a Developing Nation*, 6th Ed. (Fort Worth, TX: Harcourt College Publishers, 2000). One of the standard introductions to Indian politics.

Jayal, Niraja Gopal (Ed.) *Democracy in India* (Oxford: Oxford University Press, 2001). An edited collection that includes chapters on the relationship between democracy and different elements of life in India.

COMPARATIVE FOCUS

IDEOLOGIES

If a competition were to be held for the most commonly used and most frequently misunderstood terms in political science, *ideology* would make a strong running against terms such as *state, democracy,* and *freedom*. It is much abused, has multiple submeanings, and is often associated with partisans or zealots (if the latter are defined as people of uncompromising or extreme views). "Oh, she's an ideological liberal," we might hear it said of someone with strong left-wing political views.

Although it was coined in 1795 by the French philosopher Antoine Destutt de Tracy to describe the science of ideas, the term has since come to mean a set of ideas or values held by individuals or societies. Put another way, it means a "worldview," or an overall perception that believers have about the world around them, and is made up of a set of attitudes, moral views, and beliefs that provide believers with a set of reference points and explanations for the world around them. An ideology helps us organize the complexity of the world in which we live and helps drive our attitudes toward the events we witness and decide how we feel about those events. It is usually applied to politics but is also used in relation to other elements of the social sciences, such as religion and economics.

For purposes of easy reference, most political ideologies are classified on a spectrum running from left to right. This grew out of the practice in the French National Assembly in the late 18th century, when—to keep delegates with similar views together and to prevent the outbreak of fistfights—conservative members (pro-monarchists) were seated on the right of the chamber, moderates in the center, and radicals (who wanted an entirely new political system) on the left. We still tend to describe conservatives as right-wing and liberals as left-wing and to place all the other "isms" somewhere on that spectrum, from nationalism and fascism on the right to social democracy, socialism, and communism on the left. If we examine these closely enough, though, we find that the far left and the far right are not that different in terms of their ideologies, so we should really talk in terms of a circle rather than a spectrum.

Ideology plays a very different role in the various political systems examined in this book:

- For most Americans it has little meaning, because ideological identification is low among American voters and American political parties rarely couch their policy positions in terms of ideology. It is understood that the Republicans have conservative leanings and that the Democrats have liberal leanings, but there are many shades of ideological identification within the two parties, so much so that there is very little difference in Congress between liberal Republicans and conservative Democrats in terms of the views they hold and their positions on bills. When it comes to voters, only about one in three Americans admits to being firmly liberal or conservative or to identifying with either of the two major parties.

- Ideology in almost every other liberal democracy is associated with a variety of economic and social issues (and occasionally regional issues), there is a greater variety of positions represented on the political spectrum than in the United States, and there is more ideological distinction among parties and the voters who support them. Most mainstream parties are either conservative or liberal (as they are conventionally defined). Conservatives take the view (confusingly) that government should pursue classical liberal ideas such as promotion of the free market, a limited role in the economy, and a belief in self-reliance (but a hands-on approach to moral issues). Liberals believe that society's inequalities can best be resolved through government intervention in the form of welfare, subsidized education, and regulation.

At the same time, though, parties with more radical views have won support on the margins, notably communist parties on the left and anti-immigrant nationalist parties on the right. Western Europe has also seen notable gains being made by feminist and green political parties. The latter are commonly associated with environmental issues but actually have a much wider range of interests and often claim that they are "neither left nor right, but in front."

- For emerging countries, ideological divisions are based less on the hands-on/hands-off spectrum seen in liberal democracies, and more on differing attitudes toward reform or national identity. As Russia struggles to reinvent itself, the key division among parties relates to their positions on reform of the economic system—some advocate rapid reforms designed to turn Russia into a free-market liberal democracy, others would prefer a return to centralized state control, and yet others worry about Russia's place in the world as the reforms take place. In Mexico, the key issue is reform of the political and economic system, and left-right differences are less important than differences over the speed of political and economic reform.

- In deeply divided societies such as India, Nigeria, and Egypt, ideology is associated in most people's minds with regional, ethnic, and religious differences. The key driving force in India is the balance between Hindu and Muslim interests, and between the interests of the states versus India as a political entity. In Nigeria, attempts to build an "ideologically driven" party system (that is, a system in which parties are driven by differences over economic and social issues) have failed time and again as parties become ethnically driven, identifying with the interests of the major ethnic groups. In Egypt, the only significant opposition to the governing National Democratic party comes not from liberal or conservative opposition parties but from a banned Islamist party, the Muslim Brotherhood.

One of the eternal questions in politics is whether people are motivated mainly by their interests, their beliefs, or a combination of the two. It might be logical to assume that rich people in liberal democracies would be conservative (because, among other things, conservative parties are opposed to high taxes) and poor people would be liberal or socialist (because liberal parties are in favor of welfare), but the opposite is often true. It might also be logical to assume that all Indians and Nigerians identify with parties that promote their regional or ethnic interests, but they do not. Ideology may not be a foolproof guide to political attitudes and action, but—used carefully—it can help explain a lot.

Part IV

LESS DEVELOPED COUNTRIES

Seek ye first the political kingdom and all other things will be added unto you.

—Kwame Nkrumah, Ghanaian leader

Describing and explaining the features of liberal democracies or newly industrializing countries (NICs) is not easy, because social scientists have not yet been able to agree on a standard set of criteria to apply. Even if they could agree, the judgments they would make would unavoidably be value-laden. But at least there is a high degree of consistency in the political, economic, and social features of these two groups of countries. The same cannot be said for less developed countries (LDCs). Their features are less predictable and less consistent, many of them are plagued by instability, and social scientists have had difficulty keeping up with changes in these countries and developing theories to explain those changes.[1]

For example, why is Jamaica (a NIC), which became independent in 1962, more peaceful and stable than nearby Haiti, which had a 158-year head start on independence? Why has the West African state of Senegal never had a military coup, while nearby Burkina Faso has had six since 1960? Why is Nigeria, with all its natural and human wealth and its potential as the economic powerhouse of sub-Saharan Africa, failing in its search for political stability? Why have Argentina and Brazil become NICs, while neighboring Bolivia, with about as many years of independence, remains one of the poorest countries in the world? Why is Tanzania politically stable, when its immediate neighbors Rwanda and Burundi are not? Are there common structural explanations for the differences? Is it something growing out of the choices made by the leaders of these countries? Are they victims of a global system that has kept them immature and dependent? Or is this simply a matter of perception?

Western political science has failed to provide general answers to questions like these. Part of the problem is self-imposed: Most political scientists handicap themselves by approaching the Third World as an amorphous whole, instead of trying to understand what makes the countries of Asia, Africa, and Latin America different from one another. The task is complicated by the way in which understandings of poorer countries are driven more by economic and social factors than by political factors. Look at most of the books published on poorer countries and you will find chapters on economic structures and social change, but there will be little on their political features.

We looked at NICs in Part III and saw how they were building stronger economies and political stability by opening up their markets and investing in their people. In this section, our focus will be on less developed countries (LDCs), defined for our purposes as countries that have not yet built legitimate and stable political structures and processes and whose abilities to produce economic wealth are reduced by a heavy reliance on agriculture rather than industry or services. Some have made policy changes in recent years that may lead to long-term stability and prosperity, but most have immature political institutions, top-heavy or inefficient bureaucracies, economies that depend either on agricultural exports or on a small range of major products or services, poorly developed social services, and—correspondingly—little political or economic independence.

Broadly speaking, LDCs have five major sets of features in common.

Weak Political Institutions

In most liberal democracies, political institutions and processes have achieved high levels of legitimacy and public acceptance. There are strong and complex state systems, with executives, legislatures, constitutions, effective bureaucracies, and many channels through which people can take part in government. By contrast, most LDCs have low levels of **political institutionalization,** a process defined by one political scientist as "the effective establishment of state authority over society through specially created political structures and organs."[2] At best, LDCs have systems of government that fail to meet many of the basic needs of most of their citizens, and—at worst—they are still searching for a political system that suits their needs. Part of the reason Nigeria is having so many problems, for example, is that it has yet to develop institutions that have validity among Nigerians or that have the power and authority to compete against the other allegiances (notably ethnicity) that attract public attention. The weakness of civilian institutions in LDCs is reflected in three phenomena that most have experienced at one time or another:

- **One-party rule.** Many LDCs have seen rule by a single party or a single dominant party, most often because opposition parties have either been banned or controlled. In some cases, their leaders argue that the existence of more than one political party is too divisive for young states trying to build national unity. This explains, for example, the policies of Ugandan president Yoweri Museveni, who points out that because most Ugandans are poor, they do not have the social and economic divisions needed to encourage the development of parties with different ideological platforms. Instead, they tie themselves to ethnic differences, which creates conflict. To prevent this, he has declared Uganda to be a "no-party state."

  In other cases, leaders of LDCs have used the Leninist vanguard argument, portraying the party as an educated elite who can lead the masses out of ignorance and division. Some African leaders have claimed that the one-party system is based on an African tradition of consensus government. For example, former president Julius Nyerere of Tanzania once argued that African society lacked the class divisions that

CHECKLIST

LESS DEVELOPED COUNTRIES
What Are Their Features?

- Relatively low levels of political institutionalization, with weak, immature, poorly defined, and/or unpredictable political institutions and processes.

- Varying degrees of public loyalty to the state; in the most troubled cases, legitimacy is undermined by serious external or internal threats.

- A variety of institutionalized forms of political participation and representation, but no guarantees that the voices of citizens will be heard effectively.

- A mixed record on the protection of individual rights under the law.

- In the worst cases, elections that may be accompanied by fraud and violence and government and public services undermined by incompetence, corruption, and/or cronyism.

- Inefficient or troubled economies with low per capita GDPs, and based either on one dominant product or a variety of primarily agricultural products.

- Relatively low levels of urbanization.

- A relatively low quality of life when measured by the provision of education, health care, and other basic services.

- Middle-range to low ratings on the Freedom House Index and usually low ratings on the Human Development Index.

Where Are They?

There are 36, and they are mainly in Africa:

Belize	Guyana	Paraguay
Bolivia	Honduras	Samoa
Botswana	Kenya	Senegal
Cameroon	Kiribati	Seychelles
Cape Verde	Marshall Islands	Solomon Islands
Congo	Micronesia	Suriname
Dominican Republic	Namibia	Swaziland
Ecuador	Nauru	Tanzania
Fiji	Nicaragua	Tonga
Gabon	Nigeria	Uganda
Ghana	Palau	Vanuatu
Guatemala	Papua New Guinea	Zimbabwe

had encouraged the emergence of multiparty systems in liberal democracies.[3] Whether these are self-serving excuses or real attempts to explain a political phenomenon is debatable.

- **Personal rule.** Whereas power in liberal democracies is divided and limited, in most LDCs it is centralized and personalized. Individuals and groups rarely compete publicly to win the right to govern or to influence government policy within an overall and legitimate framework of accepted rules.[4] Instead, power often accumulates in the hands of ruling elites, in the worst cases leading to the rise of authoritarian regimes, such as those led by Somoza of Nicaragua, Stroessner of Paraguay, Trujillo of the Dominican Republic, Moi of Kenya, and Mugabe of Zimbabwe.

In the more ambitious citizens of LDCs, there are fewer opportunities in business, law, or education than in politics, which is partly why it attracts those with a thirst for power. Politics regularly consists of personal or factional struggles to win and keep power; politicians use private agreements and personal ties rather than public rules and institutions.[5] There are three main results: First, there is rarely a time limit on incumbency, and many LDC leaders stay in power as long as they can, their terms in office being ended only by murder, military coup, foreign invasion, or old age. Second, the ruler is often the pivot of state power. He manipulates the law, the police, and the military to keep and express power; he denies power to other groups; and his hold on power breeds corruption and the misuse of public office for personal gain. Finally, rulers often build a cult of personality, sometimes being given (or demanding) an almost mystic reverence. Systems of personal rule are inherently uncertain; the welfare of the rulers is critical to the welfare of the political class that supports them and to political order in general. Personal rule has led to political stagnation or instability, and even in the best cases has retarded the evolution of other political institutions.

- **Military rule.** The recent history of many LDCs is peppered with military governments. This began to change in Latin America from the late 1970s, when they were replaced by civilian systems in Ecuador (1978), Bolivia (1982), Guatemala (1985), Honduras (1986), and Paraguay (1993). But they have lasted much longer in many sub-Saharan African states. Why has there been so much military activity, and has it been a cause or a consequence of wider political problems?

The Kenyan political scientist Ali Mazrui offers four possible explanations for the frequency of military governments in Africa:

- They may reflect the weaknesses of other political institutions, which are unable to oppose the military. In states that have banned or restricted political parties, the military often becomes the only real focus of opposition to the government.
- The military offers social advancement, so many of a country's brightest and most ambitious citizens join the military, where a lack of purpose (few LDCs have been to war in recent decades) can lead to boredom and dissatisfaction with incumbent leaders.
- Many LDCs rely on the military as a tool of state power, so losing the support of the military almost inevitably leads to a loss of political power. For African LDCs, concludes Mazrui, "ultimate power resides not in those who control the means of production...but in those who control the means of destruction."[6]
- Coups are relatively easy to stage. Many LDCs have a concentration of political and economic power in one urban center, so staging a coup often means simply taking over the main military bases, the radio and television station, the main airport, and the main roads. This is especially easy if the incumbent leader happens to be out of the country at the time.

PhotoDisc

Unlike most other parts of the developing world, where economic growth is leading to industrialization and urbanization, the economies of most sub-Saharan African countries are still predominantly rural, and critical infrastructure—such as transport, education, and modern health care—is not reaching women like these.

A Limited Economic Base

While NICs have attracted foreign investment, opened their markets, and experienced broad-based export-led economic growth, LDCs' economies have grown more slowly, if at all. They are not the poorest countries in the world; that distinction is reserved for marginal states, or what the UN describes as least developed countries (LLDCs). However, most are industrializing only very slowly, rely heavily on agriculture, have few exports, and have a low per capita GDP (mainly in the range of $300 to $1,500). Some LDCs are building their industrial sectors and developing more diverse economies, but they tend to be the exceptions. Botswana, for example, has invested its earnings from diamond exports in infrastructure, meat production, and the tourist trade. However, most LDCs rely on one or two major exports: sugar from Belize; oil from Congo, Gabon, and Nigeria; and fish from Kiribati, Palau, and Tonga.

Many LDCs are quintessential **banana republics.** A pejorative label, the term was originally coined to describe countries such as Guatemala and Honduras, whose economies relied heavily on the export of bananas, whose economic policies were dominated by U.S. multinationals such as the United Fruit Company, and whose politics were prone to interference by the United States. It could now be applied to almost any country that is dependent on a small selection of agricultural products whose prices are determined by the international market. For these and other LDCs, the prospects for economic improvement are dimmed by at least four problems:

- The prices for most of their exports are determined in foreign markets, and LDCs have little influence over those prices and limited prospects of diversifying their economies to compensate.

- LDC exports are growing only slowly. For example, while Mexico's merchandise exports increased by 271 percent in the period 1991–2001 and those of Malaysia and India grew by 155 and 146 percent, respectively, Nigeria increased its exports by just 56 percent, Senegal by 35 percent, and Zimbabwe by 15 percent. In more troubled marginal states, merchandise exports in some cases actually fell.[7]

- Most LDCs have substantial debt problems, caused by heavy borrowing when commodity prices were high in the 1970s or by the need to counter their economic problems in the 1990s. Now that prices are low, LDCs are finding it hard to repay those debts, a problem compounded by their inability to expand exports and earn foreign currency.

- Many LDC governments are guilty of corruption, mismanagement, and waste and of squandering badly needed foreign aid and investment on low-priority prestige projects—such as new airports, conference centers, highways, and luxury hotels—instead of investing in education, health care, and sanitation.

To complicate the situation for many LDCs, health care has improved more quickly than economic prospects, which has led to increased population growth. The birth rate may not have changed, but infant mortality rates have declined, leading to an explosion in the number of younger people. The major demographic challenge facing liberal democracies is that their citizens are living longer and the number of elderly people is increasing, putting increased pressure on health care and social security. For LDCs, population numbers are expanding from below, increasing the demand for education and jobs and stretching the ability of the economic system to manage (see Figure IV.1).

A Weak Sense of National Identity

An important prerequisite for political stability in a country is a strong sense of national identity, something that many LDCs lack. This is mainly because their borders were often decided by competing European powers, with little regard for local ethnic, religious, or cultural realities. This is particularly true in Africa—the maps in Figure IV.2 show clearly how the borders of modern African states bear no relation at all to the territories of different ethnic groups. As a result, most African states comprise many ethnic groups that often dislike or distrust one another. Politics is often driven not by ideological differences but by ethnic differences, with different parties identifying with the interests of different ethnic

FIGURE IV.1

Comparing Population Structure

% of population in specific age groups

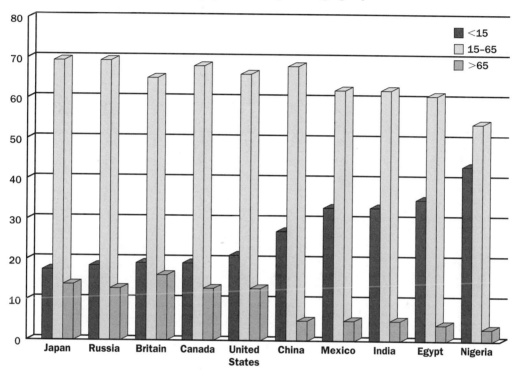

Source: From World Resources Institute, 2003, *http://www.wri.org.* Figures are for 2000.

groups and politics being driven by nepotism and discrimination. This has regularly led to internecine conflict and civil war, such as the Biafran civil war in Nigeria, the conflict in Ethiopia that led to the secession in 1993 of Eritrea, and the regular outbreaks of genocide between members of the Hutu and Tutsi tribes in Rwanda and Burundi. Although ethnic conflict does not threaten the fabric and viability of LDCs to the degree it does in countries such as Haiti or Liberia, it remains a root cause of political turmoil.

Latin American LDCs face almost no ethnic problems, because native peoples have either been exterminated or marginalized, but their sense of national identity has been weakened by the economic influence of the major powers. While NICs export manufactured goods and have been able to influence global prices and markets, LDCs export mainly agricultural goods whose prices are dictated by importing countries; this makes it difficult for food-exporting countries such as Guatemala or Honduras to take control of their own economic policies.

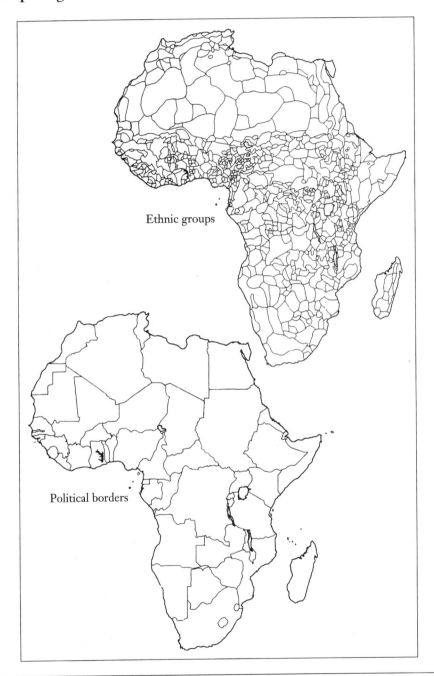

FIGURE IV.2

Comparing Traditional and Modern Boundaries in Africa

Ethnic groups

Political borders

Source: Upper map from Martin Ira Glassner and Harm J. de Blij, *Systematic Political Geography* (New York: John Wiley and Sons, 1989).

Some political scientists also argue that the national identity of Latin American LDCs has been undermined by Western neo-imperialism, such as the U.S.-sponsored coup in Guatemala in 1954 and U.S. support for Nicaraguan counter-revolutionaries (the Contras) in the 1980s. For LDCs generally, more interference comes in the form of demands made by international lending institutions. Anyone who wants to borrow money obviously has to be creditworthy, but bodies such as the World Bank and the International Monetary Fund (IMF) have become significant policy actors in many LDCs. Kenya, for example, was obliged to hold multiparty elections in 1992 because of a refusal by the World Bank and Western donors to provide any more aid. Similarly, the IMF has played a central role in compelling changes in Nigerian economic policy. Is this just common financial sense, or is it economic imperialism?

Inadequate Social Services

LDCs are typically much less urbanized than liberal democracies or NICs, with about 50 to 80 percent of their populations living in rural areas, having little political influence on urban policymakers, and being provided only with basic education and health care. Where NICs have invested in infrastructure, most LDCs have poorly developed transport and communications systems, leaving their rural areas isolated and making it difficult for goods to be moved. Among the consequences: few opportunities for farmers and small entrepreneurs to turn a profit, an undereducated workforce, high levels of illiteracy (10 to 40 percent among men), low life expectancy (40 to 60 years), and high rates of infant mortality (30 to 90 deaths per 1,000 live births). On the Human Development Index, most LDCs rank among the lower two-thirds of the countries on the list.

For many African LDCs, the absence of adequate education and health care not only has meant too many avoidable deaths from diseases such as malaria (which now kills about a million people in sub-Saharan Africa every year) but has taken on a new significance over the last 20 years with the spread of HIV/AIDS. The lack of preventive health care, coupled with migratory labor systems that oblige many working men to spend many months away from home and social norms that make it difficult to convince many of these men to practice safe sex and avoid prostitutes, has led to the rapid spread of HIV/AIDS. Of the more than 42 million people thought to be infected with HIV worldwide in 2002, about two-thirds were in sub-Saharan Africa. In the worst affected states, more than 10 percent of the population may be infected, and deaths from AIDS have begun to lead to falling life expectancy.

Global and Regional Marginalization

Their growing wealth and political stability has given NICs a new level of influence in the world, allowing some of them to act as engines of regional economic growth and drawing more attention from the leaders of the rich industrialized countries. By contrast, most LDCs lack the political or economic power to play an active role in regional affairs and have very little impact on global events. They have less control over their own destinies than do NICs and find themselves in a reactive rather than a proactive relationship with the rest of the world. Most have relatively few sources of income and rely either on one major commodity (such as

CRITICAL ISSUES

HOW POOR IS POOR?

Poverty is a problem that every society faces to one degree or another. Even rich welfare states such as the United States are faced with homelessness, malnutrition, and all the other problems that we associate with being poor. But the definition of poverty is highly contentious and means very different things in different societies.

In the United States, you are poor—says the government—if you live in a family of four that has less than $18,100 per year in household income: the so-called **poverty line**. This is determined by calculating a minimal household food budget for an urban family and multiplying by three to cover the cost of housing, clothes, and necessities. According to this standard, 35 million Americans (including nearly 15 million children) are living in poverty—this is about 12 percent of the population. Roughly half the median household income in the United States, the poverty line may not seem like very much money. But set against the income of people living in much of Africa and Asia, it is a king's ransom.

While wealth in liberal democracies is determined on the basis of income, in poor countries it is determined on the basis of expenditure because income is difficult to measure. According to the World Bank, nearly one in four humans in

the late 1990s—about 1.5 billion people—lived on less than $1 per day. True, a dollar in most parts of Africa goes a lot further than a dollar in the United States, but this is still a pitifully small amount when compared to income in the average liberal democracy. At the same time, the income gap between rich countries and poor countries is growing: In 1960 the world's wealthiest 20 percent of people were earning 30 times as much as the world's poorest 20 percent; by 1999 the ratio was up to 74:1.[8]

Poverty has much the same impact in poor countries as in rich countries. It reduces overall levels of health, with infant mortality rates being high and life expectancy being low. It is related to inadequate schooling and illiteracy, which in turn handicap attempts to build a skilled and productive workforce. This in turn undermines attempts to improve the economic productivity of society, and poor countries find themselves economically disadvantaged in the global system. It contributes to a sense of powerlessness, insecurity, and vulnerability. The poor react to circumstances rather than having the motivation to change their lives and are cut off from the political system. In the poorest societies, there is a significant gender gap, with women much worse off then men.

oil), the price of which is driven by global market forces, or on a variety of low-profit commodities, such as agricultural produce. The prospects for economic development are further compromised by poor policy choices, centralized decision making, an undereducated workforce, and social problems that undermine attempts to build political stability.

Rich countries and poor countries alike have to borrow to pay the bills, but while rich countries have abundant collateral, poor countries have few sources of income and find it much more difficult to service their debts (make the scheduled repayments). A poor country that wants to maintain a positive credit rating with international lending agencies may be required to make policy adjustments demanded by these agencies, or the agencies may demand that loans be directed at particular economic sectors. This has led to charges that these agencies, most of which are based in, and underwritten by, North America or Western Europe, are engaging in a form of neo-imperialism. Equally, though, they may be encouraging the kinds of economic changes LDCs need to build self-reliance.

Prominent among international lending agencies are the World Bank and the International Monetary Fund, both of which are specialized agencies of the United Nations, both of which were founded in 1945, and both of which are headquartered in Washington, D.C. While the World Bank provides economic development loans, the IMF promotes global monetary stability and economic development. The World Bank has been associated in recent years with so-called **structural adjustment** programs, through which it has required countries seeking loans to balance their budgets, deregulate their financial systems, adopt more liberal trade policies, privatize state-owned industries and services, and remove price controls.

Although these are the kinds of policies associated with liberal democracies, questions have been raised about whether they are the right policies for poorer countries. On other hand, they helped Asian and Latin American states become NICs, so they may offer the same possibilities for LDCs. However, among the criticisms of the World Bank and the IMF are that (1) they channel government money to poor countries, which may be better served by private investment; (2) they have been prepared to help authoritarian regimes if they are able to guarantee economic stability; and (3) they do not so much encourage self-reliance as incorporation into a Western-dominated global economy. Critics of the lending agencies argue that the best short-term prospects for LDCs may be offered by spillover from neighboring economic powers, such as Mexico, South Africa, and Southeast Asia's tiger economies. This would reduce the dependence of poor countries on Western-brokered lending agencies and move economic development more toward the free market.

EXPLAINING THE PROBLEMS OF DEVELOPMENT

Like almost every NIC, every LDC was colonized at one time or another. However, where NICs have been able to build new levels of postcolonial prosperity, most LDCs have not. Exactly why this has happened is debatable. Social scientists have offered many different theories in their attempts to explain the problems of LDCs, variously blaming such potential villains as the international economic system, the greed of Western corporations, the entrapment of LDCs in cold war competition, traditional cultural values, and the incompetence of LDC governments. None of these theories—whether orthodox or radical—have yet stood the test of time.

Orthodox Approaches

In the 1960s, many of the debates about development centered on **modernization theory.** Growing out of the process of decolonization in Africa and Asia, proponents of this theory optimistically argued that emerging countries could follow the same path as liberal democracies; they too had once been "underdeveloped," and look where they were now. Surely the Third World could follow suit—all it needed to do was to adopt modern cultural values and build modern political and economic institutions.[9] This was certainly a belief typical of the more optimistic colonial administrators as they bade farewell to their former colonies in Africa in the 1950s and 1960s. Leave these countries with good infrastructure, an educated elite, a reasonable range of exports, and Western political institutions—went the argument—and help them along with injections of foreign aid, and these countries stood a good chance of succeeding. In fact the opposite happened. Modernization turned out to be much more complex than most people thought, and the very process of modernizing often brought instability and violence,[10] making the prospects for these countries worse.

One of the orthodox approaches was spelled out in 1960 by Walter W. Rostow, an economic historian who was about to become an advisor to President Kennedy (and later national security advisor to President Johnson) and whose theories—some charge—helped encourage the United States to become involved in Vietnam. He argued that if poor countries were provided with enough capital, they could be encouraged to "takeoff" and move toward democracy and capitalism rather than communism. He suggested that countries would go through five **stages of growth:** (1) the traditional society, (2) the preconditions for takeoff, (3) takeoff, (4) the drive to maturity, and (5) the age of high mass consumption.[11] Under this analysis, liberal democracies would be at stage 5, most NICs would be between stages 3 and 4, and LDCs would be at stages 1 and 2. Useful though it is, Rostow's theory has been criticized for not explaining how societies move from one stage to another, for overlooking the extent to which the traditional and the modern coexist in many poorer countries, and for assuming that capitalism and the "age of high mass consumption" are the goals of all economic development.

Radical Explanations

Reacting to the orthodox theories, several scholars in the 1960s and 1970s began arguing that the key to understanding LDCs was to focus on underdevelopment. They talked of a global economic system in which Europeans and North Americans made all the important decisions, and they argued that the LDCs were being kept on the periphery, leading to unequal or uneven levels of development. There were several variations on this theme:

- **Imperialism.** Lenin argued that imperialism was the highest stage of capitalism, that Western capitalists exploited African and Asian workers and peasants, and that by dividing up the rest of the world among themselves, the major powers had created a new proletariat and were promoting global class antagonism.[12] He also argued that the exploited countries would eventually rise up against the exploiters (as they did, with the struggle against colonialism).

    Many Marxists have assessed colonialism along these lines and argued that colonialism and neocolonialism were and are the major obstacles to progress in the LDCs. One theory is based on the idea of a global commercial and financial system dominated by a world bourgeoisie at the center (the major industrialized countries) that influences a bourgeoisie on the periphery (the middle class of LDCs), with a peripheral proletariat (the urban and rural poor of LDCs) at the bottom of the heap.[13] No one questions the economic power of liberal democracies and Western multinationals, but neither Marxism nor Leninism have been able to explain why some African, Asian, and Latin American countries have become wealthy while others have stayed poor.

- **Vicious circle theory.** This theory argues that poverty perpetuates itself. Because incomes are low, money cannot be saved; without savings there is no capital or investment; without capital, productivity remains low, and the lack of investment leads to low productivity, low incomes, and low exports. In other words, it makes the pessimistic argument that poor countries will always stay poor. However, the theory does not explain where and how the circle began (colonialism is usually blamed),[14] says nothing about the role of government and politics, and—again—fails to explain the emergence of NICs or the fact that many LDCs have wealthy elites, emerging middle classes, and successful entrepreneurs.

- **Dependency theory.** Developed mainly by Latin American social scientists in the 1960s and 1970s (who came to be known as *dependencistas*), this theory argues that poor countries will not follow the same path as rich countries (as suggested by modernization theory) because the latter have forever changed the nature of the international system. The rich countries had no major external competition when they first emerged, whereas emerging states in the 1970s faced major competition from the Americans, the Europeans, and the Japanese. Also, the new emerging countries had to borrow money and buy technology from the rich countries, building on a dependency that began during the colonial era. The result was the creation of an unequal world, with a core of rich countries controlling manufacturing and a periphery of poor countries living off the export of raw materials on unfavorable terms. To make matters worse, the rich countries maintained the wealth and power of elites within the poor countries. In short, poverty was not the fault of the poor countries, but of an unequal international system.

  The main problem with dependency theory once again was that it failed to explain how and why countries such as Argentina, Brazil, Indonesia, Mexico, and Thailand were breaking the mold of poverty. Variations on the theme of dependency theory suggested that some of the dependent countries could become wealthier, but they would do so while still remaining dependent on banks and multinationals in the rich countries.[15] As we saw in the case study on Mexico, however, some NICs have become so important as sources of cheap manufactured goods and cheap labor that not only have they undermined key sectors of the rich economies, but their welfare has a direct impact on the overall economic welfare of liberal democracies.

Responding to the problems in all these approaches, and criticizing Western political scientists for their tendency to apply American and European experiences, values, and assumptions,[16] non-Western theorists have responded by arguing the need to look at poorer countries on their own terms. One such line of thought is offered by the Indian theorist Vrajenda Raj Mehta, who argues that

Western models take a unidimensional view of humans and society. He supports a multidimensional approach that goes beyond the objective and rational and includes the subjective, intuitive, ethical, and spiritual dimensions of our lives. He argues that "each national community has its own law of development, its own way to fulfill itself," that many of the problems of a country such as India can be linked to its attempts to apply inappropriate Western models, and that India, instead of trying to copy the West, should choose its own goals and "find its own strategy of development and nation-building suited to its own peculiar needs."[17] These are the same kinds of arguments behind the Islamic resurgence since 1979 in the Middle East (see Part V).

LDCs TODAY

Whether because of the international system, or because of their own internal weaknesses, or because of bad decisions by their leaders, or for some other reason, LDCs today find themselves struggling. And yet there are also signs that at least some of them are slowly developing traditions of political stability, which could help them build and diversify their economies.

For example, several LDCs with a history of military government are now working to build sustainable civilian government. This has happened in countries such as Guatemala and Ghana, but nowhere more dramatically than in Bolivia. During the first 155 years after its independence in 1825, Bolivia had 189 military coups, more than 60 revolutions, 70 presidents, and 11 constitutions—and yet since 1982 it has been under civilian rule. At the same time, new market-oriented economic policies helped bring its inflation rate down from a staggering 11,700 percent in 1985 to about 20 percent in 1997. The authoritarianism of most military governments has been a barrier to the development of democracy or economic liberalism, but the switch to civilian government in countries such as Bolivia and Paraguay may now allow them, like Argentina, Brazil, Portugal, and Spain before them, to build democratic institutions.

Similarly, there are signs in some LDCs that leaders are prepared to retire or hand over power to elected governments. Julius Nyerere of Tanzania retired in 1985 after 24 years in office, Jerry Rawlings of Ghana—military leader for 11 years—stood for and won freely contested civilian elections in 1992, and Daniel arap Moi of Kenya stood down in 2002 after 24 years in office. Most Latin American LDCs now have multiparty systems (in some cases with so many parties that power is fragmented), and contested elections have been held in more than two dozen African states since 1991.

These could be the first signs that some LDCs may be about to begin resolving the short-term problems that have prevented them from building political stability and economic prosperity. Without internal stability, it is difficult to see them attracting the kind of foreign investment that allowed the United States to develop its resources in the 19th century, or Japan and Western Europe to rebuild their economies after World War II, or NICs to achieve the high levels of economic growth they have seen in the past 10 to 15 years. Integration in the global economy on unequal terms is often seen as a possible cause of the continued marginalization of LDCs, yet opening their markets may be the only way of achieving long-term political stability and economic growth.

KEY TERMS

banana republic
dependency theory
imperialism
modernization theory

political
   institutionalization
poverty line
stages of growth

structural adjustment
vicious circle theory

STUDY QUESTIONS

1. Why are poor countries poor?

2. Is one-party rule an obstacle to political and economic development?

3. Comparing liberal democracies, NICs, and LDCs, what would you say were the minimum prerequisites for the construction of a stable and effective system of government?

4. Which is best for LDCs: changes to economic policies required by the World Bank and the IMF, or private investment from neighboring regional powers?

LDCs ONLINE

International Monetary Fund: *http://www.imf.org*
World Bank: *http://www.worldbank.org*
Web sites of the IMF and the World Bank; the latter includes useful information on all the countries where the bank is active.

U.S. Agency for International Development: *http://www.info.usaid.gov*
Web site of the federal agency responsible for overseeing the U.S. overseas aid program. It includes pages on all the countries where USAID is active.

FURTHER READING

Cammack, Paul, David Pool, and William Tordoff, *Third World Politics: A Comparative Introduction*, 3rd Ed. (Baltimore: Johns Hopkins University Press, 2003). Despite its unfortunate title, a useful introduction to the major political features and institutions of Africa, Latin America, and the Middle East.

Handelman, Howard, *The Challenge of Third World Development*, 3rd Ed. (Upper Saddle River, NJ: Prentice Hall, 2003). An introduction to the theories and realities of underdevelopment.

Harbeson, John W., and Donald Rothchild (Eds.), *Africa in World Politics: The African State System in Flux*, 3rd Ed. (Boulder, CO: Westview, 1999). A series of essays on the history and current problems of Africa, including economic development, democratization, and humanitarian issues.

Kamrava, Mehran, *Politics and Society in the Developing World* (London: Routledge, 2000). A useful study of issues such as democratization, economic development, and social change in poorer states. (Tellingly, it was first published in 1993 as *Politics and Society in the Third World*.)

Wiarda, Howard J. (Ed.), *Non-Western Theories of Development* (Fort Worth, TX: Harcourt Brace, 1999). An edited collection of chapters looking at the impact of Western and non-Western models of development on different regions of the world.

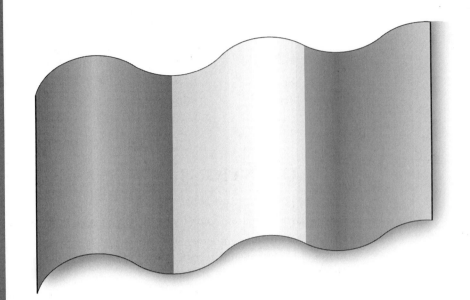

CHAPTER 8

NIGERIA

NIGERIA: QUICK FACTS

Official name: Federal Republic of Nigeria

Capital: Abuja

Area: 351,649 square miles (910,770 sq. km) (twice the size of California)

Languages: English (official), Hausa, Yoruba, Igbo, Fulani, and several other languages

Population: 129.8 million

Population density: 361 per square mile

Population growth rate: 2.9 percent

POLITICAL INDICATORS

Freedom House rating: Partly Free

Date of state formation: October 1, 1960

System type: Presidential republic

Constitution: Published May 1999

Administration: Federal; 36 states and a Federal Capital Territory

Executive: President directly elected for 4-year, renewable terms

Legislature: Bicameral National Assembly, consisting of a Senate (109 members) and a House of Representatives (360 members), both elected for 4-year renewable terms

Party structure: Multiparty, but in early stages of evolution

Judiciary: Federal Supreme Court

Head of state: Olusegun Obasanjo (1999–)

Head of government: Olusegun Obasanjo (1999–)

ECONOMIC INDICATORS

GDP (2001): $41.2 billion

Per capita GDP: $290

Distribution of GNP: Services 48 percent, industry 27 percent, agriculture 25 percent

Urban population: 28 percent

SOCIAL INDICATORS

HDI ranking: 136

Infant mortality rate: 84 per 1,000 live births

Life expectancy: 46.8 years

Literacy: 64 percent of people aged 15 and older

Religions: About 50 percent Muslim, 30 percent Christian, and 20 percent traditional beliefs (estimated)

INTRODUCTION

Nigeria is an ideal laboratory in which to study African politics, for several reasons. It is a young country struggling to develop a national identity in the face of ethnic and religious divisions. Its political problems have given rise to both civilian and military governments, which have run the gamut from authoritarian to relatively progressive. Its military power and oil wealth give it the potential to become a major regional power. It has particular interest to the United States given that many African Americans trace their roots to what is now Nigeria and that Nigeria supplies the United States with much of its oil and an estimated 40 percent of its heroin. Finally, a study of Nigeria provides insights into a continent about which most Americans know far too little.

Nigeria is the most populous country in Africa, but the exact size of the population is disputed. The deeply flawed 1991 census came up with a figure of 88.5 million, but more recent UN estimates put the total closer to 130 million. Growing annually at 2.9 percent, that figure is expected to double within 25 years, placing considerable strain on an infrastructure that is already grossly inadequate. Just more than half of all Nigerians live in the rural areas, but the urban population is growing rapidly as people move to cities such as Lagos, Ibadan, and Enugu in search of jobs.

In economic terms, Nigeria is a poor country, with a GDP of just more than $41 billion, or $290 per capita. If recalculated using purchasing power parity, however, the GDP rises to nearly $150 billion (or $1,310 per capita), a reflection of the unrealistically low exchange rate of the Nigerian currency, the naira. If the large Nigerian black market could also be factored in to calculations, the economic picture would look very different. Whatever the size of the economy, however, the biggest problem that Nigeria faces is its heavy dependence on oil, which accounts for nearly 99 percent of exports. Not only does this mean that the size and health of the entire economy is driven by the international market price of oil, but so are government revenues. To make matters worse, much of the oil wealth has been squandered and stolen, and arguments over how the balance should be spent have caused much bitterness. Nigeria also outspent itself during the oil-boom years of the 1970s and now has the biggest national debt in Africa: $32 billion.

In social terms, Nigeria suffers four critical divisions:

- **Ethnicity.** There is little agreement on how many different ethnic groups live in Nigeria, but the total is thought to be somewhere between 250 and 400. The biggest are the **Hausa-Fulani** in the north (28 to 30 percent of the population), the **Yoruba** in the southwest (about 20 percent), and the **Igbo** in the southeast (about 17 percent). Every attempt to encourage these groups to think of themselves as Nigerians has so far failed, leading a disgusted Wole Soyinka—the Nigerian novelist and 1986 Nobel laureate for literature—to dismiss the idea of a Nigerian nation as a "farcical illusion."

- **Religion.** Nigeria is divided between a mainly Muslim north and a non-Muslim south: Just more than half of all Nigerians are Muslim, 30 percent are Christian, and the rest follow traditional religions. In the north there is support in some states for the introduction of *sharia*, or Islamic law, and widespread admiration among ordinary people for the Al-Qaeda leader Osama bin Laden. Religious

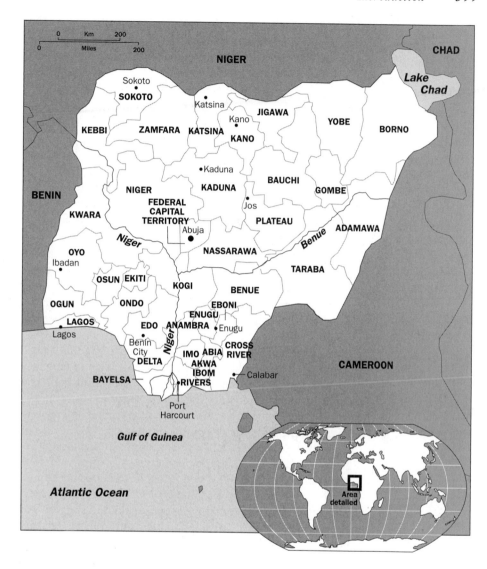

tensions repeatedly turn violent, as they did during 2002 when the Miss World beauty contest was due to be held in Nigeria and a local journalist commented that the participants were so beautiful that the prophet Muhammed might have wanted to marry one. Fighting broke out between Muslims and Christians, leaving 200 people dead and many more injured.

- **Region.** Nigeria is divided between a north that is dry and poor and a south that is better endowed in resources and basic services: The city of Lagos alone has nine times the elementary school enrollment of the northern region and five times as many hospital beds. Most of the best agricultural land is in the heavily populated south, while most of the northern half of the country is savanna or semi-desert, limiting the potential for agriculture. Regional tensions have been exacerbated by oil, most of which lies either in the southeast or off the coast of Nigeria, but the profits of which have largely been stolen or misappropriated by political elites in other parts of the country.

- **Class.** As in many African states, government and business in Nigeria are dominated by a small educated elite. The wealthiest Nigerians include the new business class, landlords, traders, and self-employed professionals, but social advancement and wealth are also tied to jobs in government and the bureaucracy, which offer high salaries and opportunities for bribery and embezzlement.

In political terms, coming to grips with Nigeria is complicated by the lack of settled and predictable political patterns. Since independence in 1960, there have been three civilian governments, five successful and several attempted military coups, a costly civil war, and nearly 30 years of military government. The first civilian government was based on the Westminster system, but Nigerians subsequently opted for the American model, with an elected president and a separate legislature. The first and second attempts at civilian government (1960–1966 and 1979–1983) broke down as leaders lost control and were unable to encourage Nigerians to set aside their ethnic differences. After being delayed several years, a third attempt was launched in May 1999 but faced the same tough challenge of encouraging Nigerians to pull together: estimates suggest that communal violence in the period 1999–2003 resulted in the deaths of a staggering 10,000 people (see Political Debates, p. 425).

POLITICAL DEVELOPMENT

Nigeria faces the challenge of trying to build a stable and united state out of a society that is divided along ethnic, religious, and economic lines and in which corruption has become a way of life. The legacy of colonialism could once be blamed for its problems, but Nigerian governments have made matters worse by failing to build a sense of national unity, by failing to tap in to the country's wealth of oil and people, by failing to build successful civilian political institutions, and by allowing incompetence to become a hallmark of the bureaucracy. The cumulative effect has been a story of unfulfilled dreams and missed opportunities, where narrow agendas have undermined the larger goals of building a stable and successful society.

Precolonial Era (900 B.C.–A.D. 1851)

As with feudal Europe, the early history of Nigeria is one of a series of states and kingdoms emerging, declining, and combining. From 900 B.C. to A.D. 200, what is now central Nigeria was dominated by the Nok, who discovered how to smelt iron and built a rich and advanced culture. Muslim traders began arriving in about 700, and by the 14th century the region was dominated by the kingdoms of Mali, Ghana, and Kanem-Bornu, connected by trade routes that stretched to Europe and the Middle East. By the 16th century, what is now northwest Nigeria was part of the Songhai empire, while southern Nigeria saw the rise of the rich and influential Benin culture.

The Portuguese were the first Europeans to explore the area, setting up coastal trading stations in the late 15th century. With the cooperation of Benin, they shipped slaves to the Americas to work in mines and on sugar plantations, and the **slave trade** became the biggest influence on the development of West Africa. The French, British, and Dutch arrived in the 17th century, setting up trading companies and building garrisons to protect their interests. Britain became the biggest slave trader, but when it banned the slave trade in 1807 (it was universally banned in 1833), the Royal Navy was dispatched to enforce the ban. Traders turned their interests to ivory and palm oil, explorers began opening up the interior, and then missionaries arrived, intent on bringing Christianity.

The Colonial Era (1861–1960)

Britain annexed Lagos in 1861 and then conquered the rest of what was to become Nigeria, driven mainly by concerns about French colonial expansion across the Sahel and North Africa. In 1900 Britain declared separate protectorates over Northern and Southern Nigeria and then combined them in 1914 into the colony and protectorate of Nigeria. Despite this, it ruled Nigeria as two colonies with different administrative systems: indirect rule in the north through traditional Muslim emirates, which were hierarchical, authoritarian, and bureaucratic,[1] and direct rule in the south through an advisory Legislative Council. The divisions were deepened in 1939 when Britain split Nigeria into three provinces, each based on a different cash crop: peanuts in the North, cocoa in the West, and palm oil in the East. Because the provinces roughly coincided with Nigeria's three major ethnic groups, they were encouraged to think in regional rather than national terms.

Opposition to British rule began to emerge as educated Nigerians railed against colonialism. In 1920 the National Congress of British West Africa was founded and began demanding greater political participation for Nigerians. Among the most active of the nationalists was Dr. Nnamdi Azikiwe, who in 1944 helped set up Nigeria's first modern political party, the National Council of Nigeria and the Cameroons.

After World War II, Britain began making arrangements for Nigerian independence. Three experimental constitutions were published, the third of which—in 1954—created the Nigerian Federation and established a federal parliament with half the seats allocated to the North. Regional elections were held that were contested by several new political parties and movements, almost all of them regionally based. Na-

TABLE 8.1

Key Dates in Nigerian History

1485	First Portuguese trading post established
1833	Abolition of the slave trade
1861	Lagos annexed by the British
1884–1885	Berlin Conference confirms British claims to the Niger Territories
1914	Creation of the colony and protectorate of Nigeria
1920	Foundation of the National Congress of British West Africa
1944	Creation of the first modern Nigerian political party
1954	Declaration of the Federation of Nigeria
1960	(October 1) Independence
1963	Nigeria becomes a republic with Nnamdi Azikiwe as president
1966	(January) First military coup, Ironsi takes power; (July) second military coup, Gowon takes power
1967–1970	Nigerian civil war
1975	(July) Third military coup, Muhammed takes power
1976	Failed military coup, Obasanjo replaces Muhammed
1979	Fifth constitution
1979–1983	Second Republic; Shagari president
1983	(December) Fourth military coup, Buhari takes power
1985	(August) Fifth military coup, Babangida takes power
1989	Sixth constitution
1991	Abuja becomes Nigeria's new capital
1993	(June) Presidential elections held, but Babangida refuses to release results; (August) Babangida steps down, replaced by transitional civilian government; (November) Abacha takes power
1995	(July) Forty people, including Olusegun Obasanjo, imprisoned on charges of complicity in a coup plot; (October) Abacha regime announces its intention to return Nigeria to civilian rule by October 1998; (November) Ken Saro-Wiwa executed; Nigeria suspended from the Commonwealth
1998	(June) Death of Sani Abacha; (July) death of Moshood Abiola
1999	(February) Olusegun Obasanjo wins presidential elections; (May) civilian rule returns with creation of Fourth Republic; (November) thousands killed in army massacre in Delta region
2000	(August) Visit to Nigeria of President Clinton
2001	(September) More than 500 people killed in religious fighting in Jos; (October) more than 300 people killed in army massacre in Benue
2002	(January) 700–2,000 people killed following explosion at Lagos army barracks
2003	(April) Olusegun Obasanjo wins election to a second term

tional elections in 1959 produced the first fully elected national government, and on October 1, 1960, Nigeria became independent under the leadership of its first prime minister, a Muslim Hausa-Fulani named Alhaji Sir Abubakar Tafawa Balewa.

Independence and the First Republic (1960–1966)

The new Nigeria was a federal parliamentary democracy. The British monarch was still head of state, but legislative power was vested in a bicameral parliament, executive power in a prime minister and cabinet, and judicial authority in a Federal Supreme Court. In 1963 Nigeria cut its remaining ties to the British Crown and became a republic with a new nonexecutive post of president, filled by Dr. Azikiwe.

Unfortunately, the new Nigerian government almost immediately became tangled in a web of ethnic and religious divisions. The census proved a heated political issue, because the allocation of seats in the federal parliament was based on the number of people in each region. It was also clear that political parties had broken down along regional lines, with each state dominated by a single party. Squabbling broke out among the parties, there were strikes by workers complaining about low pay, and charges of political corruption flew. National elections were held in 1964 amid charges of fraud, and regional elections in the west in 1965 were marred by civil unrest and riots. Meanwhile, the military had been quickly Africanized,[2] attracting some of the best and brightest members of Nigerian society, who watched the chaos of civilian politics with growing dismay.

Military Government I (1966–1979)

On January 15, 1966, Nigeria experienced its first military coup, staged by a group of Igbo officers headed by Major Johnson Aguiyi Ironsi. Senior national and regional political leaders (including Prime Minister Balewa) were murdered, and the federal system was abolished. Northerners now feared that Igbos were establishing an hegemony over Nigeria, and within days hundreds of northern Igbos had been beaten and killed in outbreaks of civil unrest. Problems reached a head in July, when northern army officers staged a second coup, killing Ironsi and replacing him with Lieutenant Colonel Yakubu Gowon, a Christian from Nigeria's central region (sometimes known as the **Middle Belt**). Gowon restored the federal structure and promised a return to civilian rule following agreement of a new constitution. The massacre of Igbos living in the north continued, however, followed by retaliation against northerners living in the south. Tensions boiled over in July 1967, when the Igbo-dominated eastern region declared its independence as the new state of **Biafra,** and civil war broke out, pitting the Nigerian federal government against the secessionist Biafrans led by Lieutenant Colonel Odemegwu Ojukwu.

The war dragged on for 27 months, the Biafrans fighting tenaciously out of fear that northern Muslims were bent on their extermination. Biafra received financial support from sympathizers outside Nigeria, but it was recognized as a sovereign state by only four African governments. Cut off by a naval blockade, it was finally all but starved into submission, with the deaths of between 500,000 and 2 million Biafrans. The war ended in January 1970, Ojukwu went into exile, and Nigeria was reunited.

Gowon was a capable leader who did much to patch up the wounds caused by the civil war, but he was slow to return Nigeria to civilian government and did too little to curb inflation, economic mismanagement, and the squandering of the profit from Nigeria's oil boom of the early 1970s. In July 1975 reform-minded senior officers seized power in a bloodless coup, replacing Gowon with Brigadier Murtala Muhammed, a Hausa-Fulani. He won public praise by purging the army, announcing a 4-year timetable for the return to civilian rule, and dismissing 10,000 government officials and 150 officers on charges of corruption. However, he also upset those who had gained illicitly from the Gowon years, and barely 7 months after coming to power, he was assassinated during an attempted coup by followers of Gowon trying to regain power. The coup failed, and Muhammed was succeeded by Lieutenant Colonel Olusegun Obasanjo, notable for the fact that he was Nigeria's first Yoruba head of state. Obasanjo promised to respect the goal of a return to civilian rule by October 1979 and work on the new constitution continued.

The Second Republic (1979–1983)

For its new system of government, Nigeria abandoned the Westminster model, opting instead for the U.S. model, with a directly elected executive, a bicameral National Assembly, and a separate Supreme Court. National elections in 1979 resulted in a clean sweep of the presidency and the legislature by Shehu Shagari and his National Party of Nigeria. Shagari won praise for pardoning Ojukwu and Gowon and allowing them both to return from exile, and—to help promote national unity—he announced plans to move Nigeria's capital from Lagos to Abuja, 300 miles to the north in the exact geographical center of the country. However, Shagari was unable to control corruption, and when the international oil price fell in the early 1980s, his government was further weakened by an economy on the verge of collapse. New elections were held in 1983 as planned, but although they were contested by five parties, and Shagari won a second term, the parties again broke down along ethnic and regional lines, and the elections were marred by charges of ballot-rigging and by clashes among supporters of rival parties.

Military Government II (1983–1999)

On December 31, 1983, 3 months after being returned to office, Shagari was ousted in Nigeria's fourth successful military coup. Although it was welcomed at first, the new leader—Major General Muhammadu Buhari, a Muslim northerner—became increasingly authoritarian and was ousted in August 1985 in yet another coup. He was succeeded by Major General Ibrahim Babangida, a Muslim from the Middle Belt (but widely perceived as a northerner).

Like several of his predecessors, Babangida made the usual promises of a new constitution, an early and orderly return to civilian rule, and economic revival. At first, he won praise both inside and outside Nigeria for his policies, even earning himself the nickname "Maradona," after Argentinean soccer player Diego Maradona, famed for his handling of the ball. Political parties were legalized in 1989, state governments and a new National Assembly were elected in 1990–1992, and the final step in the transition to the new Third Republic was to have been the presidential election of June 1993. This was apparently won by Moshood Abiola of the new Social Democratic party, but instead of handing over power, Babangida claimed that the election had been rigged and refused to release the results. The outcry that followed persuaded him to step down in August and to hand over power to a transitional civilian government, which was itself ousted within 3 months by Brigadier Sani Abacha, the defense minister. When Abiola defiantly proclaimed himself president, he was jailed. His wife was later killed, allegedly by common criminals but more likely for political reasons.

Abacha was openly contemptuous of human rights. He sentenced the respected former military leader Olusegun Obasanjo to life imprisonment in July 1995 on charges of helping plot a coup and allowed the execution the following November of Ken Saro-Wiwa and eight activists from the Ogoni tribe of southeastern Nigeria. Saro-Wiwa was a nationally famous novelist and the scriptwriter of a popular Nigerian TV soap, who in the early 1990s had became involved with a movement created to promote the interests of the Ogoni people, who live among the oil fields of the Niger delta. Few of the profits from this oil had been invested back into Ogoniland, which had suffered severe environmental problems. When four pro-government Ogoni chiefs were murdered at a political rally in 1994, Saro-Wiwa was accused of organizing the murders, by a military tribunal, and was tried and executed.

Abacha announced plans to return Nigeria to civilian rule and won qualified approval from Western governments for his efforts to control public spending and inflation and to promote privatization. However, Nigeria was suspended from the Commonwealth following the Saro-Wiwa execution, and it became clear that Abacha was manipulating the return to civilian government so as to ensure that he would be elected president. Before he could carry out his plan, however, he died in June 1998 of a heart attack (described by many Nigerians as the "coup from heaven"). When a heart attack also claimed Moshood Abiola the following month, power fell into the hands of General Abdulsalam Abubakar, who moved rapidly to return government back into the hands of the civilians.

Following a series of elections in late 1998 and early 1999, the military stepped down on May 27, 1999; the **Fourth Republic** came into being; and a civilian government took power, headed by Olusegun Obasanjo—who had stepped out of retirement—and his centrist People's Democratic party. Like many of his predecessors, Obasanjo made all the usual statements about promoting democracy, putting Nigeria back on the road to economic prosperity, overcoming ethnic and religious tensions, and dealing with corruption. Again like many of his predecessors, he launched a war against corruption by suspending or reviewing government contracts and by replacing several hundred bureaucrats. He also moved to neutralize possible opposition within the military by purging several dozen military officers who had held political office between 1984 and 1999.

On the economic front, Obasanjo moved quickly to renegotiate Nigeria's debt repayment schedule and to repair Nigeria's relations with its major trading partners and sources of lending. It was a calculated risk, because the kinds of reforms that the World Bank and the International Monetary Fund wanted in Nigeria involved the imposition of austerity measures—including a cutback on government spending—that might have undermined the popularity of the Obasanjo government at a time when it desperately needed public support. At the local level, the government was almost immediately faced with outbreaks of community violence as different ethnic groups fought with one another over access to local resources, such as land and jobs. Within months of his inauguration, hundreds of Nigerians had been killed or wounded in such violence, mainly in the south. The bloodshed continued throughout his first term in office.

Obasanjo was faced with the same structural problems that had undermined previous attempts to make civilian government work in Nigeria. To address these problems, he had to fundamentally alter the style of Nigerian politics. His first challenge was to build strong political institutions that could sustain democracy and withstand the threats posed by social and economic divisions. He also had to break the power of elites, and as well as dealing with corruption among those in power, he had to take on and defeat the kind of low-level, routine bribery and extortion that has become so much a part of daily life in Nigeria. Finally, questions emerged about the nature of the relationship between national and local governments outlined in the new constitution of the Fourth Republic, with critics calling for a looser association and weaker central government.

The prospects for success were heightened by President Obasanjo's own record in politics. As military leader in 1976–1979, he had proved among the least corrupt of all Nigeria's leaders, and he was the first to actually fulfill his promise of returning power to civilians. Unfortunately, good intentions are a very small part of the abilities that a leader of Nigeria must show if he is to help civilian government take root and if he is to help foster a sense of national unity in a country as severely divided as Nigeria. His record during his first term was widely seen as a failure, and many of Nigeria's problems worsened.

Nigeria Today

In April 2003 the second set of elections was held under the constitution of the Fourth Republic. It was surrounded by the usual charges of fraud and by the violence and destruction that has come to be a tragic hallmark of political competition in Nigeria. There were few surprises when Olusegun Obasanjo won a second term in office after having fought a spirited campaign against his main opponent, Muhammadu Buhari, another of Nigeria's erstwhile military leaders.

It was remarkable in many ways that Obasanjo should have won, given the critical problems still faced by Nigeria and the many doubts over his abilities to deal with them. Among the issues at the top of the political agenda: Nigeria's ongoing economic problems, the institutionalized corruption that pervades public and political life, the appalling record of religious and ethnic violence that is so much a feature of life in Nigeria, problems with crime in the major cities, and the dispute over the place of Islamic *sharia* courts in Northern Nigeria (see later in this chapter). A political leader running for reelection in a liberal democracy on Obasanjo's record would almost certainly lose; it says something about the quality of desperation in Nigerian politics that the majority of voters apparently believed he was still the best option.

POLITICAL CULTURE

In a society as diverse and unstable as Nigeria, it is difficult to distinguish indigenous political values from those created by the confluence of African and European political traditions. One Nigerian political scientist argues that the political culture of most countries can be traced back to "some epochal beach-head in its history," such as the American Revolution in the United States or the Bolshevik Revolution in Russia, but that the epochal events in Nigeria were the slave trade and colonialism, which left negative legacies such as corruption, violence, and mistrust.[3] Through all the problems that have been created, however, it is still possible to identify several themes in the country's political culture.

A Belief in Democracy

Despite all the military governments Nigeria has had, they have always been seen by most Nigerians as temporary, and military leaders who were slow in delivering on promises of a return to civilian government (such as Gowon, Babangida, or Abacha) quickly found themselves in trouble. Despite the difficulties experienced by civilian government, Nigerians believe that democratic civilian rule is preferable to un-elected military government and support political parties, a free press, interest groups, and social organizations. Although the First and Second Republics both failed, Nigerians are not inclined to accept failure as inevitable or enduring.[4]

A Multiethnic State

Ethnic divisions are more important to understanding Nigerian society than social or labor divisions because Nigerians differentiate themselves less by class or occupation than by ethnic group. This phenomenon (variously labeled ethnicity, ethnonationalism, or tribalism) involves adherence or loyalty to a particular region or tribe, a sense of exclusivity, and discrimination against people from other regions or tribes (see Close-Up View, p. 408). Ethnicity was not a problem in the precolonial era because different groups had worked out a balance among themselves. It became a problem only when the imposition of colonial frontiers forced different ethnic groups to live together and to develop a mutually agreeable system of government. So far, a tradition of Nigerian nationalism has not taken root, and politics routinely break down in ethnic rivalry.

The Importance of Community

Closely tied to the issue of ethnic division—and further complicating attempts by Nigeria's leaders to build a sense of national identity—is the priority given by many Nigerians to their local communities. Given the lack of a state tradition in Nigeria, and given the widespread distrust among Nigerians toward officialdom, individuals look to their communities for stability, and they believe that loyalty to the community is the paramount virtue. One of the more dangerous consequences of this attitude is the persistence of nepotism and corruption, which are distinctive in Nigeria because it is expected that public officials will enrich their constituents and that they are failures if they do not.[5]

The Dominance of the State

Ironically, while the institutions of government and the state are weak in Nigeria, control of state power has come to mean everything. Because it plays such a critical role in creating economic opportunities, winning control of the state has become more important than competing openly over policies. As long ago as 1964, John Mackintosh suggested that "politics count for too much" in Nigeria, the advantages of controlling power being so great that competing groups will use every method

CLOSE-UP VIEW

ETHNICITY AND POLITICS IN NIGERIA

The characteristic that most clearly distinguishes one African from another is **ethnicity.** When outsiders look at Nigeria, they see Nigerians, but when Nigerians look at one another, they *are* more likely to see Yorubas, Hausas, or Ogonis. The greatest barrier to the creation of a stable state, a workable system of government, and a strong economy in Nigeria is the persistent failure of so many of its people to put the national interest above narrow regional interests.

Ethnicity is a difficult notion to pin down, but it generally revolves around symbols and experiences that give a group of people a common identity and make them different from neighboring communities. It is usually marked by language, history, customs, experiences, and values. The lines between ethnicity, race, and nation are often fuzzy, but—in general terms—ethnicity and nationality can be seen as subdivisions of race. In other words, most Nigerians belong to the same race (Negroid) but are members of different ethnic groups. Similarly, most Europeans belong to the same race (Caucasian) but are members of different national groups.

Group identity is a natural inclination of many people and can help give them a sense of who they are, but problems arise when groups become exclusive and adopt attitudes of superiority toward other groups, as often as not driven by feelings of insecurity. Sociologists have long argued that racism in the United States, for example, is largely a defense mechanism driven by concerns about loss of status or opportunity. This is certainly true of ethnic tensions in Nigeria, where members of one ethnic group—no matter how much they deny it—will always have a sneaking suspicion that other groups will gain the upper hand unless their group is well represented in the power structure.

It is difficult to see how Nigeria can rise above its ethnic differences. In precolonial times, ethnic groups worked out a balance among themselves and largely governed themselves without external interference. The creation of Nigeria forced these groups to live and work together and to build shared systems of government and administration. It also set them on a path of mutual hostility as they competed for power and resources and struggled to preserve their identity. It will take considerable moral courage for them to put aside their hostility and to learn to trust one another.

available to win and keep power. Their desperation is exacerbated by the absence of enough independent sources of wealth and position to allow democratic institutions to operate the way they should.[6]

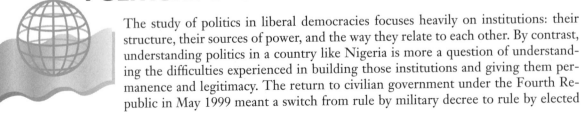

POLITICAL SYSTEM

The study of politics in liberal democracies focuses heavily on institutions: their structure, their sources of power, and the way they relate to each other. By contrast, understanding politics in a country like Nigeria is more a question of understanding the difficulties experienced in building those institutions and giving them permanence and legitimacy. The return to civilian government under the Fourth Republic in May 1999 meant a switch from rule by military decree to rule by elected bodies with constitutional powers, but the prospects for civilian government in Nigeria still depend in large part on the extent to which its institutions can develop roots and overcome the structural problems that have so long plagued Nigerian society. No civilian government has yet lasted more than a few years; it will take a combination of luck, political will, and a massive effort on the part of Nigerians to set aside their differences if the Fourth Republic is to last.

THE CONSTITUTION

Reflecting the uncertainties surrounding its political development, Nigeria has had seven constitutions since World War II. The first two (named for the British colonial administrators under whom they were drawn up) were the Richards constitution of 1947 and the Macpherson constitution of 1951. Both were flawed because Nigerians had little say in their creation and because they encouraged regionalism without giving the regions much power. The third constitution—the Lyttleton constitution of 1954—was drawn up with the input and support of Nigerians. It took powers away from the central government, created a federal system of government, and paved the way to self-government in 1956. It was then replaced by the independence constitution of 1960, which was amended in 1963 to declare Nigeria a republic and to replace the British monarch with a Nigerian head of state.

The fifth constitution was published in 1979, paving the way for the creation of the Second Republic, which was based on the American model rather than the Westminster model. It was suspended with the return to military government in 1983, and work was begun by the Babangida administration in 1988 on a replacement, in preparation for the creation of the Third Republic. Early discussions were sidetracked by a controversy about whether Islamic law should be included, with northern Muslims reviving demands that Nigeria be declared an Islamic republic. When it became clear that no agreement would be reached, Babangida banned further discussion of the issue, and the constitution of the Third Republic was finally promulgated in May 1989. But before it could be put into force it was suspended by the Abacha regime and was replaced in May 1999 by the constitution of the Fourth Republic, the seventh Nigerian constitution in 39 years.

The new document borrows heavily from its predecessors. Unlike the U.S. Constitution, which is full of ambiguities, gaps, and generalities and whose interpretation is left up to the U.S. Supreme Court and its lower courts, the Nigerian constitution is both long and detailed, considerable effort having been made by its authors to cover as many different eventualities as possible. It has 320 articles (the U.S. Constitution has just 7), several schedules, lengthy lists outlining the policy responsibilities of the different branches of government, and—just in case anyone has any doubts—includes a glossary defining the meaning of terms such as *authority*, *decision*, *government*, and *law*. Although there are many similarities with the U.S. model, it also contains several features that reflect the peculiar problems and needs of a country like Nigeria:

- National unity is a key theme, emphasized in the opening paragraphs with the argument that Nigeria is an "indivisible and indissoluble" state. The duties of the state include fostering a feeling of belonging and involvement so that "loyalty to the nation shall override sectional loyalties." Remarkably, the state is also made responsible for encouraging "inter-marriage among persons from different places of origin, or of different religions, ethnic or linguistic associations or ties." It is hard to imagine an idea like this being accepted in the United States.

- Like its predecessors, it includes elements designed to make sure that the national government does not become dominated by any one region or ethnic group. For example, the president must win at least 25 percent of the vote in two-thirds of Nigeria's 36 states, and the federal government must include ministers drawn equally from all 36 of those states.

- Seven articles discuss citizenship, and thirteen articles outline the fundamental rights of citizens. These include some unusual ideas. For example, torture, slavery, forced labor, "corrupt practices," and abuse of power are all outlawed; privacy of homes and phone conversations is guaranteed; and—going well beyond the U.S. Constitution—discrimination on the grounds of "place of origin, sex, religion, status, ethnic, or linguistic association or ties" is prohibited.

Nigeria's approach to constitutions is a good example of **constitutional engineering.** Constitutions work best if they are based on political and social realities, but in Nigeria's case the more recent constitutions have been based not only on ignoring those realities but on actively trying to change political behavior. For example, the committee appointed to write the 1979 constitution was told by the military government to draw up a document that would eliminate "cut-throat political competition," develop consensus politics, promote national interests over regional interests, and eliminate the excessive centralization of power.[7]

THE EXECUTIVE: PRESIDENT

Like almost all Britain's former African colonies, Nigeria entered independence with a Westminster-style parliamentary system: The legislature and the executive were fused, the government was headed by a prime minister and Council of Ministers, and the British monarch was head of state. Former British colonies with predominantly white populations such as Canada, Australia, and New Zealand still recognize the British monarch as head of state and still use the parliamentary system. By contrast, most predominantly nonwhite former colonies—such as India and Pakistan—rejected the monarchy. In 1963 Nigeria followed suit by becoming a republic and replacing the monarch with a nonexecutive presidency elected by parliament for a 5-year term.

As it made plans to switch back to civilian government in 1979 under the Second Republic, Nigeria went a step further by abandoning the Westminster system of having a prime minister appointed out of the legislature, and instead adopted an elected executive presidency along American lines, sharing powers with a separately elected legislature. Many other African states have done the same thing, and in many cases have seen the evolution of executives with substantial (even authoritarian) powers. What are the attractions of the presidential model for a country like Nigeria?

TABLE 8.2

Postindependence Leaders of Nigeria

Date	Head of government	Ethnicity/ region	Religion	Type of government	Reason for losing office
1960	Sir Alhaji Abubakar Tafawa Balewa	Hausa-Fulani	Muslim	Civilian	Killed in coup
1966	(Jan) Johnson Aguyi-Ironsi	Igbo	Christian	Military	Killed in coup
1966	(July) Yakubu Gowon	Middle Belt	Christian	Military	Coup
1975	Murtala Muhammed	Hausa-Fulani	Muslim	Military	Killed in coup
1976	Olusegun Obasanjo	Yoruba	Christian	Military	Retired
1979	Shehu Shagari	Hausa-Fulani	Muslim	Civilian	
1983	Shehu Shagari	Hausa-Fulani	Muslim	Civilian	Coup
1984	Muhammadu Buhari	Hausa-Fulani	Muslim	Military	Coup
1985	Ibrahim Babangida	Middle Belt	Muslim	Military	"Retired"
1993	(Aug) Ernest Shonekan	Yoruba	Christian	Interim	"Resigned"
1993	(Nov) Sani Abacha	Northerner	Muslim	Military	Died in office
1998	Abdulsalam Abubakar	Northerner	Muslim	Interim	Retired
1999	Olusegun Obasanjo	Yoruba	Christian	Civilian	
2003	Olusegun Obasanjo	Yoruba	Christian	Civilian	

- One explanation is that the Westminster model depends on a nonpolitical head of state, a role that was played until independence by the colonial administration itself, which was anything but nonpolitical.[8] The idea of a neutral figurehead was undermined from the outset, but independence left Nigeria without a strong colonial overlord, so a strong executive presidency was created to fill the void.

- Another argument is that the Westminster model is based on multiparty competition and is too divisive for a society as ethnically diverse as Nigeria. By contrast, the American model forces the candidates running for election to the presidency to draw support from across the country, and encourages political parties with different ethnic or religious bases to work together.

- A third argument is that the fusion of executive and legislature in the Westminster system increases the likelihood of a single political party dominating both branches of government. If that party has its base in a particular ethnic group, then that group will dominate government. With the American model, on the other hand, there is more chance of the president coming from one party and the legislature being dominated by another, thereby dividing power and preventing dominance by one ethnic group.

PEOPLE IN POLITICS

OLUSEGUN OBASANJO

AP/Wide World Photos

The election of Olusegun Obasanjo as the new civilian president of Nigeria in 1999 was generally welcomed inside and outside the country. He had a strong, positive reputation both among the elites within Nigerian politics and among key foreign governments, based mainly on his record as military leader of Nigeria in 1976–1979 and on the fact that he had been the first African military leader voluntarily to hand power back to civilians.

Born in 1937, Obasanjo is a deeply religious Christian Yoruba who first came to national attention as the military officer who accepted the surrender of Biafran forces following the Nigerian civil war of 1967–1970. Six years later, following the assassination of Brigadier Murtala Muhammed, Obasanjo took over the leadership of Nigeria. Following the creation of the Second Republic, he declared that he was retiring from politics and set up a pig and poultry farm in his home state in southwestern Nigeria. He nonetheless kept in touch with developments in national politics and was once considered as a possible candidate for the post of secretary-general of the United Nations.

During the Abacha years, Obasanjo became increasingly critical of the abuses of power by the military and was imprisoned in 1995 along with several dozen others on charges of plotting a coup. He was released in June 1998 following the death of Abacha. Although he initially refused to reenter politics, he changed his mind and won the People's Democratic party nomination for the presidential election in early 1999, winning the presidential election in May. Distrusted by some for being too close to the military officers who governed Nigeria in the 1980s and 1990s, he was seen by others as having the credentials of honesty and international statesmanship that were considered critical to ensuring that the Fourth Republic had the best chance of succeeding. Much like Boris Yeltsin, Obasanjo came to power at a critical juncture in the development of his country. (He is shown on the left in the photograph, as the reigns of office are handed over by the military at his inauguration.)

He moved quickly to rid the country of corrupt government officials and to put the economy back on a stable footing, and he set up a seven-member panel to look into three decades of the abuse of power by military leaders. Previously a champion of active government, he now argued instead that he wanted to put the private sector at the heart of Nigeria's revival and launched a halting program of privatization. But he was also widely criticized—at home and abroad—for his failure to control civil conflict, for his use of the army to put down unrest, and for his unwillingness to criticize the army's excessive use of force. Despite a first term marked by political, economic, and social unrest, Obasanjo was able to fight off challenges to his leadership and was elected for a second 4-year term in April 2003.

Nigeria continues to follow the American model. Under the Fourth Republic, the president is elected by direct universal vote to a 4-year term in office, renewable once, and there is a clear division of powers among the executive, legislative, and judicial arms. For example, the president has the power of appointment, but all senior nominations must be approved by the Senate. He cannot declare war without the approval of the National Assembly. He has the power of veto, but this can be overturned by the National Assembly with a two-thirds majority.

The president governs in conjunction with a Government of the Federation, consisting of senior government ministers. The number of ministers—and their portfolios—can be changed by the president without Senate approval, but there must be at least one minister from each of Nigeria's 36 states, and all ministers must be confirmed in office by the Senate. The requirement that every state be represented in the cabinet has stretched the possibilities for the number of meaningful portfolios, so along with important jobs, such as commerce, foreign affairs, defense, and justice, there are less important ones, such as the ministries of aviation, power and steel, solid minerals, and sport.

Nigeria also has a vice president, who would step into the presidency in the event of the death, resignation, or removal of the incumbent. Again with an eye to ensuring that no one ethnic group dominates government, the constitution requires that vice presidents come from a different part of the country than the president. Obasanjo chose as his vice president Abubakar Atiku, a Muslim northerner. Obasanjo's opponent in the 2003 presidential election—Muhammadu Buhari—was a Muslim northerner whose running mate who was an Igbo from southeast Nigeria.

In both the United States and Nigeria, the formal rules of government say nothing about the role of personality. The true nature of both presidencies is determined by the ability (or inability) of incumbents to manipulate public opinion and the legislative and judicial branches to achieve their goals. Nigerian leaders in particular have had to use the force of their personalities to promote national unity. Military leaders have been helped by their ability to suspend the constitution, rule by decree, and use the military as a means of control, and civilian leaders have been helped by being the only politicians elected from a national constituency. The Second Republic ultimately failed not because it was structurally flawed but because President Shehu Shagari was unable to provide the leadership needed to deal with corruption and ethnic conflict. The success of the Fourth Republic has depended in large part on the ability of Olusegun Obasanjo to lead and to avoid repeating the mistakes of the Shagari administration. Unfortunately, he has often used authoritarian methods to keep control.

THE LEGISLATURE: NATIONAL ASSEMBLY

Nigeria has had more experience with executive politics than with legislative politics. Most of its leadership has come from presidents, whether military or civilian, and during the relatively rare periods of civilian government, legislatures have been trampled in the rush to win control of the only real office that counts, the presidency. During the First Republic, Nigeria followed the Westminster model, with legislative power vested in a bicameral Federal Legislature. The lower House of Representatives had 312 members, elected for 5-year terms from single-member districts with roughly equal populations. However, it did little more than rubber-stamp govern-

The National Assembly building in Nigeria's capital city, Abuja. Nigeria does not have a strong tradition of civilian government, and during periods of military government the halls of the National Assembly have usually been empty. Until civilian politics develops roots, the Assembly building will continue to stand as a monumental symbol of the problems of government in Nigeria.

ment policy decisions and was further weakened by the fact that it met for fewer than 30 days every year. There was also a 54-member Senate elected by the federal and regional governments and consisting of tribal chiefs and elders.

Under the Fourth Republic, Nigeria has a bicameral National Assembly based on the model of the U.S. Congress, with powers to check and balance those of the executive.

Senate

Representing the states, the Senate has 109 members: three each from Nigeria's 36 states and one from the Federal Capital Territory of Abuja. Unlike the United States, where U.S. senators represent their entire state, Nigeria has opted for a system in which each state is divided into three senatorial districts, and the candidate who wins the most votes in each district is declared the winner. Senators serve fixed and renewable terms of 4 years, and they all come up for reelection at the same time. The Senate is presided over by a president elected from among its members and who is third in line to the presidency of Nigeria after the vice president.

House of Representatives

Representing the people, the lower chamber has 360 members elected on a single-member, winner-take-all basis from districts of roughly equal population size and is presided over by a Speaker elected by the House. As with the Senate, members are elected for fixed 4-year and renewable terms, and elections to both chambers are held at the same time. In line with the principle of separation of powers, any member of the National Assembly who is appointed to a position in government or wins a seat in state or local government must vacate his National Assembly seat.

Both chambers must meet for at least 6 months each calendar year; have the same powers to initiate, change, and approve legislation; and normally conduct all their business in English. Reflecting concerns about Nigeria's problems with corruption, the constitution notes that before taking up their seats, all National Assembly members must declare their assets and liabilities and must also declare any pecuniary interests they might have in any matters coming up for discussion. The constitution also bars anyone from becoming a member of the Assembly who is a member of a secret society, who is "adjudged to be a lunatic," or who is "declared to be of unsound mind."

THE JUDICIARY: SUPREME COURT

Through all the changes in Nigerian politics since 1960, only one institution has remained relatively stable: the judiciary. Although Nigerian military governments have suspended political parties, abolished civilian political institutions, and sometimes resorted to the use of military tribunals, they have usually allowed the courts to continue functioning, in some respects using them to underpin the return to civilian rule. During the Second Republic, the judiciary played exactly the same role as that played by the Supreme Court in the United States: acting as guardian and interpreter of the constitution and interceding in disputes between states or between states and the federal government. This is also its role in the Fourth Republic.

The Supreme Court has 15 members overseen by a chief justice, nominated by the president, and either confirmed by the Senate or approved by a judicial commission. Below the Supreme Court is a system of federal and state courts of appeal and high courts, and a separate system of *sharia* **courts** to deal with issues of Islamic law (for more details, see Part V). Since they were created in 2000, *sharia* courts have been controversial. Restricted to 12 northern Nigerian states, they deal only with matters of family law and petty crime, but southern Nigerians worry that their work poses a threat to civil rights across the country. Worldwide media attention was drawn during 2002 to the case of Amina Lawal, a woman who was convicted in a *sharia* court of having committed adultery and giving birth to an illegitimate daughter. In line with Islamic law, she was sentenced to be buried up to her waist and stoned to death. She initially accepted the sentence but then appealed her case to a higher court after lawyers took up the case. She was not expected to win unless the federal government intervened directly, but it was unwilling to do this, for fear of upsetting political sensibilities in northern Nigeria.

SUBNATIONAL GOVERNMENT

The question of federal-state relations was at the core of the early political development of the United States, and it took 13 years of confederation before the original states agreed to form a federation. Even then, states' rights were jealously guarded, and there were doubts that the union would last. Tensions between the North and the South led to civil war in 1861, and as recently as the 1950s violence broke out again over the issue of desegregation. Even today, interstate competition continues over the issue of federal government subsidies.

In Nigeria, federal-state tensions have been driven by ethnic hostilities and jealousies, which boiled over with the end of the colonial hegemony in 1960. During its 40 years of independence, Nigeria has seen a civil war, the breakdown of civilian po-

FIGURE 8.1

Internal Boundary Changes in Nigeria

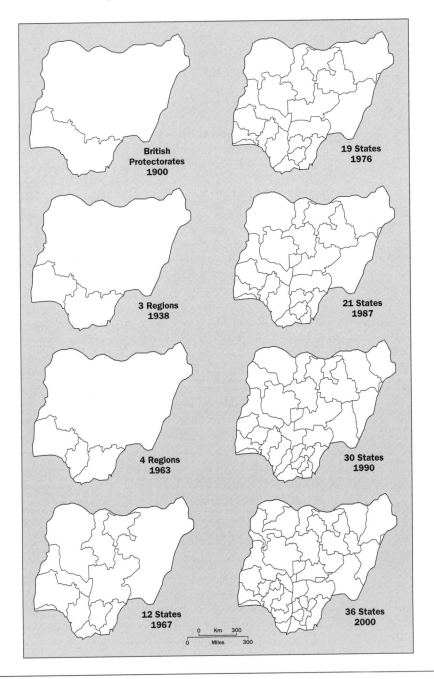

litical systems into ethnic and religious rivalry, and an almost routine pattern of civil violence. In their attempts to reduce regionalism, Nigerian governments have changed internal boundaries so often that the map of Nigeria has frequently had to be redrawn.

The problems arguably date back to colonial times and to Britain's decision to rule Nigeria first as two separate territories, and then as three regions. Because southerners have always been worried about the power of the predominantly Muslim north (which has produced seven of Nigeria's 11 political leaders), successive governments have divided Nigeria into ever smaller local government units: A fourth region was created in 1963, the four regions were replaced by 12 states in 1967, and the number of states was subsequently increased in increments to its present total of 36 (see Figure 8.1). Although the multistate structure has been described as an attempt to break up the power of the major ethnic groups and to make sure that none of the states is dominated by a single ethnic group, the government of the Fourth Republic has still had to work hard to prevent regionalism interfering with attempts to build a unified Nigerian state (and has not done a very good job so far).

Under the Fourth Republic, every state is governed by an elected governor serving renewable 4-year terms and a unicameral House of Assembly. The House of Assembly has between three and four times as many seats as the state has in the national House of Representatives—it must have at least 24 and no more than 40. Governors have the power of veto, but this can be overruled by a two-thirds majority in the House of Assembly.

THE MILITARY

Of the nine countries discussed in this book, Nigeria is the only one in which the military plays an important political role. Whereas the political influence of the military in Mexico and Egypt has declined, the Nigerian military has been centrally involved in politics from the outset, and there are few signs of it being marginalized. Weaknesses in the conduct of civilian politics have combined with the zest for power of some of Nigeria's military leaders to ensure that in its first 43 years of independence (1960–2003), Nigeria spent just 14 years under civilian rule. It saw nine changes of leadership, five of which were violent and two of which involved the overthrow of a civilian government by the military. The Shagari government was returned to office in 1983 through a popular vote, but in more than 40 years, no civilian president has yet been removed from office through a popular vote.

Given the divisions in African civil society, the military is often the only institution with any kind of strength and continuity. In Nigeria, only one coup (in 1976) was an attempt by a deposed regime to win back power; most of the others were responses to political crises, and most were initially welcomed by Nigerians. In every case, the military stepped in supposedly to restore order, and although Nigeria's military governments routinely suspended the constitution and abolished civilian political institutions, they allowed the judiciary, the courts, the bureaucracy, the police, and public and private businesses to carry on as usual[9] (although "business as usual" typically meant continued corruption and incompetence).

Not surprisingly, Nigeria's military governments have been centralized and hierarchical and have permitted few significant alternative sources of power. Although most Nigerian military leaders have generally shied away from autocracy, they have never pretended to be democratic, arguing that the breakdown of civilian government has demanded an authoritative response. Their definitions of authority have varied:[10]

- The Buhari regime (1983–1985) decided that military-style discipline was the best way of correcting Nigeria's problems, so orderly queues were enforced, the flying of the national flag in public places was mandated, all Nigerians had to stay at home one day per month to help clean up their neighborhoods, and any bureaucrats who arrived late for work were forced to do the frog-jump (jumping up and down in a squatting position with their hands on their ears).

- Concerned about the possibilities of a countercoup, the Babangida regime (1985–1993) in 1990 ordered the execution of 69 army officers, each tried before a military tribunal.

- The Abacha regime (1993–1998), undoubtedly the most despotic and corrupt of all Nigeria's military governments, forced confessions by beating dissidents, hanging them upside down, or starving them; refused public trials for political prisoners; and arranged for convicted criminals to be shot to death without the right of appeal. Abacha's record was so extreme that, ironically, it offers some hope for the future: it gave the military such a bad name that the prospects of a return to military government are weaker now than they have ever been.

In order to rule, Nigeria's military governments have created their own subculture of administrative institutions, which paralleled civilian institutions but were based on rule by decree. Early military administrations (1966–1979) governed through two bodies:

- A Supreme Military Council (SMC), made up of selected senior officers and which functioned as the principle policymaking forum

- A Federal Executive Council, made up of senior federal bureaucrats and which was responsible for implementing the decisions of the SMC

During the Gowon years (1966–1975), Nigeria was effectively ruled by a joint military-bureaucratic government, with civil servants achieving so much influence over the SMC that many were compulsorily retired after the 1975 coup.[11] The Muhammed regime (1975–1976) added three new bodies:

- A National Council of Ministers, which functioned like a cabinet

- A Council of States, consisting of the military governors of the then 12 states and charged with overseeing federal-state relations

- A National Security Organization (NSO), charged with controlling "opponents of the state," but which became a quasi-political organization that intimidated the critics and opponents of the Muhammed and Obasanjo regimes[12]

During the second military era (1983–1999), all five institutions were initially revived, the only substantial difference being that during the Buhari regime the NSO was given greater latitude, and Nigeria came dangerously close to becoming a police state. (The Buhari regime overstated the degree of Nigeria's problems and rapidly degenerated from being seen as the provider of salvation to being at war with its own people.[13]) Upon taking power in 1985, Babangida changed the name of the SMC to the Armed Forces Ruling Council (AFRC) and expanded its membership to 28, all of them military officers. He went on to split the NSO into three agencies responsible for national defense, overseas intelligence gathering, and internal security, and he created bodies responsible for public security and the territorial integrity of Nigeria.

Abacha replaced the AFRC with a 26-member Provisional Ruling Council, which was different from its predecessor only in name. Like all military leaders, Abacha was careful to watch out for opposition and to prevent anyone building too much power or offering too much opposition to his policies. In April 1996, for example, he dismissed the heads of the army and the air force, allegedly for failure to support some of his more hard-line policies. However, it was clear by then that Abacha was one of the exceptions to the general rule of military leaders who claimed that they had no long-term aspirations to hold onto power. He used the governing institutions to strengthen his own grip on power and to make sure that when Nigeria returned to civilian rule, it would do so under his control.

REPRESENTATION AND PARTICIPATION

Nigerians take politics seriously, sometimes *too* seriously, given how often their disagreements lead to ethnic and religious conflict. Urban Nigerians tend to be more politically active than those in rural areas, partly because they are closer to the centers of power, partly because of their higher levels of education and standards of living, and partly because the more unscrupulous among them have the most to gain from abusing power. Rural Nigerians have neither the personal mobility nor the access to the channels of participation or communication available to urban Nigerians. Many also value local and community politics over national politics and come under the influence of traditional ethnic and clan leaders.

ELECTIONS AND THE ELECTORAL SYSTEM

The electoral system of the Fourth Republic is fairly simple and straightforward. From local councils to the federal presidency, all elected officials win office through a winner-take-all vote, and all officials serve the same 4-year terms, with the president alone being limited to two terms. The last round of elections was held in 2003, beginning with legislative, gubernatorial, and presidential elections in April and finishing with regional legislative elections in May.

There are no primaries in the Nigerian system; the candidates for the presidency from each of the major parties are instead chosen by a vote among senior party members. The successful candidate must win at least half the vote; otherwise a second round is called between the two top-placed candidates in the first round. Although Obasanjo claimed to have won the nomination for his party in 2003 relatively fairly, questions were raised about his opponent, former military dictator Muhammadu Buhari. Twelve candidates contested the nomination for the opposition All Nigeria People's party, but 11 either withdrew or failed to attend the nominating convention, and Buhari won with 4,328 votes in his favor and just 30 against.

To ensure that the successful candidate wins a broad base of support at the presidential election itself, he must win a majority of all votes cast and at least 25 percent of the vote in at least two-thirds of Nigeria's 36 states. Similarly, state governors must win at least 25 percent of the vote in at least two-thirds of the local government districts within their state. In the event that no candidates meet the terms of this formula, runoff elections are held between the two top finishers, and if neither of them meets these terms, a third runoff is held that requires a simple majority for the winner.

Elections in Nigeria have traditionally been overseen by government commissions, which have come under a variety of different names; the body currently responsible is the Independent Election Commission. Like its predecessors, its job is to oversee the electoral process and ensure that vote rigging and intimidation are minimized, and—on the basis of the census—to redraw electoral districts every 10 years as necessary.

POLITICAL PARTIES

Nigerian party politics has had a checkered history. The evolution of the party system has three times been interrupted by the intervention of the military, which in each case banned existing parties and insisted on the creation of completely new parties free of allegiances to regions and ethnic groups. Few parties have been able to develop a truly national platform, most have been built on regional differences rather than ideological differences, and none has so far lasted more than a few years.

Phase I: Before and After Independence (1944–1966)

The roots of the Nigerian party system can be traced to the early 20th century nationalist movement. Among its leaders was Herbert Macaulay (1884–1946), often described as the "father of Nigerian nationalism." Macaulay came under the influence of the Pan-African movement, which met at periodic congresses in Europe and the United States between 1919 and 1945. (The first leader of the movement was the American W. E. B. Dubois.) Nationalism was given an early boost by the foundation of the National Congress of British West Africa, whose first meeting in 1920 was attended by delegates from Nigeria, Gold Coast (now Ghana), Sierra Leone, and Gambia. In 1923 Macaulay founded the Nigerian National Democratic party, a Lagos party that was active until the late 1930s, espousing the cause of African freedom from colonialism.

Party formation moved into a new phase in the 1930s with the return to Nigeria of a growing number of students educated abroad, where they had met one another and been exposed to ideas of democracy and self-determination. The most celebrated was Nnamdi "Zik" Azikiwe (1904–1996), an Igbo who joined with Macaulay in 1944 in founding the first party with a national platform, the National Council of Nigeria and the Cameroons (or NCNC, which later changed its name to the National Convention of Nigerian Citizens). The NCNC led the opposition to the 1947 colonial constitution, and Azikiwe developed such a strong following that *Zikism* became synonymous for many with Nigerian nationalism, even though the NCNC drew most of its support from eastern Nigeria.

Meanwhile, Obafemi "Awo" Awolowo (1909–1987) founded the Yoruba-based Action Group (AG) in 1948, and northern interests were represented by the Northern People's Congress (NPC), founded in 1949 and led by Alhaji Sir Ahmadu Bello, the religious leader (or Sardauna) of Sokoto in northwest Nigeria. All three claimed to reject tribalism, but they all swept their respective states in the 1951 regional elections, beginning a tradition of close identification between party, region, and ethnic group.

The 1959 federal elections were contested by the same three parties. When none won a clear majority, the NPC and NCNC agreed to form a coalition. NPC leader Ahmadu Bello would have been expected to become prime minister of Nigeria, but he opted to remain prime minister of the Northern Region, feeling that it was a more important job. In his place, the deputy leader of the NPC, Alhaji Sir Abubakar Tafawa Balewa, became the first prime minister of Nigeria, and AG leader Awolowo became leader of the opposition.

Many other smaller parties were also formed, but it was with this tripartite NCNC-AG-NPC system that Nigeria entered independence. Hopes for the perpetuation of a multiparty democracy rapidly disappeared as the Action Group became bogged down by internal divisions and as a crisis developed over the 1962 census and the 1964 federal elections, when northern and southern parties accused each other of rigging the results and the NPC refused even to take part. The chaos that followed led to the January 1966 military coup and the banning of all political parties.

Phase II: The Second Republic (1979–1983)

During the preparations for the return to civilian government in the late 1970s, the Obasanjo regime set out to avoid ethnic politics by laying down detailed rules on party formation. Membership had to be open to all Nigerians, party names and emblems could not reflect regional or ethnic interests, and party headquarters could be situated only in Lagos, the federal capital. A Federal Election Commission (FEDECO) was created to screen all parties, to make sure they met the terms of the new rules, and to oversee the elections. Nineteen associations applied to be recognized as parties, of which only five were allowed to contest the 1979 elections. Despite this, the party system once again boiled down to a tripartite contest strongly reminiscent of the First Republic.

The 1979 presidential election was won by Shehu Shagari of the National Party of Nigeria (NPN), which was seen by many as the successor to the NPC. The NPN also won a plurality in the new National Assembly and the State Assemblies.

Meanwhile, Obafemi Awolowo came a close second in the presidential election at the head of the Unity Party of Nigeria (UPN), which looked remarkably like his old Action Group and was ideologically to the left of the NPN. Finally, the spirit of the NCNC was revived in the Nigerian People's party (NPP), which ran Nnamdi Azikiwe as its presidential candidate.

In the lead-up to the 1983 elections, the NPN was accused of using FEDECO to manipulate the election, of changing the timetable to its own advantage, and of refusing to register new parties. The new electoral register drawn up for the election showed a hard-to-believe 34 percent increase in the number of voters, and the elections themselves were marred by charges of abuse and cheating. When Shagari won reelection with a greatly increased share of the vote (up from 34 percent in 1979 to nearly 48 percent in 1983), the credibility of the new administration suffered a fatal blow. Three months later, it was ousted by a military coup.

Phase III: The Third Republic (1989–1993)

Preparations for the return to civilian rule under the Third Republic closely paralleled those for the Second Republic. In a new attempt to break the regionalism of political parties, the Babangida regime prevented anyone with experience in politics from running for election, hoping (as he put it) to replace **"old brigade"** politicians with a "new breed" of leaders driven by ideology and unencumbered by the regional ties that had caused so many problems for earlier civilian governments. Announcing his transition plans in 1987, Babangida said he would allow only two parties to contest the new elections. FEDECO was replaced by the National Electoral Commission (NEC), to which 13 political groups applied during 1989 for registration as parties. They were required to show that they had offices and support in every Nigerian state and that membership was open to all, regardless of race or religion. Babangida himself had little respect for parties, describing them as "natural grounds for the idle and illiterate who over the years have failed to qualify for any reputable profession."

The NEC concluded that six of the 13 groups might qualify. But amid suspicions that most were being manipulated behind the scenes by former politicians, Babangida rejected all their applications and instructed his government to draw up manifestos for two new parties, the Social Democratic party (SDP) and the National Republican Convention (NRC), "one a little to the left, and the other a little to the right of center," as he described them. Neither was allowed to depart from Babangida's free-market economic policies, and he even went so far as to provide each with offices, official colors, and election symbols. The two new parties almost immediately developed regional biases; the NRC had a northern tilt, attracting former supporters of Shagari's NPN, while the SDP had a southern tilt, deriving its support from Yoruba and Igbo areas.

The results of local elections in December 1990 seemed to allay fears of a continuation of regionalism. Only 20 percent of voters turned out, but many genuinely made choices between competing candidates, each party won at least one-third of the vote in most states, and each party won local councils outside their region. In October 1991, state gubernatorial primaries were held, but once again it was suspected that old brigade politicians were pulling the strings. The following month, the NEC canceled the results of primaries in 13 states because of suspicions about manipulation, arrested several old brigade politicians, and arranged new primaries in the affected states.

In December 1991 elections were held for state assemblies and governors. To prevent ballot rigging, secret votes were not allowed; instead, voters at each polling station had to line up behind photographs of their preferred candidates. They were then counted and the results announced immediately. The elections passed off peaceably, with about 20 million Nigerians turning out to vote. The SDP won the governorship and state assemblies in 14 states, including 3 in the north; the NRC won the governorship and state assemblies in 13 states, including 6 in the south; and in 3 states, the NRC won the governorship and the SDP the assembly.

The results seemed to bode well for Babangida's attempts to create parties with national appeal, although optimism was tempered by the emergence of factions within both parties, which suggested that they might eventually break down into regional subparties. Among the most radical of the factions was the People's Front, led by the SDP's vice presidential candidate, Babagana Kingibe; it was the object of particular criticism for being manipulated by the old brigade in the lead-up to the state elections. Presidential primaries were held in August 1992, and contested by 23 candidates, but the NEC declared that nearly all of them had cheated and ordered that new primaries be held.

The presidential elections, finally held in June 1993, were apparently won by Moshood Abiola of the SDP. Although a Muslim, Abiola would have been the first civilian president to come from the predominantly Christian south, breaking the traditional hold on power of predominantly Muslim soldiers and civilians from the north. Babangida annulled the election amid suspicions that the NRC candidate, Bashir Tofa, had been the army's favored candidate. With the crisis that led to Babangida's resignation in August 1993, the party system once again went into suspension.

Phase IV: The Fourth Republic (1998–)

The Abacha regime convened a constitutional conference, which reported in April 1995. Its findings were not released but were thought to include a recommendation for a return to multiparty civilian politics as quickly as possible. Abacha set up a new national electoral commission, and municipal elections were held in March 1996 on a nonparty or "zero-party" basis. The seeds of new parties, meanwhile, had begun to sprout, much of the opposition to Abacha forming around the National Democratic Coalition (NADECO), formed in May 1994 and led by former state governor Michael Ajasiu. During 1996, 15 new political parties were formed to contest the 1998 elections, but 10 were immediately disqualified by the Abacha regime and it became clear that he planned to manipulate the remaining 5 to his own ends.

Following Abacha's death in 1998, the new Abubakar regime decided to wipe the slate clean and—yet again—encourage the development of a new party system. This was to be overseen by a new Independent National Electoral Commission (INEC), founded in August that year. The result was the development of three major new parties, with which Nigeria went into the elections for the government of the new Fourth Republic:

TABLE 8.3

Results of Recent Presidential Elections in Nigeria

Candidate	Party	% vote
1999		
Olusegun Obasanjo	People's Democratic Party	62.8
Olu Falae	All Nigeria People's Party/Alliance for Democracy	37.2
2003		
Olusegun Obasanjo	People's Democratic Party	61.9
Muhammadu Buhari	All Nigeria People's Party	32.2
Odemegwu Ojukwu	All People's Grand Alliance	3.3
Other		2.6

- **People's Democratic party (PDP).** Describing itself as a centrist party, the PDP was led mainly by veteran politicians, including several former military officers brought together by their mutual opposition to the Abacha regime. It did well in local elections in 1998, prompting the two opposition parties to form an electoral pact. The PDP then also did well in elections to the National Assembly in 1999, and its candidate Olusegun Obasanjo rounded off the results by winning the presidency with a solid 62.8 percent share of the vote. Its successes were repeated in 2003.

- **All Nigeria People's party (ANPP).** The second largest party and therefore the major opposition, the ANPP took moderately conservative positions and was backed by wealthy businesspeople brought together by their support of Sani Abacha and his plans to become the elected president of Nigeria—hence the jibe by its opponents that it should be called the Abacha People's party. The pact formed with the Alliance for Democracy was one mainly of convenience, given that the latter is a moderately liberal party. The ANPP/AD ticket for the 1999 presidential election was won by Olu Falae, a bureaucrat and former finance minister who—ironically—was jailed by Sani Abacha.

- **Alliance for Democracy (AD).** The AD was a regional party with a firm base of support among the Yoruba in southwestern Nigeria, where it won local and state elections in six states. It very quickly became embroiled in controversy, however, when members of the party in the Lagos state legislature broke into two factions supporting different leaders. When they began throwing chairs and tables at each other during a meeting, the police had to be called in to restore order.

In the lead-up to the 2003 elections, there was no certainty that Obasanjo would be nominated once again as the candidate for the PDP. Nigeria had become more democratic under his tenure, but economic problems persisted, thousands of people had died during his term in factional violence and conflict of various kinds (see

HOW MUCH IS A HUMAN LIFE WORTH?

Imagine if, during the 4-year-term of an American president, several thousand people were killed in the United States in a combination of religious and racial conflict, manmade disasters, and army massacres. Imagine some of those massacres taking place after the president himself had sent in troops to restore order, and the president refusing even to issue an apology. Imagine the political and legal ramifications, and the nonstop media analysis. Imagine the chances of that president being reelected.

Consider, then, that an estimated 10,000 people died in Nigeria in violence of one kind or another during the first 4-year term of President Olusegun Obasanjo (1999–2003). Examples include the following:

- In November 1999, after 12 policemen were killed in the Niger Delta region, Obasanjo dispatched tanks and soldiers to restore order, and several thousand people were massacred. Obasanjo refused to apologize, instead promoting the local army commander.
- In June–July 2001, fighting broke out between two ethnic groups in the south central state of Benue, during which perhaps as many

as 200 people were killed and 50,000 displaced from their homes. In October, after 19 of their colleagues involved in putting down the fighting were killed, Nigerian soldiers went on a 3-day rampage through local villages, killing at least 300 people.[14]

- In September 2001, as many as 500 people were killed and 900 injured in the city of Jos after Muslims and Christians attacked one another with axes, clubs, and machetes. President Obasanjo described the killings as a "disgrace."
- In January 2002, munitions carelessly stored at a Lagos army barracks exploded. People living near the barracks panicked and many ran toward a nearby canal, where they were trampled or drowned. The official death toll was put at 700, but unofficial estimates went as high as 2,000.

The international press pays remarkably little attention to such incidents. In Nigeria, carnage of this scale is deeply criticized, to be sure, but—remarkably—it was not enough to prevent the reelection of Olusegun Obasanjo in 2003. What does this tell us about the relative value of human life in different societies?

Political Debates, above), and Obasanjo had lost much of the support from the Muslim north that had won him the presidency in 1999. Many political leaders also felt that it was time for the election of a president from another part of the country, and Obasanjo was challenged by a former vice president, an easterner named Alex Ekwueme. But Obasanjo safely won the PDP nomination.

According to the Independent Election Commission, some 60 million Nigerians were eligible to vote in 2003 and were faced with choosing among 22 registered political parties. Given the low levels of literacy in Nigeria, each party had to be represented on the ballot by a symbol (much like the arrangement in India). The elections were a major test for the credibility of the government because, unlike the military, no Nigerian civilian government had *ever* organized successful elections.

Reflecting the continuing influence of the military even over the civilian political process, four of the presidential candidates were former Army generals: They included Obasanjo himself, his chief opponent—Buhari of the ANPP—and even the former Biafran rebel leader Odemegwu Ojukwu. Meanwhile, rumors were rife that a fifth former military leader—Ibrahim Babangida—was using his money and influence behind the scenes to influence the outcome of the election. Despite the usual charges of fraud and the usual violence that accompanies Nigerian elections, Obasanjo was elected to a second term in a process regarded as relatively fair.

LOCAL AND TRADITIONAL POLITICS

In their attempts to achieve a balance between state and federal government, the United States and Nigeria have much in common. Tip O'Neill, a one-time Speaker of the U.S. House of Representatives, once famously quipped that "all politics are local." However, given the repeated failures of national government in Nigeria, the importance of ethnic allegiances, and the identification of many Nigerians with their local community, local politics has much greater significance in Nigeria than is the case in the United States. It not only revolves around the elected members of local and state assemblies but is given another dimension by the role of traditional leaders.

As a colonial power, Britain strengthened the position of traditional leaders in many of its colonies by ruling through them; the result in Nigeria is that traditional leaders still have much local influence. Nowhere is this more clear than in the **caliphate of Sokoto.** Created in the 19th century, the caliphate replaced the many city-states that had existed for centuries in what is now northern Nigeria and brought together emirates from the different ethnic groups. The caliphate still has its own administrative structure, which coexists with that of federal Nigeria. The leader is the sultan, responsible for the administration of Islamic law, enforcing orthodox Islamic practice, and supervising local taxes.

As happens in many tribal units elsewhere in West Africa, Nigeria's sultans are appointed by a selection council that operates on the basis of consensus to appoint a successor acceptable to the other contenders and to the community. Each has a chief political advisor known as a **sardauna;** among the most influential sardaunas of this century was Ahmadu Bello (1909–1966).[15] Showing how traditional and modern politics often overlap, Bello founded the Northern People's Congress and became prime minister of the Northern region before being murdered during the January 1966 coup. A recent sultan of Sokoto, Sheikh Ibrahim Zakzaky, said that he hoped to promote an "Islamic awakening" in Nigeria and to work toward the creation of an Islamic republic.

Although their power has been greatly reduced in the past century, traditional political units have the advantages over modern, postcolonial units of longevity, legitimacy, and deep roots in local culture.[16] By contrast, elected legislatures and competing political parties are alien and so have had trouble developing a firm foundation. Nigerian federal governments face a dilemma: Should the special place of traditional leaders in the community be exploited to extend the reach of federal government and to support programs of modernization and democratization (which might then weaken the power of traditional leaders), or should traditional leaders be bypassed and their powers reduced, thereby risking the anger of local communities and reducing the credibility and popularity of the federal government?

INTEREST GROUPS

Although politically significant interest groups are relatively rare in LDCs, Nigeria is one of the notable exceptions. It has labor unions (such as the Nigerian Railway Workers Union and the Nigerian Union of Dockworkers), employers associations (such as the various Chambers of Trade and Commerce), and more specialized interests (such as the Market Women's Association, which has long represented the interests of traders in Lagos city markets). Interest groups have a longer history of political activity than political parties; because they emerged earlier, they have persisted where parties have come and gone, and have often been more effective at articulating citizen demands in a society in which political institutions have not yet developed deep roots. At the same time, with the rise of political parties since independence, interest groups have lost some of their influence, mainly because they are seen as a threat to the power of parties and as sources of opposition.

The most consistently successful of Nigeria's interest groups are those that are ethnically or religiously based. The ethnic groups are particularly important in urban areas, where they will often be the first port of call for newcomers arriving from the rural areas in search of jobs. By helping the newcomers and earning their obligation, they also become powerful recruiting agents for political parties.

Perhaps the least successful of Nigeria's interest groups have been the labor unions, which for many years were coordinated by the Nigeria Labour Congress (NLC). The NLC only once has been able to organize a general strike (in 1964), and although many subsequent sectoral strikes have led to pay raises for workers, unions have had only fitful influence and usually have been inexpert and ineffective in negotiations.[17] The power of the unions has been further weakened by serious internal divisions within the NLC and by an economic recession that has made those with jobs unwilling to strike or confront employers. The weakness of the NLC was illustrated in mid-1994 when it called off a general strike that was to have been held in support of oil workers striking in favor of the installation of Moshood Abiola as president.

Given the stakes, competition for influence between groups representing Muslim and non-Muslim interests is perhaps greater than that of any other area of public interest. The Muslim lobby in northern Nigeria has been active in ensuring the preservation of *sharia* courts, and one group, the Islamic League, is a powerful voice for Nigerian Muslims. The Muslim lobby has also pressed Nigerian foreign-policymakers to take a pro-Islamic and pro-Arab line.

One of Ibrahim Babangida's first decisions upon taking power in 1985 was to change Nigeria's status in the international Organization of the Islamic Conference (OIC) from observer to full member. This was an important concession to the Muslim lobby, but it greatly increased the tensions between Christians and Muslims. The main aim of the OIC—which is headquartered in Saudi Arabia (see Part V)—is to promote solidarity among its 48 members. The Christian Association of Nigeria, which represents Christian interests against what it sees as the threats posed by northern Muslims, lobbied hard to prevent Nigeria from joining the OIC.

The combination of a weak party system, a prevailing lack of faith in the bureaucracy, and the failure of government to respond to the needs of the average Nigerian has produced a culture in which direct action has been commonly used to achieve change, particularly by the poorest Nigerians. In October 1998, for example, demonstrators from the Ijaw ethnic community in Nigeria's delta region, demanding more say in local government, took over local fuel pumping stations and cut off one-third of Nigeria's oil exports. Events turned tragic when a valve at a local pumping station on the pipeline carrying fuel to northern Nigeria was allegedly opened by young men to siphon off fuel, but jammed open. Hundreds of local people took the opportunity to fill buckets and bottles with fuel, and when a spark apparently caused a huge fireball to erupt from the valve, more than 700 people were killed and hundreds more were burned.

THE MEDIA

Nigeria has one of the biggest and most vibrant mass media establishments in sub-Saharan Africa. Although it was heavily controlled and censored during the military era, it has become much freer during the Fourth Republic and more than willing to publish stories critical of the government. Nigerians can choose from more than 20 daily newspapers (such as *The Guardian, The Champion, Vanguard, This Day,* and the government paper *The Daily Times*), several authoritative weekly news magazines (some with an international circulation, like *The African Concord*), and several radio and television stations; the latter include the state broadcaster—the Nigerian Television Authority (NTA)—and the commercial Degue Broadcasting Network (DBN). Nigeria also has an active book publishing industry; Western students researching African states will find most English language books written by Western scholars and published by Western presses, but most of the works on Nigerian politics are written by Nigerian scholars and published in Nigeria.

Nigeria's cultural identity and influence has meanwhile been strengthened by its juju and Afro-Beat musicians, such as King Sunny Ade and the late Fela Anikulapo-Kuti (who was arrested more than 200 times for his political activities and died of AIDS-related illness in 1997), who have developed a reputation well outside their homeland. For their part, Nigerian playwrights and novelists such as Chinua Achebe and the outspoken Nobel laureate Wole Soyinka have enhanced Nigeria's literary reputation and have occasionally used their international reputation as a platform for involvement in politics. For example, Soyinka emerged as one of Babangida's most ardent critics, noting in 1993 that Nigeria was "being wound round the finger of a master player whose mental state is seriously in question." He kept up the pressure with his 1996 book *The Open Sore of a Continent,* a diatribe in which he described Sani Abacha variously as an outlaw, a despot, and a man with "a minuscule being and matching mind, but with a gargantuan ego."[18]

A combination of widespread illiteracy, lack of the necessary funds and technology, the poor service provided by the Nigerian state telephone company, and frequent interruptions in electricity supply has meant that access to the Internet and email is still very limited in Nigeria. Most people still rely on the printed press, radio, and television for most of their political information, which has meant that they do not yet have access to the variety of sources and opinions that citizens of more technologically advanced societies enjoy.

POLICIES AND POLICYMAKING

The policymaking structures of liberal democracies are relatively stable and consistent. By contrast, these structures in Nigeria are very changeable, and since independence in 1960 have taken three forms:

- Between 1960 and 1966, policymaking structures were based on the Westminster model of a fused executive and legislature, with power divided by a federal system.
- During its periods of military government, Nigeria has been a dictatorship, with all effective decision-making power centered in the military leader and his advisors, the key institutions based around a military-bureaucratic structure, and no substantial alternative or competing sources of power.
- Now, under the Fourth Republic (as before during the Second Republic), it is based on the U.S. presidential model, with power shared at the national level among an executive president, a legislature, and an independent judiciary, and further divided between the federal government and state governments.

With all these changes, it is difficult to find any consistent patterns in the policymaking process (other than a high degree of centralization) or to pin down the rules of the process. Superficially, the structure outlined in the 1999 constitution almost exactly follows that of the United States. The powers of the federal government are shared and limited through a system of checks and balances. The presidency is supposed to provide national unity and to place national interests above those of regions or ethnic groups, the National Assembly provides both the states and the people with representation, and the Supreme Court provides a judicial check. At the state level, 36 state governments take care of local administration, represent local interests, and further limit the powers of the federal government.

However, just as in a liberal democracy, the bare outline of government overlooks many of its important nuances, and theory and practice do not always coincide. The success of Nigerian government must ultimately be measured in terms of its ability to balance the conflicting demands of the many sectors of Nigerian society, to steer a careful course through the minefield of ethnic and religious divisions, and to limit corruption and opportunism. Effective government also depends heavily on the legitimacy of the system of government. In contrast to liberal democracies, where the legitimacy of government is rarely seriously questioned, Nigerian governments have had to struggle as much with issues of their own legitimacy as with responding to the everyday needs of simply running the country.

Underlying the challenges of state-building, one of the recurring features of politics in LDCs is the existence of a political elite, which often is cut off from direct contact with the people. Nigeria has been no exception, its problems exacerbated by the relatively small pool of qualified and experienced individuals from which government and the bureaucracy can draw. Nigeria's elite tends to come mainly from three groups: educated or ambitious individuals who win influence through their own efforts (legal or otherwise), people who have won influence through traditional clan or village positions, and senior officers in the military.

The concentration of power in the hands of these elites has limited citizen access to the policy process. Members of the elites set up **patron-client relationships** with networks of political supporters who are obligated to them through the exchange of favors. This description might equally apply to the United States, Japan, and Mexico, but leaders in these countries must build a wider base of support. Also, there are many independent channels through which political views can be expressed and opposition exerted that counterbalance the accumulation of power by the elites.

In liberal democratic terms, elitism might be dismissed as working against the interests of democracy (even though every liberal democracy has its own elite). However, should liberal democratic criticisms of elitism be applied to Nigeria? Are patron-client relationships an aberration, or do they simply perpetuate traditional clan and tribal hierarchies? Whatever the case, they will continue to exist as long as education and the opportunities for the accumulation of wealth are restricted to a minority, as long as ethnic differences persist, and as long as traditional political leaders continue to have influence. Under these circumstances, policymaking in Nigeria will be based more on limited networks than on any broader notion of the "national interest."

ECONOMIC POLICY

When Nigeria became independent, there was reason to be optimistic for its economic prospects. Not only had it undergone a careful transition to self-government, but it was self-sufficient in food; had nine major exports (a good range by most African standards); had a good network of British-built roads, railroads, and harbors; and had considerable natural and human resources. To add to the optimism, major reserves of good-quality, low-sulfur oil were discovered in the 1950s, setting Nigeria on the road to becoming a major oil producer. (By 2000 it had known reserves that would last about another 25 years at existing rates of consumption and large natural gas deposits that had not yet been fully exploited.)

In the mid-1970s, prospects improved even more as the world oil price rose from about $3 per barrel to $15 per barrel. Nigerian oil exports grew rapidly, and Nigeria enjoyed a balance-of-trade surplus. Although most of the exploration and production was undertaken by foreign companies, Nigeria kept a majority shareholding in the oil industry through the state-owned Nigerian National Petroleum Corporation (NNPC) and so was able to restrict the proportion of the profits that left the country. The economy grew by about 8 percent annually, and as a member of the Organization of Petroleum Exporting Countries (OPEC), Nigeria helped engineer the oil price increases of the 1970s that resulted in huge profits for the government.

Nigeria's annual oil income grew from $400 million in 1965 to $9 billion in 1970; in 1980 it reached $26 billion. With money flowing into its coffers, the Gowon government launched the biggest development plan ever considered by an African country, planning to spend $100 billion on nothing less than transforming Nigeria from a traditional society into a modern, unified state in 5 years. The minimum wage was doubled, all civil servants were given a 60 percent pay raise, 50,000 Nigerians were sent to the United States and Europe to learn new skills, and con-

The heat, dirt, smell, chaos, and congestion of Lagos—former capital of Nigeria and still its commercial capital—is captured in this scene of a local market. Nigeria has considerable economic potential but lacks the organization and infrastructure fully to capitalize on its assets.

struction plans were announced for seven universities, three airports, 13 television stations, and a new federal capital at Abuja. The United States, the USSR, and Western Europe showed new interest in closer ties with Nigeria, which was now seen as a major regional economic power.

Then the bottom fell out of Nigeria's ambitions. OPEC unity collapsed, the price of oil fell from its all-time high of nearly $40 per barrel to $12 per barrel,[19] and Nigerian oil revenues fell from $26 billion to $10 billion between 1980 and 1983, just as its foreign debt came due. Nigeria had squandered most of its oil profits, and hopes for economic and social transformation were dashed by political instability, bad planning decisions, waste, hoarding, and profiteering. Instead of investing oil wealth in other economic sectors to prepare itself for the rainy day when the oil price would inevitably fall, the government allowed the agricultural sector to decline. In 1970, oil and cocoa accounted for nearly three-fourths of all exports. Today, oil accounts for nearly 99 percent of exports and 12 percent of GDP. Not only has Nigeria become a single-product economy, its prospects almost entirely dependent upon changes in the price of oil on the international market, but receipts from oil have proved erratic, making it impossible to predict income and to plan development. This dependence on a single valuable product is known in Nigeria and other comparable countries as "the resource curse."

During the 1980s, Nigeria went from boom to slump. Its currency was overvalued, its foreign exchange reserves fell alarmingly, inflation grew from 20 percent (1980–1984) to 70 to 100 percent (1993), it became a net food importer, and its national debt overtook its GDP. The GDP fell from $1,100 per capita in 1980 to about $250 in 1989, and even today languishes at just $290. Oil profits also perpetuated inequalities in the distribution of national wealth, so that the richest 1 percent of the population of Nigeria now controls 75 percent of the national wealth.

In short, Nigerians were poorer in real terms after the oil boom than they had been in 1970. Rather than becoming a rich country during the oil years, Nigeria, like Mexico, amassed a substantial national debt. By 2002, its foreign debt stood at about $32 billion (the biggest in sub-Saharan Africa), and servicing the debt accounted for nearly one-third of Nigeria's export earnings.

Under the Obasanjo administration, Nigeria has faced a host of severe economic and social problems:

- **Decaying infrastructure.** Roads and railroads are in a bad state of repair, heavy traffic in major cities often leads to severe traffic jams, water and electricity supplies break down daily, the postal service is slow, and there is only one phone per 500 people (compared with more than one per person in the United States). So few telephones work properly that most people find it simpler to make personal visits. A step forward was taken in 2000 with the auction of the first cell phone licenses; since then cell phone use has grown rapidly.

- **Fuel shortages.** Absurd as it may seem in a major oil-producing country where government subsidized fuel is sold at 90 cents (U.S.) a gallon, finding fuel is difficult: Gas stations often lack supply or oblige their customers to wait in line for up to 48 hours. This not only is a political irritant but wastes time, creating more economic problems as workers miss valuable time at their desks. One of the biggest pressures on the government is to deregulate the fuel market, but this is opposed by the less scrupulous members of the elite who have benefited from siphoning off oil profits. The fuel shortage is caused mainly by the smuggling of fuel to neighboring countries, where it is sold at much higher world market prices.

- **A prosperous black market.** Known euphemistically as the "parallel market" or the **informal sector,** the black market can be seen in some ways as a healthy form of free-market economics based on supply and demand, but its existence makes it difficult for the government to collect taxes or to control economic development. Most Nigerians make their livings wholly or partly from the black market, in part because there are so few who are employed on a conventional basis. The foreign

OIL AND NIGERIA

As the world's sixth-largest producer of oil, generating about 2 million barrels of crude oil per day and about $18 billion annually from oil exports, Nigeria should be a wealthy country. It should be using the oil money to invest in broadening the base of its economy, building new roads and schools, creating the foundations of a welfare system, and—at the very least—bringing wealth and opportunity to the thousands of Nigerians who work for the oil industry and in related segments of the economy. But oil has proved to be a source of many of Nigeria's biggest problems. It contributed to the civil war in 1967, and it continues to cause national tensions by pitting the interests of the six oil-producing southern states against those of nonoil states demanding a cut of the profits. Income from oil exports has proved an irresistible lure to corrupt politicians and military leaders, and oil production has caused major environmental problems in southern Nigeria.

Ironically, economic development problems are among their worst in the oil-producing regions themselves, where little investment has been made in roads, electricity, safe water supplies, or telephones. Particular criticism has been directed at the Dutch British multinational corporation Royal Dutch/Shell, which produces most of Nigeria's oil. But Shell points the finger of blame at the Nigerian federal government, which collects all of Nigeria's oil revenues. Much goes into paying salaries and overheads, and much of the rest has been siphoned off by corrupt

officials. Little has been invested in Nigeria's own oil refineries, which are now in such an advanced state of neglect and disrepair that fuel shortages are common, and Nigeria must import 70 percent of its fuel needs. Meanwhile, the government subsidizes fuel to keep the cost low and remembers that fuel price increases in the past have led to strikes.

Nigeria also has other nonfuel mineral resources, such as tin, bauxite, iron ore, and gold, but it needs the investment to develop these resources, little of which is available locally and little of which will be forthcoming from abroad until foreign investors believe that there is less risk of losing their investments to corruption or to another military government. Unlike many other African countries, Nigeria earns little from tourism. Despite the fact that it has one of the most vibrant cultures on the continent, and a long and fascinating history, little is done to preserve its heritage (most of its best artifacts were either taken by the British or have since been sold, usually illegally, for the profit of corrupt leaders), and there has been almost no investment in building the infrastructure—including hotels, roads, airports, and communication systems—that tourists demand. Tourists are also put off by crime, corruption, and the challenge of even entering the country. Novelist Chinua Achebe once quipped that "Only a masochist with an exuberant taste for self-violence will pick Nigeria for a holiday."[21]

exchange black market is estimated to be worth as much as $5 billion annually, or about one-sixth of Nigeria's GDP.[20]

- ■ **A large state sector.** Ever since independence, the government has dominated the business sector; state ownership has meant monopolies and easy pickings for corrupt politicians and bureaucrats, and many of these businesses—such as NITEL, the state telephone company, and NEPA, the electricity company—are infamous for their incompetent management and bad service. The Obasanjo administration promised that it would address this issue, but it privatized just 14 of 107 state-owned companies in its first 3 years in office. Part of the problem has been a lack of capital within Nigeria to buy these companies, and part has been a lack of confidence in the Nigerian market by potential foreign investors.

- **Widespread poverty.** An estimated two-thirds of Nigerians—nearly 90 million people—live below the poverty line, a problem that feeds into ethnic conflict to produce social unrest. Although liberal democracies also have large numbers of their citizens living in poverty, they have large welfare programs that provide their recipients with money and services that poor Nigerians would define as immense wealth. Americans, for example, are poor if they live in households that earn less than $18,100 (for a family of four). This works out to about $12 per person per day. Those Nigerians who are defined as poor are earning less than $1 per day.

- **Institutionalized corruption.** Nigeria is one of the most corrupt countries in the world, routinely placed near the bottom of a Corruption Perceptions Index developed by Transparency International.[22] The abuse of power for personal gain in Nigeria poses a threat to political stability on a par only with ethnicity. In the period 1993–1998, for example, it was estimated that Sani Abacha, his family, and his senior advisors and ministers embezzled at least $1 billion, and perhaps as much as $3 billion to $6 billion.[23] President Obasanjo moved quickly within weeks of coming to office to launch an anticorruption crusade: He suspended all contracts, licenses, and appointments made in the 5 months before he took office; replaced the heads of several public agencies; and gave compulsory retirement to more than 200 government officials, including 99 customs officers. However, it has been normal procedure for every new Nigerian leader to launch an anticorruption drive upon coming to office, without much effect. The only way to remove institutionalized corruption is to ensure that power in the Nigerian political system is shared and checked as widely as possible.

- **An inadequate education system.** Although Nigeria has ostensibly been able to provide free secondary education, there are too few teachers and classrooms, and the provision of education has been uneven: Southerners have better facilities and more graduates than northerners, and there are too few scientists and professionals being turned out by universities. About 36 percent of Nigerian adults are illiterate, hindering Nigeria's hopes of building a modern, successful society.

- **An inadequate health care system.** Nigeria has 10 doctors and 40 nurses for every 100,000 people (compared with nearly 280 doctors and more than 830 nurses in the United States),[24] infant mortality is 12 times the rate in the United States, life expectancy is just under 47 years, and only one in five rural people has access to safe drinking water. As with many other African states, AIDS is a critical problem in Nigeria. It arrived later in West Africa than in southern and eastern Africa, but the response has been handicapped by the same social taboos about discussing sex (to which are added religious taboos). In 1999 it was estimated that about 3 million Nigerians were infected, but this was probably an underestimate, and there are fears that Nigeria could soon overtake South Africa as the country with the biggest proportion of AIDS cases on the continent. The Obasanjo administration has done little in response.

Nigerian economic policy has been driven in recent years by the demands of the major international lending organizations: such as the World Bank and the International Monetary Fund (IMF). As noted in Part IV, both have typically demanded structural adjustment (fundamental changes to the economy, cuts in public spending, and a reduction of the budget deficit) before providing countries like Nigeria with the "seal of approval" needed to win their support and have its debt repayments rescheduled. In the late 1990s the World Bank was talking of new levels of economic growth in parts of sub-Saharan Africa, with GDP in the previous year having grown by an average of nearly 4 percent and income per person by 1 percent. Unfortunately, Nigeria was not among the higher achievers: its manufacturing output was down, its foreign exchange reserves were low, and it was falling behind on its debt repayment schedule. There were a few hopeful signs, however, notably a fall in inflation from 56 percent to 22 percent, a balanced budget, and an accelerated program of privatization. With its large population and considerable oil wealth, Nigeria has the potential to be the economic rival of South Africa, but only if it can find some means to achieve political stability.

FOREIGN POLICY

Generally speaking, the richer a country and the more its economy is geared toward trade, the more active an interest it will take in foreign relations and the more complex its foreign policies will be. Most liberal democracies have extensive economic and security interests beyond their borders, with the result that most emphasize foreign relations and maintain policies on issues as varied as trade, defense, immigration, and communications. Foreign policy becomes almost as complex as domestic policy, and liberal democratic leaders are judged as much by their foreign policies as by their domestic policies.

Poorer countries tend to be more introverted, their attention and resources diverted by pressing domestic issues. For countries like Nigeria, which face no major external security threats, foreign policy is driven by the need to promote economic development and trade. Some political scientists argue that countries such as Nigeria have become so dependent on loans, aid, trade, and foreign investment that the political dependence of the colonial era has been replaced by a postcolonial economic dependence. But simply by virtues of its size and relative wealth, Nigeria is the dominant regional power in sub-Saharan Africa, and since the return to civilian government, it is one of the two African states (along with South Africa) that is taken seriously by foreign governments. Nigeria's participation is sought in regional economic and security matters, and there has been much more two-way traffic of government leaders to and from Nigeria.

Good relations with Nigeria are now seen as important to any external power looking for influence in the region, and many other African leaders see Nigerian stability as critical for the future development of the entire region. Notable here has been Nigeria's role in the **Economic Community of West African States** (ECOWAS), which was founded in 1975 and is headquartered in Lagos. With 16 member states and a total population of more than 210 million, ECOWAS set out to achieve first a customs union and then a full common market along the lines of the European Union. To promote cooperation, a development fund was created through which the wealthier ECOWAS members could channel investment funds to the poorer members.

With its growing oil revenues in the late 1970s, Nigeria was initially an active member of ECOWAS, exerting substantial regional influence through grants, loans, and technical assistance. During the 1980s, however, as Nigeria began tightening its belt and putting domestic economic priorities above those of regional cooperation, the cracks in the ECOWAS structure began to show. ECOWAS has suffered from the instability of several of its members (such as Liberia and Burkina Faso), but the major problem has been the unequal size of its members. With 60 percent of the population of ECOWAS, Nigeria is by far the biggest, wealthiest, and most powerful member, which not only makes smaller and poorer members (such as Benin, Burkina Faso, and Cape Verde) nervous but has also caused resentment among Nigerians who feel that their country has borne too much of the burden of building ECOWAS.

Nigeria is a large and valuable market for the smaller member states, but they have been unwilling to reciprocate by opening their markets to Nigeria and have long suspected Nigeria of working toward regional domination.[25] ECOWAS members also have often conflicting economic and trade policies, have made little progress in stabilizing exchange rates among themselves, and regularly fail to pay their membership dues. One of the organization's few tangible achievements to date has been its role in peacekeeping operations in countries such as Liberia and Sierra Leone. Nigeria has played an active role, and has even contributed to UN operations in Somalia and Bosnia.

Nigerian foreign policy has gone through spells of assertiveness and reticence. During the 1970s it was an active supporter of regional economic cooperation through ECOWAS, felt confident enough to publicly disagree with U.S. involvement in Angola and Belgian involvement in what was then Zaire, became critical of apartheid in South Africa, actively supported liberation movements in Zimbabwe and Angola, and tried to reduce its dependence on multinational companies, notably when it nationalized British Petroleum interests in 1979. It also campaigned for a permanent seat on the UN Security Council.

As its economic problems worsened in the early 1980s, however, Nigeria became more introverted, and by the mid-1990s was too concerned with internal political and economic issues to be an assertive regional power. But international leaders have nonetheless courted Nigeria. In 1992 there was the remarkable visit to Nigeria by South African president, F. W. de Klerk. U.S. President Bill Clinton visited in 2000, and British prime minister Tony Blair in 2002. Meanwhile, President Obasanjo has several times visited the United States, meeting with both Bill Clinton and George W. Bush. Such contacts serve to underline Nigeria's potential importance in the region, and its value to non-African states.

Nigeria has taken on a new economic significance for the United States in recent years, as the dependence of energy-hungry Americans on imported oil grows. As part of its strategy to decrease dependence on Persian Gulf oil, the Bush administration in 2002 held talks with the leaders of 11 African oil-producing states, prominent among them being Nigeria. There is a concern that, unless U.S. relations with the Arab world improve—and of late there has been little sign of that happening—oil supplies from the Gulf could be disrupted. Thus, the United States is looking to increase imports of "secure" oil from African and other oil-producing nations. Some estimates suggest that the United States could be importing as much as 25 percent of its oil from West Africa within the next 15 to 20 years, with Nigeria being the major source.

NIGERIAN POLITICS IN TRANSITION

"The trouble with Nigeria" wrote the novelist Chinua Achebe, "is simply and squarely a failure of leadership. There is nothing basically wrong with the Nigerian character. There is nothing wrong with the Nigerian land or climate or water or air or anything else. The Nigerian problem is the unwillingness or the inability of its leaders to rise to the responsibility, to the challenge of personal example which are the hallmarks of true leadership."[26] He was writing in 1983, just as another of Nigeria's experiments in civilian government was about to collapse. His sentiment still applies today, but—to be fair—Nigeria's problems are so severe that it will take more than strong leadership to solve them. The Obasanjo administration has addressed several of the core issues relating to corruption, investor confidence in Nigeria has improved under the Fourth Republic, and Nigeria is slowly being taken more seriously in international affairs.

To make Nigeria "work," however, will take a fundamental transformation in the way Nigerians relate to one another, and will demand that they set aside ethnic and religious differences and try to think of themselves more actively as Nigerians. The worsening level of communal violence suggests that there is still a long road to be traveled. It will also take a fundamental transformation of the economy, with Nigeria moving away from its dependence on oil and broadening the sources of its income, and moving away from the tradition of monopoly and incompetence that characterizes its state-owned businesses, which are in urgent need of being privatized.

Nigeria's future remains frustratingly uncertain. It is the biggest and most powerful country in sub-Saharan Africa (excepting South Africa), has a large and energetic population that favors democracy over military government, has oil wealth that could provide the basis for sound economic development, and could become an engine for regional economic and political growth. If it can find a way to rise above ethnic and religious division, to channel its oil wealth into building infrastructure and education, and to rid itself of its dependence on military arbitration, it could become Africa's first world power.

KEY TERMS

Biafra
caliphate of Sokoto
constitutional
  engineering
Economic Community of
  West African States
ethnicity

Fourth Republic
Hausa-Fulani
Igbo
informal sector
Middle Belt
National Assembly
old brigade

patron-client relationships
People's Democratic
  party
sardauna
sharia courts
slave trade
Yoruba

KEY PEOPLE

Sani Abacha

Nnamdi Azikiwe

Ibrahim Babangida

Muhammadu Buhari

Yakubu Gowon

Olusegun Obasanjo

Ken Saro-Wiwa

Shehu Shagari

STUDY QUESTIONS

1. Is Nigeria worth saving?

2. How do Nigeria's experiences in nation-building compare with those of the United States, and is there anything that Nigeria could learn from the U.S. experience?

3. Would divided societies such as Russia, India, and Nigeria be better off as confederations?

4. What is the difference between race and ethnicity?

5. Is military government a necessary evil for a country such as Nigeria?

6. If you were Olusegun Obasanjo, what would you be doing to ensure the success of the Fourth Republic?

7. Should Nigeria accept its ethnic divisions and build a political system that accommodates them rather than subverts them?

8. Should Nigeria respect and build upon traditional local political models, or keep on trying to make Western models work?

9. Are political parties the best option for divided societies such as Nigeria, or are there more efficient channels through which citizens can express themselves and be governed?

NIGERIA ONLINE

The Presidency: *http://www.nopa.net*

Web site of the office of the President, with links to sites for other government departments.

The Guardian: *http://www.ngrguardiannew.co*m

Nigeria.com: *http://www.nigeria.com*

NigeriaWEB: *http://odili.net/nigeria.html*

Useful sources of news and information on Nigeria, the first being the Web site of a Lagos-based independent newspaper and the last including a series of links to government Web sites.

allAfrica.com: *http://allafrica.com*

Panafrican News Agency: *http://www.panapress.com*

Good sources of news on Africa in general, both with regular stories on Nigeria.

Economic Community of West African States: *http://www.ecowas.int*

Home page of the regional integration organization.

FURTHER READING

Achebe, Chinua, *Things Fall Apart* (New York: Anchor Books, 1994). The classic novel by the acclaimed Nigerian novelist (first published in 1958), which looks into the heart of a family in a small village in Nigeria.

Aborisade, Oladimeji, and Robert Mundt, *Politics in Nigeria*, 2nd Ed. (New York: Longman, 2002). A patchy but useful introduction to Nigerian politics, with chapters on political culture, political structure and processes, and public policy.

Maier, Karl, *This House Has Fallen: Midnight in Nigeria* (New York: Public Affairs, 2000). A narrative and interpretation of recent events in Nigeria, written by a journalist.

Osaghae, Eghosa, *Crippled Giant: Nigeria Since Independence* (Bloomington, IN: Indiana University Press, 1998). A history of political changes in Nigeria from 1960 to 1996.

Soyinka, Wole, *The Open Sore of a Continent: A Personal Narrative of the Nigerian Crisis* (New York: Oxford University Press, 1996). A personal and occasionally grumpy set of reflections on Nigeria's political problems, written by the Nobel laureate.

COMPARATIVE FOCUS

SYSTEMS OF ADMINISTRATION

One of the fundamental problems facing Nigeria is how to achieve a balance between the powers of national and local government. It could decide that its internal divisions are so great that the concept of Nigeria should be abandoned and the country should be split up into smaller states based around different ethnic groups or religions. This is unlikely to happen though, so the only alternative is to try to build national unity, and the nature of its administrative system is the key to winning the battle.

Different administrative systems are distinguished from one another by the relative balance of power between national and local levels of government:

- In **unitary systems,** most significant power rests with the national government, while local units of government have little independence. National government is responsible for almost all key policy areas, taxes are almost all national taxes, national elections are far more significant than local elections in determining the distribution of power, and local government units can be redesigned and abolished by national government. The vast majority of countries have unitary administrative systems, including Britain, France, Japan, China, and Egypt.

- In **federal systems,** local government has more power. There are many competing theories about the nature and the goals of federalism, which comes in many different forms, but its defining characteristic is a system of government in which national and local governments have independent powers, and neither level is subordinated to the other. Federal systems involve the division of powers: national government is typically responsible for broad economic policy issues, foreign policy, and defense, and local government is usually responsible for policing and education. Both levels of government also have their own taxing and lawmaking powers. There are less than two dozen federations in the world, including the United States, Canada, Australia, Brazil, Germany, Russia, Mexico, India, and Nigeria.

- An even looser arrangement would be found in a **confederation,** an unusual kind of administrative system that was used in the United States in 1781–1789 and in Germany in 1815–1871. Although Switzerland calls itself a federation, the relationship between its cantons is very loose and the Swiss national government has very limited powers, pushing the country close to the definition of a confederation. The European Union also has many of the features of a confederation. The focus of political power in a confederal system rests at the local level, which is responsible for all policy areas except those that local governments agree are better dealt with jointly, such as foreign, defense, and monetary policy.

Unitary systems work best in small or homogeneous societies where there are too few political and social divisions to make minorities fearful of the hegemony of the majority. Federalism works best in countries that are either big, heterogeneous, or based on the voluntary union of previously independent groups of people. For the United States, federalism was seen as the only arrangement that could unite 13 mutually suspicious colonies that had tried several years of confederalism before they agreed to a closer union. Support for small government in the United States was driven at first by fear of tyranny, but then by desires for self-determination. American federalism has been so successful that there is very little of substance today that differentiates residents of California from those of Arizona, Indiana, or New Hampshire.

In other parts of the world, federalism plays an essential role in providing order and in uniting communities with very different characteristics.

In Belgium, there is a southern region based on French and a northern region based on Flemish.

Each region has its own subgovernment, the capital city of Brussels is bilingual neutral territory in the middle, and visitors wonder what it means to be "Belgian." Belgium has remained intact because the constitution has been amended to give the two language-based regions more power.

In Canada, French-speaking Quebecois see themselves as so different from their English-speaking compatriots that many want complete independence. Since 1987, the provinces have had new powers over appointments to the Canadian Senate and Supreme Court and veto power over certain constitutional amendments.

Soviet federalism was little more than a cover for imperialism, and its underlying fragility was illustrated by the speed with which the 15 Soviet republics declared sovereignty following the collapse of the Gorbachev government. Even today, Russia finds itself struggling with demands for self-determination or independence from ethnic minorities living on its borders, developments that could threaten the viability of the entire Russian state.

In Nigeria, the only attempt to create a unitary state led to the overthrow of the Ironsi government in 1966. The number of states has tripled since 1975 in an increasingly desperate attempt to ensure the unity of Nigeria by breaking up the major ethnic groups and by addressing the fears of minority ethnic groups that one of the larger groups would dominate national government. Ironically, Nigerian national identity is weak, but poorer regions of Nigeria are disinclined to see the country break up because they would then lose access to their current share of the profits from the oil-rich states in the south. Debates continue about the nature of Nigerian federalism and the relationship between national and local government. Among the particular criticisms of the constitution of the Fourth Republic is that it gives the federal government too much power. History may reveal that Nigeria needs a looser confederal relationship in which the balance of power lies with the states, leaving the "national" government responsible for foreign, defense, and monetary policy and for trade issues affecting the country as a whole. A number of Nigeria's ethnic groups are strongly in favor of such a system.

Part V

ISLAMIC COUNTRIES

Islam is the solution.

—Slogan of the Muslim Brotherhood, Egypt

The cold war between communism and the West may be over, but there is now every indication that a new cold war—between Islam and the West—has emerged to take its place. The old threats of nuclear conflict have seemingly been replaced by a new kind of ideological conflict, between two protagonists whose failures to understand each other seem to constantly worsen. This is no new war: the West and Islam have been at odds with each other in various ways for 1,200 years or more. Not even the methods are new; terrorism and conventional state-on-state violence have been elements in the conflict before. What is new is the scale of the conflict and its potential reach in terms of the number of people threatened, the instability promised, and the economic costs involved.

Islam has long been a factor in global politics, but—at least until the attacks of September 11, 2001—mainstream Western political science had failed to give much serious thought to its broader political significance. (Symptomatic of this problem is that this is the only introductory comparative politics textbook published in English—or possibly any language—that treats Islam as a distinct political system type.) Many political scientists have been arguing the need to pay more attention since the **Islamic resurgence** that followed the overthrow of the regime of the Shah of Iran in 1979 (see later in this chapter); they have been joined by many more since September 2001, and there is now a growing literature that argues that we should approach Islamic states as members of a distinct system type. These states are socially quite different from the rest of the "Third World," and although Islamism as a political ideology is more a theory than a reality in most Islamic states, it gives most of them a political identity that makes them quite distinctive from their non-Islamic neighbors.

The most common mistake made by the West is its failure to appreciate that Islam is much more than a religion, and this leads us to misunderstand the complex interplay between Islamic law, social rules, and politics in countries throughout North Africa and the Middle East. Whereas Western liberal democracy supports a

443

FIGURE V.1

Distribution of Muslims in the Islamic World

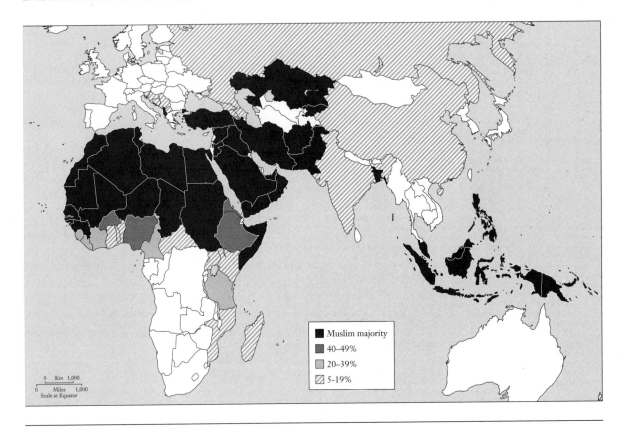

Muslim majority
40–49%
20–39%
5-19%

0   Km   1,000
0   Miles   1,000
Scale at Equator

separation of church and state, Muslims argue that there is no separation of religion *(islam)* and state *(dawla)*, and that the followers of Islam are all part of a larger community of the faithful *(umma)* that transcends race, language, and national borders. Unlike any other major religion except perhaps Judaism, Islam provides theories of government and the state and a comprehensive body of law that can guide the lives of Muslims if properly applied. In short, Islam (unlike, say, Christianity) contains a complete program for ordering society.

To be fair, the misunderstandings have also stemmed from the failure of Islamic societies to institutionalize politics. Islamic theory provides detailed guidance on goals and values but leaves it up to Muslims to decide what form political institutions should take. The absence of such institutions is often blamed by Muslims on the problems caused by European colonialism and the imposition of political borders and Western institutions, which caused Islam to lose its way. But Muslims themselves have also disagreed about the role of Islam in politics, which varies from one state to another, not least because of differences in interpreta-

ISLAMIC COUNTRIES
What Are Their Features?

- The majority of their populations are Muslim.
- A dominant role—actual or potential—for Islam in the forces that drive politics.
- A tendency toward authoritarianism and paternalism.
- Inconsistent and often unpredictable political institutions and processes.
- A high degree of public loyalty to the Islamic community.
- Most forms of political participation and representation directly or indirectly influenced by Islamic values.

- Most countries have a poor record on human rights, including gender discrimination and little protection for minorities.
- The only significant opposition is often the Islamic opposition.
- Free-market economies.
- A relatively poor quality of life when measured by the provision of education, health care, and other basic services.
- Low ratings on the Freedom House, Economic Freedom, and Human Development indexes.

Where Are They?

There are 26, and they are mainly in the Middle East and North Africa:

Afghanistan	Iraq	Pakistan
Algeria	Jordan	Qatar
Bahrain	Kuwait	Saudi Arabia
Bangladesh	Lebanon	Sudan
Brunei	Libya	Syria
Comoros	Maldives	Tunisia
Djibouti	Mauritania	United Arab Emirates
Egypt	Morocco	Yemen
Iran	Oman	

tion.[1] One school of Islamic thought sees Islam as an ideology, argues that it needs to become more political, and believes that religion should be tailored toward more radical political ends.[2] Others argue that church and state should be kept separate and that a dominant role for Islam runs the danger of creating a powerful group of religious leaders who would offset the authority of the secular government or could make the people fatalistic and easy to dominate and manipulate.

One of the results of these divisions is that political structures in Islamic countries vary, from the **theocracy** (rule by religious leaders) of Iran to the absolute monarchies of the Arabian peninsula and Brunei, from constitutional monarchies such as Jordan to emergent democracies like Egypt, and from countries officially designated as Islamic republics (Pakistan, the Comoros, and Mauritania) to states that are legally secular but where Islam is still a central issue in politics (Algeria, Iraq, Morocco, and Syria). At the same time, there is no denying that the Islamic resurgence since the 1970s has been accompanied—as one political scientist puts it—by the reassertion of Islam in public life: "an increase in Islamically oriented governments, organizations, laws, banks, social welfare services, and educational institutions. Both governments and opposition movements have turned to Islam to enhance their authority and muster popular support."[3] In other words, there has been a rediscovery of political Islam, and it has exerted an increasingly important influence in several Middle Eastern and North African states. Unfortunately, we tend to hear about it largely in relation to the extremism of groups such as Al-Qaeda, Hamas in Palestine, Islamic Jihad in Egypt, and Hizbollah in Lebanon. This draws attention away from the much more important role played by Islam in mainstream politics.

Islamic countries have five major sets of features that make them distinctive.

Patrimonialism

In theory, Islamic government should be based on mutual consultation *(shura)* involving the community and on rule by the "competent," defined as rulers with faith, a clear vision of Islam, trustworthiness, initiative, and leadership.[4] Islam also teaches that all humans (Muslim and non-Muslim) are born free; cannot be denied their religious, cultural, social, economic, or political freedom; have rights to personal safety, property, and privacy; have freedom of faith, association, and expression; and are to be considered innocent until proven guilty and given a fair trial. In other words, it is very democratic.

In practice, most Islamic states have a mixed record on human rights. It has been argued that only Malaysia and Iran have "Islamically legitimate" governments, that few Muslim leaders could be described as competent, and that the concept of *shura* has been distorted to mean that leaders can consult key advisors or experts of their choice.[5] The result in many Islamic states has been a tradition of patrimonialism, where leadership develops around a dominant figure who becomes the source of all important ideas, strategies, and policies, and will even occasionally go so far as to describe his subjects as "my children" or "my people." Leadership is also often underpinned by a cult of personality, like those surrounding the sultans, sheiks, and emirs of the Middle East, or Nasser and Sadat in Egypt, Saddam Hussein in Iraq, and Ghaddafi in Libya.

There is a fine line between patrimonialism and authoritarianism; as the 19th century British historian Lord Action famously noted, "Power tends to corrupt, and absolute power corrupts absolutely." Many Islamic leaders have developed an unfortunate reputation for accumulating and abusing power and for using Islam as a cloak. Although no Islamic leader since Muhammad has been exclusively a religious leader, many have tried to express their power in religious terms. Anwar Sadat, for example, in a failed attempt to offset criticism that Egypt had become too Westernized and secularized, tried to portray himself as the Believer President and made sure that television news gave prominent coverage to his visits each Friday to the mosque.

Personalism

Because power in a patrimonial system depends on access to the leader, he becomes the most important element in the system and tends to govern through an extended network of personal ties that are based on informal links rather than formal contracts or constitutions.[6] Networks are a part of politics everywhere, but they are almost institutionalized in Islamic societies. The royal families of Saudi Arabia and the Gulf emirates are obvious examples; less well known are the many family and personal links in Saddam Hussein's government in Iraq or the network of elites that underpins the Egyptian government. Family and kinship ties have occasionally turned into extensive bureaucracies and elites based on the military, business, academia, and the mass media.

Islamic Law

Islam has its own body of law, known as the ***sharia***, which tends to make the news in the West only when someone has been sentenced to have their hand cut off for stealing or to be stoned to death for committing adultery. The result is a very narrow and misleading conception of how it works. In fact, Islamic law is deep and sophisticated, with its own system of courts, legal experts, and judges and its own long tradition of jurisprudence.

Muslims believe that God, through Muhammad, outlined universal laws that govern not just human behavior but also explain how nature works. Unlike Western law, where lawbreakers must account only to the legal system, lawbreakers in the Islamic tradition must account to God and all other Muslims. Also unlike Western law, the *sharia* outlines not only what is forbidden for Muslims but also what is discouraged, what is recommended, and what is obligatory. So, for example, Muslims should not drink alcohol, gamble, steal, commit adultery, or commit suicide, but they *should* pray every day, give to charity, be polite to others, dress inoffensively, and—when they die—be buried in anonymous graves.

The *sharia* is not universally applied, and in most Islamic countries there is an ongoing argument about the relationship between the *sharia* and Western law. It is widely used in countries such as Iran, Jordan, Libya, Mauritania, Oman, and Saudi Arabia, but the majority of Islamic countries use a mix of Western and Islamic law, using the former for serious crime and the latter for family issues. When Muslims have any doubts about whether something they are considering doing is acceptable, they are encouraged to speak to a Muslim judge, called a *mufti*, who will issue a legal judgment known as a *fatwa*.

A Divided Community

The ideal Islamic state should be based on the sovereignty of the *sharia* and on **universalism** (unity of the Muslim community). However, the *sharia* is not universally applied in any Islamic country, and universalism is undermined in several different ways:

- **Political.** Muslims are politically divided by boundaries developed during the colonial era, which have encouraged Islamic states to put national interests above those of the *umma*, causing deep and sometimes costly divisions.

- **Doctrinal.** Islam is divided into two major sects: the **Shi'ah,** or party of Ali, and the orthodox and conservative **Sunni.** The Shi'ah believe they are the true Muslims in the model of Muhammad and that he was semi-divine. For their part, the Sunni believe Muhammad was an ordinary human being; they are mostly non-Arabs, make up about 80 percent of all Muslims, and do not believe in religious leaders on earth. With the exception of Iran, Iraq, and Yemen, most Muslim countries are predominantly Sunni.

- **Religious.** Muslim countries are divided over the role of religion in national life, with some—such as the Comoros, Iran, Mauritania, and Pakistan—claiming to be true **Islamic republics,** based on an Islamic constitution and full application of the sharia. Others—such as Albania, Indonesia, and Turkey—are more secular, and believe in a true separation of religion and state. (This is why the latter three countries are not classified in this book as Islamic countries.)

- **Social.** Muslims are divided over whether they should follow traditional values or adopt Western values. In Saudi Arabia, for example, women are increasingly rejecting their inferior role in society, but in Egypt they have been encouraged to adopt traditional habits, such as the wearing of the *hijab* (veil). Modernization is often equated with Westernization, but standard theories of modernization do not really help explain what is happening in the Islamic world, which is less a process of modernization than of **Islamization.** This can be defined not as wholesale Westernization but as Islamic modernization, or change that borrows from other systems but that embodies Islamic principles and values and is not contrary to Islam.[7]

Social and Economic Inequalities

Islamic theory includes ideas about wealth and the economy that reflect elements of both capitalism and socialism. As well as encouraging honesty and criticizing cheating, hoarding, and theft, Islamic economic theory supports material progress and the right to private property (although only in trust from God) and disapproves of monopolies. At the same time, it is also hostile to materialism, encourages the equitable distribution of wealth, and emphasizes the importance of placing wider community needs above personal gain.[8] Islam also emphasizes the value of education; criticizes illiteracy and ignorance; and encourages brotherhood, community values, the family, and concern for the poor.

In practice, however, illiteracy and poverty are widespread in the Islamic world, there are often considerable and obvious gaps between the wealthy and the poor, education is handicapped by competition between Western and Islamic ideas, many people lack basic services, and there is little interstate economic cooperation. Militant Islamists have been quick to exploit the dissatisfaction of the poor and to identify the wealthy in the Middle East with Western culture and mass consumption. They have also been keen to promote divisions between men and women. Even though it goes against the teachings of Islam, women are generally treated as inferiors by men, were long denied the right to vote, and do not play a very prominent role in politics even today; social inequalities mean that levels of literacy vary between men and women.

Young boys learning the Quran at an Islamic school in the northern Pakistani town of Peshawar. Islam is the fastest-growing religion in the world, there has been a resurgence of Islamic consciousness since 1979, and the links between politics and religion play an increasingly important role in countries such as Pakistan.

THE EVOLUTION OF ISLAM

Most Westerners think of Islam as monolithic and homogeneous, associate it mainly with the Middle East, often associate it with fanaticism, assume that all Muslims are Arabs, and assume that all Arabs are Muslim. They are wrong on every count.

With an estimated 1.2 billion adherents, Islam is the second biggest religion in the world after Christianity and is rapidly on its way to becoming the biggest. "Islam" means submission to God (or Allah) and is based on taking the **Quran** (the book of revelations supposedly made to the prophet Muhammad by the archangel Gabriel) as the literal word of God. Collected and written down after Muhammad's death, the revelations now constitute the final authority on the religious beliefs and the social system of Islam. Islamic law consists of codes of behavior that evolved over time out of the Quran and the *hadith*, the collected sayings and hearsay statements of Muhammad.

The Founding of Islam (622–632)

Islam was founded by the prophet Muhammad in the seventh century. Although he features prominently in the Islamic faith, he was simply one of a series of prophets supposedly sent from God, among them Abraham, Moses, John the

Baptist, and Jesus Christ. For Muslims, Muhammad is the most important of all the prophets because they believe that his revelation was God's last message to humankind.

Muhammad was born in about A.D. 570 in Mecca in present-day Saudi Arabia, at a time when the Middle East was in economic and political turmoil, divided by tribal rivalries. Raised an orphan, he made a name for himself as a trader before marrying a wealthy widow at the age of 25. When he was about 40, he claimed to have been visited by the archangel Gabriel, who gave him the first of many messages from God. He began preaching in Mecca, but he met with local hostility and left in 622 with some followers for Medina, 250 miles to the north. This *hijra* (or exodus) is regarded as the beginning of the Muslim era.

In Medina, Muhammad became both the political and religious leader, thereby emphasizing from the outset the fusion of religion and the state in Islam. Using Medina as a base, he launched a war against paganism and foreign religions. Within 6 years he had raised an army of 10,000, and in A.D. 628 he captured Mecca. By the time he died in 632, most of the Arabian Peninsula had come under the influence of his faith. The main attraction of Islam was that it was a homegrown religion with mass appeal and with more relevance to the lives of local people than imported religions such as Christianity. Distinctively Arab, it united the Arabs for the first (and so far only) time in their history.

The Caliphate (632–1258)

Muhammad died without appointing a successor. His father-in-law was eventually designated as the new leader, becoming the first of the many caliphs who would lead Islam for the next 600 years. Within 25 years of Muhammad's death, the Muslims had conquered all of the present-day Middle East. By 750, the Arab empire stretched from Tashkent in central Asia to Marrakech in Morocco. Muslims even conquered Spain and parts of France and southern Italy; the Arab influence can still be seen today in some of the architecture of southern Spain. The turning point came in 732, when the Arabs were defeated by Charles Martel, the Holy Roman emperor, at the battle of Poitiers, just 100 miles from Paris. Had Martel lost, the subsequent history of the West might have been very different.

At its height, the **Arab empire** was one of the great cultural centers of the world. The **Pax Islamica** covered an area greater than that of the Roman Empire at its height. Trade routes grew, towns flourished, political systems evolved, and Arabic became the lingua franca. In the eighth century, the world's best universities, libraries, architects, musicians, scientists, and scholars were Arab. We still feel their influence in our use of Arabic numerals, the decimal system, algebra, geometry, and the concept of zero, which was borrowed by the Arabs from India. Many of the words used in Western science come from Arabic, such as *nadir, zenith, alkali,* and *alcohol.*[9]

The Arab empire reached its zenith in about 950, and then began declining as a result of internal dissension and division. Although Arab political unity ended, the spread of Islam did not. By 1500, under the leadership of several competing administrations and empires, Islam had spread south into Africa, north into central Asia, and east into what are now India, Bangladesh, and parts of Indonesia. The era of the caliphate ended in 1258, when the Mongols captured Baghdad, then the center of the empire, and killed the last caliph.

The Ottoman Empire (c. 1300–1922)

If the Arabs were the first major influence on the evolution of Islam, the Ottomans were the second. Arriving from central Asia, the Ottoman Turks from the late 13th century embarked on an expansionist policy, establishing their first capital at Bursa in what is now western Turkey. In 1453 they took the eastern Christian bastion of Constantinople (renaming it Istanbul), and from there moved as far north as what is now Hungary, south into Egypt, and west along the North African coast. The Ottoman Empire eventually covered almost the entire Middle East and remained the major power in the region until well into the 19th century. It outlasted the other two Islamic empires, the Safavid, which was based in what is now Iran and collapsed in the 18th century, and the Mogul, which covered the Indian subcontinent and lost power in the early 19th century to expanding British influence. In all three, Islam was the major source of law, ideology, and political legitimacy. The Ottoman sultan ruled by divine right and was seen as defender and protector of Islam, and the *sharia* was the official law of the Ottomans.

Modernization and Nationalism (1798–1945)

Ottoman power began declining in the 17th century, the beginning of the end coming in 1798 when Napoleon invaded Egypt. Anglo-French influence spread through North Africa, Russian expansionism reached down into central Asia, and Islam itself went through an identity crisis. Ottoman rule in the Balkans ended, Egypt was occupied by Britain in 1882, and all that remained for the Ottomans was to carve out a new secular existence in Turkey, which was declared a republic in 1923.

Surrounded by all these threats, Islamic leaders such as Muhammad Ali in Egypt began arguing that Islam needed to modernize. This was an attempt to respond to, rather than simply react against, Western imperialism. In other words, these leaders believed that they could strengthen their countries by modernizing their military and bureaucracy along European lines, while looking to the Quran and the *sharia* for their guidance.[10] The new policies immediately caused a split between modernists and traditionalists that even today influences politics in Egypt and Iran.

Interestingly, the experience of Muslim countries directly contradicts Western theories of modernization, which argue that the process of modernization leads to a reduction in the influence of religion. Although this was certainly true in many Western countries, it was not true with Islam, emphasizing once again the close connections between state and religion in the Islamic world.

The post–World War I settlement gave Britain a mandate over what is now Iraq, Jordan, and Israel; gave the French a mandate over present-day Syria and Lebanon; and—through the 1917 **Balfour Declaration**—supported the establishment of a Jewish national homeland in Palestine. Central Arabia (Saudi Arabia from 1932) was independent, but most of Persia (Iran from 1935) was under

British and Russian control, and the small Gulf states such as Kuwait and Qatar were British protectorates. In short, most of Islam was under European occupation or subject to European and Russian influence. The British and the French began treating their mandates more like colonies, and plans for a Jewish homeland went ahead despite Arab opposition, further deepening resentment against colonialism and promoting a new sense of Arab nationalism and Islamic revival.

During and after World War II, European influence in the Middle East waned, and Islamic states were given their independence: Lebanon in 1941, Syria in 1945, Jordan in 1946, Pakistan in 1947, and Libya in 1951. The British pullout from Palestine in 1948 was accompanied by the creation of Israel, and the hostility between the Israelis and the Arabs immediately became one of the defining influences in the region (see Political Debates, p. 495). Although British influence in Egypt and Iraq had ended by 1958, and France completely withdrew from North Africa in the period 1958–1962, the United States and the Soviet Union began taking a new interest in the region, or at least in its oil supplies. Some would argue that European colonialism was simply replaced by American neocolonialism, and the U.S. presence came to be seen by many Muslims as just the latest chapter in the history of Western interference in the affairs of Islam.

The Islamic Resurgence (1979–)

The wave of independence gave the Muslim states confidence and a renewed desire to end their subordination. Nasser's defeat of Anglo-French attempts to retain control of the Suez Canal in 1956 (see Chapter 9) made him a hero to Arabs, but it also represented a wider Islamic reaction against Western influence. In few countries was that Western influence more troubling than in Iran. An attempt by Prime Minister Mohammed Mussadeq to nationalize the Iranian petroleum industry in the early 1950s led to his being deposed with U.S. connivance in a 1953 coup and replaced by Shah Mohammed Reza Pahlavi. Iran enjoyed stability and growth under the shah, but he was a tyrannical leader dismissed by his opponents as a puppet of the United States, and opposition eventually emerged around the exiled religious leader Ayatollah Ruhollah Khomeini.

Pressures for a return to Islam forced the shah into exile in 1979, paving the way for the creation of an Islamic republic under Khomeini and capping a resurgence of political Islam which had begun in the early 1970s. Some saw the revolution as symbolic of Muslim disillusionment with Western values and influence and as evidence that revolutionary endeavor had grassroots support in many Islamic states. In December 1979 Islamic militants in Saudi Arabia rebelled, occupying the Great Mosque in Mecca. In October 1981 President Anwar Sadat of Egypt was assassinated by militants critical of the peace treaty he had signed in 1979 with Israel and Sadat's failure to establish an Islamic state in Egypt. In December 1981 militants launched a coup attempt in Bahrain, and in 1985 an attempt was made on the life of the emir of Kuwait. Islamic radicals took several Westerners hostage during the late 1980s and threatened to launch a terrorist offensive against the West. Although the Western media preferred to use the term "Islamic fundamentalism," a new term began to creep into debates about these events: **Islamism** (see Critical Issues, p. 453).

ISLAMISM: RELIGION OR IDEOLOGY?

Particularly since the oil crisis of 1973, there has been a resurgence in parts of the Islamic world of a phenomenon described in the West as fundamentalism or revivalism. Application of the term *fundamentalism* to Islam has at least two problems. First, it comes out of the Protestant Christian ethic and describes a belief that the Bible should be taken literally. But because Islam is based on taking the Quran literally, it is by definition a fundamentalist religion, so the term is redundant. Second, the term is often used to suggest a restoration of a pure and authentic form of religion, but most Islamic "fundamentalists" are actually looking to revitalize and re-Islamize modern Muslim societies,[11] which is something quite different.

Because of these problems, an increasing number of scholars prefer the term *Islamism*, implying that it should be seen as a rival to "foreign" ideologies such as socialism, fascism, or liberalism.[12] Islamism is usually described either as a movement advocating a revitalization of political Islam or as an attempt to translate the original meaning of the Quran into something like a constitution for a new kind of political movement, with government-sponsored programs that reassert Islam as a primary ideological force.[13]

In general, Islamists argue that Western technology, political ideas, and moral standards have corrupted Islam, have taken away the dignity of Muslims, and are used by their followers to keep power by force and deceit. Once Muslims go back to the basics of Islam, argue the Islamists, everything else will fall into place. Exactly how this will happen is irrelevant; what matters is that Muslims have faith. Islam has decayed mainly because it has ceased to be seen as a whole, according to the Islamists. Once Muslims return to the basics of their faith, Islam will be regenerated, and politics will have been "spiritualized."[14] Islamism has had its greatest impact in Iran, where the late Ayatollah Khomeini spearheaded the 1979 revolution against the regime of the shah, who was overtly secular and pro-Western.

On the political front, Islamism has had a notable impact in several countries:

- In Algeria, sweeping gains by the Islamic Salvation Front in elections in 1990–1991 led to a military coup in January 1992 and the suspension of democratic reforms. Free elections were subsequently postponed, the government suspecting that they would easily be won by Islamists. Civil unrest throughout the 1990s claimed the lives of more than 40,000 people.

- In Afghanistan, Islamist rebels called the Taliban capped several years of mounting conflict with their capture in September 1996 of the capital, Kabul. They said their goal was to establish the world's purest Islamic state, to which end they banned television, music, and cinema; introduced public executions for crimes; and prevented men from shaving or women from working. Their actions were met with widespread criticism from most other governments, including those of the United States, Russia, and Iran; Russia was concerned that their ideas might spread to other Central Asian Islamic communities, and Iran called their policies "medieval." (The Taliban were removed from power by the U.S.-led invasion that followed the September 2001 terrorist attacks.)

- As we will see in Chapter 9, Islamism has been the only significant opposition force in Egypt, where it has been carefully kept under control, but has been active both in the form of a mainstream political party—the Muslim Brotherhood—and of militant Islamist groups that have sometimes used violence to achieve their ends.

- In the Sudan, a civil war broke out in the early 1980s following the imposition on the non-Muslim south of the *sharia* by the government in the Muslim north. Despite the advent of a new military government in 1991 that reversed this decision, the war has continued, so far claiming an estimated 1.2 million lives and raising questions about the continued viability of Sudan as a united state.

ISLAMIC COUNTRIES TODAY

Islamic politics is influenced at one level by concerns about Western involvement in the affairs of the Islamic world. At other levels, it is influenced by the continuing internal debate about the nature of Islam, worries about its social and moral decline, and the gaps that some Muslims see between the will of Allah and the historical development of Islam.[15] In this sense, the Islamic resurgence is really only the latest in a series of revivalist movements that have tried to transform the political, religious, and social life of Islam.

Many Islamic countries were united first by their opposition to Israel (although almost all now recognize its right to exist) and more recently by criticism of Israeli policy toward Palestinians. However, the Islamic world has not been bound more closely by the common thread of Islam. Just as the earlier Islamic empires competed with one another, so Islamic countries are often at odds with one another today. The 1980–1988 Iran-Iraq war, one of the most brutal and costly in modern history, was at heart a conflict between Islamic nationalism (Iran) and secular Arab nationalism (Iraq), and it exemplified the ideological disagreements that still exist between Islamic states. Similarly, several Islamic states fought on the allied side against Iraq during the 1990–1991 Gulf crisis, while others took a pro-Iraqi line. Opinion was divided in 2002–2003 over the issue of how to deal with Iraq and charges that it had developed weapons of mass destruction, with opposition to U.S. policy—ironically—providing many Islamic states with something in common.

There is a sentimental attraction among many Muslims for the "Islamic cause" and among Arabs for the "Arab cause," but both are difficult to define and neither has had much success. Just as the concept of the Islamic *umma* has been undermined by the imposition of the nation-state, so Arab nationalists have been torn between *wataniyya* (loyalty to a particular country) and *qawmiyya* (loyalty to pan-Arabism). Economic logic suggests that the countries of the Middle East should work more closely together, if only because of their very different sizes.[16] Despite this, and despite the fact that so many Middle Eastern states are oil exporters, regional cooperation has made little progress.

Three particular organizations play an important role in pan-Islamic or pan-Arab affairs:

- The **Arab League** (founded in 1945) has promoted Arab nationalism, but its members are divided. Despite being a founding member, Egypt broke ranks in 1979 by signing the peace treaty with Israel and was temporarily expelled from the League. In 1990 the ranks of the League again broke over the Iraqi invasion of Kuwait, when an emergency summit of the League criticized the Iraqi invasion, an event that was itself symptomatic of Arab disunity.

- The Arab world plays a key role in the **Organization of Petroleum Exporting Countries** (OPEC), founded in 1960 by several Middle Eastern and Latin American oil-producing countries in an attempt to win greater control over their oil resources and to break the dominance of the major Western oil companies, which until then had controlled capital resources, technology, and distribution. By 1970, OPEC had 11 members who among them controlled 90 percent of the world's oil exports. Following the outbreak of war in 1973 between the Arabs and the Israelis, OPEC's Arab members imposed an embargo on exports to Israel's major allies in the West. The consequence was a sharp increase in oil prices, huge new profits for OPEC states, a global oil crisis, and major energy problems for the industrialized countries. However, OPEC has never been able to match that kind of power since, and not all Arab oil producers are members.

- Attempts to promote Islamic solidarity and consciousness have been made by the Muslim League (founded in 1962), the Islamic Pact (1966), and the **Organization of the Islamic Conference** (OIC). The OIC was founded in 1971, 2 years after an arsonist inflicted damage on the Al-Aqsa mosque in Jerusalem. Its immediate goals included the protection of Islamic holy sites and the creation of a Palestinian homeland, but its interests quickly expanded to focus on the promotion of Islamic solidarity. In 1975 it established the Islamic Development Bank, which provides interest-free loans to the OIC's poorer members and encourages investments and joint ventures within and among OIC states. Headquartered in Jeddah, Saudi Arabia, it now has 48 member states, including most of the states of the Middle East, of Africa north of the equator, and of central Asia.

  The OIC has been unable to overcome the focus by its members on their national interests at the expense of the collective interest of the Islamic *umma*. Its richer members tend to have more influence in the world than the OIC as a collective, its members have often conflicting economic and foreign policy interests, its regular conferences tend to consist of little more than a repetition of the rhetoric of Islamic solidarity, and it has been able to do little to address the problems of poverty and human rights abuses in many of its member states.[17] In many respects, its plight is reflective of the divisions within Islam more generally.

The absence of a common purpose—other than the negative philosophy of hostility to (or distrust of) the West—denies the Islamic world many of the threads that pull liberal democracies together. The latter have the common objectives of promoting democracy and capitalism, but critics charge that the Islamic world has lost direction and is failing either to completely rediscover the core values of Islamic philosophy or to adopt the more attractive elements of Western politics and economics. Unless and until it rises above political, doctrinal, religious, or social divisions, Islam will continue to face the identity crisis that has caused it so many problems over the last few centuries.

KEY TERMS

Arab empire
Arab League
Balfour Declaration
Islamic republic
Islamic resurgence
Islamism
Islamization
Organization of the
    Islamic Conference

Organization of Petroleum
    Exporting Countries
Ottoman Empire
patrimonialism
Pax Islamica
personalism
Quran
sharia
Shi'ah

shura
Sunni
theocracy
umma
universalism

KEY PEOPLE

Saddam Hussein
Ayatollah Khomeini

Osama bin Laden
Muhammad

STUDY QUESTIONS

1. How do the gaps between theory and practice in political Islam compare with those between theory and practice in liberal democracies?

2. Who is to blame for Islam's political problems: Islam, the West, or both?

3. The confrontation between the West and Islam has been likened to that between liberal democracy and communism during the cold war. What are the similarities, and what are the differences?

4. Is Islamism a religion or an ideology?

ISLAM ONLINE

It is difficult to find English-language sites on Islam that do not proselytize and difficult always to know the motives behind these sites. The following provide an interesting variety of options, although they emphasize Arab politics and culture.

ArabNet: *http://www.arab.net*
Owned by a Saudi research company, this includes links to sites on a wide variety of Arab-related topics, including news in English.

Arabia.com: *http://www.arabia.com/english*
Mainly information on business and culture, with country links (including some to Egypt), political news, links to English-language newspapers in the Middle East, and a link to the Paris-based newsletter *Issues.*

Islamic Gateway: *http://www.ummah.org.uk*
A British-based site that contains an interesting set of links to sites relating to Islam.

FURTHER READING

Bill, James A., and Robert Springborg, *Politics in the Middle East*, 5th Ed. (New York: Longman, 2000). The standard introduction to the politics of the region.

Anderson, Roy R., Robert F. Seibert, and Jon G. Wagner, *Politics and Change in the Middle East*, 6th Ed. (Upper Saddle River, NJ: Prentice Hall, 2001). A study of the role of Islam in the Middle East, including its history and its impact on politics and economics.

Esposito, John L., *Political Islam: Revolution, Radicalism or Reform?* (Boulder, CO: Lynne Rienner, 1997), and Esposito, John L., and John O. Voll, *Islam and Democracy* (New York: Oxford University Press, 1996). Two surveys of politics and democracy in Islamic societies; the latter includes case studies from six countries, including Egypt.

Husain, Mir Zohair, *Global Islamic Politics*, 2nd Ed. (New York: Longman, 2003). A study of the causes, meaning, and implications of the Islamic revival, with case studies from throughout the Islamic world.

EGYPT

EGYPT: QUICK FACTS

Official name: Arab Republic of Egypt (*Jamhuriyat Misr al-Arabiya*)

Capital: Cairo (*el-Qahira*)

Area: 382,865 square miles (991,620 sq. km) (three times the size of New Mexico)

Languages: Arabic (official), English and French widely understood by educated classes

Population: 64 million

Population density: 167 per square mile (64 per sq. km)

Population growth rate: 2.2 percent

POLITICAL INDICATORS

Freedom House rating: Not free

Date of state formation: February 28, 1922 (nominal independence from British protection established 1922; legal independence 1936, effective independence 1952)

System type: Presidential, limited democracy

Constitution: Published 1971

Administration: Unitary

Executive: President, serving 6-year renewable terms

Legislature: Bicameral: People's Assembly of 454 members, elected for 5-year terms, and a Consultative Assembly of 264 members

Party structure: Multiparty; 14 parties now recognized, but party activity controlled and system dominated by National Democratic party

Judiciary: Supreme Constitutional Court

Head of state: Hosni Mubarak (1981–)

Head of government: Atif Ebeid (1999–)

ECONOMIC INDICATORS

GDP (2001): $97.5 billion

Per capita GDP: $1,530

Distribution of GNP: Services 50 percent, industry 33 percent, agriculture 17 percent

Urban population: 45 percent

SOCIAL INDICATORS

HDI ranking: 105

Infant mortality rate: 42 per 1,000 live births

Life expectancy: 67.5 years

Literacy: 55 percent of people aged 15 and older

Religions: Islam is the state religion; 94 percent of the population is Muslim, the rest Christian and other religions

INTRODUCTION

Egypt has been the dominant political and economic actor in the Middle East for most of the 20th century. This is due partly to its size (there are about 64 million Egyptians), but mainly to its strong national identity and the fact that Egypt has been a distinct polity for nearly 5,000 years. The Egyptian nationalism that brought Gamal Abdel Nasser to power in a 1952 military coup had a long history, and Nasser went on to inspire at least two generations of Arab leaders. Between 1948 and 1979, Egyptian-Israeli hostility was at the heart of international relations in the region, and although Egypt and Israel are now at peace, Egypt remains a power broker between warring factions in the Middle East and a key point of contact for the West. Egypt also exerts a strong cultural influence: Its television programs, films, and music are watched or heard throughout the Arab world.

Egypt occupies a strategically important position at the conjunction of Asia and Africa and at the crossroads of the Middle East, the Arab world, and Islam. The heart of Egyptian culture and society has always been the fertile Nile River valley and delta, a ribbon of green and brown that bisects the country and supports 99 percent of the population. The major cities of Egypt—Cairo, Alexandria, Giza, Mansoura, and Zagazig—are all within 160 miles of one another at the mouth of the Nile. With more than 10 million people, Cairo is one of the biggest and most crowded cities in the world, and the Egyptian population, which is growing at 2.2 percent annually, is expected to double in the next 25 years.

In economic terms, Egypt is not a rich country. It has the second biggest economy in the Arab world after Saudi Arabia, but its per capita GDP of $1,530 makes it one of the poorest countries in the Middle East. The contribution of agriculture to national wealth has fallen since the mid-1960s as the contribution of industry and manufacturing has grown, but Egypt's major handicap is its lack of natural resources. About 95 percent of Egypt is too barren and dry to be habitable or cultivable, and although Egypt is an oil producer, its oil reserves are small. The only other major sources of revenue are foreign aid, tourism, revenues from the Suez Canal, and remittances from Egyptian workers living abroad. To complicate matters, Egypt has accumulated a national debt of $28 billion, and no government has succeeded in giving Egypt a strong economic base or in closing the wealth gap between the masses and the urban elite. There have been some signs of a modest economic upturn in recent years, but many problems remain.

In social terms, Egypt has none of the disruptive ethnic divisions of countries such as India or Nigeria. Most Egyptians are Arab, speak Arabic, and follow Islam. The only significant minority are the Copts, direct descendants of the early Christian Egyptians, who make up 6 percent of the population. But while Islam may give most Egyptians a strong common bond, it is also at the heart of the country's political divisions. There is an ongoing tension between secularism and Islamism, and militants have done their best to undermine government. They assassinated President Anwar Sadat in 1981, have made several attempts on the life of President Hosni Mubarak, and have launched attacks on tourists in an attempt to hit at one of Egypt's major sources of foreign income. One of the key militant groups declared a cease-fire in March 1999 (see Close-Up View, p. 486), but Islamism remains at the heart of a

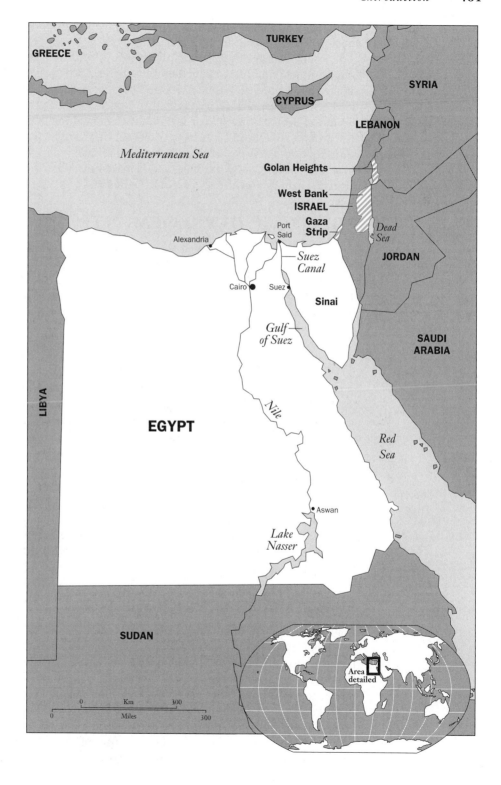

GREECE

TURKEY

CYPRUS

SYRIA

LEBANON

Mediterranean Sea

Golan Heights

West Bank

ISRAEL

Gaza
Strip

*Dead
Sea*

JORDAN

Port
Said

Alexandria

*Suez
Canal*

Cairo   Suez

Sinai

*Gulf
of Suez*

SAUDI
ARABIA

Nile

EGYPT

*Red
Sea*

LIBYA

Aswan

*Lake
Nasser*

SUDAN

Area
detailed

0   Km   300

0   Miles   300

debate over the goals of economic development and modernization and has had much influence on social values.

In political terms, Egypt has evolved since 1952 into a multiparty civilian system of government, but one in which power is centralized in the office of the president; supported by political, business, and military elites; and underpinned by a large and cumbersome bureaucracy. Egypt today is more democratic than before, but the process of democratization has been limited and halting and the control of opposition groups has left most Egyptian voters cut off from the political process. Political centralization has been heightened by Egypt's geography, which has concentrated most of its people along the Nile, and has been promoted by a tradition of personalism and rule by an elite rather than rule by law.

POLITICAL DEVELOPMENT

Despite its long and rich history, Egypt has spent most of the last 2,500 years under foreign domination. Only in 1952 did it finally establish political independence, but even then it found itself caught in rivalries involving first the British and the French, then the USSR and the United States, and then the West and Islam. For all these reasons, the emergence of the nation-state in Egypt has been a recent phenomenon, and state-building is still a work in progress.

The Era of the Pharaohs (3100–525 B.C.)

What we loosely define as civilization began in the fertile valley of the River Nile about 7,000 years ago. Nomadic peoples were attracted to the region by the rich silt deposited along the banks of the Nile. As more people arrived, an organized political and social system emerged. In about 3100 B.C., the first of many dynasties of pharaohs was established at Memphis, near present-day Cairo. This led to the unification of the country from the Nile Delta to Upper Egypt and the creation of one of the most sophisticated and successful cultures in history.

The era of the independent pharaohs ended in 525 B.C. with Egypt's defeat by the Persians. Except for a short break between 380 and 343 B.C., Egypt was to be dominated for the next 2,400 years by one alien power after another: First came the Persians, then the Greeks under Alexander the Great, the Romans, the Byzantines, and in 642 the Arabs, who brought with them Islam.

From the Arabs to the Ottomans (642–1875)

Arab rule lasted for about 600 years, established the Arabs as the majority ethnic group in Egypt, and led to the conversion of Egyptians from Christianity to Islam. In the tenth century a group of Shi'ah Muslims based in what is now Tunisia attacked Egypt and set up a new capital at el-Qahira (Cairo). In the face of growing external threats to Egypt, one of the last of the Arab rulers created a new regiment of Turkic slaves known as Mamluks (the owned). In 1250 the Mamluks became the new rulers of Egypt, which became the new center of Islamic culture and political power.

In 1517 the lower Nile valley became part of the growing Ottoman Empire. The Ottomans ruled indirectly through a corrupt and despotic group of Mamluks who took Egypt to the edge of ruin. In 1798 Napoleon arrived in Egypt, presenting himself as a liberator but actually aiming to establish a foothold in the Middle East as a means of threatening British power in India. Despite cloaking his administration in Islamic principles, Napoleon was not widely welcomed and had to put down two uprisings before finally being driven from Egypt in 1802 by the British and the Ottomans.

Egypt now came under the rule of Muhammed Ali (1769–1849), an Albanian who had risen through the ranks of the Egyptian army. He became governor in 1805, launching a dynasty that would rule Egypt until 1952. He tried to modernize Egypt by building a Western-trained army; introducing cotton in 1820; reforming local agriculture; building canals and dams to provide transport and a steady supply of water; and building iron foundries, munitions plants, a shipyard, and textile plants. His administration also marked the beginning of the state system in Egypt, which was unified for the first time in 300 years under a central authority based in Cairo.

The modernization was not to last, however, because there were too few qualified Egyptians to maintain the new economic system and because Europeans (the British in particular) worked to undermine the monopolies created by Muhammed Ali. He died in 1849, leaving behind a durable administrative system that gave Egypt a new prominence in the Middle East and reduced its allegiance to the Ottoman Empire. That prominence grew in 1854 when the French engineer Ferdinand de Lesseps was given a concession to build the **Suez Canal.** Opened to shipping in 1869, it was owned by Egypt and managed by French operators, but most of the shipping going through the canal was British.

The Era of the Europeans (1875–1952)

In the early 1870s, Egypt faced bankruptcy as cotton prices fell after the U.S. Civil War and a series of extravagant economic development schemes failed. Unable to pay its foreign debts, Egypt agreed in 1875 to sell its shares in the Suez Canal to Britain. To protect its new interests, Britain landed troops in 1882, and Egypt became to all intents and purposes a British protectorate, despite the fact that it was still technically a province of the Ottoman Empire. Britain continued to modernize Egypt but spent little on education or industry and gave Egyptians little say in government. A nationalist undercurrent developed, but its adherents disagreed on the role of Islam. In any case, Egypt was never declared an Islamic state, and its politics, government, and law have always leaned toward the secular and the Western.

In 1914 Britain went to war with the Ottoman Empire, which sided with Germany in World War I, and formally declared Egypt a protectorate. With British control over Egypt expanding, nationalists led by Saad Zaghlul (1857–1927), a high-ranking civil servant, formed *Wafd al-Misri* (the Egyptian Delegation) and began agitating for independence. When Zaghlul was deported in 1919, a mass insurrection grew, leading to an agreement by Britain to end the protectorate in 1922. Egypt now became a monarchy under King Fuad I, but British troops remained in the Suez Canal zone and Britain still controlled foreign and defense policy. A new constitution was drawn up, giving the king extensive powers but giving the new Egyptian parliament the power of veto. The Wafd party won a majority in the 1924 elections, and Zaghlul became prime minister.

TABLE 9.1

Key Dates in Modern Egyptian History

1798	Invasion by Napoleon
1805–1848	Muhammed Ali
1854–1869	Construction of the Suez Canal
1875	Egyptian shares in the Suez Canal sold to Britain
1914	British protectorate declared
1922	Independence granted under a League of Nations mandate
1936	Anglo-Egyptian Treaty
1937	Farouk succeeds to the throne
1948	Creation of Israel; first Arab-Israeli war
1952	Military coup (July 23); King Farouk abdicates
1953	Egypt becomes a republic
1954	Nasser becomes president
1956	(July) Suez Canal nationalized by Nasser; (October) invasion by Israeli, British, and French forces; Israel occupies Gaza strip
1958–1961	United Arab Republic (Egypt and Syria)
1967	(June) Six-Day War with Israel; Suez Canal closed; Israel occupies Sinai Peninsula
1970	Death of Nasser; succeeded by Anwar Sadat
1971	Corrective Revolution; new constitution; completion of Aswan High Dam
1973	Yom Kippur War with Israel
1979	(March) Peace treaty with Israel signed; Sinai returned to Egypt; Egypt suspended from the Arab League
1981	Assassination of Anwar Sadat; succeeded by Hosni Mubarak
1989	Egypt readmitted to the Arab League
1990	Egypt forges Arab coalition to free Kuwait following Iraqi invasion and takes part in the subsequent allied offensive
1991	Egypt signs agreements with the IMF and the World Bank in response to continuing debt problems
1993	Islamic militants make attempts on the lives of Egypt's information and interior ministers, and—in November—on Prime Minister Atef Sidqi
1995	Assassination attempt on Hosni Mubarak
1997	Construction begins on $1 billion Peace Canal to irrigate Sinai; (November) 48 tourists killed by Islamic militants in attack at Luxor
1999	(September) Assassination attempt on Hosni Mubarak, who is reelected for fourth term
2002	(July) Egypt celebrates 50th anniversary of Free Officers coup

In 1936 King Fuad died and was succeeded in 1937 by his son Farouk. An Anglo-Egyptian Treaty was signed and brought an end to the British military occupation, except along the Suez Canal. With the outbreak of World War II, however, British troops returned when Egypt was used as a base for the war against the Germans in North Africa. One of the most decisive battles of the war was fought in October 1942 at El Alamein, 70 miles west of Cairo, when the German Afrika Korps was turned back by British and Empire troops. Egypt benefited from Allied spending on industry and labor, but the new wealth was unevenly spread and land ownership was concentrated in the hands of Farouk and his supporters. Farouk made matters worse by developing a reputation as a playboy with a taste for food, yachts, and fast women.

Anti-British sentiment was strongest among the new corps of professional officers coming out of the Egyptian Military Academy, founded in 1936. The creation of Israel in 1948 sparked the first Arab-Israeli war, aimed at preventing the creation of the Jewish state. Israel survived, however, and nationalists blamed Egypt's poor showing on the weakness of the Farouk government and the incompetence of his commanders. Secret societies began plotting against the monarchy, among them the **Free Officers,** a group of about 300 junior military officers. On July 23, 1952, they overthrew Farouk, meeting little resistance.

Nasser and the Arab Republic (1952–1970)

The military emerged from the 1952 coup in a strong position, but the Free Officers had no particular plans about how to proceed. Farouk was sent into exile (he died in Italy in 1965), and the monarchy was abolished in 1953. All political parties were banned, and a nine-member Revolutionary Command Council (RCC) took power. General Mohammed Naguib became the first president of the republic in June 1953, but it soon became obvious that the real power behind the throne was Colonel Gamal Abdel Nasser. In November 1954, Naguib was arrested and Nasser became president.

Nasser saw a continued division between Islam and the state, but he increasingly used Islam as a means of legitimizing his brand of Arab socialism and of underpinning Egypt's claims to be leader of the Arab world.[1] Those claims were given new credibility with the **Suez crisis** of 1956, one of the major turning points in the history of international relations since 1945. The crisis grew out of Nasser's plan to build the $1.4 billion **Aswan Dam,** on the upper Nile. Britain and the United States agreed to provide part of the financing, but when Nasser bought arms from Czechoslovakia in 1955, the United States withdrew its financial support. Looking for another source of funding, Nasser nationalized the Suez Canal in July 1956, guaranteeing freedom of shipping and compensation for the mainly British and French stockholders. Apparently egged on by Britain and France, Israel attacked Egypt in October and Britain and France responded in November by invading the canal zone, supposedly to protect their interests. The Soviet Union, which had approved the nationalization of the canal, strongly criticized the invasion, and the United States demanded a withdrawal of all three armies. They were finally pulled out in March 1957 and replaced by a UN peacekeeping force.

The Suez crisis had several consequences: It led to the resignation of British prime minister Anthony Eden; hammered the last nails into the coffin of the ailing

GAMAL ABDEL NASSER

Not only is he widely regarded as the founder of modern Egypt, but Gamal Abdel Nasser (1918–1970) is still revered by many in the Middle East as one of the great heroes of the Arab cause. He led a coup that (he argued) gave Egypt its first truly Egyptian government since the fifth century B.C., and he was also responsible for a program aimed at modernizing Egypt and ending its subservient position in the global system. By so doing, he symbolized Arab resistance to the West.

Born in Alexandria in 1918, Nasser graduated from the Egyptian Military Academy, becoming an army officer in 1938. Almost immediately, he began plotting to overthrow the government and remove the British. He fought in the 1948 Arab-Israeli war, and in the same year helped form the Free Officers Movement, which elected as its leader General Mohammed Naguib and launched the coup of July 1952. In 1954 Nasser replaced Naguib first as prime minister and then as president. In June 1956 he was "elected" president and in 1958 became leader of the short-lived United Arab Republic.

Nasser not only built enormous popularity among Egyptians but was also popular in the wider Arab world for his stand against the West with the 1952 coup, for the 1956 nationalization of the Suez Canal, and for his hostility toward Israel. He played a leading role in the creation of the Non-Aligned Movement in 1955, coming to be regarded as one of its leaders alongside Yugoslavia's Marshal Tito, India's Jawaharlal Nehru, and China's Zhou Enlai. Despite his "nonalignment," however, he accepted military aid from Czechoslovakia in 1955, a move that the United States saw as an unwelcome extension of Soviet influence in the region.

Nasser died of a heart attack on September 28, 1970, at the early age of 52, and was succeeded by Anwar Sadat. Despite his authoritarianism, his occasional arrogance toward his Arab neighbors, and his unwillingness to tolerate dissent or opposition, Nasser's stature in the Arab world remains virtually unassailable. Just as many Americans and Europeans who were alive in 1963 remember where they were when they first heard of the assassination of John F. Kennedy, many Arabs who were alive in 1970 remember where they were when they first heard the news of Nasser's death.

French Fourth Republic; ended Anglo-French control over the canal; symbolized the end of Britain and France as major world powers; and bolstered Nasser's reputation in the Arab world, where his actions were seen as a slap in the face to the West. It also led to an increase in Soviet influence in the Middle East when the Soviets gave Nasser the aid he needed to build the Aswan Dam, which finally went into operation in 1971.

Nasser's reputation was further strengthened by an invitation from Syria in 1958 to become leader of a new Syrian-Egyptian federation, the **United Arab Republic (UAR)**. Syrian political parties were abolished, Cairo became the capital of the UAR, and Nasser became president of the new state. The marriage was not to last long, however. It was patently unequal, and the physical distance between the two countries made it impractical. The union collapsed after antiunionists took control in Syria in 1961.

In 1962 Nasser created the **Arab Socialist Union** (ASU), which had all the outward appearances of a political party but actually was little more than an institution he could use to extend his control. Through the Union, he promoted a philosophy of "scientific Arab socialism," which he argued was compatible with Islamic principles and would allow the Arab world to build a political and economic position independent of either superpower. (Despite his claims that Egypt was nonaligned, Nasser bought weapons from the USSR and invited thousands of Soviet military advisors into Egypt, causing many sleepless nights in the U.S. State Department.)

If the 1950s had seen Nasser's rise as a leader of the Arab cause, the 1960s saw his credibility diluted, notably when Egypt was defeated in the 1967 Arab-Israeli war, otherwise known as the **Six-Day War.** Responding to border incidents, acts of sabotage, verbal threats, and the signing of a mutual defense treaty between Egypt and Jordan, Israel launched a preemptive strike on June 5 against Egypt, Jordan, Syria, and Iraq. Within hours, the air forces of all four Arab states had been virtually destroyed, and by June 10 the Israelis had overrun the **Sinai Peninsula** and forced a cease-fire. The defeat left Egypt battered and demoralized, and—for some—seemed to confirm Islam's impotence. Nasser took responsibility for the defeat and resigned, but such was his popularity that he was persuaded to return to office.

In March 1969 Nasser launched a War of Attrition against the Israelis in the Sinai, which brought costly counterattacks by Israeli artillery and jets. Nasser accepted Soviet military aid but said he would also accept a U.S.-sponsored cease-fire. With his death in September 1970, plans for the cease-fire were suspended.

Peace with Israel (1979–)

Egypt since 1970 has been led by two men: Anwar Sadat (1970–1981) and Hosni Mubarak (1981–). A veteran of the Free Officers Movement who was driven by a concern to move out from under the shadow of Nasser, Sadat continued Egypt's economic development. He also made it his priority to take back the Sinai Peninsula and reduce Egyptian dependence on the USSR. In October 1973, during **Yom Kippur** (the Jewish Day of Atonement), he launched a surprise attack against Israel. Crying "Allahu Akbar!" ("God is Great!"), Egyptian troops crossed the canal and took some Israeli fortifications. Israel immediately counterattacked and recrossed the canal within hours, but Egypt's moment in the sun was enough to earn Sadat the title "Hero of the Crossing." A cease-fire was arranged, but the exchange gave Sadat the opportunity to look for a diplomatic resolution of the Arab-Israeli impasse.

The failure of U.S.-mediated negotiations in 1974–1976 prompted Sadat to make the bold and ultimately fatal gesture of flying to Jerusalem, becoming the first (and still only) Egyptian leader ever to visit Israel. Negotiations led to the **Camp David Accords** of 1978, agreed to under the sponsorship of President Jimmy Carter. When Egypt and Israel signed a peace treaty in 1979, the Sinai was finally returned to Egypt. Despite this, Sadat was accused by other Arab leaders of selling out to the United States and Israel, and he never won the same level of trust and admiration in the Arab world as Nasser.

The Egyptian economy improved little during Sadat's tenure, despite his policy of liberalizing the economy (known as *Infitah*) and allowing new foreign investment in Egypt. On the political front, he tried to offset criticisms of the peace treaty with

Israel by allowing three factions to emerge within and eventually supersede the ASU. He also allowed Islamic opposition groups to operate, but when they openly criticized the peace treaty, he cracked down. Their response was deadly. On October 6, 1981, while reviewing a military parade on the outskirts of Cairo, Sadat was shot to death by members of a group of Islamic radicals. Showing how he had become more popular outside Egypt than within, three U.S. presidents attended his funeral, but he was barely mourned in the Arab world.

Egypt Today

Sadat was smoothly succeeded by Hosni Mubarak, who was confirmed to a second term as president in 1987, a third in 1993, and a fourth in 1999. As well as continuing to promote economic growth, Mubarak has had to walk a fine line between restoring Egypt's reputation among its Arab neighbors and maintaining good relations with Israel. Careful diplomacy led to Egypt's readmittance to the Arab League in May 1989, 10 years after it was expelled in retaliation for signing the peace treaty with Israel. In August 1990 Egypt played a pivotal role in organizing an Arab response to the Iraqi invasion of Kuwait and sent 32,000 troops to the region, a contingent second in size only to that of the United States.

At home, Mubarak has had to balance the demands of Islamists with his plans to promote a secular Egyptian state. He has continued to democratize Egypt in a carefully controlled process, and most opposition parties consider him preferable to a more authoritarian or radical Islamic alternative.[2] Egypt has been under a state of emergency since the assassination of Sadat, and Mubarak used his emergency powers to clamp down on Islamic militancy during the 1990s; more than 1,200 people were killed in acts of violence between 1992 and 1999, the worst being an attack on tourists at Luxor in the Nile valley in November 1997, which left 52 people dead. Militants also tried to assassinate Mubarak during a visit to Ethiopia in June 1995, but following the declaration of a cease-fire in March 1999, the government became more lenient toward the militants, despite another attempt on Mubarak's life in September 1999.

The economic news has been mixed, with falling inflation, growing unemployment, not enough foreign investment, and a halting program of privatization. Meanwhile, Mubarak has clamped down on political corruption and has allowed opposition parties to expand their activities. However, the pace of political reform has not kept up with economic reforms, and there is a growing impatience for change at the top. With his reelection for a fourth term in September 1999, Mubarak became the longest-serving Egyptian leader in more than 150 years, and there were no obvious successors in sight (unless one believes gossip that he is grooming his son Gamal to take over). Pressure has recently grown for him to appoint a vice president to help ensure the continuity of government and of his policies.

POLITICAL CULTURE

When the Free Officers took power in 1952, there was little in the way of an established political structure that they could build on, reform, or even abolish. There had been little popular participation; there were few organized economic, social, or political groups; and there was no tradition of political accountability. However, there had been a tradition of centralization and a strong, bureaucratized state.

A Dominant State

For most of its history, Egypt has been governed by strong leaders using authoritarian methods. It has been argued that Egyptians during the Sadat years came to expect "harsh government as almost a natural phenomenon about which little could be done except to adapt or to evade its exactions."[3] Having become used to a strong state system with little public accountability, Egyptians see themselves as separated from the state. There is little sense of belonging or of mutual responsibility between the governors and the governed, creating a political gulf that limits the growth of political consciousness and participation. An example of the lengths to which the Mubarak administration is prepared to go to stifle opposition came in June 2002, when Dr. Saadeddin Ibrahim—an American-educated sociology professor—was jailed for 7 years, charged with tarnishing Egypt's image abroad. One of Egypt's best-known champions of clean government, Ibrahim ran an independent research institute and was deeply critical of the way recent elections had been managed. He was held initially under the state of emergency that has been in force in Egypt since 1981.

A Patrimonial Society

Patrimonialism and personalism have always been important features of Islamic society, building on the patriarchal system at the core of all traditional societies. While the patriarch operates at the family level with no machinery in place to enforce his will, the patrimonial leader sets up an identifiable administrative structure and rules through an extensive bureaucratic network.[4] Patrimonialism has been a theme in Egyptian political leadership since the pre-coup days, monarchs and presidents alike portraying themselves as father figures and using networks of supporters to keep a grip on power and limit the growth of autonomous political institutions. Before 1952, the king was at the hub of the system. With Nasser, army officers became the new elite, and they were subsequently joined by the bureaucracy, business leaders, and party leaders. Sadat and Mubarak have both exploited the patrimonial tradition and the attendant shortcuts it provides to authoritarian government.

Localism and the Peasant Society

More than half of all Egyptians are peasants (or *fellahin*) and live in 7,000 villages scattered along the Nile. Much like Indian villagers, their lives are tied to the land, reach no more than a few miles from the village, and are inherently conservative. Recent studies have shown a growing awareness among peasants about events in Cairo and beyond, but those studies have also shown little inclination among peasants to respond or take part. Even Nasser realized that the traditional mistrust of the *fellahin* toward government would make it dangerous to give the impression that the government wanted to make them into state functionaries by nationalizing or collectivizing farms. Nasser's interest in improving the quality of life for the peasants, combined with the changes he made with land reform and the expansion of social services, made him a hero among the *fellahin*.[5]

As economic development and urbanization change the social structure of Egypt, the *fellahin* population is declining in relative terms, and the new urban middle class and working class are growing. As this happens, traditional culture is being undermined, forcing the government to respond by allowing more public access to the political process. Centralization and patrimonialism are becoming less acceptable, and although they are still weak, autonomous political institutions such as the legislature, political parties, and the media are winning more power.

Religious-Secular Tension

Islam is the state religion of Egypt, and all three of its modern presidents have claimed to be true believers and have felt obliged at least to go through the motions of identifying themselves with Islam. In fact, there has been a tendency toward secularism in government and public policy, even though Islamists have worked hard to encourage Egyptians to adopt traditional Islamic values. There were signs during the late 1980s that these values were slowly spreading—notably as more women wore veils or completely covered their bodies—but they now seem to be on the wane. The shift has been a result of the ongoing debate within Islam about the nature of modernity. Physical signs of that modernity are everywhere, with fast food, cell phones, satellite dishes, early signs of a Muslim feminist movement, and more Egyptians hooked up to the Internet. This does not mean that Muslims are rejecting the religion, but rather that they are increasingly adapting it to modern pressures.

POLITICAL SYSTEM

Egypt is an emerging democracy in the sense that political power has been devolved since 1952 from a military elite to a broader, popular constituency. This is still a very limited constituency, however, and the average Egyptian has little influence over politics or government. Opposition groups are controlled, political institutions are still evolving, and the pace of democratization has been carefully regulated. Anwar Sadat spoke of his support for the rule of law and his desire to create a "state of institutions," but he was not prepared to give these institutions autonomy. Hosni Mubarak has allowed the creation of new political parties, but government control of the electoral system has prevented them from winning more than a handful of seats. The constitution describes Egypt as a "democratic socialist state" and condemns exploitation and income differences, yet levels of personal income vary widely.

It has been argued that a common feature of politics in poorer states is the dominance of policy-implementing institutions (such as the military and bureaucracy) over policymaking institutions (such as legislatures and parties).[6] This is certainly true of Egypt, where politics revolves around personalities rather than institutions and where power is expressed through an unwieldy bureaucracy, creating a phenomenon described as "bureaucratic feudalism."[7] The 1952 coup was not a popular revolution but instead was carried out by a small group of army officers working in what they thought was the public interest. Once in power, the Free Officers were driven less by ideology than by a belief in change, a concern to avoid the worst mistakes of capitalism and communism, and a desire to end Egypt's subordination to the West.

Arguing that discipline rather than democracy was the key to changing Egypt,[8] and worried about opposition from every quarter, the officers created a political system that remains authoritarian, centralized, bureaucratic, and elitist and that revolves around personality politics, nepotism, and patronage. The president sits at the center and rules through personal networks rather than through well-defined institutions. His power is underpinned by a network of elites, whose influence radiates in concentric circles. Closest to the president is the **core elite.** Under Nasser this elite consisted mainly of the military and a few influential civilians, but it has since expanded to include ministers, military commanders, senior civil servants, managers of public sector businesses, newspaper editors, religious and academic leaders, heads of syndicates and chambers of commerce, members of parliament, and party leaders.

The support of the elite has been encouraged under Mubarak with rewards and inducements such as job offers in government, the bureaucracy, joint-venture business enterprises in which the government has a stake, public organizations, or the governing National Democratic party.[9] Dissent and opposition are contained, notably through the state security apparatus and other government ministries. Given the extent to which political participation is controlled, Islamists have become the only significant source of opposition to the government.

THE CONSTITUTION

Egypt's first constitution—published in 1923—created a limited democracy that might have laid the foundations of a lasting parliamentary democracy had it not been changed to give the monarch the right to appoint the prime minister, dismiss the cabinet, and dissolve parliament. It was suspended in 1952 and replaced in 1956 by a new document that made Egypt a republic, gave considerable power to the president, and included a commitment to economic planning and social welfare. During his 16-year tenure, Nasser drew up five more constitutions, the 1964 version of which described Egypt as a "democratic socialist" state and declared Islam to be the state religion.

The eighth (and most recent) constitution was drawn up in 1971, and—like constitutions in most authoritarian states—it includes ideas that are still not put into practice. For example, it declares that the *sharia* is the "principal" source for law and the legal system, yet Egypt remains a secular state. Opposition parties have called for a new constitution that would guarantee human rights, give the legislature more powers, and limit the president to two 4-year terms, but few changes of a democratic nature have been made.

THE EXECUTIVE: PRESIDENT

The Egyptian political system is often compared with that of France or Russia, which have a **dual executive:** a powerful president, separately elected from the legislature, and a prime minister, who is appointed and dismissed by the president. The French and Russian presidents tend to act as guides and arbiters, while prime ministers roll up their sleeves and jump into the fray of day-to-day politics. The Egyptian system has some of the features of a dual executive (with a president and a prime minister), but the balance of power lies much more with the president, and—predictably—the system is often described as having a pyramidal structure with the president sitting at the peak in the role of a modern-day pharaoh. He so dominates the system that all other institutions are peripheral, although the legislature and political parties are becoming more important.

The Egyptian president is not directly elected by the people. Instead, the president must be nominated by at least one-third of the members of the People's Assembly, confirmed by at least two-thirds of the members, and then "elected" by a popular referendum for an unlimited number of 6-year terms. The referendum is not so much an election as confirmation of the choice of the legislature, which is dominated by the governing party; its choice is automatically confirmed, and voters are faced with a simple choice: yes or no to the legislature's nominee. In the 1999 "election," President Mubarak had the support of 98 percent of the members of the legislature and was allegedly confirmed by nearly 94 percent of the nearly 80 percent of registered voters who took part in the referendum.

Once in office, the president has an array of powers greater than those of any other leader covered in this book:

- He can hire and fire a large number of people, including his vice president, prime minister, the cabinet, the governor of the Central Bank, senior military leaders, managers of publicly owned businesses, newspaper editors, party leaders, judges, university presidents, and provincial governors. He can even make himself prime minister, as Mubarak did in 1981–1982.

- He suggests all major legislation, has the power of veto, determines all major policies, and effectively handpicks members of parliament. Through favors, appointments, and rewards, the president can make sure that his legislation is accepted. If he finds the People's Assembly uncooperative, he can dissolve it and call new elections, provided only that he wins the approval of a majority in a referendum.

- He can issue decrees and decisions that have the power of law, he can call and chair meetings of the Council of Ministers, and he can call public referenda to change the constitution, as did Sadat in 1980 when he gave himself an unlimited number of 6-year terms in office.

- He can use emergency powers if "national unity or safety" is threatened (notions which are open to wide interpretation) or if the "Constitutional role of state institutions" is obstructed or threatened. An emergency was declared in 1981 following the assassination of President Sadat and has since been renewed every 3 years.

- He is commander-in-chief, can declare war with legislative approval (which is guaranteed), has complete control over foreign and defense policy, and can conclude treaties with other countries, not all of which need legislative approval.

Given all these powers, understanding the presidency is less a question of appreciating the formal rules of the office than of understanding how incumbents have defined the office. Each Egyptian president has stamped a unique character on the job.

The Nasser Presidency (1956–1970)

The Nasser administration could be described as a "benevolent dictatorship." He and the other Free Officers had no clear plan for Egypt, but they were convinced that the old regime would mean continued social divisions and poverty for the majority of Egyptians. They believed that a new system based on equality and justice would somehow evolve out of the ashes of the old regime. When this did not happen, and when it seemed clear that the old elite was being replaced by a new one, Nasser argued the need for a transitional phase in which changes could be generated by his leadership; he called this "guided democracy."[10]

Tolerating no overt criticism, Nasser—popularly known as *El-Rais*, or the Boss—surrounded himself with a core elite recruited mainly from the military. To some extent this elite worked as a communal leadership; policy was made within the elite and imposed through the military and the bureaucracy. The army was the basis of his support, but Nasser also controlled the internal security apparatus and the one protoparty (the Arab Socialist Union, or ASU), and he regularly reshuffled ministers and other senior officials to prevent anyone from building an independent base of support. His power was underpinned by a cult of personality, reflected in the many titles by which he was known, including "Father Gamal," "Destroyer of Imperialism," and "Hero of Heroes."

Because he depended so much on his charisma and on the personal link between him and his followers, power was not institutionalized. The stability that Nasser himself provided stood in sharp contrast to the instability of other institutions; his parliaments lasted 2 years on average and his cabinets 13 months, and he promulgated six constitutions in 16 years.[11] And despite his criticism of the Farouk regime and its elitism, military leaders during the Nasser years began to take on many of the trappings of the old elite. They became less interested in the wider needs of Egyptians and more concerned with personal power. Egypt's humiliation in the 1967 Arab-Israeli war seemed to confirm just how ineffectual and corrupt the system had become. Despite the defeat and mass demonstrations in 1968 that seemed to suggest that the people wanted a greater say in politics and government, Nasser himself survived, his popularity barely dented. This could be partly explained by the fact that most Egyptians did not know just how badly their country had been beaten in the war; had they known, they might have been less charitable toward the Boss.

The Sadat Presidency (1970–1981)

The centrality of Nasser to the Egyptian political system was reflected in the power struggle that followed his death. He had made few plans for the succession, and there was no formal process in place by which a new president could be elected. The office of vice president had been abolished in 1968, but it was revived in 1969 and given to Sadat, who became such a trusted lieutenant of Nasser's that he earned the nickname "Colonel Yes-Yes." Sadat succeeded Nasser, and although he inherited the strength of the presidency, little was known about him, few Egyptians even knew what he looked like, and few expected him to last long. They were to be proved quite wrong.

TABLE 9.2

Modern Leaders of Egypt

Head of state	Prime minister
1936 Farouk	(12 in the period 1944–1952)
1952 Ahmad Fouad II	1952 Mohammed Naguib
1953 Mohammed Naguib	
1954 Gamal Abdel Nasser	1954 Gamal Abdel Nasser (February–March)
	Mohammed Naguib (March–April)
	Gamal Abdel Nasser (April–)
	1962 Ali Sabri
	1965 Zakariya Mohieddin
	1966 Muhammad Sedki Sulayman
	1967 Gamal Abdel Nasser
1970 Anwar Sadat	1970 Mahmoud Fawzi Desoqi Gohari
	1972 Aziz Sedki
	1973 Anwar Sadat
	1974 Abdel-Aziz Hejazi
	1975 Mahmoud Muhammad Salem
	1978 Mustafa Khalil
	1980 Anwar Sadat
1981 Sufi Abu Talib (acting)	1981 Hosni Mubarak
1981 Hosni Mubarak	
	1982 Ahmad Fuad Mohieddin
	1984 Kamal Hassan Ali
	1985 Ali Mahmoud Lufti
	1986 Atef Sidqi
1987 Hosni Mubarak	
1993 Hosni Mubarak	
	1996 Kamal al-Ganzouri
1999 Hosni Mubarak	1999 Atif Ebeid

Born the same year as Nasser, Sadat had been a member of the Free Officers and from 1961 to 1969 was speaker of the Egyptian legislature. Regarded by many Nasserites as a usurper, the way in which Sadat confirmed his position and made the presidency his own says much about how Egyptian politics works. Although Sadat was quickly confirmed as president by both the ASU and the National

Assembly, his position was far from secure, and he faced opposition from his vice president, Ali Sabri, and from the Central Committee of the ASU. The army and the legislature were on his side, though, and Sadat was able to bide his time and build support. His authority was finally confirmed in a series of rapid-fire events in May 1971, described by Sadat as the **Corrective Revolution:** He fired Sabri; purged senior members of the military, the police, the ASU, and the intelligence service; reorganized the cabinet; appointed key governors; had street demonstrations in his support; disbanded the ASU Central Committee; and set up a committee to carry out elections to the ASU.[12] By the end of May, Sadat was firmly established in power. Within months, a new constitution was published on his instructions, and the anniversary of the Corrective Revolution subsequently became a national holiday.

Sadat may have been more liberal than Nasser, but his methods regularly bordered on autocratic. His tenure has been described as a "presidential monarchy": He wanted political institutions to function, but if they deviated from his definition of the public interest, he saw it as his job to set them right. Whereas Nasser addressed the Egyptian people as "brothers," Sadat was more overtly paternalistic. He saw himself as *rabb alaila al-misriya* (head of the Egyptian family), described the people as "my children," and talked about "my constitution," "my parties," and "my opposition."

Although Sadat had removed his opponents, he also believed that it was important to build a popular base of support and to give his government legitimacy. Claiming to abhor the personalism and mistrust that surrounded Nasser, he began devolving power to the legislature, the press, and a multiparty system, while at the same time making sure that the presidency monitored and controlled all these other centers of power. In May 1980 he took the job of prime minister for himself, arranged a referendum to end the constitutional limit of two terms for a president, and effectively became president for life. He also created a new upper house designed to strengthen his control of the legislature.

The Mubarak Presidency (1981–)

Mubarak became president by virtue of being vice president when Sadat died, and he represented a new generation of political leaders, having been only 24 at the time of the Free Officers coup. He has been more low-key, cautious, pragmatic, and conciliatory than his predecessors; claims to be a religious moderate; has avoided the cult of personality; and argues that he is an exception to traditional Islamic paternalism. (See People in Politics, p. 476.)

In policy terms, Mubarak's options have been limited by Egypt's severe economic and social problems, by the need to contain the Islamic opposition, and by Egypt's position at the hub of the Arab world. Mubarak has maintained a state of emergency during his entire term, although he has won the confidence of opposition parties by including them in policy debates.[13] He has allowed an opposition press to operate and has increased the number of parties from 4 to 14. He initially showed little inclination for holding on to power indefinitely, but he stood for—and won—a third 6-year term in October 1993. He said it would be his last, but then allowed himself to be "elected" unopposed to a fourth term in September 1999.

PEOPLE IN POLITICS

HOSNI MUBARAK

AP/Wide World Photos

Hosni Mubarak has been president of Egypt since 1981, making him one of the longest-serving heads of state in the world. Despite his longevity, and despite the importance of Egypt to U.S. interests in the Middle East, Americans know much less about him than they did about his predecessor, Anwar Sadat. While Sadat became a world statesman, both praised and pilloried for his overtures to Israel, Mubarak has kept his head below the barricades and is not known for bold initiatives.

Born in 1928 in the Nile delta village of Kafr-El Meselha, Mohamed Hosni Mubarak was one of five children of an inspector in the ministry of justice. He graduated from the national military academy in 1947 with degrees in military and aviation sciences, trained as an air force fighter pilot and instructor (spending time in the Soviet Union), was appointed director of the air force academy in 1968, was made air force chief of staff in 1969 by Nasser, and was elevated to commander of the air force by Sadat in 1972. He led the air force during the 1973 Yom Kippur War and—to the surprise of many—was made vice president in 1975, probably because he was competent and dependable without being a political threat to Sadat; Nasser had made Sadat his vice president for similar reasons.

Mubarak was sitting beside Sadat when he was assassinated in October 1981 but was only slightly wounded. Within a week he had been nominated as president, and his "election" was confirmed in a national referendum. Mubarak subsequently made the office his own but used less authoritarian methods than his predecessor. His priorities have included greater freedom for opposition parties; taking on—and ultimately defeating—Islamic militancy during the 1990s; keeping on good terms with Israel, the United States, and the Arab world; and maintaining a steady program of privatization aimed at strengthening the private sector in Egypt. He has survived at least four assassination attempts and was "reelected" to his fourth term in office in 1999. Given that he will be 77 when his current term runs out in 2005, pressure has been growing on him to appoint a vice president and groom a successor. Although he repeatedly denied it, speculation mounted in early 2003 that he was grooming his son Gamal when the latter was appointed political secretary of the NDP, the third most senior position in the party.

THE LEGISLATURE: PEOPLE'S ASSEMBLY

The legislative arm of the Egyptian government consists of three elements: a prime minister, a Council of Ministers (or cabinet), and a quasi-bicameral legislature. The prime minister and other ministers are all appointed and removed by the president, do not need to be members of the legislature, and are often chosen more for their loyalty than for their abilities. To prevent anyone from developing enough power to oppose the president, cabinet posts are regularly reshuffled.

Prime ministers tend to be functionaries of the president, overseeing the government's legislative program, focusing on domestic issues, coming and going very quickly, and being little known outside Egypt. The most notable holder of the office was Atef Sidqi, who also was the longest holder of the office: 1986–1996. Much like Viktor Chernomyrdin in Russia, Sidqi was loyal, dull, and dependable; posed no threat to Mubarak's position; and overall was a safe choice for the post. He pushed Egypt steadily toward a market economy before being replaced in 1996 by Kamal al-Ganzouri. In an attempt to inject some new blood into the cabinet at the beginning of his fourth term in 1999, Mubarak replaced al-Ganzouri with Atef Ebeid. American-educated (with a Ph.D. from the University of Illinois) and a longtime member of the Council of Ministers (to which he was first appointed in 1984), Ebeid was centrally involved in Mubarak's privatization program, and his promotion was seen as an indication of the centrality of that program to Mubarak's new term in office.

Egypt has had a legislature since 1923, when a bicameral parliament was created, with a Senate and a Chamber of Deputies. It could override the king with a two-thirds majority, but the king appointed the ministers and 40 percent of the senators and could dissolve parliament and rule by decree, so it was little more than a legislative façade. Under the 1956 constitution, a unicameral National Assembly was created, with 350 members. It was replaced in 1958 with the National Assembly for the United Arab Republic (with 400 members from Egypt and 200 from Syria), which did little more than rubber-stamp Nasser's policies.

Changes made by Sadat created the current arrangement.

Consultative Assembly (*Majlis al-Shura*)

Established by Sadat in 1980, the Consultative Assembly is not a full-fledged upper chamber, but it has many of the trappings of a legislative body. Although its powers are limited and it was once dismissed as "a retirement haven for burned-out top-level bureaucrats, ministers, and politicians,"[14] it must be consulted on constitutional amendments, treaties, draft laws referred by the president, and any policy issues referred by the president. It has 264 members, of whom 176 are elected to renewable 6-year terms and the rest appointed by the president. Half come up for reelection or reappointment every 3 years, and half of the elected members must be workers or farmers. In recent elections, the ruling National Democratic party has won a monopoly in the chamber.

People's Assembly (*Majlis al-Shaab*)

Replacing the National Assembly in 1971, the People's Assembly has 444 elected members (deputies) and 10 members appointed by the president. Between 1983 and 1990, 400 deputies were elected using proportional representation; the remaining 44

Prime Minister Atef Ebeid (right) addresses the People's Assembly in Cairo. Unlike dual executives in countries such as France, the Egyptian version is heavily weighted toward the president, and the People's Assembly has been little more than a rubber-stamp and a safety valve to keep opposition parties under control.

seats were reserved for independents. This was deemed unconstitutional by the Constitutional Court, so the electoral system was changed for the 1995 elections to one based on 222 districts, with the top two vote winners in each district being elected. As with the Consultative Assembly, half the members must be workers or farmers. The Assembly is elected for 5-year terms, but it can be dissolved by the president before the 5 years are up if he wins public support in a referendum, which he always does. New elections must then be held within 60 days.

The legislature was relatively weak under Nasser but became stronger under Sadat. Sadat not only gave it greater freedom of expression but also allowed the emergence of opposition groups and parties and used the Assembly as a source of policy ideas, from changes in land tenure to suggestions that shares in public companies be sold off to private investors. It also became a link between the government and the people.

The People's Assembly has several constitutional powers that seem to limit those of the president: It can reject laws proposed by the government or decreed by the president, can propose laws of its own, and has close control over the national budget. It also has the power of oversight: It can monitor the performance of the government, ask ministers to appear before it to be questioned, relay problems or grievances from citizens, and hold investigations and hearings into government activities. Finally, it can debate government policy, although this means little in real terms. Parliamentary debates in Egypt were once described as follows: "The normal pattern . . . has been to tear a given policy to pieces in committee. . . , to give ample newspaper . . . coverage to the findings, and then to have the Assembly as a whole approve the policy with marginal modifications."[15]

The lack of independence of the Assembly is reflected clearly in election results; at no time has the governing National Democratic party ever won less than 70 percent of the seats. Because the president controls the party, sets the legislative program for the Assembly, and can bypass the Assembly any time he likes, it is clearly no more than a legislative façade designed to bolster the authority of the presidency.

THE JUDICIARY: SUPREME CONSTITUTIONAL COURT

Despite the weaknesses of the constitution, Egypt has a Supreme Constitutional Court that is responsible for interpreting the constitution and occasionally influences government policy. The work of the Court is undermined by at least two major problems: First, Egyptian law is confusing by nature; it consists of a mixture of Islamic, French, British, and Soviet-inspired influences and can easily be negated by presidential decrees and states of emergency. Second, judges are overworked and underpaid.

The Court has played an important role in revealing the weaknesses in the Egyptian definition of democracy. It has been particularly active on the issue of elections, beginning when it voided the 1984 and 1987 elections to the People's Assembly on the grounds that electoral law discriminated against independent candidates. This led to changes in the electoral law and the holding of new elections in December 1990, nearly 18 months early. But the Court declared that the governing National Democratic party had interfered in the outcome of the 1990 and 1995 elections as well, casting doubts on the legitimacy of the entire legislative process. These decisions exemplify the role of the Court as the only significant opposition to the powers of the government. Critics of those powers argue that there is so much confusion in the existing system that nothing less than a new constitution will solve Egypt's legal problems.

THE MILITARY

Since the 1952 Free Officers coup, the military has played an important supporting role in Egyptian government and society, not least because all three of its presidents have been former military officers (the army for Nasser and Sadat, the air force for Mubarak). Nasser claimed that he saw the military as a vanguard in the vein of Lenin's Bolsheviks: a group that would take power on behalf of the people and then hand over that power when the people wanted it.[16] In fact, power in Egypt from 1952 until 1967 lay in a mutually supportive relationship between the government and the military, which was without doubt the strongest institution in the political system.

Sadat continued to promote the power of the military over that of civilian institutions, using the success of the armed forces in the 1973 crossing of the Suez Canal to restore the prestige of the military (but keeping the full truth of their performance from the Egyptian people). He also gave officers promotions, secondments to the government, and salary increases. Part of the reason Hosni Mubarak was chosen as vice president was so Sadat could be sure that the air force was controlled by the government.[17]

A major challenge for Mubarak when he came to office was to give the military a sense of purpose in the aftermath of the 1979 peace treaty. The military had been almost halved during the late 1970s (from 900,000 personnel to 500,000), and its mission was altered from preparing for war with Israel to becoming a rapid strike force with the ability to intervene in other regional trouble spots. Mubarak ended the reductions and appointed as chief of staff—and eventually minister of defense and deputy prime minister—a former classmate named Abd al-Halim Abu Ghazala. In recent years, the military has expanded its interests into the civil sphere, even going so far as to build highways, clean polluted beaches, and run new farms. The military is still a key institution in the political system, compelling the government to maintain a balance between the civilian and military sectors of society.

SUBNATIONAL GOVERNMENT

Given that Egypt is a unitary state, that almost all Egyptians live in the vicinity of a single river, and that its rulers have long favored centralized control, local government is a relatively minor element in the political system. This is not to say that the local community—particularly the peasant community—has no importance; it just has little independence. In the rural areas, the village is the basic social unit, and villagers have traditionally owed their allegiance to the village headman, or *umdeh*. Clientelism is still so strong in these communities that an *umdeh* might be able to deliver the entire vote of his village to the governing party, in return for policies that support his position and his privileges.

The highest level of local government in Egypt is the governorate (or *muhafazah*), of which there are 26, each with its own governor appointed by the president. Below these are 133 districts and hundreds of villages, each with an appointed executive officer and executive council. The higher-level executives are hired and fired at the discretion of the president of Egypt.

REPRESENTATION AND PARTICIPATION

The average Egyptian has little influence on politics. Several legal political parties exist, but none have enough power to overrule the government-sanctioned National Democratic party. There are elections, but turnout is low and the results prove little beyond the regime's control of the electoral system.[18] Egypt has a poor record on human rights, and Egyptian leaders have little public accountability, ignoring, except in the most limited way, the principle of *shura* (consultation). At the same time, some recent trends point toward democratization, and public opinion is taken more seriously than before. The Mubarak era in particular has seen the rise of opposition political parties and an opposition press, and more leniency has recently been shown toward the Islamist opposition.

ELECTIONS AND REFERENDA

Egyptian elections are neither free nor fair. Official turnout figures are inflated, the results lead to few changes in policy or the makeup of government, and the choices facing Egyptian voters have been controlled by the government. The 1956 constitution created the National Assembly, but all candidates had to be screened by the only legal party, the National Union, and official electoral turnout figures were high only because voting was compulsory or the figures were exaggerated. No competing parties ran in the election, and the Assembly was little more than a rubber stamp for the policies of the Nasser government.

The choice for Egyptian voters broadened during the Sadat administration, when three officially sanctioned parties were created. However, they were so patently manipulated by the government that the 1976 elections could hardly be described as competitive. Hosni Mubarak has allowed more parties to be licensed during his administration, and although the governing party wins a near monopoly of seats in the legislature, elections are at least contested by groups that look like political parties.

The election process is controlled by state agencies, and banks and agricultural loan agencies are used in rural areas to provide incentives to voters to turn out. State control goes so far as regulating the flow of information, intimidating voters and candidates, and "correcting" results. Candidates are selected less on the basis of what they know than whom they know, with members of the elite often stepping in to make sure that friends or relatives are nominated. According to official figures, turnout at People's Assembly elections is 80 percent or more, but the figures are probably inflated by the government. In 1990, with most of the opposition parties boycotting the election in protest at government controls over the process, only 15 percent of eligible voters turned out and only one opposition party won enough votes to be represented in the People's Assembly. At the 1995 elections, turnout was back up to 48 percent but only 13 opposition deputies were elected. In more than half the districts, opposition candidates challenged the results in court.

Following a speech in 1999 by President Mubarak in which he indicated that he wanted more democracy and opposition participation in politics, rumors began to circulate that he might change the electoral system to allow more opposition deputies to be elected in the 2000 People's Assembly elections. It was thought that this might be a reward for the support given him by several parties in the 1999 presidential referendum, but cynics suggested that the proposal was aimed simply at improving Egypt's international image and that the number of opposition deputies would still be restricted. In fact, the NDP did remarkably badly, and although its share of seats went up by 11 percent, this was only because the party was able to encourage 218 "independent" candidates to declare themselves as NDP members. Meanwhile, the number of opposition deputies grew by just one, to a paltry total of 14.

In addition to elections, Egyptians also take part in referenda or plebiscites, whose results are also engineered. The president has the power to call a public referendum on issues of national importance, such as changes to the constitution, and his own position in office has also been confirmed in recent years by a referendum.

If the figures are to be believed, turnout at referenda is always 85 percent or more, and presidents always win at least 90 to 95 percent of votes. No surprise, then, that the referendum has been described as "a government tool of extreme cynicism."[19]

POLITICAL PARTIES

Egypt has a long history of party politics, but parties have always been carefully manipulated by the governing regime to suit its objectives. A multiparty system was in place between 1923 and 1953, but real power was centralized in the monarchy, and the Wafd party (formed in 1918 to campaign for independence) was the only organization with the support, resources, and local branches to be able to function like a party. The legislature also contained independent members, a Communist party founded in 1922, and a Wafdist breakaway party (the Saadists). The only other significant political groups were the Muslim Brotherhood and the right-wing Young Egypt (*Misr al-Fatat*, founded in 1933), neither of which operated as formal political parties.

Following the 1952 coup, political parties were abolished and replaced by mass membership movements. Designed to rally support for Nasser's government, these movements encouraged people to back his policies rather than debate them; meanwhile, all other political activity was banned. The first of the movements was the Liberation Rally, which was created in 1953 and then replaced in 1957 with the National Union. Much like a Soviet-style vanguard party, the National Union was used by Nasser as a means of generating public approval, stifling opposition, excluding other groups from politics, and building a "national consciousness."[20]

In 1962, following the collapse of the United Arab Republic, Nasser proclaimed that Egypt would be a revolutionary model for the rest of the Arab world and created the Arab Socialist Union (ASU). Modeled on the Communist Party of the Soviet Union (CPSU), its higher levels were locked into the government structure in much the same way as the CPSU related to the Soviet government, and it had a National Congress (equivalent to the People's Congress of the CPSU), a central Committee, and a 10-member Supreme Executive Committee that looked much like a politburo. At the apex of both party and government was Nasser himself, who so dominated the "party" that it never really took root in Egyptian society. There were signs in later years that Nasser was prepared to tolerate more criticism and dissent so long as it took place within the one-party system. Dying before he was able to develop his ideas, he bequeathed to Sadat an immature political system.

Once Sadat had consolidated his power after the 1973 war, he allowed opposing political views to be more freely expressed, seeing this as a way of making his administration different from Nasser's, satisfying public demand for greater participation, winning support from the liberal elements of the Egyptian bourgeoisie that formed the basis of much of his power, pleasing the United States, and encouraging his economic liberalization program.[21]

Although he was opposed to a multiparty system, Sadat announced in July 1975 that he would allow more debate and a greater diversity of viewpoints within the ASU and he encouraged the establishment within the party of what he called "pulpits" or "platforms." By the end of 1975, more than 40 platforms had been declared,

TABLE 9.3

Legislative Electoral Trends in Egypt

Party	Number of seats			
	1987	1990	1995	2000
National Democratic party	346	383	317	353
Socialist Labor Coalition: Muslim Brotherhood	38	—	—	—
Socialist Labor party	16	—	—	—
Socialist Liberal party	6	—	1	1
New Wafd party	35	—	7	7
National Progressive Unionist party	—	6	5	6
Independents and others	3	55	114	77
TOTAL	444	444	444	444

but Sadat approved only 3, and these now became "organizations," supposedly representing the right, center, and left of the ASU. The centrist Arab Socialist Organization (ASO) took over the structure and policies of the ASU, while the right was represented by the Socialist Liberal Organization and the left by the National Progressive Union Organization. All three organizations were allowed to compete in the 1976 elections, which resulted in a landslide for the ASO.

The three organizations were now allowed by Sadat to become full-fledged parties; the word *Organization* in their titles was replaced with *Party*. However, he made sure that the center dominated; the right-wing and left-wing parties (and independent deputies) were allowed to act only as safety valves for government opponents. When Sadat announced in July 1978 that he was organizing his own party, the National Democratic party, it immediately absorbed the Arab Socialist party, which it mirrored in everything but name.

Hosni Mubarak has continued to encourage the development of this multiparty system, allowing ten more parties to be licensed. Although Egypt now looks like a true multiparty system, no opposition party has been able to develop a firm social base, so they all remain to some extent artificial. Mubarak has continued to defend the constitutional ban on parties based on religion, class, or region, and he has banned parties opposed to the peace treaty with Israel. His government has also undermined the strength and credibility of opposition parties, notably by exploiting their internal divisions.[22] The opposition is further handicapped by restrictions placed on its activities, by its lack of access to state-run radio and television, by its lack of new ideas, and by its aging leadership; in 1999 the leader of the New Wafd party was Fouad Serageddin, an octogenarian who had served as a minister in the Farouk government.

There are now 14 legal parties in Egypt, of which the most important are as follows.

The National Democratic Party (NDP)

Successor to Nasser's Arab Socialist Union and Sadat's Arab Socialist party, the National Democratic party has been more streamlined in ideological terms than the catch-all ASU, but its position is difficult to pin down. It calls itself pro-Arab, pro-Palestinian, and nonaligned, and yet it is also overtly pro-Western. The NDP supports some of the socialist elements of the Nasser revolution, yet it has also stood for Mubarak's policy of strengthening the private sector. It claims to be concerned less with ASU-type propaganda and indoctrination and more with recruiting leaders and mobilizing the people, yet it is still dominated by the core elite, contributes little to government policy, and has little sense of purpose or ideological identity. Despite these contradictions, the NDP has dominated the People's Assembly, winning 80 percent of the seats in the 2000 election. (To be accurate, though, many of its Assembly members are independents who have allied themselves with the NDP.)

Socialist Labor Party

Although not very different ideologically from the NDP, this oddly named party is in fact conservative and was once something like an authentic opposition. It criticized the warming of Egyptian relations with Israel and became so critical of Sadat's style of leadership that its leaders were arrested in a 1981 purge. It became part of the coalition opposition in 1987, but it boycotted the 1990 elections and lost its 16 seats in the People's Assembly, winning none of them back in 1995 or 2000.

Socialist Liberal Party

Despite their name, the Socialist Liberals were the successors to the right-wing platform of the ASU. Once again, they were ideologically little different from the NDP, and Sadat even arranged for some of his supporters to join the party to limit its powers of opposition. It has since become more firmly centrist, emphasizing the importance of free enterprise and arguing in favor of privatization and political liberalization. It joined the opposition coalition in 1987, boycotted the 1990 elections and lost its six seats, and won only one of its seats back in 1995 and 2000.

New Wafd Party

The New Wafd is a liberal party that was founded in 1978, quickly banned, then revived in 1983. It favors political and economic liberalization and is strongly nationalist and secularist, although it confused its followers by joining in a brief alliance with the Muslim Brotherhood in 1984. The New Wafd won nearly 11 percent of the vote and 35 seats in 1987, and it was one of the few parties not to denounce the Iraqi invasion of Kuwait in 1990. It boycotted the 1990 elections, but 14 of its members ignored the boycott and won seats as independents. It won seven seats in the 1995 elections and retained them in 2000.

Smaller Parties

In addition to the four larger parties, Hosni Mubarak has allowed ten smaller parties to be licensed, including these three:

- A revived left-wing National Progressive Unionist party, which became the only opposition party represented in the People's Assembly after the 1990 elections, although it had only six seats.

- The Umma party, a religious grouping with a very small following, which was licensed in 1984.

- The Green party, the Arab world's first. Licensed in 1990, it promotes environmental issues, consists mainly of academics and scientists, and has been unable to build either support or a strong profile.

The Muslim Brotherhood

Although the constitution makes it illegal to form parties based on religion, this has not stopped the Muslim Brotherhood—the nearest thing in Egypt to a bona fide Islamic political party—from being a major force on the margins of Egyptian politics. The Brotherhood bypassed the law by first making an electoral pact with the New Wafd party and then running in the 1987 elections in an alliance with the Socialist Labor and Socialist Liberal parties. The alliance campaigned under the slogan "Islam is the Solution" and called for the abrogation of the 1979 treaty with Israel and full application of the *sharia*. It won 17 percent of the vote and 60 seats and—as the Socialist Labor Coalition—briefly constituted the opposition to the NDP.

The Brotherhood was founded in 1928 by a schoolteacher named Hasan al-Banna (1906–1949). Members argued that because Islamic principles were not being followed in the government of Muslim countries, Islam had been vulnerable to outside influences from the days of the Crusades right up to the 20th century. They argued that there was too much Western orientation in the thinking of Islamic leaders, that neither capitalism nor communism provided the answer, and that only a return to Islamic principles promised any future for the Muslim world. They advocated an Islamic revolution, the use of the Quran as a constitution, and the creation of a new political order based on the *sharia*, although they did not spell out the details of how the new Islamic government would work.

Accused of complicity in the 1948 assassination of the Egyptian prime minister, the Brotherhood was banned, and al-Banna was murdered by Egyptian secret police in 1949. The Brotherhood was further marginalized in 1952 by the success of the Free Officers coup and the popularity of Nasser's brand of Arab socialism. When a member of the Brotherhood fired six shots at Nasser while he was addressing a crowd in Alexandria in October 1954, Nasser arrested several thousand of its members. The Brotherhood was further weakened by internal divisions and a lack of leadership, and it was finally driven underground in 1965 following charges that it was implicated in an attempted coup.

CLOSE-UP VIEW

ISLAM AND RADICALISM

The Muslim Brotherhood and pro-government clergy are the mainstream representatives of Islamist ideas in Egypt, but the opposition also includes two more militant strands: underground groups known as *jamaat* and local associations known as *jamiyat*.[23]

The *jamaat* have won the most publicity in recent years and between 1992 and 1999 were at the heart of a campaign of violence aimed at overthrowing the Mubarak administration; as many as 1,300 people died and 30,000 were imprisoned. Arguing that the Brotherhood has sold out to the secular system, that state and society have become un-Islamic, and that Muslims must rise in a *jihad* (holy war) that would lead to a new Islamic state, the *jamaat* vary considerably in terms of numbers, size, and methods.

One group that won particular notoriety was *Jamaat al-Jihad* (Holy War Society). One of its members, Lieutenant Khalid Islambuli, was one of the assassins of Anwar Sadat in 1981. The assassination was supposed to have preceded the foundation of an Islamic caliphate; the preparations included the infiltration of the armed forces by several members of Jihad. Nearly 300 members of Jihad were put on trial, and 5 conspirators were executed in April 1982. In 1986 Jihad was implicated in a plot to overthrow the Mubarak government; among the 30 conspirators arrested were several army officers, a fact that raised concerns about the extent to which radicals had infiltrated the military. Jihad went on to claim responsibility for attempts on the lives of Prime Minister Atef Sidqi in 1993 and of President Mubarak in June 1995.

The mid-1990s saw radicals attacking tourists in an attempt to undermine one of Egypt's major sources of income. During 1992–1993, attacks on tourists left 290 people dead and 670 wounded, contributing to a falloff in tourist arrivals from 3.2 million in 1992 to 2.6 million in 1993.[24] One of the most active of the organizations targeting tourists was *Jamaat Islamiya* (Islamic Group), founded in the late 1970s as the student wing of the Muslim Brotherhood. They were behind an attack in November 1997 at Luxor, during which 48 tourists and four Egyptians were machine-gunned and stabbed to death. The attack was widely condemned by Islamist groups outside Egypt, lost *Jamaat Islamiya* much of its following, and led to a split within its ranks about the policy of tourist attacks. In 1998 it started developing links with the Al-Qaeda leader Osama bin Laden, and its name was regularly mentioned in the "war on terrorism" launched by the Bush administration in the United States.

Sadat apparently encouraged the revival of an Islamic opposition, but only as a means of providing an ally against his left-wing opponents. The Brotherhood initially supported Sadat, was allowed to openly hold prayer meetings in Cairo, and was allowed to revive its journal *Al-Dawa* in 1976. Following Camp David, however, the Brotherhood began to criticize Sadat's overtures to the West, his rapprochement with Israel, and the isolation from the Arab world that followed. It warned of the dangers of more Western involvement in Egyptian affairs in the wake of economic liberalization, and it continued to argue that only the introduction of Islamic principles based on the *sharia* could end corruption and contamination from the West. Brotherhood members became particularly active on university campuses, encouraging women to wear more modest dress, recruiting new members, encouraging the segregation of sexes in lectures, and exploiting the frustration among recent graduates unable to find jobs or afford adequate housing. By 1986 the Brotherhood was claiming a membership of 1 million, although other estimates were in the region of 250,000 to 400,000.[25]

Today the Muslim Brotherhood is a political party in all but name. It has a strong institutional base, rejects violence, and even refuses to take part in demonstrations. Despite this, it remains frustrated by the unwillingness of the government to give it formal recognition as a political party. How long it takes for this frustration to be transformed into militancy remains to be seen. Mubarak initially tolerated limited political activities by the Brotherhood, but he began to crack down on it in the mid-1990s as part of his government's program to contain militant Islam, and hundreds of its members were imprisoned or tried.

INTEREST GROUPS

In a political system based on personalism, access to policymakers by definition depends on personal contacts and influence. Those with close links to the president are the most powerful, those without such links are marginalized, and the minimum requirement for anyone who wants to influence politics is high office in government, the bureaucracy, or the military. The needs, demands, and even political support of groups outside the elite count for relatively little.

There are more than 14,000 interest groups in Egypt, but the government closely monitors their activities. All new organizations must be officially registered, and since a controversial new law was passed in 1999, the Ministry of Social Affairs has had considerable powers to interfere in the work of groups: it can hire and fire board members, cancel board decisions, and even dissolve a group by court order. Groups are also barred from taking part in political activity, and their members are subject to imprisonment for a variety of vague and general crimes, including "undermining national unity." Groups affiliated with religious organizations and those working on human rights issues have been particularly affected by the new law.[26]

Mainstream interest groups fall into the following three categories:

- **Business and Agricultural Interests.** With the economic liberalization of the *Infitah* (see section on Economic Policy), the number of Egyptian entrepreneurs grew, and so did the voice of the private sector. Groups such as the Chamber of Commerce and the Federation of Industries lobbied for more liberalization and more incentives to private enterprise, particularly the removal of fixed prices. Elitist agricultural interests meanwhile lobbied against the land reform that had benefited peasants at the expense of larger landowners.

- **The Professions.** As in many liberal democracies, professional groups in Egypt are represented by associations, such as the Journalists Syndicate, the Lawyers Syndicate, and the Engineers Syndicate. Each of the syndicates uses personal contacts in government to win concessions for its members, and in that sense they are not very different from professional associations in the United States, like the American Medical Association. Academics also wield influence, and university faculties have been regularly used as personnel pools for recruitment into the higher levels of the bureaucracy.

- **Religious Elites.** In addition to the continuing challenge of controlling the Islamic opposition, Egyptian leaders have had to respond to the needs of the religious elite. While most religious leaders have supported the government and have often endorsed economic and foreign policy decisions, they have been less willing to toe the line on social issues. While some clergy have taken a liberal approach to issues such as women's rights, apostasy (abandonment of religious faith), and the availability of alcohol, others have placed greater emphasis on Islamic principles.

THE MEDIA

Despite government control over the political process, there are several areas in which opposition parties and movements can function relatively freely and pass on their message to the public. One of these is the mass media. Large parts of it are government-owned, and the rest is subject to restrictions and censorship; however, editors and journalists can be surprisingly candid, and the Egyptian press in particular is the most substantive, respected, and widely read in the Arab world. Egyptians can choose from several government and opposition newspapers and magazines, among them the mass-circulation government dailies *Al-Ahram* and *Al-Akhbar*, opposition papers such as *Al-Wafd* (associated with the New Wafd party) and *Al-Ahali* (associated with the National Progressive Union party), and the English-language *Middle Eastern Times*. Even though *Al-Ahram* (the Pyramids, founded in 1876) is state-owned, it has been known to be critical of government policy.

The government will occasionally censor or ban an opposition periodical, as it did with the Muslim Brotherhood weekly *Al-Dawa*, but officials usually depend on more subtle methods of undermining the authority of the opposition press, such as denying it access to officially generated news or harassing its journalists.[27] This prevents opposition papers from becoming authoritative sources of news and information, but they can still deal with rumor and supposition, which may not help their credibility, but at least offers readers an alternative source of analysis. Just as parliamentary debates often seem lively but result in few changes in policy, so apparently lively debates in the press often end up being little more than an exposition of government policy.

The state-owned Egypt Radio and Television Union (ERTU) has a monopoly on radio broadcasting in the country, and until recently it monopolized television with its Egyptian Space Channels 1 and 2, which are broadcast throughout the Arab world. But in 2001 the first privately-owned satellite network—Dream TV—was launched. An estimated 600,000 Egyptians were Internet users in 2002, giving them the opportunity to bypass government censors.

POLICIES AND POLICYMAKING

The policymaking process in Egypt is relatively simple. Policy is made almost entirely by the president and the core elite, influenced by groups with access to that elite, and implemented by a large and mainly inefficient bureaucracy. Institutions outside the center—such as the legislature, opposition political parties, and the opposition media—tend to be controlled by the core elite, have little independent freedom of action, and have only a marginal effect on policymaking. Despite the emphasis on the Islamic theory concerning consultation, the input of "the people" is severely limited, and citizens have tended to follow rather than lead in the design of public policy. Nevertheless, policies do change from one administration to another.

- Under Nasser, the public sector was given priority, the government intervened heavily in economic planning and management, and Egypt pursued a supposedly nonaligned foreign policy. Nasser tried to impose his brand of Arab socialism on Egypt and to marginalize the Islamic opposition.

- Under Sadat, state control over the economy was reduced, foreign investment was encouraged, and—toward the end—Egypt followed a more conciliatory policy toward Israel and a more pro-Western foreign policy.

- Under Mubarak, Egypt has seen slow democratization and economic liberalization, and the centrality of the president and the elite in the political structure has been reduced. The trend in policymaking continues to be toward greater input by other institutions, and Egypt plays an important role in bringing together different parties in Middle Eastern political disputes.

All three presidents had at least one common problem: a bureaucracy that is big, overworked, and riddled with corruption, inertia, and inefficiency. It is a large part of the reason why Egypt was ranked 62 out of 102 on Transparency International's Corruption Perceptions Index for 2002. The bureaucratization of modern Egypt began with Nasser's policies of nationalization and centralization. In 1952 there were only 250,000 bureaucrats in Egypt. Thanks to a guarantee made by Nasser of a job in government for every university graduate, the numbers rose so rapidly that by 1985 public employees made up one-third of the labor force. The guaranteed-job policy has been quietly ignored since then, but there are still about 6 million public employees today, making up about 25 percent of the labor force. (In the United States, bureaucrats at all levels make up about 15 percent of the labor force.) Most bureaucracies are inherently conservative, but the Egyptian bureaucracy has proved particularly cumbersome and resistant to change. Under the circumstances, presidents and ministers alike have often found their efforts to change Egypt hampered by a bureaucracy unable or unwilling to change itself.

Sadat missed several opportunities to reform the system, being too preoccupied with foreign policy to provide the leadership needed for economic reform and too naively optimistic that simply returning Egypt to market policies would bring prosperity. Without the necessary drive and cohesion that strong leadership would have brought, decision making was fragmented among many agencies and committees.[28]

In short, the good of Egypt as a whole has been sacrificed to interagency rivalries and empire building, and these problems have been compounded by the effects of bribery, corruption, and the demands of special interests. The cumbersome bureaucracy is both a cause and an effect of the tendency for policymaking and implementation to bypass established channels. The process of government tends to bypass the bureaucracy, relying instead on decrees and personal contacts.

ECONOMIC POLICY

In economic terms, Egypt is both poor and vulnerable. Many Egyptians live in crushing poverty, especially those who have moved to Cairo in search of work. About 18 to 20 percent of the labor force is unemployed (according to unofficial estimates; the government claims the rate is only 9 percent), another 30 to 35 percent is underemployed, and many of those with work are paid minimal wages: 75 to 80 percent of Egyptians have family incomes of less than $50 per month, forcing many to take second jobs, often as laborers or taxi drivers. The contribution of agriculture to GNP has fallen, but it still accounts for 17 percent, while industry accounts for 33 percent and half comes from services. As with many poorer countries (and even some richer ones), there are big gaps in income between the rich and the poor, promoting resentment among the poor, which has been exploited by the Islamist opposition.

Throughout its modern history, Egypt has depended almost entirely on a single export at a time. Cotton was king until the worldwide collapse of the cotton market in 1951–1952. Since then oil has taken over and now accounts for about 25 percent of exports, with cotton, textiles, and agricultural goods making up much of the rest. Like Nigeria, the dominance of oil makes Egypt vulnerable because its economy is affected by changes in the price of oil on the international market. To make matters worse, Egypt is a relatively small oil exporter compared with some of its Arab neighbors, oil production has been developed only relatively recently, and the level of production will fall as Egypt's limited reserves are used up.

Apart from oil, Egypt has little in the way of natural resources. Only 3 to 5 percent of its land is cultivable, the rest being desert and semi-desert. It has a few small mineral resources and some natural gas, and it meets about 15 percent of its energy needs with hydroelectricity from the Aswan Dam. Without oil, Egypt would have only four significant sources of income: revenues from tourism (about $4.3 billion in 2000–2001), $2.4 billion in annual foreign aid (about 80 percent of it from the United States), revenues from the Suez Canal (about $2 billion annually), and remittances from more than 4 million Egyptians who work in nearby oil-exporting countries (such as Libya and the Gulf states, where they can often earn ten times as much as they would at home).[29] These are all modest sources of income, so Egypt needs to diversify its economic base and look for new sources of domestic income. The problem is made all the more urgent by the population growth rate of 2.2 percent (up from 1.9 percent in 1999), which adds 1 million more people to the total every 9 months. There is also a steady movement of people from rural areas to the cities, exerting growing pressure on urban infrastructure.

The dominance of the Egyptian political system by the president means that the evolution of the country's public policies must be seen in relation to the personal objectives of Nasser, Sadat, and Mubarak. In many ways, Egyptian economic policy today is still influenced by Nasser's early priorities of heavy centralization and ridding Egypt of foreign domination and dependence upon the West. That influence can be summarized as follows.

- **Economic centralization and bureaucratization.** Nasser created a large public sector and introduced Soviet-style economic plans, which led to a rapid increase in the size and power of the bureaucracy. The problems of a cumbersome bureaucracy spilled over into the inefficiencies of the state-run industries, which made over-priced goods of inferior quality. Unable to export these anywhere outside the Soviet bloc, Egypt was unable to earn much hard currency.

- **Nationalization of the Suez Canal.** Following nationalization in 1956, the canal almost immediately became a major source of revenue for Egypt, a source that was temporarily cut off when the canal was closed following the 1967 Arab-Israeli war. Revenues increased sharply following the reopening of the canal in 1975, but they are unlikely to grow much beyond present levels. If the government were to try to increase its profits by raising tariffs, it would discourage shippers from using the canal.

- **The building of the Aswan Dam.** The help given by the USSR in building the dam reinforced the tendencies toward centralized economic planning. The dam quickly paid for itself, created an inland fishery, and became a valuable source of electricity and water for irrigation, but the demands of energy generation and irrigation often conflict; depending on the season, the flow of water needed for irrigation is either too low or too high for electricity generation. The dam has also cut the flow of silt to land downstream, increasing Egypt's need for artificial fertilizers, causing a dangerous accumulation of salt in neighboring soils, and leading to a deterioration of the Nile delta and its fishing industry.

To complicate Egypt's economic development plans, conflicts with Israel were expensive, not only in the direct costs of maintaining a large military and going to war but also in the revenues lost while the Suez Canal was closed to shipping, oil fields in the Sinai were under Israeli occupation, and tourists stayed away. The 1979 peace treaty with Israel at least reduced the costs of defense and gave Egypt a "peace dividend."

Whereas Nasser believed in centralized government control over the economy, Sadat took a more liberal approach. Soon after becoming president, he expelled Soviet military advisors, and with them went significant Soviet influence over Egyptian economic policy. Having won a psychological victory in foreign policy with the crossing of the Suez Canal, Sadat turned his attention to the domestic front, where he had plans for an economic "crossing." The result was the *Infitah*, an attempt to open the Egyptian market and combine its basic strengths with the benefits of foreign investment and technology.

The **Infitah** (*al-infitah al-iqtisadi*, or economic opening) proved to be one of the most controversial initiatives of the Sadat years. Under this policy, Sadat allowed a dramatic increase in foreign investment in Egypt, relaxed currency and import restrictions, and encouraged a growth in the private sector. His hope was that Western technology could be combined with Arab capital and Egypt's natural resources and abundant labor to promote economic development.

In many ways, the *Infitah* had exactly the opposite effect. First, foreign investment did not reach the levels hoped for by Sadat. Second, while that investment should have promoted industrial development, industrial activity as a percentage of total economic activity actually declined. Capital was instead invested in the financial sector, tourism, and construction, all of which benefited tourists and the middle class. Third, the most profitable imports were luxury and consumer goods, which could be afforded by only a few and raised questions about how long Egypt could support a

Mark Henley/Panos Pictures

A group of Japanese tourists visiting the Sphinx and the pyramids at Giza, near Cairo. Tourism is one of the major sources of income for Egypt, a point that Islamic extremists exploited in the 1990s when they launched a series of attacks on tourists—a policy that backfired when the death toll became too great.

consumer market without increasing its domestic levels of consumption.[30] The output of goods and services in Egypt could not meet the growing demand, so Egypt had to borrow to pay for imports, leading to the rapid growth of its national debt.

As Egyptian workers began to realize that there would be few benefits in the *Infitah* for them, labor unrest grew, and the Sadat administration was compelled to act to forestall Egypt's growing debt problems. In 1976 the United States and the International Monetary Fund (IMF) convinced Sadat to end the subsidies on basic commodities such as flour, rice, sugar, beans, and bread, which made them cheap to Egyptians but which drained the national treasury. Sadat lifted the subsidies in January 1977, the price of bread doubled, and for two days in mid-January, Egypt was torn by riots that brought the country to a halt. Officially, 80 people were killed during the riots and 800 injured, although the true figures were probably much higher. Sadat immediately reintroduced the subsidies, but his political reputation had been irreparably damaged.

Hosni Mubarak has continued to liberalize the economy, directing more investment toward industry and agriculture and trying to broaden Egypt's economic base. He has been driven in part by economic reforms forced on Egypt by the terms of debt-relief programs agreed with the IMF and the World Bank in 1987, 1991, and 1993. The IMF has encouraged Egypt to move to a market-oriented economy and to sell off some of its more than 314 largely inefficient state-owned industries. By mid-1999, 124 had been privatized, and the government was making plans to sell off

7 regional electricity companies and the telecommunications company Telecom-Egypt. The public sector now accounts for 70 percent of GDP.

Much of Egypt's industry is linked to agriculture, through food processing and textile manufacture, for example. More investment is now being geared toward energy generation and the development of heavier industries, such as vehicle manufacture. Agricultural growth is limited by the shortage of arable land, a problem that is worsening in the face of urban sprawl. The only options available are investments in mechanized farming techniques and new technology or land-reclamation schemes, either of which will be expensive. The biggest and most controversial example of land reclamation was launched in 1997; nearly 20 years after it was first proposed by Anwar Sadat, construction began on the 190-mile Peace Canal, aimed at using wastewater to irrigate 500,000 acres of desert in the Sinai at an estimated cost of $800 million to $1 billion. An even more ambitious project in southern Egypt—the New Delta scheme—proposes taking water from the Aswan Dam and transporting it along a canal linked by a series of oases into the center of Egypt, creating a "parallel Nile."

Prospects for the Egyptian economy began to improve in the 1990s. Inflation was down from a high of 20 percent to just 2 percent in 1999, the economy grew at a healthy 5 to 6 percent annually during the second half of the decade, industrial production was up 8 percent in 1999, foreign investment was pouring in to the country, and the quality of public services and infrastructure was improving. The campaign against militant Islamism meant that more effort was being expended on the tourist industry, more money was being spent in the poor urban areas that were long hotbeds of discontent, and there was an expansion of electricity and water supply to villages.

Then came the events of September 11, 2001. The global economic downturn that followed had a particularly damaging effect on Egypt, as reliant as it is on foreign sources of income. Oil revenues fell, and so did tourist arrivals as jittery foreigners cancelled their vacations. The impact of 50 years of central planning continues to be felt, limiting the attractions of government-owned industries to private investors. Unemployment is growing, capital is leaving the country, exchange rates are falling, property values were halved in 1999–2002, and although government figures show a growth in GDP, independent economists have cast strong doubt on the official calculations.[31] A combination of long-term structural problems and short-term international problems raise many questions about Egypt's economic future.

FOREIGN POLICY

Egypt is the closest ally of the United States in the Arab world and has always been an influential force in the Middle East, not least because of its size and location. This was made clear once again in 2002–2003 as the United States increased the pressure on the Iraqi regime of Saddam Hussein and Hosni Mubarak found himself once again playing an important role in the debate over whether and when the United States should attack Iraq or whether a peaceful resolution to the problem could be brokered.

Egyptians see themselves as the natural leaders of the Arab world, but that role has been expressed in different ways. During the Nasser era, Egypt was officially nonaligned, hostile to Israel, and lukewarm toward the United States. Since then, it has reached an accommodation with Israel and become closer to the United States—helped, of course, by the large amounts of aid given to Egypt by the United States. The Middle East has been one of the most volatile regions in the world for more than two generations now; there are still many unresolved problems, and thus—to understand Egyptian foreign policy today—we have to review events going back several decades.

Foreign Policy Under Nasser

Nasser's priorities in foreign policy were twofold. First, he worked to end Anglo-French control over the Suez Canal and to establish an independent position for Egypt in the global system. To this end, he attended the founding meeting of the Non-Aligned Movement in Bandung, Indonesia, in 1955; sought Soviet military and economic assistance; and ultimately sparked the 1956 Suez crisis. By 1970, there were an estimated 15,000 to 20,000 Soviet military advisors in Egypt, leading some to argue that Egypt had simply replaced dependence on the West with dependence on the Soviet bloc.

Second, Nasser worked to establish Egypt as the leader of the Arab world, building on the praise he won at Suez in 1956. He set up the abortive union with Syria in 1958, sent Egyptian troops to Yemen to back up a republican military regime that took power in 1962, and pursued an aggressively anti-Israeli policy. Egypt's defeat in the 1967 Six-Day War led Nasser to tone down his revolutionary stance in foreign policy. Not only did the war leave the Sinai Peninsula and half of Egypt's oil resources under Israeli occupation, but revenues from the Suez Canal came to a halt and nearly 25 percent of national income was being spent on the military.[32]

Foreign Policy Since Nasser

Sadat's foreign policies stood in stark contrast to those of Nasser, in several respects. Within a year of coming to power, Sadat had expelled all Soviet advisors and other personnel and had begun working toward a closer alliance with other richer Arab states. In 1973 he launched the attack on the Israeli occupation of the Sinai, which resulted in the much-vaunted crossing of the Suez. Sadat subsequently felt that Egypt had regained enough of its self-esteem for his government to embark on a policy of accommodation with Israel. His historic visit to Jerusalem in November 1977—the first by an Egyptian leader—heralded the Camp David meetings between Israel and Egypt in September 1978 and the signing of the Egypt-Israel Peace Treaty in March 1979. Sadat's supporters say his actions were an example of statesmanship; others argue that Egypt's economic problems left him with no choice but to make a deal with Israel and the West. The bread riots of 1977 emphasized the importance of redirecting military spending into investment in economic growth at home.

Hosni Mubarak has followed a more overtly pro-U.S. policy than Sadat, irritating the Islamist opposition. Mubarak has had to maintain a fine balance between peace with Israel and ensuring that he is not seen by the Arab world as having sold out to the West. Significantly, he has never visited Israel, but he has always made sure that he is seen to be open to overtures from progressive Israeli governments. During the Reagan and first Bush administrations, the United States shifted its foreign policy interests in the Middle East from Egyptian-Israeli relations to the Gulf region but continued to underwrite the Camp David Accords with aid to both Israel and Egypt: Given on a 3:2 ratio, Israel receives nearly $3 billion and Egypt nearly $2 billion. (It is slowly being phased out, but still accounts for one-third of U.S. foreign aid.) Much of the aid to Egypt is used to subsidize prices on basic food needs, helping stave off a

POLITICAL DEBATES

CAN THE ARABS AND ISRAELIS LIVE TOGETHER?

The dominating foreign policy concern of Egypt for the last two generations—and one of the most troubling issues in Middle Eastern politics generally—has been the relationship between Israel and its Arab neighbors. The creation of the Jewish state of Israel in 1948 had an effect much like throwing a large rock into a pond: There was a large splash, waves were sent out in all directions, and the ripples continue to move back and forth even today.

Calls for an independent Jewish homeland in **Palestine** date back to the 19th century, and Jews began to immigrate to the region in 1870. In 1920 Palestine was placed under the administration of the British, who quickly found themselves caught between Jews wanting to settle there and indigenous Arabs opposed to the idea. A plan to partition the region was accepted by the Jews and the new United Nations but not by the Arabs, and when the British mandate ended in May 1948, Jewish leaders immediately proclaimed an independent state of Israel in Palestine.

While Israel was widely recognized in the non-Arab world, there were four wars between Arabs and Israelis (in 1948, 1956, 1967, and 1973). Meanwhile, Jews immigrated in growing numbers to the new state, and many of its Arab residents fled into exile. President Nasser led the opposition to Israel, and the 1967 Six-Day War

was designed to be the fatal blow. Rather than destroying Israel, however, the war left Egypt's military in disarray and left Israel in occupation of Egypt's Sinai Peninsula (it had taken over the Gaza strip during the 1956 Suez crisis) as well as Jerusalem, the Golan Heights in southern Syria, and the West Bank area of Jordan.

Israel had withdrawn completely from the Sinai by 1982, but the Israeli-Palestinian conflict continued to destabilize the region, as did the decision by Israel to move illegal settlers into the territories it had occupied since the Six-Day War. Meanwhile, the Palestinians continued to lobby for their own homeland in the West Bank and Gaza, the pressure increasing in 1987–1991 with the *intifada*, an uprising among Palestinians. In September 1993, an agreement was reached in Oslo, Norway, under which the Palestinians recognized the right of Israel to exist, and Israel recognized partial Palestinian self-rule. Following the failure of an attempt by the Clinton administration to broker a treaty that would have created a Palestinian state, violence between the two sides escalated. Palestinian suicide-bombers launched attacks on Israel, which responded with aggressive military action. Yet another attempt at peace was being made as this book went to press—the so-called road map approach, sponsored by the United States, the EU, the UN, and Russia.

repetition of the 1977 bread riots. Egypt today has a more influential role in Arab politics than it has had since the 1970s; its new confidence came through in the active support it gave to the allied coalition in the 1990–1991 Gulf War (in return for which $15 billion in foreign debt was written off).

The relationship between Egypt and the United States was put to its sternest test in 2002–2003, as the Bush administration increased the pressure on Iraq to come clean on whether it had developed weapons of mass destruction. Unlike the 1990–1991 Gulf crisis, when there was a high degree of support both within the Arab world and outside for an attack on the Iraqi regime following its invasion of Kuwait, there was much less support for the attack that came in March–April 2003.

American policy was widely criticized within Egypt, where many asked why the United States did not first use its influence to compel Israel to withdraw from its illegal occupation of the West Bank. President Mubarak downgraded relations between Egypt and Israel, accused the latter of "state terrorism" and of "perpetuating horrific human rights abuses" in Palestinian territories, and lobbied the United States and other Western governments to adopt a peace plan by which a Palestinian state would be created and Israel would withdraw from the occupied territories. The two crises once again placed Egypt in a difficult position, torn between pleasing its American allies and its Arab neighbors.

EGYPTIAN POLITICS IN TRANSITION

Egypt is a poor and overpopulated country that walks a fine line between Islamism and secularism, between tradition and modernity, between the Arabs and the West, and between democracy and authoritarianism. It has maintained a balance of sorts and earned a reputation for itself as the most influential state in the Arab world, but at the cost of sluggish democratic and economic progress.

It is a nation of Muslims, but although Islamists influence social and moral issues in Egypt, it is still far from being an Islamic state of the kind they want. Islamism continues to feed off the poverty of Egypt and off concerns about the influential role that the West (and the United States in particular) plays in Middle Eastern affairs. Egypt has been the key power broker in Middle Eastern and Arab relations over the last two generations, but it has not yet reaped the kind of economic rewards that often come to powerful regional actors. There has been a gradual process of democratization over the last 20 years, and attempts have been made to deal with Egypt's pressing economic problems, but these have had mixed results. The future is likely to see Mubarak continuing the process of democratization, but he will need to move more quickly and effectively if he is to provide the kind of sustained political stability, bureaucratic efficiency, and economic growth needed to address the plight of the Egyptian people. Meanwhile, all attempts at political and economic change in the region continue to be impacted by the tensions between Islam and the West.

KEY TERMS

Arab Socialist Union	Free Officers	People's Assembly
Aswan Dam	*Infitah*	Sinai Peninsula
Camp David Accords	*jamaat*	Six-Day War
core elite	Muslim Brotherhood	Suez Canal
Corrective Revolution	National Democratic	Suez crisis
dual executive	party	United Arab Republic
fellahin	Palestine	Yom Kippur War

KEY PEOPLE

Muhammed Ali	King Farouk	Anwar Sadat
Hasan al-Banna	Hosni Mubarak	Atef Sidqi
Atef Ebeid	Gamal Abdel Nasser	Saad Zaghlul

STUDY QUESTIONS

1. Of the many historical influences on Egypt, which are the most politically prominent today?

2. Egypt had a relatively limited experience of colonialism. Compare and contrast the effects of that experience with the effects of the much longer and deeper history of colonialism in India and Nigeria.

3. Does Egypt need a strong, centralized government?

4. Compare and contrast the role of personality in the presidencies of the United States and Egypt. Why—and in what ways—does the personality of the incumbent influence the character of the office?

5. Compare and contrast the dual executive in Russia and Egypt. How are the roles of the legislatures different?

6. Why is the military so much more politically significant in Nigeria than in Egypt?

7. What does Hosni Mubarak have to fear from honest and fair elections?

8. Compare and contrast the relative roles in their respective countries of strong political parties such as the LDP in Japan, PRI in Mexico, and the NDP in Egypt.

9. Why has the party system in Egypt been more enduring than it has in Nigeria?

EGYPT ONLINE

The Egyptian Presidency: *http://www.presidency.gov.eg*
An official government site with information on the presidency and on Egypt.
People's Assembly: *http://www.assembly.gov.eg*
The home page for the People's Assembly, which includes information on Assembly members and the text of the Egyptian constitution.
Egyptian State Information Service: *http://www.sis.gov.eg*
An official government site that provides links to information on Egyptian politics, current events, and economic matters.
Egypt WWW Index: *http://ce.eng.usf.edu/pharos*
Megasite maintained by the University of South Florida, with links to sites on politics, business, history, and news about Egypt.
Middle East Times: *http://metimes.com*
Cairo Times: *http://www.cairotimes.com*
Sources of English-language news on Egypt and the Middle East.

FURTHER READING

Goldschmidt, Arthur, *Modern Egypt: The Formation of a Nation-State*, 2nd Ed. (Boulder, CO: Westview Press, 2003). A history of Egypt, with an emphasis on the modern era (post-1850s).

Long, David E., and Bernard Reich (Eds.), *The Government and Politics of the Middle East and North Africa*, 4th Ed. (Boulder, CO: Westview, 2002). An introduction to the politics of the Middle East, placing Egypt in the context of regional political, economic, and social change.

Rubin, Barry, *Islamic Fundamentalism in Egyptian Politics* (New York: Palgrave Macmillan, 2002). A study of Islamic fundamentalism in Egypt, looking at the different groups and their policies and philosophies.

TERMS OF OFFICE

Hosni Mubarak's "reelection" to office for a fourth 6-year term as president in 1999 made him one of the longest-serving heads of state in the world, and raised once again the issue of the appropriate limits that should be placed on the terms of office of elected officials. Questions continue to be asked—in Egypt and elsewhere—about how many terms government officials should be allowed to serve, how long each term should be, and whether the terms should be of fixed or of flexible duration. Those opposed to the Mubarak administration in Egypt would favor a limited and fixed number of short terms for the Egyptian presidency, but its supporters probably argue that Mubarak should be allowed to stay in office as long as he continues to do a good job.

Different governments have developed different combinations of limits on different offices, with varying results.

- **Limited vs. unlimited terms.** The United States—and other systems that have adopted the American model—has opted for a combination of limited and unlimited terms in its executive and legislature: The president can serve a maximum of two 4-year terms, while members of Congress can serve an unlimited number of 2- or 6-year terms. The U.S. Constitution said nothing about limits on the terms of the presidency, but George Washington set a precedent by stepping down after two terms. All his successors honored that precedent until Franklin Delano Roosevelt, who was reelected twice to the office, serving a total of 13 years as president. The 22nd amendment to the constitution, ratified in 1951, limited subsequent presidents to two terms in office.

  The main advantage of term limits is that they encourage regular turnover in office. Not only

does this avoids the dangers of authoritarian tendencies, complacency, or the development of a ruling elite, but it also ensures that new ideas and policies are brought into government. Term limits also cancel out the sometimes unfair advantages of incumbency, which include name recognition and the ability to attract greater media attention and more campaign funding.

The arguments against term limits include the following: they prevent good leaders and legislators from staying in office; they are undemocratic in the sense that they restrict the ability of voters to elect whomever they like to office; they do not allow for the development of "career politicians" who can develop the experience, contacts, and reputation needed to do the best possible job for their constituents; and they weaken the powers of elected officials relative to lobbyists and bureaucrats, who can build many years of experience in government and thus can be at an advantage over elected officials.

With their restriction on executives to a single 6-year term in office and their ban on consecutive terms in legislative office, the Mexicans have developed something of a compromise. However, it has the confusing effect of encouraging politicians to move back and forth among different offices.

- **Short vs. long terms.** Terms in office vary substantially, from as little as 2 years to as much as a lifetime appointment that can result in a leader staying in office for several decades. The U.S. House of Representatives is at the low end of the scale, its 2-year terms being among the shortest in the world. Just down the street in Washington, D.C., however, justices of the U.S. Supreme Court enjoy appointments for life, and can be removed only for committing "high crimes and misdemeanors" (which are not defined in the constitution). Elsewhere, the most common terms of office are in the range of 4 to 6 years, the length increasing for constitutional courts, whose members are commonly appointed for anything between 12 years and life.

The main advantage of short terms is that they ensure that voters often have the opportunity to comment through the ballot box on the performance of their elected officials. They also keep representatives accountable and discourage them from taking voters for granted. The disadvantages, however, are many: Frequent elections court the danger of promoting voter apathy; unless elections are paid for out of the public purse, they force parties and candidates to spend less time on government business and more time raising campaign funds; they interfere with the development of long-term views on public policy; and they heighten the danger of high turnover in public office.

Lifetime appointments to constitutional courts reduce the political pressures on the work of the judiciary and make it more likely that courts will develop more consistent positions on judicial issues. At the same time, however, they reduce the introduction into the courts of new ideas, raising the danger that courts might fall out of step with the prevailing views of government and society.

- **Fixed vs. flexible terms.** While the United States and other countries using the U.S. model have opted for fixed terms for elected officials—2 years for representatives, 4 years for presidents, and 6 years for senators—most

parliamentary systems have adopted a system of maximum terms, where elections can be held any time within an agreed limit, which is typically 4 or 5 years.

The main advantage of fixed terms is that they allow both voters and elected officials to plan around a predictable timetable, and to know how much time is left for a legislative program before the next election. The use of staggered terms also allows voters to change the makeup and direction of government in increments and reduces the likelihood of temporary emotions producing a massive switch in the makeup and direction of government.

Flexible terms inject a note of uncertainty into the electoral process, which affects elected officials, parties, and voters alike. Everyone knows the final permissible date for an election, but no one except the leader and his or her advisors know when it is most likely to come. Cynics who argue that elected officials think only about elections would probably conclude that flexible terms compel those officials constantly to be thinking about being responsive to the needs of constituents, rather than only in the weeks or months leading up to the election. Finally, flexible terms allow leaders to manipulate the electoral system by calling elections only at times when there is the greatest likelihood of their party winning.

Although there is universal agreement that representative democracy demands that limits be placed on the terms in office of elected officials, there is no agreement concerning the number and length of those terms.

CONCLUSIONS

There is a famous Chinese curse: "May you live in interesting times." The opening years of the 21st century have certainly been "interesting," although it is debatable just how the sentiment of that curse now applies. The times are changeable certainly, dangerous in some ways, challenging and uncertain in many ways, encouraging for some and discouraging for others. When the first edition of this book was written in the early 1990s, the word *transition* was included in the title to illustrate the shift from the cold war era to President George Bush Sr.'s idea of a "new world order." In fact, the process of transition never ends. As the case studies in this book have revealed, our understanding of politics is constantly changing, the priorities of leaders and citizens are always being amended to fit new circumstances, and even the structures of governments change.

There is nothing predictable about life except change, but perhaps no generation has seen quite such all-encompassing changes in its time as ours. Advances in science, technology, and communications have dramatically redefined our relationships with others; news from thousands of miles away reaches us the instant it happens; we can travel to another continent—and even to the other side of the earth—in a matter of hours; political events in one part of the world can have immediate implications in another; financial markets are affected around the clock by developments all over the world; and the Internet has turned the way we do business on its head and has given us instant access to a huge new storehouse of information that once took days or even weeks to collect, assuming we could find it at all.

In political, economic, and social terms, many of the changes have been positive. Consider the following:

- The collapse of Soviet-style communism and the spread of democratic, free-market ideas in Russia and its former Eastern European satellites.
- The economic and political integration of Western Europe, which has now enjoyed its longest spell of peace since medieval times.
- The expansion of free-market principles in China and India, potentially the consumer giants of the new century.
- The emergence of newly industrializing countries with new political stability and economic confidence.
- The expansion of democracy in Latin American states, as exemplified by the end of PRI's 71-year monopoly on power in Mexico in July 2000.
- The end of nearly five decades of apartheid in South Africa, of 16 years of military rule in Nigeria, and of a generation of political violence in Northern Ireland.

Unfortunately, there are just as many—if not more—examples of new and ongoing problems:

- Conflicts in many parts of the world—including Israel/Palestine, Kashmir, and many parts of Africa—that almost seem to defy resolution.
- An almost perpetual cycle of poverty and instability that grips much of sub-Saharan Africa, to which has been added the worsening specter of HIV and AIDS.
- Religious and ethnic strife in India, Nigeria, the Balkans, and many other parts of the world.
- Global and regional environmental problems caused by a combination of the thoughtless overconsumption of wealthy states and the desperate struggle for existence of poor states.
- A resurgence of nationalism in parts of Eastern Europe, Asia, and Africa.
- The persistence of authoritarian governments in Africa and Latin America.

Most troubling of all at the beginning of the new century is the regrowth of the age-old misunderstandings between Islam and the West. The attacks of September 11, 2001, were just the most deadly and violent of a string of terrorist attacks in the United States, East Africa, Southeast Asia, and the Middle East that have represented a new iteration of an old war, using old methods but at a greatly heightened level. The uneasy peace that prevailed during the cold war was always ultimately protected by the certainty of mutually assured destruction: If one side launched its weapons on the other, the other would respond in kind—and both sides could be sure that the costs of war would greatly outweigh the benefits. Today, we live in a world where states are terrorized by people and groups that are happy to die for their cause and are difficult to identify and pin down and whose operations cannot easily be related to national boundaries.

Whether good or bad, the importance of understanding all these political and economic changes remains. When events on another continent can have a direct and almost immediate impact on our own lives, it is critical that we try to understand those events. Unfortunately, too many of us insist on living in splendid isolation and allow our interests to reach little further than our homes, our families, and our neighborhoods. Many of us watch changes unfolding in Iraq, Russia, the Koreas, the Balkans, South Africa, Israel, Kashmir, and Mexico without the ability to put them in perspective, or even to understand their causes or significance.

The United States is a large, rich, powerful, generous, dynamic, and well-endowed country that has become used to leading rather than following. However, one of the problems with power is that it can breed complacency. Time after time, the dominant actors in the world have assumed that they are the keepers of their own destinies, only to find that the world has changed around them more quickly than they realized.

The challenges to the superpower status of the United States reveal themselves in many ways. They can be seen in the way that traditional American export markets are being undercut by cheaper and often better-manufactured goods from East Asia. They can be seen in the way that jobs are being lost to economic competition and cheaper labor. They can be seen in the way that the best military technology in the world is not always able to stand up to the sheer determination of a community to pursue its own goals.

Closer to home, challenges to the power of the United States are posed by the persistence of poverty, violence, and discrimination; by falling SAT scores; by reduced opportunities; and by dulled ambition. The United States has the best medical technology in the world, yet many people lack health insurance and so are denied the benefits of that technology. The United States has some of the most innovative entrepreneurs in the world, yet many Americans are still denied access to the opportunities they create. The United States has some of the best colleges and universities in the world, yet thousands of its citizens can do little more than read a road sign. Ethnic minorities suffer low life expectancy, poor education, high murder rates, and high rates of illiteracy.

These two sets of developments—abroad and at home—are intimately linked. For nearly two generations, the place of the United States in the world was determined by cold war thinking. Americans were raised to think of global relations as a struggle between the forces of capitalism and socialism, or good and evil, and to think of the United States as the major actor in the Western response to the Soviet challenge. But the world is no longer quite so neatly predictable (assuming it ever was), and the military tensions of the cold war have been replaced by an increasingly complex web of political, economic, and social tensions, spearheaded by—but by no means restricted to—the war on terrorism.

You have just finished reading a book designed to introduce you to the variety of political systems in the world, and—by comparing their political structures, values, and processes—to illustrate the differences and similarities among political systems with a view to shedding light on the changes the world is undergoing. There are 193 independent countries in the world, and although we have looked at just nine of them, the examples used in this book were picked because they underline several themes that comparativists have been able to identify through their study of different societies:

1. All societies are interrelated. The only way that each of us as individuals can effectively relate to our social environment is to understand how we fit in and what drives others. The same is true of countries. Domestic policy of every kind in every country is influenced by outside political, economic, and social forces and we cannot develop effective policies without understanding those forces. We saw the impact of colonialism on Africa, Asia, and Latin America, and—more recently—we have seen how even the world's biggest economies have come to be affected by developments in the newly industrializing countries.

2. Political, economic, and social issues are intimately and inextricably interlinked. Systems of government are the product of the societies in which they function, and no study of those systems would be complete without an understanding of the links between government, markets, and people. We saw how political culture has brought significant differences to the expectations of government in liberal democracies such as the United States, Britain, and Japan and how it resulted in different interpretations of Marxism-Leninism in the USSR and China.

3. The fundamental measure of the legitimacy and efficiency of a system of government is the extent to which it meets the needs, values, and wishes of its citizens. We saw how political systems that fail to take root and respond to the changing needs of their peoples (such as the USSR and former colonies such as Nigeria) will ultimately collapse under the weight of their internal contradictions. We saw that the United States and Britain enjoy high levels of legitimacy, while Russia, China,

and India struggle to find a workable formula and Nigeria and Egypt still have large gaps between the goals of government and the needs of the people.

4. No political system is perfect, and it would be dangerous to argue that one is necessarily better than another. Each meets different needs in different ways and with different levels of efficiency. Americans often talk about the United States as the epitome of democracy; Britons assume that their political system has endured because it was built on more solid foundations than those of their European neighbors; Westerners look on the apparent chaos of politics in countries like Nigeria and Egypt with horror and wonder why liberal democracy does not take root in those societies. However, the way things are done in liberal democracies is not necessarily the way they are done or even should be done in other kinds of systems. The competitive multiparty democracy used by liberal democracies, for example, may not be the best option for societies that put a premium on consensus.

5. Nothing is predictable about politics except its unpredictability. Political scientists have worked for decades to try to understand human society and to draw up predictive rules about politics, but they find themselves frustrated by the vagaries of human relationships. The environment in which politics takes place constantly changes, making it difficult always to accurately predict the outcome of political change. Imagine, for example, a political science professor in 1970 making forecasts about the world in 2005. Is it likely he or she would have foreseen the reunification of Germany, the emergence of the European Union, or economic liberalization in China and India?

6. Social divisions are a fact of life in virtually every political system. Whether they are based on class, ethnicity, religion, gender, region, or wealth, these divisions play a major role in determining how well a political system meets the needs of its citizens. We saw how politics in countries such as India and Nigeria is driven in large part by the need to address social conflict, but even relatively stable democracies such as the United States and Britain are faced with resolving internal ethnic, religious, and economic divisions.

As we begin the new millennium, opinion is divided on what the future holds. Optimists argue that we are headed toward global democracy and that government after government is improving its ability to respond to the needs of its citizens. They argue that peace has broken out in many nations that have a tradition of instability and war (like those of Western Europe) and that economic prosperity and political stability are coming to other nations that were once destabilized by colonialism (like those in Southeast Asia).

Pessimists point to the regional and local wars that continue to afflict many parts of the world; at the continued disruption caused by nationalism; at questions about the transition to democracy in Russia, Eastern Europe, and other parts of the world; at the social problems that trouble societies on every continent; at the widespread poverty in sub-Saharan Africa and Latin America; at global population growth and environmental problems; and at the repeated inability of political leaders to meet the needs of all their citizens. Wherever we are headed, comparative politics can give us insight into the paths we are taking and perhaps help us make decisions that will make the world a better, safer, and more fulfilling place in which to live.

GLOSSARY

Many of the terms used in political science have meanings that are both debatable and changeable, either because they have taken on new meanings as political systems have evolved or because they have been misused over time. This glossary contains brief definitions of key terms and concepts used in the text, defined according to the way they are generally applied today.

absolute government   A system in which there is no limit to what government may do.

anarchy   Literally, an absence of government. Although this is a term usually used to describe chaos, anarchism is actually a political theory based on the arguments that society does not need government and that no government is legitimate unless based entirely upon the consent of the governed.

autocracy   Self-rule, or rule by one person who usually exercises power without reference to anyone else. Compare with *monarchy*.

bourgeoisie   Literally "town-dwellers" (from the French). A term appropriated by Karl Marx to describe the class of property owners created by the capitalist system. Coincides roughly with the middle or upper-middle class.

bureaucracy   A collective term for all those employed directly by a government to implement policy and to carry out the daily administration of a society.

cabinet   The group of heads of government departments and senior administrators who act collectively as the government in parliamentary systems of government (such as Britain or Japan) or as administrators and advisors to the executive in presidential systems (such as Mexico or the United States). Also sometimes known as a council of ministers.

capitalism   An economic system characterized or dominated by private ownership of services, industry, and agriculture, where production and distribution are driven by the profit motive, prices are set by supply and demand, and employees sell their labor for wages.

civil liberties   The rights that protect individuals from the arbitrary acts of government. These include freedom of speech, movement, association, and religion.

civil rights   The rights that protect individuals from exploitation or harm by other individuals. These include the right not to be discriminated against on the basis of being a member of a group (for example, gender, race, age, religion, or sexual orientation).

cold war   The war of words, ideas, ideologies, and threats that took place between the Western bloc (the United States, Canada, and Western Europe) and the Soviet-Chinese bloc between 1945 and 1990. The war involved very few direct military conflicts between the two sides, but many conflicts between their clients.

collective responsibility   An understanding that all decisions taken by a group are taken collectively and that all members must stand or fall by those decisions. It applies, for example, to the cabinet in Westminster-style government.

colonialism   The theory and practice by which citizens of one territory or political unit have a physical presence in another territory, and—while sustaining themselves in the new territory—show allegiance to and retain the language and customs of the mother territory.

communism   A social, economic, and political system in which power and property are held in common, all decisions are taken communally, and all members of the system are equal in the eyes of the law.

comparative politics   One of the major branches of the academic study of politics. It involves the systematic study of the differences and similarities between and among political systems, with the goal of understanding those systems and of making generalizations and drawing up rules about politics.

consensus   Common understanding. A decision-making system in which all opinions converge to reach a common conclusion with which everyone can agree.

conservatism   A political ideology that sprang from a desire to maintain or conserve the status quo, but has gone on to include a belief in "traditional" customs and values, a limited economic role for government, self-reliance, and the exercise of power through a strong legal system.

constitution   A set of rules (usually written in a single document) outlining the structure, operating rules, and powers of a government; defining the responsibilities of government; and stating the relative rights of the governors and the governed.

corporatism   A political system based on corporate bodies or associations playing an intermediary role between their members and the state. This was a key feature of Mussolini's Italy and Franco's Spain, and elements remain today in countries such as Mexico.

coup d'etat   Literally "blow against the state" (from the French). A term describing the sudden and forcible overthrow of a government, usually by the military or other armed opponents.

cult of personality   A program through which a leader perpetuates his power by ensuring that he is omnipresent in the consciousness of his subjects and by ensuring that he is strongly associated in their minds with images of the state. The cult is usually promoted by making sure that his image is everywhere, that stories about him lead the daily news, and that children are trained to think of him as a father figure.

culture   A sociological or anthropological term referring collectively to the customs, habits, beliefs, norms, and values of a group of people.

democracy   Literally "government by the people as a whole" (from the Greek). An immensely complicated concept generally understood to mean a political system in which government is based on a mandate from the people and in which power is constitutionally limited, and is given to—or taken from—leaders at the behest of those they lead. The features of democracy in practice are debatable.

democratic centralism   A Leninist concept describing a society governed by a single, strictly hierarchical party operating on democratic principles, with free political discussion and free elections, but only within the party. Each level of the party would be elected by the level below and would be accountable to that lower level.

dependency   A theory describing a relationship in which a former colony has achieved political independence but is still economically dependent on the Western capitalist powers.

dictatorship   A system of government in which all political power is held by one person or group of people who is/are accountable to no other person or group and who is/are able to use that power to direct and govern society and compel obedience.

divine right   A belief largely peculiar to medieval Europe, arguing that a monarch or sovereign rules by the consent of God and may even be a god himself or herself. The sovereign, answerable only to God, rules without a contract or the common consent of the people.

dual executive   A political system in which executive power is shared between an elected president and a prime minister appointed out of the legislature. Used in Russia, France, Poland, and Egypt, among others.

ethnocentrism   A view of the world based on a belief in the cultural or ethnic superiority of the observer and the culture or race to which he or she belongs.

executive   The element of government responsible for implementing policy and executing laws passed by the legislature (for example, the presidency of the United States).

fascism   A political ideology characterized by a belief in strong, centralized leadership, a cult of personality, nationalism, collective organization, social discipline, and hostility to democracy (all features of Nazi Germany or Italy under Mussolini). "Fascist" is now widely used as a term to describe anyone supposedly hostile to liberal or democratic ideas.

federalism   An administrative system in which local units of government have powers independent of those of the national government and in which authority is divided between the two.

feudalism   A heavily hierarchical political, social, and economic system (usually associated with medieval Europe or Asia) in which the majority of people own little or nothing and are subservient to an aristocracy that owns most of the land (and has most of the political power) and grants access to land in return for service (usually military).

free trade   An arrangement in which there is a free flow of goods and services between two or more trading partners, and trade is not subject to tariffs, quotas, or any other limits.

glasnost   Literally "openness" (from the Russian). A term used to describe Soviet President Mikhail Gorbachev's policy of encouraging more open debate about the problems facing the USSR and of showing a greater willingness to acknowledge the problems of the Soviet government and economy.

government   The exercise of influence over a group of people, either through law or coercion. Also used (as a noun) to describe the body that exercises that control.

green politics   A political ideology based on a holistic view of the place of humanity in the world and advocating a nonviolent and sustainable way of life.

gross domestic product   The basic measure of economic output of a country, expressed as the sum value of the final goods and services produced within the borders of a country.

gross national product   The sum value of the final goods and services produced by a country, both domestically and through investments abroad.

head of government   The individual who directs the government of a country and in whom executive power is normally vested. In liberal democracies, this would be a partisan politician elected to that position for a fixed term.

head of state   The individual who symbolically represents the state and all the citizens of that state, irrespective of their backgrounds and beliefs. This is usually a nonexecutive, figurehead position. In the United States, Mexico, and Egypt, the president is both head of state and head of government; in Britain, the prime minister is head of government and the monarch head of state.

human rights   Rights that are determined by mutual agreement to belong to all humans, whether or not the rights are protected by law. Examples: freedom from hunger, want, persecution, and discrimination.

ideology   A systematic, consistent, and hopefully coherent set of political beliefs, ideas, and values.

imperialism   The extension of power (political, economic, social, or even cultural) through superior force.

industry   Any economic activity that involves the transformation of raw materials, such as minerals and wood, into tangible and usable products.

interest group   A group of people who use their collective power to influence public policy, opinion, or behavior toward a particular end.

Islam   The political, social, and economic values and goals associated with adherents to Islamic religious beliefs. Also describes the worldwide community of Muslims.

Islamism   The term preferred by some Muslims to describe their belief in a return to the basic ideas of the Islamic faith, including those relating to government and society.

judiciary   The collective body of judges within a legal system. Their powers vary from one system to another, but they are commonly involved in interpreting and applying constitutional law.

legislature   The part of government concerned with "making" law, that is, introducing, discussing, and voting on new laws. In a democracy, this would be an assembly of elected officials (such as Congress in the United States, the Diet in Japan, and the Federal Assembly in Russia).

Leninism   An ideology associated with Lenin's revolutionary principles, which included the establishment of a vanguard party, the promotion of democratic centralism, and the furtherance of worldwide revolutionary activity aimed at the overthrow of capitalist imperialism.

less developed country   A country at an early stage of political and economic development, whose recent history may have been disrupted by colonialism and that has yet to develop consistent political institutions or to build economic or social stability.

liberal democracy   A political system built around a belief in representative and limited government, regular and competitive elections, the rule of law, multiple channels for political participation, limited state control over the economy, and the protection of civil rights and liberties.

liberalism   A political philosophy based on a belief in limited government, the freedom of the individual, toleration in matters of morality and religion, and the redistribution of resources to the equal benefit of all in a society.

limited government   A form of government in which sovereign power is limited by law. The opposite of *absolute government*.

Maoism   Mao's interpretation of communism, influenced by application to the needs and circumstances of predominantly rural societies such as China in the 1950s.

Distinguished by a rejection of elitism, hierarchy, and technical expertise and by a stress on communalism, small-scale organization, and social experimentation.

martial law The imposition of military rule over a civilian population. Sometimes imposed during a state of emergency or during military occupation of a foreign territory.

Marxism The philosophy of Karl Marx, who argued that the structure and inequalities of industrialized societies could be explained by understanding the tensions arising out of class struggle, which would ultimately lead to the overthrow of capitalist society.

Marxism-Leninism A combination of the economic theories of Marx and the revolutionary methods espoused by Lenin, the latter being used to bring about the end of the political and social inequalities resulting from capitalism.

modernization The process by which traditional societies are transformed by scientific, technological, social, economic, and political change. The term usually implies a transition toward the model provided by Western liberal democracies.

monarchy Literally rule by one, but generally applied to an institution characterized by nobility, aristocracy, and heredity. Most monarchs are heads of state (and occasionally even of government), inherit their position from a parent, and hold power for life or until they voluntarily renounce that power. Their power is usually constitutionally limited.

nation A cultural concept describing a group of people sharing a common cultural heritage, language, customs, and traditions, and usually inhabiting a fixed territory.

nation-state A state organized for the government of a nation. In practice, most nation-states consist of a single state system bringing together two or more nations.

nationalism The promotion of ideas associated with the nation, or putting national values and interests above those of the wider community. May spill over into an aggressive posture against anything considered a threat to the identity of a national community.

newly industrializing country A country that has undergone recent, relatively rapid, and sustained economic growth, largely as a consequence of the development of manufacturing and of exports. This economic growth is underpinned by—and promotes—political stability.

nonalignment A philosophy generated by the leaders of a number of newly independent African and Asian countries in the 1950s to promote mutual solidarity, to refuse to take sides in the cold war, and to reduce their dependence on the superpowers.

oligarchy Literally "rule by a few" (from the Greek). A political system in which all real power is held by a group. Could be used to describe the relationship between administrators and students in a university.

orientalism The tendency of Westerners to use misleading stereotypes and generalizations in describing the East (or the Orient).

parliament The legislative body in the Westminster system of government (derived from the French word *parler*, to talk). Normally consisting of elected members, its primary function is to debate and vote on proposals for new laws.

parliamentary system A political system, based on the Westminster model, in which supreme legal authority is vested in parliament, of which all elected government officials are members. Distinct from the separation of powers used in the U.S. system of government.

patrimonialism   A political system based on the concept of the leader as a father figure who has limited accountability to his people but who claims to understand their interests and needs. Many Middle Eastern societies and African tribal societies are based on this idea.

perestroika   Literally "restructuring" (from the Russian). The policy instituted by Mikhail Gorbachev of restructuring the Soviet Union's political and economic system to reduce the control of central government and promote efficiency.

personalism   A system of government in which power revolves around personal links between the rulers and the ruled. Occasionally also known as cronyism.

pluralism   A belief in the distribution of power among several institutions and in allowing government to be influenced by competition among competing groups, systems of values, and sets of demands.

plurality   Term used to describe the outcome of an election in which the candidate with the most votes wins, without having a majority.

police state   A state in which power is distributed and stability maintained by force, usually through the police. It commonly involves the use of secrecy and the granting to the police of almost unlimited powers over the lives of citizens.

political culture   The political norms and values of a society. Political culture helps explain what citizens and leaders regard as acceptable or unacceptable behavior.

political party   A group of like-minded individuals formed to put forward a set of ideas and objectives concerning government and to compete for power in open elections.

political science   The systematic study of politics, with the objective of drawing up rules about government, political culture, representation, participation, and public policy.

politics   The process by which individuals compete for power and resources and by which competing interests are reconciled. The process that determines who gets what, when, and how.

polity   A politically organized society, or the structure and form of government in that society.

polycentrism   The division of a political organization into competing centers of power. Usually applied to describe the many competing interpretations of communism and to indicate the emergence of competing communist parties in different countries.

postindustrial society   A society that has undergone agricultural and industrial revolutions and where most economic activity is based around the provision of services (such as retailing, financial services, transport, and information).

power   The ability to have another person or group act in accordance with one's wishes. Power comes in many forms, including political, social, economic, military, personal, psychological, ideological, legal, and inspirational.

privatization   The process by which government-owned businesses, industries, and services are sold to private owners and/or shareholders.

proletariat A term associated with Marxism, describing the class of workers in a capitalist industrial society who have little or nothing to sell other than their labor and so have little or no political or economic power.

proportional representation An electoral system in which political parties win seats in a legislature in direct proportion to their share of the popular vote. Used in a number of European countries, such as Italy and Sweden. Contrast with the *winner-take-all* or *plurality* system.

public policy The deliberate actions and inactions of governments and elected officials; whatever they do (or do not do) to govern or change society. The concept usually assumes a set of logically planned objectives, but it is often driven by inspiration and opportunism and characterized by incremental change and muddling through.

purchasing power parity A different method of calculating the GDP or GNP of a country, by which the total is expressed not in absolute terms but according to the purchasing power of the national currency.

republic Literally "the public thing" (from the Latin). A political system in which all members of the government are elected (as opposed to a *monarchy*, where at least one is not).

revolution Political, economic, or social change that represents a marked break with what came before. It may happen suddenly and be accompanied by violence (as with the American, French, and Russian revolutions), or may take longer and be achieved through changes in law or policy (as with the Thatcher and Gorbachev revolutions).

rule of law A system of government in which the distribution of power is determined and limited—and conflicts resolved—according to a mutually agreed-upon body of laws, to which every citizen is equally subject.

services Any economic activity that does not result in the production of a physical commodity, but rather in the provision of an intangible service (such as retailing, banking, transport, and communication).

single-member districts Legislative districts represented by a single person in a local or national legislature (as opposed to multimember districts, which are represented by more than one person).

social democracy A political and economic ideology seeking social change and the redistribution of wealth and political power through democratic rather than radical means. A less radical form of *socialism*.

socialism A political and economic ideology based on a redistribution of wealth, political power, and social services; the promotion of social and economic equality; and the elimination of social control (notably through ownership of property).

sovereignty An attribute possessed by a person or institution, giving them power over a particular constituency. In the United States, sovereignty is shared by the three major arms of government. In parliamentary systems, sovereignty rests largely with the legislature. All nation-states have sovereignty over the lands within their borders (provided they are recognized in international law).

Stalinism The political, economic, and social values, methods, and policies associated with the administration of Joseph Stalin in the USSR. These included centralized economic planning, the systematic elimination of all opposition, a cult of personality, a police state, and mass terror and propaganda.

state   One of the most hotly debated concepts in political science. Generally connotes a community of individuals living within recognized frontiers, adhering to a common body of law, and coming under the jurisdiction of a common government. Also used to describe collectively the officials, laws, and powers of that community.

state of emergency   A situation in which normal legislative and judicial powers—and perhaps even the rights of citizens—are suspended or bypassed in order to deal with an emergency situation, such as a threat to government or the state.

state-building   The process by which a community of individuals builds a state system and an identity, to which they feel common allegiance.

state socialism   A system in which the state owns the means of production and in which government and party institutions encourage the people toward the ultimate goal of creating a classless communist society.

structural violence   As distinct from physical violence, this term connotes social and economic oppression built into a system of government. Anyone suffering political, economic, or social discrimination or hardship as a consequence of prevailing conditions becomes the victim of structural violence.

terrorism   The use of physical or psychological violence for political ends. It is usually aimed against civilian targets with the goal of arousing fear and achieving political change.

Third World   The group of countries that, during the cold war, supposedly took the side of neither the Western alliance nor the Soviet bloc. More generally used to describe the countries of Latin America, Africa, and Asia, most of which were at one time or another European colonies.

totalitarianism   A political system in which all institutions and activities are subject to total state control and in which no individual rights or privileges are formally recognized (for example, the USSR under Stalin or Germany under Hitler).

unitary state   A state in which all significant executive power is vested in the national government, with little or no independent power vested in local units of government.

vanguard party   The Leninist concept of a revolutionary party created to bring change or revolution on behalf of the masses.

welfare state   A state that provides through law for people in need, such as the poor, the elderly, the handicapped, or anyone otherwise economically or physically disadvantaged.

Westminster model   The system of government associated with the British parliamentary model, the key features of which are: a fused executive and legislature, two legislative chambers representing different constituencies, a cabinet exercising key executive powers, an elected head of government, and a separate head of state.

winner-take-all   An electoral system in which the candidate winning the most votes (a plurality) wins office.

ACRONYMS

AFRC	Armed Forces Ruling Council (Nigeria)	ODA	official development assistance
ASU	Arab Socialist Union (Egypt)	OECD	Organization for Economic Cooperation and Development
CCP	Chinese Communist party		
CNN	Cable News Network	OIC	Organization of the Islamic Conference
CPC	communist and post-communist countries	OPEC	Organization of Petroleum Exporting Countries
CPSU	Communist Party of the Soviet Union	PAN	National Action party (Mexico)
ECOWAS	Economic Community of West African States	PLA	People's Liberation Army (China)
EU	European Union	PPP	purchasing power parity
G-8	Group of 8	PR	proportional representation
G-77	Group of 77		
GATT	General Agreement on Tariffs and Trade	PRC	People's Republic of China
GDP	gross domestic product	PRD	Party of the Democratic Revolution (Mexico)
GNP	gross national product		
IMF	International Monetary Fund	PRI	Institutional Revolutionary party (Mexico)
LDC	less developed country	SCAP	Supreme Commander for the Allied Powers (Japan)
LDP	Liberal Democratic party (Japan)	SDP	Social Democratic Party
MNC	multinational corporation	SDPJ	Social Democratic Party of Japan
MP	Member of Parliament (Britain)	SMC	Supreme Military Council (Nigeria)
NAFTA	North American Free Trade Agreement	UAR	United Arab Republic
NATO	North Atlantic Treaty Organization	UK	United Kingdom
		UN	United Nations
NDP	National Democratic party (Egypt)	UNAM	National Autonomous University (Mexico)
NIC	newly industrializing country	UNCTAD	United Nations Conference on Trade and Development
NIEO	New International Economic Order	USSR	Union of Soviet Socialist Republics
NPC	National People's Congress (China)	WTO	World Trade Organization
NRC	National Republican Convention (Nigeria)		

ENDNOTES

Introduction

1. Dogan, Mattei, and Dominique Pelassy, *How to Compare Nations: Strategies in Comparative Politics* (Chatham, NJ: Chatham House Publishers, 1984), p. 5.

2. See, for example, Gabriel Almond et al., *Comparative Politics Today*, 7th Ed. (New York: Longman, 2000).

3. Weber, Max, *The Theory of Social and Economic Organizations* (Glencoe, IL: Free Press, 1947).

4. Moore, Barrington, *Social Origins of Dictatorship and Democracy* (London: Methuen, 1967).

5. Safire, William, *Safire's Political Dictionary: The New Language of Politics* (New York: Random House, 1978).

6. Wolf-Phillips, Leslie, "Why Third World?" in *Third World Quarterly* 1:1, February 1979, pp. 105–114.

PART I: Liberal Democracies

1. Bloom, Alan, *The Republic of Plato*, 2nd Ed. (New York: Basic Books, 1991).

2. Dahl, Robert, *Polyarchy: Participation and Opposition* (New Haven, CT: Yale University Press, 1971).

3. Moore, Barrington Jr., *Social Origins of Dictatorship and Democracy: Lord and Peasant in the Making of the Modern World* (Boston: Beacon, 1967), p. 417.

4. Hobbes, Thomas, *Leviathan* (Oxford: Oxford University Press, 1998).

5. Landes, David, *The Unbound Prometheus: Technological Change and Industrial Development in Western Europe from 1750 to the Present* (Cambridge, UK: Cambridge University Press, 1969), pp. 42–54.

6. Smith, Adam, *The Wealth of Nations*, Ed. Edwin Cannan (New York: Modern Library, 1994).

7. Landes, *op. cit.*, p. 10.

8. Mill, John Stuart, *On Liberty* (New York: W.W. Norton, 1975).

9. Tucker, Robert (Ed.), *The Marx-Engels Reader* (New York: W.W. Norton, 1978), p. 287.

10. Landes, *op. cit.*, pp. 35–36.

Chapter 1: United States

1. U.S. Bureau of the Census, *Projections of the Population of the U.S. by Age, Sex and Race: 1995 to 2050* (Washington, DC: U.S. Bureau of the Census, 1996).

2. Federal Election Commission Web site, 2003, *http://www.fec.gov.*

3. *Ibid.*

4. Burns, James MacGregor, J. W. Peltason, Thomas E. Cronin, and David B. Magleby, *Government by the People*, 18th Ed. (Upper Saddle River, NJ: Prentice Hall, 2000), p. 362.

5. Greenstein, Fred I., *The Presidential Difference: Leadership Styles From FDR to Clinton* (New York: The Free Press, 2000).

6. *Ibid.*, p. 369.

7. Hibbing, John and Elizabeth Theis-Morse, *Congress as Public Enemy* (Cambridge, UK: Cambridge University Press, 1995).

8. All data from Federal Election Commission Web site, 2003, *http://www.fec.gov.*

9. University of Michigan Survey Research Center figures.

10. Welch, Susan, John Gruhl, John Comer, Susan M. Rigdon, and Jan Vermeer, *Understanding American Government*, 5th Ed. (Belmont, CA: West/Wadsworth, 1999), p. 143.

11. Federal Election Commission, *op. cit.*

12. Putnam, Robert D., "Bowling Alone: America's Declining Social Capital," in *Journal of Democracy* (January 1995), pp. 65–78.

13. Welch et al., *op. cit.*, pp. 116–117.

14. For a discussion of the structure of policy making in the United States, see B. Guy Peters, *American Public Policy: Promise and Performance*, 5th Ed. (Chappaqua, NY: Chatham House Publishers, 1999), Chapter 2.

15. See for example Princeton Survey Research Associates, as reported in *The Polling Report*, October 27, 1997.

Chapter 2: Britain

1. Jacobs, E., and Robert Worcester, *We British* (London: Weidenfeld and Nicolson, 1990), pp. 138–139.

2. Jones, Bill, and Dennis Kavanagh, *British Politics Today*, 6th Ed. (Washington, DC: CQ Press, 1998), pp. 179–185.

3. Norton, Philip, *The British Polity*, 4th Ed. (New York: Longman, 2001), p. 44.

4. World Bank figures quoted in McCormick, John, *Understanding the European Union*, 2nd Ed. (New York: Palgrave, 2002), pp. 42–44.

5. Hart, Vivien, *Distrust and Democracy* (Cambridge, UK: Cambridge University Press, 1978), pp. 202–203.

6. Dahl, Robert (Ed.), *Political Oppositions in Western Democracies* (New Haven, CT: Yale University Press, 1966), p. 353.

7. Almond, Gabriel A., and Sidney Verba (Eds.), *The Civic Culture Revisited* (Newbury Park, CA: Sage Publications, 1989).

8. Wallace, M., and J. Jenkins, "The New Class, Postindustrialism and Neocorporatism: Three Images of Social Protest in the Western Democracies," in J. Jenkins

and B. Klandermans (Eds.), *The Politics of Social Protest* (London: University College London Press, 1995).

9. Office for National Statistics, *UK 2002: The Official Yearbook of Great Britain and Northern Ireland* (London: The Stationery Office, 2001), p. 238.

10. Kavanagh, Dennis, *British Politics: Continuities and Change*, 4th Ed. (Oxford: Oxford University Press, 2000), pp. 47–49.

11. Norton, *op. cit.*, p. 57.

12. Bagehot, Walter, *The English Constitution* (Ithaca, NY: Cornell University Press, 1963).

13. Norton, *op. cit.*, p. 308.

14. *Ibid.*

15. Kavanagh, *op. cit.*, p. 50.

16. For more details, see Hennessy, Peter, *The Prime Minister: The Office and its Holders Since 1945* (New York: Palgrave, 2001).

17. Fielding, Steven, "A New Politics?" in Patrick Dunleavy, Andrew Gamble, Ian Holliday, and Gillian Peele (Eds.), *Developments in British Politics 6* (New York: Palgrave, 2000), p. 27.

18. For more discussion, see Sanders, David, "Voting and the Electorate," in Patrick Dunleavy, Andrew Gamble, Ian Holliday, and Gillian Peele (Eds.), *Developments in British Politics 5* (Basingstoke, UK: Macmillan, 1997).

19. *Ibid.*

20. Dunleavy, Patrick, "Introduction: 'New Times' in British Politics," in *ibid.*

21. Kavanagh, Dennis, *British Politics: Continuities and Change*, 4th Ed. (Oxford: Oxford University Press, 2000), p. 183.

22. *Ibid.*, p. 197.

23. Young, Hugo, *One of Us* (London: Pan Books, 1990), p. 371.

24. Figures from Riddell, Peter, *The Thatcher Decade* (Oxford: Basil Blackwell, 1989), pp. 53, 72, 75, 118.

25. *Ibid.*, pp. 93–94.

26. Kaltesky, Anatole, "Sour noises, but what a sweet taste" in *The World in 2003* (London: The Economist, 2002).

Chapter 3: Japan

1. Miyamoto, Masao, *The Straitjacket Society: An Insider's Irreverent View of Bureaucratic Japan* (New York: Kodansha International, 1994).

2. Umegaki, Michio, *After the Restoration: The Beginning of Japan's Modern State* (New York: New York University Press, 1988), p. 54.

3. Fukui, Haruhiro, "Postwar politics, 1945–1973," in Peter Duus (Ed.), *The Cambridge History of Japan, Vol. 6* (New York: Cambridge University Press, 1988), p. 155.

4. Hrebenar, Ronald J., *Japan's New Party System*, 3rd Ed. (Boulder, CO: Westview, 2000).

5. *The Economist*, "What Ails Japan? A Survey of Japan," April 20, 2002.

6. Mouer, Ross, and Yoshio Sugimoto, *Images of Japanese Society: A Study in the Social Construction of Reality* (London: Kegan Paul International, 1990).

7. Berry, Mary Elizabeth, *Hideyoshi* (Cambridge, MA: Harvard University Press, 1989), p. 111.

8. Hayao, Kenji, *The Japanese Prime Minister and Public Policy* (Pittsburgh: University of Pittsburgh Press, 1993).

9. *The Economist*, April 28, 2001, p. 39.

10. Stockwin, J. A. A., "Parties, Politicians and the Political System," in J. A. A. Stockwin et al., *Dynamic and Immobilist Politics in Japan* (Honolulu: University of Hawaii Press, 1988), p. 42.

11. *Ibid.*, p. 53.

12. *Ibid.*, p. 54.

13. Hayes, Louis D., *Intoduction to Japanese Politics* (New York: Paragon House, 1992), p. 112.

14. Krauss, Ellis S., *Japan's Democracy: How Much Change?* (New York: Foreign Policy Association Headline Series No. 305, 1995), p. 37.

15. *The Economist*, January 10, 1998, p. 34.

16. Stockwin, *op. cit.*, pp. 36–37.

17. Uchida, Mitsuru, "The Disintegration of Japan's Party System of 1955 and After," in *Waseda Political Studies*, March 1986, p. 6.

18. Krauss, *op. cit.*, pp. 39–40.

19. Hayes, *op. cit.*, p. 117.

20. *Ibid.*, pp. 126–127.

21. Hoye, Timothy, *Japanese Politics: Fixed and Floating Worlds* (Upper Saddle River, NJ: Prentice Hall, 1999), p. 110.

22. van Wolferen, Karel, *The Enigma of Japanese Power: People and Politics in a Stateless Nation* (London: Macmillan, 1989).

23. Johnson, Chalmers, *MITI and the Japanese Miracle: The Growth of Industrial Policy 1925–75* (Stanford: Stanford University Press, 1985), p. 154.

24. Hayao, *op. cit.*, pp. 7–8.

25. *The Economist*, *op. cit.*, note 5.

26. *The Economist*, July 6, 2002, p. 49.

27. *The Economist*, *op. cit.*, note 5.

28. *The Economist*, May 19, 2001.

PART II: Communist and Postcommunist Countries

1. Barry, Donald B., and Carol Barner-Barry, *Contemporary Soviet Politics: An Introduction* (Englewood Cliffs, NJ: Prentice Hall, 1982), p. 362.

2. Lieberthal, Kenneth, *Governing China: From Revolution Through Reform* (New York: W.W. Norton, 1995), pp. 293, 329.

3. Lane, David, *The Socialist Industrial State: Towards a Political Sociology of State Socialism* (London: George Allen & Unwin, 1976), p. 73.

4. Lenin, Vladimir Ilyich, *What Is To Be Done?* (New York: Penguin, 1988).

5. Lenin, Vladimir Ilyich, *Imperialism: The Highest Stage of Capitalism* (New York: International Publishers, 1939).

6. Schram, Stuart, *The Thought of Mao Tse-Tung* (Cambridge, UK: Cambridge University Press, 1989).

7. Bernstein, Eduard, *Evolutionary Socialism: A Criticism and Affirmation* (London: Independent Labour Party, 1909).

Chapter 4: Russia

1. Pipes, Richard, *The Russian Revolution 1899–1919* (London: Harrill, 1989).

2. Arendt, Hannah, *The Origins of Totalitarianism* (New York: Harcourt Brace, 1968).

3. Hammer, Darrell P., *The USSR: The Politics of Oligarchy* (Boulder, CO: Westview Press, 1990), p. 36.

4. Lucas, Edward, "Putin's Choice: A Survey of Russia," in *The Economist*, July 21, 2001.

5. White, Stephen, *Political Culture and Soviet Politics* (New York: St. Martin's Press, 1979), p. 64.

6. Rhodes, Mark, "Political Attitudes in Russia," in *RFE/RL Research Report*, January 15, 1993, pp. 42–44.

7. Barry, Donald D., and Carol Barner-Barry, *Contemporary Soviet Politics: An Introduction* (Englewood Cliffs, NJ: Prentice Hall, 1982), p. 13; White, *op. cit.*, pp. 110–111.

8. Biryukov, Nikolai, and V. M. Sergeev, *Russia's Road to Democracy: Parliament, Communism and Traditional Culture* (Aldershot, England: Edward Elgar, 1993).

9. Cohen, Stephen R., *Rethinking the Soviet Experience: Politics and History Since 1917* (New York: Oxford University Press, 1986), Chapter 5.

10. For details, see Sakwa, Richard, *Russian Politics and Society*, 3rd Ed. (London and New York: Routledge, 2002), pp. 55–60.

11. Oleynik, Igor, *Introduction to Russian Government Today* (Washington, DC: Carroll Publishing, 1993), p. v.

12. Hughes, James, "From Federalization to Recentralization," in Stephen White, Alex Pravda, and Zvi Gitelman (Eds.), *Developments in Russian Politics 5* (Durham, NC: Duke University Press, 2001).

13. *The Economist*, February 16, 2002, p. 48.

14. Sakwa, Richard, *op. cit.*, p. 112.

15. See Nichols, Thomas M., *The Russian Presidency: Society and Politics in the Second Russian Republic* (New York: Palgrave, 2000), Chapter 7.

16. Government figures quoted by Remington, Thomas F., "Parliamentary Politics in Russia," in White et al. (2001), *op. cit.*

17. McFaul, Michael, *Post-Communist Politics: Democratic Prospects in Russia and Eastern Europe* (Washington, DC: Center for Strategic and International Studies, 1993), p. 55.

18. Willerton, John P., "The Presidency," in White et al. (2001), *op. cit.*

19. Remington, Thomas F., "Towards a Participatory Politics?" in Stephen White, Alex Pravda, and Zvi Gitelman (Eds.), *Developments in Soviet and Post-Soviet Politics* (Durham, NC: Duke University Press, 1992), p. 151.

20. Lampert, Nicholas, "Patterns of Participation," in Stephen White, Alex Pravda, and Zvi Gitelman (Eds.), *Developments in Soviet Politics* (Durham, NC: Duke University Press, 1990).

21. Kelley, Donald R., *Politics in Russia and the Successor States* (Fort Worth, TX: Harcourt Brace, 1999), pp. 261–264.

22. Oates, Sarah, "Politics and the Media," in White et al. (2001), *op. cit.*

23. Jensen, Donald, How Russia Is Ruled, RFE/RL Web page at *http://www.RFERL. org/nca/special/ruwhorules*, October 1999.

24. *The Economist*, "Putin's Choice: A Survey of Russia," July 21, 2001, p. 12.

25. Harvard economist Jeffrey Sachs, quoted in *The Economist*, March 23, 2002, p. 67.

26. Transparency International Web site, 2003, *http://www.transparency.org*.

27. Shaw, Denis J. B., *Russia in the Modern World: A New Geography* (Oxford: Blackwell Publishers, 1999), p. 58.

28. Truscott, Peter, *Russia First: Breaking with the West* (Ilford, UK: Frank Cass, 1997).

29. *The Economist*, December 1, 2001, pp. 46–47.

Chapter 5: China

1. Derbyshire, Ian, *Politics in China: From Mao to the Post-Deng Era* (Edinburgh, Scotland: W & R Chambers Ltd., 1991), p. 1.

2. Schram, Stuart, *The Thought of Mao Tse-Tung* (Cambridge, UK: Cambridge University Press, 1989), p. 195.

3. Mao Zedong, *Quotations from Chairman Mao Tse-Tung* (Beijing: Foreign Languages Press, 1972).

4. Lin, Nan, *The Struggle for Tiananmen: Anatomy of the 1989 Mass Movement* (Westport, CT: Praeger, 1992), pp. 1–17.

5. Harding, Harry, "Political Development in Post-Mao China," in A. Doak Barnett and Ralph N. Clough, *Modernizing China: Post-Mao Reform and Development* (Boulder, CO: Westview Press, 1986), p. 33.

6. *The Economist*, November 23, 2002, p. 40.

7. Pye, Lucian, *China: An Introduction* (New York: Longman, 1991), p. 72.

8. Lieberthal, Kenneth G., and Michel Oksenberg, *Policy Making in China: Leaders, Structures and Processes* (Princeton, NJ: Princeton University Press, 1988), pp. 162–163.

9. Shirk, Susan L., "The Chinese Political System and the Political Strategy of Economic Reform," in Kenneth G. Lieberthal and David M. Lampton, *Bureaucracy, Politics and Decision-Making in Post-Mao China* (Berkeley, CA: University of California Press, 1992).

10. *Ibid.*

11. Townsend, James R., and Brantly Womack, *Politics in China*, 3rd Ed. (Chicago: Scott Foresman, 1998), p. 352.

12. Shirk, *op. cit.*, p. 61.

13. Long, Simon, "Leadership Politics Since 1989," in Robert Benewick and Paul Wingrove (Eds.), *China in the 1990s* (Basingstoke, UK: Macmillan, 1999).

14. Saich, Tony, *Governance and Politics of China* (New York: Palgrave, 2001), p. 110.

15. Wang, James C. E., *Contemporary Chinese Politics: An Introduction*, 7th Ed. (Upper Saddle River, NJ: Prentice Hall, 1999), p. 117.

16. Moody, Peter, *Tradition and Modernization in China and Japan* (Belmont, CA: Wadsworth, 1995), p. 214.

17. Saich, *ibid.*, p. 114.

18. Jencks, Harlan W., "The Chinese People's Liberation Army: 1949–89," in David Goodman and Gerald Segal (Eds.), *China at Forty: Mid-Life Crisis?* (Oxford: Clarendon Press, 1989), pp. 93–94.

19. For example, they are barely mentioned at all by either Saich, *op. cit.*, or Wang, *op. cit.*

20. Saich, *op. cit.*, p. 76.

21. Wang, *op. cit.*, p. 98.

22. *The Economist*, June 1, 2002, p. 40.

23. See Saich, *op. cit.*, pp. 81–85.

24. Houn, Franklin, *A Short History of Chinese Communism* (Englewood Cliffs, NJ: Prentice Hall, 1967), p. 89.

25. Hamrin, Carol Lee, "The Party Leadership System," in Kenneth G. Lieberthal and David M. Lampton, *op. cit.*

26. Wang, *op. cit.*, p. 82.

27. Chang, Parris, "The Last Stand of Deng's Revolution," in *Problems of Communism* 30 (January–February 1981), pp. 3–19.

28. *Ibid.*

29. Wang, *op. cit.*, p. 102.

30. Rosen, Stanley, "Prosperity, Privatization and China's Youth," in *Problems of Communism* 24:2 (March–April 1985), p. 26.

31. Saich, *op. cit.*, p. 171.

32. *The Economist*, October 26, 1996.

33. Lieberthal and Oksenberg, *op. cit.*

34. Lampton, David M., "The Implementation Problem in Post-Mao China," in David Lampton (Ed.), *Policy Implementation in Post-Mao China* (Berkeley, CA: University of California Press, 1987), pp. 7–8.

35. *Ibid.*, pp. 49–51. Samuel S. Kim (Ed.), *China and the World: New Directions in Chinese Foreign Relations* (Boulder, CO: Westview Press, 1989).

36. *The Economist*, "A Survey of China," June 15, 2002, p. 3.

37. Warshaw, Steven, *China Emerges* (Berkeley, CA: Diablo Press, 1991), p. 93.

38. Levine, Steven I., "Sino-American Relations: Renormalization and Beyond," in Kim, *op. cit.*

39. Cumings, Bruce, "The Political Economy of China's Turn Outward," in Kim, *ibid.*

40. Wang, *op. cit.*, pp. 319–320.

41. *Ibid.*, pp. 363–364.

PART III: Newly Industrializing Countries

1. Shaw, Timothy M., and Jerker Carlsson, "Newly Industrialized Countries and South-South: Concepts, Correlates, Controversies and Cases," in Carlsson and Shaw (Eds.), *Newly Industrialized Countries and the Political Economy of South-South Relations* (New York: St. Martin's Press, 1988), p. 7; Mortimer, Robert A., *The Third World Coalition in International Politics* (Boulder, CO: Westview Press, 1984).

2. Denoon, David B. H., "Facing the New International Economic Order," in David B. H. Denoon (Ed.), *The New International Economic Order: A U.S. Response* (New York: New York University Press, 1979).

3. Garten, Jeffrey, *The Big Ten: The Big Emerging Markets and How They Will Change Our Lives* (New York: Basic Books, 1997), pp. 70–71.

4. Sauvant, Karl P., *The Group of 77: Evolution, Structure, Organization* (New York: Oceana Publications, 1981).

5. Karl, Terry Lynn, "Dilemmas of Democratization in Latin America," in Dankwart A. Rustow and Kenneth Paul Erickson, *Comparative Political Dynamics: Global Research Perspectives* (New York: HarperCollins, 1991), p. 168.

6. Lipset, Seymour Martin, "Some Social Requisites of Democracy: Economic Development and Political Legitimacy," in *American Political Science Review* 53:1 (March 1959).

7. Karl, Terry Lynn, "Dilemmas of Democratization in Latin America," in Dankwart A. Rustow and Kenneth Paul Erickson, *Comparative Political Dynamics: Global Research Perspectives* (New York: HarperCollins, 1991), p. 168.

Chapter 6: Mexico

1. Needler, Martin C., *Mexican Politics: The Containment of Conflict* (New York: Praeger, 1990), p. 13.

2. Paz, Octavio, "Reflections: Mexico and the United States," in *New Yorker*, September 17, 1979.

3. Purcell, Susan Kaufman, "Mexico," in Howard J. Wiarda and Harvey F. Kline (Eds.), *Latin American Politics and Development* (Boulder, CO: Westview Press, 1990), p. 397.

4. Wiarda and Kline, *ibid.*, p. 15.

5. Wiarda, Howard J., "Constitutionalism and Political Culture in Mexico: How Deep the Foundations?" in Daniel P. Franklin and Michael J. Bann, *Political Culture and Constitutionalism: A Comparative Approach* (Armonk, NY: M. E. Sharpe, 1995).

6. For more discussion on this, see George W. Grayson, *Mexico: From Corporatism to Pluralism?* (Fort Worth, TX: Harcourt Brace, 1998).

7. Camp, Roderic A., *Politics in Mexico: The Decline of Authoritarianism* (New York: Oxford University Press, 1999), pp. 135–138.

8. *Ibid.*, p. 11.

9. Camp, Roderic A., *Mexico's Leaders: Their Education and Recruitment* (Tucson: University of Arizona Press, 1990), p. 11.

10. Needler, *op. cit.*, p. 92.

11. Needler, Martin C., "The Government of Mexico," in Michael Curtis (Ed.), *Introduction to Comparative Government*, 4th Ed. (New York: Longman, 1997), pp. 530–531.

12. Camp, Roderic A., "Mexico's Legislature: Missing the Democratic Lockstep," in David Close (Ed.), *Legislatures and the New Democracies in Latin America* (Boulder, CO: Lynne Rienner, 1995).

13. *The Economist*, January 5, 2002, p. 32.

14. Avalos, Francisco A., *The Mexican Legal System* (Westport, CT: Greenwood Press, 1992), p. 16.

15. *Ibid.*, p. 12.

16. Ugalde, Antonio, *Power and Conflict in a Mexican Community: A Study of Political Integration* (Albuquerque: University of New Mexico Press, 1970), p. 95.

17. Camp, *op. cit.*

18. Alcocer, V. Jorge, "Recent Electoral Reforms in Mexico: Prospects for a Real Multiparty Democracy," in Riordan Roett (Ed.), *The Challenge of Institutional Reform in Mexico* (Boulder, CO: Lynne Rienner, 1995).

19. Mendez, Guadalupe Pacheco, "Voter Abstentionism," in Grayson, *op. cit.*, p. 71.

20. Teichman, Judith A., *Policymaking in Mexico: From Boom to Crisis* (Boston: Allen and Unwin, 1988), p. 13.

21. Cornelius, Wayne A., and Ann L. Craig, "Politics in Mexico," in Gabriel Almond and G. Bingham Powell, *Comparative Politics Today: A World View* (Glenview, IL: Scott, Foresman/Little, Brown, 1988), pp. 444–445.

22. *The Economist*, August 11, 2001, p. 30.

23. *The Economist*, January 11, 2003, p. 27.

24. *The Economist*, May 12, 2001, p. 42.

25. Transparency International, Corruption Perceptions Index 2003, *http://www. transparency.org/surveys/index.html.*

26. For more details, see Camp, 1999, Chapter 6.

27. Purcell, *op. cit.*, p. 412.

28. Grayson, *op. cit.*, p. 121.

29. Needler, *op. cit.*, p. 118.

30. *The Economist*, "After the Revolution: A Survey of Mexico," October 28, 2000.

31. Levy, Daniel, and Gabriel Szekely, *Mexico: Paradoxes of Stability and Change* (Boulder, CO: Westview Press, 1987), p. 131.

32. Smith, Geri, "The Decline of the Maquiladora," in *Business Week Online*, April 29, 2002, *http://www.businessweek.com.*

33. *The Economist*, July 13, 2002, p. 31.

34. Levy and Szekely, *op. cit.*, p. 189.

35. Smith, Peter H., *Mexico: The Quest for a U.S. Policy* (New York: Foreign Policy Association, 1980), pp. 6–7.

36. Quoted by Grayson, *op. cit.*, p. 242.

37. *The Economist*, July 21, 2001, p. 31.

Chapter 7: India

1. Government of India, *Report of the Backward Classes Commission* (Delhi: Government of India, 1981).

2. Lall, Arthur, *The Emergence of Modern India* (New York: Columbia University Press, 1981), p. 2.

3. *Ibid.*, p. 3.

4. *Ibid.*, p. 6.

5. Nandy, Ashis, "The Political Culture of the Indian State," in *Daedalus* 118:4 (Fall 1989), pp. 1–26.

6. Hardgrave, Robert L., and Stanley A. Kochanek, *India: Government and Politics in a Developing Nation*, 6th Ed. (Fort Worth, TX: Harcourt Brace, 2000), pp. 11–13.

7. Huntington, Samuel P., *Political Order in Changing Societies* (New Haven, CT: Yale University Press, 1968), p. 5.

8. Brass, Paul R., *A New Cambridge History of India*, Vol. I, V:I (Cambridge, UK: Cambridge University Press, 1990), pp. 10–13.

9. *Ibid.*, p. 9.

10. Hart, Henry C., "Political Leadership in India," in Atul Kohli (Ed.), *India's Democracy: An Analysis of Changing State-Society Relations* (Princeton, NJ: Princeton University Press, 1988), p. 55.

11. Brass, *op. cit.*, p. 36.

12. For more details, see Hardgrave and Kochanek, *op. cit.*, p. 301ff.

13. Wheare, Kenneth, *Federal Government* (New York: Oxford University Press, 1951), p. 28.

14. Chanda, Asok, *Federalism in India* (London: George Allen & Unwin, 1965), p. 124.

15. For more details, see Hardgrave and Kochanek, *op. cit.*, pp. 318–319.

16. Brass, *op. cit.*, p. 83.

17. *Ibid.*, p. 86.

18. For more details, see Hardgrave and Kochanek, *op. cit.*, Chapter 6.

19. Shah, Ghanshyam, "Grass-Roots Mobilization in Indian Politics," in Kohli, *op. cit.*

20. Hardgrave and Kochanek, *op. cit.*, p. 275.

21. *The Economist*, April 17, 1999, p. 44.

22. Shah, *op. cit.*

23. *The Economist*, May 22, 1999.

PART IV: Less Developed Countries

1. Kamrava, Mehran, *Politics and Society in the Developing World* (London: Routledge, 2000), p. 209.

2. *Ibid.*, p. 2.

3. Nyerere, Julius, *Freedom and Unity* (Dar-es-Salaam and London: Oxford University Press, 1966), p. 198.

4. Jackson, Robert H., and Carl G. Rosberg, *Personal Rule in Black Africa* (Berkeley, CA: University of California Press, 1982), p. 1.

5. *Ibid.*, p. 1.

6. Mazrui, Ali A., *The Africans: A Triple Heritage* (London: BBC Publications, 1986), pp. 182–183.

7. Figures from World Trade Organization Web site, 2003, *http://www.wto.org*.

8. Figures from UN Fund for Population Activities Web site, 2003, *http://www.unfpa.org*.

9. Handelman, Howard, *The Challenge of Third World Development*, 3rd Ed. (Upper Saddle River, NJ: Prentice Hall, 2003), p. 14.

10. Moore, Barrington, *The Social Origins of Dictatorship and Democracy* (Boston: Beacon Press, 1966), p. 418.

11. Rostow, Walter W., *The Stages of Economic Growth: A Non-Communist Manifesto* (New York: Cambridge University Press, 1960).

12. Lenin, Vladimir Ilyich, *Imperialism: The Highest Stage of Capitalism* (London: Lawrence and Wishart, 1948).

13. Amin, Samir, *Accumulation on World Scale: A Critique of the Theory of Underdevelopment* (New York: Monthly Review Press, 1974); and *Unequal Development: An Essay on the Social Transformations of Peripheral Capitalism* (New York: Monthly Review Press, 1976).

14. Reitsma, H. A., and J. Al. G. Kleinpenning, *The Third World in Perspective* (Assen, Netherlands: Rowan and Allanheld, 1985), p. 215ff.

15. See, for example, Fernando Henrique Cardoso and Enzo Falletto, *Dependency and Development in Latin America* (Berkeley, CA: University of California Press, 1979).

16. Chilcote, Ronald, *Theories of Comparative Politics: The Search for a Paradigm* (Boulder, CO: Westview Press, 1981), p. 287.

17. Mehta, Vrajenda Raj, *Beyond Marxism: Towards an Alternative Perspective* (New Delhi: Manchar Publications, 1978), p. 92.

Chapter 8: Nigeria

1. Whitaker, C. S., "Second Beginnings: The New Political Framework in Nigeria," in Richard L. Sklar and C. S. Whitaker, *African Politics and Problems in Development* (Boulder, CO: Lynne Reinner Publishers, 1991), p. 230.

2. Aborisade, Oladimeji, and Robert J. Mundt, *Politics in Nigeria*, 2nd Ed. (New York: Longman, 2002), pp. 13–15.

3. Ekeh, Peter, "Nigeria's Emergent Political Culture," in Peter Ekeh et al. (Eds.), *Nigeria Since Independence: The First Twenty-Five Years* (Ibadan, Nigeria: Heinemann Educational Books, 1989), pp. 2–6.

4. Diamond, Larry, "Nigeria: Pluralism, Statism, and the Struggle for Democracy," in Larry Diamond et al. (Eds.), *Democracy in Developing Countries, Vol. 2: Africa* (Boulder, CO: Lynne Reinner Publishers, 1988), p. 60.

5. Ekeh, *op. cit.*, p. 4.

6. Mackintosh, John, "Nigeria Since Independence," in *World Today* 20:8 (1964), p. 337.

7. Graf, William D., *The Nigerian State: Political Economy, State Class and Political System in the Post-Colonial Era* (London: James Currey, 1988), pp. 65–66.

8. Oyinbo, John, *Nigeria: Crisis and Beyond* (London: Knight, 1971), p. 9.

9. Graf, *op. cit.*, p. 41.

10. *The Economist*, January 15, 2000, Nigeria Survey, p. 4.

11. Elaigwu, J. Isawa, "The Political Trio on Nigeria's Military Government: The Dynamics of Inter-Elite Relations in a Military Regime, 1967–75," in *The Nigerian Journal of Public Affairs*, VI:2 (1976).

12. Dudley, Bill, *An Introduction to Nigerian Government and Politics* (Bloomington, IN: Indiana University Press, 1982), p. 103.

13. Joseph, Richard A., "Principles and Practices of Nigerian Military Government," in John W. Harbeson (Ed.), *The Military in African Politics* (New York: Praeger, 1987), pp. 83–84.

14. *The Economist*, July 7, 2001, p. 45 and November 3, 2001, p. 54.

15. Paden, John N., *Ahmadu Bello: Sardauna of Sokoto* (Zaria, Nigeria: Hudahuda Publishing, 1986).

16. Graf, *op. cit.*, p. 186.

17. Kirk-Greene, Anthony, and Douglas Rimmer, *Nigeria Since 1970: A Political and Economic Outline* (London: Hodder and Stoughton, 1981), p. 106.

18. Soyinka, Wole, *The Open Sore of a Continent: A Personal Narrative of the Nigerian Crisis* (New York: Oxford University Press, 1996), p. 13.

19. For a chronology of world oil prices, see the U.S. Department of Energy Web page at *http://www.eia.doe.gov/emeu/cabs/chron.html.*

20. *The Economist*, August 3, 2002, pp. 59–60.

21. Achebe, Chinua, *The Trouble with Nigeria* (Oxford: Heinemann, 1983).

22. For the latest rankings, based on the extent to which corruption is perceived to exist among politicians and public officials, visit Transparency International's Web site at *http://www.transparency.org.*

23. Economist Intelligence Unit Country Report, *Nigeria*, 3rd quarter 1999, p. 19.

24. Nigerian data from World Bank, 2003, *http://www.worldbank.com*; U.S. data from Bureau of Health Professions, quoted by Centers for Disease Control, 2003, *http://www.cdc.gov.*

25. Aluko, Olajide, *Essays on Nigerian Foreign Policy* (London: George Allen & Unwin, 1981), p. 17.

26. Achebe, *op. cit.*

PART V: Islamic Countries

1. Bannerman, Patrick, *Islam in Perspective: A Guide to Islamic Society, Politics and Law* (London: Routledge, 1988), pp. 60–82.

2. Piscatori, James P., *Islam in the Political Process* (Cambridge, UK: Cambridge University Press, 1983), p. 4.

3. Esposito, John L., *The Islamic Threat: Myth or Reality?* (New York: Oxford University Press, 1992), p. 12.

4. The information here on the theoretical features of Islamic politics and economics is drawn from Ismail Raji al Faruqi, "The Islamic Critique of the Status Quo of Muslim Society," in Stowasser, Barbara Freyer (Ed.), *The Islamic Impulse* (London: Croom Helm, 1987).

5. Rahman, Fazlur, "The Law of Rebellion in Islam," Paine Lecture in Religion, published by the University of Missouri-Columbia, 1983, p. 8.

6. Bill, James A., and Robert Springborg, *Politics in the Middle East* (New York: Longman, 2000), p. 152ff.

7. Esposito, John L., *Islam and Politics* (Syracuse, NY: Syracuse University Press, 1991), p. 296.

8. Bannerman, *op. cit.*, pp. 97–98.

9. Peretz, Don, *The Middle East Today* (Hinsdale, IL: The Dryden Press, 1971), pp. 40–41.

10. Esposito, *op. cit.*, p. 42.

11. Beinin, Joel, and Joe Stork, *Political Islam* (Berkeley, CA: University of California Press, 1997), p. 3.

12. Khalid, Detlev, "The Phenomenon of Re-Islamization," in *Aussenpolitik XXIX* (Winter 1978), pp. 433–453.

13. Husain, Mir Zohair, *Global Islamic Politics*, 2nd Ed. (New York: Longman, 2003), p. 53.

14. Piscatori, James P., *Islam in the Political Process* (Cambridge, UK: Cambridge University Press, 1983), pp. 3–4.

15. Esposito, *op. cit.*, p. 32ff.

16. Bill and Springborg, *op. cit.*, p. 415.

17. Husain, Mir Zohair, *op. cit.*, pp. 212–215.

Chapter 9: Egypt

1. Esposito, John L., *Islam and Politics* (Syracuse, NY: Syracuse University Press, 1991), p. 128.

2. Beattie, Kirk, J., "Prospects for Democratization in Egypt," in *American-Arab Affairs* 36, Spring 1991, pp. 31–47.

3. Hinnebusch, Raymond A., *Egyptian Politics Under Sadat* (Cambridge, UK: Cambridge University Press, 1985), p. 223.

4. Weber, Max, *The Theory of Social and Economic Organization* (New York: The Free Press, 1947).

5. Hopwood, Derek, *Egypt: Politics and Society 1945–1991* (London: George Allen & Unwin, 1982), p. 172; Ibrahim, Saadeddin, "Religion and Politics Under Nasser and Sadat, 1952–81," in Barbara Freyer Stowasser (Ed.), *The Islamic Impulse* (London: Croom Helm, 1987), pp. 123–124.

6. Bill, James A., and Robert Springborg, *Politics in the Middle East* (New York: Longman, 2000), p. 230.

7. Baker, Raymond William, *Egypt's Uncertain Revolution Under Nasser and Sadat* (Cambridge, MA: Harvard University Press, 1978), p. 70ff.

8. Hinnebusch, *op. cit.*, note 3, pp. 12–13.

9. Springborg, Robert, *Mubarak's Egypt: Fragmentation of the Political Order* (Boulder, CO: Westview Press, 1989), pp. 30–33.

10. Andersen, Roy, Robert Seibert, and Jon Wagner, *Politics and Change in the Middle East*, 6th Ed. (Upper Saddle River, NJ: Prentice Hall, 2001), pp. 88-89.

11. Vatikiotis, P. J., *The History of Egypt* (Baltimore: Johns Hopkins University Press, 1985), p. 422.

12. Cooper, Mark N., *The Transformation of Egypt* (Baltimore: Johns Hopkins University Press, 1982), p. 70.

13. McDermott, Anthony, *Egypt from Nasser to Mubarak: A Flawed Revolution* (London: Croom Helm, 1988), p. 73ff.

14. Springborg, *op. cit.*, p. 139.

15. Waterbury, John, *The Egypt of Nasser and Sadat: The Political Economy of Two Regimes* (Princeton, NJ: Princeton University Press, 1983), p. 16.

16. Nasser, Gamal Abdel, *The Philosophy of the Revolution* (Cairo: The National Publication House, 1954), pp. 33–34; Springborg, *op. cit.*, p. 96.

17. Marsot, Afaf Lutfi Al-Sayyid, *A Short History of Egypt* (Cambridge, UK: Cambridge University Press, 1985), p. 143.

18. Beattie, *op. cit.*

19. McDermott, *op. cit.*, p. 102.

20. Hopwood, *op. cit.*, p. 89.

21. Hinnebusch, *op. cit.*, pp. 158–159.

22. Springborg, *op. cit.*, pp. 198–202.

23. Rubin, Barry, *Islamic Fundamentalism in Egyptian Politics* (New York: Palgrave Macmillan, 2002).

24. *New York Times*, February 3, 1994; tourist arrival figures from Egyptian Tourism Authority, quoted in Economist Intelligence Unit, *Egypt Country Profile 1995–96* (London: Economist Intelligence Unit Ltd., 1995).

25. Beattie, *op. cit.*

26. Economist Intelligence Unit Country Report, Egypt, 3rd Quarter 1999, pp. 13–14.

27. Springborg, *op. cit.*, p. 193.

28. Hinnebusch, *op. cit.*, p. 259.

29. Economist Intelligence Unit, *op. cit.*

30. Marsot, *op. cit.*, p. 142.

31. *The Economist*, January 5, 2002, p. 36.

32. Vatikiotis, *op. cit.*, p. 409.

NAME INDEX

SUBJECT INDEX